Handbook of Housing
and the Built Environment
in the United States

Handbook of Housing and the Built Environment in the United States

EDITED BY
Elizabeth Huttman
and Willem van Vliet—

FOREWORD BY
Sylvia F. Fava

GREENWOOD PRESS
New York • Westport, Connecticut • London

363,5
H 236

Library of Congress Cataloging-in-Publication Data

Handbook of housing and the built environment in the United States /
  edited by Elizabeth Huttman and Willem van Vliet ; foreword by
  Sylvia F. Fava.
      p.   cm.
    Includes indexes.
    ISBN 0–313–24874–5 (lib. bdg. : alk. paper)
    1. Housing—United States—Handbooks, manuals, etc.   2. Housing
  policy—United States—Handbooks, manuals, etc.   3. Housing
  subsidies—United States—Handbooks, manuals, etc.   I. Huttman,
  Elizabeth D., 1929–   .   II. Van Vliet, Willem.
  HD7293.H236   1988
  363.5′068—dc19   87–36093

British Library Cataloguing in Publication Data is available.

Library of Congress Catalog Card Number: 87–36093
ISBN: 0–313–24874–5

First published in 1988

Greenwood Press, Inc.
88 Post Road West, Westport, Connecticut   06881

Printed in the United States of America

The paper used in this book complies with the
Permanent Paper Standard issued by the National
Information Standards Organization (Z39.48–1984).

10   9   8   7   6   5   4   3   2   1

Contents

Figures and Tables

FIGURES

TABLES

Foreword

In 1987 the Census Bureau reported that there were 100 million housing units in the United States. How appropriate that this milestone is followed within a year by the publication of the first handbook on housing in the United States. The study of housing has come of age.

Among the disciplines represented in this volume are sociology, planning, economics, and political science. Accordingly, the first part of the volume is concerned with the broad social setting of housing and the impact of housing, including, for example, neighborhood quality, the "building" of community, and residential density. The second and third parts deal with the supply, demand, and affordability of housing and with housing subsidy programs, and are essential for an understanding of housing in the United States, where housing is a commodity rather than an entitlement. The fourth part deals with the housing needs of "special groups": women, minorities, young people, the elderly, and those with no housing at all—the homeless. These groups, which are ill-served in our housing system, underscore the system's defects and also imply the need for comparative analysis of housing systems. Inequality of housing outcomes is not confined to capitalist systems. The fifth and final part presents the social changes underway in urban and suburban housing.

Housing is a multifaceted subject, encompassing elements of sociology, planning, architecture, political science, economics, geography, anthropology, and psychology. No single volume can cover all the various disciplines or be complete even within one discipline. This handbook, for example, has little coverage of mobile homes, which, while still a small percentage of total housing units, have tripled since 1960. However, for social science this handbook sets the parameters for housing theory and research. It presents current findings and provides the framework for cumulative further research.

Sylvia F. Fava
Senior Research Scholar

Graduate Center,
City University of New York

Acknowledgments

We wish to thank Roger Montgomery, Dean of the College of Environmental Studies, University of California, Berkeley, for suggesting to Greenwood Press our involvement in this project. We would like to express appreciation to Mary Sive and Loomis Mayer at Greenwood Press for their editorial encouragement and assistance in this massive project. We both also wish to thank Neil Kraner, Todd Adkins, and Charles Eberline of the Greenwood Press staff for all their assistance. Elizabeth Huttman would like to express thanks for typing assistance to Vreni Lembo of Zermatt, Darlean Cole, and Ginny Juzapavicus, Shelter Island; and to Peter Föhn, director, Zermatt Mengis, and Walter Juon, for xeroxing help. She would also like to express appreciation for those providing a comfortable atmosphere in which to work, including the Familie Furrer of Beny, H. Taugwalder of the Victoria, and the Biner Cafe staff; to those giving useful information, Joan Nixon, Isabel Haigh, Phil and Lil Sturgeon, Ann Biner, Corrine Corra, Lenita Robbins, and Eleanor Gurewitsch; and last of all to her husband, John Huttman, and to Ulrich Inderbinden. At the Pennsylvania State University and later at the University of Colorado, indispensable and expert secretarial assistance was provided by, respectively, Monica Allebach and Lorraine Self. Finally, we are grateful to the contributors for their patience and their willingness to work with a set of guidelines intended to promote a more or less uniform format of the diverse chapters.

Introduction

ELIZABETH HUTTMAN

The chapters that follow show the field of housing to be multidimensional. The various contributors view housing as a sociopsychological phenomenon, as a part of the urban environment, as an economic activity, as a policy issue, and as an architectural and planning activity. Housing must be looked at as an ever-changing demand, or need, and its provision, or supply, as a dynamic process involving many actors. One of these actors is the state. Its degree of involvement can vary, as can the goals it wants to meet and the strategies it uses to meet them.

SCOPE OF THIS BOOK

Because housing is a broad, multidisciplinary, and fragmented field of research, a core of basic, state-of-the-art knowledge is not easily assembled. Yet such background material is necessary for any academic researcher, student, or practitioner, whether housing specialist, general planner, architect, or developer. At present, information is scattered in many journals, government reports, and books, and is seldom comprehensive. Rather, it is contained in narrow reports of specific research or of a very specific aspect of a program, which are often hard to obtain due to limited circulation or limited knowledge of their existence. In addition, the reports are written for a specific audience, such as government officials or academics in a particular discipline.

In order to overcome these problems, this handbook provides all-inclusive chapters on particular subfields, written by experts knowledgeable about research in that special topic. Each chapter covers historic developments, the present situation or program, and future trends in the United States in that field. These uniform comprehensive reports also include extensive bibliographies.

The topics chosen for coverage are those of current importance to planners, urbanologists, environmental psychologists, architects, and political policymakers, as well as economists researching housing supply and demand issues. Not all of the relevant subjects in the housing field can be covered in a single volume, so selection has been necessary.

The first part of this book establishes a context for housing in sociopsychological terms. It covers the societal function of housing, indicators of neighborhood quality, and spatial arrangements and housing form as a basis for community. Other aspects, such as the relationship between behavior and architecture and the effects of residential crowding, are also considered. In Part II the focus shifts to supply, demand, and affordability of housing, including their economic components. Chapters discuss affordability of housing, private-sector rental housing, house purchase and foreclosure potential, and cooperative condominium conversions. Part III deals with housing subsidy programs and tenant concerns. An overview chapter on American housing policy and subsidy programs is followed by chapters on public housing, tax subsidies, housing allowances, and the local approach to housing regulation, rent control. The last chapter concerns the tenants' movement in the United States. The fourth part focuses on the needs for housing of special groups, including women, minorities, young people, the elderly, and the homeless. The last part covers housing needs and housing developments in different geographic settings, first in the suburban environment, and then in the inner city in the areas of urban redevelopment and gentrification, revitalization, and displacement. Finally, new towns are discussed. While these chapters do not cover all aspects of housing, they do treat those topics that are of current concern, those that are widely researched and discussed in the literature and in policymaking circles. This book covers the main subjects found in any of the books of readings on housing, but it differs from those books in that each chapter is a comprehensive coverage of developments in its field, not a report on a narrow piece of research within that field.

MULTIFIELD CONCERNS WITH HOUSING

Specialists in many fields have an interest in housing because of its many aspects. Housing is more than shelter. It has sociopsychological meanings for the user of the home; it is a financial asset; and it is a major element of the total urban and rural environment. Housing construction and the overall housing stock are major factors in the country's economic life. Housing is a dynamic and complex subject with demand and supply ever changing and is a policy issue with subsidy approaches continually fluid (Struyk, Mayer, and Tuccillo, 1983).

The types of demands for housing are complex; needs are based on demographic factors such as size of the household and its composition, the degree of residential mobility (Kendig, 1984), internal and international migration, and levels of affluence of different consumer groups, as well as degree of segregation and other societal conditions (Helper, 1986; Sternlieb and Hughes, 1985). The supply of housing provided is the result of complex economic factors. It is influenced by a variety of conditions including the price of land and land availability, mortgage interest rates, the efficiency of the construction industry, and types of subsidies available (Downs, 1983; Cooke and Hamilton, 1984; Fare and Yoon, 1984).

The level of state involvement in meeting these needs or demands varies, as do the particular strategies for coping with the demand of the variety of groups with their diverse housing needs (Donnison and Ungerson, 1982). The multidimensional aspects of housing are discussed in the following sections. Then the major issues of demand, supply, and state intervention are covered in detail.

Housing as Home: Its Sociopsychological Meaning

Housing is a basic element in our everyday living. Housing provides shelter, but more than that it is the primary component of the total environment in which we live (Michelson, 1986). The forms and conditions of the housing shape the urban environment, whether as slum housing, suburban tract developments, or new towns. In this book housing is broadly defined as including its surrounding neighborhood and amenities (Adams, 1984; Altman and Werner, 1985).

Housing has a psychological aspect as one's home (Hummon, 1985); the housing structure itself meets the individual's needs for privacy, security, adequate health conditions, and even green space through its spatial features and amenities; or, conversely, the housing does not meet these needs due to crowding and inadequate plumbing (Kain and Quigley, 1970). Housing must have congruence; that is it must provide sufficient spatial opportunity for the life-style or action/behavior system of the user (Michelson, 1986). For example, for the elderly the environment must be congruent with their health needs at a particular stage in their life (Lawton, Brody, and Turner-Massey, 1978); for younger people, with their child-rearing activities. Other psychological meanings of housing also relate to the setting.

Housing has a sociopsychological meaning in giving status to the user and providing a safe environment in which to function; in giving the person a sense of place (Blum and Kingston, 1984); and in giving the person a financial asset and thus making him or her feel financially well-off. It is also a consumer good, with an interior and exterior, influenced by interior designers on the one hand, and landscapers on the other (Lindamood and Hanna, 1979).

The housing unit is set in a neighborhood that provides an infrastructure of services, such as schools. The setting can have such positive features as parks, prestigious surroundings, and a desirable location, or such negative features as unkept streets, crowding, and crime (Newman, 1976).

In this book psychological aspects of housing are discussed by William Michelson in his opening chapter, by Raymond Studer in relation to housing design, Charles Connerly and Robert Marans in relation to neighborhood and housing satisfaction, and Mark Baldassare in relation to crowding.

Housing and the Urban Environment

Housing is a major component of the overall plan of urban areas. Its present conditions, its use, its location, and its shape are dominant features of the urban environment (Rosenthal, 1984); its future characteristics due to revitalization projects (Gale, 1984) in the inner city and development projects in the suburbs are a constant focus of planners. The relationship of residential use of land to commercial and industrial use and to open space is another main focus of the planning profession. No urbanologist or planner can avoid dealing with the many ramifications and complexities of housing provision. In this book many aspects of the urban environment are covered. Baldassare examines residential crowding today and in the past. Connerly and Marans cover neighborhood quality, and Suzanne Keller discusses satisfaction with land use, spatial arrangement, and housing form by townhouse users. The urban environment of the inner city is detailed in terms of three types of changes: urban redevelopment, by Norman and Susan Fainstein; gentrification, revitalization, and displacement, by John Palen; and condominium conversion, by Brian O'Connell. The suburban environment today is detailed by David Popenoe.

Housing as Planned Space

Use of space in any city is planned; residential housing of various types, such as apartments, single-family dwellings, or institutional living, is allocated to certain spatial locations. Whole new towns are planned (Huttman and Huttman, 1973). Code enforcement laws, zoning regulations, and other provisions apply to housing. Planners must deal with housing in light of all these considerations; so must regional scientists (Claval, Forrester, and Goldsmith, 1980; Meier, 1983; Kmiec, 1986). In this book planning is discussed in relation to a PUD (planned unit development) by Keller, suburban and new-town development by Popenoe and by Elizabeth Huttman, urban renewal by the Fainsteins, and segregation by Diane Pearce.

Housing and Architectural Design

Housing as a structure is of concern to architects. Its design and aesthetic and technical aspects concern members of this profession and persons in the building field. Design in relation to user preference, life-style, and need is of increasing importance (Regnier, 1986; Duffy and Wilson, 1984). In this book Studer details the environmental design field. In the past, design features have sometimes been so unsatisfactory for users that the subsidized programs using this type of architecture have failed. Such is the negative impact in the case of design features of some high-rise public housing (Yancey, 1971; Priemus, 1986) and some European new-town architecture (Huttman, 1985b). Fenna Pit and Willem van Vliet— discuss these architectural failures for public housing.

Housing and Health

Housing needs to be designed to fit those with health problems, whether the disabled (Roston, 1984), the elderly (Newcomer and Frise, 1979; Struyk, 1985; Struyk and Zais, 1982; Lawton, Greenbaum, and Liebowitz, 1980), or the mentally ill homeless (Bassuk, 1986). In this book Elizabeth Huttman and Eleanor Gurewitsch discuss the housing needs of frail elderly people and the housing arrangements, or continuum of care, needed for different health categories of the elderly. Charles Hoch and Mary Jo Huth discuss the mentally ill and the alcoholic homeless and the types of housing they require, including city-subsidized single-occupancy residences (see also Felton, Lehmann, and Adler, 1981).

Housing and the Law

Various aspects of housing provision are subject to law and disputed in the courts; thus legal centers for the poor and the law profession in general have had members concerned with housing, whether in relation to rent control and eviction laws, civil rights, housing discrimination, environmental impact reports on land use, or home ownership disputes (Roisman, 1983; Hartman, 1983). Kenneth Baar and Dennis Keating cover law in relation to rent control, and Diane Pearce in relation to housing discrimination. John Gilderbloom discusses the impact of tenants' movements on laws concerning renters' rights. Housing laws supporting subsidy programs are detailed in many chapters in this book.

Housing and the Economy

Housing is an economic issue involving economic forecasting and analysis as well as economic model building. The economic aspects of the housing field are determined to a large degree by general societal economic trends such as economic growth and income elasticity of consumers, as well as alternative investment opportunities for developers and fluctuations in the money market (Kane, 1984). Other economic aspects affecting the degree of building are incentives, the cost efficiency of the building industry, and the health of lending institutions (Downs, 1983, 1985; Florida, 1986; Sternlieb and Hughes, 1983). Housing is used as a source of employment in recession and depression periods, supported by government subsidies (Mitchell, 1985; Starr, 1985; Mills, 1985). Housing is also an economic asset that owners can convert into cash through home-equity programs and second mortgages (Jacobs, 1986).

In this book the economic aspects of housing are covered by Lily Hoffman and Barbara Heisler in regard to mortgages and foreclosures; by Chester Hartman on lending institution activities; by Irving Welfeld on tax subsidies and government financial activities; and by Brian O'Connell on financing condominium conversion. Huttman and Gurewitsch in their chapter on the elderly cover home-equity conversion. R. Allen Hays in his general subsidy overview chapter covers economic trends and subsidy provision.

Housing as Policy

Subsidization of housing is a policy issue whose priority or lack of priority must be assessed by politicians. Its availability is increased by legislative actions and other government directives; its forms of tenure and location are partially determined by political values. In northern Europe after the war, provision of social housing was one of the highest-priority issues of government; in the late 1940s this was somewhat true in the United States. Legislative policy in the United States promoted a location preference for the suburbs. Federal programs such as mortgages insured by the Federal Housing Administration (FHA) and the Veterans Administration (VA) started the massive suburban migration; highway policy further encouraged workers to relocate there (Hays, 1985; Huttman, 1985a; Starr, 1985). In this book Hays, Hartman, and others discuss subsidy policy, while Popenoe discusses suburbs. Welfeld and others discuss legislative support of homeownership through allowable tax deductions for mortgage interest and property taxes—a policy that encouraged this tenure form (Quigley, 1978; Swan, 1984; U.S. Congressional Budget Office, 1981).

Housing as a Welfare Service

Subsidized housing for the poor can be seen as a welfare benefit. A subsidy is given to take care of a basic need. The constructed unit, whether public housing for families or the elderly, or nonprofit housing for the elderly or disabled or other groups, provides a standard unit at an affordable rent and also a suitable unit for those displaced by urban renewal (Huttman, 1981). For the elderly it also provides services (Struyk and Zais, 1982). Shelters for the homeless not only provide meals in many instances, but also offer counseling for those who are mentally ill, alcoholic, drug abusers, or the like (Bassuk, 1986).

Hoch and Huth provide a detailed account of the homeless situation today. Hartman discusses the increasingly severe affordability problem of the lower-income part of our population. Michael Harloe also illustrates the inability of the poor to find cheap rental housing. Karen Franck indicates the serious problems for women in poverty; Huttman and Gurewitsch, for the elderly poor; and Pearce, for the minority poor (also see Sternlieb and Hughes, 1983; Hoover, 1981).

HOUSING AS A DEMAND, SUPPLY, AND STATE-INTERVENTION ISSUE

Housing as a Demand Issue

The demand for housing is a major concern in any society. In general, housing demand is determined by such basic demographic factors as the number of households in the population, the size and composition of these households, the ages of household members, and other characteristics. Demand is also determined by the degree of household formation, which today is increasing at a much faster rate than population growth. The traditional housing demand groups are also changing. First of all, there are many more single-person households, including the elderly, the never-married, and divorced persons (Sternlieb and Hughes, 1985; Huttman, 1982; Quigley, 1978; Michelson, 1986). In addition, there is an increase in households of newly arrived immigrants. Willem van Vliet— discusses demand by young people and their household formation; Huttman and Gurewitsch do the same for the elderly; and Hoch and Huth examine various homeless groups. Hartman considers the increase in poor households that have serious housing affordability problems. Franck covers a group especially notable for this problem, the growing number of female heads of household, many of whom are recent divorcees.

A factor influencing the effective actual demand is the ability of either the consumer or the state to pay for housing of decent quality; the extent of poverty, now increasing (Sternlieb and Hughes, 1983), and the degree of government subsidies influence demand for a standard unit. In the United States cheap rental units are in great demand, and their supply is limited, as Harloe details in his chapter.

Demand also relates to the condition of the present housing stock, including the number of substandard units, the degree of overcrowding, and the degree of existence of undesirable slum areas. While overcrowding is in general no longer a problem in the United States, and substandard housing, by some criteria, is minimal, building code violations data and other evidence still indicate quality problems, as Baldassare states. City neighborhoods today possess many undesirable features, such as high crime and drug addiction rates and lack of decent amenities (Bajic, 1984; Clark, Deurloo, and Dieleman, 1984).

Americans demand higher-quality units today (Apgar, 1985), preferably new suburban housing, and a higher standard for size and number of rooms (Morris, Crull, and Winters, 1976). They want such amenities as modern bathrooms and kitchens, extensive landscaping, and three-car garages. They require quality not only in the house, but in the surrounding environment, such as found in planned new developments and adult living complexes. There is also demand for renovated inner-city dwellings close to urban cultural activities, as in gentrification areas, as Palen describes in his chapter (also see Gale, 1984).

Another factor that influences demand is type of tenure, that is, owner-occupied units versus rental units (Swan, 1984). Since World War II there has been an accelerating demand in the United States for private owner-occupied units, first for freestanding units with a lawn, and more recently for condominiums. While there has always been the assumption in the United States that housing would be private rather than a subsidized social unit, as prevalent in Europe, private rental housing has been an acceptable accommodation for many urban and lower-class and lower middle-class households. However, in the postwar period this

8   Elizabeth Huttman

has changed for many in this group; homeownership has become the predominant tenure for most families (see the chapters by Popenoe, Hartman, and Hoffman and Heisler; also see Huttman, 1985b; Clark, Deurloo, and Dielemann, 1984).

After the war new, more lenient mortgage arrangements that reduced the entry cost of purchasing single-family units were one factor that turned consumers to this suburban housing that so definitely met their tenure preference for an American dream house; another was their increased affluence in the postwar period of economic growth. The extensive postwar construction of federally supported highways increased the accessibility of this suburban location to their work. By the 1980s suburban home ownership was so much the tenure norm that housing problems of the poor in inner-city slums or of the whole inner-city rental sector seemed remote to most American homeowners. Their concern instead was centered on mortgage interest rates and production of new affordable houses for purchase, that is, on the new housing supply. Popenoe describes this suburban scene in his chapter.

The Supply Side: Provision of Housing Stock

Continual provision of a supply of new housing to meet demand is of course the basic issue in the housing field (Sternlieb and Hughes, 1983; Grebler and Mittelbach, 1979; Downs, 1985). This is covered in several of the following chapters, including those by Hays, Frieden, Harloe, Pit and Van Vliet— and Hartman. The demand for homeownership in the suburbs in the postwar years was answered because of improvement of several supply-side factors, such as more lenient mortgage terms. In the postwar period these allowed homeownership in suburban tract developments to become more possible for even manual-worker families. Since the war there has been a revolution in building and mortgage lending practices. Large-scale capital investment underwrote development of massive suburban housing estates with cheap home purchase prices, low down payments, and feasible mortgage arrangements. The 30-year mortgage replaced the 5- to 10-year one, and the 10 to 20 percent down payment replaced the 50 percent or more down payment. This improved lending arrangement was partially the result of FHA and VA policies of insuring mortgages and thus removing the risks from the lending institutions (Downs, 1985), making them both more willing to lend to lower middle-class households and to do this on better terms. Cheaper prices were a result of the developer's ability to assemble tracts of cheap land in the suburbs. This development phenomenon was also due to investors' preference for this type of housing investment rather than that of landlord-managed rental investment with its problems of long-term responsibilities for the property and of meeting city rental housing regulations such as building codes and tenant rights, even rent control, as Baar and Keating's chapter details.

Housing Supply as a Dynamic Process

The cyclical and anticyclical effects of the economy play a part in construction of housing. The interplay between this new supply of housing and the total housing stock, as Harloe and others point out in their chapters (also see Downs, 1983), and the aggregate of demand from a wide variety of groups of users present a varying and dynamic situation. The many stakeholder groups on the housing scene, from the consumer groups of the elderly, single-family households, and the newly married to the production-sector groups of developers and contractors, financial lending institutions, realtors, and government subsidy interventionists, interact in different time periods in different ways to produce a dramatically fluid, ever-changing housing situation. Always influencing this process is the configuration of such dynamic factors on the demand side as demographic trends, disposable income levels, and the changing urban landscape, and on the supply side, the abundance of or restraints on economic resources, the general money market situation, land availability, construction technology, and costs. Also dynamic are shifting political allegiances and political orientations to housing provision and the type of intervention by government (Struyk, Mayer, and Tuccillo, 1983).

Supply and Finance

The housing industry operates within the larger economic framework. Economic conditions and government policies influence the flow of credit to the construction industry based on the situation in the money market, on interest rates, and on the position of the mortgage lending institutions (Florida, 1986). Other economic factors, such as the price of materials and of land for residential housing use, also influence supply (Fare and Yoon, 1984).

There is a crisis in the housing industry today caused by costs of building, land, labor, and, until very recently, money due to double-digit interest rates. The industry is largely countercyclical, for when interest rates rise (normally with improvement of economic conditions), housing investment becomes less popular because of competing attractive alternative investments. Thus as interest rates rise, money available for mortgage lending declines and consumer demand drops; housing starts often decline due to high interest rates (see the chapters by Hartman and by Hoffman and Heisler).

These disruptions make the supply of housing a fluctuating commodity. Fiscal monetary policies affect both monies to build a supply of housing and the cost of new units; this cost and mortgage interest rates influence demand for such units. Housing starts at any particular time have an impact on the number of older units available to filter down from households buying new units. Not only investment policies and the cost of money, but disposable income levels and economic growth rates influence the degree of housing construction and purchase, as do tax incentives. These factors can also determine the financial profitability of building apartments (multi-family units) versus single-family owner-occupied dwellings or alternative investment in other enterprises. In the 1960s there was a boom in apartment building, but today there is a reluctance by investors to invest in apartments due to the unprofitability related to many of these factors and the recent tax law change with its lengthened depreciation period (this is covered in Harloe's rental housing chapter; see also Huttman and Huttman, 1986).

Of these economic factors, the cost of building plays a major part in determining the supply of new housing. Today, labor and materials as well as land prices and up-front developmental expenses make costs high (see Van Vliet—on young people buying). The average cost of building a new single-family dwelling in the United States was over $122,000 in 1986 (selling price), and over $135,000 in the Los Angeles and San Francisco areas (see Hartman's chapter).

Attempts to cut costs have not been very successful. A continuing attempt has been made to increase the use of industrialized prefabricated parts. However, because the housing construction industry is so fragmented, with many small builders constructing 10 or fewer units a year, this industrialization is difficult. As a major government report on the housing industry states, there are many subgroups involved in housing production and sale:

These housing assemblers include homebuilders, contractors, home manufacturers (and their dealers) and mobile home producers. These firms procure their materials from an extraordinary range of building products managers, from tiny millwork plants to some of the nation's largest corporations . . . acquisition and preparation of land for the ultimate construction of housing commonly involves real estate brokers, lawyers, title insurance companies, surveyors, and civil engineers and possibly land planners and landscape architects. Engineers and architects are sometimes involved in design. Much on-site construction work is characteristically performed by special subcontractors: painting, plumbing, and electrical work, for example. Financing, needed by both the builders to complete construction and development, and by buyers to finance purchase of completed units, is available through a battery of lending institutions. Operation of apartments may involve superintendents or management firms. Maintenance of housing adds to the cast of characters—for example, repair men, janitors, remodeling firms and domestic workers. (President's Commission on Housing, 1968: 13)

With all these actors in the housing industry, it is hard to keep costs down (Fare and Yoon, 1984). The large-scale developers, increasingly present in the postwar period, do have better ability to utilize industrialized methods because of their massive building of units on large acreages of assembled land, but even here there has been a slow evolution to industrialized methods. Unlike auto production, building of houses is hardly a uniform nationwide activity limited to a few dozen models; even the individual developer has to offer a number of models, each built to that particular city's building codes and the customer's local style preferences, with some individuality of house appearance made apparent to the buyer. Industrialization is usually limited to certain components being factory-made, such as sectionalized rooms and wall panels or bathroom units, and this cost-efficiency component is often offset by costs of getting the industrialized segment to the site. On the site itself there has been cost-saving industrialization such as planned patterns of assembly and joining, operations that narrow the specialization of the work that a construction worker does. From this and other factors overall cost savings have evolved due to optimum scheduling of on-site work and control of the process. However, the kind of modules futurists discuss as cost savings are not now in wide use and are often not manufactured to be compatible with other parts. Only in the manufacture of mobile homes has industrialization reached a high level of realization (Pastalan, 1984). Over one-fourth of annual housing starts are mobile homes.

Another trend to cut costs in a few projects of subsidized housing is self-building of homes, with use of subcontractors for specialty work. We may see this trend increase. Another cost cutter some special developers that serve the low end of the housing-purchase market are trying is to reduce the size of the house, but at the same time designing it for later expandability. However, many American consumers will not accept fewer than three bedrooms (though perhaps smaller in size), two baths, and a two- or three-car garage. Some building ordinances and zoning codes, in fact, insist on certain amenities such as off-street parking and certain house and lot sizes.

Availability and Price of Land

House costs also include land costs, and this cost is increasing as a proportion of total cost (National Association of Home Builders [NAHB], 1982). Availability of vacant urban land and cost of land affect the supply of housing (the number of new housing starts) and the character of the housing (whether it is low-density or cluster housing, or high-rise; see Keller's chapter on PUDs). Local government regulations on land use also have an effect on numbers and characteristics of units built.

In the postwar period the supply of vacant land in inner cities greatly decreased; the land available has been in-filling sites, including those opened by demolition, and much of this land has been used for office buildings and other non-residential purposes. More plentiful supplies of vacant land are found on the metropolitan fringes; this has meant that new residential building has had to be concentrated there. In these suburban areas large vacant parcels have been assembled by developers who have gone through the process of developing this raw land, putting in such up-front amenities as sidewalks, roads, and sewage hookups, and making these expenditures (varying with the size of the lot) part of the total house purchase price. These developer costs today often include costs for extra amenities demanded by city planning departments in exchange for approval of environmental impact reports (EIRs); these include parks and other open space that the limited-growth opponents to development demand.

Land costs are also influenced by local zoning ordinances that specify the size of the plot and of the house on it. Many experts see these zoning restrictions as major inhibitors of production of low-cost housing units and of multi-family housing in general (see Harloe's chapter on rental housing and Hartman's on affordability).

The Filtering Process

A part of the housing market dynamics is the filtering or trickling-down process, whereby a household moves up to a better-quality or higher-priced house or a better location—a more desirable house in the public's mind—and its former house filters or trickles down to some other household. One move leads to another, and this constant flow of people through the housing stock represents a major dynamic aspect of the housing market (Braid, 1984).

The idea is that as new housing is built, that is, as the housing supply is enlarged, households at the higher-income spectrum will move into these new units and open up their older and presumably cheaper units to others; the older housing will trickle down in price, thus becoming available to somewhat poorer families. Filtering (Braid, 1984) is associated with technological obsolescence, style obsolescence, and deterioration. Besides these quality and age variables, the desirability of a location also causes filtering, with those of higher income willing to pay a higher price for the most desirable location. In fact, location can mean "filtering up" of older housing, now desirable after rehabilitation, with higher-income groups moving in, as in gentrification areas (see Palen's chapter).

Household characteristics such as income and race influence the degree to which the household can take advantage of filtering possibilities and determine where households are located in the housing stock (Palm, 1985). Households can only take advantage of changes in the housing market if their income allows it; this income elasticity is an important factor. Researchers such as Smith (1973) have studied the filtering response to changes in income composition. Grigsby (1973) has postulated in relation to this income variable and price of housing that

the farther down the scale [in housing values] that new construction can be injected [into the market], the larger the excess of units, absolutely, needed to check further building, and the greater the ultimate effect at the bottom of the market. Equally the effect of low-priced construction will be felt much sooner at the bottom since the impact is transmitted a shorter distance. Regardless of the initial level, the impact will be felt much more rapidly in the rental market since more frequent occupancy changes cause the influence of new construction to travel faster throughout this sector of the supply. (p. 85)

The filtering theory has been found to be very imperfect and has caused much debate. First, the housing market is very segmented, with the black population and other minorities often finding it difficult to take advantage of units made vacant by moves of whites to new housing. The vacated units do not open up to them due to exclusionary housing market situations and their income limitations. In an early study of black movers, Lansing and Morgan (1973) stated that they were forced to conclude "that Negroes benefited less than whites from new construction. There is some shifting of dwellings from whites to Negroes as sequences of moves develop, but not enough for Negroes to benefit in proportion to their numbers.'' This finding is confirmed by recent data (Kmiec, 1986; Palm, 1985). Aspects of this are covered in Pearce's chapter on housing segregation.

Another limitation to the filtering theory relates to a landlord's ability to drop the rent for older, less adequate units to a level that allows the very poor to afford them. Costs of maintenance, property taxes, insurance, and mortgage indebtedness force ''slum'' landlords to abandon buildings instead (Sternlieb, 1973; Lawson, 1986). Mandelker and Montgomery (1973) state that ''as the filtering process was supposed to work, all housing was eventually to filter down. But in many cities in the country, especially in poor housing areas, thousands of units filtered out of the housing market altogether . . . what happened was that costs simply exceeded rent income, and the owner walked away from this investment.'' In New York City, for example, Sternlieb (1973) found that many landlords were low-income owners who could not even take advantage of the depreciation allowance for the building on their tax form due to their income bracket. Rent control, he found, limited the rent income they got from buildings. Their solution was abandonment, here defined as landlords ''no longer providing services to an occupied building and allowing taxes and mortgages to go unpaid, and thus the building becomes uninhabitable by all but depreciation standards'' (Sternlieb 1973: 105). In many cities, block after block of such abandoned structures are found, usually related to a decline of the neighborhood and often to ethnic/racial and income change in the composition of the renter population, causing disinvestment in the property (Lawson, 1986).

The fact is that rents can only go so low before investors find profitability lacking and negative cash flow high. Then these investors/landlords move out of the rental housing business, leaving poor households with fewer affordable rentals. This situation increases the demand for more subsidized housing. The degree to which the state intervenes to alleviate this situation varies (see Hartman's chapter on rental affordability and Harloe's chapter on rental housing).

The State's Role in Housing

The state can play different roles in meeting housing demand and increasing the supply. The levels of state intervention in the housing sector can be categorized as (1) minimal involvement; (2) a moderate level of involvement with emphasis on provision of social housing and an orientation to social equality in housing; or (3) comprehensive or inclusive planning and engineering of most housing production and management (Donnison and Ungerson, 1982). These levels of state involvement have a relationship to the political orientation of the government in power, especially regarding values on state intervention, and to its leaders' perception of housing as a major priority, first in terms of need and in relation to other demands on the federal budget, and then in terms of the economic climate of the day.

A minimal level of state involvement in housing has been the orientation of the Reagan administration. Limited resources have been devoted to housing compared to defense and other budget categories. The consensus is that dwelling units should be privately built and owned; production of public housing is considered undesirable. The government no longer considers subsidization of the housing industry necessary to decrease unemployment, as it did in the late 1930s. Nor is the national government willing to take major steps to address the affordability problem or the homeless issue. The Reagan administration is also uninterested in providing subsidies for a more planned environment, as the chapter by Hays on subsidies points out.

The picture is somewhat different at the state and local government levels. State housing agencies display variations in approach; some states with a conservative political orientation see no necessity for major state intervention in the housing market, while other states feel an obligation to respond to demand for affordable housing and housing for specific groups such as farm workers and the elderly. Local governments have done likewise. Seeing housing as a basic interest, they have intervened to provide social housing, especially to groups that cannot easily have their housing needs satisfactorily met in the open market. Historically this role has been taken by our national government when the Democratic party has controlled the legislative outcome. The role has always been a residual one, however, of mainly providing social housing, with the government allowing supply and demand forces of the private market to operate for most residents (see Frieden's chapter on the housing allowance approach). This has been felt to be possible because of a substantial national private lending apparatus as well as a lively private building industry, both operating in a growth economy situation in most of the postwar period (see the chapters of Hays and Hartman on subsidies).

In some policy contexts this social housing role is considered too limited. Second, with social housing (publicly built units and subsidized nonprofit housing) only about 3 percent of all American units, our commitment to social housing is very weak compared to that of other countries such as Britain, with 30 percent council housing (although under the Thatcher government this is decreasing). Pit and Van Vliet— detail public housing in the United States. This limited role of government is also criticized for producing a dual housing market or two housing classes, those few in social housing and the rest in private-market units, even though in reality this latter middle-class market is subsidized through indirect tax subsidies, mortgages at below-market interest rate in some cases and government-insured mortgages (FHA- and VA-insured mortgages) in others. Welfeld in his chapter covers these tax subsidies as do Pit and Van Vliet—.

The comprehensive housing policy level, whereby government plans, regulates, and subsidizes the whole housing sector, is the level that some suggest that American housing policymakers should move toward, a level that exemplifies the Swedish and even more the Eastern European governments' approach to housing policy. To some degree American policies do have some attributes found in the comprehensive approach; for example, in a minor way we develop estimates and projections of the country's housing requirements through the U.S. Department of Housing and Urban Development (HUD) and through local housing assistance plans, and we do draw up long-term plans, though seldom of a comprehensive nature encompassing all forms of house building. We also seldom include detailed statements on the government's own contribution to this projection. Ours is a more marginal state intervention and not a major aspect of any national planning. Second, the federal and state governments do not make a major effort to marshal a substantial amount of savings and other capital for new building, though till recently they designated savings and loan associations as lending institutions to carry on this role as their major function; in addition, they have allowed tax investment shelters in low-income housing. Nor does the federal government actively control the total output of new housing through regulations or subsidies or relate its subsidy programs to its activities in other sectors of the economy except in some minor ways, encouraging housing production in recession periods (such as the Johnson administration's heavy subsidization of housing in the mid-1960s). Nor does the U.S. government determine housing size, standards, and cost in the way many Western and Eastern European countries do for their large subsidized housing sectors; yet our local governments do have housing standards controlled by building departments and zoning ordinance enforcers. For existing units our local governments also have some control over rents where rent control laws have been enacted, though again hardly to the degree existing in countries classified as comprehensive housing types. Baar and Keating cover rent controls in detail in this book. The U.S. government has some effect on interest rates on mortgages through the Federal Reserve Bank's role in setting the prime rate. Hoffman and Heisler in this volume discuss the government's role in home financing.

Housing Goals for State Provision

In the classification of the different state approaches to housing, the goals of these state housing subsidy programs were mentioned. Governments subsidize housing for a wide variety of reasons. A basic reason is to insure that everyone has a dwelling to live in. Another goal that is prominent is provision of a standard uncrowded unit with plumbing; in the United States the slogan from 1949 on was "a decent home for all Americans" (Starr, 1985). A goal of greater prominence today is provision of housing that is affordable, housing that is not too high a financial burden in relation to income. Another goal is provision of this housing to all comers, regardless of race, ethnic background, sex, family composition, or age (Huttman, 1976). The desired consequence government policymakers want from realization of these goals is greater equality in housing quality and location between different groups. As part of this goal they want dispersal of low- and moderate-income households and ethnic/racial groups throughout the whole area, rather than concentrations in slum areas.

Other goals often concern improvement of blighted areas, with reversal of trends toward abandonment and deterioration. Goals may be even broader and aim at provision of a large planned environment with amenities, such as a new town, or at a large area urban renewal or rehabilitation project, such as those mentioned by the Fainsteins in their urban renewal chapter or Keller in her discussion of PUDs.

Government policymakers over the years have had a variety of other goals or aims in subsidizing housing. Policymakers may use housing as a reward for key workers or as an incentive to encourage workers to work in undesirable areas or in growth industries. The goal may be to give workers cheaper shelter in high-priced areas like the computer industry area of Silicon Valley, California, by providing such incentives for construction as a tax shelter for investors. Or the goal may be to locate new development outside a sprawling suburban area (the 1970 subsidy of U.S. new communities). Government goals have been simply to rehabilitate cities or increase the postwar quantity of housing (FHA-insured mortgages) or to help the building industry work in a period of unemployment (during the 1930s depression period). The goals may be to lessen social unrest, to provide a social wage in a low-wage area, or to eradicate potential health problems (Donnison and Ungerson, 1982). Pit and Van Vliet— in this volume give reasons for building public housing.

Strategies for Provision of Subsidies

Governments provide subsidies in a variety of different forms; many are mentioned briefly here and in more detail in the chapter by Hays. There is continual debate not only on the most efficient way to provide the subsidies, but on the degree to which these strategies accomplish their desired goals. There is also debate over which groups in society intentionally should or unintentionally do benefit from particular strategies (Donnison and Ungerson, 1982); and over the type of tenure group (renters or owners) that should be subsidized (Huttman, 1985a). There is discussion as to whether the subsidy should go for new building or for rehabilitation, whether it should be given in terms of placing people in buildings, as in conventional public housing, or given to the person, as with a housing allowance (see Frieden's chapter), and whether the subsidy should be used to improve a whole area, as in urban renewal or rehabilitation, or even to develop a whole new area, as with new-town subsidies (see the chapters by Palen on rehabilitation, the Fainsteins on urban renewal, O'Connell on condominium conversion, and Huttman on new towns).

One long-term debate regarding subsidies is at what level in the housing stock the state should intervene. Many economists have argued that the state should assist the middle class to purchase new units; they conceptualize that this means that the vacated older housing will filter down to the poorer-income groups. However, filtering has proved to be an unreliable process because of segregated housing markets and because of the low income of many families (Braid, 1984).

Some experts believe that subsidies should be targeted directly to those most in need, the inadequately housed, but these experts disagree among themselves on whether new units should be built for these poor or working-class groups or whether the poor instead should be subsidized to live in older units as in the Section 8 program. The government usually will try several routes simultaneously, such as support of public housing and Section 8 (see the chapter by Hays).

Policymakers differ as to whether the strategy should be for the state itself to provide the subsidized housing, to subsidize through nonprofit groups, or to let the subsidized user of a housing allowance look for housing on the private market (Section 8). Strategies can also involve the consumer in the housing program, whether by building housing (self-help low-income projects) or by managing it. Subsidies can take a variety of forms, such as a grant or loan for rehabilitation; mortgages at below-market interest rates for purchase of new housing, either to an individual or to a nonprofit organization; a rent allowance to pay part of the rent; an outright capital grant to an organization to build units; and other government measures such as tax incentives, rent controls, and zoning.

This discussion of the many demand and supply factors and the possible roles and strategies of governments in meeting demand, enhancing supply, and promoting certain goals should provide a framework for the chapters to follow, as should the detailing of the many dimensions of the housing field, from sociopsychological to environmental (including architecture and planning), health, welfare and policy considerations.

REFERENCES

Adams, John. 1984. "Presidential Address: The Meaning of Housing in America." *Annals of the Association of American Geographers* 74, no. 4: 515–526.

Altman, Irving, and Carol Werner (eds.). 1985. *Home Environments*. New York: Plenum Press.

Apgar, William C., Jr. 1985. *Recent Trends in Housing Quality and Affordability: An Assessment*. Working Paper no. W85–1. Cambridge, Mass.: Joint Center for Housing Studies.

Bajic, Vladimir. 1984. "An Analysis of the Demand for Housing Attributes." *Applied Economics* 16:599–610.

Bassuk, Ellen (ed.). 1986. *The Mental Health Needs of Homeless Persons*. New Directions for Mental Health Services, no. 30. San Francisco: Jossey-Bass.

Blum, Terry C., and Paul Kingston. 1984. "Homeownership and Social Attachment." *Sociological Perspectives* 27, no. 2:159–180.

Braid, Ralph M. 1984. "The Effects of Government Housing Policies in a Vintage Filtering Model." *Journal of Urban Economics* 16: 272–296.

Clark, W. A. V., M. C. Deurloo, and F. N. Dieleman. 1984. "Housing Consumption and Residential Mobility." *Annals of the Association of American Geographers* 74, no. 1: 29–43.

Claval, Pierre, John Forrester, and William Goldsmith. 1980. *Urban Planning in an Age of Austerity*. New York: Pergamon Press.

Cooke, Timothy, and Bruce Hamilton. 1984. "Evolution of Urban Housing Stocks: A

Model Applied to Baltimore and Houston." *Journal of Urban Economics* 16: 317–338.

Donnison, David, and Clare Ungerson. 1982. *Housing Policy*. Harmondsworth: Penguin Books.

Downs, Anthony. 1983. *Rental Housing in the 1980's*. Washington, D.C.: Brookings Institution.

———. 1985. *The Revolution in Real Estate Finance*. Washington, D.C.: Brookings Institution.

Duffy, Michael, and Victor Wilson. 1984. "The Role of Design Factors of the Residential Environment in the Physical and Mental Health of the Elderly." *Journal of Housing for the Elderly* 2, no. 3: 37–45.

Fare, Rolf, and Bong Joon Yoon. 1984. "Technological Change in Urban Housing Production." *Journal of Urban Economics* 16: 351–356.

Felton, Barbara, Stanley Lehmann, and Arlene Adler. 1981. "Single-Room Occupancy Hotels: Their Viability as Housing Options for Older Citizens." In M. Powell Lawton and Sally Hoover (eds.), *Community Housing Choices for Older Americans*. New York: Springer.

Florida, R. L. 1986. "The Political Economy of Financial Deregulation and the Reorganization of Housing Finance in the United States." *International Journal of Urban and Regional Research* 10, no. 2: 207–231.

Gale, Dennis. 1984. *Neighborhood Revitalization and the Postindustrial City*. Lexington, Mass.: Lexington Books.

Grebler, Leo, and Frank Mittelbach. 1979. *The Inflation of House Prices*. Lexington, Mass.: D. C. Heath.

Grigsby, William. 1973. "Housing Markets and Public Policy." In Daniel Mandelker and Roger Montgomery (eds.), *Housing in America*. Indianapolis: Bobbs-Merrill.

Hartman, Chester (ed.). 1983. *America's Housing Crisis: What Is to Be Done*. Boston: Routledge & Kegan Paul.

Hays, R. Allen. 1985. *The Federal Government and Urban Housing*. Albany, N.Y.: State University of New York Press.

Helper, Rose. 1986. "Success and Resistance Factors in the Maintenance of Racially Mixed Neighborhoods." In John Goering (ed.) *Housing Desegregation and Federal Policy*. Chapel Hill: University of North Carolina Press.

Hoover, Sally. 1981. "Black and Spanish Elderly: Their Housing Characteristics and Housing Quality." In M. Powell Lawton and Sally Hoover (eds.), *Community Housing Choices for Older Americans*. New York: Springer.

Hummon, David M. 1985. "House, Home, and Identity." *Sociological Inquiry*, 23–34.

Huttman, Elizabeth. 1976. *Class Mix in New Towns: Report on NIMH-Sponsored Research*. Hayward: California State University.

———. 1981. "Social Work Services in the Housing Field." In Neil Gilbert and Harry Specht (eds.), *Handbook of the Social Services*. Englewood Cliffs, N.J.: Prentice-Hall.

———. 1982. "Housing Formation and Life Style as Indicators of Housing Need." Paper presented at the World Congress of Sociology meetings, Mexico City, August 18.

———. 1985a "Policy Approaches to Social Housing in Northern and Western Europe." In Willem van Vliet—, Elizabeth Huttman, and Sylvia Fava (eds.), *Housing Needs and Policy Approaches: Trends in Thirteen Countries.* Durham, N.C.: Duke University Press.

————. 1985b "Transnational Housing Policy." In Irving Altman and Carol Werner (eds.), *Home Environments.* New York: Plenum Press.

Huttman, Elizabeth, and John Huttman. 1986. "An Economic and Social Analysis of the International Private Rental Housing Crisis." Paper presented at the International Research Conference on Housing Policy, Gävle, Sweden, June.

Huttman, John, and Elizabeth Huttman. 1973. "Dutch and British New Towns: Self-Containment and Socio-Economic Balance." *Growth and Change*, January, 30–37.

Jacobs, Bruce. 1986. "The National Potential of Home Equity Conversion." *Gerontologist* 26, no. 5: 496–504.

Kain, John, and John Quigley. 1970. "Evaluating the Quality of the Residential Environment." *Environment and Planning* 2 (January): 23–32.

Kane, Edward. 1984. "Change and Progress in Contemporary Mortgage Markets." *Housing Finance Review* 3, no. 3: 257–284.

Kendig, Hal. 1984. "Housing Careers, Life Cycle, and Residential Mobility Implications for the Housing Market." *Urban Studies* 21: 271–283.

Kmiec, D. W. 1986. "Exclusionary Zoning and Purposeful Racial Segregation in Housing." *Urban Lawyer* 18, no. 2: 393–422.

Lawson, Ronald (ed.). 1986. *The Tenant Movement in New York City, 1904–1984.* New Brunswick, N.J.: Rutgers University Press.

Lawton, M. Powell, E. Brody, and P. Turner-Massey. 1978. "The Relationship of Environmental Factors to Changes in Well-Being." *Gerontologist* 18, no. 3: 137.

Lawton, M. Powell, Maurice Greenbaum, and Bernard Liebowitz. 1980. "The Lifespan of Housing Environments for the Aging." *Gerontologist* 20, no. 1: 56–63.

Lindamood, S., and S. Hanna. 1979. *Housing, Society, and Consumers.* St. Paul, Minn.: West Publishing.

Mandelker, Daniel, and Roger Montgomery (eds.). 1973. *Housing in America.* Indianapolis: Bobbs-Merrill.

Meier, Ron. 1983. "Code Enforcement and Housing Quality Revisited: The Turnover Case." *Urban Affairs Quarterly* 19, no. 2: 255–273.

Michelson, William. 1986. "Housing in a Way of Life." In Leon Deben and Dick van der Vaart (eds.), *International Conference on Housing Research and Policy Issues in an Era of Fiscal Austerity.* Amsterdam: Gestructureerde Samenwerking.

Mills, Edwin S. 1985. "Open Housing Laws as a Stimulus to Central City Employment." *Journal of Urban Economics* 17: 184–188.

Mitchell, J. Paul. 1985. "Historical Overview of Direct Federal Housing Assistance." In J. Paul Mitchell (ed.), *Federal Housing Policy and Programs, Past and Present.* New Brunswick, N.J.: Center for Urban Policy Research, Rutgers University.

Morris, Earl, S. R. Crull, and Mary Winters. 1976. "Housing Norms, Housing Satisfaction, and the Propensity to Move." *Journal of Marriage and the Family* 38: 309–320.

National Association of Home Builders. 1982. *Land Use and Construction Regulations: A Builder's View.* Washington, D.C.: NAHB.

Newcomer, Robert, and L. Frise. 1979. "Housing in the Continuum of Care." *Generations* 3: 13–14.

Newman, Oscar. 1976. *Design Guidelines for Creating Defensible Space*. Washington, D.C.: Law Enforcement Assistance Administration.

Palm, Risa. 1985. "Ethnic Segmentation of Real Estate Agent Practices in the Urban Housing Market." *Annals of the Association of American Geographers* 75, no. 1: 58–68.

Pastalan, Leon. 1984. "Manufactured Homes for the Elderly." *Journal of Housing for the Elderly* 2, no. 3: 89–92.

President's Commission on Housing. 1968. *Report*. Washington, D.C.: Government Printing Office.

Priemus, Hugo. 1986. "Post-War Public High-Rise Estates: What Went Wrong with Housing Policy, with Design, and with Management." *Netherlands Journal of Housing and the Environment* 1, no. 2: 157–186.

Quigley, John M. 1978. "Housing Markets and Housing Demand: Analytic Responses." In Larry Bourne and John Hitchcock (eds.), *Urban Housing Markets: Recent Directions in Research and Policy*. Toronto: University of Toronto Press. 23–44.

Regnier, Victor. 1986. "Design Trends and Resident Preferences in Congregate Housing." *Gerontologist* 26, no. 10: 239A. Abstract.

Roisman, Florence. 1983. "Legal Strategies for Protecting Low Income Housing." In Chester Hartman (ed.), *America's Housing Crisis: What Is to Be Done?* Boston: Routledge & Kegan Paul.

Rosenthal, Donald. 1984. "Joining Housing Rehabilitation to Neighborhood Revitalization: The Section 8 Neighborhood Strategy Area Program." In R. Eyestone (ed.), *Public Policy Formation*. Greenwich, Conn.: JAI Press.

Roston, J. 1984. "The Physically Disabled: An International Audit of Housing Policies." *Public Health* 98: 247–255.

Smith, Wallace. 1973. "The Income Level of New Housing Demand." In Daniel Mandelker and Roger Montgomery (eds.), *Housing in America*. Indianapolis: Bobbs-Merrill.

Starr, R. 1985. "Twenty Years of Housing Programs." *Public Interest* 81 (Fall): 82–93.

Sternlieb, George. 1973. "The Tenant Landlord." In Daniel Mandelker and Roger Montgomery (eds.), *Housing in America*. Indianapolis: Bobbs-Merrill.

Sternlieb, George, and James W. Hughes, 1983. "Housing the Poor in a Post-Shelter Society." *Annals of the American Academy of Political and Social Science* 465 (January): 109–122.

———. 1985. "Demographics and Housing in America." *Population Bulletin* 41, no. 1: 1–34.

Struyk, Raymond. 1985. "Future Housing Assistance Policy for the Elderly." *Gerontologist* 25, no. 1: 41–46.

Struyk, R., and J. Zais. 1982. *Providing Special Dwelling Features for the Elderly with Health and Mobility Problems*. Washington, D.C.: Urban Institute Press.

Struyk, R., N. Mayer, and J. Tuccillo. 1983. *Federal Housing Policy at President Reagan's Midterm*. Washington, D.C.: Urban Institute Press.

Swan, Craig. 1984. "A Model of Rental and Owner-Occupied Housing." *Journal of Urban Economics* 16: 297–316.

U.S. Congressional Budget Office. 1981. *The Tax Treatment of Home Ownership: Issues and Options*. Washington, D.C.: Government Printing Office.

Yancey, William L. 1971. "Architecture, Interaction, and Social Control: The Case of a Large-Scale Public Housing Project." *Environment and Behavior* 3, no 1: 3–21.

PART I

THE CONTEXT OF HOUSING

1

The Societal Functions of Housing

WILLIAM MICHELSON

This handbook provides dramatic testimony to the diversity of considerations inherent in housing. These considerations represent many aspects of the spaces in which people live and the contexts in which they are found. Included are many types of processes by which housing is created and managed, and the insights and findings of many disciplines. This variety of factors presents the well-intentioned housing analyst with the burden of making progress while simultaneously dealing honestly with untold complexity. Not only do we have a legacy of considerations inherited from the past, but the times are always a-changin'!

For anyone who has assimilated the complexities of this literature, nothing that anyone would write here could make housing appear simple again. Nonetheless, the kaleidoscopic development of housing research might be to some extent clarified by an examination of the circumstances under which certain of the emphases emerged. The arrival of complexity was not like spontaneous combustion. Rather, it occurred over time and within societal contexts.

In this chapter I would like to examine some of the societal functions of housing. The aim is to show that particular interests in housing research were given priority in view of emergent societal issues. This not only helps put some order into the host of factors but alerts us to the onset of additional factors in the future.

BACKWARD

In their book *Housing and Residential Structure* (1980), Keith Bassett and John Short provide both a historical and critical approach to the different perspectives brought to bear by researchers on housing. Their coverage includes the Chicago School's explanation of residential patterning, other more recent sociological views incorporating considerations of life cycle and life-style (that is, demographic and behavioral considerations), geographic views focusing heavily on accessibility, and, at greater length, the nearly contemporary explanations leaning heavily on Marxist theory. While the foci chosen are, in the context of the present book, extremely selective, they do illustrate clearly how scholarly attention can vary over time. Yet there is an attitude expressed that is typical to science: one must determine which perspective is most fruitful, as if they were mutually exclusive and one therefore had to select among them rather than to benefit from their respective contributions.

When undertaking basic research, scientists have the latitude to play with theories and their respective merits. But when one applies the scientific outlook to tangible phenomena, complexity of explanation is more pertinent, because the different aspects of the phenomena are not kept in watertight compartments in the real world. Housing, whether a product or a process, is surely tangible and the function of many forces.

The argument of this chapter is that the various explanatory approaches to housing did not appear over time as a reflection of scientific superiority concerning a static problem or phenomenon (like theories of the universe). Rather, the scientific agenda followed developments in society that made certain approaches appear necessary and desirable. The argument is therefore that these approaches concerning housing are inherently complementary but have been brought into the limelight at fixed moments in history by the societal problems of the time. Like those of Bassett and Short, my examples are a sample, as are the works cited. This is not a one-chapter history of housing, but an illustration of a point.

The Industrial Revolution and Its Wake

Advances in technology begot both mechanized industry and rationalized agriculture, which in turn begot cities with unprecedentedly large populations. The rules of the game in the emergent societies of the industrial revolution were those of free-market capitalism. Thus housing for the huge numbers of persons attracted to the growing cities was a subsidiary sector of an economy based on supply and demand, profit and loss, and the invisible hand presumed to coordinate by common logic the actions of countless individual entrepreneurs.

No one claimed that typical rural living conditions were wonderful. Privacy and sanitation were not household words. Living conditions for the great urban masses in England, the Continent, and the largest American and Canadian cities were dreadful by our modern standards, but at the time they were accepted as part of the progress of the industrialized society—for a while. Then some of the dysfunctions of the urban, industrial society became evident, no doubt magnified and exacerbated by the highly visible critical mass of affected persons. Contrasts between wealth and poverty became apparent. The latter appeared to accompany problems with health and moral turpitude.

Housing was part of this societal system. No one could claim that most housing was good, and many hypothesized that it was bad, but what is indisputable is that it was visible. Thus whether the critical observer tried to explain social problems from a liberal or socialist point of view, housing could be fair play (that is liberal analysts could discuss it without questioning free enterprise in the larger sense). Marx ([1867–94] 1967) and Engels ([1845] 1973, [1873] 1975), for example, put housing explicitly into their observations and discussions (see Dear and Scott, 1981). Charles Booth's surveys of poverty in London (1889–1903) included the documentation of housing conditions. In America the journalistic muckraking at the turn of this century was very critical in its attribution of ills to poor housing (for example, Riis, 1890; Steffens, 1931); this approach left the reader with the resolve to do something about housing standards in order to solve social and health problems.

The most organized academic research of the time offered no such message, but did tie living conditions to the underlying societal structure. The Chicago School of sociology, so maligned now for its supposedly uncritical approach to urban problems (Castells, 1977), nonetheless did tie the nature and distribution of residential districts to the larger and presumably unchangeable capitalist system of land valuation and land use (Park, Burgess, and McKenzie, 1925). These so-called subsocial forces, which thrust population subgroups together in particular kinds and locations of neighborhoods, were thus thought responsible for many novel behavioral outcomes of particular agglomerations of population, even though the researchers at the same time eschewed consideration that something could be done about the conditions spawned.

Public housing was an offspring of those in society who felt that housing did play a role in its health and that intervention in housing markets was possible. To them, housing was not only an economic aspect of the larger society, but a factor in societal welfare. On the latter ground one could justify public-sector intervention beyond the apparent limits of the private market to make available safe and sanitary housing to those unable to get it through normal market channels. Thus the industrial revolution and its wake successively brought economic and welfare functions of housing to the fore. Large, central-city public housing projects came to complement private-market activities, reflecting the expanded societal viewpoints.

Suburbanism

Suburbs go back to the Renaissance. But the housing research questions that accompany the building of large numbers of homes in relatively low-density settings removed from traditional central cities (Popenoe, 1977, 1985) depended on the societal conditions responsible for the great growth of this form and location of dwelling. Transportation technology was necessary so that suburbanites could get to employment, commerce, and recreation despite the absence of the traditional densities supporting customary urban transit. Yet the shape, form, and dominance of the suburbs we know reflected two other functions that housing fulfills. One is to support family formation and the accompanying raising of children. Where housing is in short supply, leading to overcrowding or the occupancy of units considered inappropriate, life-cycle flexibility and mobility are constrained. Suburban housing was an answer to the needs of millions of World War II veterans who had largely delayed normal family activity and were returning to a housing supply made stagnant by the war. Second, government housing bureaucrats wanted security for the investments that banks and other financial organizations were making in housing and that they themselves were guaranteeing. To be secure, such investments had to be made away from the deteriorating central cities and in accord with the site and design criteria that we now associate with suburbs.

Research now focused on aspects of life in new, relatively homogeneous housing areas (Dobriner, 1958; Whyte, 1956; Clark, 1965; Gans, 1967). It dealt with interaction patterns, child rearing in demographically and socially homogeneous areas, the development of social infrastructure in new areas, and the consequences of peripheral location. It dealt also with consumption styles and voting patterns (Berger, 1960).

These were "new" housing issues. People had consumed, voted, developed an infrastructure, and so on before this time; but now explicit government actions spurred housing development that had the effect of turning the peripheral into the societal mainstream by expanding explicity recognized societal functions of housing.

The effect of this charge to the suburbs, recognized only after many years, was the formation of nearly separate societies, with housing reflecting very different societal functions. Because the suburban movement was new, modern, and relatively optimistic, however strange and puzzling, the immediate research focus centered on the central-city residues.

Responses to the Residues

The field of housing had to cope with the reality of central cities that reflected the products of much earlier free-market activities, now having largely filtered down to a less-than-affluent, often minority-background population, together with the occasional public housing nod to conscience (all too often just a wink, because public housing was explicity not to create any competition to the private sector). Housing now took on another function, as one of several land uses to be employed in urban renewal to stop the so-called cancer of central-city deterioration. Operationally, cancer surgery meant that property tax values had to be raised, that dilapidated buildings and blocks had to be repaired or replaced, and that minorities should be removed. These several goals of urban renewal could be achieved simultaneously by replacing older, minority-group neighborhoods with upscale, multiple-occupancy dwellings, not to speak of shopping centers, office buildings, and the like. The alternative of new public housing on the site of the older dwellings and for its residents became less and less popular, not only because it did not serve all the desired surgical functions, but because of literature and observations indicating that public housing did not have the curative functions previously hypothesized (for example, Wilner et al., 1962) and that many additional dysfunctions accompanied the building of large, dense ghettoes of lower-income, minority residents by public authorities (Moore, 1969; Rainwater, 1970). Thus housing, in its role as a form of potentially high-value land use, was entrusted with the function of helping to upgrade older central cities in a way that, because of its specificity, was not directly or overtly racist.

Hindsight, of course, has shown that neither the facade nor the process had great validity (Wilson, 1966; Pynoos, Schafer, and Hartman, 1973). Most central-city renewals were seen not to substantially help either the original residents or the cities. The sociodemographic and economic balance between central city and suburb did not change. While the suburbs grew larger, more plentiful, and more heterogeneous, the city trends did not change radically; hence there was a reasonably continuous balance.

The function of housing as a factor in more general urban land-use viability is not entirely off base, however. What was clearly wrong was the belief that land-use deterioration could be halted by the expropriation of specific sites, the purging of certain numbers of hapless residents, and the parachuting in of higher-income consumers. In some cities, not least in New York, trends to abandonment of residential properties have shown how disastrous housing destruction can be to the land use and infrastructure of large areas (for example, the South Bronx). Research in this genre has focused on both macroeconomic and microeconomic factors (for example, rent controls, investment strategies, and the balance sheets of rental housing) together with their impact on the housing market and urban structure (Salins, 1980).

Within the context of the neighborhoods struggling to continue within the central city, some housing research turned to the difference various forms of rental management could make to building viability. This outlook by no means conflicted with any other, but delved more deeply into the functions that different forms of ownership and management have for building maintenance and social control (Krohn, Fleming, and Manzer, 1977). Such alternate forms (for example, on-site versus absentee ownership or management), in turn, ebb and flow according to the economic and legal trends in the larger society. The intricacies of municipal policies, economic considerations, management prerogatives and concerns, and investment time frames now militate against the creation of rental housing of any kind (though they do not as yet eliminate it). But for many housing researchers in older metropolitan areas, these are the overriding issues in housing research.

Another response to the residues cast housing in a societal role concerning residential segregation. Because housing costs, allocation patterns, discriminatory policies, and newly produced markets tend to segregate elements of the population geographically, it becomes difficult for schools based on local districting to integrate disparate population subgroups. When American society proceeded to emphasize the importance of school integration, the spotlight then turned not only to school board policies but, once these had been liberalized, to the dynamics of housing segregation, which produced school segregation through indirect means. Included are such processes as blockbusting, redlining, and gatekeeping. When school board busing practices addressed intracity segregation patterns, even more families moved across municipal or county boundaries, the pattern called white flight. It is a relatively subtle question how much white flight had racist roots and how much was an extension of ongoing suburbanism to yet another group of urbanites seeking improved housing (Frey, 1979). But subcultural integration is certainly another societal function of housing brought to attention by developments in society.

Responses to the Solutions

Historians seldom agree on the temporal delimitations of periods or trends. Societal activities are diverse and scattered, seldom dovetailing neatly. The societal functions of housing noted so far have been accorded attention in a rough order, but the periods illuminated by them are by no means mutually exclusive. The overlaps are appreciable. The same can be said about the timing of many responses to these phenomena, which have not waited for the completion of any fuzzy period of emphasis on particular housing problems, programs, or research. But such responses have nonetheless indicated even more awareness of the functions in society played by housing.

One kind of response to the various difficulties found in central and suburban settings is to pursue the general consideration of how well the built environments serve human needs and desires. This is a matter of how well the housing and its larger contexts support people's everyday behavior and feelings. It came as a shock to many that behavioral functions had only on rare occasions been elevated to the same priority as the functions discussed to this point. This so-called person-environment relations approach to housing did not dismiss other perspectives, but its import was that solutions that did not incorporate such behavioral considerations would always be found wanting by users, even if they were politically and economically satisfactory to others.

My own work on housing emphasized the need to understand the degree of "congruence" between built spaces and human preferences and behaviors (Michelson, 1976a), but stressed also the need to understand housing satisfaction in terms of both personal and societal aspirations and the degree to which these are thought reachable during a reasonable period of one's lifetime (Michelson, 1977, 1980). Anthropologists considered housing design in terms of proxemics, the culturally defined distances people keep from each other for stated kinds of activity (Hall, 1966). Other cultural researchers considered housing in terms of customary solutions to common problems within given cultures (Rapoport, 1969). Psychologists have been deeply involved from many angles, including human development, perception, cognition, and evaluation (Ittelson et al., 1974; Rapoport, 1977; Moore, Tuttle, and Howell, 1985; Stokols and Altman, 1987; Bechtel, Marans, and Michelson, 1987). These various social science approaches, involving both behavior and subjective human considerations, came about in the context of the apparent failure of the previously acknowledged functions of housing to evolve solutions that satisfied people. The period in history (the late 1960s and 1970s) when society responded more fully to individual desires and quality of life made this kind of response seen rational and justifiable.

A very specific consideration pursued by some social scientists was the effects of density and crowding in housing. If confirmed by empirical research, these causes of malaise in housing could be easily rectified by design reforms without having to wait for more general societal reforms. However, despite some suggestive lines of evidence (Baum and Paulus, 1987), consistent and theoretically grounded findings of practical relevance have not as yet emerged (Baldassare, 1979).

In contrast, architectural programming and postoccupancy evaluation have become two more practical outcomes of this general approach to housing. The former addresses what designers might need to learn about users and their needs in preparation for making their drawings (Spreckelmeyer, 1987), while the latter follows up empirically how built environments work in practice in order to get hints for betterment (Zimring, 1987).

At a greater level of scale, this function of housing as contributing to behavioral and subjective optimization has led to the consideration of housing within the context of neighborhood and city land use. This brings in a degree of explicit and sometimes centralized control of a number of land uses in conjunction with housing that was not envisaged by those dealing with housing purely as a laissez-faire economic commodity. Although the thinking about planned communities (Reiner, 1963) and cities (Howard, 1898) goes back to earlier centuries, systematic work on how these can and do function has recently gained favor (Hallman, 1984; Banerjee and Baer, 1984; Lansing, Marans, and Zehner, 1970; Burby and Weiss, 1976; Zehner, 1977). Central to recent thinking on this subject are the concepts of time and space, together with how these interact as people try to accomplish their daily needs and wants within the contexts and social organizations of particular communities (Carlstein, Parkes, and Thrift, 1978; Michelson, 1985).

Whether at the micro or macro levels, researchers and policymakers taking this approach have often been concerned with residential mobility as a process critical to housing. The ability to move throughout one's life span has been shown to be essential to making adjustments in the match of housing to the demands on it. Residential mobility is essential to much job mobility, to changing life-cycle stages and life-styles, and to the avoidance in the United States of undesirable neighborhood and municipal trends (Clark and Moore, 1980). Even the perception that a person or family has the opportunity for future mobility (or the lack thereof) has been shown to be important in how people evaluate their current housing and what they think of it (Michelson, 1977).

A second response to the solutions is complementary, but takes a very different approach. While the previous response addresses the failures of generalized physical fixes (with some degree of environmental determinism implied) by turning to an attempt at understanding the more subtle and varied processes by which improved environments can better accommodate human life, this response turns to the matter of social participation. Housing, in this view, is not a passive object for use, but rather something to be actively planned and managed by its residents. Involvement in the process of housing would give people both more appropriate housing in terms of design, cost, and context and more subsequent satisfaction with it. Planning would therefore turn from a process based on the ingenuity of the planner with pencil, paper, and facts to a conception of the planner as social activator and facilitator (Michelson, 1976b). Users would contribute in ways ranging from total control over projects to, at the minimum, assent (Arnstein, 1969). Applications of citizen participation range from the dwelling (self-building) to the complex (cooperative or condominium) to the neighborhood (local control) and to the planning of even larger entities (communes and communities, towns, cities, and regions) (Simmie, 1974; Thorns, 1976). Not least in this thinking is the concept of advocacy planning, in which planners act in traditional roles as professional experts, but on behalf of indigenous populations against bureaucracies (Davidoff, 1965).

The recent process of gentrification is in some respects consistent with this second response. Inner-city neighborhoods have gained valuation and some visual appeal (and lost the presence of some minority populations) through the piecemeal but steady counterinvasion by more affluent populations of neglected housing having some degree of structural soundness or historical value. Gentrification does not typically occur through formal programs or bulldozer tactics, but rather through an accumulation of personal or realtor actions. Gentrification is usually consolidated, however, through associational activities by gentrifiers in the same area, subsequently supported by municipal planning officials. In St. Louis, for example, a typical process culminates in neighbors privatizing city streets so as to better exercise control over their surroundings. Although many find gentrification positive for cities, others worry about the fate of the populations displaced, often without any provision for future residence; these latter populations do not enter the dialogue of housing and planning (Rosenthal, 1980; Palen and London, 1984).

The squatter settlements of the Third World represent a vastly different scene than the trendy areas of gentrification in the United States. Yet both situations are being informed by a conception of housing fulfilling a function of providing a locus for citizen participation. Certainly, housing has long been problematic in the Third World in terms of availability, location, and quality (Payne, 1977; Van Vliet— and Fava, 1987). What is interesting to contemplate is that it took until the most recent past for the respective societies to be regarded as having indigenous populations with needs and sensitivities as human beings, not merely as impersonal figures indirectly serving imperial interests or shrouded in romantic but removed mystery. Instead of continuing previous patterns of either ignoring local population needs or arbitrarily providing the housing accoutrements in favor in the developed world, it became possible under more sensitive views of the local societies to assist with the most basic infrastructure but then to facilitate community development by those on the spot. Although not an instant cure, this is felt to lead to more secure, appropriate development over time, providing local populations an incentive to take control over their living conditions—a great contrast to either dictating or threatening such conditions.

It was in this latter context that Turner (1976) suggested that housing should be treated as a verb, not just as a noun. By this he meant that the process by which housing is created and maintained should be at least as central a part in people's lives as the resultant physical artifacts. Turner's point is tantalizing and potentially fruitful for a number of settings. But its main contribution to the current discussion is to further illustrate how conceptions of housing reflect the functions housing is seen to play in given societies and over time. One of the difficult matters to deal with during the International Year of the Homeless was (and remains) that the developed societies do not formally allow for homelessness as a rational possibility. Hence housing for such persons does not fit an agreed-upon role for housing endeavors. Remedial action (and even research on the problem) has largely fallen through the cracks, with selected charitable organizations acting to plug as many holes in the dike as possible.

A third response to the solutions is new and old at the same time. Critical analysis of housing and related urban contexts has again, despite its protestations, taken up the reliance of the Chicago School on economic factors as the basic form of explanation behind residential patterning and related phenomena. What is new is the emphasis on a wide range of economic actors functioning in their own self-interest, taking potent actions that have direct effects not only on the nature and distribution of housing, but on the location and nature of urban development much more generally. Developers, banks, city officials, land speculators, and a wide range of entrepreneurs have been shown to have profound effects on the continued development of new areas and the inflated values of even older ones as a function of the modern economic ethos of nonstop reinvestment and increasing profit levels (Harvey, 1973; Dear and Scott, 1981; Saunders, 1981; Fainstein and Fainstein, 1982).

In this genre Castells (1976) held that there is no distinct urban sociology. Until the mid-1980s he and a number of practitioners of a "new" urban sociology argued that the economic factors and motives that prevailed in society operated equally well on all subsidiary aspects, like housing and urban affairs. What you had to know about housing was what makes the larger society go round, which, in their estimation, was found in the works of Marx ([1867–94] 1967), but as interpreted by a number of more recent European thinkers.

One allure of this form of analysis of housing is that there is never any doubt as to the explanation for a problem. Specifics of cases may vary, but not ultimate causes and factors. On the other hand, experience has shown that other kinds of knowledge and considerations are necessary to deal constructively with many other aspects and ramifications of housing, such as those treated earlier.

Thus the argument of this chapter, on the functions of housing within and for society, is quite different from one that sees housing and society as identical. Housing involves physical and social considerations that are different in substance from other commodities, and its economic superstructure has different ramifications from those of, for example, automobiles and beer.

Yet there is no denying the usefulness of understanding and dealing with economic strategizing. Nevertheless, like the other functions of housing in society, the value of this approach depends on the nature of the particular society. The same dynamics simply do not hold in societies based on different economic principles and processes, such as the USSR or China (UNESCO and UNEP, forthcoming).

Thus there are at least three complementary responses to previous conceptions of housing and the rough but pervasive "solutions" to earlier problems. None of these are better or worse in any absolute sense. Indeed, except for the fact that current examples are selective, the number of approaches could be greatly widened. Economists, for example, spend considerable effort analyzing the potential effects of many ways of tinkering with housing supply, demand, and forms of pricing, payment and subsidy (Bourne and Hitchcock, 1978). This growing welter of approaches, reflecting a growing realization of the numbers of functions in society played by housing, leaves us with the dilemma as to what is to be done with it all. Where do we go from here?

FORWARD

The relative validity and potential fruitfulness of different approaches to housing have been established. These bring in different disciplinary perspectives, levels of scale, conceptions of the dynamics of housing itself, and societal contexts. Surely the path forward is not strewn with disciplinary or professional mudslinging to the effect that "my theory's better than your theory."

Yet the complexity facing anyone who could consider dealing with every approach put forward to date is staggering. Furthermore, it is very likely that societies will continue to evolve, contributing new housing considerations, pressures, and problems. This will compound the dilemma. Housing, the subject, must consider all these factors. Once found relevant, an intellectual approach is not easily dismissed.

Any particular housing question or problem, however, need not be hung on all the potential horns of the dilemma. In this respect housing is similar to other applied social research topics, generally called "social ecology." The crucial aspect of explanation in this genre is to start with a clearly defined problem rooted in a tangible situation (including the societal context). The various perspectives, theories, and concrete angles form a pool from which to draw plausible contributions to explanation. Many items in the pool simply drop by the wayside when confronted by the demands and setting of the given problem. Indeed, it is to be expected that most problems will draw a unique configuration of plausibly relevant factors.

Those remaining as relevant are not necessarily equally pertinent. The actual pattern of explanation is as unique as the problem and combination of variables. Not only is the nature of explanation complex, but it is likely to involve an interaction among factors. For example, the combination of socioeconomic class and ethnic background of residents of an area may be more important to local behavior than each of these factors taken separately. Furthermore, while some units of analysis of housing may be in dollars and sense, others of equal value may be in daydreams and sentiment, depending on the question.

What is essential is being certain that sufficient factors are in the pool for consideration and that these are assessed fairly and ably. Special attention to the characteristics and changes in society is necessary. For example, my own assessment of recent trends in the housing market centered on family housing (Michelson, 1977); 10 years later, the function of housing placing priority on nest formation and maintenance appears relatively trivial in view of alternate family structures and life-styles.

This suggests as well that the potential substantive coverage of individual researchers or teams ought to be considerable. If an individual hopes to tackle a succession or range of housing issues, he or she must be familiar with various perspectives on the subject and with different methodologies. Mastery of a highly sophisticated but narrowly applied methodology is not helpful if unique problems require continually varying research techniques.

Similarly, in the absence of well-grounded Renaissance people, the ability of persons to work effectively on a cross-disciplinary basis is essential to responsive research and practice. Nonetheless, for members of such groups to function suitably, the problem must be explicit and its solution considered more pressing than the logic and techniques of a home discipline or profession. A major component of this problem is its societal context.

In short, housing and the research that informs it are made more complicated with the evolution and increasing sophistication of modern societies. This surely makes work on the subject challenging—but not impossible. Our conceptual and methodological approaches in turn must come to grips with the evolution of society and the increasing functions placed on housing.

REFERENCES

Arnstein, Sherry. 1969. "A Ladder of Citizen Participation." *Journal of the American Institute of Planners* 35: 216–224.

Baldassare, Mark. 1979. *Residential Crowding in Urban America*. Berkeley and Los Angeles: University of California Press.

Banerjee, Tridib, and William C. Baer. 1984. *Beyond the Neighborhood Unit*. New York: Plenum Press.

Bassett, Keith, and John Short. 1980. *Housing and Residential Structure*. Boston: Routledge & Kegan Paul.

Baum, Andrew, and Paul Paulus. 1987. "Crowding." In Daniel Stokols and Irwin Altman (eds.), *Handbook of Environmental Psychology*. New York: Wiley Interscience. 533–570.

Bechtel, Robert B., Robert Marans, and William Michelson (eds.). 1987. *Methods in Environmental and Behavioral Research*. New York: Van Nostrand Reinhold.

Berger, Bennett. 1960. *Working-Class Suburb*. Berkeley and Los Angeles: University of California Press.

Booth, Charles. 1889–1903. *Life and Labour of the People in London*. 17 vols. London.

Bourne, L. S., and John Hitchcock (eds.). 1978. *Urban Housing Markets: Recent Directions in Research and Policy*. Toronto: University of Toronto Press.

Burby, Raymond, and Shirley Weiss. 1976. *New Communities U.S.A.* Lexington, Mass.: Lexington Books.

Carlstein, Tommy, Don Parkes, and Nigel Thrift (eds.). 1978. *Human Activity and Time Geography*. New York: Halsted.

Castells, Manual. 1976. "Is There an Urban Sociology?" In C. Pickvance (ed.), *Urban Sociology: Critical Essays*. London: Tavistock. 33–59.

———. 1977. *The Urban Question*. London: Edward Arnold.

Clark, S. D. 1965. *The Suburban Society*. Toronto: University of Toronto Press.

Clark, William, and Eric Moore. 1980. *Residential Mobility and Public Policy*. Beverly Hills: Sage.

Davidoff, Paul. 1965. "Advocacy and Pluralism in Planning." *Journal of the American Institute of Planners* 31: 331–338.

Dear, Michael, and Allen J. Scott. 1981. *Urbanization and Urban Planning in Capitalist Society*. New York: Methuen.

Dobriner, William (ed.). 1958. *The Suburban Community*. New York: Putnam.

Engels, Friedrich. [1845] 1973. *The Condition of the Working Class in England in 1844*. Moscow: Progress.

———. [1873] 1979. *The Housing Question*. Moscow: Progress.

Fainstein, Norman, and Susan Fainstein. 1982. *Urban Policy under Capitalism*. Beverly Hills: Sage.

Frey, William. 1979. "Central City White Flight." *American Sociological Review* 44: 425–448.

Gans, Herbert J. 1967. *The Levittowners*. New York: Pantheon.

Hall, Edward T. 1966. *The Hidden Dimension*. Garden City, N.Y.: Doubleday.

Hallman, Howard. 1984. *Neighborhoods: Their Place in Urban Life*. Beverly Hills: Sage.

Harvey, David. 1973. *Social Justice and the City*. London: Edward Arnold.

Howard, Ebenezer. 1898. *Tomorrow: A Peaceful Path to Real Reform*. London: S. Sonnenschein.

Ittelson, William, et al. 1974. *An Introduction to Environmental Psychology*. New York: Holt, Rinehart & Winston.

Krohn, Roger G., Berkeley Fleming, and Marilyn Manzer. 1977. *The Other Economy*. Toronto: Peter Martin Associates.

Lansing, John, Robert Marans, and Robert Zehner. 1970. *Planned Residential Environments*. Ann Arbor: Institute for Social Research, University of Michigan.

Marx, Karl. [1860–94] 1967. *Capital*. 3 vols. New York: International.

Michelson, William. 1976a. *Man and His Urban Environment: A Sociological Approach*. Reading, Mass.: Addison-Wesley.

————. 1976b. "Planning and the Amelioration of Urban Problems." In Kent Schwirian et al. (eds.), *Contemporary Topics in Urban Sociology*. Morristown, N.J.: General Learning Press. 185–197.

————. 1977. *Environmental Choice, Human Behavior, and Residential Satisfaction*. New York: Oxford University Press.

————. 1980. "Long and Short Range Criteria for Housing Choice and Environmental Behavior." *Journal of Social Issues* 36, no. 3: 135–149.

————. 1985. *From Sun to Sun: Daily Obligations and Community Structure in the Lives of Employed Women and Their Families*. Totowa, N.J.: Rowman & Allanheld.

Moore, Gary, D. Paul Tuttle, and Sandra Howell. 1985. *Environmental Design Research Directions: Process and Prospects*. New York: Praeger.

Moore, William. 1969. *The Vertical Ghetto*. New York: Random House.

Palen, J. John, and Bruce London. 1984. *Gentrification, Displacement, and Neighborhood Revitalization*. Albany: State University of New York Press.

Park, Robert, Ernest Burgess, and R. D. McKenzie. 1925. *The City*. Chicago: University of Chicago Press.

Payne, Geoffrey K. 1977. *Urban Housing in the Third World*. Boston: Routledge & Kegan Paul.

Popenoe, David. 1977. *The Suburban Environment*. Chicago: University of Chicago Press.

————. 1985. *Private Pleasure, Public Plight*. New Brunswick, N.J.: Transaction Books.

Pynoos, Jon, Robert Schafer, and Chester Hartman (eds.). 1973. *Housing Urban America*. Chicago: Aldine.

Rainwater, Lee. 1970. *Behind Ghetto Walls: Black Families in a Federal Slum*. Chicago: Aldine.

Rapoport, Amos. 1969. *House Form and Culture*. Englewood Cliffs, N.J.: Prentice-Hall.

————. 1977. *Human Aspects of Urban Form*. New York: Pergamon Press.

Reiner, Thomas. 1963. *The Place of the Ideal Community in Urban Planning*. Philadelphia: University of Pennsylvania Press.

Riis, Jacob. 1890. *How the Other Half Lives*. New York: Scribner.

Rosenthal, Donald (ed.). 1980. *Urban Revitalization*. Beverly Hills: Sage.

Salins, Peter. 1980. *The Ecology of Housing Destruction*. New York: New York University Press.

Saunders, Peter. 1981. *Social Theory and the Urban Question*. London: Hutchinson.

Simmie, J. M. 1974. *Citizens in Conflict: The Sociology of Town Planning*. London: Hutchinson.

Spreckelmeyer, Kent. 1987. "Environmental Programming." In Robert B. Bechtel, Robert Marans, and William Michelson (eds.), *Methods in Environmental and Behavioral Research*. New York: Van Nostrand Reinhold. 247–269.

Steffens, Lincoln. 1931. *Autobiography*. New York: Harcourt, Brace, and World.

Stokols, Daniel, and Irwin Altman (eds.). 1987. *Handbook of Environmental Psychology*. New York: Wiley Interscience.

Thorns, David. 1976. *Quest for Community*. London: George Allen & Unwin.

Turner, John. 1976. *Housing by People: Towards Autonomy in Building Environments*. London: Marion Boyars.

UNESCO and UNEP. Forthcoming. *Urban Planning in Ecological Perspective* (Edited proceedings of a conference under the Man and the Biosphere Program in Suzdal, USSR, September 1984).

Van Vliet—,Willem, and Sylvia Fava (eds.). 1987. "Housing in the Third World." *Environment and Behavior* 19, no. 3, special issue.

Whyte, William H., Jr. 1956. *The Organization Man*. Garden City, N.Y.: Doubleday Anchor Books.

Wilner, Daniel, et al. 1962. *The Housing Environment and Family Life*. Baltimore: Johns Hopkins Press.

Wilson, James Q. (ed.). 1966. *Urban Renewal: The Record and the Controversy*. Cambridge, Mass.: M.I.T. Press.

Zehner, Robert. 1977. *Indicators of the Quality of Life in New Communities*. Cambridge, Mass.: Ballinger.

Zimring, Craig. 1987. "Evaluation of Designed Environments: Methods for Post-Occupancy Evaluation." In Robert B. Bechtel, Robert Marans, and William Michelson (eds.), *Methods in Environmental and Behavioral Research*. New York: Van Nostrand Reinhold. 270–300.

2

Neighborhood Quality: A Description and Analysis of Indicators

CHARLES E. CONNERLY AND ROBERT W. MARANS

Real estate appraisers often say that the three most important concepts in real estate are "location, location, location," meaning that value estimation requires an assessment of the property's location. In the case of residential real estate, not only does a house's location affect its monetary value, but the quality of living in the house is affected by many other locational attributes to be discussed in this chapter.[1]

In examining the residential environment, therefore, it is impossible to ignore the impact of location and the impact of the neighborhood as an important determinant of housing quality. In fact, it can be argued that the neighborhood is actually an extension of the dwelling, as it is difficult to experience the qualities of a house without also being sensitive to those of the surrounding neighborhood.

But what is a neighborhood and what do we mean by neighborhood quality? From the perspective of the researcher, planner, or designer, the neighborhood is an aggregation of dwellings and the physical, social, political, and economic systems that bind these dwellings together. Although the variety of residential areas discourages a precise definition of neighborhood, there is strong evidence (Hunter, 1979; Connerly, 1985) to show that neighborhoods are not only identifiable as geographic entities, but in varying degrees perform important social, political, administrative, economic, and symbolic functions. More specifically, neighborhoods continue to assume varying importance as places in which people experience the surrounding built, natural, and social environments, socialize with neighbors, invest in property, receive or use local public services, organize to protect property values and otherwise defend the neighborhood from forces that affect the neighborhood's collective welfare, shop or work, and generally develop a sense of neighborhood identity.

In turn, these aspects of neighborhood life can be evaluated in terms of what we call neighborhood quality, which is simply the degree of excellence or goodness that is found in each of these aspects as well as in the neighborhood as a whole. Specifically, neighborhood quality, as will be discussed more fully, can be described in terms of four primary dimensions: (1) the quality of the physical environment; (2) proximity and convenience to various activity nodes, such as shopping or work; (3) the quality of local services and facilities; and (4) the quality of the neighborhood's sociocultural environment. Collectively, judgments on these dimensions are assumed to relate to an overall or global evaluation of neighborhood quality.

The purpose of this chapter is to describe, analyze, and make suggestions for using the various indicators of neighborhood quality that have appeared in the social science, planning, and design literature on neighborhoods. The primary source of information is an extensive survey of this literature as well as the authors' own research and experience in evaluating neighborhood quality. The primary utility of this chapter is for students, researchers, planners, and designers engaged in neighborhood quality research or evaluation who want both to extend their knowledge of neighborhood quality indicators and to improve their ability to use these indicators.

TYPES OF INDICATORS OF NEIGHBORHOOD QUALITY

Before beginning any assessment of neighborhood quality, it is important to think about the types of indicators to be analyzed. Our review of the literature shows that an extensive variety of indicators have been used to record neighborhood quality. Most fundamentally, neighborhood quality indicators can be distinguished by whether they are objectively or subjectively measured. Objective data are primarily derived from governmental reports, physical measurement, and direct observation, and by their nature provide descriptive information on neighborhood conditions.

Objective Indicators of Neighborhood Quality

Physical and Mental Health

One major group of objective indicators covering a neighborhood focuses on the physical and mental health of its residents and draws heavily on the urban ecological studies begun in the 1920s (Park, Burgess, and McKenzie, 1967). These studies considered the degree of social disorganization or pathologies within various neighborhoods by examining such variables as crime, suicide, and illness rates. Subsequent studies using physical and mental health data have examined relationships between physical health and pathology variables on the one hand and characteristics of individuals and their housing on the other (Schmitt, 1966; Dunham, 1965; Bagley, Jacobson, and Palmer, 1973). Other studies have used crime records of local police departments to infer neighborhood quality (Rogers et al., 1975; Taub, Taylor, and Dunham, 1981). City census tracts with high incidences of tuberculosis, infant mortality, venereal disease cases, suicide, and crime rates have been by inference viewed as low-quality areas in contrast to those areas where the incidences of physical disorders or pathologies are less prevalent.

Condition and Market Value of Housing

A second category of objective indicators implying overall neighborhood quality centers on the physical condition and market value of housing units. Whereas health measures have been used by social scientists, indicators of physical condition have been used with regularity by city planners over the past 40 years. Characteristic of this category has been the work carried out by local urban renewal agencies in the 1950s that focused on assessing residential areas for their slum clearance and redevelopment potential. Areas where the physical condition of dwellings was structurally unsound, where vacancies were prevalent, where rents were low, and where building coverage was high were considered poor in quality and therefore eligible for clearance and renewal.

Sources of such data were the U.S. census or inspections made by "trained" observers who rated dwelling units on such dimensions as the condition of stairs, the adequacy of plumbing, and structural soundness. On occasion, the American Public Health Association appraisal technique, incorporating an assessment of environmental quality beyond the house, was used (1960). The use of housing-condition data has been made more costly, however, since the U.S. Bureau of the Census discontinued, after 1970, any attempt to measure the overall quality of housing.

In more recent years economists and planners have sought to measure housing and neighborhood quality by employing housing-market indicators. Market values, it is believed, represent the sum of the values housing consumers impute to specific residential attributes, such as the quality of local public schools or lot size (see, for example, Quigley, 1978). Several studies have examined specific neighborhood and environmental amenities in order to determine their relationship to property values. Kain and Quigley (1970), for example, demonstrated that the value of housing was significantly related to the physical conditions of surrounding properties and two neighborhood characteristics—school quality and incidence of crime. Ridker and Henning (1967) found relationships between levels of air pollution and aggregated property values. In each of these studies selected attributes of the neighborhood were measured, and together with characteristics of the dwellings and households in the neighborhood, an overall measure of residential quality was imputed in the form of aggregated property values. Finally, Koebel (1983) has shown how the statistical analysis of market values, using hedonic regression techniques, can be used to infer housing and neighborhood quality.

Because market value is based on a broad variety of housing and neighborhood quality variables, it is more global than the other objective indicators described here. Whereas neighborhood data on health or housing condition measure individual attributes of the neighborhood, market value, when aggregated at the neighborhood level, is a measure of the neighborhood's excellence as a whole.

Market value measures housing and neighborhood demand and their relation to the supply of residential services. Other indicators, such as rents, turnover rates (how frequently people move in and out of dwellings), vacancy rates, absorption rates (how quickly new construction units are purchased or rented), the amount of private lending, the level of government-insured lending, ownership rates, the amount of absentee ownerhsip, tax delinquency rates, the incidence of property abandonment, and the amount of conversion from one property use or form of tenure to another, also provide information on the degree to which housing in a neighborhood is in demand and hence are imputed indicators of neighborhood quality. Such variables can be used to compare different neighborhoods as well as to measure change in a single neighborhood over time. Goetze and Colton (1983), in particular, advocate that market indicators such as these be used in conjunction with housing quality data to monitor the degree to which housing demand is rising or falling for a particular neighborhood. By knowing in which way demand is turning, it will be easier, they argue, to anticipate changes in housing and neighborhood quality.

Similarly, data on household income, age, race, tenure, size, and family structure can be used to determine the type of demand that exists for a neighborhood (Myers, 1983). Although such variables do not indicate neighborhood quality per se, changes in these indicators may reflect changes in neighborhood quality as well as anticipate or determine further changes.

Direct Observation

In addition to using observers to measure the quality of individual dwellings, planners and designers have used observation techniques to record qualities of the neighborhood. "Windshield" or "sidewalk" surveys have been frequently used as a "quick and dirty" method of assessing various aspects of a neighborhood, including housing quality, yard upkeep, street and sidewalk condition, amount and type of pedestrian activity, traffic volume and noise, type and mix of land uses, evidence of abandoned properties, evidence of changes in types of residents, construction and rehabilitation activity, evidence of property use or tenure conversions, number of "for sale" or "for rent" signs, and graffiti.

Unfortunately, observing such indicators has rarely been taught or used in a systematic fashion, and hence observations often become impressionistic and partial. Nevertheless, recent works by Clay (1980) and Jacobs (1985) attempt to develop a more systematic method for directly observing neighborhoods and other parts of cities. Because direct observation is relatively inexpensive, it can be used as a technique for selecting neighborhoods or problems that require more intensive and expensive examination.

Subjective Indicators of Neighborhood Quality

Rationale for Subjective Indicators

Although there is little doubt that these objective indicators are useful in understanding the condition of neighborhoods, several researchers have argued that exclusive use of such data to describe the goodness (or badness) of an area may not be totally appropriate since they are not indicative of the quality of neighborhood life as experienced and perceived by the people living there (Campbell and Converse, 1972; Marans and Rodgers, 1975; Scharf, 1978; Brudney and England, 1982). Even the most encompassing or global of these objective indicators, market value, tends to imply that only more affluent people can live in better neighborhoods and that lower-income households will live in lower-quality neighborhoods. By assuming that all factors relevant to neighborhood quality are reflected in value, we may minimize those characteristics that distinguish, for example, a safe, socially close-knit, low-income neighborhood from a low-income neighborhood in which people feel alone and afraid.

Moreover, it is unclear how objective "objective" indicators of neighborhood quality really are. The use of housing condition indicators, for example, has been found to be unreliable because independent, trained observers frequently cannot agree on whether a particular house or neighborhood is deteriorated or dilapidated. For this reason the U.S. Bureau of the Census discontinued its attempts to measure overall housing quality (Weicher, 1980). Furthermore, the urban renewal program's use of housing condition data to determine whether a neighborhood should be rehabilitated or razed has been described as reflecting middle-class notions of what constitutes a good neighborhood while ignoring other indicators of a community's viability (Gans, 1982).

Dissatisfaction with the negative impacts of urban renewal and highway construction on neighborhoods helped lead in the 1960s to a greater emphasis on citizen participation in various neighborhood assistance programs (Rohe and Gates, 1985). In turn, this increased emphasis on citizen input into local decisionmaking has led to increased reliance on subjective assessments of neighborhood quality. If we are to plan with neighborhoods, it has been argued, then it makes good sense to obtain citizen opinions on what problems exist in their neighborhoods and what should be done about them.

As a result of these considerations, much research on neighborhood quality has used data collected from sample surveys of neighborhood residents. However, sample surveys are not the only means of obtaining information on neighborhood quality from residents. Other subjective assessment techniques include various small-group decisionmaking and conflict-resolution techniques, such as nominal group technique, brainstorming, Delphi, or policy capturing. While such techniques are often preferable to sample surveys for helping residents set policy goals or make choices (Hester, 1984), survey sampling is more useful for obtaining a representative cross section of opinion on existing neighborhood quality (Milbrath, 1981). For this reason much of the remaining discussion will focus on sample surveys.

Types of Subjective Data

Sample surveys have been used to obtain four basic types of subjective data: perceptual, evaluative, preferential, and behavioral. Perception and evaluation can be regarded as the two psychological stages that intervene between any object in an individual's environment and his or her assessment of that object's quality (Marans and Rodgers, 1975). Perceptual data are based on an individual's awareness of neighborhood conditions. Hence respondents may be asked about perceptions of their neighbors' characteristics: for example, are neighbors primarily white or black, rich or poor, educated or uneducated? Differences, of course, often occur between peoples' perceptions and objective reality. Consequently, individuals' views on neighborhood crime sometimes differ from the "objective" reports on crime produced by police departments (Lee and Marans, 1980).

The second stage in the assessment process is evaluation itself. In neighborhood quality research, evaluation has generally been measured by asking residents about their level of satisfaction with specific aspects of the neighborhood as well as the neighborhood as a whole. Specific neighborhood evaluative indicators are discussed later in this chapter.

In examining subjective evaluations of neighborhood quality, some researchers have attempted to determine whether there are any relationships between objective and subjective quality of life indicators. Early research on this topic (Schneider, 1975; Kuz, 1978) found little association between citywide objective and subjective quality-of-life indicators. More recent research, however, has shown that when quality of life is measured at the subarea or neighborhood level, objective and subjective indicators are more likely to be correlated (Dale, 1980; Van Vliet—, 1981). This latter finding is important because it indicates that changes in the objective neighborhood environment, over which urban planners and designers have some control, can affect subjective evaluations of the neighborhood (Van Vliet—, 1981).

The measurement of residential preferences is also prevalent in housing and neighborhood quality research. As a way of identifying attributes of neighborhoods considered to be most desirable, a number of researchers have had survey respondents choose from an array of neighborhood attributes. That is, trade-off games or forced-choice situations have been used to identify attributes of neighborhood quality that people would be willing to forgo in favor of other attributes (Wilson, 1962; Michelson, 1966; Hoinville, 1974; Knight and Menchik, 1974; Cooper, 1975; Robinson et al., 1975; Marans and Wellman, 1978; Dowall and Juhasz, 1979; Johnson, 1980; Banerjee and Baer, 1984). These trade-off situations have been introduced in the context of social surveys involving either face-to-face contact between interviewer and respondent or through mail questionnaires.

Surveys have also been used to examine the behaviors or activities of people within their residential settings, and in some instances inferences have been made about neighborhood quality from the reported activities. Studies involving face-to-face interviews have focused on neighboring (Festinger, Schachter, and Back, 1950; Gans, 1982; Suttles, 1968; Michelson, 1977), on recreation and play (Lansing, Maransa, and Zehner, 1970; Marans and Fly, 1981), or on experiences with crime (Newman, 1972; Taub, Taylor, and Dunham, 1981; Greenberg, Rohe, and Williams, 1981). Other researchers have examined an entire spectrum of resident behaviors by using time budgets within the context of surveys (Zehner and Chapin, 1974; Michelson, 1977). Finally, studies have used participant observation to record neighborhood behavior (Gans, 1982, 1967; Suttles, 1968; Howell, 1973).

Moving behavior, when interpreted as an indicator of neighborhood quality, has also been examined within the context of social surveys. A number of studies have reported on the reasons people have moved from one dwelling to another (Lansing, Mueller, and Barth, 1964; Butler et al., 1969; Wolf and Lebeaux, 1969; Speare, 1974; Duncan and Newman, 1976; Newman and Duncan, 1979; Varady, 1983) or on factors associated with their desire to move (Rossi, 1955; Hamovitch and Peterson, 1969; Kasl and Harburg, 1972; Newman, 1974; Cadwallader, 1979; Heaton et al., 1979; Kirschenbaum, 1983; Connerly, 1986).

Despite these studies on neighborhood preferences and behavior, the bulk of neighborhood quality research has focused on people's evaluations of their existing neighborhoods. Hence the remainder of this chapter will focus primarily on neighborhood evaluation issues.

SURVEY METHODS FOR EVALUATING NEIGHBORHOOD QUALITY

Defining the Neighborhood

In evaluating neighborhoods it is important to remember that residents, even those living near one another, may have differing definitions of the neighborhood. Research examining the mental image of neighborhoods has had residents describe or draw on a map the boundaries of their neighborhood and has shown that people in the same neighborhood often draw highly divergent maps (Lee, 1968; Sanoff, 1973). Other research, however, has shown that residents of the same neighborhood draw maps with similar boundaries (Haney and Knowles, 1978). While the evidence is therefore mixed, it seems safe to say that researchers should expect to find instances where local residents disagree with each other about what constitutes their neighborhood. Moreover, research has also shown that neighborhood definitions vary extensively from one neighborhood to another and depend on a variety of physical and social factors (Hunter, 1974; Banerjee and Baer, 1984).

Consequently, resident neighborhood evaluations are partly contingent on how the neighborhood is defined. Unfortunately, many surveys of neighborhood quality (including the American Annual Housing Survey) have ignored this by simply asking respondents to evaluate their neighborhood, without any discussion of what neighborhood the respondent is describing. One alternative is first to solicit the resident's personal definition of his or her neighborhood. Several techniques for obtaining neighborhood cognitive maps have been developed (Pacione, 1984; Rodgers et al., 1975) that typically involve asking respondents to draw their neighborhood on a city base map or to select from a list of neighborhood sizes the one that best fits their neighborhood.

But the delineation of cognitive maps does not negate the fact that comparisons of quality among several neighborhoods are confounded by differences in respondents' personal neighborhood definitions. An alternative that has been employed in several sample surveys (Lansing, Marans, and Zehner, 1970; Rodgers et al., 1975) is to specify a consistent spatial reference that is used throughout a series of questions on neighborhood conditions and services. Lansing, Marans, and Zehner's (1970) survey of new-town residents defined the neighborhood for the respondent as the 10 or 15 homes nearest to the respondent's dwelling, or in the case of apartments, the apartment building and the area around it.

In this instance the neighborhood definition roughly corresponds to the block face. The block face is a useful definition because (1) it is a common referent with which most people are familiar (although it has less utility in superblock and rural situations); (2) while the block face is not coterminous with all neighborhood definitions, it is often the primary "building block" comprising neighborhoods; and (3) various aspects of neighborhood quality are most salient at the block level.

For those neighborhood issues, such as the quality of local schools and other public services, that affect a broader area than the block, the researcher should probably supply a spatial referent, such as the school district, that is appropriate to the neighborhood issue being addressed. Also, when doing research on a single multiblock neighborhood, researchers may want respondents to focus on the entire neighborhood in answering questions.

Measuring Overall Neighborhood Quality

Beginning in the 1960s and early 1970s, a number of studies using social surveys contained specific questions aimed at measuring people's overall evaluation of their neighborhood. In a national study of residential location and urban mobility, Lansing and his colleagues Mueller and Barth asked respondents how well they liked their neighborhoods (1964). Since then a large number of surveys have been conducted, using a variety of questions to measure overall neighborhood quality. Typical neighborhood quality questions are shown in Table 2.1. These have been used as global indicators because each attempts to obtain from the respondent an assessment of overall neighborhood quality. They are distinguished from evaluations of specific neighborhood quality attributes, such as traffic noise or crime. Measures of these specific attributes will be discussed later in this chapter.

Survey questions using a satisfaction-dissatisfaction format have dominated the neighborhood quality literature. Beginning with Wilson (1962), designers of community, regional, and national surveys have asked people to evaluate their neighborhoods using satisfaction-dissatisfaction scales ranging from 2 to 11 categories (Butler et al., 1969; Rodgers et al., 1975; Campbell, Converse, and

Table 2.1
Global Measures of Perceived Neighborhood Quality, with Frequency Distributions

"All things considered, how satisfied or dissatisfied are you with this neighborhood as a place to live?" (Rodgers et al., 1975; Campbell et al. 1976) (Asked of Detroit area residents; USA residents)

		Rodgers et al.	Campbell et al.
1.	Completely satisfied	36.3%	46.0%
2.		30.0	21.0
3.		10.4	13.0
4.	Neutral	12.7	11.0
5.		4.6	4.0
6.		2.9	2.0
7.	Completely dissatisfied	3.1	3.0

"How do you feel about: This particular neighborhood as a place to live?" (Andrews and Withey, 1976) (Asked of USA residents)

1.	Delighted	18.0%
2.	Pleased	39.0
3.	Mostly satisfied	24.0
4.	Mixed	10.0
5.	Mostly dissatisfied	4.0
6.	Unhappy	2.0
7.	Terrible	3.0

"Do you think of this neighborhood as your home, or just as a place you happen to live in?" (Rodgers et al., 1975) (Asked of Detroit area residents)

1.	Home	76.9%
2.	Just place to live	23.1

"When you think of your attachment to this neighborhood, are you": (Ahlbrandt, 1984) (Asked of Pittsburgh residents)

1.	Very strongly attached	23.0%
2.	Strongly attached	40.0
3.	Undecided	12.0
4.	Not strongly attached	18.0
5.	Not at all attached	7.0

Rodgers, 1976; Hall and Ring, 1974; United Kingdom, Department of the Environment, 1972; Francescato et al., 1979; Michelson, 1977; Marans and Wellman, 1978; Gollin, Dixon, and Golden, 1975). An alternative approach that has been commonly used, both in face-to-face and telephone surveys, is to ask respondents to rate their neighborhoods as either excellent, good, fair, or poor (U.S. Bureau of the Census, 1984; Ahlbrandt, 1984).

These global measures are examples of "cognitive" measures of neighborhood quality. Research on subjective well-being (Campbell, Converse, and Rodgers, 1976; McKennell, 1978; Andrews and McKennell, 1980; McKennell and Andrews, 1980, 1983) has differentiated between affective measures, which are often expressed in terms of emotions such as happiness or pleasure, and cognitive measures that imply an evaluative judgment based on the satisfaction of some standard or aspiration.[2]

Several types of questions have been developed to measure the affective content of neighborhood quality. The first of these, used in Bradburn, Sudman, and Gockel (1970), attempts to directly tap the affective dimension by asking people how happy they are with their neighborhood. The original testing of the happiness measure was done in conjunction with mental health studies (Bradburn and Caplowitz, 1965). While happiness is clearly relevant to mental health, it is not apparent that it is of primary concern or even relevant to assessments of neighborhood quality, such as quality of schools or upkeep of nearby houses. Instead, as Campbell, Converse, and Rodgers (1976) noted, satisfaction and dissatisfaction appear more appropriate as descriptors of positive and negative neighborhood quality.

Nevertheless, neighborhood quality probably has both cognitive and affective dimensions, and consequently Andrews and Withey (1976) proposed that neighborhood quality, as well as the quality of other life domains, be measured with a delighted-terrible scale (see Table 2.1). This scale asks people to say whether they are satisfied or dissatisfied with their neighborhood, but also gives them the opportunity to report whether they feel delighted, pleased, unhappy, or terrible about their neighborhood.[3]

Overall neighborhood quality has also been conceptualized and measured by tapping people's sense of attachment or belonging to the place they live. Several researchers have asked residents whether they think of their neighborhood as their real home or just a place to live (Barton, 1975; Rodgers et al., 1975; Fried and Gleicher, 1961; Kasarda and Janowitz, 1974; United Kingdom, Royal Commission, 1969), how proud they are of it (Wilner et al., 1962; United Kingdom, Department of the Environment, 1972), and whether they feel a part of or attached to the local area (Gollin, Dixon, and Golden, 1975; Hunter, 1974; Ahlbrandt, 1984) (see Table 2.1 for several examples). Similarly, quality has been implied by people's expressions of disappointment with having to leave their neighborhood (Bradburn, Sudman, and Gockel, 1970; United Kingdom, Royal Commission, 1969) and their expressed desire to move (Kasl and Harburg, 1972;

Nathanson et al., 1976; Speare, 1974; Connerly, 1986), although desire to move can be stimulated by many non-neighborhood reasons, such as a job transfer.

In contrast to neighborhood satisfaction, attachment to the neighborhood has been shown to be more closely related to the affective component of perceived neighborhood quality (Connerly and Marans, 1985). Hunter (1974) has argued that emotional involvement with a neighborhood produces a sense of attachment that can transcend any evaluative judgment of the neighborhood. Such involvement is often produced via interaction with friends, relatives, and acquaintances living in the neighborhood. Although both satisfaction and attachment are affected by social relations with neighbors, attachment is more affected by such interaction than is satisfaction.

Defining the Dimensions of Neighborhood Quality

The discussion thus far has focused on global or overall indicators of neighborhood quality, but a review of the neighborhood literature reveals that specific dimensions of neighborhood quality have received at least as much attention as that given to the global measures. Dimensions of neighborhood quality can be generally categorized into four groups: (1) indicators of physical environmental conditions; (2) indicators of the neighborhood's location relative to various nodes, services, and amenities; (3) indicators of the quality of local services and facilities (public and private); and (4) indicators of the sociocultural environment. The types and sources of data for each dimension are shown in Table 2.2.

Physical Environment Conditions

The physical environment of the neighborhood represents those attributes that are most visible to residents in the neighborhood and that are subject to alteration by design and physical improvement. As discussed earlier, a number of these attributes have been recorded and measured by trained observers. While this has been especially true for housing conditions, other physical attributes of the neighborhood have also been measured in this way. Traffic (Appleyard, Gerson, and Lintell, 1976), pollution (Jacoby, 1971), density (Rodgers et al., 1975; Marans et al., 1976; Marans and Wellman, 1978), and public litter (Hatry, Winnie, and Fisk, 1981) have also been recorded through direct observation. More often, however, the quality of a neighborhood's physical condition has been measured with sample survey questions.

Overall physical appearance has been assessed in several studies that have asked residents to indicate whether or not they thought the area in which they lived was attractive or well planned. Many studies, however, also examine the quality of specific physical or environmental attributes. Residents' evaluations of neighborhood housing conditions, for example, have also been obtained through survey research. Surveys have asked residents about abandoned housing (Rodgers et al., 1975; U.S. Bureau of the Census, 1984) and occupied housing

Table 2.2
Dimensions, Types, and Sources of Neighborhood Quality Data

DIMENSIONS	TYPES	SOURCES

Physical Environment Conditions	Housing
	  condition
	  market value
	  density
		field visits
		resident surveys
		Annual Housing Survey
		U.S. Census
		assessors' records
		maps, aerial photos

	Traffic and Streets
	  counts
	  noise
	  safety
	  lighting
	  street conditions
	  pollution
		traffic surveys
		noise measurement devices
		traffic accident records
		resident surveys
		field visits
		government pollution data
		Annual Housing Survey

	Neighborhood Conditions
	  building upkeep
	  yard upkeep
	  abandoned housing
	  trash, litter, junk
	  incompatible land uses
	  pollution
	  amount and quality of
	    open space
		field visits
		resident surveys
		government pollution data
		Annual Housing Survey

Locational Characteristics	Proximity,
	Convenience to
	  work
	  schools
	  shopping
	  recreation
		maps, aerial photos
		resident surveys
		Annual Housing Survey

Local Services, Facilities	recreation schools police protection fire solid waste disposal libraries road and highways mass transit health care	resident surveys department records field visits Annual Housing Survey

Sociocultural Environment	neighborhood social
	  relations
	number and type of
	  community
	  organizations
	crime
		resident surveys
		interviews with
		  key informants
		police records

units that are poorly kept up or vandalized (Zehner and Chapin, 1974; Campbell, Converse, and Rodgers, 1976). Indicators of residents' perception of their own dwelling's quality can also be used to obtain information on housing quality throughout a neighborhood. The measures used in the Annual Housing Survey provide a fairly complete inventory of questions on specific attributes of the dwelling unit, such as structural quality, quality of maintenance, and performance of heating and plumbing systems.

Questions focusing on the measurement of residents' perceptions and evaluations of street noise, traffic, street lighting, road conditions, and odors and smoke in their neighborhoods have been incorporated into household surveys conducted at the national level (U.S. Bureau of the Census, 1984; U.S. Department of Housing and Urban Development [HUD], 1978), at the regional or community level (Wilson, 1962; Rodgers et al., 1975; Marans and Wellman, 1978), and in public housing (United Kingdom, Department of the Environment, 1972; Sanoff, 1973). In particular, the research of Appleyard, Gerson, and Lintell (1976, 1981) on the impact of traffic and traffic noise on neighborhood quality demonstrates the richness of information that is available on how neighborhood physical conditions can affect residents' quality of life.

Although density has often been measured with census data or by independent observers, residents' perceptions and evaluations of density have been used as indicators of neighborhood quality. Several studies have asked people the degree to which their residential settings are crowded and the extent to which crowded conditions are disruptive to their lives (Wilson, 1962; Lansing, Marans, and Zehner, 1970; Zehner and Marans, 1973; Baldassare, 1975; Cooper, 1975).

The residual amount of open space associated with a neighborhood has also been considered an indicator of neighborhood quality. In addition to the quantity of open space, the types of open space in the neighborhood are an important indicator of neighborhood quality. Open space has been described in terms of vacant lots, wooded areas, parks, school yards, playgrounds, bodies of water, and hard-surfaced open areas such as plazas (Knight and Menchik, 1974; Campbell, Converse, and Rodgers, 1976).

Locational Characteristics

Another dimension of neighborhood quality is the neighborhood's location and convenience relative to places used by residents in performing their day-to-day activities. Convenience has been measured in terms of the actual distance between a neighborhood and various activities centers such as work, school, shopping, and recreation. Residents have been asked in surveys for the location of these activities, so that researchers can actually measure the distance between residence and these activities (Marans and Fly, 1981). In other surveys convenience is measured in the time estimates respondents give for the travel to various activity centers (Lansing, Marans, and Zehner, 1970; Michaelsen et al., 1976). In both instances, however, the researcher must decide what distances or times are convenient.

Since the definition of locational convenience can vary across individuals, other researchers (Butler et al., 1969; Cooper, 1975; Campbell, Converse, and Rodgers, 1976) have preferred to ask residents how conveniently located they are to various activities. For example, Campbell, Converse, and Rodgers asked respondents whether their neighborhood is very convenient, convenient enough, not very convenient, or not convenient at all to a variety of places. In this case the definition of convenience is left up to the respondent.

Local Services and Facilities

A third group of neighborhood quality attributes focuses on the quality of public services provided or funded by local government and the quality of nearby private services such as shopping. Perhaps the most comprehensive attempt to catalog indicators of local public services is the compendium prepared by Hatry et al. (1977) at the Urban Institute. The Urban Institute report illustrates, for such services as solid waste collection and disposal, recreation, libraries, crime control, fire protection, transportation and mass transit, water supply, and complaint handling, how efficiency and effectiveness have been measured, either in terms of objective indicators, such as usage rates of parks, or subjective attitudes of residents.

Other sources of public service measures include the American (Annual) Housing Survey (U.S. Bureau of the Census, 1984), which has asked questions on a variety of public and private services, and studies that examine specific services, such as schools (Bradburn, Sudman, and Gockel, 1970; Rodgers et al., 1975), public transportation (Rodgers et al., 1975), police and fire protection (Marans and Wellman, 1978; Brown and Coulter, 1983), health care (Becker, 1974; Dear and Taylor, 1979), and the responsiveness of local government officials in meeting neighborhood needs (Rodgers et al., 1975).

Sociocultural Environment

The quantity and quality of social relations are a fourth dimension of neighborhood quality. Numerous studies have asked residents to rate their neighbors in terms of whether they are friendly, trustworthy, helpful, and generally supportive (Zehner, 1971; Lansing, Marans, and Zehner; 1970; Becker, 1974; Cooper, 1975; Rodgers et al., 1975; Andrews and Withey, 1976). Other studies have examined the degree and type of contact among neighbors in racially integrated neighborhoods (Bradburn, Sudman, and Gockel, 1970), in public housing (United Kingdom, Department of the Environment, 1972; Cooper, 1975; Wilner et al., 1962), and in broader community settings (Fried, 1973; Chapin, Butler, and Patten, 1972; Lansing, Marans, and Zehner, 1970; National Opinion Research Center [NORC], 1978). Still others have asked people whether they had friends or family living nearby (Rodgers et al., 1975; Cooper, 1975; Michelson, 1977) or whether they would like their neighbors as friends (Lansing and Hendricks, 1967; Zehner and Chapin, 1974; Zehner, 1971). A number of studies have questioned respondents about their ability to recognize or name the people who live in the neighborhood (Lansing, Marans, and Zehner, 1970; Becker, 1974; Rodgers et al., 1975; Cooper, 1975). Finally, studies have been done to determine residents' willingness to assist strangers (Korte, 1978, 1980).

Another aspect of the neighborhood's social environment deals with the extent to which people are involved or participate in community institutions, such as parent-teacher associations, church groups, and neighborhood organizations. Often, questions within surveys are aimed at first identifying whether or not such institutions exist or are perceived to exist by the respondent (Kain and Quigley, 1970; City of Cincinnati, 1978) and whether the resident is a member (Ahlbrandt, 1984). For residents who report the presence of a community organization and their affiliation with it, they are often asked about their level of involvement (Lansing, Marans, and Zehner, 1970; HUD, 1978) or whether the organization holds meetings within the neighborhood (Wilner et al., 1962). Research on neighborhood organizations has also been performed using direct observation and interviews with key informants (Henig, 1982; Mayer, 1984).

Although no research has fully tested the hypothesis, it appears that the degree and type of social interaction and involvement in neighborhood organizations may be important indicators of residents' commitment to improve their neighborhood. In turn, commitment to the neighborhood may be indicative of a neighborhood's willingness to support revitalization efforts. If so, efforts to promote neighborhood revitalization, particularly through upgrading by incumbent residents (Clay, 1979), should look not only at neighborhood conditions and perceived neighborhood quality but also at indicators of personal and collective commitment to shaping the neighborhood's quality. In particular, researchers should examine homeownership as it relates to commitment to neighborhood improvement.

Another component of the social environment of the neighborhood is the degree of crime, delinquency, or vandalism that pervades the area. Crime indicators based on police statistics have been incorporated into metropolitan area studies (Rodgers et al., 1975). Other crime indicators have been based on people's reports of crimes against themselves, their properties, or their neighbors, or on people's perceptions of the amount of crime in the neighborhood (Dubow, McCabe, and Kaplan, 1979) and the degree to which they feel it is safe for them during the day and at night (Andrews and Withey, 1976; Appleyard, Gerson, and Lintell, 1976; NORC, 1974; Cooper, 1975).

Using Neighborhood Quality Indicators

In addition to research, there are a variety of uses to which neighborhood quality indicators can be put. First, local governments can use indicators to monitor neighborhood quality in various neighborhoods with the object of identifying those neighborhoods with a greater number of problems or undergoing changes that might require public action. Second, many cities have used surveys to obtain citizen evaluations of neighborhood public services. Third, cities and neighborhood organizations have used surveys of residents to identify key problems in areas targeted for action as well as to identify possible solutions to these problems. Finally, surveys tapping residential preferences can be used for designing new neighborhoods or redesigning older neighborhoods or their facilities. Whether neighborhood quality is being measured for purposes of addressing research questions or for planning and design purposes, there are a number of general methodological (or measurement) issues that need to be considered.

General Measurement Issues

In addition to the issues of neighborhood definition and the validity of global neighborhood quality indicators, several other measurement issues warrant consideration. First, in the interests of increasing measurement validity, it is important that researchers employ specific measures of neighborhood attributes. Given the great variety of these attributes, it is tempting to simply measure each one in terms of a common scale, such as satisfaction. On such a scale respondents are asked whether they are satisfied with public transit, local schools, the friendliness of their neighbors, and so on.

By only having one indicator of each of these attributes, however, the researcher will be unable to interpret why someone is dissatisfied with, say, local public transit. Instead, if there are specific indicators of satisfaction with the different dimensions of local public transit service, relating to such areas as proximity of transit stops, frequency of service, and timeliness of service, it will be much easier to infer why a particular neighborhood attribute may be problematic. Moreover, if the particular aspect of the attribute being evaluated is specified, the respondent is less likely to randomly respond to a general question on public transit. Consequently, increased specificity will also increase measurement reliability. Finally, the importance of each dimension of public transit can be assessed by calculating the statistical relation between each dimension and an overall assessment of public transit.

Another technique for increasing measurement reliability is to combine responses to related questions into a scale or index that captures the multidimensional aspects of the concept or construct of interest. For example, an overall measure of perceived public transit quality can be obtained from combining the scores on the individual measures for each aspect of transit quality. These scores can be weighted equally, or they can be weighted based on theory or on empirical results, such as those produced in factor analysis. For an illustration of the latter, using neighborhood quality data, consult Angrist (1974), Carp, Zadawski, and Shokrkon (1976), or Carp and Carp (1982).

Because greater specificity can increase the number of questions employed in a survey, researchers may want to limit the focus of their research to a few neighborhood quality attributes or dimensions. In order to select attributes to concentrate upon, the researcher may wish to meet with neighborhood and community leaders and residents to obtain an impression of what neighborhood issues are likely to be most important. This technique is recommended by Hester (1984), who sees survey research as the second step, following neighborhood "listening," in a sequence of steps necessary to neighborhood planning and design.

In addition to increasing the specificity of neighborhood quality measures, it is also important to obtain information, wherever feasible, of the resident's knowledge of a particular neighborhood attribute. This is particularly true with regard to local public services, especially those services that many people do not regularly use. For example, in obtaining assessments of local public transit, it is important to find out how often, if ever, the respondent uses public transportation. Similar information should be obtained in order to evaluate other neighborhood public services, such as police, fire, recreation, schools, and libraries.

Issues for Neighborhood Planning and Design

Aside from the issues just described, it is important to consider specific ways in which neighborhood quality research can be used in neighborhood planning and design. Two situations are discussed in this context: (1) planning for a single neighborhood and (2) planning for a number of neighborhoods.

In planning for a particular neighborhood, the task often centers on either preparing a comprehensive plan or designing a particular facility for the neighborhood, such as a community building or a park. In either situation problems must be identified, goals must be established, and choices about which goals will be given priority and which actions will achieve these goals need to be determined. As previously discussed, surveys addressing neighborhood quality can be used to identify the problems that disturb residents. In most cases the problems that are frequently cited will be those upon which planning and design efforts will be concentrated.[4]

But planners and designers also may want to obtain information on the importance residents attach to correcting specific neighborhood problems. In multiproblem neighborhoods there will frequently be insufficient resources to adequately address all the problems identified by residents. Consequently, choices must be made about which problems are the most important. Sample surveys can be used in which residents are given a list of neighborhood concerns and asked to state the importance or priority each should receive. Respondents can then be asked to rank each of the most important concerns or to nominate the two or three most important that should be addressed immediately.

Multiple regression analysis of survey data is another approach to ranking priorities. Researchers can employ regression analysis to determine which assessments of various neighborhood attributes are most important (have the highest coefficients) in predicting some global indicator of neighborhood quality, such as satisfaction. This procedure may reveal latent priorities that were not manifested in the rating of individual neighborhood attributes as being problematic or important.

Multiple-neighborhood planning is similar in many respects to single-neighborhood planning. The major difference, of course, is that multiple-neighborhood planning will often require making choices about the level and type of resources that should be channeled to each neighborhood. In the context of our discussion, such decisions would involve comparing neighborhoods in terms of expressed need. Hence neighborhoods in which the highest proportion of residents report crime problems, for example, would be given highest priority in the allocation of resources for public safety.

Some analysts have argued against employing subjective indicators in this way to assess relative need. In particular, Stipak (1979) contends that subjective assessments of a neighborhood's attributes are influenced not only by objective conditions, but also by resident expectations about their neighborhood.[5] Given a low level of neighborhood quality, therefore, residents with higher expectations are likely to express greater dissatisfaction than those with lower expectations about their neighborhood. Hence lower levels of neighborhood satisfaction may not correspond to inferior objective conditions.

In Stipak's view, this lack of complete correspondence between objective and subjective indicators decreases the value of the latter. He therefore recommends that subjective indicators be used in conjunction with objective measures and that subjective indicators be adjusted, using multiple regression techniques, for the impact individual expectations have upon overall evaluations.

By performing such adjustments, however, Stipak, in effect, negates the primary utility of subjective indicators: their usefulness in providing the subjective views of neighborhood residents that are not represented by so-called objective indicators. As noted earlier, "objective" indicators, such as crime statistics or expert housing quality assessments, are not completely valid or reliable measures of the dimensions they purport to represent. Consequently, when subjective indicators are employed, they should be used to complement objective data, rather than exorcised of their subjective content.

NOTES

1. This chapter draws extensively from a report prepared for the U.S. Department of Housing and Urban Development (Marans, Scharf, and Connerly, 1982).

2. It should be noted that although cognitive and affective dimensions of well-being can be defined as distinctive, it is also expected that there will be considerable overlap between the two dimensions, since people who are happy with some aspect of their life are also likely to be satisfied and vice versa. In fact, Campbell, Converse, and Rodgers (1976) found that the Pearson correlation coefficient between satisfaction and happiness with life as a whole was .50.

3. Andrews and Withey (1976) prefer this scale over the seven-point satisfaction scale because the latter does not distinguish between the "merely" satisfied and those who derive more enjoyment from their neighborhood. Moreover, unlike the satisfaction scale, all categories of the delighted-terrible scale are labeled. This presumably helps to better define for the respondents what each response category means.

Despite the merits of the delighted-terrible scale, it may not be preferable to the satisfaction or excellent-poor scales. First, it has apparently been used in only two neighborhood quality studies (Andrews and Withey, 1976; U.S. Department of Housing and Urban Development [HUD], 1978). The other scales have been applied more frequently and thus provide more opportunity for comparison than does the delighted-terrible scale. Second, as discussed earlier, the strong emotional content of feeling delighted or terrible may simply be inappropriate to evaluations of neighborhood quality.

Andrews and Withey (1976) also expected to get a distribution with their delighted-terrible scale that was less skewed than that obtained with the seven-point satisfaction scale. Indeed, the study of Campbell, Converse, and Rodgers (1976) found that 67 percent of their sample of the U.S. population selected either of the top two categories of satisfaction, while Andrews and Withey (1976) reported that 57 percent of their sample of the U.S. population selected either of these categories. Nevertheless, both scales are fairly skewed. This does not mean, however, that relatively few people identify problems in their neighborhoods. The literature has generally shown that when people evaluate specific neighborhood attributes, they are more likely to identify problems than when they are asked to give an overall evaluation. This suggests, as Campbell, Converse, and Rodgers (1976) have noted, that people place a small "positive edge" on their general assessment of the neighborhood, and this edge is less likely to affect their evaluation of specific neighborhood attributes.

4. For further information on integrating survey research on neighborhood quality into the broader context of neighborhood planning and design, consult Hester (1984) and Smith and Hester (1982).

5. Stipak's research (1979, 1983) focuses on subjective evaluation of urban public services, but his ideas can easily be extended to subjective evaluation of other aspects of neighborhood quality.

REFERENCES

Ahlbrandt, Roger S., Jr. 1984. *Neighborhoods, People, and Community*. New York: Plenum Press.

American Public Health Association. Committee on the Hygiene of Housing. 1960. *Planning the Neighborhood*. Chicago: Public Administration Service.

Andrews, Frank M., and Aubrey C. McKennell. 1980. "Measures of Self-Reported Well-Being: Their Affective, Cognitive, and Other Components." *Social Indicators Research* 8: 127–155.

Andrews, Frank M., and Stephen B. Withey. 1976. *Social Indicators of Well-Being: Americans' Perceptions of Life Quality*. New York: Plenum Press.

Angrist, Shirley S. 1974. "Dimensions of Well-Being in Public Housing." *Environment and Behavior* 6: 495–516.

Appleyard, Donald, with M. Sue Gerson and Mark Lintell. 1976. *Liveable Urban Streets*. Washington, D.C.: Federal Highway Administration.

———. 1981. *Livable Streets*. Berkeley and Los Angeles: University of California Press.

Bagley, Christopher, Solomon Jacobson, and Clare Palmer. 1973. "Social Structure and the Ecological Distribution of Mental Illness, Suicide, and Delinquency." *Psychological Medicine* 3: 177–187.

Baldassare, Mark. 1975. "The Effects of Density on Social Behavior and Attitudes." *American Behavioral Scientist* 18: 815–825.

Banerjee, Tridib, and William C. Baer. 1984. *Beyond the Neighborhood Unit*. New York: Plenum Press.

Barton, Allen H. 1975. "Observations on Neighborhood Satisfaction in New York City." Unpublished paper, August.

Becker, Franklin D. 1974. *Design for Living: The Residents' View of Multi-Family Housing*. Ithaca, N.Y.: Center for Urban Development Research, Cornell University.

Bradburn, Norman M., and David Caplovitz. 1965. *Reports on Happiness*. Chicago: Aldine.

Bradburn, Norman M., Seymour Sudman, and Galen Gockel. 1970. *Racial Integration in American Neighborhoods*. Chicago: National Opinion Research Center, University of Chicago.

Brown, Karin, and Philip B. Coulter. 1983. "Subjective and Objective Measures of Police Service Delivery." *Public Administration Review* 43 (January/February): 50–58.

Brudney, Jeffrey L., and Robert E. England. 1982. "Urban Policy Making and Subjective Service Evaluations: Are They Compatible?" *Public Administration Review* 42 (March/April): 127–135.

Butler, Edgar W., F. Stuart Chapin, Jr., George C. Hemmens, Edward J. Kaiser, Michael A. Stegman, and Shirley F. Weiss. 1969. *Moving Behavior and Residential Choice: A National Survey*. Washington, D.C.: Highway Research Board.

Cadwallader, M. T. 1979. "Neighborhood Evaluation in Residential Mobility." *Environment and Planning A* 11: 393–401.

Campbell, Angus, and Philip E. Converse (eds.). 1972. *The Human Meaning of Social Change*. New York: Russell Sage Foundation.

Campbell, Angus, Philip E. Converse, and Willard L. Rodgers. 1976. *The Quality of American Life: Perceptions, Evaluations, and Satisfactions*. New York: Russell Sage Foundation.

Carp, Frances M., and Abraham Carp. 1982. "Perceived Environmental Quality of Neighborhoods: Development of Assessment Scales and Their Relations to Age and Gender." *Journal of Environmental Psychology* 2: 295–312.

Carp, Frances M., Rick T. Zawadski, and Hossein Shokrkon. 1976. "Dimensions of Urban Environmental Quality." *Environment and Behavior* 8 (June): 239–264.

Chapin, F. Stuart, Jr., Edgar W. Butler, and Frederick C. Patten. 1972. *Blackways in the Inner City*. Chapel Hill: Center for Urban and Regional Studies, University of North Carolina.

City of Cincinnati. 1978. *Service Monitoring Survey: Instrumentation*, January.

Clay, Grady. 1980. *Close-Up: How to Read the American City*. Chicago: University of Chicago Press.

Clay, Phillip. 1979. *Neighborhood Renewal*. Lexington, Mass.: Lexington Books.

Connerly, Charles E. 1985. "The Community Question: An Extension of Wellman and Leighton." *Urban Affairs Quarterly* 20: 537–556.

———. 1986. "The Impact of Neighborhood Social Relations on Prospective Mobility." *Social Science Quarterly* 67, (March): 186–194.

Connerly, Charles E., and Robert W. Marans. 1985. "Comparing Two Global Measures of Perceived Neighborhood Quality." *Social Indicators Research* 17 (July): 29–47.

Cooper, Clare. 1975. *Easter Hill Village*. New York: Free Press.

Dale, Britt. 1980. "Subjective and Objective Social Indicators in Studies of Regional Social Well-Being." *Regional Studies* 14: 503–515.

Dear, Michael, and S. Martin Taylor. 1979. ''Community Attitudes toward Neighborhood Public Facilities.'' Hamilton, Ontario: Department of Geography, McMaster University, September.

Dowall, David E., and J. B. Juhasz. 1978. ''Trade-Off Surveys in Planning: Theory and Application.'' *Environment and Planning A* 10 (February): 125–136.

Dubow, F., E. McCabe, and G. Kaplan. 1979. *Reactions to Crime: A Critical Review of the Literature*. Washington, D.C.: U.S. Department of Justice.

Duncan, Greg J., and Sandra J. Newman. 1976. ''Expected and Actual Residential Mobility.'' *Journal of the American Institute of Planners* 42 (April): 174–186.

Dunham, H. W. 1965. *Community and Schizophrenia*. Detroit: Wayne State University Press.

Festinger, L., S. Schachter, and K. Back. 1950. *Social Pressures in Informal Groups*. New York: Harper & Brothers.

Francescato, Guido, Sue Weidemann, James R. Anderson, and Richard Chenowith. 1979. *Residents' Satisfaction in HUD-Assisted Housing: Design and Management Factors*. Urbana-Champaign: Housing Research and Development Program, University of Illinois, March.

Fried, Marc. 1973. *The World of the Working Class*. Cambridge, Mass.: Harvard University Press.

Fried, Marc, and Peggy Gleicher. 1961 ''Some Sources of Residential Satisfaction in an Urban Slum.'' *Journal of the American Institute of Planners* 27 (November): 305–315.

Gans, Herbert J. 1967. *The Levittowners*. New York: Free Press.

———. 1982. *The Urban Villagers*. Revised ed. New York: Free Press.

Goetze, Rolf, and Kent W. Colton. 1983. ''The Dynamics of Neighborhoods: A Fresh Approach to Understanding Housing and Neighborhood Change.'' In Phillip L. Clay and Robert M. Hollister (eds.), *Neighborhood Policy and Planning*. Lexington, Mass.: Lexington Books. 57–76.

Gollin, Albert E., Mary Eileen Dixon, and Andrea E. Golden. 1975. *Social Patterns and Attitudes in Greater Washington, 1973–1975*. Washington, D.C.: Bureau of Social Science Research.

Greenberg, Stephanie, William Rohe, and Jay Williams. 1981. *Safe and Secure Neighborhoods: Physical Characteristics and Informal Territorial Control in High and Low Crime Areas*. Research Triangle Park, N.C.: Research Triangle Institute.

Hall, John F., and A. James Ring. 1974. *Indicators of Environmental Quality and Life Satisfaction: A Subjective Approach*. London: Survey Unit, Social Science Research Council.

Hamovitch, M., and J. Peterson. 1969. ''Housing Needs and Satisfaction of the Elderly.'' *Gerontologist* 9: 30–32.

Haney, Wava S., and Eric S. Knowles. 1978. ''Perceptions of Neighborhoods by City and Suburban Residents.'' *Human Ecology* 6: 201–214.

Hatry, Harry P., Richard E. Winnie, and Donald M. Fisk, 1981. *Practical Program Evaluation for State and Local Governments*. 2d ed. Washington, D.C.: Urban Institute Press.

Hatry, Harry P., Louis H. Blair, Donald M. Fisk, John H. Greiner, John R. Hall, Jr., and Philip S. Schaenman. 1977. *How Effective Are Your Community Services? Procedures for Monitoring the Effectiveness of Municipal Services*. Washington, D.C.: Urban Institute Press.

Heaton, Tim, Carl Fredrickson, Glenn V. Fuguitt, and James J. Zuiches. 1979. "Residential Preferences, Community Satisfaction, and the Intention to Move." *Demography* 16 (November): 565–573.

Henig, Jeffrey R. 1982. *Neighborhood Mobilization*. New Brunswick, N.J.: Rutgers University Press.

Hester, Randolph T., Jr. 1984. *Planning Neighborhood Space with People*. 2d ed. New York: Van Nostrand Reinhold.

Hoinville, Gerald. 1974. "Evaluating Community Preferences." In J. T. Coppock and C. B. Wilson (eds.), *Environmental Quality: With Emphasis on Urban Problems*. New York: Halstead Press.

Howell, Joseph T. 1973. *Hard Living on Clay Street: Portrait of Blue Collar Families*. Garden City, N.Y.: Anchor Books.

Hunter, Albert. 1974. *Symbolic Communities: The Persistence and Change of Chicago's Local Communities*. Chicago: University of Chicago Press.

———. 1979. "The Urban Neighborhood: Its Analytical and Social Contexts." *Urban Affairs Quarterly* 14: 267–288.

Jacobs, Allan B. 1985. *Looking at Cities*. Cambridge, Mass.: Harvard University Press.

Jacoby, Louis R. 1971. *Perception of Air, Noise, and Water Pollution in Detroit*. Michigan Geographical Publication no. 7. Ann Arbor: Department of Geography, University of Michigan.

Johnson, Robert E. 1980. *Assessing Housing Preferences of Low Cost Single Family Home Buyers*. Ann Arbor: Architectural Research Laboratory, University of Michigan.

Kain, John F., and John M. Quigley. 1970. "Evaluating the Quality of the Residential Environment." *Environment and Planning* 2 (January): 23–32.

Kasarda, John D., and Morris Janowitz. 1974. "Community Attachment in Mass Society." *American Sociological Review* 29: 322–339.

Kasl, S., and E. Harburg. 1972. "Perceptions of the Neighborhood and the Desire to Move Out." *Journal of the American Institute of Planners* 38 (September): 318–324.

Kirschenbaum, Alan. 1983. "Sources of Neighborhood Residential Change: A Micro-Level Analysis." *Social Indicators Research* 12 (February): 183–198.

Knight, Robert, and Mark Menchik. 1974. *Residential, Environmental Attitudes and Preferences: Report of a Questionnaire Survey*. Institute for Environmental Studies, Report No. 24. Madison: University of Wisconsin, October.

Koebel, C. Theodore. 1983. *Housing Quality in Louisville and Jefferson County*. Louisville, Ky.: Urban Studies Center, University of Louisville.

Korte, C. 1978. "Helpfulness in the Urban Environment." In A. Baum, J. E. Singer, and S. Valins (eds.), *Advances in Environmental Psychology*, vol. 1, *The Urban Environment*. Hillsdale, N.J.: Lawerence Erlbaum. 85–110.

———. 1980. "Urban-Nonurban Differences in Social Behavior and Social Psychological Models of Urban Impact." *Journal of Social Issues* 36: 29–51.

Kuz, Tony J. 1978. "Quality of Life: An Objective and Subjective Variable Analysis." *Regional Studies* 12: 409–417.

Lansing, John B., and Gary Hendricks. 1967. *Living Patterns and Attitudes in the Detroit Region*. Ann Arbor: Institute for Social Research, University of Michigan, January.

Lansing, John B., Robert W. Marans, and Robert B. Zehner. 1970. *Planned Residential Environments*. Ann Arbor: Institute for Social Research, University of Michigan.

Lansing, John B., E. Mueller, and N. Barth. 1964. "Residential Location and Urban Mobility." Ann Arbor: Institute for Social Research, University of Michigan.

Lee, Terrence R. 1968. "Urban Neighborhood as a Socio-Spatial Schema."*Human Relations* 21: 241–268.

Lee, Trevor, and Robert W. Marans. 1980. "Objective and Subjective Indicators: Effects of Scale Discordance on Interrelationships."*Social Indicators Research* 8: 47–64.

McKennell, Aubrey C. 1978. "Cognition and Affect in Perceptions of Well-Being."*Social Indicators Research* 5: 389–426.

McKennell, Aubrey C., and Frank M. Andrews. 1980. "Models of Cognition and Affect in Perceptions of Well-Being."*Social Indicators Research* 8: 257–298.

———. 1983. "Components of Perceived Life Quality."*Journal of Community Psychology* 11: 98–110.

Marans, Robert W., and J. Mark Fly. 1981. *Recreation and the Quality of Urban Life: Recreational Resources, Behaviors, and Evaluations of People in the Detroit Region*. Ann Arbor: Institute for Social Research, University of Michigan.

Marans, Robert W., and Willard Rodgers. 1975. "Toward an Understanding of Community Satisfaction." In Amos Hawley and Vincent Rock (eds.) *Metropolitan America in Contemporary Perspective*. New York: Halsted. 295–354.

Marans, Robert W., S. J. Newman, J. D. Wellman, and J. Kruse. 1976. *Waterfront Living: A Report on Permanent and Seasonal Residents in Northern Michigan*. Ann Arbor: Institute for Social Research, University of Michigan.

Marans, Robert W., and John D. Wellman. 1978. *The Quality of Nonmetropolitan Living: Evaluations, Behavior, and Expectations of Northern Michigan Residents*. Ann Arbor: Survey Research Center, Insititute for Social Research, University of Michigan.

Marans, Robert W., Stephanie Scharf, and Charles Connerly. 1982. *The Concept and Measurement of Neighborhood Quality*. Ann Arbor: Institute for Social Research, University of Michigan.

Mayer, Neil S. 1984. *Neighborhood Organizations and Community Development*. Washington, D.C.: Urban Institute Press.

Michaelsen, Larry K., Donald A. Murray, Neal J. Dickerman, Jr., Howard E. VanAuken, and Marjorie Early. 1976. "Quality of Life in Oklahoma—Preliminary Results." Norman: Center for Economic and Management Research, University of Oklahoma, November.

Michelson, William. 1966. "An Empirical Analysis of Urban Environmental Preference."*Journal of the American Institute of Planners* 32: 355–360.

———. 1977. *Environmental Choice, Human Behavior, and Residential Satisfaction*. New York: Oxford University Press.

Milbrath, Lester W. 1981. "Citizen Surveys as Citizen Participation Mechanisms."*Journal of Applied Behavioral Science* 17 (October–December): 478–496.

Myers, Dowell. 1983. "Population Process and Neighborhoods." In Phillip L. Clay and Robert M. Hollister (eds.), *Neighborhood Policy and Planning*. Lexington, Mass.: Lexington Books. 113–132.

Nathanson, Constance A., Jeanne S. Newman, Elizabeth Moen, and Helen Hiltabiddle. 1976. "Moving Plans among Residents of a New Town." *Journal of the American Institute of Planners* 42 (July): 295–302.

National Opinion Research Center. 1974. *Continuous National Survey: A Compendium of Questionnaire Items, Cycles 1 through 12.* Chicago: University of Chicago.
————. 1978. *General Social Surveys, 1972–1978: Cumulative Codebook.* Chicago: University of Chicago.
Newman, Oscar. 1972. *Defensible Space.* New York: Collier Books.
Newman, Sandra J. 1974. *The Residential Environment and the Desire to Move.* Ann Arbor: Institute for Social Research, University of Michigan.
Newman, Sandra J., and Greg J. Duncan. 1979. "Residential Problems, Dissatisfaction, and Mobility." *Journal of the American Planning Association* 45 (April): 154–162.
Pacione, Michael. 1984. "Local Areas in the City." In D. T. Herbert and R. J. Johnston (eds.), *Geography and the Urban Environment,* vol. 6. Chichester, England: John Wiley. 349–392.
Park, Robert, E. Burgess, and R. McKenzie. 1967. *The City.* 4th ed. Chicago: Univeristy of Chicago Press.
Quigley, John M. 1978. "Housing Markets and Housing Demand: Analytic Responses." In Larry S. Bourne and John R. Hitchcock (eds.), *Urban Housing Markets: Recent Directions in Research and Policy.* Toronto: University of Toronto Press. 23–44.
Ridker, Ronald G., and John A. Henning. 1967. "The Determinants of Residential Property Values with Special Reference to Air Pollution." *Review of Economics and Statistics* 49: 246–257.
Robinson, Ira, W. C. Baer, T. K. Banerjee, and P. G. Flachsbart. 1975. "Trade-off Games." In W. Michelson (ed.), *Behavioral Research Methods in Environmental Design.* Stroudsburg, Pa.: Dowden, Hutchinson & Ross.
Rodgers, Willard L., Robert W. Marans, Stephen D. Nelson, Sandra J. Newman, and Orian Worden. 1975. *The Quality of Life in the Detroit Metropolitan Area: Frequency Distributions.* Ann Arbor: Institute for Social Research, University of Michigan.
Rohe, William M., and Lauren B. Gates. 1985. *Planning with Neighborhoods.* Chapel Hill: University of North Carolina Press.
Rossi, P. H. 1955. *Why Families Move: A Study in the Social Psychology of Urban Residential Mobility.* Glencoe, Ill.: Free Press.
Sanoff, Henry. 1973. *Integrating User Needs in Environmental Design.* Washington, D.C.: National Technical Information Service, U.S. Department of Commerce, January.
Scharf, Stephanie Ann. 1978. "The Social Psychology of Neighborhood Satisfaction." Ph.D. diss., University of Chicago.
Schmitt, R. C. 1966. "Density, Health, and Social Organization." *Journal of the American Institute of Planners* 32: 38–40.
Schneider, H. 1975. "The Quality of Life in Large American Cities: Objective and Subjective Social Indicators." *Social Indicators Research* 1: 495–509.
Smith, Frank J., and Randolph T. Hester, Jr. 1982. *Community Goal Setting.* Stroudsburg, Pa.: Hutchinson Ross Publishing.
Speare, A., Jr. 1974. "Residential Satisfaction as an Intervening Variable in Residential Mobility." *Demography* 11: 173–188.
Stipak, Brian. 1979. "Are There Sensible Ways to Analyze and Use Subjective Indicators of Urban Service Quality?" *Social Indicators Research* 6: 627–649.

———. 1983. "Interpreting Subjective Data for Program Evaluation." *Policy Studies Journal* 12 (December):305–314.

Suttles, Gerald D. 1968. *The Social Order of the Slum*. Chicago: University of Chicago Press.

Taub, Richard P., D. Garth Taylor, and Jan D. Dunham. 1981. "Crime, Fear of Crime, and the Deterioration of Urban Neighborhoods." Chicago: National Opinion Research Center.

United Kingdom. Department of the Environment. 1972. *The Estate outside the Dwelling*. London: Her Majesty's Stationery Office.

———. Royal Commission on Local Government in England. 1969. *Research Studies: Community Attitudes Survey*. London: Her Majesty's Stationery Office.

U.S. Bureau of the Census. 1984. *Annual Housing Survey: 1983*. Washington, D.C.: Government Printing Office.

U.S. Department of Housing and Urban Development. 1978. *The 1978 HUD Survey on the Quality of Community Life: A Data Book*. Washington, D.C.: Government Printing Office.

Van Vliet—, Willem. 1981. "Neighborhood Evaluations by City and Suburban Children." *Journal of the American Planning Association* 47 (October): 458–466.

Varady, David P. 1983. "Determinants of Residential Mobility Decisions: The Role of Government Services in Relation to Other Factors." *Journal of the American Planning Association* 49 (Spring): 184–199.

Weicher, John C. 1980. *Housing: Federal Policies and Programs*. Washington, D.C.: American Enterprise Institute.

Wilner, Daniel M., Rosabelle Walkeley, Thomas C. Pinkerton, and Matthew Taybeck. 1962. *The Housing Environment and Family Life*. Baltimore: Johns Hopkins Press.

Wilson, R. L. 1962. "Liveability of the City: Attitudes and Urban Development." In F. S. Chapin, Jr., and S. Weiss (eds.), *Urban Growth Dynamics: In a Regional Cluster of Cities*. New York: Wiley & Sons.

Wolf, Eleanor, and Charles Lebeaux. 1969. "Newcomers and Oldtimers in Lafayette Park." In Eleanor Wolf and Charles Lebeaux (eds.), *Change and Renewal in an Urban Community*. New York: Praeger.

Zehner, Robert B. 1971. "Neighborhood and Community Satisfaction in New Towns and Less Planned Suburbs." *Journal of the American Institute of Planners* 37: 379–385.

Zehner, Robert B., and F. Stuart Chapin, Jr. 1974. *Across the City Line: A White Community in Transition*. Lexington, Mass.: Lexington Books.

Zehner, Robert B., and Robert W. Marans. 1973. "Residential Density, Planning Objectives, and Life in Planned Communities." *Journal of the American Institute of Planners* 39: 337–345.

3

The Townhouse: A Basis for Community

SUZANNE KELLER

Many in our time are concerned about the fate of territorial communities in the era unfolding. Some fear, others welcome, the possibility that the electronic society will make such communities obsolete, since in that view instant communication permits the creation of instantaneous communities independent of any given site. This notion strikes me not only as premature, with potentially destructive effects on existing communities, but as based on a misreading of contemporary trends. On the contrary, place, space, and territory cannot be dispensed with quite so easily. Twentieth-century humans still need to reside somewhere, if not to strike up permanent roots, then at least to create some kind of home base between moves. Even outer space colonies will be settlements in place. The question is which type of spatial arrangements will be acceptable to diverse contemporary populations.

In the postconstruction evaluation of new communities, such as the case study discussed here, a key objective has been to be attentive to the role of space, land, privacy areas, and place in the development of a sense of community. These new communities, or PUDs (planned unit developments), with their higher densities and shared land uses (often in townhouse or apartment house form), differ from conventional suburbs in their efforts to break down the splendid isolation of suburban life and move toward some form of shared living that constitutes a compromise between urban conviviality and suburban privatism.

A PUD both reflects and attempts to foster a new sense of collective responsibility. As the twentieth century goes forward, the shrinkage of households both in terms of size and the activities centered there creates a need to reach beyond the cocoon of the family to a wider social terrain. With the rise of divorce, single parenthood, and smaller families, erstwhile suburban privacy and self-containment all too readily become suburban isolation and vulnerability to crime and loneliness, further promoting a reaching out to others. PUDs represent a built environment for doing so.

OPPOSING VIEWPOINTS OF THE ROLE OF SPATIAL ARRANGEMENTS IN STRENGTHENING SOCIAL TIES

In the current commentaries on the changing housing market, one finds two antithetical views. One attributes to the rise of new housing developments a propensity for stronger social and neighborhood ties, while the other prophesies a weakening of such ties. The "stronger" position rests on the sharing of facilities and land, while the "weaker" position refers to the transiency and brevity of social contacts in new developments that preclude deeper social bonds. The data presented below supports the "stronger" position in that emerging housing forms are shown to engender patterns of social solidarity with varying degrees of communal cohesion.

THE AMERICAN CONSUMER'S ACCEPTANCE OF THIS TOWNHOUSE HOUSING FORM

A question that has surfaced repeatedly over the past decade is whether and how middle-class suburban and exurban Americans will be able to let go of the single-family house ideal and adapt to multifamily and townhouse living. The contrary ideal, though not as ancient as we like to believe, has been extolled long enough to constitute a firm article of faith for most Americans. To that end, countless zoning boards have passed restrictive zoning ordinances, and building codes have specified lot sizes to accommodate the traditional single-family house that was the badge of middle-class respectability and at the apex of the hierarchy of desirable residential land uses.[1]

Yet research findings such as those given in this chapter indicate that many young Americans are buying the townhouse idea and are satisfied with it. In this period of lessened affordability of freestanding homes, the question arises whether Americans are downgrading not only their spartial requirements to fit their financial ability to pay the mortgage, but also their ideals of what constitutes a desirable housing environment.

PRESENT RESEARCH EVALUATIONS OF THE PUD/TOWNHOUSE SPATIAL ARRANGEMENTS

This section centers on the author's longitudinal study of one PUD with a view to evaluating the role of the townhouse, privacy areas, and place in developing a sense of community and satisfaction with life. Twin Rivers, the community selected, was created in the mid-1960s and opened its doors to the first of a prospective 10,000 residents in 1970. It was the first planned unit development (PUD) in the state of New Jersey, 15 miles east of Princeton, with a population mix that was fairly typical of modern suburbia. So were the motives that propelled newcomers there. Most had to do, in one way or another, with land and space: "The 'good life,' 'clean life,' a home of your own, a lawn, a back yard, a place for your children to play and be safe. These were the things most people wanted when they moved to this community'' *(Twin Rivers Periscope*, September 1975: 32).

All told, there were 3,000 dwellings on 719 acres for a population of 10,000. I have monitored the development of this PUD from its inception to the present with a view to charting its course and identifying the critical features in its emergence. The research discussed is based on an in-depth monitoring of residents and institutions over a 15-year period, with a before-and-after design, some 500 in-depth interviews, a Gallup survey of 1,000 households, and a repeat study of 50 residents a decade apart. A precise dating of the community's start permitted the construction of a baseline against which to chart its pattern of growth and change.

THE HOUSE: PROPERTY, SHELTER, AND PRIVATE DOMAIN

A part of what unites residents in this community is their ownership of townhouses that satisfy the need for separateness yet also give to each of them a joint stake in each other's lives and the land they possess in common. Townhouses, by not being self-sufficient in principle, challenge the ideal of the house as one's castle and private refuge, an ideal hard to sustain where dwellings are physically linked and involve owners in shared financial and territorial responsibilities.

Twin Rivers permitted an exploration of the response to townhouse living for Americans quite traditional in their orientation to family and homeownership. Such a traditional population would normally have aspired to live in a traditional freestanding house. Instead, they found themselves unwilling pioneers for a new mode of living as another frontier draws to a close—namely, the ''average American's ability to own a free-standing single-family house on a substantial plot of land'' (Wald, 1984: 1).

In Twin Rivers outreach was mandated by a number of design decisions involving the house, the land, and novel spatial arrangements. Most significant was the townhouse, which links residents physically, visually, and aurally and makes every homeowner automatically a land sharer bound up with the private and domestic space of unknown other residents. The sections that follow examine the townhouse and its impact on this community.

POSITIVE ATTITUDES TO THE TOWNHOUSE HOUSING FORM

Given the continued idealization of the freestanding single-family house, it comes as a surprise that the townhouse turned out to be basically a positive experience for these young couples. Whichever indicator we examined—the reactions to the house as a whole, desired improvements, demands for privacy, or responses to density, noise, and neighbors—the house came out as a plus.

Table 3.1
What Is the Key Ingredient of an Ideal Community?

	1980s Respondents		1980s Twice-Interviewed Sample	
"A detached house" (first response)	27%	(5%)*	21%	(0%)
Did not mention a detached house	73%	(95%)	79%	(100%)
	N = 71		N = 44**	

*Numbers in parentheses refer to the 1970s.
**These are residents interviewed both in 1973 and 1983.

None of the prophesied fears—from ruthless invasion of privacy to horrendous neighbors—materialized for more than a fraction of the population. This contradicts the conventional wisdom that Americans are not ready to give up the single-family house cum front lawn and private backyard or must experience extreme stress in doing so.

The facts show otherwise. On a 15-item index of housing satisfaction based on liking the house overall and on specific ratings of various dimensions, the large majority of Twin Rivers residents liked the house (two-thirds), one-third being enthusiastic and only a minority having mixed feelings. A minuscule proportion (2 percent or less) disliked the house.

Moreover, townhouses, though sharing walls and common spaces, are connected in the minds of their owners not with apartments, which they resemble somewhat, but with freestanding houses. Indeed, there is a rather consistent pattern of association between housing type and life satisfaction: apartment dwellers are noticeably low on both, townhouse residents, high.

The house is seen not only as a haven for shelter but as a provider of outdoor play space for children with adult supervision nearby, and of space where adults may gather for gossip or social celebrations. On all these counts, the townhouse proved more than adequate. Even the high densities turned out to be acceptable provided that they also allowed for some private space and amenities close by. Contrary to much expert opinion, therefore, residents were both receptive and adaptable to what must still be considered a novel form of housing in suburbia.

Nonetheless, erstwhile ideals die hard. Despite living in attached housing, and even ready to acknowledge its advantages, a minority of residents remained faithful to the idea of a freestanding house. Some residents (5 to 10 percent) knew almost immediately that a townhouse was not for them and left the community as soon as feasible. A larger proportion stayed but may have clung to the ideal of a detached house someday.

Comparative data prove especially useful here (Table 3.1). In the 1970s, in the flush of high expectations about the community, virtually none of the residents considered a detached house as a key ingredient of an ideal community. By the 1980s one-fourth gave this as their first response and 31 percent as a second response.

This suggests that the ideal of a detached house is still compelling, albeit for only a minority, at least in fantasy, but for the majority this does not detract from the considerable satisfaction with the townhouse already inhabited.

A more instructive comparison stems from the homeowners interviewed twice, a decade apart, still occupying the same houses they had initially purchased. Here we see that none mentioned a detached house as a significant ingredient of an ideal community in the early 1970s. By the early 1980s 21 percent did so, and they hoped to move away from the community. But the large majority stuck with their townhouses.

Research has shown that residential satisfaction reflects four main land- and space-related factors: (1) maintenance and upkeep of property and grounds; (2) external appearance of the dwellings; (3) the shape and layout of buildings; and (4) landscaping (Becker, 1977: 22). The fact that the townhouses of Twin Rivers proved very satisfactory to most residents suggests that it is possible to find satisfactions in a housing type that may not live up to one's ultimate ideal. Indeed, the data suggest further that housing preferences are not held to once and for all but are flexible and modifiable on the basis of experience.

A good deal seems to depend on skillful design. Design can provide the illusion of spaciousness, thereby enlarging what Becker has called "the psychological size of the house" (1977: 27). Design can make a small house appear spacious, even luxurious, by the use of skylights, high ceilings, windows above eye level, light-colored walls, mirrors, and open floor plans (Kerr, 1982: 1–8). In our image-conscious culture, appearance is all, and the illusion of space is apparently as effective as the actual provision of space. By and large, the Twin Rivers townhouses seem to have provided both the space needed by the inhabitants and the spaciousness desired by them.

TOWNHOUSE LIVING AND PRIVACY

There are many who believe that with townhouse living, privacy, that coveted nugget of well-being in an impersonal mass society, becomes an endangered species. High densities, as well as the visual and auditory proximity of neighbors, are seen to affect privacy adversely.

This in-depth study provides some needed answers about the availability of personal space in a dense settlement in which most of the space left to individual control is collectively shared. Privacy fared very well in Twin Rivers (Table 3.2). Both in the 1970s and the 1980s the large majority of residents thought privacy was quite satisfactory, and one-third thought it especially good. The minority who gave it low marks decreased over the decade suggesting either changing needs for privacy or habituation to the townhouse versions of it. Privacy has been associated with user satisfaction in general, and this is true for Twin

Table 3.2
Ratings of Privacy by Time Period

	1970s	1980s
Privacy is		
Particularly good	32%	31%
Adequate	35%	44%
Bad	33%	24%
	$N = 167^*$	$N = 71^*$

*Totals include townhouse dwellers only.

Table 3.3
Satisfaction with Twin Rivers Community by Rating of Privacy

Rating of Privacy	% of 1980s Townhouse Residents Saying They Like Twin Rivers Very Much
Particularly good	50%
Adequate	32%
Poor	10%
	N = 71
	X^2 = 10.17
	df = 4
	sig. = 0.031

Rivers as well. There is a clear-cut relationship between high ratings on privacy and strong liking for the community (Table 3.3).

Indeed, ratings on privacy improve with length of time in the community. The twice-interviewed residents, for example, gave privacy higher ratings in the 1980s, when 90 percent were satisfied with it, than in the 1970s, when only 57 percent were satisfied. This again suggests that people adapt on the basis of experience and can learn to adjust their needs for privacy to new conditions.

Privacy is a function not only of density but of visibility and observability. For example, the parking areas in Twin Rivers, located in front of the houses, generate a high degree of visibility. They show which residents go in and out of their houses frequently, who has visitors, and who gets packages, all of which makes some residents feel that they are living in a fishbowl (O'Toole, 1971: 10). On the other hand, witnessing the daily routines of their court neighbors can be quite compelling, and, at the start, residents are fascinated with and enjoy them. In time, however, they come to protect their privacy by ignoring much of what they see and spontaneously generate a privacy based on inattention.

However privacy was defined and obtained, it was not a problem but a very satisfactory aspect of Twin Rivers life. This further reinforced the acceptability of townhouse living for this quite typical modern population.

NEIGHBORS IN TOWNHOUSE DEVELOPMENTS

One meaning of community is good fellowship and neighborliness. An environment experienced as friendly and supportive enlists positive in-group feelings and loyalties, whereas one experienced as deficient in these respects diminishes the sense of community by bringing negative and uncooperative feelings to the fore.

High densities, by increasing physical proximity, can promote interpersonal friction or closeness. In Twin Rivers closeness was more common. The large majority of residents gave their neighbors a very positive rating both in the 1970s and the 1980s. Two determinants of neighborly feeling could be identified: (1) housing tenure and (2) spatial design.

As regards housing tenure, Twin Rivers confirms an oft-noted social division between those who own their own dwellings and those who rent them, the former living in the main in houses, the latter in apartments. Such a division creates disunity in an emerging community and rigidifies social stereotypes.

Twin Rivers homeowners tended to look down on apartment renters as being less desirable neighbors and less responsible citizens. In turn, apartment renters resented these slights and felt isolated and excluded from the incipient community. The social distance between owners and renters was sharp and definite from the earliest days. The two formed separate worlds and stayed within their borders. Adult homeowners, especially, tended to confine their range of sociability to other homeowners, either within their own courts or outside them. These patterns, once started, continued on their own momentum. Housing tenure was thus a significant determinant of patterns of sociability.

Spatial design affected sociability in a somewhat different way. For the residents in general, and for ex–New Yorkers in particular, major sites for sociability were the common parking areas in front of the townhouses. These become spaces where the neighbors' comings and goings could easily be observed. The high visibility made the area a convenient place for surveying one's immediate surroundings. Usually children played there as well—the danger of cars notwithstanding—and insiders could readily be distinguished from outsiders, as residents were able at a glance to determine who belonged and who did not.

This spatial visibility seems to have exercised a positive effect on sociability. Ex–New Yorkers, for example, used the small front lawns for conviviality and gossip. That this was a reflection of siting rather than merely the availability of open space is indicated by the fact that the grassy common areas at the rear of the houses were not used for such socializing at all. Residents found them unsuited or unappealing. They seemed to lack the necessary spatial ambiance for sociability.

Thus high densities made for high visibility, while the sharing of public spaces, parking areas, and services such as lawn maintenance and garbage disposal made for a high degree of interdependence. It was hard to avoid neighborly contact, and most residents desired not less but more such contact. The closed cul-desac arrangements also gave the housing courts a sense of spatial, if not always of social, cohesion. The visual awareness generated there made for a gradual development of mutual recognition followed by verbal greetings, and these led to whatever further social contacts seemed agreeable.

In sum, house-related land and space were significantly related to privacy as well as to sociability. In addition to the spaces they shared, residents also cherished spaces of their own in the form of small patios fenced off at the rear of their townhouses. These small spaces, only between 200 and 400 square feet, were of great personal and symbolic significance. In addition to the outdoor space they provided, they distinguished the townhouse from an apartment, thereby bringing it closer to the traditional image of a detached house. Part of the charm of this space was that it permitted the residents to express themselves freely, without the social controls that operated throughout the community. They found varied uses for their relished little corners of solitude. Some residents created beautiful gardens there, communed with nature, enjoyed barbecue family suppers in good weather, or contemplated the eternal verities in private. It was a delicious space of freedom in a community of shared spaces and ubiquitous architectural controls, the latter arousing strong, often negative passions.

In conclusion, a major lesson gained from this close look at a community in the making is that a population wedded to the single-family house in principle can nonetheless learn to appreciate, and even prefer, a form of shared housing in practice. This learning proceeded more rapidly than one would have thought and suggests that a well-designed townhouse can satisfy aspirations for privacy as well as for community. Given current U.S. economic and demographic trends toward smaller families, single-parent and two-job households, prolonged singlehood, high divorce rates, and an aging population, townhouse living may well become the housing ideal of the future.

NOTE

1. According to Gans, most Levittowners were not interested in living in a row house ever. Indeed, he warns, that "unless future row houses are designed to maximize privacy and can also overcome their present low-status image, they will be not be very popular with the next generation of house buyers" (Gans, 1976: 274). Zelinsky refers to the American "aversion" to inhabiting multifamily structures (Zelinsky, 1973: p.93).

REFERENCES

Becker, Franklin. 1977. *Housing Messages*. Stroudsburg, Pa.: Dowden, Hutchinson & Ross.

Gans, Herbert J. 1976. *The Levittowners*. Rev. ed. New York: Columbia University Press.

Kerr, Peter. 1982. "House Trend Downsized." *New York Times*, September 23.

O'Toole, Michael 1971. "Physical Features and Social Relations in a Planned Community." Senior thesis, Department of Sociology, Princeton University.

Twin Rivers Periscope, September 1975.

Wald, Matthew L. 1984. "The American Dream is Changing." *New York Times*, October 28, section 12.

Zelinsky, Wilbur. 1973. *The Cultural Geography of the United States*. Englewood Cliffs, N.J.: Prentice-Hall.

4

Design of the Built Environment: The Search for Usable Knowledge

RAYMOND G. STUDER

As is amply documented in various chapters of this book, the built environment can no longer be viewed as a background phenomenon in understanding sociobehavioral processes. The built environment has a conceptually independent ontological status, and while its influence relative to other classes of variables has not been clearly documented, few would deny its role in influencing human affairs. The simple fact is that design and management of the built environment is an act not only of invention, but of intervention in sociobehavioral processes. As such, physical design and management functions are an integral aspect of sociogenesis and are thus of considerable societal concern. Given this reality, what kinds of issues must be addressed, and what kinds of information and procedures are required to enter into such an enterprise generally, and in the case of the housing environment in particular?

Whatever economic and social analyses, policies, or programs are effected to guide development of housing in the aggregate, the success or failure of the housing environment obviously depends on its congruence with the specific needs, goals, and day-to-day behaviors of its inhabitants. The responsibility for realizing and maintaining this state of congruence ultimately falls on those who organize the built environment: physical designers. The focus of this chapter is upon the issues and processes involved in organizing built environments, particularly those of housing, with emphasis on the status of sociophysical knowledge and its utilization in design and decisionmaking processes. The perspective will be that of the architect seeking sociophysical knowledge that can be directly utilized in designing housing environments responsive to their user's sociobehavioral needs and goals. We will begin with a brief historical overview of the relatively new field of environmental design, as well as the agenda and current status of environmental design research. This will be followed by an attempt to identify major knowledge-generation and utilization issues with respect to the design of physical settings, concluding with suggestions for alternative strategies that might be considered for coming to grips with these issues.

HISTORICAL CONTEXT

Current sociophysical knowledge-generation and utilization issues in housing must be seen in the context of certain evolutionary developments in the fields of design and planning. These developments involve a unique interplay of the artistic, humanistic, and scientific traditions. Indeed, a well-documented sociology and social history of the architectural profession, that is, a systematic examination of the traditions, values, norms, and practices (behaviors) of architectural designers and educators, would provide important insights into sociophysical knowledge-generation and utilization issues. In the absence of such documentation, identification of several evolutionary developments relative to the processes of organizing, producing, and maintaining built environments may shed some light on current issues.

A major evolutionary threshold was reached with the transformation of physical problem solving from unself-conscious to self-conscious processes (Alexander, 1964; Studer and Van Vliet—, 1987). The unself-conscious physical organizing processes of indigenous cultures were guided by certain covert rules of physical organization that produced built environments integrally linked to the builder-inhabitant's sociocultural norms (and attendant sociobehavioral requirements) on the one hand, and to the physical and technological constraints on the other. No formal planning or design process per se was involved. The resultant spatial arrangements and structures exhibited little variation, and norms for organizing and constructing these structures evolved over an extended period. The builders were close to their materials and techniques, usually inhabited the shelters they produced, and subsequently altered them as required by unanticipated events and emerging dysfunctions. In short, the unself-conscious process was one wherein user-builders responded directly to slowly evolving sociophysical requirements.

When cultures experienced a transformation from unself-conscious to self-conscious processes, responsibility for organizing and constructing built environments was assumed by specialist master craftspersons. The process of incremental, adaptive change was replaced by one of simultaneous comprehension and conceptual organization of built environments prior to their construction; that is, the idea of self-conscious design emerged. Accompanying this form of decisionmaking was the introduction of new building technologies, thus elaborating and complicating the range of possible solutions.

Faced with the far more complex organizational task, the self-conscious designers began to formulate guiding principles, prescriptive theories to render their problems tractable. Guilds, special educational requirements, and other institutionalized arrangements eventually evolved, and the need to attain status within the guild produced a striving for identity and competition among prescriptive theories regarding how best to proceed and succeed. While success of the unself-conscious form makers depended on their integral role in and the norms operating in their sociocultural context, success of the self-conscious designers depends on the viability of the prescriptions guiding their efforts in the context of the norms of their guild.

The scientific and technological revolution produced vast changes in social organization and greater differentiation and division of labor. Larger-scale housing projects were required to accommodate rapidly growing urban populations. Both tenement and middle-class apartment dwellings were constructed on a massive scale without benefit of formal planning processes, knowledge of the human social and health consequences, or adequate understanding of interdependencies among physical, economic, and social dimensions in the built environment. The increasingly complex functions of conceptualizing, organizing, and producing built environments led to more specialized professionals, technicians, entrepreneurs, organizations, and processes. Landscape architecture, a field that addressed larger-scale environmental issues, gained an independent identity from architecture in the late nineteenth century. Widespread housing and public health problems spawned by industrialization led to a series of developments and reforms that eventually produced an independent profession of city planning. The field of city or urban planning emerged in response to the need to deal more comprehensively with large-scale physical problems and the infrastructural aspects of larger population aggregates, such as housing, transportation, and land use. While architecture continued its development under the umbrella of the visual arts, planning developed in a manner explicitly incorporating social, economic, and political variables into physical decisionmaking processes, drawing on methodological and substantive knowledge from relevant social and other scientific disciplines.

In the 1960s and early 1970s attempts to rationalize and formalize physical design processes were accompanied by research programs to bring the resources of the social and behavioral sciences to bear on physical problem solving. A significant epistemological transformation emerged that challenged traditional norms of architectural designers and educators. The term ''environmental design'' was introduced to differentiate new precepts, new axiological commitments (akin to the positive sciences)[1] from the more traditional view of architecture as an extension of the visual arts. Environmental design

1. focuses on general properties of the built environment, which are analyzed and synthesized in terms of their relationship to human (social, psychological, and biological) variables, goals, and outcomes;

2. is predicated on an approach to organizing the built environment that is quite concrete but conceptually independent of changing architectural styles, the dispositions of individual designers, or historically conditioned norms of the enterprise; and

3. is integrally linked to a program of scientific inquiry committed to the organization and generation of cumulative knowledge regarding (a) the relationship between built environmental and sociobehavioral phenomena and (b) procedures for relating sociobehavioral ends to built environmental means.

Many practicing architects and architectural educators have not fully embraced the precepts of environmental design. Indeed, postmodernism questions not only the precepts of the modern movement in architecture, but implicitly rejects the precepts of environmental design (Harris and Lipman, 1986). In spite of such counterforces, development of the field of environmental design has continued and its influence has widened. An accompanying research agenda is in place, a significant literature has been developed, and the institutional supports (academic programs, research organizations, journals) suggest a viable future. However, a serious knowledge-generation and utilization issue remains. To begin an examination of this issue, let us look briefly at the field of environmental design research.

MAJOR THEMES IN ENVIRONMENTAL DESIGN RESEARCH

The goal of environmental design research is to provide an empirically based, intellectually rigorous rationale for physical invention and intervention. Research literatures bearing on design of the built environment, and housing environments in particular, are extensive and expanding, as evidenced by other chapters of this book (see also, for example, Stokols, 1978; Dunlap and Catton, 1979; Foley, 1981). To properly characterize and critique this vast literature in any detail is quite beyond the scope of this chapter. Useful to this discussion is an overview developed in a recent volume (Moore, Tuttle, and Howell, 1985) that attempts to explicate the mission, goals, organization, and accomplishments of the field labeled environmental design research. This work claims to represent consensus of a broad spectrum of researchers from several disciplines.

The field is defined in the Moore, Tuttle, and Howell volume as ''basic and applied research and research utilization dealing with environment-[person]-behavior relations and applications [directed toward] improving the quality of life through better informed environmental policy, planning, design and education.'' (p. 3.) The status of this field, according to the authors, is admittedly preparadigmatic (Kuhn, 1962) and features the inclusion of a variety of major fields, several of which are themselves multidisciplinary in nature, for example, urban planning research, social geography, resource management, architecture, and landscape architecture research. Research issues include those that emerge along the entire aggregate-disaggregate continuum and are seen to be organized around four dimensions: places, people, sociobehavioral phenomena, and time. Each dimension, alone or in combination with others, has been the prime focus of various environmental design research efforts, the bulk of which relate directly or indirectly to the design of housing environments. Let us briefly characterize some of these efforts.

Place-focused investigations are seen to deal with particular types of settings, such as residential, industrial, commercial, or recreational, and these are further classified according to macro, mezzo and micro scale, for example, natural environments, regional areas, metropolitan areas, communities, housing, work places, other building types, and types of spaces within various building types. These "places" may be inhabited or utilized by many types of people, thus the issues investigated derive from the characteristics and requirements of the type of physical setting and its effectiveness in supporting the sociobehavioral goals and requirements of various users.

Housing is predictably a major "place type" investigation since it constitutes a major unresolved societal problem, is the product of the major building effort, and is the most sociobehaviorally salient and complex class of built environments (Ross and Campbell, 1978; Cooper, 1975; Weideman et al., 1982). The complexity of sociophysical issues in housing, together with the highly descriptive methodology of housing research, makes their application to new situation-specific housing settings and housing types quite difficult. The atheoretical nature of ex post facto sociophysical analyses of housing studies (for example, indices of satisfaction), indeed the methodology of postoccupancy evaluations (POEs) generally, produces at best only general recommendations for housing design. Theoretical models of housing (for example, Rapoport, 1969; Morris and Winter, 1978) seek to provide more generalizable design directives. Michelson's work appears to provide a most promising empirically based theoretical framework for housing designers (1973, 1976, 1977).

People-focused investigations involve issues related to user groups with particular environmental requirements. Life-span developmental issues figure heavily in this category, and environmental research activity concentrating on children (Altman and Wohlwill, 1978) and the elderly (Zeisel, Epp, and Demos, 1978, 1984) has been extensive. Handicapped populations have also received considerable attention (Steinfeld, 1979), as have other user groups with particular dependence on physical support systems. Included are investigations of underrepresented minorities as affected by distribution of resources in the built environment. Obviously the categories of user groups are almost boundless, and the particular subject populations tend to vary with the nation's changing social agenda (and research funding priorities).

A focus on issues related to sociobehavioral phenomena relative to the built environment is most closely linked to the basic social and behavioral science disciplines. These issues range from physiological needs and responses to sociocultural world views, values, norms, and life-style patterns as related to the built environment. Investigations of sociobehavioral phenomena are generally categorized as physiological or psychological responses to built environmental stimuli. Physiological investigations include those assessing the impacts of built environmental conditions (such as light, sound, heat, and cold) on human health, comfort, stress, and various other performance measures. In this category the effect of noise on human stress and performance has been a major topic at macro, mezzo, and micro scales (Glass and Singer, 1972; Cohen, Glass, and Singer,

1973), as has the acoustical performance of living environments, theaters, and work settings. Microepidemiological studies of built environments document various health effects of building materials and micropollutants.

Investigations of psychological responses to aspects of the built environment include those involving perception, cognition, meaning and symbolism, psychological stress, development, learning, and emotions/affect. These investigations build upon a vast body of basic research to examine the influence of the built environment on these states and processes. The areas of environmental perception and cognition have perhaps received the greatest attention (for example, Moore and Golledge, 1976).

Behavioral (overt) responses to built environments have been investigated along the entire aggregate-disaggregate continuum. These investigations are wide-ranging and include such areas as adaptation to environmental stimuli (Wohlwill, 1974), orientation and wayfinding (Passini, 1984), environmental preferences and attitudes (Craik and Zube, 1976), and human performance and productivity. Major topics of this category relative to housing include investigations of human privacy (Altman, 1975), density and crowding (Stokols, 1972), territoriality and criminal behavior (Newman, 1972), and safety (Archea, 1977; Ventre, Stahl, and Turner, 1982).

Investigations of interpersonal and group behavior in the context of variables in the built environment include group dynamics, proxemics, and organizational behavior. Relocation behavior relative to properties of the built environment figures heavily in the category, as do changing familial patterns, life-style, and "opportunity fields" with respect to different social groups (Van Vliet—, 1985). Macro-scale investigations executed in the context of the built environment include influences of relevant cultural norms, rules, attitudes, roles, class structures, and group memberships examined in cross-cultural and historical studies (Rapoport, 1969, 1979).

Clearly the field of environmental design research is a wide-ranging knowledge-generating enterprise. Indeed, it has been characterized as "data rich" but difficult to comprehend with respect to its utilization in environmental design and decisionmaking. While this work gives the practicing architect a great deal to think about, procedures for integrating and utilizing this information in design processes have not been adequately documented.

The most successful knowledge-utilization efforts are in areas where (1) physical support is most critical, for example, the elderly (Lawton, 1980) and the handicapped (Canter and Canter, 1979); (2) performance criteria are most clearly specified, for example, work environments (Sundstrom, Kastenbaum, and Konar-Goldband, 1978), health facilities (Clipson and Wehrer, 1974), and urban crime (Newman, 1972); or (3) research efforts are integral to situation-specific design and decisionmaking issues and processes. This last category suggests a key arrangement in addressing the impasse that seems to exist between the knowledge-generation and utilization components of the enterprise. John Zeisel's perspective on "inquiry by design" (1981) has provided a promising direction for overcoming the impasse, as have his efforts to utilize this approach in practice (Zeisel and Griffin, 1975). Similar efforts to integrate research with design and decisionmaking (see Brill, 1982; Schneekloth and Shibley, forthcoming) support the view that the more closely tied an investigation is to issues as they arise in design and decisionmaking processes, the narrower is the gap between knowledge generation and utilization. We will return to this theme later.

We have traced in a historical context the emergence of the field of environmental design as one closely linked to, but differentiated in certain respects from, the traditional profession of architecture. The field of environmental design research has been identified as the knowledge-generating instrumentality to support design activities. Our characterization of the field was drawn from a consensus statement developed under the auspices of the Environmental Design Research Association. This is a very useful description of how the field views itself, but the explication leaves unanswered critical questions regarding its status. It is in certain respects a field that is indeed not only "preparadigmatic," but aparadigmatic in that it is not clear what kind of engination would move the enterprise toward something approaching paradigmatic status. An ex post facto framework consisting of categorization and cataloging of a collection of investigations (regardless of their quality) does not constitute a research discipline. One cannot readily distinguish the "leading" or "trailing" edge; there is no sense of cumulative knowledge to address agreed-upon major questions. More importantly, there is limited documentation of how the bulk of this generated knowledge can be utilized in design and decisionmaking processes, the only conceivable rationale for such a field. In short, this program, one committed to the generation of a significant body of usable knowledge, has been difficult to consummate. At the very heart of the matter is the frequently posed rhetorical question: Are physical designers asking the wrong questions, are social scientists providing the wrong answers, or both? After several decades of sociophysical inquiry we have no clear answer to this question. Let us examine some of the underlying problems and issues attendant to this challenge.

MAJOR PROBLEMS AND ISSUES

Given the historic antecedents of the physical design enterprise vis-à-vis the artistic, humanistic, and scientific traditions, organization of the built environment is predictably approached from several conflicting axiological platforms. This, together with conflicting perspectives operating in the sociophysical research community, not to mention historically conflicting norms of social science and physical design, produces a rather snarled array of propositions. With no intent to exacerbate such impediments to communication and collaboration, these axiological conflicts among knowledgeable actors must be seen as background to any examination of the knowledge-generation and utilization issue.

The intrinsic disparities between the goals of social science and sociophysical design are quite obvious. Social scientists seek general knowledge, while designers must solve situation-specific sociophysical problems (Altman, 1973). Social scientists can select and bound their problems as suits their interests, while designers must take problems as they come. Social scientists seek to document what is (and possibly what will be) and generalize this to a wider population and context. Designers necessarily deal with what is, what will be, and what ought to be in a particular problem context.

Fundamental differences between the perspectives, goals, and norms of social scientists and designers, although problematic, are to be expected. It is also well known that significant differences prevail among various social scientists, including those involved in sociophysical research. These differences include not only what is studied and how it is studied, but also the theoretical posture upon which research problems are formulated and executed. Within the community of social and behavioral science these differences have been accommodated via a division of labor and a general framework of understanding. These differences among social scientists are not, however, so well understood or easily accommodated by designers seeking resources from the social and behavioral sciences.

Differences within the community of physical designers have already been described, particularly as these have been played out via the emergence of environmental design with its differentiated axiological commitments. Also problematic is the conflict between norms of the design community and those of user-stakeholders. William Michelson's aptly titled article "Most People Don't Want What Architects Want" (1969) characterizes this dilemma. Finally, the differences in values and goals among user-stakeholders in collective decision-making contexts round out the complexity of problem spaces encountered in sociophysical design.

The field of architecture has always been supported by a constantly refined physical technology that provides systematic means for responding to natural physical forces. As a result, buildings that fail to accommodate physical forces are a rarity; those that fail to respond to human requirements are all too frequent (Marans and Spreckelmeyer, 1981). In essence what we are engaged in is the search for some sort of sociophysical technology that links the social and behavioral sciences to the practical problems of environmental design. To even approach such an undertaking, we must be able to identify or develop directly usable knowledge, as contrasted with general (background) knowledge. This requires a firm understanding of how questions and issues emerge in design and decisionmaking processes involved in realizing built environments. Setting aside differences among particular models of design and decision-making, let us briefly, but critically, review the major questions and issues that must be addressed in designing the built environment (see Figure 4.1).

What is? The act of intervening in the built environment is predicated on the presumption or perception on the part of a population of stakeholders that something is amiss (or will be if extant trends continue).[2] Since the enterprise is directed toward changing the state of human sociobehavioral affairs (via inter-

Figure 4.1
Built Environmental Decisionmaking Issues

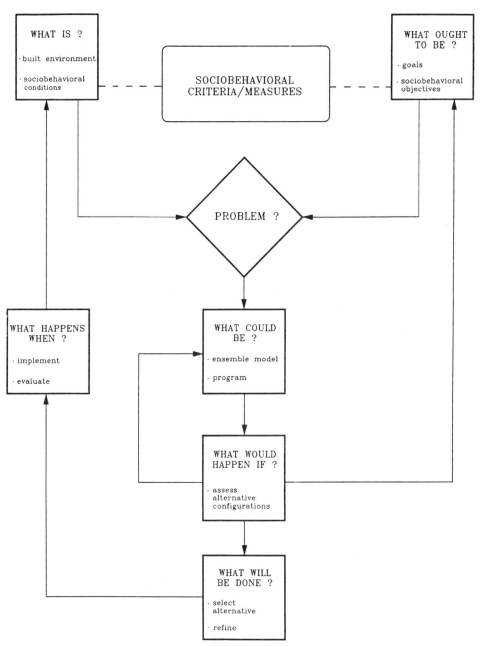

vention in the built environment) from an existing to a more desirable condition, the process logically begins with an assessment of the existing conditions.

Tasks

• Identify the stakeholders.
• Describe the stakeholders, for example, roles, dispositions, expectations, socioeconomic status, behaviors, built environmental needs.
• Describe the social organization of user-stakeholders.
• Describe stakeholder perceptions of built environmental dysfunctions and incongruities.
• Describe the existing built environment(s) of user-stakeholders.
• Describe relationships between user-stakeholders' behaviors and the aspects of the existing built environment(s).
• Describe relevant aspects of the impinging external environment, for example, economic, social, political, and physical (built and natural), detailing constraints and opportunities that condition organization of the built environment.

Assessment of the existing state of sociophysical affairs translates to "what are the facts?" The response is clearly linked to the axiological posture of one who would observe (and model) the situation. The objective of such an analysis is intendedly empirical. However, to the extent that any observation is biased by the axiological predicates underlying such observations (Dunn, 1982), the data that emerge can be challenged. The model of man embraced by the analyst will determine the units of analysis, that is, the elements and structure of the model or analytical framework that guides observation of the system or setting. Beyond these analytical (ontological, epistemological, theoretical) biases, whose ideological and practical interests are involved and implicated in the outcomes of such an ostensibly factual analysis? The point to be made here is that while assessment of what is (and what will be, given the present built environmental structure) may be "intendedly empirical," there are any number of realities depending on the assumptions underlying them. In short, facts and values are not so simply disentangled. Moreover, while documentation of the existing sociophysical state of affairs informs decisions regarding future states, it cannot produce such decisions. Indeed, "facts as such have no meaning; they can gain it only through our decisions" (Popper, 1962: 278).

What ought to be? It is the disparity between what is and what ought to be that defines a built environmental problem—confirms that one actually exists and clarifies its nature. Externalizing, assessing, and documenting the values (preference orderings) of the participating stakeholders, that is, establishing the goals of a population or setting, is of a fundamentally different order than assessing the existing state of affairs.

Tasks

• Define the purpose (mission) of the setting.

- Externalize and describe the (built environmentally relevant) goals of various stakeholders.

- Identify and resolve goal conflicts among various stakeholders.

- Operationalize goals in terms of performance (sociobehavioral) objectives.

- Develop performance (sociobehavioral) criteria and measures for assessing extant and requisite built environmental states.

Whatever the nature of the fact-value dichotomy (ontologically), the establishment of goals involves the issue of value, pure and simple. Goal setting is a normative function. Although the proposition would seem plain enough, its implementation in practice has, in one way or another, led to some of the major difficulties emerging from instrumental rationalism, that is, the implementation of means, the ends of which are taken for granted (Leiss, 1975; Dunn, 1982). The difficulties of goal setting are essentially definitional (what is a goal?) and methodological (how are goals to be externalized, assessed, and consensually ordered?).

Goals are attained through some form of human behavior and must ultimately be operationalized in these dimensions. Defining requisite states of sociobehavioral affairs is an extension of the goal-setting function, but involves a technical (design) dimension. Both technical and practical knowledge come to bear on the issue of defining sociobehavioral states required to attain goals. Clearly, there is more than one way to "skin a cat" or consummate a goal, but it suffices to say here that requisite behaviors are lower-order, operationally defined goals (sometimes called performance objectives) on the part of participating stakeholders.

As noted, this is a continuation of the goal-setting function, but involves an instrumental (empirical/technical) component. First, the units of defining requisite behaviors are tied to particular axiologies. Second, which set or system of requisite behaviors best operationalizes the goals is a matter of considerable interpretation. Various competing organizational models might suggest one or another set or system of requisite behaviors. Human behavior and social structure are, after all, the means of attaining human goals, and since alternative requisite states might be technically indicated, we have a means-ends, fact-value, normative-empirical dichotomy requiring resolution.

What is the problem? Since human environmental problems are ultimately sociobehavioral problems (disparities between is and ought states), the problem is formulated via (1) assessment of the disparity between existing and requisite sociobehavioral states, and (2) identification of those aspects of the user-stakeholder's existing housing environment(s) that are maintaining existing sociobehavioral states. The purpose of intervention in a population's housing environment is to facilitate the change of goal-related sociobehavioral outcomes from where they are to where they ought to be. This is the problem.

Tasks

- Identify existing sociobehavioral states (utilizing performance and sociobehavioral criteria and measures).
- Compare existing and requisite sociobehavioral states.
- Identify aspects of the built environment related to extant sociobehavioral states.
- State the sociobehavioral problem, for example, increase x, decrease y, maintain z.

Assessment of the disparities between existing and requisite behaviors is an ostensibly empirical issue. But conflicts in the axiological posture, the underlying assumptions guiding such an analysis, impact this function precisely as they do assessing the existing system in the first place. Moreover, developing criteria for classifying a disparity as sufficiently critical to indicate intervention is yet another kind of decision issue. There are problems and there are problems; the decision to define a situation as a problem is itself a normative one. Moreover, the manner of defining a problem establishes the universe of discourse within which both normative and empirical issues will be addressed.

What could be? If the existing housing environment is ill-related to the goals, it is because aspects thereof need reorganization. The task is to describe characteristics of an environment required to facilitate the change of relevant sociobehavioral affairs from existing to requisite states. Necessary at this point is development of some sort of sociophysical program describing the quantitative, qualitative, and relational requirements of a new built environmental–sociobehavioral ensemble. Embedded in this program is a predictive or functional model that carries the assertion: "If a particular built environmental configuration is implemented, certain behaviors (the requisite behaviors) will emerge."

Tasks

- Review appropriate literatures to identify comparable documented sociophysical problem settings and sociobehavioral outcomes, as well as applicable general models of sociophysical phenomena.
- Review findings of the analyses of "what is" and "what ought to be."
- Prescribe quantitative spatial requirements.
- Prescribe the qualitative requirements of various elements and components of the requisite built environment.
- Prescribe the relationships among elements and components of the requisite built environment.
- Document the prescribed program in a manner that facilitates conceptual transformation into a built environmental system.

The properties of this sociophysical program are obviously predicated on the axiological posture, for example, the model of man invoked. Specification of a requisite environment, in essence, involves the development of a predictive model of a system yet to be realized. A handy resource to support this task would be nomological knowledge of human sociobehavioral processes relative to the built environment. As things stand, there is little agreement among knowledgeables about how such predictive models should be formulated; not only is there a great deal of axiological conflict among relevant experts, but there are limits on the predictive capabilities of any known system of sociobehavioral science. Whatever the difficulties of assessing the "facts" regarding an existing state of sociophysical affairs, these are compounded when we attempt to render reliable predictions regarding new system states. Given the lack of universal agreement on how to go about consummating this task, the issue is: What are the assumptions underlying a set of requisite environmental specifications and their predicted sociobehavioral impacts?

What would happen if? Having specified the general characteristics of the requisite system, the task is then to transform these specifications into a real functioning system. The issue here is that while the basic characteristics of the requisite system have been described, many solutions or possible system configurations could be hypothesized. There are no algorithms for solving this class of problems, and direct implementation of untested models of complex sociophysical interventions may carry considerable social, economic, political, and even physiological risk. We are thus committed to a process of heuristic search— a process of generating and pretesting proposed concrete solutions. At this point the technical demands of real-world constraints (economic, physical, social, and political) impinging on the proposed solution come into play. The development and assessment of various alternative environmental arrangements and the selection of that particular configuration deemed most effective in realizing the goals established for the setting generally involve, among other things, the utilization of various techniques available to facilitate this process (such as simulation, cost-benefit analysis, and other assessment procedures). The conclusion of this search/assessment process is the selection of the instrumental means, a built environment, to achieve the ends, the sociobehavioral goals, of the population under analysis.

Tasks

- Develop *n* alternative built environment configurations based on program specifications.
- Assess each alternative configuration in terms of the probabilities of achieving stakeholder goals and sociobehavioral objectives.
- Assess each alternative configuration in terms of constraints imposed by and its impacts on the external environment, for example, economic, political, social, and physical.
- Organize valuative and factual assessment data in a manner that will effect a comparison of alternative built environmental configurations proposed.
- Based on a comparative assessment of proposed alternatives utilizing defined performance criteria and measures, select that built environmental configuration to be implemented.

• Implement required technical procedures for realizing the selected built environment, for example, technical refinements, technical documents, various construction arrangements, and construction procedures.

Appropriate built environments, including those of housing, are thus organized via heuristic search processes, aspects of which are not well understood beyond recognition that these involve invention and comparative assessment of alternative configurations (see Simon, 1957, 1973; Rittel and Weber, 1973). In any event, the characteristics of the means selected to facilitate requisite stakeholder goals and sociobehavioral objectives are, again, predicated on the axiological postures of those generating and evaluating various alternatives. Within any population of stakeholders these are generally conflicting both technically and practically. Moreover, the configuration selected can only be seen as one hypothesized to support the needs and goals of stakeholders.

What happens when? Assuming that both the goals and the instrumental means have been consensually formulated, the act of placing the selected system in the larger environment presents only technical and logistical problems. That is, the appropriate, specified technical procedures are employed to bring the selected built environment into reality and then to evaluate its performance.

If there is consensus among stakeholders regarding both the ends (goals) and the means (built environment) implemented, the process of evaluating the new sociophysical system is straightforward and involves no issues beyond those encountered in assessing the existing system initially. Implementation can appropriately be viewed as the realization of a sociophysical "experiment" to field-test a hypothesized solution. What is required here is assessment of emergent sociobehavioral states and comparison of these with the stakeholder's sociobehavioral goals—a confirmation of the effectiveness of the implemented built environment.

Tasks

• Describe the sociobehavioral responses of user-stakeholders utilizing previously defined performance criteria and measures.
• Compare emergent and requisite sociobehavioral states.
• Describe stakeholder perceptions of built environmental–sociobehavioral incongruities.
• If there is significant disparity between requisite and emergent sociobehavioral states, identify built environmental elements and components influencing the latter.

This function embodies precisely the same issues, that is, axiological conflicts among investigators, as those encountered in assessing a sociophysical system prior to intervention. In any event, if there is a disparity between is and ought states, or if and when stakeholder goals or external conditions change, this would (theoretically) call for reiteration through the entire decisionmaking process until requisite and resultant states reach consonance. Extant physical technologies make this kind of dynamic responsiveness highly problematic (Studer, 1970, 1987).

It is clear from this very brief review that (1) the procedures for realizing housing or any other class of built environments involve an amalgamation of two distinct ontological classes: (probabilistic) facts and values (Michalos, 1980; Studer, 1982); (2) our knowledge of both sociophysical problem and solution spaces is highly limited; and (3) effectuation of these procedures is predicated on the axiological postures of those involved in the enterprise.

DESIGNER AND SOCIAL SCIENTIST COLLABORATION

This brief depiction of the kinds of issues that are encountered in environmental design and decisionmaking suggests a challenging agenda not only for designers, but also for sociophysical researchers, and implicitly argues for the need to integrate both procedural and substantive knowledge from the social and behavioral sciences into environmental design and decisionmaking processes. Direct involvement of social and behavioral scientists in design and decisionmaking contexts is indicated in order to address truly relevant questions and to apply the needed test of relevance or usability of knowledge provided. This leads to a consideration of the problems encountered in the collaboration of social and behavioral scientist and designer.

The architect's power to effect viable housing solutions has traditionally rested in his knowledge and expertise; but when certain large-scale sociophysical failures, for example, the Pruitt-Igoe public housing project in St. Louis, are documented by experts from other fields, that is, social and behavioral scientists (Rainwater, 1966; Yancey; 1971), this tends to undermine his role and gives him a great deal to think about generally. In response to this, many designers simply retreat to one or another mode of traditional formalism (citing, with some justification, the naivete of sociobehavioral scientists regarding the nature of design products and processes). Other designers have responded more reflectively, probing deeper into the human problems they seek to solve. In the process they often turn to those specialists who uncovered the problems in the first place. What designers soon discover is that social scientists are more effective in documenting what went wrong than in predicting how to make things right environmentally. There are a number of historical, conceptual, and even epistemological reasons why this is so; nevertheless, it remains the case that precious little in the way of predictive models of sociophysical phenomena has been consummated. The more competent the sociobehavioral scientist interrogated, the more likely he or she is to respond to a designer's question with another question.

Such an enterprise first requires an epistemological shift on the part of physical designers along the lines discussed earlier. Beyond this, designers must become more knowledgeable regarding the objectives, substance, and methods of the social and behavioral sciences and must truly internalize a great deal of this information, especially what kinds of questions are appropriate to an empirical inquiry and what kinds of sociobehavioral theories, strategies, and methods are available to answer these. As designers become knowledgeable regarding the modes of inquiry in the sociobehavioral sciences, they soon realize that what we have is not an integrated science of human affairs but an array of "schools," conflicting epistemologies (models of man), and research paradigms. Each of these offers convincing empirical evidence and powerful methods to support its position.

Although one may elect to specialize (for example, in certain building types or populations), a designer is, for better or worse, a designer. By contrast, there is not a social scientist but varieties of them. What virtually all of them share is a commitment to empirical methodologies and a form of knowledge we generally label "scientific." Beyond this, they are more easily identified by their differences than their similarities. Social and behavioral scientists not only specialize in the classical areas of basic inquiry, but also identify with highly divergent "schools" within these.

The productivity of social scientist–designer collaborations is thus directly related to the "fit" or compatibility between the way each formulates the problem under analysis. It is likely that a team of social scientists is required to effectively deal with a problem of any complexity, but even then such a team must be gathered from an epistemologically compatible population. For obvious reasons social scientists have been rather laggard in pointing out this reality. After all, not only does each of them feel his or her orientation to be the "correct" one, but also each would tend to suggest that his or hers is precisely the set of skills most needed in the planning and design disciplines. While these differences among social scientists may be overstated, the point is that unless the designer becomes more knowledgeable regarding the issues involved in applying the methods and findings of social science to environmental design problems, prospects for truly effective collaboration appear problematic.

Conversely, social scientists, if they are to be effective in the design enterprise, must come to better understand designers and design processes. They must, of course, respect the fact that the fully trained designer, the good one at least, is a product of years of arduous, competitive, and rigorous training and is highly selected for creative or synthetic abilities. Social scientists cannot be one of these professionals unless they qualify in kind.

Designers cannot, by the same virtue, become fully trained sociobehavioral analysts, but the issue regarding level of competence is less clear. Designers may require more knowledge of the social sciences than the reverse. This is due, in part, to the fragmented nature of the social sciences on the one hand and to the synthetic nature of the design enterprise on the other. They must, for example, understand both the necessity and the characteristics of sociophysical hypothesis formulation (although such formulations and their validation undoubtedly require more specialized technical competence). The problem here is that the information and skill required of designers already fills extant curricula to overflowing, suggesting that it is a new kind of specialist that may be needed. Be this as it may, many designers have been disappointed with the inputs of social scientists, but the fact is that these designers have not engaged the proper issues. Social scientists can only help when designers learn to ask appropriate questions, to formulate their problems in a manner that makes the knowledge and skills of the social scientist relevant.

SUGGESTIONS FOR FUTURE RESEARCH

This attempt to illuminate sociophysical knowledge-generation and utilization issues is intended neither to portray the problem as intractable nor to devalue the strides that have been made in bringing social science knowledge to bear on physical design processes. The challenge at this juncture is to build on the developments to date in realizing more effective linkages between knowledge generation and utilization in the interest of significantly improving housing environments in the future. In this regard, Horst Rittel (forthcoming) has proposed a useful three-part typology: research on design, research for design, and research in design. Building on this proposal, we will characterize these three aspects from the perspective of housing design, together with a fourth, generative decisionmaking, in suggesting alternative metastrategies for dealing with the knowledge-generation and utilization issue.

Research on Design is predicated on the assumption that the sociophysical design enterprise embodies a set of unique procedural and substantive issues that define a discrete field of fundamental inquiry. Modeled after fields of basic (deductive) science, the objective of research on design is realization of a body of nomological knowledge, a science of sociophysical design, that "trickles down" to areas of application. This level of inquiry is highly theoretical and deals with "essences" arrived at through reductive processes characteristic of other fields of basic research.

Basic inquiry in the procedural realm draws from such areas as mathematical decision theory, artificial intelligence, and topology in the development of formal design and decisionmaking models applicable to all sociophysical design problems. Formal logics, as well as mathematical and computer modeling, figure heavily in this level of procedural inquiry.

Basic substantive inquiry can be seen to include two foci: general theories of physical system organization and general theories of sociophysical phenomena. Based in great part on formal linguistics, investigations of physical phenomena characteristically explore the combinatorics of physical organization via computer-generated configurations of components and basic elements that make up the built environment (Mitchel, 1977). At more advanced levels of development these configurations would be driven by formal models of sociophysical phenomena (structures and processes). Investigations of sociophysical phenomena would generally take the form of theoretical, transdisciplinary modeling. General systems theory would figure heavily in conceptualizing sociophysical phenomena, and the resultant product might be seen as a system of functional, rather than discursive, sociophysical systems models. In any event, at this highly theoretical level of inquiry substantive and procedural phenomena tend to merge in that the resultant models not only depict dynamic sociophysical systems, but the processes (functional relationships between independent and dependent variables) of their organization and evolution.

Characterized thusly, research on design sounds more like science fiction than contemporary social science. While elements of such a program are ongoing, its realization in terms of providing usable knowledge within any reasonable time frame is highly problematic. It is well known that formal theoretic models of decisionmaking have been successfully applied to only a small class of highly improverished problems to date (Kickert, 1980), and the introduction of sociobehavioral variables severely compounds complexity. Development of functional models of sociophysical phenomena of the sort needed to implement systematic design processes seems even less tractable, given our present knowledge base. What all of this comes down to is that commitment to this level of basic inquiry, unencumbered by real-world complexities in realizing built environments, is predicated on the hope that a theoretical breakthrough might occur that would "trickle down."

Research for Design is essentially what we are involved in at the present. It is an arrangement in which a wide variety of research programs generate knowledge assumed to be relevant to housing design and decisionmaking. The assumption is that although executed in the context of a variety of interests, foci, and axiological platforms, the building up of a massive knowledge base will, in time, surely lead to more effective, congruent housing environments (Zeisel and Griffin, 1975).

Procedural research in this category generally involves appropriation of decision models from the so-called systems sciences in an attempt to rationalize conventional design and decisionmaking processes. All design and decisionmaking models are normative, being essentially more or less formal arguments for the most effective procedures for linking ends to means. We have a plethora of these normative models competing for recognition and adoption. Since normative models cannot be verified empirically, their merits must be argued in terms of their utility vis-à-vis rival variants.

Substantive research for design consists of a collection of primarily descriptive investigations, usually unconnected directly to design and decisionmaking processes. Attempts to catalog and organize the findings of these investigations into a general framework (Moore, Tuttle, and Howell, 1985) help to illuminate their potential relevance, but no amount of cataloging and classifying will overcome the problems of utilizing the findings of these various studies in situation-specific problem settings. The underlying issue is, of course, generalization. We have a large collection of descriptive investigations (focusing on place, people, and sociobehavioral variables), the findings of which, while relevant, are generalizable only within the limits of the studies. The prospects that any one or a combination of these investigations will match a particular problem setting (for example, population sample, place type, or sociobehavioral variables) is quite remote. Moreover, it is simply not feasible to develop a comprehensive catalog of investigations from which could be selected one (or even a combination of them) that precisely matches a particular problem context. In short, notwithstanding the value of generating a body of sociophysical knowledge for widening and deepening our social scientific understanding, the direct impacts on designing built environments, including those of housing, are not likely to be significant in the near future.

Research in Design characterizes an arrangement wherein sociophysical knowledge is produced within, and in response to, a situation-specific design and decisionmaking context. This direct, situation-specific knowledge-generating process, of course, produces highly usable, that is, instrumental, knowledge; but its generalizability across a wide range of problem settings is unlikely. What are generally appropriated are the methods of sociophysical inquiry rather than its substance, with the probable result that more effective (that is, congruent) housing environments are realized. In any event, such an arrangement has the advantage of selecting from the social sciences knowledge that is useful in organizing built environments. It also suggests close collaboration and a mutual learning opportunity for both designers and social scientists. Over time the result would be a cumulative, relevant instrumental knowledge base, perhaps eventually leading to a technology of sociophysical design and decisionmaking via an integration of empirical and design and decisionmaking methodologies.

Notwithstanding the positive impacts of this instrumental knowledge-generating enterprise, there is the inevitable trade-off with respect to participating social scientists. Few situation-specific design and decisionmaking contexts lend themselves to quality research within the norms of social science. The controls required (for example, sample selection or numbers of subjects) to assure validity (Campbell and Stanley, 1963) are not readily implementable. In short, research in design must generally be seen as applied social science. This is no problem for environmental designers or user-stakeholders, but it may be for potential social science collaborators.

Generative Decisionmaking, a variant of research in design, constitutes a fourth metastrategy, one based on an alternative, postpositivist axiological platform (Dunn, 1982; Mason and Mitroff, 1981). In this arrangement user-stakeholders are directly involved in decisionmaking processes, and it essentially bypasses major aspects of the knowledge-generation and utilization problem. In generative (collective, participatory) decisionmaking processes user-stakeholders' values, goals, needs, and preferences are played out directly as a function of reaching collective decisions. Generative processes require a supporting instrumentality that guides and manages the decision processes, analyzes stakeholder responses to various decisionmaking issues, and illuminates consequences of alternative environmental configurations. While this arrangement does not overcome all of the problems associated with incomplete sociophysical knowledge, it does have the advantage that built environmental ends and means are identified, analyzed, and selected via direct responses of user-stakeholders engaged in structured intersubjective, dialectical discourse. Over time, these kinds of decisionmaking contexts are likely to produce generalized sociophysical knowledge unattainable through other means. In any event, the challenge here is in the development of a generative methodology (Mason and Mitroff, 1981; Dunn, 1982; Studer, 1982, 1987) and the instrumental support necessary to effect collective, intersubjective decisionmaking processes.

CONCLUSION

These characterizations of alternative metastrategies for approaching the knowledge-generalization and utilization issue in housing design are offered to further illuminate problems and opportunities as well as some of the trade-offs involved in dealing with the problem of generating usable knowledge to support design of housing environments. Given the plurality of interests and goals among various members of the sociophysical research community, we can perhaps advance the cause of more effective housing environments by acknowledging and supporting all of these approaches and variants or combinations thereof.

The problem of built environmental sociobehavioral congruence in housing comes down to a problem of supply and demand, a major unsolved problem in all political economies (Studer and Van Vliet—, 1987). Neither the free-market mechanisms of capitalist economies nor the resource-allocation mechanisms of socialist economies have been fully effective in dealing with the supply and demand problems in housing. Aggregate supply and demand problems in housing cannot be solved solely by physical designers, since the problem is linked to societal priorities and power politics—to major economic and social policies, programs, and processes. On the other hand, the etiology and dynamics of housing supply and demand are closely linked to the issues and processes involved in organizing the built environment. Pruitt-Igoe and similar sociophysical (and economic) failures result not so much from social and economic policies and programs per se as from an inadequate understanding and accommodation of user-stakeholder sociophysical requirements. It is at this level of analysis, however, that usable sociophysical knowledge becomes problematic, in spite of the high level of competence that generally exists among physical designers with respect to organizing physical settings.

In this chapter we have attempted to illuminate, from the perspective of the physical designer, some of the major problems encountered in utilizing the resources of the social and behavioral sciences in organizing housing environments. Emergence of the field of environmental design was identified as an important development, explicitly focusing as it does on human sociobehavioral variables in designing and evaluating built environments. Environmental design research was characterized as an enterprise that has produced a broad range of findings relevant to the built environment, yet lacking in terms of generating directly usable knowledge. Arguments have been made for direct collaborative involvement of social and behavioral scientists in design and decisionmaking processes as a means of identifying and generating more usable forms of knowledge, and integrating sociobehavioral methods into these processes. Some of the intrinsic problems encountered in designer and sociobehavioral scientist collaboration were identified, and four alternative metastrategies for dealing with the knowledge-generation and utilization problem were outlined. The major purpose of this analysis has been to argue that a serious knowledge-generation and utilization problem exists and needs to be systematically addressed. In doing so we might well reconsider Karl Popper's suggestion (1959) that although we mortals may differ widely in the bits of knowledge we have, in our infinite ignorance we are all about equal.

NOTES

1. Anxiology refers to the ontological, epistemological, and theoretical platform upon which investigations of phenomena are predicated (see, for example Sutherland, 1974).

2. Stakeholders are "all parties who will be affected by or who affect an important decision" (Mitroff, Emshoff, and Kilmann, 1979), that is, user, nonuser decisionmakers, and technicians.

REFERENCES

Alexander, C. 1964. *Notes on the Synthesis of Form*. Cambridge, Mass.: Harvard University Press.

Altman, I. 1973. "Some Perspectives on the Study of the Man-Environment Phenomenon." *Representative Research in Social Psychology* 4: 109–186.

———. 1975. *Environment and Social Behavior*. Monterey, Calif.: Brooks/Cole.

Altman, I., and J. F. Wohlwill (eds.). 1978. *Children and the Environment*. New York: Plenum.

Archea, J. 1977. "Behavioral Science Impact on Environmental Policy: Applications to Stairs." In P. Suedfeld, J. A. Russell, L. M. Ward, F. Szigeti, and G. David (eds.), *The Behavioral Basis of Design*, vol. 2. Stroudsburg, Pa.: Dowden, Hutchinson & Ross.

Brill, M. 1982. *Do Buildings Really Matter? Economic and Other Effects of Designing Behaviorally Supportive Buildings*. New York: Educational Facilities Laboratories, Academy for Educational Development.

Campbell, D. T., and J. C. Stanley. 1963. *Experimental and Quasi-Experimental Designs for Research*. Chicago: Rand McNally.

Canter, D., and S. Canter (eds.). 1979. *Designing for Therapeutic Environments: A Review of Research*. New York: Wiley.

Clipson, C., and J. Wehrer. 1974. *Planning for Cardiac Care: A Guide for Planning and Design of Cardiac Care Facilities*. Ann Arbor, Mich.: Health Administration Press.

Cohen, S., D. C. Glass, and J. F. Singer. 1973. "Apartment Noise, Auditory Discrimination and Reading Ability in Children." *Journal of Experimental Social Psychology* 9: 407–422.

Cooper, C. C. 1975. *Easter Hill Village: Some Social Implications of Design*. New York: Free Press.

Craik, K. H., and E. H. Zube (eds.). 1976. *Perceiving Environmental Quality: Research and Applications*. New York: Plenum.

Dunlap, R. E., and W. R. Catton. 1979. "Environmental Sociology." *Annual Review of Sociology* 5: 243–273.

Dunn, W. N. 1982. "Reforms as Arguments." In E. R. House, S. Matheson, J. A. Pearsol, and H. Proskill (eds.), *Evaluation Studies Review Annual*, vol. 7. Beverly Hills, Calif.: Sage. 117–128.

Foley, D. C. 1981. "The Sociology of Housing." *Annual Review of Sociology* 6: 457–478.

Glass, D. C., and J. E. Singer. 1972. *Urban Stress*. New York: Academic Press.

Harris, H., and A. Lipman. 1986. "A Culture of Despair: Reflections on 'Post-Modern' Architecture." *Sociological Review* 34: 837–854.

Kickert, W. 1980. *Organization of Decision-Making*. Amsterdam: North Holland.

Kuhn, T. 1962. *The Structure of Scientific Revolutions*. Chicago: University of Chicago Press.

Lawton, M. P. 1980. *Environment and Aging*. Monterey, Calif.: Brooks/Cole.

Leiss, W. 1975. "The Problem of Man and Nature in the Work of the Frankfurt School." *Philosophy of Social Science* 5: 163–172.

Marans, R. W., and K. F. Spreckelmeyer. 1981. *Evaluating Built Environments*. Ann Arbor: University of Michigan Press.

Mason, Richard O., and Ian I. Mitroff. 1981. *Challenging Strategic Planning Assumptions: Theory, Cases, and Techniques*. New York: John Wiley.

Michalos, Alex C. 1980. "Facts, Values and Rational Decision-Making." *Policy Study* 9: 544–551.

Michelson, W. 1969. "Most People Don't Want What Architects Want." *Trans-Action* 5: 282–301.

———. 1973. "Reconciliation of 'Subjective' and 'Objective' Data on Physical Environment in the Community: The Case of Social Contact in High-Rise Apartments." *Sociological Inquiry* 43, no. 3–4: 147–173.

———. 1976. *Man and His Urban Environment*. Reading, Mass.: Addison-Wesley.

———. 1977. *Environmental Choice, Human Behavior and Residential Satisfaction*. New York: Oxford University Press.

Mitchel, W. 1977. *Computer-aided Architectural Design*. New York Petrocelli/Charter.

Mitroff, I., J. Emshoff, and R. Kilmann. 1979. "Assumptional Analysis: A Methodology for Strategic Planning." *Management Science* 25, no. 6: 1–12.

Moore, G. T., and R. G. Golledge (eds.). 1976. *Environmental Knowing: Theories, Research and Methods*. Stroudsburg, Pa.: Dowden, Hutchinson & Ross.

Moore, G. T., D. P. Tuttle, and S. C. Howell. 1985. *Environmental Design Research Directions*. New York: Praeger.

Morris, E. W., and M. Winter. 1978. *Housing, Family and Society*. New York: Wiley.

Newman, O. 1972. *Defensible Space: Crime Prevention Through Urban Designs*. New York: Macmillian.

Passini, R. 1984. *Wayfinding in Architecture*. New York: Van Nostrand Reinhold.

Popper, K. 1959. *The Logic of Scientific Discovery*. New York: Basic Books.

———. 1962. *The Open Society and Its Enemies*, vol. 2. New York: Harper & Row.

Rainwater, L. 1966. "Fear and the House-as-Haven in the Lower Class." *Journal of the American Institute of Planners* 32, no. 1: 23–31.

Rapoport, A. 1969. *House, Form and Culture*. Englewood Cliffs, N.J.: Prentice-Hall.

————. 1979. "Cultural Origins of Architecture." In J. C. Snyder and A. J. Cahanese (eds.), *Introduction to Architecture*. New York: McGraw-Hill.

Rittel, H. W. J. Forthcoming. "Saying What You Do and Doing What You Say." *Design Methods and Theories*.

Rittel, H. W. J., and M. M. Weber. 1973. "Dilemmas in a General Theory of Planning." *Policy Sciences* 4: 155–169.

Ross, R. P., and D. E. Campbell. 1978. "A Review of EDRA Proceedings." In W. E. Rogers and W. H. Ittelson (eds.), *New Directions in Environmental Design Research*. Washington, D.C.: Environmental Design Research Association.

Schneekloth, L. H., and R. G. Shibley. Forthcoming. "The Tasks of a Research/Practitioner." *Design Theories and Methods*.

Simon, H. A. 1957. *Models of Man*. New York: Wiley.

————. 1973. "The Structure of Ill-Structured Problems." *Artificial Intelligence* 4: 181–201.

Steinfeld, E. 1979. *Access to the Built Environment*, 7 vols. Washington, D.C.: U.S. Government Printing Office and U.S. Department of Housing and Urban Development.

Stokols, D. 1972. "On the Distinction Between Density and Crowding: Some Implications for Future Research." *Psychological Review* 79: 275–278.

————. 1978. "Environmental Psychology." *Annual Review of Psychology* 29: 253–295.

Studer, R. G. 1970. "The Dynamics of Behavior-Contingent Physical Systems." In H. M. Proshansky, W. H. Ittelson, and L. G. Rivlin (eds.), *Environmental Psychology: Man and His Physical Setting*. New York: Holt, Rinehart & Winston.

————. 1982. "Normative Guidance, for the Planning, Design and Management of Environment-Behavior Systems." Ph.D. diss., University of Pittsburgh.

————. 1987. "The Prospects for Realizing Congruence in Housing Environments." In W. van Vliet—, H. Choldin, W. Michelson, and D. Popenoe (eds.), *Housing and Neighborhoods: Theoretical and Empirical Contributions*. Westport, Conn.: Greenwood Press. 29–41.

Studer, R. G., and W. van Vliet—. 1987. "Sociophysical Congruence as a Problem of Supply and Demand." *Archetecture et Comportement* 3, no. 2: 159–173.

Sundstrom, E., D. Kastenbaum, and E. Konar-Goldband. 1978. *Physical Office Environments, Employee Satisfaction*. Buffalo, N.Y.: Buffalo Organization for Social and Technological Innovation.

Sutherland, J. 1974. "Axiological Predicates of Scientific Research." *General Systems* 19: 3–13.

Van Vliet—, W. 1985. "The Role of Housing Type, Household Density and Neighborhood Density in Peer Interaction and Social Adjustment." In J. F. Wohlwill and W. van Vliet— (eds.), *Habitats for Children: Impacts of Density*. Hillsdale, N.J.: Erlbaum. 165–201.

Ventre, F. J., F. I. Stahl, and G. E. Turner. 1982. Crowd Ingress to Places of Assembly." Washington D.C.: National Bureau of Standards, NBSIR 81–2361. Unpublished report.

Weideman, S., J. R. Anderson, D. I. Butterfield, and P. M. O'Donnell. 1982. "Residents' Perception of Satisfaction and Safety: A Basis for Change in Multifamily Housing." *Environment and Behavior* 14: 615–724.

Wohlwill, J. F. 1974. "Human Adaptation to Levels of Environmental Stimulation." *Human Ecology* 2: 127–147.

Yancey, W. L. 1971. "Architecture, Interaction and Social Culture: The Case of a Large-Scale Public Housing Project." *Environment and Behavior* 3: no. 1: 3–21.

Zeisel, J. 1981. *Inquiry by Design: Tools for Environment-Behavior Research.* Monterey, Calif.: Brooks/Cole.

Zeisel, J., and M. Griffin. 1975. *Charlesview Housing: A Diagnostic Evaluation.* Cambridge, Mass.: Harvard University, Architecture Research Office.

Zeisel, J., G. Epp, and S. Demos. 1978. *Low-Rise Housing for Older People.* Washington, D.C.: U.S. Government Printing Office and U.S. Department of Housing and Urban Development.

————. 1984. *Mid-Rise Elevator Housing for Older People.* Washington, D.C.: U.S. Government Printing Office and U.S. Department of Housing and Urban Development.

5

Residential Crowding in the United States: A Review of Research

MARK BALDASSARE

DEFINITION AND BASIC INFORMATION

Residential crowding is a major issue to those who study housing and the built environment. In this chapter I will review the theories guiding this work and the research evidence, which now spans two decades. I will also demonstrate that the issues involving residential crowding have their roots in classic theories about urban life in sociology.

Residential crowding refers to the ratio of people to their amount of living space. It is a topic that has attracted considerable attention in academic, planning, policy, and public arenas. The major focus of the research on high-density living is to determine the attitudinal, social, psychological, and health outcomes of living in conditions in which there is too little space. The two places in which residential crowding has most often been studied are the home and the neighborhood.

Household crowding is usually defined in terms of persons per room in the dwelling. The Census Bureau considers "overcrowded" households as those with more than one person per room. But few people today in the United States live under these conditions, so most studies use less stringent definitions. In some rare instances researchers have also defined household crowding as the floor-area space per person. While this may yield a more accurate measure of residential crowding, it is highly impractical to gather such statistics in large studies of the general population.

Neighborhood crowding is almost always defined as the population density of some geographically defined locality. From census figures and maps the numbers of persons per square acre or square mile are calculated. More sophisticated measurements are sometimes used that consider the number of people per residential acre in a neighborhood. These exclude the uninhabited land that is open space, industrial, and commercial. There is no absolute definition of what is a high-density or a low-density neighborhood. Relative comparisons within a specific population are made instead.

There are subjective measures of residential crowding as well as the objective definitions mentioned thus far. Subjective crowding is the individual's attitude or perception of not having sufficient space. Some researchers place greater importance on the subjective dimension, considering it as the true definition of crowding and the most important object of study. Most agree that the feeling of crowding is largely a result of actual household crowding and neighborhood density (Stokols, 1972). There are instances, however, when the functions, characteristics, and expectations of a social group can intensify the perceptions of limited space. Subjective crowding can then influence the extent and types of difficulties individuals have with high-density living.

HISTORICAL DEVELOPMENT

The interest in residential crowding can be traced to the grand theories of early twentieth-century sociology. In *The Division of Labor in Society* ([1893] 1964) Durkheim stated that population density was one of several causes of the formation of modern society. Durkheim believed that high densities allowed for industrialization and urbanization to take place. These phenomena, in turn, created more unhappiness for individuals in modern times compared with preindustrial society. The large and dense communities with workers in specialized jobs, according to Durkheim, caused feelings of normlessness and alienation and an increase in deviant behavior.

The theme of dense urban areas causing social and psychological problems was elaborated on in the pre–World War II writings of the Chicago School. Louis Wirth's essay "Urbanism as a Way of Life" (1938) best summarized the concerns of his contemporaries. He defined urbanism as the combination of high population density, large population size, and social heterogeneity. He posited that these conditions of city life combined to cause serious problems of living for residents. As Georg Simmel ([1905] 1969) had stated earlier, Wirth argued that high density could produce a situation of psychic overstimulation and social overload. In order to avoid the daily barrage of social contacts, urban residents coped by avoiding public interactions.

Wirth also stated that adjustments to dense urban areas had repercussions on social life and individual well-being. He believed that what relations did exist were predominantly of a superficial, transient, and functional character. Close social bonds and feelings of attachment to the community were thus rare. As a result, residents became withdrawn, isolated, and unhappy in the midst of crowded conditions.

Academic interest in urban living then diminished for several decades, though Wirth's statements about high density were still viewed as common knowledge. An era of intense concern about residential crowding began in the early 1960s. This was caused by both dramatic research evidence and current events.

A study of rats allowed to overpopulate a laboratory cage provided a terrifying description of the effects of interior-space crowding. The widely noticed research article by John Calhoun (1962) reported that overcrowding caused a long list of pathologies. These included infant mortality, poor nest building, aggression, sexual perversions, extreme social withdrawal, and high levels of anxiety. Analogies were quickly drawn between the conditions of mice and men.

Overcrowding in urban areas and homes became the popular explanation for the urban crisis underway in American cities. This included the racial violence, civil unrest, and high crime rates that were evident during the 1960s. Social commentators and the media noted that the large and crowded cities were in explosive times. The situation seemed to replicate the findings in rat cages. Hence many concluded that there was in fact a relationship between high-density living and social problems. Few at that time reasoned that while social inequalities cause crowding and social problems, the relation between crowding and these urban events may be spurious.

Stanley Milgram soon after published an essay titled "The Experience of Living in Cities" (1970), which was widely read and influential. In many ways it was an attempt to explain the apathy evident in urban areas. Milgram's reasoning was similar to that of Wirth and Simmel. He argued that the demographic facts of urban areas, especially high density, produced excess social stimulation. As an adjustment to these conditions, residents learned to filter and block unpleasant social situations. In the article Milgram provided evidence for this hypothesis from field studies in the urban setting. There were some findings that suggested that an urban life-style and personality type exists that includes dehumanization, aloofness, impersonality, social withdrawal, and superficial relations.

Academic researchers during the next decade became intensely involved in empirically linking crowding in urban areas and homes with psychological stress and social problems. This issue was of concern to policy analysts as well because of the evolution of building codes, interior-space standards, and housing norms by the American Public Health Association (Baldassare, 1979). The studies sought to understand exactly what consequences overcrowding had for the individual, why these effects occurred, and ultimately, whether humans ought to live under high-density conditions.

MAJOR THEMES AND APPROACHES

Several approaches to understanding residential crowding can be found in the empirical literature. They are reviewed in this section (see also Baldassare, 1978). They include the biological, the cultural, the design, and the social structural perspectives. These perspectives have influenced the research in many ways. The choice of hypotheses that are tested and the use of experimental settings, field observations, or public opinion surveys are guided by the approach taken. The groups studied, settings observed, questions asked, and interpretations derived from the findings are obviously also affected.

In order to accurately portray residential crowding research, one important fact must be conveyed. No one approach to understanding residential crowding has dominated the field. There are two reasons why this has occurred. One is that the findings as a whole have been inconsistent and somewhat ambiguous. There is no consensus as to what the overall or specific effects of residential crowding actually are. The other is that the field is multidisciplinary in nature. Researchers with widely varying styles of investigation and from very different theoretical backgrounds have converged on the topic of residential crowding. The research thus suffers from not having collaborative and interdisciplinary work and from the lack of attention to integrating the current streams of thought and empirical work.

The biological perspective is the one most frequently utilized. The biological view is simply that overcrowding causes stress manifested in physiological and psychological symptoms. The stress is believed to have its roots in hereditary responses to territoriality and invasions of personal space (Sommer, 1969). There are some specific biological responses to stressful overcrowding, most notably aggression. An inability to escape overcrowding also causes physical, psychological, and social pathologies since the human organism is placed in an unnatural situation.

A second view is that culture dictates the experience of residential crowding. In his widely read book *The Hidden Dimension* (1966), Edward Hall argues that cultures vary in the densities and interpersonal distances that are considered appropriate. Some cultures, such as those in Latin America, have a greater tolerance for overcrowding than other cultures, such as those in North America. The learning of acceptable levels of density occurs through early childhood socialization and becomes a fixed attribute of members of the culture. Situations that deviate from the culturally prescribed norm, such as extreme overcrowding for North Americans, are avoided and are reacted to with hostility when they occur. It is possible for members of a culture to change their norms over time and tolerate higher densities, but as with other social rules, this is not an easy nor necessarily a successful process.

The design perspective offers another way of understanding residential crowding. This view suggests that how we place objects and partition space in physical settings has very strong implications for whether or not overcrowding is experienced. Certain designs result in forced contacts and congestion, while other designs lead to fewer interactions and relative social isolation. Oscar Newman's discussion of public housing projects in *Defensible Space* (1972) and Jonathan Freedman's suggestions for high-rise living in *Crowding and Behavior* (1975) represent this kind of perspective. The notion that there are ''good designs'' and ''bad designs'' in high-density settings implies that there are physical adjustments that can be made to avoid the health, psychological, and social problems that may be associated with overcrowding. Of course, even the proponents of this viewpoint recognize that there are practical limitations as to how many people can be placed in a residential space even with the best-conceived designs.

The social structural perspective is a sociological viewpoint that suggests that whenever we inhabit residential space, we simultaneously have a social position in a group. These social positions have attributes such as social rank, status, and certain rights vis-à-vis other group members. This simple fact has two important implications for the experience of residential crowding. First, there is a social order that can make rules about how space and social interactions are organized in the crowded residential setting. This may limit the group's stresses and strains with overcrowding. For instance, families in crowded dwellings can adjust to this situation if the elders decide and then enforce rules for the timing and use of limited space (Anderson, 1972). Second, since individuals in a group are not of equivalent social rank, we can then assume that there is inequality in the distribution of limited space. In the crowded home adult parents may give themselves more rights to privacy and space than children or boarders and thus have less stress (Mitchell, 1971).

The social structural perspective seems most consistent with the somewhat weak and contradictory findings reported in studies of the general population. Only some residents may have problems with high density because of their social status relative to others. Marginal associations between residential crowding and personal problems in the general population may thus really reflect strong effects on certain types of individuals and no effects on others. Many groups are probably sheltered from adverse experiences since their households and communities develop socially prescribed adjustments to overcrowding. Thus the influences of residential crowding may vary between study sites, leading to an overall pattern of ambiguous results.

CURRENT STATUS

Scores of studies have sought to determine the effects of residential crowding. In retrospect, few are relevant and appropriate for testing issues relating to household and neighborhood crowding. A very brief description of early research is presented here (see Fischer, Baldassare, and Ofshe, 1975, for more detail). Then the results from more recent studies using random population surveys are reviewed.

Research was first carried out by psychologists who crowded human subjects into laboratory settings and measured their stress levels. In extreme situations there were psychophysiological responses that were somewhat abnormal, but no evidence of serious hostility or aggression was reported. The results across studies were not only inconclusive but can be questioned for their invalidity in residential situations.

Other psychologists observed urban residents in crowded public places. They watched for signs of peculiar behavior and adjustments to overcrowding. There were some results that pointed to the avoidance of interactions, but there were no indications of major social disruptions. The findings, in any event, are only of limited relevance since they provide a glimpse of populations in outdoor settings rather than people in their home environments.

Urban sociologists used government statistics from neighborhood areas to calculate the correlations between urban densities and rates of crime, mental health, and physical diseases. In only some cities were there associations between residential crowding and reported social problems. These studies were met with skepticism because of methodological problems. Most noteworthy is the high correlation between poverty and overcrowding in the United States. It is thus difficult to determine the factor that really predicts social problems.

In *Residential Crowding in Urban America* (1979) I used a contextual approach to test hypotheses concerning the effects of overcrowding. Existing national surveys that contained "quality-of-life" questions were reanalyzed with information including the neighborhood densities of the respondents. The measure of urban density was the number of persons per residential acre within the census tract of residence. Ratings of satisfaction with the residence, reports on friendship and neighboring, and mental and physical health symptoms were examined. Correlations between neighborhood density and the attitude measures were calculated using multiple regression techniques that controlled for social and economic factors. Residents of higher-density areas were significantly more dissatisfied with the places in which they lived. They also tended to know their neighbors less well, though they had as many and as satisfying friendships as did others. Residential crowding in the neighborhood context was not, however, associated with more unhappiness, stress, or physical illness. Neighborhood crowding seemed to have limited but important effects on the quality of urban life.

In the same book I also examined the effects of household crowding on residential satisfaction, family interactions, and physical and mental well-being. The number of persons per room in an individual's home was correlated with the attitude questions in the national surveys. Social and economic factors were again controlled using multiple regression methods. Residents of more crowded homes were more dissatisfied with their dwellings, were more likely to want to move, and were more likely to perceive their dwellings as having inadequate space. There was some evidence that marital problems were greater in crowded homes, though parent-child relations and family ties in general were not affected by household crowding. Physical health, happiness, and mental health symptoms were unrelated to the number of persons per room.

The most recent and perhaps, most comprehensive analysis of household crowding is reported in a book by Walter Gove and his colleagues titled *Overcrowding in the Household* (1983). The study involves a random sample of households in the Chicago area from which 2,035 adults were interviewed. Each individual was asked over 300 questions in a session that was over an hour long. The measure of household crowding, which was the number of persons per room, correlated with subjective crowding and well-being. This included an increased perception of a lack of privacy and social demands by housemates and self-reports of increased physical health, mental health, and family problems. The statistical approach they used was to examine the relationship between household crowding and attitudes, controlling for social and economic factors with multiple regression techniques. They also explored the mediating role of subjective crowding. The conclusion, in the authors' words, is that "household crowding, as measured by persons per room and experienced lack of privacy and an excess of social demands, has substantial pathological effects across a wide range of variables" (Gove, Hughes, and Galle, 1983: 227).

There are studies that reach different conclusions based on similar research designs. For instance, Booth in *Urban Crowding and Its Consequences* (1976) reports on a large survey he conducted in the Toronto area. He could find almost no evidence that residential crowding, either in the household or the neighborhood, had significant effects on social, psychological, or physical health attributes. It is possible, however, that limited ranges of the density variable accounted for the lack of effects.

The pattern of findings suggests that fears expressed about the effects of residential crowding are not warranted. In both the household and the neighborhood context there is little indication that crowding per se consistently causes serious problems. This is true, at least, for the levels of density experienced in the United States today. Thus the question that set off the recent flurry of research activity seems to have been answered.

SUCCESSES AND FAILURES

Despite the conflicting evidence in the residential crowding literature, there have been notable accomplishments. There have been advances in the methods used to study residential crowding. Early studies were discounted because of the invalid use of experimental subjects, inappropriate field observations, and limited government statistics. Later research responded to these criticisms and employed random survey techniques. Further, the use of multivariate statistics insured that the many factors that are related to crowding measures and to the potential effects of high-density living could be controlled. Thus methodological improvements insured that the information gathered in later crowding studies was both more valid and reliable than in the past.

Still, there are many shortcomings of the research that has thus far been reported. These include the lack of standardization of crowding measurement across studies. This has made attempts to replicate, at best, guesswork for those who have tried. In fact, this may be the cause of the inconsistent and contradictory findings in the field. The appropriate measurements of household crowding and neighborhood density have been subjects of disagreement. As a result, researchers have used a variety of measures that may not be comparable. There is also no agreed-upon definition of what exactly constitutes overcrowding in the home and the neighborhood. Because of this, researchers have relied upon correlation analysis. The distributions of actual densities experienced varies across study sites, and therefore so does the possibility of significant associations between residential crowding and self-reported problems.

Another failure of the residential crowding literature is one that was inherited from social surveys. This is the lack of agreement on the appropriate measurement of sociopsychological dimensions. These are, of course, important since they constitute the effects of residential crowding. There are numerous questions and scales that are used to assess an individual's psychological state, neighborhood satisfaction, housing evaluations, subjective crowding, social relations, family life, health, and personal happiness. There is no consensus concerning the best survey items to use. Researchers who have studied residential crowding have rarely repeated the same questions in more than one survey. This again creates difficulties in comparing findings across studies and drawing more general inferences about the effects of residential crowding.

MAJOR PROBLEMS AND ISSUES

There remain several important and unresolved issues in the residential crowding literature. Some are derived from the initial questions that guided early research. Others originate from the empirical findings thus far reported in the literature. The major issues are summarized here.

The relative significance of household crowding versus neighborhood density has yet to be addressed. Some suggest that household crowding is more problematic. This is because the household realm has more importance for the individual due to the amount of time spent in the dwelling and the intimacy of activities that occur in the home. Yet others point to the problems of living in high-density neighborhoods. In such conditions the resident is unable to escape the constant press of large numbers of surrounding people. One reason why this important issue remains unresolved is that few studies have been designed to contrast the effects of housing and neighborhood densities on the same measures of social and personal problems.

The role of subjective crowding is also in question. There are several findings that suggest that subjective crowding is strongly related to experiencing high density in the residential setting. But there must be numerous other social, personal, cultural, and design factors that contribute to the perception of feeling crowded. These have yet to be systematically examined. The unique effects of subjective crowding on personal well-being have also not been explored. The combined effects of experiencing both objective crowding and subjective crowding, as a separate and more difficult circumstance than either separately, still need to be investigated.

One of the largest problems with the existing research is its inability to empirically document the ways in which groups adjust to overcrowding. There is some evidence that certain groups and individuals adapt to high density more effectively than others (Baldassare, 1981, 1982). One assumes that over time some groups develop ways to adjust while others are not able to, but this has not been verified in the research thus far. There has been insufficient use of longitudinal designs or panel surveys that follow individuals in the course of their residential life. Surveys that have used retrospective questions about how space and social activities were initially arranged and then reorganized are almost nonexistent. In-depth field observations of household units or urban neighborhoods are also lacking. How people adjust, why, when, and for what reasons remain unanswered. These are important questions, perhaps as important as the initial concern about how serious the effects of crowding actually are for residents. Until these topics are addressed by appropriate study designs, one is left to speculate, perhaps inaccurately, about the mechanisms that are used to avoid serious social and personal problems.

EVALUATIONS AND SUGGESTIONS FOR FUTURE RESEARCH

Many of the most fundamental questions about the effects of residential crowding have already been studied. The knowledge to date is that the levels of high density experienced by Americans in their homes and neighborhoods show no consistent patterns of serious consequences. As with many new topic areas, the next stages of research will be much more costly and complex. Some suggested directions for future studies are presented here.

One important possibility has been overlooked in search of significant correlations between residential crowding and measures of social and personal problems. This is that there may be threshold levels at which overcrowding does have adverse effects. In random surveys of the general population, relatively few individuals live in very high density neighborhoods or high persons per room ratios. For this reason it has been virtually impossible to establish whether extreme overcrowding causes health, psychological, or social problems. Future studies ought to use stratified sampling techniques that would overrepresent those living in very crowded homes or very dense neighborhoods. Only then can valid comparisons between average and unusual levels of crowding and valid statements about threshold effects be made.

Thus far there have only been hints of the possibility that certain groups may have more difficulties than others when experiencing high densities. This is because, again, the statistical analyses have had to rely upon limited samples of at-risk groups drawn at random from the general population. New studies ought to be conducted that involve quasi-experimental designs. For instance, these would include equal representation of random samples from four groups: low-density and low-risk, low-density and high-risk, high-density and low-risk, and high-density and high-risk. The latter group should have more difficulties than any other. Such a design would be applicable to issues regarding neighborhood density and household crowding. At-risk groups should be defined in terms of income, occupation, tenure status, life cycle, household social composition, and status within the family unit.

More complete self-reports taken from residents in surveys over time are also needed. Typically only a few questions, at one point in time, of a very general nature have been used. These should be replaced with batteries of survey items on the perceptions of residential environments taken at several points over time. Further questioning is also needed on the ways in which households and neighborhoods have avoided problems with overcrowding. There has been little information about the problems experienced, adjustments made, and the successes of these rearrangements for social groups and individuals. Also, while there has been much attention to the issue of subjective crowding, there has been relatively little advance in the measurement of this concept.

RECOMMENDATIONS AND ASSESSMENTS
OF FUTURE TRENDS

Residential crowding today commands much less attention as a research topic than it did in the 1970s. Practical concerns, however, will force residential crowding to the forefront in future housing research. First, current demographic and housing trends point to the increasing densities of homes and neighborhoods. Second, groups that are most vulnerable to the effects of crowding will most likely live at high densities in greater proportions than they do today.

For the last 25 years the densities of homes and neighborhoods in the United States declined. But the cost of purchasing and renting a dwelling has risen so sharply in recent years that crowding is once again on the increase (Baldassare, 1986). This is because land prices, mortgage rates, construction costs, and the demand for housing have risen in many metropolitan regions. The recent influx of immigrants and the redistribution of population from the Frostbelt to the Sunbelt and from the cities to suburbs also favor the trend of increasing densities. In the suburbs apartments and condominiums with minimal interior space and little residential outdoor space are replacing the dominance of spacious dwellings and large lots. The supply and cost of available housing are thus leading many consumers to choose residences that are more crowded (Baldassare, 1986).

The rising cost of housing is resulting in changes in the social composition of household units. This will inevitably increase the subjective crowding experienced in certain groups. For instance, many single adults cannot afford to live alone, so they are more frequently choosing to live with unrelated individuals. Their social structure is less stable than that of family households, and as a result, their abilities to adjust to overcrowding are limited. Also, many young adults are remaining in their parents' dwellings because they cannot afford their own residences. The likelihood is that these households have more stress than those composed of nuclear families with minor children. These trends in housing composition are now evident in growing suburbs with tight housing markets and should soon spread to other regions (Baldassare, 1985).

The elimination of certain housing programs and severe cutbacks in others can only mean more residential crowding for the disadvantaged. A reduction in housing subsidies and public housing construction results in more limited choices and higher costs for poor people. Public sentiment and social policy have, in an era of fiscal strain, turned against government housing-assistance programs. However, the adverse effects may be greater when vulnerable groups such as the poor experience residential crowding than when more advantaged groups do. As a result, the cost of public health and social service programs may increase when the household and neighborhood densities rise precipitously. The long-term burden of increased health, psychological, and social problems is undoubtedly greater than the immediate costs of providing adequate housing. It is thus of the highest priority to continue allocating resources that will reduce residential overcrowding in the lowest socioeconomic groups.

REFERENCES

Anderson, E. N. 1972. "Some Chinese Methods of Dealing with Crowding." *Urban Anthropology* 1: 141–150.

Baldassare, Mark. 1978. "Human Spatial Behavior." *Annual Review of Sociology* 4: 29–56.

———. 1979. *Residential Crowding in Urban America*. Berkeley and Los Angeles: University of California Press.

———. 1981. "The Effects of Household Density on Subgroups." *American Sociological Review* 46: 110–118.

———. 1982. "The Effects of Neighborhood Density and Social Control on Resident Satisfaction." *Sociological Quarterly* 23: 95–105.

———. 1985. "The Housing Crisis in Suburbia." Paper presented at the American Sociological Association meetings, Washington, D.C., August 27.

———. 1986. *Trouble in Paradise*. New York: Columbia University Press.

Booth, Alan. 1976. *Urban Crowding and Its Consequences*. New York: Praeger.

Calhoun, John 1962. "Population Density and Social Pathology." *Scientific American* 206: 139–148.

Durkheim, Emile. [1893] 1964. *The Division of Labor in Society*. New York: Free Press.

Fischer, Claude, M. Baldassare, and R. Ofshe. 1975. "Crowding Studies and Urban Life: A Critical Review." *Journal of the American Institute of Planners* 41: 406–418.

Freedman, Jonathan. 1975. *Crowding and Behavior*. San Francisco: W. H. Freeman.

Gove, Walter, M. Hughes, and O. Galle. 1983. *Overcrowding in the Household*. New York: Academic Press.

Hall, Edward T. 1966. *The Hidden Dimension*. New York: Doubleday.

Milgram, Stanley. 1970. "The Experience of Living in Cities." *Science* 167: 1461–1468.

Mitchell, E. T. 1971. "Some Social Implications of High Density Housing." *American Sociological Review* 38: 18–29

Newman, Oscar. 1972. *Defensible Space*. New York: Macmillan.

Simmel, Georg. [1905] 1969. "The Metropolis and Mental Life." In Richard Sennett (ed.), *Classic Essays on the Culture of Cities*. New York: Appleton-Century-Crofts. 47–60.

Sommer, Robert. 1969. *Personal Space: The Behavioral Basis of Design*. Englewood Cliffs, N.J.: Prentice-Hall.

Stokols, Daniel. 1972. ''A Social Psychological Model of Human Crowding Phenomena.'' *Journal of the American Institute of Planners* 38: 72–84.

Wirth, Louis. 1938. ''Urbanism as a Way of Life.'' *American Journal of Sociology* 44: 1–24.

PART II

SUPPLY, DEMAND, AND
AFFORDABILITY OF HOUSING

6

Affordability of Housing

CHESTER HARTMAN

Housing affordability, definitionally, is the relation of a consumer's housing costs to his or her available resources. It is an issue that encompasses both facts and standards, often in conflicting fashion. The fewer the available resources, the more likely that affordability is a perceived and real problem, particularly in an economy where housing costs have been rising rapidly. Let us deal first with the facts—the relationship of housing costs to consumers' incomes (the most widely available surrogate for resources), how this relationship has varied over time in recent years, and how it varies by race and income.

THE AFFORDABILITY PICTURE FOR RENTERS

It is clear from Table 6.1 that renters are devoting ever-higher proportions of their income to housing.[1] By 1983 (the latest year for which such data are available), more than one-third of renter households were paying 35 percent or more of their income for housing, and more than one-fifth were paying half or more. These proportions have been increasing year by year, and one suspects that when the 1985 American Housing Survey data are finally published there will be an even larger jump than the 3 percent increase in both categories that characterized the period between 1981 and 1983. Only two out of every five renter households in 1983 were paying less than the most commonly used 25 percent rule of thumb.

Minority (black and Hispanic) households fare even worse. The proportion of such households paying 35 percent or more of their income for housing was 43–44 percent, and 26–28 percent were paying half or more in 1983. Only 35–36 percent were paying less than the 25 percent rule of thumb. At the other end of the scale, a staggering 20–22 percent were paying 60 percent or more of their income for housing (a data category reported only for minority households). The median rent-to-income ratio as of 1983 was 29 percent for all renter households and 32 percent for black and Hispanic renter households.

Table 6.1

Distribution of All Renter Households, Black Renter Households, and Hispanic Renter Households by Rent-to-Income Ratio, 1973–83

	Total # hhs (millions)	-25% (%)	25-34% (%)	35+% (%)	50+% (%)	35-49%[d] (%)	50-59%[d] (%)	60+%[d] (%)	Median
	All renter households								
1973	24.3	54	15	23	NA	NA	NA	NA	NA
1974	24.3	54	16	24	NA	NA	NA	NA	NA
1975	25.0	52	16	26	NA	NA	NA	NA	23
1976	25.4	50	17	27	NA	NA	NA	NA	24
1977	25.8	49	17	29	NA	NA	NA	NA	25
1978	26.1	48	18	29	16	13	NA	NA	25
1979	26.6	45	19	30	17	13	NA	NA	26
1980	26.7	44	18	31	18	13	NA	NA	27
1981	28.1	43	19	32	19	13	NA	NA	27
1983	29.3	40	19	35	22	14	NA	NA	29
	Black renter households								
1973	3.9	54	14	25	NA	NA	NA	NA	NA
1974	4.0	51	16	29	NA	NA	NA	NA	NA
1975	4.2	47	16	32	NA	NA	NA	NA	25
1976	4.3	46	18	31	NA	NA	NA	NA	26
1977	4.4	44	18	34	NA	NA	NA	NA	27
1978	4.5	45	18	32	19	13	6	13	26
1979	4.6	43	18	33	20	13	6	14	27
1980	4.8	41	18	36	22	14	5	17	29
1981	4.8	42	19	39	24	15	6	18	29
1983	4.7	35	21	44	28	16	7	22	32
	Hispanic renter households								
1973	1.6	51	19	25	NA	NA	NA	NA	NA
1974	1.6	52	18	27	NA	NA	NA	NA	NA
1975	1.7	47	18	29	NA	NA	NA	NA	25
1976	1.9	46	17	32	NA	NA	NA	NA	26
1977	2.0	45	19	32	NA	NA	NA	NA	27
1978	2.1	49	19	33	17	16	5	12	26
1979	2.2	42	21	32	20	12	6	14	28
1980	2.3	42	18	35	22	13	6	16	28
1981	2.5	38	18	40	24	16	5	19	30
1983	2.5	36	17	43	26	17	6	20	32

[a]In an effort to keep up with the realities of astronomical rent-to-income ratios not foreseen at the time such data collection began, the AHS in 1978 started reporting these ratios in finer categories at the upper end, especially for minority households. Thus from 1973 to 1977 all those at the upper end of the ratio scale were grouped in the 35 + % category. Starting in 1978 black and Hispanic households were reported in 35–49%, 50–59%, and 60 + % categories, and for all households the upper catch-all category became 50 + %.

Source: U.S. Bureau of the Census, 1973–83.

A 1985 U.S. General Accounting Office (GAO) report provides the most useful data set relating rent burdens to incomes (GAO, 1985). Annual (American) Housing Survey (AHS) data on rents and incomes were recalculated on the basis of household income relative to area median family income, and rent burdens

Table 6.2
Rent Burden of Households with Incomes 80 Percent or Less of Area Median Family Income

Rent burden[a]	1975 Housing units (in thousands)	Percent of total	1983 Housing units (in thousands)	Percent of total
30% or less	6,694	46	6,533	36
Over 30%	7,824	54	11,853	64
Total	14,518	100	18,386	100

[a]Rent burden, or rent-to-income ratio, equals gross annual household rent divided by gross annual household income.
Source: U.S. General Accounting Office, 1985.

Table 6.3
Rent Burden of Households with Incomes 0–50 Percent of Area Median Family Income

Rent burden[a]	1975 Housing units (in thousands)	Percent of total	1983 Housing units (in thousands)	Percent of total
30% or less	2,777	29	2,695	22
Over 30% to 40%	1,670	18	1,897	15
Over 40% to 50%	1,309	14	1,635	13
Over 50% to 60%	982 ⎤	10 ⎤	1,339 ⎤	11 ⎤
Over 60% to 70%	589 ⎟ 3,566	7 ⎟ 38	935 ⎟ 5,955	8 ⎟ 49
Over 70%	1,995 ⎦	21 ⎦	3,681 ⎦	30 ⎦
Total[b]	9,322	99	12,182	99

[a]Rent burden, or rent-to-income ratio, equals gross annual household rent divided by gross annual household income.
[b]The percentages do not total 100 due to rounding.
Source: U.S. General Accounting Office, 1985.

are presented for households with incomes 50 percent or less and over 50 up to 80 percent of the area median income from 1975 to 1983.

Tables 6.2 and 6.3 present selected portions of these data. For all renter households with incomes 80 percent or less of the area median, the number of households paying more than 30 percent of their income for rent ("the U.S. Department of Housing and Urban Development [HUD] often uses the figure of 30 percent or less of gross income," the GAO report notes, "as a benchmark for a reasonable or affordable rent burden for a lower income household") rose by 4.1 million, from 7.8 million (54 percent of all such households) in 1975 to 11.9 million (64 percent of all such households) in 1983. In the very lowest income category—those with incomes 50 percent or less of the area median— the number of households with rent burdens in excess of half their income rose from 3.6 million (38 percent of all such households) in 1975 to 6.0 million (49 percent of all such households) in 1983. (The GAO report deals only with rents and renters. Renter households who reported no positive income were excluded; since such households may well include the most rent-burdened of all, the reported findings may actually understate the seriousness of the nation's rent-burden problem.)

Although these massive increases in rent burden doubtless were accompanied by improvement in housing conditions (as measured by a HUD classification scheme using six specified deficiencies, data which were unavailable for the 1983 AHS at the time the GAO report was done), the extent of physical improvement, even using this rough measure, was far short of the dramatic increase in rent burdens and was an artifact of general upgrading in the quality of the housing stock, mainly via removal of obsolete units, over which lower-income households have neither control nor choice.

THE AFFORDABILITY PICTURE FOR HOMEOWNERS

Homeowners too are facing increasing housing-cost burdens, although their situation is inherently more complex to analyze than that of renters, and (relatedly) the data collected reveal less. Since 1974 the AHS has collected information on the monthly housing payments of homeowners. (These generally are defined as the sum of: mortgage and similar debt payments; real estate taxes; fire and hazard insurance; utilities; and fuel.) But for mortgaged homeowners, some two-thirds of such payments are for mortgage interest and principal repayment, and no account is taken of the amount of down payment the homeowner has made and thus of the proportion of total capital costs for a given house represented by the loan. The owner of a $100,000 home bought with a $20,000 down payment and an 80 percent mortgage will have far higher monthly payments than the owner of a home of similar value who has paid 50 percent down and has a 50 percent mortgage; and to carry this to the extreme, someone who has paid all cash for his or her home (which many persons "trading down" will do) has no principal repayments or interest. No data collection methods have been developed at the national level that take into account the opportunity costs of money that homeowners put into equity investment. The eventual capital gain profits the homeowner may make upon sale of the residence—which often make a high monthly payment more acceptable and a good investment—also are not factored in. These caveats must be kept in mind as one examines the data.

Table 6.4 shows an increasing proportion of income being devoted to housing by homeowners. The rise in median cost-to-income ratio for housing has been slight but steady, from 17 percent in 1974 to 20 percent in 1983 for homeowners with mortgages and from 11 percent to 13 percent over this same period for homeowners without mortgages. Nearly one-third of the former group in 1983 paid one-quarter or more of their income for housing, while more than one-

Table 6.4
Housing Costs of Homeowners, with and without Mortgages, as a Percentage of Income, 1974–83

	Total # hhs (millions)	-25% # hhs (millions)	%	25-35% # hhs (millions)	%	35+% # hhs (millions)	%	Median %
				Homeowners with Mortgages				
1974	23.0	15.8	69	2.7	12	1.8	8	17
1975	23.5	15.7	67	2.9	12	2.1	9	18
1976	24.1	15.8	66	3.3	14	2.3	10	18
1977	24.9	16.1	65	3.6	14	2.6	10	19
1978	25.6	16.2	63	3.9	15	2.8	11	19
1979	26.4	16.6	63	4.1	16	3.1	12	19
1980	27.1	16.9	62	4.1	15	3.6	13	19
1981	27.9	17.3	62	4.3	15	3.8	14	19
1983	27.8	16.4	59	4.6	17	4.3	15	20
				Homeowners without Mortgages				
1974	13.2	10.0	76	0.8	6	0.8	6	11
1975	13.9	10.3	74	0.9	6	0.9	6	11
1976	13.9	10.2	73	0.9	6	0.9	6	11
1977	13.9	10.3	74	1.0	7	1.0	7	12
1978	14.5	10.6	73	1.0	7	1.1	8	12
1979	14.9	11.0	74	1.0	7	1.2	8	12
1980	14.9	10.8	72	1.1	7	1.3	9	13
1981	15.4	11.3	73	1.1	7	1.4	9	12
1983	15.8	11.4	72	1.2	8	1.4	9	13

Note: Totals do not equal 100% because of exclusion of "not reported" and "not computed" households.
Source: U.S. Bureau of the Census, 1974–83.

seventh paid 35 percent or more. Among homeowners without mortgages, the corresponding proportions were one out of 6 and one out of 11.

Somewhat over one-third (36 percent) of all homeowners (1983 data) have no mortgage (for the most part, these are probably elderly persons who have paid off their mortgage, although there has been almost no study of the characteristics of nonmortgaged homeowners). Such persons of course have far lower monthly housing costs: in 1983 the median monthly housing cost for nonmortgaged homeowners ($166) was 36 percent of the median monthly cost for mortgaged homeowners.

Although the American Housing Survey does not publish data on housing-cost burdens of homeowners by race, such data are available in the decennial U.S. Housing Census. The most recent such census (U.S. Bureau of the Census, 1982) shows that among homeowners with mortgages, the median housing cost-to-income ratio is 19.0–19.8 (for owners of one-unit detached and attached units, respectively) for whites, 21.0–20.1 for blacks, and 20.0–22.2 for Spanish-origin homeowners. For owners of unmortgaged homes, the comparative median ratios are 11.2–12.1 for whites, 14.9–14.1 for blacks, and 9.5–11.5 for those of Spanish origin. These data are, however, quite old, and of course minority owners have generally lower incomes and worse housing conditions, meaning their cost burdens are in fact more onerous and their housing dollars are buying less.

Yet another index of homeowners' affordability problems is mortgage delinquency and foreclosure rates. As Table 6.5 indicates, in the second quarter of 1986, 5.71 percent of all loans were delinquent (30 or more days past due). This is down somewhat from the historic high of 6.13 percent in the first quarter of 1985 (collection of such data, by the Mortgage Bankers Association, was begun in 1953), but higher than the late 1970s–early 1980s period. The foreclosure rate (foreclosure actions started in a given quarter as a percent of all loans), as well as the (related) rate of loans 90 or more days past due, has been rising steadily.

It is becoming increasingly important for households to have a second income in order to support their mortgage payments. The percentage of households with two adults in which income contributed by a second earner accounts for 10 percent or more of total household income rose from 47.2 percent in 1977 to 56.6 percent in 1985 (U.S. League of Savings Institutions, 1986).

Another sign of the nation's housing affordability problem is the slight decline in the homeownership rate, which began in 1981. The high point in the nation's homeownership rate was attained in the third quarter of 1980, when it reached 65.8 percent. In 1981 the third-quarter rate dropped to 65.5 percent; in 1982, to 64.9 percent; in 1983, to 64.8 percent; and in 1985, to 63.9 percent (U.S. Bureau of the Census, various years). The slow but steady decline in the homeownership rate has recently been halted, but the rate is still below those of the peak years. While homeownership is not per se a desideratum, nor (as the mortgage foreclosure data indicate) synonymous with absence of affordability problems, in our culture it is the dominant and generally preferred form of tenure, and data correlating income with tenure status show that the overwhelming majority of those who can afford to own do. Thus the drop in the nation's homeownership rate, while small, has been taken as a sign, not that fewer people want to own their own homes, but that fewer are able to afford the down payments and monthly costs.

Both the National Association of Home Builders (NAHB) and the National Association of Realtors (NAR) publish affordability indexes, the former naturally for new (single-family) homes, the latter for existing (single-family) homes. The NAHB index measures the ratio of household incomes to prevailing costs for new single-family housing, "incorporat[ing] mortgage payments (with their associated tax implications), property taxes, depreciation expenses, maintenance expenses, and the opportunity costs associated with the down payment" (*Economic News Notes*, 1983). The NAR index shows the relationship between median family income and the income needed to qualify (according to lenders' criteria, to be discussed later) for the purchase of an existing single-family home.[2]

Table 6.6 shows these two indexes from 1977 to 1985. While the recent

Table 6.5
Mortgage Delinquency and Foreclosure Rates, 1977–86

Year	Delinquency Rates, All Loans				New Foreclosures Started	
	Total Past Due	30 Days Past Due	60 Days Past Due	90 Days Past Due	All Loans	Conventional
1977						
Q1	4.54	3.23	0.76	0.55	0.19	0.09
Q2	4.60	3.28	0.78	0.54	0.18	0.08
Q3	4.46	3.19	0.75	0.52	0.17	0.07
Q4	4.56	3.29	0.76	0.51	0.16	0.07
1978						
Q1	4.59	3.29	0.78	0.52	0.15	0.07
Q2	4.51	3.23	0.76	0.52	0.16	0.06
Q3	4.56	3.29	0.76	0.51	0.16	0.06
Q4	4.64	3.38	0.76	0.50	0.16	0.07
1979						
Q1	4.43	3.24	0.73	0.46	0.15	0.07
Q2	4.47	3.26	0.73	0.48	0.14	0.06
Q3	4.83	3.57	0.78	0.48	0.13	0.06
Q4	4.77	3.47	0.79	0.51	0.15	0.06
1980						
Q1	4.89	3.53	0.83	0.53	0.13	0.07
Q2	4.99	3.60	0.84	0.55	0.14	0.07
Q3	5.00	3.55	0.85	0.60	0.16	0.08
Q4	5.02	3.53	0.87	0.62	0.15	0.09
1981						
Q1	5.23	3.73	0.86	0.64	0.16	0.09
Q2	5.23	3.71	0.88	0.64	0.17	0.11
Q3	5.31	3.76	0.90	0.65	0.15	0.11
Q4	5.20	3.68	0.88	0.64	0.16	0.11
1982						
Q1	5.30	3.70	0.90	0.70	0.20	0.13
Q2	5.53	3.82	0.96	0.75	0.20	0.13
Q3	5.54	3.80	0.95	0.79	0.22	0.14
Q4	5.72	3.93	0.96	0.83	0.22	0.14
1983						
Q1	5.75	3.94	0.98	0.83	0.20	0.13
Q2	5.61	3.84	0.94	0.83	0.23	0.16
Q3	5.31	3.59	0.88	0.84	0.22	0.16
Q4	5.69	3.91	0.93	0.85	0.21	0.17
1984						
Q1	5.42	3.66	0.90	0.86	0.19	0.13
Q2	5.51	3.75	0.88	0.88	0.22	0.15
Q3	5.87	4.02	0.95	0.90	0.24	0.18
Q4	5.81	3.95	0.95	0.91	0.19	0.15
1985						
Q1	6.13	4.17	1.01	0.95	0.24	0.17
Q2	5.83	3.97	0.94	0.92	0.23	0.18
Q3	5.68	3.79	0.97	0.92	0.23	0.17
Q4	5.71	3.81	0.94	0.96	0.21	0.16
1986						
Q1	5.80	3.85	0.97	0.98	0.24	0.18
Q2	5.71	3.70	0.94	1.07	0.25	0.18

Note: Rates are seasonally adjusted.

Delinquency Rate = percent of loans past due by given period.

Foreclosure Rate = foreclosures started in quarter as a percent of all loans.

Source: National Association of Home Builders, 1986. Reprinted with permission.

Table 6.6
National Association of Realtors and National Association of Home Builders Affordability Indexes, 1977–85

	Affordability Indices	
Year	NAR	NAHB
1977	117.4	100.0
1978	106.8	93.5
1979	93.0	87.0
1980	77.9	83.3
1981	67.4	73.6
1982	68.5	75.5
1983	82.1	81.9
1984	86.2	79.3
1985	93.2	84.5

Source: National Association of Home Builders, 1986. Reprinted with permission.

Table 6.7
Affordability of Housing, Based on a 30-year Fixed Rate Mortgage of $90,000 ($100,000 Purchase; 10% Down Payment)

Interest Rate	Monthly Principal & Interest Payment	Property Taxes & Insurance	Total Monthly Expenses	Annual Income Needed to Afford	Number of Families w/ Income Needed	Percent
9%	$ 725	$145	$ 870	$37,271	16,136,000	26.0%
11	858	145	1003	42,969	11,828,000	19.1
13	999	145	1144	49,009	8,324,000	13.4
15	1143	145	1288	55,178	6,085,000	9.8
17	1287	145	1432	61,347	4,265,000	6.9

Note: Figures are based on a 1986 estimate of 62,000,000 families in the United States. A 1983 family income distribution estimated by the NAHB Economics Division is applied. Expenses are assumed to equal 28% of income.
Source: *Housing Backgrounder*, 1986. Reprinted with permission.

picture is better than that of the period of extremely high interest rates in the early 1980s, the figures show as well a serious decline in affordability of homes for sale compared with the mid- to late 1970s. The centrality of mortgage interest rates to affordability is shown in Table 6.7, which illustrates the sharp decline in numbers of families with incomes sufficient to afford a house of a given price (in this example, $100,000) as interest rates rise. Each increase of a single point in the mortgage interest rate can price several million families out of the market.

OTHER INDEXES OF THE HOUSING AFFORDABILITY CRISIS

Other important aspects or indexes of the country's housing crisis are in essence affordability problems as well. One is the need to double up or otherwise over-crowd existing space. This is a difficult area in which to collect accurate data (particularly on doubling up), because of understandable fears on the part of respondents that such reporting will cause problems with landlords, code en-forcement agencies, welfare administrators, and immigration officials. Wide-spread anecdotal reports of this phenomenon exist, as well as scattered numerical estimates from public housing officials. The New York City Housing Authority, for example—by far the nation's largest—estimates, based on utility consump-tion, visual observation, elevator breakdowns, and so on, that 50,000 of the 174,000 apartments it manages are illegally occupied by more than one household (Hartman and Robbins, 1986). Two years earlier, the authority's estimate was that 17,000 units were being illegally occupied in this fashion, the later figure confirming the 1983 statement by the authority's chair that "the problem is growing geometrically" (Rule, 1983).

Another index is the fact that some 2.5 million Americans are displaced annually from their homes due to gentrification, undermaintenance, evictions, arson, rent increases, property tax delinquency, mortgage foreclosures, specu-lation, conversions, demolitions, "planned shrinkage," and historic preservation (HUD, 1981; LeGates and Hartman, 1981; Hartman, Keating, and LeGates, 1982).

Third, the number of outright homeless Americans, by all accounts, is on the rise. While there exists a range of estimates as to the actual number of homeless nationally (in part a function of inherent difficulties in counting homeless persons, in part a function of the motivations of the estimators), from a low of 250,000–350,000 (by HUD; see U.S. House of Representatives, 1982, 1984) to 2–3 million (by advocacy groups such as the Community for Creative Non-Violence; see Hombs and Snyder, 1982), there is consensus that the problem is rapidly growing and that the homeless more and more are a representative slice of the society in terms of age and family composition (Hopper and Hamberg, 1986). While a disproportionate number of deinstitutionalized mental hospital patients and persons with severe alcoholism and drug dependency problems appear among the homeless (which observation in no way detracts from the fact that they also have severe housing problems; see Hartman, 1986), for the most part people in the United States become homeless because they cannot afford the housing that is available.

Finally, rapidly rising utility costs, which can rival rent and mortgage payments, lead to eviction for nonpayment or produce unsafe and uncomfortable living con-ditions. The Consumer Price Index (CPI) for fuel, oil, coal, and bottled gas rose from 110.1 in 1970 to 646.0 in mid-1984; in the same 14-year period gas and electricity prices rose by 343 points, compared with a 194-point rise in the CPI for all items (U.S. Bureau of the Census, 1984: 475). Permanently high oil and electricity prices, deregulation of natural gas, and aggressive rate-increase campaigns by utility companies indicate that these costs will continue to consume a growing proportion of the family budget, although some assistance is provided to the elderly and to low-income households under various government programs.

AFFORDABILITY STANDARDS

What people "ought" to pay for housing has always been a somewhat murky matter. The usual expression applied to such standards, "rules of thumb," captures the imprecise, ad hoc quality of the concept and measure. What proportion of income people pay for housing is subject to factors well beyond their control—what they can earn, what the market charges for housing—and, where income levels or the nature of the housing market permit, to personal choice. As is to be expected, the data consistently show that the higher one's income, the lower the proportion (although not the absolute amount) of one's income that is actually spent on housing and on basic needs generally (what high income buys is the ability to consume nonbasic items and services).

The rules of thumb that exist therefore serve, for some, as a vaguely applicable guideline to personal patterns of expenditure. They also are used by lending institutions to place a cap on the mortgage amount that will be granted; by rental agents to judge whether an applicant for a given apartment can afford the rent being asked; and in government-aided housing programs that either (as in public housing) base the rent charged on the resident's income or (as with programs like Section 8) base the subsidy to the private owner on the difference between the (capped) market rent and a given percentage of the low-income resident's income.[3]

There have been all too few writings on ability-to-pay standards, perhaps because, at least for people at the lower end of the income scale, the concept of "ought" is almost meaningless in the face of the overwhelming realities of income and housing costs and the growing gap between them. To postulate seriously that people ought to pay no more than 25 percent or 30 percent of income for housing, if they are to have enough left over for other basics and for those nonbasics that are considered part of "the American standard of living," leads one into paths that few wish to tread: extraordinarily costly demands and programs capable of turning this desideratum into reality.

The fact is that as realities of housing costs and incomes inexorably change in the direction of the former outpacing the latter for ever-larger segments of the population, "standards" and "rules of thumb" shift to accommodate and rationalize those facts. Thus the federal government's low-rent housing program began in the 1930s with a 20 percent standard as the portion of residents' income to be charged, the remainder coming from federal subsidies designed to cover capital costs only (through annual payments to retire local housing-authority bonds), with operating costs paid for by rental revenues. As tenants' income-based rents increasingly were unable to cover sharply rising operating costs in public housing, housing authorities were forced to dip into reserve funds, with the threat of bankruptcy, and to increase tenants' rents, which in some cases rose to 50 percent or more of their incomes. In the face of this untenable situation, Congress, in a series of legislative steps in 1969–71 known as the Brooke amendments, introduced federal operating and modernization subsidies and at the same time placed a 25 percent cap (in effect, a floor as well for most families) on the amount of the tenants' income that could be charged for rent. The cost of such subsidies, given both the extensive maintenance and repair needs of the older projects and the constantly growing gap between public housing tenants' incomes and the costs of materials, utilities, wages, and other components of the operating budget, grew so fast that the Reagan administration, when it took office in 1981, raised the maximum (and, for most families, minimum) rent-to-income ratio for all low-rent subsidized housing to 30 percent, originally by Office of Management and Budget fiat, later codified by congressional action. Thus the Reagan administration's solution to the problem was simply to change the standard—in essence, to extract money from the poorest tenants of all in order to reduce the need for government subsidies.[4]

In one of the few conceptual treatments of the rent-to-income ratio, applicable for the most part to homeowners as well, Rapkin (1957) observes about an older rule of thumb—one month's rent should approximate one week's salary—that "it has never been quite clear to me whether this statement purports to be a statistical observation or whether it is a 'folkloristic' exhortation to husbandry. . . . How this homily has survived in the minds of men, despite a century or more of statistical research on the patterns of consumption, is for others to determine." That statistical research, as noted earlier, shows that the proportion of income spent on rent declines, on the average, as income increases (Table 1 of Rapkin's article shows this relationship clearly, using 1950 data). But while the pattern of averages is clear, it is equally clear that within any given income class there is considerable variation in the actual proportion of income devoted to rent, based on factors other than income (Rapkin reports a correlation coefficient of .41 between rent and income based on 1950 data). Besides size of household, other factors are the length of time a household has been at a given income (consumption expenditures generally, and housing more than most other consumption items, adjust slowly to changes in income), the household's wealth/asset position, consumer preferences (housing versus vacations, for example), the length of time one has been in a given residence, regulatory controls on housing costs, and regional variations in income and housing costs.

Regional variations in incomes, housing costs, and housing payments as a percentage of income are quite striking. For the selected cities in Table 6.8, average household income in 1984 ranged from a low of less than $30,000 to highs of $41,000–44,000; average home prices (for conventionally financed new and existing homes sold) ranged from lows of $78,000–97,000 to highs of

Table 6.8
Housing Affordability in Selected Markets, 1984

Market	1984	Market	1984
Atlanta		Miami-Fort Lauderdale	
Average household income	$37,250	Average household income	$35,000
Average home price[a]	$98,300	Average home price	$84,700
Payment as percent of income	29.7%	Payment as percent of income	27.8%
Boston		Minneapolis-St. Paul	
Average household income	$41,750	Average household income	$40,200
Average home price	$102,500	Average home price	$103,400
Payment as percent of income	32.1%	Payment as percent of income	27.9%
Chicago		New York City area	
Average household income	$39,800	Average household income	$44,300
Average home price	$90,700	Average home price	$126,500
Payment as percent of income	26.9%	Payment as percent of income	36.6%
Dallas-Fort Worth		Phoenix	
Average household income	$38,950	Average household income	$35,400
Average home price	$109,200	Average home price	$101,400
Payment as percent of income	32.7%	Payment as percent of income	30.9%
Denver		San Francisco Bay area	
Average household income	$41,000	Average household income	$43,750
Average home price	$115,400	Average home price	$143,400
Payment as percent of income	31.1%	Payment as percent of income	36.7%
Houston		Seattle-Tacoma	
Average household income	$41,650	Average household income	$35,250
Average home price	$94,800	Average home price	$97,800
Payment as percent of income	27.1%	Payment as percent of income	30.2%
Los Angeles-Orange Co.-Riverside		Tampa-St. Petersburg	
Average household income	$39,200	Average household income	$29,700
Average home price	$132,000	Average home price	$78,100
Payment as percent of income	37.2%	Payment as percent of income	27.5%

[a]Refers to conventionally financed new and existing homes sold.
Source: Lomas and Nettleton Co., 1985. Copyright 1987 BUILDER Magazine, Hanley-Wood, Inc., Washington, D.C. Reprinted with Permission.

$126,000–143,000; and payment-to-income ratios ranged from lows around 27 percent to highs around 37 percent.

Rapkin also notes the ambiguity in definitions of both income and rent; the former, for example, can be before- or after-tax income and can include or exclude in-kind income; the latter can be contract rent (which may or may not include some or all utilities), gross rent, or total housing expenditures. (A particular problem pertains to income from lodgers or subtenants: whether to treat it as additional income or a lower rent, each of which yields very different results for the rent-to-income ratio.) Employing very different concepts of both the numerator and denominator of the rent-to-income ratio fraction, Rapkin, using 1950 data, shows that for the lowest-income range, where variations in definition can have the greatest influence, "a twist of the tongue can shrink the housing expenditure ratio from 50.9 to 19.3 percent" (p. 168). (One other good treatment of the conceptual ambiguities of rent-to-income ratios is Newman, 1971.)

For people in the middle- and upper-income ranges, affordability is of course a somewhat different notion, having more to do (for homebuyers at least) with lenders' perceptions of risk—the risk that such people, through dramatic changes in their economic status (loss of job, disability, and so on) may not be able to meet their mortgage commitments, or the risk that other forms of consumption or borrowing may lead to a crisis in debt-paying ability. Lenders, and the secondary mortgage markets they depend on, establish maximum loan amounts according to some relatively arbitrary rule of thumb—say, 28 percent of the potential borrower's income—as the maximum monthly payment the borrower can "afford." While persons with substantial incomes obviously can afford to make higher monthly payments, lenders are worried that in the event of an economic squeeze the borrower will choose to default on the loan. In times of high interest rates, when the pool of eligible borrowers/home purchasers shrinks through application of these rules of thumb, there is a tendency to substitute more relaxed standards in order to perk up the homebuilding and mortgage lending industries, even at the price of greater risk. For example, during the peak mortgage interest rate period of the early 1980s an article in *Builder* magazine by a senior economic analyst for the Federal Home Loan Bank of San Francisco noted:

Setting a standard for housing affordability is an arbitrary process. . . . Given the many changes that have taken place in the home finance field in recent years, it is time to take a fresh look at standards for gauging affordability and mortgage risk. Traditional rules of thumb are outdated, and perhaps no other standards should take their place. Affordability can probably best be determined on a case-by-case basis, through a wide range of payment-income terms that are related to the probability of repayment and to the value and marketability of the property. (Vickroy, 1982)

A two-edged innovation by the real estate industry in the late 1970s and early 1980s has had a large impact on the housing affordability question for middle-

and upper-income homebuyers. During inflationary periods lenders are reluctant to make fixed interest rate loans, as the dollars that repay such loans are worth far less at the times of repayment, and lenders want to avoid tying up for long periods funds that could be loaned out a short time later at higher prevailing interest rates. In order to revive the housing and mortgage lending industries, so-called adjustable rate mortgages (in various forms) were introduced to replace the traditional fixed interest rate, level payment mortgage that had been the standard instrument since the restructuring of the home finance industry during the depression. At its high point (August 1984), 68 percent of all mortgage originations were of the adjustable rather than the fixed rate variety, although the proportion has fallen sharply with the drop in inflation rates ("Outlook for Homeownership," 1986). Under the latter type of mortgage, the interest rate is fixed for the life of the mortgage, and monthly payments are for a constant amount (although composed of very different proportions of interest and principal repayment at different stages in the life of the mortgage). Adjustable rate mortgages have in essence shifted the burden of inflation from the lender to the borrower, creating a larger pool of homebuyers and borrowers, but putting them at the disadvantage of having to shoulder any costs of inflation via higher monthly payments. Should the borrower's income not keep pace with the various indexes (such as the Treasury borrowing rate) used in determining this floating interest rate, true affordability problems and eventual mortgage delinquency and foreclosure may well occur.[5] But these new instruments have enhanced the appearance of affordability, as illustrated by the figures given by the National Association of Home Builders' "affordability index," using fixed versus adjustable rate mortgages. For 1984 the index was 84.6 using the former measure, 92.1 using the latter; for 1985 (preliminary data) the comparative index numbers were 94.0 and 105.5, respectively (Crellin, 1986).

An important conceptual and policy critique of the affordability standard, whatever the actual figure used, has been raised by Michael Stone (1983). Stone points out that such ratios realistically are and ought to be a function both of household size and household income. That is, the larger the number of people in the household, the more that household must spend for food, clothing, transportation, medical care, and other nonshelter necessities; therefore, at any given income level, the proportion of income devoted to housing should decrease as household size increases.[6] The household's income level must similarly be considered in arriving at an acceptable housing expenditure-to-income ratio. The higher one's income, the more one has left to devote to housing once nonshelter basics have been taken care of; conversely, lower-income households (holding size constant) can afford to devote less of their income to housing if they are to satisfy the household's basic needs for food, clothing, and so on.

Whereas across-the-board housing cost-to-income ratios—notwithstanding the fact that over time there has been a constant upward shift in the actual rule of thumb in use at any given time—have been well institutionalized in government programs, lending standards, and management practices, the compelling logic of Stone's argument suggests a very different approach. He writes: "Any attempt to reduce the affordability of housing to a single percentage of income—no matter how low or high—simply does not correspond to the reality of fundamental and obvious differences among households" (1983: 102–03). In place of traditional fixed rules of thumb, Stone suggests a sliding scale of affordability related to both household size and income level. He also offers a concrete proposal on how to operationalize this, both in general form and in modified fashion for existing government housing programs, via a system of deductions related to household size from the income base on which rent is calculated.

The impact of Stone's analytic work in this area, were his proposals to be followed—as they should—would be profound for all aspects of affordability, from the ways we collect and analyze data, to lending and management practices, the formulation and administration of government housing, income support, and social service programs, and our perception of the magnitude of the nation's affordability crisis. Stone's basic analytic concept, which he terms "shelter poverty," suggests that the nation's housing problem is far greater than has been accepted in conventional literature and political thinking. Using the Bureau of Labor Statistics' lower budgets as a standard for what families must at a minimum expend for nonshelter basics, and comparing these figures with data on actual household incomes, Stone shows that in 1980 over 25 million households (owners as well as renters)—32 percent of all households—were "shelter poor," that is, were paying more than they could afford for housing if they were to have enough left to purchase the minimum nonshelter basics they need, according to the Bureau of Labor Statistics; and that that number had increased by 6.4 million during the 1970s.

WHAT CAN BE DONE?

Logically, there are two ways of ameliorating the affordability problem: by dealing with the numerator (lowering housing costs) or with the denominator (raising the disposable income). In theory, the nation could adopt a policy of providing everyone (via any of a number of direct and indirect means) with income sufficient to afford the going market cost of decent housing. Needless to say, such a massive redistributive policy is not likely. Furthermore, without controls on the housing market, such a policy, even if adopted, would not prevent housing costs from constantly inflating to a degree that would make income catch-up unfeasible. (It also should be noted that an income policy alone would not be able to deal with the multiple forms of housing-market discrimination—by race, life-style, family composition, and so on—that prevent access to otherwise available housing on the part of groups against whom this discrimination is practiced by the various "gatekeepers," such as real estate agents, building managers, sellers, and developers.)

In recent years, and to the extent that such programs have not been cut back or eliminated, the nation's approach to the affordability crisis for low-income households has been to provide payments (Section 8, housing allowances, vouchers, and so on) to bridge the gap between what housing costs and what consumers can afford. Approaches of this sort do nothing to lower the cost and price of housing, and without market controls and in the face of a widening housing affordability gap, the cost of and consequent political opposition to such programs become enormous.

Any substantial reduction in the cost of housing, thereby increasing its availability to and affordability by the millions of American households presently living in shelter poverty, can come about only through radical changes in the nation's system of providing housing. At the heart of the affordability dilemma lie two principal features of that system: the role of profit maximization at all stages in the process, and the role of credit. The fact that housing gets built and managed only if it brings profit to the myriad actors along the way—landowners, developers, lenders, materials providers, speculators, landlords, managers, realtors, and rental agents—increases the cost of developing and operating the final product well beyond the reach of increasing numbers of American households. The central role of credit costs—the essentially permanent burden all occupants must shoulder of repaying the capital used to build the units, transformed into the selling price for future occupants—must be tackled as well. For owners of single-family mortgaged homes, mortgage repayment costs on the average represent 65 percent of total monthly housing costs (U.S. Bureau of the Census, 1984). While parallel data on how much of monthly housing payments goes to repay loans are not available for renters, it is likely that, given the use of multiple mortgages by apartment house owners, this percentage is even higher for the one-third of American households who are tenants.

Detailed treatment of alternative, fundamental approaches to solving the affordability crisis is beyond the scope of this chapter. One such program is offered in Hartman and Stone, 1986. In essence, it calls for increasing amounts of new housing construction and housing rehabilitation to be financed via capital grants rather than credit, under the control of a range of public and private "social housing agencies." It also provides for the transfer of substantial amounts of the existing housing stock to such agencies, with one-time retirement of the outstanding debt, as an alternative to foreclosure proceedings, as a form of lifetime annuity for the elderly, as an option for lower-income homeowners, and as a means of dealing with multifamily housing that either is tax-delinquent or in violation of local health and safety codes.

A precondition to dealing with the nation's growing housing affordability problem is to recognize its true magnitude and trends, analyze correctly its root causes, and create programs that derive from such analysis. The costs of such programs must, by definition, be many times what the society now devotes to ameliorating its housing ills.[7] Choices on how to allocate the nation's resources are rooted in values and political processes. If and when achieving the goal of decent, affordable housing for all Americans is taken seriously, we then will face the realities of the price tag for attaining that plateau and the kinds of systemic changes needed to bring it into existence.

NOTES

1. Rent-to-income ratios conventionally are expressed in terms of gross rent (the contract plus the estimated average monthly cost of utilities and fuels, if these are paid by the renter in addition to the rent) and before-tax household income (the sum of money income of all persons 15 years and older occupying the housing unit.

2. The accuracy and usefulness of the NAR measure have been criticized, because prices of existing houses, which, by comparison with prices of new homes, are much more elastic, will drop if an insufficient number of buyers are able to afford the asking price. As formulated by Peter Salins, "Over the long run, the ratio of median incomes to median housing prices is stable and must be stable. . . . If it is calculated correctly, it should only go above or below a one-to-one ratio as a fluke" (quoted in Johnson, 1985). The NAHB currently is revising its index (phone interview, Dean Crist, NAHB, February 25, 1987).

3. Other, smaller government programs employ such percentages as well. For example, under the Uniform Relocation Act, a (capped) payment is made to tenants displaced by federal action, computed as the difference between 25 percent of the displacee's income and the actual rent charged on the apartment into which he or she relocates.

4. When the Office of Management and Budget announced this upward shift in the proportion of low-rent subsidized tenants' income that would be charged, the announcement was accompanied by data showing how much it would save the government: nearly $6 billion over five years. Of course, the other way of looking at this policy change was that those least able to afford the costs were being required to come up with that amount in order to relieve the government's budget problems.

5. A range of other nonconventional arrangements (known by the euphemism "creative financing") were introduced during this period to reduce apparent entry costs for the homebuyer, even though this often led to subsequent problems for incautious buyers: seller "buydown" of the interest rate for the initial few years of the loan, interest-only mortgage payments, "wraparound loans," lowered down payment requirements, and so on. Various marketing techniques also were and are employed to induce home purchasers to opt for the adjustable rate version of the mortgage, such as a very low interest rate— sometimes three to four points under the rate for a fixed interest rate mortgage—for the first year or two.

6. Because of the fixed nature of housing costs (as compared with, say, food, the other major expense item for most households, expenditures for which can be rapidly and substantially altered by altering the amount, frequency, quality, and composition of meals), lower-income households especially seek to keep housing costs to a minimum, as rent or mortgage payments represent the overriding claim on disposable income, and the consequences of not meeting that claim (eviction, foreclosure) are drastic.

7. The largest government housing subsidy by far is the indirect one embedded in the income tax system, the homeowner deduction, by which virtually all mortgage interest and property tax payments can be deducted from the taxpayer's taxable income base. Because of rapidly rising home prices and mortgage amounts and high interest rates, as

well as rising property tax bills, these deductions have been increasing steeply, and now are in the range of $40–50 billion annually. They are also extremely regressive, since these tax expenditures are available only to homeowners (who as a class have far higher incomes than renters) and since homeownership rates increase with income; they are available only to those who itemize deductions, a practice that in general makes sense only for middle and upper-income taxpayers; they have no dollar limit, and the higher one's income, the more dollars one generally spends on housing; and they are worth more to higher-income taxpayers whose marginal tax rate is higher (see Dolbeare, 1985). A more equitable and rational housing system designed to insure all Americans decent, affordable shelter, while costly, would appear less so when compared with this hidden subsidy.

REFERENCES

Crellin, George. 1986. "Residential Real Estate, 1985: The Housing Year in Review." *Real Estate Quarterly*, Winter.

Dolbeare, Cushing 1985. *Federal Housing Assistance: Who Needs It? Who Gets It?* Washington, D.C.: National League of Cities.

Economic News Notes. 1983. "Housing Affordability Index." Washington, D.C.: National Association of Home Builders, January.

Hartman Chester. 1986. "The Housing Part of the Homelessness Problem." In Ellen Bassuk (ed.), *The Mental Health Needs of Homeless Persons*. New Directions for Mental Health Services, no. 30. San Francisco: Jossey-Bass.

Hartman, Chester, and Tom Robbins. 1986. "No Vacancy: The Disappearance of Affordable Housing." *Village Voice*. April 1.

Hartman, Chester, and Michael Stone. 1986. "A Socialist Housing Alternative for the United States." In Rachel Bratt, Chester Hartman, and Ann Meyerson (eds.), *Critical Perspectives on Housing*. Philadelphia: Temple University Press.

Hartman, Chester, Dennis Keating, and Richard LeGates. 1982. *Displacement: How to Fight It*. Berkeley: National Housing Law Project.

Hombs, Mary Ellen, and Mitch Snyder. 1982. *Homelessness in America: A Forced March to Nowhere*. Washington, D.C.: Community for Creative Non-Violence.

Hopper, Kim, and Jill Hamberg. 1986. "The Making of America's Homeless: From Skid Row to New Poor, 1945–84." In Rachel Bratt, Chester Hartman, and Ann Meyerson (eds.), *Critical Perspectives on Housing*. Philadelphia: Temple University Press.

Housing Backgrounder. 1986. Washington, D.C.: National Association of Home Builders, Public Affairs Division, May.

Johnson, Kirk. 1985. "Rate Decline Aids Affordability." *New York Times*. November 17.

LeGates, Richard, and Chester Hartman. 1981. "Displacement." *Clearinghouse Review*. July.

Lomas and Nettleton Co. 1985. "U.S. Housing Markets." *Builder*, April.

National Association of Home Builders. 1986. "The Current Housing Situation." Washington, D.C.: Economics, Mortgage Finance, and Housing Policy Division. Vol. 7, no. 3 (November). News release.

Newman, Dorothy. 1971. "Housing the Poor and the Shelter to Income Ratio." Paper submitted to the Subcommittee on Housing Panels of the House Committee on Banking and Currency. 92d Cong., 1st sess. June.

"The Outlook for Homeownership Seems on the Upswing." 1986. *Savings Institutions*, September.

Rapkin, Chester. 1957. "Rent-Income Ratio." *Journal of Housing* 14 (January).

Rule, Sheila. 1983. "17,000 Families in Public Housing Double Up Illegally, City Believes." *New York Times*, April 21.

Stone, Michael. 1983. "Housing and the Economic Crisis." In Chester Hartman (ed.), *America's Housing Crisis: What Is to Be Done?* Boston: Routledge & Kegan Paul.

U.S. Bureau of the Census. 1973–83 (various years). *Annual (American) Housing Survey*. Washington, D.C.: Government Printing Office.

————. 1982. *Census of Population and Housing*. Washington, D.C.: Government Printing Office.

————. 1984. *Statistical Abstract of the United States*. Washington, D.C.: Government Printing Office.

U.S. Department of Housing and Urban Development, Office of Policy Development and Research, 1981. "Residential Displacement—An Update." Washington, D.C.: Government Printing Office.

U.S. General Accounting Office. 1985. *Changes in Rent Burdens and Housing Conditions of Lower Income Households*. GAO/RCED-85–108, April 23.

U.S. House of Representatives. Subcommittee on Housing and Community Development. 1982. *Homelessness in America*. Serial no. 97–100. Washington, D.C.: Government Printing Office, December 15.

U.S. House of Representatives. Subcommittee on Housing and Community Development and the Subcommittee on Manpower and Housing. 1984. *HUD Report on Homelessness*. Joint Hearing. Banking Committee serial no. 98–91. Washington, D.C.: Government Printing Office, May 24.

U.S. League of Savings Institutions. 1986. "Homeownership: Return of Tradition." Chicago: The League.

Vickroy, Connie. 1982. "What Does 'Affordable' Mean?" *Builder*, September.

7

Private Rental Housing

MICHAEL HARLOE

Despite the domination of homeownership in the United States, private rental housing still accommodates more than one-third of all households, and a far higher proportion of the population pass through it at some time in their housing careers. This makes the tenure more significant in America than in, for example, many of the more developed Western European societies. It is particularly important as a houser of low-income households. Especially in urban areas the private landlord is often the only option for these households.

However, despite the mass of federal, state, and local programs that impact on the tenure, it has been much less important as a subject for housing policy than homeownership. This reflects the relative political weakness of the tenure. Although there has been some involvement by large-scale capital in rental housing, most landlords remain small-scale, locally based operators—able to make some impact, for example, regarding rent controls (and other locally regulated aspects of the tenure)—but much less effective in lobbying the federal government for support and financial assistance. A similar conclusion applies in the case of private tenants, who consist increasingly of those whose incomes and other characteristics make them among the politically and economically weakest and most exploited sections of the population (on these issues see Dreier, 1984; Mollenkopf and Pynoos, 1980).[1] Many aspects of this situation are discussed in detail in other chapters in this book. Here we shall provide a broad review of the development and nature of the private rental sector in the United States. We begin by outlining the historical development and current state of the tenure. Then some of the more important policies affecting the tenure will be described. We then consider a question that has recently been much discussed: Is there a rental crisis? The next section examines private rental developments in other countries, helping to show that this crisis is deep rooted and is not confined to the United States. The final section highlights some research issues and discusses the prospects for private renting.

HISTORY AND CURRENT CHARACTERISTICS

Before the mid-nineteenth-century development of capitalist industrialization and urbanization there were various forms of housing provision, often of a nonmarket character, although private landlords certainly existed (see Woods, 1979a, 1979b). But the emergence of private rental as a mass tenure was the product of the distinctive social relationships that both resulted from and helped to mold capitalist urbanization. In this new world housing became a commodity offered for profit on the market, and the private rental form was well adapted to the requirements of those who provided it, the landlords, and, if not well adapted, at least accessible to those who needed it. The landlords, drawn from the expanding ranks of petty traders, manufacturers, and professionals, found that investment in rental housing that they also often managed was one of the few relatively secure and often highly profitable outlets for their money. At the same time, the newly arriving urban masses, highly mobile, in insecure employment, with low and unstable levels of earnings, could rarely afford the sizable and continuing financial costs of homeownership and were forced to accept what the landlord offered, together with the insecurities and deprivations that accompanied this form of housing (for a detailed account of this period in one city, New York, see Jackson, 1976). It was not until the 1920s, and more emphatically after 1945, when full employment and rising real incomes became a reality for the majority of the population, that the transition to the currently dominant form of capitalist housing provision, homeownership, became a reality for most Americans, aided of course by massive federal support.

This pattern of development is reflected in the historical statistics measuring the rise and decline of the tenure (U.S. Bureau of the Census, 1961: 395). In 1890, at a time when urbanization was still proceeding rapidly, the share of all occupied housing units that were privately rented (52.2 percent) was growing. By 1920 the share was 54.4 percent. Since then, allowing for a temporary reversal in the depression decade of the 1930s, the decline has been continuous, paralleling the rise in the share of homeowner units. By 1983 renter-occupied units amounted to 35.3 percent of the stock, of which about 3 percent consisted of public rather than private rental housing (a further 1.5 percent were private units with federal rent subsidies) (U.S. Bureau of the Census, 1984: Table A-1). However, this decline has not been constant. It was particularly rapid in the fifties, a time of massive, federally aided suburbanization, full employment, and rising real incomes. In the late sixties and the early seventies it was slowed by the provision of considerable numbers of federally subsidized units, the products of the urban programs of the Kennedy and Johnson administrations. In the eighties the decline may slow even further as homeownership becomes more difficult for many Americans to achieve. However, rental construction, except in limited submarkets, is likely to remain at quite low levels in the next few years (Downs, 1983a: 80–81).

Of course, growth or decline also depends on rates of stock loss. While the figures cannot be discussed in detail here, these have been at levels that are far in excess of additions to the stock by new building, so the aggregate growth in the stock of rental housing has been dependent on conversions from nonresidential use, subdivision, and the return to the inventory of previously withdrawn property (see Downs, 1983b: 73–83; Nenno and Sears, 1985: 4). Many of these losses have occurred as a result of urban renewal and, more recently, abandonment. By no means all of these units were past their useful life span. Over 300,000 of the units existing in 1973 but lost from the inventory by 1983 were built in 1960 or later (U.S. Bureau of the Census, 1984: Table A-5). In some areas gentrification, sometimes involving the establishment of condominiums or higher-income cooperatives, has also severely depleted the rental stock (for a study of the displacement of tenants by revitalization see DeGiovanni, 1984; for a discussion of the relationship between gentrification, displacement, and abandonment in the context of New York City, see Marcuse, 1985).[2] Gentrification and abandonment are responses to the changing economics of private landlordism and will be discussed later.

In line with the history of its development, the stock of private rental housing is concentrated in core cities rather than in suburban areas. The proportion of this housing is highest in the older industrial regions and cities, but much of the newer stock is located in the Sunbelt cities. Like the northern cities in an earlier era, these settlements have grown rapidly and attracted mobile workers, many of whom have at first rented rather than bought. In comparison with the owner-occupied stock, the private rental stock is older, smaller, and less adequate. But by international standards it is in relatively good condition, and its quality has improved in the last decades (the most defective housing is concentrated in rural rather than urban areas). Perhaps more importantly, there has been a considerable decline in the physical, social, and economic conditions of many of the inner-city neighborhoods in which much rental housing is located.

Some of the most important distinctions between private rental and home-ownership become clear when we examine who lives in each of these tenures. For many decades private rental housing accommodated much of the urban working class and also considerable numbers of the middle class. In the postwar period this has changed as the middle class, especially the white middle class and those with "normal" family structures, has opted for suburban homeownership (reports of a "back-to-the-city" trend by this group are much exaggerated, although the gentrification that accompanies this trend does, as stated earlier, impact greatly on some neighborhoods; see, for example, the detailed study of areas of Manhattan in Marcuse, 1985).

Data from the 1983 Annual Housing Survey (AHS) highlights some of the principal differences between renter and homeowner households (U.S. Bureau of the Census, 1984: Table A-1). Thus in 1983 about one-third of all the former were single-person households, compared with one-sixth of the latter. The two tenures contained similar proportions of two- and three-person households, but large households of five or more persons were far less common in the rental sector. However, it is interesting to note that the general trend toward smaller households is affecting both tenures, and the median size of homeowner households is approaching that of tenants.

A more detailed and revealing picture is obtained from the AHS data on household composition. This shows that about 70 percent of the homeowners were members of "normal" households, that is, married couples with or without children. Only 38 percent of renter households fell into this category. Single-person households, far more common in rental than owned housing, were also far more frequently below retirement age if they were tenants. One of the most striking differences concerns the concentrations of female-headed households. Despite the much larger number of owned units, the majority of all female-headed households live in rental housing, and far more of them are below retirement age. In general, a far higher proportion of tenants than of homeowners fall into the younger age groups.

There are equally striking differences in the incomes of homeowners and tenants. In 1983 the median income of tenants was 51 percent of the homeowner median (U.S. Bureau of the Census 1984: Table A-2). Significantly, the income gap between the two tenures has been widening; in 1970 the ratio was 65 percent. Given the facts outlined so far, it is hardly surprising to find that over half of all black- and Hispanic-headed households rent; in fact, since 1970 there has actually been a slight increase in the proportion of Hispanic households that rent (U.S. Bureau of the Census 1984: Tables A-7, A-9).

These figures show that the rented sector contains a high concentration of those whose position is weakest in the housing market (for more detailed analyses see, for example, Nenno and Sears, 1985: 9–11; Sternlieb and Hughes, 1981: 17–35). Increasingly, households with greater purchasing power have been drawn into homeownership, both for the greater satisfaction it provides (or promises to provide) in terms of housing services and because of its attraction as a heavily subsidized investment good. Private renting is increasingly confined to accommodating lower-income households who face a rising burden of rent payments. This latter point is highlighted by an examination of trends in rent-to-income ratios. Aggregate rent-to-income ratios have risen sharply in the last few years. In 1976 the median gross rent paid by tenants in unsubsidized units was 24 percent of their income; by 1983 this had risen to 29 percent (U.S. Bureau of the Census, 1978 and 1984: Table A-2). A part of this rise in the aggregate figure is due to the overall shift in the composition of the tenure toward low-income households (as such households generally pay more in housing costs than those who are better off). But medians have also risen for specific groups, and most rapidly for some of the poorest households, such as those headed by females (see Downs, 1983b: 31–2; National Low Income Housing Coalition, 1982), so the growing problem of affordability is not just a consequence of the changing income mix of those in the tenure.

All this means that the supply of affordable rental housing is declining. According to calculations made in 1982, based on the (far too optimistic) convention that all households, however poor, can afford to spend 25 percent of their income on housing, there was only enough affordable rental housing in 1980 for about 50 percent of the renter households in the bottom quartile of the income distribution (National Low Income Housing Coalition, 1982). Moreover, the continuing loss of low-rent units and the addition of new, higher-rent units to the stock exacerbates this mismatch. The median gross rent of units added to the stock between 1970 and 1983 was 20 percent higher than the overall median and the median income of those who occupied them was about 25 percent higher (U.S. Bureau of the Census, 1984: Table A-5).

Therefore, affordability is the most important constraint on housing access for would-be tenants. But it is important to note, although we cannot explore the topic in detail, that landlord selection is biased not only by the applicant's ability to pay but also by other aspects of their status. The most frequently researched basis for discrimination is race/ethnicity. However, recent studies have highlighted the existence of other exclusionary practices, for instance against low-income female-headed households and, generally, families with children (Marans and Colten, 1985; Ahrentzen, 1985). Another type of constraint on access to affordable housing is geographical. Some areas have a relatively more adequate supply of affordable housing than others.

Of course, the private rental sector still contains significant submarkets of higher-quality, newer, and high-income housing (especially in cities that contain many high-income, professional workers who have not yet formed or may never form "conventional" households). There are localities in which there has recently been something of a boom in new rental construction for such groups, especially in areas where there is a combination of relatively high incomes, severe housing shortages, no legislative restraint on the rents that can be charged, very high homeowner costs, and some tax subsidies for developers.[3] But such situations are very limited, and the housing that is produced—apart from the fact that it may well be turned into condominiums in a few years—is for the well-off. The general trend has been very different. This tenure has increasingly lost middle- and upper-income households to homeownership and has become the houser of those with low incomes and with other characteristics that make them among the weakest and most exploitable persons in the housing market. At the same time, the declining aggregate purchasing power of those in the market for rental accommodation (as well as the fact that those at the bottom of the income distribution, who are overrepresented in this tenure, have experienced a slower growth of incomes than more prosperous groups) means that new or continuing investment by landlords, except in the limited submarkets referred to above, has become much less attractive than it was in the heyday of this tenure. Again, there are exceptions to this conclusion. For example, some landlords have bought tenanted property in recent years very cheaply and then profited by charging rents that in value-for-money terms are high. Some have also made considerable profits in the medium term by realizing appreciating capital values, obtaining tax shelters, and benefiting from the period in the seventies when real interest rates were very low, a situation that no longer exists. But as a medium for long-term, stable investment, mass rental housing is now a poor option.

Two forms of disinvestment have been mentioned. Many landlords have cashed in on rising homeowner property values by selling out (in some cases via condominium or cooperative conversions; for a now rather dated nationwide analysis of this, see U.S. Department of Housing and Urban Development [HUD] 1980). While this process of tenure conversion is more likely in areas where the property is of relatively good quality and where there is a strong demand from middle- and higher-income groups, it has also involved poorer-quality, lower-value property and lower-income buyers—and the payment by them of artificially inflated prices (for a case study, see Harvey, 1985). In areas where these options do not exist, such as the declining neighborhoods of the older cities, disinvestment has taken the form of the large-scale abandonment of property after the landlords have milked every last drop of profit by, for example, reducing services, neglecting maintenance, and failing to pay property taxes.[4] Although there have been some governmental initiatives to stem the decline of the tenure, these have been insignificant in relation to the size and complexity of the problem. In particular, they are dwarfed by the impact of other policies that have increased the relative advantages of homeownership. We shall now briefly discuss these policy trends.

POLICY DEVELOPMENTS

There are many different ways of classifying the policies that impact on the private rental sector. They can be divided by function (those affecting the supply of new units, the quality of existing units, and their affordability); by source (those emanating from the federal government, from the states, and from local government); and so on. In this section we cannot discuss all these matters, let alone provide an overall assessment of their impact. We cannot, for example, examine the many ways in which localities seek to maintain the quality of existing units, by means of code enforcement, programs of rehabilitation, and so on (see, for example, Hartman, Kessler, and LeGates, 1980; Meier, 1983; DeGiovanni and Paulson, 1984). The major topic of rent control is passed over here, as it is discussed in another chapter in this book. Nor can we examine the many and varied legal provisions governing tenants' and landlords' rights and duties and the ways in which some jurisdictions have sought to reduce the imbalance that often exists between the duties of tenants and the rights of landlords (see Harloe, 1985a). Instead, we shall concentrate on reviewing how federal subsidies have affected the tenure, especially in relation to homeownership, as this is the single most important aspect of governmental action in relation to private renting.

Despite the diversity of federal housing programs, historically the most significant have been, first, the guaranteeing of private housing finance, which yields better terms than those that would have been offered by the private market acting alone; second, the provision of direct and indirect (tax) subsidies to stimulate housing production; and third, the provision of both these forms of subsidy to support housing consumption. As in most countries, tax subsidies for housing developed as a by-product of the general treatment of interest payments and certain other expenses as tax deductible. Explicit federal intervention in the mass housing market began in the 1930s with the establishment of the Federal Housing Administration (FHA) and other bodies to underpin and stimulate the provision of private mortgage finance on terms that made it accessible to a far greater proportion of the population than hitherto. As has been well described elsewhere, FHA programs have above all aided the expansion of homeownership (for a detailed history, see Fish, 1979, and the more analytical accounts in Aaron, 1972; Stone, 1980). Although they also supported a considerable production of new rental housing for a few years in the late forties and early fifties, it was not until the sixties that they were combined with direct subsidies, thus enabling the production of low- and moderate-income rental housing to occur (notably under the Section 236 and 221(d)(3) programs). This phase of development ended with President Nixon's suspension or cancellation of most federal direct subsidy programs in early 1973.

In 1974 these programs were largely replaced by the Section 8 program, which contained elements of both demand- and supply-side subsidies (for an outline, see HUD, 1976). The program aimed to stimulate the production of new and substantially rehabilitated units for low- to moderate-income households, as well as to reduce the housing costs of such households in existing units. The scale of the program has been large in relation to its predecessors and, particularly given the limited number of years in which it has operated, large in relation to the other major program of low-income rental housing—public housing. But in relation to the overall scale of the private rented sector and the size of the demand for affordable housing it is much more modest. By 1980 there were in all about 3 million renters receiving direct assistance through subsidy programs. About 1.8 million were in the private rented sector (4 percent of the total in this tenure), of whom about 1.2 million were in Section 8–assisted units (Struyk, Mayer, and Tuccillo, 1983: 16–17). Initially, the program mainly assisted existing units, but during the Carter administration there was a growing proportion of new and substantially rehabilitated units.

The picture has radically changed since 1981. Subsidized housing programs have been severely cut back by the Reagan administration. These cuts are discussed in greater detail elsewhere in this book, but starts of new and substantially rehabilitated Section 8 units had fallen from about 132,000 in 1980 to an estimated 15,500 in 1986. There had also been a decline, though less sharp, in the number of existing units assisted with Section 8 subsidy. But such figures greatly underestimate the severity of the cuts now being imposed because they relate to budget decisions taken some years ago. A much clearer view of the prospects for rental assistance programs is provided by the trends in new budget authority. For all HUD low-income housing programs (mainly Section 8 and public housing plus a much smaller amount for programs such as Section 202 housing for the elderly and handicapped), net new budget authority in 1980 was a little over $30 billion; by 1985 this was cut to a little less than $10 billion, and the administration's 1986 budget proposals aimed to virtually eliminate new commitments in 1986 (although Congress did not agree to such drastic cuts, the administration renewed its proposals for 1987) (Low Income Housing Information Service, 1985).

There have also been changes in the conditions for the receipt of low-income housing subsidies aimed at reducing eligibility and increasing the housing-payments burden of those households in the programs. In addition, there have been cuts in the federal funds available for low- and moderate-income housing rehabilitation through the Community Development Block and Urban Development Action grants as well as proposals to eliminate all the assisted housing programs of the Farmers Home Administration (some of which have been used for rental housing).

In comparison, the assistance for homeownership is on a massive and increasing scale. The nature of these subsidies, being indirectly provided through the tax system, and the political importance of the interests that they sustain—homeowners, the housing development and real estate brokerage industries, and the housing finance institutions—has made them immune from serious attack, despite the fact that they are grossly inequitable and inefficient (for an analysis, see U.S. Congressional Budget Office, 1981). In 1986 housing-related tax subsidies amounted to $45.6 billion. Under 3 percent of this total consisted of assistance for rental housing. Additionally, it should be noted that these tax subsidies went to investors in this housing; how much of it ultimately benefited tenants is unknown. In contrast, most of the tax subsidy for homeownership was claimed by homeowners, not developers (although it must be added that a good deal of this expenditure ultimately benefits property and finance capital rather than consumers). This huge total of tax subsidies contrasts with the federal housing payment outlay of just under $11 billion in 1986 for public housing and Section 8 (plus a further small amount for Section 202) (all these figures are taken from Low Income Housing Information Service, 1985).

The main tax subsidies for homeownership have been long established. They are the deduction of interest payments and property taxes (and an absence of any tax on imputed income) plus deferral or avoidance of capital gains (for a review, see U.S. Congressional Budget Office, 1981). Traditionally, the tax treatment of rental housing was straightforward. As with other business assets, landlords could deduct expenses, including a depreciation allowance. They were then taxed on their net revenue. There were various rules that allowed a benefit to be obtained by depreciating assets at a faster rate than would be justified by their economic life. Before 1969 the law governing the deductibility of depreciation contained no bias in favor of housing investment, although incentives for investment in new property were greater than those in existing property, thus in fact encouraging commercial developments that were marketed to syndicates of higher-income individuals for the tax shelter that they provided. But in 1969, as a result of the desire to encourage low-income housing, new rules—especially some relating to the arrangements for the recapture of "excess" depreciation by the tax authorities if a property was sold—were introduced for federally subsidized low-income projects. There were also new incentives for the rehabilitation of housing for low-income households. Studies showed that these tax shelters could provide very substantial subsidies for projects, but there has also been criticism of the costs and inefficiencies of these measures and the fact that there is very little real interest on the part of the higher-income investors, who in effect own the projects, in their effective management and maintenance (Einhorn, 1982: 32, estimates that professional fees amount to about 12 percent of the amount of a mortgage loan on syndicated projects; see also Harloe, 1985b: 195–200). By the late seventies there was in fact a growing problem of foreclosures on the federally insured mortgages that these projects obtained as the tax benefits ran out and revenues proved insufficient to cover liabilities (Stegman, 1978). The rehabilitation measures were probably of marginal value, since they gave the greatest help to landlords in higher tax brackets, but little assistance to lower-income landlords who probably needed the most help in upgrading their properties (Price, Waterhouse and Co., 1973).

Subsequently, various changes have been made in these provisions (a detailed discussion and analysis is contained in Einhorn, 1982). But the general situation was that special tax benefits were available for real estate that were not available for other assets, and low-income rental housing was especially favored. In 1981 the Economic Recovery Tax Act liberalized the benefits for rental housing but also increased incentives for investment in commercial buildings and equipment. This meant that relative to investment in homeownership development, investment in rental housing became more attractive. But given the new rules for nonhousing assets, the effects of this reform were uncertain. Moreover, in 1985 the federal administration proposed a new tax reform that, among other effects, would remove most of the special provisions for rental housing. This proposal will be further discussed later.

Accelerated depreciation (including the rapid write-off of rehabilitation costs) of rental housing cost about $925 million in 1986, a very modest sum compared with homeowner allowances (Low Income Housing Information Service, 1985). About another $1.1 billion was accounted for by the provision of tax-exempt state and local bonds for rental housing. The expansion of this form of subsidy accompanied the 1970s expansion of state activity in housing and enabled new projects to be built with the aid of cheap finance. Although such bonds had first been issued in the 1920s, when their issue expanded in the 1970s, they were at first mainly used for rental housing, often in conjunction with other subsidies such as Section 8; but after 1978 new issues boomed as they began to be used for homeowner projects too, so that by 1986 twice as much tax subsidy was provided for this purpose as for rental housing. Concern at the tax losses led to moves to end this form of subsidy (Einhorn, 1982; President's Commission on Housing, 1982: 169–73). However, the bonds have continued to grow in importance. According to the Real Estate Research Corporation, over 50 percent of new rental units in many parts of the country benefit from such financing. Most of this housing is, however, not for low-income households; indeed, the subsidy from tax-free financing alone is insufficient for this purpose. Commonly it is used in schemes where the vast majority of the housing is at market rents, with perhaps only 20 percent at below-market rents (a recent proposal in New York is for the issue of $400 million of such bonds to be used in such ''80/20'' schemes, with 80 percent of units let at slightly above-market rents to cross-subsidize 20 percent of lower-rent units). But as a part of the tax reform already mentioned, the federal administration now proposes to end the issue of these bonds. Together with the other proposed changes in the tax treatment of rental housing, this will, according to real estate interests, sharply reduce the production of the (relatively) affordable rental units that have been built in recent years and lead to considerable increases in the rents of existing housing (Nenno and Sears, 1985).

In sum, despite the plethora of mainly small-scale federal, state, and local policies relating to private rental housing, the most important feature of policy development concerns the differential treatment of this tenure and homeownership. In comparison with the assistance given to homeownership, subsidies for the production and consumption of rental housing are extremely modest. Moreover, even these subsidies are now being sharply reduced.

IS THERE A RENTAL HOUSING CRISIS?

We have seen how the private rental stock has housed an increasing concentration of tenants who have declining purchasing power relative to the national mean and how subsidies have encouraged the loss of middle- and upper-income households from this tenure. From the seventies onward, costs have risen faster than tenant incomes. One consequence of this has been the sharp rise in rent-to-income ratios that we have noted, but there have been some limits on the extent to which margins could be protected by passing along all cost rises to the tenant. A recent comparison of trends in apartment operating costs and renter incomes from 1976–83 shows that the former have grown almost 50 percent faster than the latter in this period (Nenno and Sears, 1985: 28). During the same period rent-to-income ratios have risen by about a one-third of this percentage. As already explained, this is not to say that landlords have not been making profits, but the availability of tax benefits and other subsidies plus the other factors noted in the last section have evidently been crucial for many operators.

From the late seventies, as the production of new unsubsidized rental housing fell sharply and as other indicators suggested a growing shortage of rental units in some areas, there was talk of a rental housing crisis and even suggestions that new subsidies should be provided for middle-income households (U.S. General Accounting Office, 1979). This case was rejected by many housing analysts and by the federal government (HUD, 1981). They argued that if there was a shortage, there would, in time, be a rise in rents, bringing about a fresh supply of housing. They also claimed that the affordability problem had been exaggerated—rising rent-to-income ratios were simply a consequence of rising housing quality and the fall in average tenant incomes as those who were better off increasingly opted for homeownership.

In a recent study Anthony Downs (1983b) has provided a detailed analysis of the current circumstances of rental housing and an assessment of these opposing points of view. His findings confirm the point stressed in this chapter. He writes that the future rental housing market will be increasingly constrained by the low purchasing power of tenants (a similar conclusion is contained in U.S. Congressional Budget Office, 1981). Downs shows that between the early 1960s and 1982 residential rents rose slower than (all) consumer incomes, operating costs, or construction costs. Much faster rent rises will be needed in the future if the output of new rental units is to grow substantially. The problem is made worse by the high real interest rates now charged for housing finance, a factor that is not likely to change in the near future and that has adversely affected the profits gained in the seventies from appreciating capital values, cheap loans, and high debt-to-equity ratios (see Downs, 1983b: 113–114).

Obviously, high real interest rates also affect the prospects for homeownership. In the future some households who would have bought will rent instead, although how many is uncertain. This will add to the demand for rental housing, inflate rents, and encourage some new output. However, a recent study, while acknowledging that this new demand may well occur, notes that there are serious affordability and financing obstacles to significantly increased production of rental units. Unless these are solved, a high level of unsubsidized starts is unlikely, and new federally subsidized housing, as we have seen, has virtually been ended (Nenno and Sears, 1985: 35). Even if there is much new building, the households who occupy it are unlikely to be among those who face the most severe problems of affordability, the low- and moderate-income households already paying very high proportions of their income in rent. For them, in the absence of adequate housing subsidies or other forms of income support, there is clearly a rental housing crisis.

SOME INTERNATIONAL COMPARISONS

Popular explanations of the declining fortunes of private rental housing often focus on national or even locally determined factors as the prime causes—rent controls are a favorite target. However, cross-national comparisons suggest that the problems of this tenure are widely experienced and that they relate to broad trends in capitalist housing provision, not simply to detailed local variations in this provision.

Thus a recent paper discussing the current state of Canadian housing revealed a private rental sector in much the same difficulties as those faced by its U.S.

counterpart. Hulchanski (1986: 5) writes, "The private rental sector is in extremely bad shape . . . very little supply of new unsubsidised rental housing is being produced, renters are increasingly becoming a low-income residual group, and serious affordability problems persist." He adds that costs have been increasing while the income profile of renters has been decreasing, so private investment in rental housing has become economically unviable. As a result of these trends in incomes and costs, there is now growing social need but a lack of effective market demand.

Very similar conclusions emerged from a study by this author of the long-term development of private rental housing in Britain, the Netherlands, West Germany, Denmark, and France, plus the United States (Harloe, 1985b). An authoritative British report concluded, "Private renting is now in decline at least in proportional, and, in the majority of countries, in absolute terms. Inflation, stagnating incomes and support for other tenures are all playing a part in bringing about the decline" (U.K. House of Commons Environment Committee, 1982: xxxv).

As in the United States, many governments have given enormous assistance to homeownership and have been unwilling to provide the scale of support necessary to sustain continuing commercial investment in decent low-income rental housing. This differential treatment reflects the political strength of homeownership and the weakness of the rental tenure. But the fact that these policies have been so similar in so many countries suggests that there are some underlying common features shaping the choices made by differing sets of national politicians.

The common features of these societies are that their economies and systems of housing provision are capitalist.[5] To understand why this is significant, we must abandon the conventional perspective from which we often view housing provision, as an activity carried out to satisfy social needs, and examine it from a capitalist point of view, as an activity of commodity production carried out for profit. From such a perspective, other things being equal, the provision of this commodity in the form of housing for sale rather than for rental is an attractive prospect. Building for sale reduces the turnover time of the capital employed, does not involve the continuing expenses and risks of housing management, and, in general, is likely to be a more attractive proposition than rental housing, especially for larger-scale capital (for a more detailed discussion of these points, see Harloe, 1981).

But in order for a mass market in homeownership to develop, there needs to be a mass market of consumers able to take on the long-term financial burdens of a mortgage. The precondition for this to occur is the emergence of full employment and rising real incomes, as well as innovations in mortgage finance that make long-term, high loan-to-value ratio loans possible at relatively low and stable interest rates. Such conditions began to emerge in the United States and the United Kingdom before World War II. But since 1945, as other countries have caught up with and even surpassed the prosperity of these two nations, the growth of homeownership has followed, although not always immediately or, as yet, always to the same extent as in the United States and the United Kingdom (the rise of homeownership is not determined purely by economics; political, cultural, and institutional factors also have some effect). In many other countries, as in the United States, governments have played major roles in helping to bring about this state of affairs, but economic expansion has been fundamental, an expansion that has been fueled to a considerable extent by the very development of homeownership that it has also facilitated.

To conclude, any account of the development of housing policies in general, and the differential treatment by politicians of homeownership and rental housing in particular, that ignores the link between the politics of housing and the changing conditions and possibilities for its production, exchange, and consumption as a market commodity is likely to be defective. It follows that while it would be foolish to reject the proposition that purely local and sectoral developments, such as rent controls, do have some effect on the state of private rental provision, it is misleading to suggest that dramatic changes are likely to occur in its situation by housing policies that focus narrowly and exclusively on legislation that only seeks to affect conditions in this tenure. The type of changes necessary to make a significant impact on the current status of private rental housing would require intervention in the circumstances of the tenure that now stands at the heart of commodified housing provision—homeownership. This would fundamentally affect the political and economic interests of far better entrenched and more powerful groups than landlords or tenants.

CONCLUSION: THE PROSPECTS FOR PRIVATE RENTING

This chapter has concentrated on examining some broad trends in the development of private rental housing in the United States and on accounting for its decline. Even to attempt this in the available space has required the omission of much important empirical detail and analysis (for a fuller statement of the central arguments of this chapter, see Harloe, 1985b). In addition, many aspects of the tenure and its problems have had to be omitted altogether.

While there is a considerable literature on many aspects of private renting, there is still a large research agenda, especially regarding sociological and political issues, as many aspects of the tenure's development and dynamics remain obscure. For example, we still know little about the ways in which different groups obtain access to rental housing; the actuality of landlord/tenant relations, as opposed to the formal legal provisions to which they are, in theory, subject (for a pioneering case study, see Nelken, 1983); the less visible ways in which accommodation becomes available for renting (the letting out of rooms by homeowners, the creation of accessory apartments, and so on); and the changing characteristics of the owners of the rental stock, their modes of operation, their economics, and so on.

All these points raise a more general issue for research. There are many studies that examine trends and characteristics in the aggregate, as this chapter does, and numerous studies of rental housing in specific localities, catering to specific population and other groups. But there is no systematic body of work, encompassing the types of research listed above, that would enable us to adequately understand the private rental market for what it really is: a collection of differentially constituted submarkets, differing greatly in their economic, social, and physical characteristics. Yet without such work it is not possible to develop an adequate understanding of how changes in the economy, society, and the political system affect the status of and the prospects for private rental housing (for a recent attempt to do this in the United Kingdom, see Bovaird, Harloe, and Whitehead, 1985a, 1985b). Without this, policy debates are all too apt to degenerate into a series of claims and counterclaims based on selective appeal to whichever set of ''facts'' best suits the protagonists' purposes.

However, we do know enough to predict that the current era of mass unemployment, growing poverty, severe reductions in public expenditures, and high real interest rates will continue to make the prospects for much of the private rental sector, and many low- and moderate-income tenants, a grim one. Downs (1983b) concludes his analysis by suggesting that in the next few years, while there will be a growth in demand for renting by those who, in better times, would have become owner-occupiers, lenders will not supply the capital required for new construction until rents have risen greatly. Given that there must be severe limitations on the extent to which many lower-income households can stretch their budgets to meet sharply increased rents, various adaptations are likely to occur. Downs itemizes some of these, including intensifying pressure to economize on the use of space, resulting in the creation by new building or subdivision of more small units; a decline in the quality of existing units; an increasing proportion of households ''doubling up''; and the use of older units for longer periods before they are renovated or removed from the inventory.

At the end of his book Downs discusses what the policy response should be to the crisis of U.S. rental housing. Here the conflict between the economic realities of the private housing market and the existence of a growing mass of households unable to comply with the terms set by this market for access to affordable and decent housing becomes very clear. He states that if decline is to be stemmed, profitability has to be increased, so rents must go up. If the price of rental housing then becomes too expensive for many to afford, they must be encouraged to consume less of it, so policies should be enacted to aid this reduction in standards to occur. So far the economist's response to the problem of matching supply to effective demand is simple and follows from the logic of the market situation. However, Downs accepts that reducing consumption is unlikely to provide a total solution. Rents will still rise, and this will place intolerable burdens on low-income households; so rents must be subsidized. Downs suggests a nationwide housing allowance system open to all households in the bottom quartile of the income distribution. When he discusses how to finance this, the limitations of the conventional economist's analysis of housing provision are clearly exposed. He proposes that the inefficient and inequitable homeowner subsidies be cut to pay for this housing assistance. He does not evaluate the political feasibility of this suggestion. Yet it is the political economy of U.S. housing that determines when and how change occurs, not simple considerations of an economist's logic or social justice, however clearly they seem to point to what ought to occur.

NOTES

Thanks are due to Chester Hartman, Elizabeth Huttman, and Peter Marcuse for their help with this chapter, including comments on an earlier draft.

1. Atlas and Dreier (1983) have recently argued that the changing prospects for homeownership in the 1980s may well result in an influx of the middle class into rental housing, and this may offer new prospects for effective political action. Even if such action occurs, it remains to be seen whether it will materially improve the prospects for the mass of low- and moderate-income tenants.

2. Marcuse (1985) defines gentrification as the displacement of older, lower-income residents by newer, better-off residents from older and previously deteriorated inner-city housing in a spatially concentrated manner.

3. Such areas exist in states such as California. According to a recent article by Del Vecchio in the *San Francisco Chronicle* (July 8, 1985), the Bay Area is now seeing a boom in rental construction after a decade of depressed production. Among the factors that are listed as responsible for this boom are rising rents (uncontrolled), tax subsidies, and the growing unaffordability of homeownership for better-off households. The article notes that the boom will quickly be killed off if interest rates rise, tax subsidies are cut, or rent controls are imposed. This has all the characteristics of a short-term, speculative development, not a return to higher levels of rental construction that are likely to persist in the longer run.

4. One myth about abandonment is that rent controls are a major reason for its occurrence. In fact, abandonment has occurred in many jurisdictions that do not have controls. Also, there is clear evidence now that where controls do exist, many buildings have been abandoned whose tenants are paying less than the maximum permissable rents— even the rents set by these laws being unaffordable by those in the areas in which these properties are located (for a fuller discussion, see Harloe, 1985: 166–167). There is evidence from other countries too that administratively set rents are sometimes above levels that would be set in a freely operating market.

5. The following argument is not intended to imply that in noncapitalist societies conventional analyses of housing provision and policies are any more satisfactory than they are in capitalist societies. For example, it is often suggested that housing provision is more closely aligned to social needs in socialist societies. However, while allocation may be more related to social need criteria in such societies, it has also been strongly influenced by labor supply considerations. Moreover, the quantity of investment in housing and its sources (individual savings, state funds, and so on) has often been affected by the wish to minimize "unproductive" investment. So the distinctive mode of production plays as central a role in determining housing provision in these societies as it does in capitalist societies.

REFERENCES

Aaron, Henry. 1972. *Shelter and Subsidies*. Washington, D.C.: Brookings Institution.
Ahrentzen, Sherry. 1985. "Residential Fit and Mobility among Low-Income, Female-Headed Family Households in the United States." In Willem van Vliet—, Elizabeth Huttman, and Sylvia Fava (eds.), *Housing Needs and Policy Approaches*. Durham, N.C.: Duke University Press. 71–87.
Atlas, John, and Dreier, Peter. 1983. "Mobilise or Compromise? The Tenants' Movement and American Politics." In Chester Hartman (ed.), *America's Housing Crisis*. Boston and London: Routledge & Kegan Paul. 151–185.
Bovaird, A., M. Harloe, and C. Whitehead, 1985a. "Private Rented Housing: Its Current Role." *Journal of Social Policy* 14, no. 1: 1–23.
———. 1985b. "Prospects and Strategies for Housing in the Private Rented Sector." *Journal of Social Policy* 14, no. 2: 151–74.
DeGiovanni, Frank. 1984. "An Examination of Selected Consequences of Revitalization in Six US Cities." *Urban Studies* 21:245–59.
DeGiovanni, Frank, and N. Paulson. 1984. "Household Diversity in Declining Neighborhoods." *Urban Affairs Quarterly* 20, no. 2: 211–232.
Del Vecchio, Rick. 1985. "Bay Builders Rushing after Rental Market." *San Francisco Chronicle*, July 8, p. 21.
Downs, Anthony. 1983a. "The Coming Crunch in Rental Housing." *Annals of the American Academy of Political and Social Science* 465: 76–85.
———.1983b. *Rental Housing in the 1980s*. Washington, D.C.: Brookings Institution.
Dreier, Peter. 1984. "The Tenants' Movement in the United States." *International Journal of Urban and Regional Research* 8, no. 2: 255–279.
Einhorn, David. 1982. *Federal Tax Incentives and Rental Housing*. Washington, D.C.: Government Printing Office.
Fish, Gertrude (ed.). 1979. *The Story of Housing*. New York: Macmillan.
Harloe, Michael. 1981. "The Recommodification of Housing." In M. Harloe and E. Lebas (eds.), *City, Class, and Capital*. London: Edward Arnold. 17–50.
———. 1985a. "Landlord/Tenant Relations in Europe and America: The Limits and Functions of the Legal Framework." *Urban Law and Policy*.
———. 1985b. *Private Rented Housing in the United States and Europe*. London: Croom Helm.
Hartman, Chester, Rob Kessler, and Richard LeGates. 1980. "Municipal Housing Code Enforcement and Low-Income Tenants." In Jon Pynoos, Robert Schafer, and Chester Hartman (eds.), *Housing Urban America*, 2d ed. New York: Aldine. 560–573.
Harvey, David. 1985. *The Urbanisation of Capital*. Oxford: Basil Blackwell.
Hulchanski, David. 1986. "Canadian Housing in the Mid-1980's: Market Trends and Policy Developments." *Newsletter of the American Sociological Association Environmental Sociology Section*, Spring issue, 5.
Jackson, Anthony. 1976. *A Place Called Home*. Cambridge, Mass.: MIT Press.
Low Income Housing Information Service. 1985. *The 1986 Low Income Housing Budget*. Washington D.C.: LIHIS.
Marans, Robert, and Mary Colten. 1985. "United States Rental Housing Practices Affecting Families with Children: Hard Times for Youth." In Willem van Vliet—,

Elizabeth Huttman, and Sylvia Fava (eds.), *Housing Needs and Policy Approaches*. Durham, N.C: Duke University Press. 41–58.

Marcuse, Peter. 1985. "Gentrification, Abandonment, and Displacement: Connections, Causes, and Policy Responses in New York City." *Journal of Urban and Contemporary Law* 28: 195–240.

Meier, Ron. 1983. "Code Enforcement and Housing Quality Revisited." *Urban Affairs Quarterly* 19, no. 2: 255–73.

Mollenkopf, John, and Jon Pynoos. 1980. "Boardwalk and Park Place: Property Ownership, Political Structure, and Housing Policy at the Local Level." In Jon Pynoos, Robert Schafer, and Chester Hartman (eds.), *Housing Urban American*, 2d ed. New York: Aldine. 57–76.

National Low Income Housing Coalition. 1982. "Meeting Our Low Income Housing Needs." Washington, D.C. Mimeo.

Nelken, D. 1983. *The Limits of the Legal Process*. London: Academic Press.

Nenno, Mary, and Cecil Sears. 1985. *Rental Housing in the 1980s: Prospects for Low-Income Households*. Washington, D.C.: National Association of Housing and Redevelopment Officials.

President's Commission on Housing. 1982. *Report*. Washington D.C.: Government Printing Office.

Price, Waterhouse and Co. 1973. *A Study of the Real Estate Property Tax Incentive Programs on Property Rehabilitation and New Construction*. Washington, D.C.: Government Printing Office.

Stegman, Michael. 1978. "Trouble for Multi-Family Housing: Its Effects on Conserving Older Neighborhoods." *Occasional Papers in Housing and Community Affairs*, vol. 2. Washington, D.C.: HUD. 233–271.

Sternlieb, George, and James Hughes. 1981. *The Future of Rental Housing*. New Brunswick, N.J.: Center for Urban Policy Research, Rutgers University.

Stone, Michael. 1980. "Federal Housing Policy: A Political-Economic Analysis." In Jon Pynoos, Robert Schafer, and Chester Hartman (eds.), *Housing Urban America*, 2d ed. New York: Aldine. 448–458.

Struyk, R., N. Mayer, and J. Tuccillo. 1983. *Federal Housing Policy at President Reagan's Midterm*. Washington, D.C.: Urban Institute Press.

U.K. House of Commons Environment Committee. 1982. *The Private Rented Housing Sector*. London: Her Majesty Stationary Office.

U.S. Bureau of Census. 1961. *Historical Statistics of the United States from Colonial Times to 1957*. Washington, D.C.: Government Printing Office.

———. 1978. *Annual Housing Survey: Part A*. Washington, D.C.: Government Printing Office.

———. 1984. *Annual American Housing Survey: Part A*. Washington, D.C.: Government Printing Office.

U.S. Congressional Budget Office. 1981. *The Tax Treatment of Homeownership: Issues and Options*. Washington, D.C.: Government Printing Office.

U.S. Department of Housing and Urban Development. 1976. *Housing for Low Income Families: HUD's New Section 8 Housing Assistance Payments*. Washington, D.C.: HUD.

———. 1980. *The Conversion of Rental Housing to Condominiums and Cooperatives*. Washington, D.C.: Government Printing Office.

———. 1981. *Rental Housing: Condition and Outlook*. Washington, D.C.: HUD.

U.S. General Accounting Office. 1979. *Rental Housing: A National Problem That Needs Immediate Attention.* Washington, D.C.: Government Printing Office.

Woods, Margaret. 1979a. "Colonial Housing, Towns, and Cities." In Gertrude Fish (ed.), *The Story of Housing.* New York: Macmillan. 6–42.

———. 1979b. "Housing and Cities, 1790 to 1890." In Gertrude Fish (ed.), *The Story of Housing.* New York: Macmillan. 43–122.

8

Home Finance: Buying and Keeping a House in a Changing Financial Environment

LILY M. HOFFMAN AND BARBARA SCHMITTER HEISLER

In advanced industrial societies high rates of homeownership are generally regarded as a desirable goal. This is particularly true in the United States, where homeownership is frequently referred to as the American dream, and the rate of homeownership increased steadily after the depression to reach a high of 65.6 percent in 1980.

By the late 1970s inflation and recession had begun to threaten the continued viability of homeownership. Between 1970 and 1982 the average price of new houses increased 190 percent; that of existing houses, 230 percent (Boleat, 1985b: 63). Mortgage interest rates rose from 7.23 percent in 1970 to 14.37 percent in 1981 (Carron, 1982: 17). At the same time, mortgage delinquencies and foreclosures increased steadily and in 1982 surpassed those of the depression (Mortgage Bankers Association, 1983). Beginning in 1981, the rate of homeownership declined for the first time since World War II; the figure for 1985 was 63.9 percent (U.S. Bureau of the Census, 1970, 1980, 1980–85).

The recent decline and continued stagnation of the homeownership rate have elicited considerable concern, most of which has focused upon the difficulties of buying a home (affordability). The problems of delinquent homeowners who face possible foreclosures and of foreclosure itself as an increasingly common phenomenon have received comparatively little attention.[1] This reflects, in part, the congruence of interests between those seeking to buy homes and powerful lobbies such as housing construction, real estate sales, and financial institutions. It also reflects a pervasive tendency to equate homeownership with buying (and selling).[2]

Because few people purchase a home outright, homeownership depends on a home finance system that enables homebuyers to finance their homes over a relatively long time period. At the heart of this system are the institutions that make money available, mortgage lending institutions, and the instrument that defines the manner of repayment, the mortgage. This means that in reality, homeownership is a process of home purchase that consists of two analytically separable components: (1) buying (and selling) and (2) keeping a home. Policies and programs that aim at supporting the first do not necessarily support the second. The first involves insuring buying affordability, that is, encouraging people to buy by making houses and money available and by providing financial incentives for homeowners. Keeping a home involves policies that permit households to continue to make monthly mortgage payments even though their income and general revenues may suffer temporary setbacks. The continued viability of homeownership is dependent upon both processes, buying and keeping.

This chapter will focus upon keeping a home, since it has received less attention, and since buying (affordability) will be treated elsewhere in this book. We will first identify the components of the home finance system and describe how they have changed over time and under the impact of financial deregulation; then we will examine the implications of these changes for buying and in particular for keeping a home. Last, we will discuss the policy implications of increased threats to homeownership. In the following pages we argue that deregulation and the resulting structural changes in the home finance system are making keeping a home an increasingly significant policy issue.

HOMEOWNERSHIP IN ITS INSTITUTIONAL FRAMEWORK

To understand past and present trends in homeownership, we must locate homeownership in its institutional context—the policies and financial institutions that support homeownership. Although government involvement has been relatively indirect in the United States, compared to other advanced industrial countries, the government has played an important role in encouraging and facilitating homeownership, particularly with regard to home finance (Heidenheimer, Heclo, and Adams, 1983; Boleat, 1985b: 63–65; Kemeny, 1981).[3] In addition to fiscal policies that favor homeownership (for example, income tax deductions of mortgage interest, property tax deductions, and the exclusion of capital gains), government efforts have shaped the home finance system by separating financial institutions according to specialized function, establishing regulatory agencies, underwriting mortgages, and insuring the availability of funds.

As already noted, homeownership depends upon long-term financing. This means that the buyer typically pays a proportion of the purchase price as the down payment and takes out a loan for the remainder—the mortgage. The mortgage pledges property or buildings as security. If the borrower defaults on his obligation, the lender can start foreclosure proceedings and claim title to the property.

Mortgage payments frequently combine the payment of interest and principal; that is, they are amortized, gradually repaying the principal together with the interest. There are two basic mortgage types, the fixed rate mortgage, which became the mainstay of the American system, and the variable rate mortgage, commonly in use in European countries. The latter varies as interest rates rise or fall, while the former remains fixed over its lifetime.

Although it is possible for individuals with surplus assets to lend money directly to homebuyers (a practice that reemerged during the mid-1970s when rising interest rates often made it impossible for sellers to find buyers), in the vast majority of cases the homebuyer obtains the necessary funds from intermediary financial institutions. These institutions, which include banks, savings banks, specialist savings banks, contractual institutions, and mortgage banks, transfer funds from the ultimate lender to the ultimate borrower and generally earn their profits by paying a lower interest rate for acquiring the funds than they charge for lending (Boleat, 1985b).

While fiscal policies directed at homeownership have been relatively stable in the post–World War II period, the home finance system has undergone considerable change in the past decade and is still in transition. In order to examine the implications of these changes for homeownership, we must describe both the "old" and newly emergent home finance systems.

The Historical Development of the Home Finance System

Prior to the 1930s homes were most typically purchased with large down payments (50 percent of the purchase price) and short-term unamortized loans (three to five years) that were frequently renegotiated (Wright, 1983: 240; Jacobs et al., 1982: 170; Agnew, 1982; Stone, 1978: 190–192). Homeownership grew along with the burgeoning savings and loan associations (S&Ls), which had originated as cooperatives to enable their members to purchase homes (Bodfish, 1931; Davis and Payne, 1958; Ritter and Silber, 1983: 116). Historically, mortgage lending was specialized, locally based, and unregulated (Boleat, 1985b: 67).

The federal government's involvement in home finance dates from the Great Depression, when, in the wake of the general economic crisis, financial institutions failed by the thousands and millions of homes were foreclosed.[4] In the 1930s a series of legislative acts—the Glass-Steagall Act (1933), the Securities Exchange Act (1935), and the Federal Home Loan Bank Act (1932)—laid the foundations for a well-defined and regulated home finance system. The first characteristic of this system was the separation of financial institutions according to function. Investment banking was separated from commercial banking, and residential mortgage lending became the primary domain of specialized institutions, the thrifts (S&Ls and mutual savings banks). Although commercial banks were permitted to lend residential mortgage loans, the thrifts were solely restricted to taking in short-term savings and lending long-term residential mortgage loans. Other legislation contributed to the specialized and fragmented nature of the banking and thrift industry. The McFadden Act of 1927 restricted branch offices to individual states as well as limiting branching within states, and beginning in the 1930s, S&Ls could choose whether to be state or federally chartered (Ritter and Silber, 1983: 111; Boleat, 1985b: 68–71).[5]

Second, to prevent a repetition of large-scale financial failure in the future,

Congress set up special federal agencies to oversee the activities of financial institutions. The Federal Home Loan Bank Act of 1932 established the Federal Home Loan Bank Board (FHLBB) to regulate the major mortgage lenders, the thrifts. The FHLBB charters federal S&Ls, sets reserve ratios and maximum deposit interest rates, approves mergers, and extends advances to member associations to ease seasonal, regional, and cyclical deficits (Aaron, 1972: 97–104). The FHLBB also insures the deposits of member associations through the Federal Savings and Loan Insurance Corporation (FSLIC).[6]

Third, the federal government put the mortgage market on a sound footing by insuring mortgages, and thus lenders, against default. The Federal Housing Administration (FHA), created by the National Housing Act of 1934, initiated a mortgage insurance program for low-equity loans that set interest rate ceilings and established uniform lending criteria (Hartman, 1975: 27–33). By insuring low-equity loans the government dramatically extended the potential market for mortgages and therefore the possibility of homeownership. In 1944 the Veterans Administration (VA) broadened federal support for mortgages by establishing a similar program for veterans of the U.S. armed services.[7]

Fourth, the FHA was instrumental in originating and standardizing the long-term self-amortizing fixed rate mortgage, the instrument that became the hallmark of the American home finance system. This instrument marked a sharp break with prior short-term high-equity loans. It also differs from the variable rate mortgages popular in other advanced industrial countries in that interest rates are fixed at the time of origin, thus placing the risk of interest rate volatility upon lenders as opposed to borrowers (Boleat, 1985b: 78).

Fifth, the FHA also created a secondary mortgage market by establishing the Federal National Mortgage Association (Fannie Mae) in 1938. Its original objectives were to draw more funds into the residential housing market, to redistribute them regionally, and to insulate housing markets from monetary and fiscal policy (Aaron, 1972: 94). In contrast to the primary market, "where buyer and seller deal directly with each other," the secondary market "is a market place in which lenders can sell or trade the loans they originate, thus lowering their risk while allowing them to retain fees for continuing to service the loans" (Boleat, 1985b: 77). The secondary market gave rise to new financial institutions—the mortgage companies. Unlike the thrifts, mortgage companies do not take deposits; they only make loans. Initially, mortgage companies specialized in originating FHA/VA loans.

The resulting home finance system had the following characteristics: (1) Mortgage lenders were functionally discrete and heavily regulated institutions. The sole function of the major lenders, the thrift institutions, was to lend out mortgage money at long-term fixed rates and to take in savings. These institutions operated exclusively at a local level. In addition to the thrifts, banks and mortgage companies also originated residential mortgages. Mortgage bankers originated FHA/VA loans; conventional banks issued few residential mortgages. (2) The mortgage instrument was the long-term self-amortizing fixed rate mortgage. (3) A federally sponsored and funded secondary mortgage market enabled low-equity home purchasing and redistributed funds regionally.

With the exception of an expanding and increasingly privatized secondary mortgage market, this system remained relatively static in the post–World War II period. Fannie Mae's success in making mortgage securities attractive to institutional investors such as insurance companies and pension funds led to the creation of two additional government agencies, the Government National Mortgage Association (Ginnie Mae) and the Federal Home Loan Mortgage Corporation (Freddie Mac). Ginnie Mae was established in 1968 as part of the Department of Housing and Urban Development (HUD). Unlike its predecessor, Fannie Mae, which buys FHA/VA mortgages and issues securities on these mortgages, Ginnie Mae buys and packages FHA/VA-insured mortgages and sells them directly to investors, creating a ''pass-through'' by guaranteeing principal and interest to the ultimate investor and servicing fees to the originator (Ritter and Silber, 1983: 117, 550; Downs, 1985: 235). Freddie Mac was established in 1970 as a subsidiary to the Federal Home Loan Bank System to establish a pass-through program for conventional mortgages.

The Emergent New System

Federal deposit insurance, federal mortgage insurance, the creation of a standardized mortgage instrument and lending criteria, and the emergence of a government-sponsored secondary market all contributed to the stability and growth of the thrift industry. This home finance system seemed to work well in the post–World War II period, characterized by high rates of growth, low inflation, and relative economic well-being. The result was an overall secular trend of increasing homeownership.

In the mid-1970s, however, an inflationary spiral threatened the survival of the system by jeopardizing the major mortgage lenders, the thrifts. Until then thrifts had been able to operate profitably in the margin between their long-term fixed rate mortgage loans and the regulated interest rates on their short-term deposits. As interest rates surged and the thrifts were unable to raise their own regulated rates, they lost depositors to money markets bearing higher interest and were left with low-interest long-term mortgages. The net result was that S&Ls and mutual savings banks, whose primary assets were residential mortgage loans (79.8 percent and 59.0 percent respectively in 1980) rapidly lost profitability. By the early 1980s more lenders were facing bankruptcy than at any time since the depression, and the thrift industry as a whole was close to insolvency (Carron, 1982: 12; Boleat, 1985b: 85–89; Downs, 1985: 198).

Financial deregulation, the primary response to the crisis of the thrift industry, has been supported by a general political climate favoring deregulation as well as by the large commercial banks, which had long lobbied for deregulation. The first major legislation toward deregulation, the Depository Institutions Deregulation and Monetary Control Act (DIDMCA) of 1980, gradually removed interest rate ceilings on thrift deposits and gave thrifts functions similar to those of commercial banks. Thrifts could establish checking accounts, issue credit cards, invest in consumer loans, and engage in trust operations (Boleat, 1985b: 87–88).

In 1981 the Federal Home Loan Bank Board permitted S&Ls to offer new mortgage instruments, the adjustable rate mortgages (ARMs). In contrast to the traditional long-term fixed rate mortgage, ARMs allow interest rates to change periodically according to some index of inflation. ARMs thus shift the burden of volatile interest rates from institutions to consumers (Goetze, 1983: 21). The Garn–St. Germain Act of 1982 represented an even further departure from the old system. It permitted thrifts to compete more directly with other financial institutions by offering money market funds and by making commercial loans. Garn–St. Germain also eased existing requirements for conversion from state to federal charter and removed restrictions that limited S&Ls to lending only on first mortgages. In addition, limited-service banks have emerged and have engaged in interstate banking.

The emergent new system differs substantially from the old. (1) The functionally discrete division of labor among financial institutions has been replaced by a highly competitive market in which all financial institutions (banks, savings and loans, mortgage companies, and investment companies) have become potential competitors for the same services and consumers. (2) An additional instrument, the variable rate mortgage, has been added to the fixed rate mortgage and has rapidly increased its market share. ARMs peaked in 1984, accounting for 68 percent of residential mortgages. This figure has since declined to fluctuate between 45 and 50 percent during 1985–86 (Federal Home Loan Bank Board, 1986). (3) The secondary mortgage market has both expanded rapidly and changed character. Not only has the proportion of mortgages going into the secondary market increased; mortgage securities and trading have become a growth industry on Wall Street. Ginnie Mae marked the start of the mortgage trading industry, which has rapidly expanded and privatized as private firms have begun to issue pass-throughs backed by conventional (non-FHA/VA) mortgages. Trading in residential mortgages has quadrupled since 1980 to compete for investors with the stock market. As mortgage securities and trading have grown, federally sponsored activity in residential housing markets has declined. The net effect of the expansion and privatization of the secondary market has been that an ever-increasing number of mortgages change holders frequently and are neither federally guaranteed nor totally insured (Grebler, 1986).

BUYING AND KEEPING IN A NEW FINANCIAL ENVIRONMENT

How has the dramatic change in the home finance system affected buying and keeping a home? While the emergent system has been credited with helping the thrifts survive and has introduced new funds into the residential mortgage market,

Table 8.1
Foreclosure and Delinquency Rates, 1954–85

Year	% Loans in Foreclosure (all loans)	% Loans 90 + days loans
1954	(1)	.19
1955		.16
1956		.18
1957		.18
1958		.23
1959		.24
1960		.30
1961		.42
1962	.32	.28
1963	.34	.34
1964	.40	.31
1965	.38	.33
1966	.37	.32
1967	.34	.28
1968	.28	.23
1969	.26	.25
1970	.32	.32
1971	.41	.42
1972	.50	.40
1973	.n.a. (2)	.45
1974	.48	.44
1975	.44	.49
1976	.37	.54
1977	.39	.53
1978	.34	.51
1979	.29	.49
1980	.34	.58
1981	.43	.64
1982	.59	.77
1983	.68	.84
1984	.68	.88
1985	.77	.93

Note: Rates are an annual average of the percentage of loans for four quarters.
(1) Data were not collected prior to 1962.
(2) During 1973, the data were reported in the category of "foreclosures started during quarter" only.
Source: Mortgage Bankers Association of America, 1986.

the new system does not appear to have reduced delinquencies and foreclosures, which have continued to rise.

Delinquencies and foreclosures have always been a part of mortgage lending activities. In the post–World War II period the general pattern has been for delinquencies and foreclosures to fluctuate in response to general economic conditions. Table 8.1 reveals some significant changes in the patterns of both delinquency and foreclosure rates within the past three decades. During the 1960s both rates fluctuated within a relatively narrow range. Between 1969 and 1979 they fluctuated more widely and generally rose. Beginning in the 1980s, both rates have climbed steeply and have not dropped even as economic conditions have improved.

While the recent sharp rise in delinquency and foreclosure rates can be traced to numerous social and economic factors not directly associated with changes in the home finance system—among them inflation accompanied by high real estate prices, family dissolution, and unemployment—the changes in the home finance system outlined here have not helped to alleviate these trends. On the contrary, they have contributed to exacerbating existing social and economic trends.

On the whole, the new home finance system favors buying over keeping. The deregulated and more competitive mortgage market permits potential homebuyers to "shop around" among a wider choice of lenders, rates, and instruments. In addition, the revolution in communications technology has created and made available computerized systems that serve as electronic bulletin boards to locate, display, and simulate differing terms and conditions. Competitive pressures also encourage lenders to "sell" rather than award mortgages. First, deregulation has removed the ceilings on origination fees charged by lenders and made them subject to market competition. This means that profits made at the point of loan origination have become more important. Thrifts are also increasing their revenues from fees for servicing mortgages, as opposed to interest rate spreads that have proved so volatile (Downs, 1985). At the same time, the increased risk associated with selling is diffused as lenders can sell mortgages into the secondary market while keeping the fees associated with origination, as well as servicing the loan.

Several aspects of the new system exacerbate the problems of homeowners who confront mortgage repayment difficulties. First, mortgage lenders are no longer mostly small and locally operated institutions. There were 5,669 S&Ls in 1970; 4,613 in 1980; and 3,513 in 1983. At the end of 1983 the five largest S&Ls earned 10.65 percent of total industry assets, compared with 8.04 percent in 1982 (Boleat, 1985b: 69, 71). Although still the predominant lenders, S&Ls have lost market share and become more diversified as well as less local, fewer in number, and more concentrated. Mortgage bankers have registered the largest gain in the residential market share. Before deregulation, they only originated FHA/VA loans. In the brief period since the beginning of deregulation they have captured an increasing share of conventional mortgages, so that by 1982 they originated 29 percent of residential loans (Boleat, 1985b: 80). As of June 1985 commercial banks had 23 percent of residential mortgages; S&Ls, 45 percent; mortgage bankers, 24 percent; and mutual savings banks, 6 percent (Federal Home Loan Bank Board, 1985). In addition to the change in the relative market share of mortgage lenders, increased competition, continued failures, forced mergers, the new ability to branch (interstate and within state), and trends toward vertical and horizontal integration have meant that an ever-growing number of mortgage lenders are larger corporate structures that are functionally diverse and heterogeneous and operate in a wider geographic range. Thus decisionmaking is likely to be more centralized.

Second, the growth of the secondary market means that most mortgages leave home and become nonlocal. The proportion of mortgages going into the secondary market increased significantly from 36.7 percent of all original mortgages for family housing of one to four units in 1970 to 50 percent in 1980–81 and to 75 percent in 1982 (Downs, 1985: 237). This means that they are frequently neither held nor serviced by the institutions that originate them. Both characteristics (size and corporate character of lenders along with the growth of secondary market activity) have increased the distance between buyers and lenders, both geographically and organizationally.

The fact that an increasing number of mortgages are obtained from and ultimately held by nonlocal institutions (both S&Ls and mortgage bankers) means that lenders have less of a financial investment in these loans. It also means that homeowners often do not know who is holding their mortgage (Horwitz, 1986; Bogdanich, 1986). Even in cases where they do, communications are likely to be impersonal and electronic. Because decisionmaking has become more centralized and less responsive to local or regional economic conditions, and because the risk associated with individual loans has been diffused by secondary market activities, delinquent homeowners have more difficulty negotiating forbearance agreements (Heisler and Hoffman, 1987).

Size, corporate character, and nonlocality also affect the relation between buyer and lender. This relation is changed when lenders are encouraged to be salesmen of potentially risky loans rather than careful assessors of risk. Attracted by fee income and by the ability to sell loans off quickly for profit on the secondary market, many lenders have tended to inflate their assessment of property value and downplay the borrower's income, thereby increasing the possibility of future default. This is particularly true in the case of second and third mortgages, which are based on the accumulated equity in the home ("home-equity" loans) and which have grown rapidly in the wake of deregulation. These loans, which bear higher interest rates and have been promoted by aggressive lenders stressing equity rather than the ability to pay, have become a major contributor to the growth of foreclosures (Bogdanich, 1986).

The privatization of mortgage insurance can have a similar negative effect upon the ability to keep. Unlike the FHA program, which required an economically sound loan as a condition for insurance elegibility, private insurance companies do not examine each loan but issue insurance contracts for specified groups of loans and for a limited time period—not the life of the loan but the first few years (Grebler, 1986).[8] For the homebuyer, purchase without a reasonable chance of being able to keep the home represents a loss of fees and, in some cases, of equity and credit ratings. Investor confidence in the secondary mortgage market is also hurt by relaxed underwriting standards (Thompson, 1985).

Third, the new variable rate instruments (ARMs) may have introduced additional liabilities that independently affect the continued payment of mortgage loans by transferring the risk of volatile interest rates from lending institutions to buyers. Unlike fixed rate mortgages of the past, ARMs have varied in terms of interest rates, ceilings, repayment schedules, and the period of the loan. This makes it more difficult for borrowers to foresee their future financial responsibilities. Introduced at a time when mortgage interest rates were high and expected to rise, ARMs have also been associated with low equity or inflated property assessments and credit evaluations. Although systematic data do not exist (U.S. League of Savings Institutions, 1985), some analysts have expressed concern that variable rates will be associated with increased foreclosures. In periods of rapid inflation and rising interest rates, for example, ARMs may lead to negative amortization—the situation in which higher interest is added to the outstanding loan and the borrower pays interest without reducing the principal. Rather than increasing borrowers' investment in their property, negative amortization decreases this investment and encourages them to walk away.

In the recent past the home finance system made mortgage lending a two-track system: conventional mortgages were offered by local and specialized lenders to homebuyers with some capital for a down payment, and government-backed loans (FHA/VA), drawn from a national market, were sold by local agents (mostly mortgage bankers and some S&Ls) to purchasers with little capital. For those who could afford to shop for conventional mortgages, locally based and restricted lenders tended to more carefully appraise both properties and potential borrowers (Perin, 1977). Those who could not qualify for the generally more stringent requirements for credit evaluation (in the 1960s the figure was 20 percent, but was reduced to 5 percent in 1974) or afford the down payment and rates set by local lenders could turn to FHA/VA loans.

Although two-track in that the old home finance system separated homebuyers by income and assets, the relation between lender and borrower extended beyond the purely economic in both situations. In the conventional nongovernment-insured mortgage market the relation between borrower and lender was generally more direct. Home mortgages were a major source of profit for local lenders. Profits were based upon a combination of mortgage origination, servicing, and the gradual repayment of interest over time. Market rationality dictated some responsiveness to changing local and individual needs, and the interests of mortgage borrowers and lenders tended to coincide. In the government-sponsored market federal agencies provided built-in mechanisms to help homeowners in difficulty. HUD, for example, has a mortgage assistance program under which it can take over the mortgages of defaulting homeowners and give them more time or better terms. Federal agencies are also generally accountable to political mandates and constituencies.

In contrast, the emergent new system has introduced additional financial intermediaries and transactions. Profits are made by several actors and at different stages in the process of home purchase. By losing their once-sheltered position in the credit market, home mortgages have become more and more of a commodity. This has made for a greater separation between mortgage originators and homeowners, not only in terms of the number of intermediaries and the geographical distance, but in terms of interests. Because they can sell their home mortgages on the secondary market, lenders do not have the same incentive to avoid delinquencies and foreclosures. The net effect of the new home finance system has been to dissociate the two components of homeownership—buying and keeping.

POLICY IMPLICATIONS AND SOLUTIONS

In the face of decreasing housing affordability and continuing high rates of foreclosures, homeownership remains the preferred form of housing tenure in the United States (Tremblay and Dillman, 1983; Wall, 1985; Downs, 1985: 130). Furthermore, as the embodiment of the American dream, homeownership is imbued with considerable social and political significance. Political leaders and social analysts have voiced concern over the possibility of diminishing access to homeownership because homeownership is generally believed to neutralize inequalities related to occupation and income and to establish an increased stake in the local community (Janowitz, 1976; Perin, 1977; Sternlieb and Hughes, 1982).

Deregulation and the emergence of a new home finance system have indirectly helped homeownership, or, as we have argued, buying. Although monetary policies aimed at reducing inflation and decreasing interest rates account for much of the recent increase in homebuying, the new home finance system has also been a factor. By helping to bail out the thrift industry, it has contributed, indirectly, to making funds available for home purchase. But deregulation has not helped the second component of homeownership—keeping (Mariano, 1986).

The differential impact of deregulation upon buying and keeping raises the possibility that delinquencies and foreclosures will become a more significant policy issue in the future. If homeownership remains an important societal goal, and if the continued viability of homeownership depends upon both the ability to buy and the ability to keep, then the failure to address this differential impact will increasingly endanger the reality of that goal.

Given both preference and problem, what solutions exist to deal with the threats posed by high and continuing rates of delinquencies and foreclosures? The surge of delinquencies and foreclosures in the past five years has produced a number of responses ranging from formal legislation to informal agreements and arrangements between the various actors involved. While the first responses have come from homeowners, institutions have increasingly initiated their own actions. The former, homeowners, have tried to negotiate individual or collective forbearance agreements, or in some cases moratoria, or have supported the introduction and passage of bills in state and federal legislatures. The latter, lenders and insurance companies, including the FSLIC, have more recently sought ways to identify, contact, and negotiate with delinquent homeowners. To evaluate and explore possible solutions, we will first briefly examine existing efforts, and then turn to a comparative example, Great Britain, to see how another Western industrialized country has dealt with the issue of keeping homes.

Threatened Homeowners

The first response to threats to keeping homes has come from homeowners and organized groups acting on their behalf. Their principal activities have been directed at local targets such as financial institutions, the courts, and the state legislatures. Their primary strategies have been to negotiate forbearance agreements on an individual basis with lenders, to put pressure on local courts and sheriffs to stay foreclosures, and to urge the legislature to pass bills aimed at helping threatened homeowners. These efforts have met with limited success. In some cases judges have stayed foreclosures or established criteria to screen properties set for foreclosure. Attempts to seek legislative solutions at the state level have included selective moratoria that give power to local judges to stay foreclosures in cases where the foreclosure is due to "no fault of one's own" (for example, plant closings); the provision of temporary financial assistance at low interest rates; and the provision of statewide mortgage insurance schemes. Selective moratoria have been passed in Minnesota and Connecticut as well as in several cities, including Philadelphia. Programs for financial assistance at low interest rates have been legislated in Pennsylvania, Maryland, and the District of Columbia.

Institutional Action

Although the national debate over deregulation has centered upon the continuing difficulties of the thrifts, these difficulties have spread so as to affect the ultimate losers—the insurers of mortgages, both federal and private companies. Lending institutions and mortgage insurance institutions have begun to systematically contact delinquent homeowners to offer financial counseling as well as plans that involve partial repayment and the restructuring of debt. Proposals by the FHLBB to rescue the thrifts (bank forebearance) include new accounting procedures, lower capital reserves, and changes in reporting and disclosure regulations that will allow thrifts to restructure problem loans. This has the potential to help delinquent homeowners by encouraging thrifts to contact and devise repayment policies for delinquents along the lines outlined by the mortgage insurance companies (Nash, 1986; Langley and McCoy, 1986).

Although these efforts may have had some impact, they have been aimed at symptoms, not causes. Furthermore, they tend to offer short-term relief and apply to only a small proportion of home mortgage foreclosures. For example, the Pennsylvania program, currently under debate in Ohio, has received some 13,798 applications since its inception in March 1984 and has approved 4,410 of these, with average payments of $12,540 per case (Ohio Legislature Budget Committee, 1986).[9] This includes arrears and monthly mortgage charges. While the program has clearly helped some families to keep their homes, those helped constitute only one-fourth of those facing home foreclosure. Furthermore, the long-term effects of the program can not be assessed at this early point, since "saving the home" ultimately depends upon increased family income, and the time limit for relief is 36 months.

Other measures such as reregulation and more stringent lending criteria might reduce rates of delinquencies and foreclosures. However, they would also affect buying. Another alternative would be the expansion of government mortgage guarantees to cover all mortgages. This would necessitate complex reorganization of the secondary mortgage market and would probably meet with opposition from several sectors, in particular, private mortgage insurance companies.

Some critics of the American system have argued for the socialization of the home finance system, the conversion of homes to public ownership (Stone, 1983; Hartman, 1983). While such a proposal would address both buying and keeping, it seems highly unlikely to be adopted, given the political climate in the United States. Short of socialization, further insight into possible solutions may be gained by a comparative perspective. Great Britain offers an interesting comparison for several reasons. Like the United States, Great Britain has made homeownership an important societal goal. The rate of homeownership in Great Britain has increased significantly in recent years to a level approaching that of the United States. In 1982, 59 percent of houses in Britain were owner-occupied (Boleat, 1985a). As in the United States, delinquencies (arrears) and foreclosures (possessions) have risen in the past decade along with deteriorating economic conditions. However, increases have been less pronounced. The delinquency rate remains significantly lower, and the foreclosure rate has been only half of that in the United States (Boleat, 1985a).

While the British and American home finance systems share some characteristics, they also differ in important respects. The differences, together with the characteristics of the British welfare system, account for a substantial part of the observed differences in delinquencies and foreclosures in the two countries. As is the case in the United States, the British home finance system has been traditionally dominated by specialized lending institutions—the building societies—that draw funds from short-term savings and lend mortgage money. Like their U.S. counterparts, the S&Ls, the building societies are highly regulated and have the largest market share of residential mortgages (local authorities and commercial banks are additional mortgage lenders). The British home finance system differs in that the mortgage instrument has always been the variable rate mortgage, and a secondary mortgage market has been virtually absent.

Unlike the American home finance system, the British system has only recently begun to change. Although some of the difficulties associated with keeping a home have been quite similar (divorce, unemployment, and rising house prices), the British home finance system still disposes lenders to be more flexible and forbearing. First, the variable mortgage interest rate has permitted building societies to adapt to changing financial markets. Therefore, they have not shared in the general crisis mentality of the American thrifts. Second, the virtual absence of a secondary mortgage market has meant that the building societies have had to take a greater interest in negotiating with delinquent homeowners.

The most important factor in protecting homeowners, however, is the nature of the British welfare system. Among the 40 different benefits available in Britain, the supplementary benefits (SB)—paid to anyone over age 16 who does not have full-time work or enough money—cover housing costs as part of the living allowance. In cases where the recipient owns a home, SB pays the interest, disregarding the value of the house itself. This applies even on second mortgages, provided that they were taken out for home repairs. The only restriction is that one cannot have more than 3,000 pounds in savings. In the words of Mark Boleat, supplementary benefits have been important "for borrowers, for Building Societies and owner-occupied housing" (Boleat, 1985a:37). In contrast to the British system, the welfare system in the United States penalizes homeowners. Although the limits on a welfare applicant's equity vary from state to state, they remain consistently low, making it difficult if not impossible for an unemployed homeowner to receive welfare benefits. Furthermore, the level of welfare payments would not permit recipients to pay off their interest, let alone to stay in their homes.

SUMMARY

Since few people have enough capital to buy a home outright, homeownership depends on long-term financing. This means that homeownership is in reality a process by which people purchase a home over time. It has two analytically distinct components: buying (and selling) and keeping a home. Although most analysts and most social and political concern have focused on issues relating to buying (affordability), we argue that homeownership depends on both the ability to buy and the ability to keep.

Deregulation has brought significant changes to the home finance system first put in place in the 1930s. Key among these have been the growth and privatization of the secondary mortgage market and the growth of lenders. While these changes have helped to bail out the ailing thrift industry and have indirectly helped buying, they have not helped the second component of homeownership, keeping. Rather, the greater distance between buyers and lenders has exacerbated the problems of delinquent homeowners and has made delinquency and foreclosure increasingly important issues. As already noted, the continued viability of homeownership is a function of both buying and keeping. If keeping a home is not addressed by the emergent home finance system, then it remains to be addressed politically. At the present time, however, programs and policies aimed at helping delinquent homeowners have remained regional and have not gained widespread political support.

NOTES

This article is part of ongoing work by the two authors. The sequence of their names has been determined by a throw of the dice.

1. Except for farming, which is a different case. Farming has a long history of government subsidies, and farms are both a business and a home.

2. Although many analysts, among them Downs, Perin, and Kemeny, point out the reality of long-term payments for "homeownership," they tend to conflate buying and keeping in their discussions.

3. In the United States the government has been a more direct actor in the home finance sector than in the provision of housing stock (public housing), particularly with regard to the development of the secondary market (Boleat, 1985b: 15, 62). We might note that although the home finance system has helped to extend homeownership to include a broad spectrum of the working class as well as the middle class, it has not been class neutral. The excluded include blacks, women heads of households, and the poor in general.

4. Between 1931 and 1933 half of all residential mortgages were in default, and there were 1,000 foreclosures each day (Jacobs et al., 1982: 4).

5. Historically, the United States has had a dual banking system with commercial banks and thrifts chartered and supervised by federal and state governments side by side. State institutions are chartered under state statutes and supervised by agencies of the state government. State-chartered institutions are more numerous, while federally chartered banks are larger (Ritter and Silber, 1983: 101).

6. The FSLIC was established by the National Housing Act of 1934. Not all savings and loans are FSLIC insured. Four states permitted S&Ls to contract with private insurance companies. Privately insured S&Ls in Maryland and Ohio were instrumental in the recent S&L crisis in these two states. In the wake of the crisis, financially sound S&Ls have joined the FSLIC.

7. FHA insurance and VA insurance differ. The government underwrites all risk for FHA loans, whereas VA loans are only partially guaranteed. The lender remains liable for that part of any loss that exceeds the guaranteed amount (Jacobs et al., 1982: 156).

8. Private insurance companies generally insure the portion of the loan usually at risk. This is the amount that exceeds the stipulated loan-to-value ratio. Since repayments usually eliminate this portion in the first few years, the insurance contract is relatively short. The underlying rationale is that since defaults are concentrated in the initial years of a long-term mortgage, it makes sense to limit the insurance protection offered to lenders to the critical period.

9. The Ohio and Pennsylvania bills differ in that the current Ohio proposal includes farms.

REFERENCES

Aaron, Henry J. 1972. *Shelter and Subsidies: Who Benefits from Federal Housing Policies?* Washington, D.C.: Brookings Institution.

Agnew, John. 1982. "Home Ownership and Identity in Capitalist Societies." In James S. Duncan (ed.), *Housing and Identity*. New York: Holmes & Meier. 60–97.

Bodfish, H. M. 1931. *History of Building and Loans in the United States*. Chicago: University of Chicago Press.

Bogdanich, Walt. 1986. "Home-Equity Loans Grow in Popularity—and in Their Problems." *Wall Street Journal*, January 29.

Boleat, Mark. 1985a. *Mortgage Repayment Difficulties*. London: Building Societies Association.

————. 1985b. *National Housing Finance Systems: A Comparative Study*. London: Croom Helm.

Carron, Andrew S. 1982. *The Plight of the Thrift Institutions*. Washington, D.C.: Brookings Institution.

Davis, L. E., and P. L. Payne. 1958. "From Benevolence to Business: The Story of Two Savings Banks." *Business History Review*. 30: 386–391.

Downs, Anthony. 1985. *The Revolution in Real Estate Finance*. Washington, D.C.: Brookings Institution.

Federal Home Loan Bank Board. 1985–86. *Federal Home Loan Bank Board News*.

Goetze, Rolf. 1983. *Rescuing the American Dream*. New York: Holmes & Meier.

Grebler, Leo. 1986. "Deal the FHA out of the Housing Market." *Wall Street Journal*, March 20.

Hartman, Chester W. 1975. *Housing and Social Policy*. Englewood Cliffs, N.J.: Prentice-Hall.

———— (ed.). 1983. *America's Housing Crisis: What Is to Be Done?* Boston: Routledge & Kegan Paul.

Heidenheimer, Arnold, Hugh Heclo, and Carolyn Teich Adams. 1983. *Comparative Public Policy*. 2d ed. New York: St. Martin's Press.

Heisler, Barbara S., and Lily M. Hoffman. 1987. "Keeping a Home: Changing Mortgage Markets and Regional Economic Distress." *Sociological Focus* 20, no. 3: 227–241.

Horwitz, Sari. 1986. "Will the Real Owner of This House Please Stand Up?" *Washington Post*, January 27.

Jacobs, Barry G., Kenneth R. Harney, Charles L. Edson, and Bruce S. Lane. 1982. *Guide to Federal Housing Programs*. Washington, D.C.: Bureau of National Affairs.

Janowitz, Morris. 1976. *Social Control of the Welfare State*. New York: Elsevier.

Kemeny, Jim. 1981. *The Myth of Home-Ownership*. London: Routledge & Kegan Paul.

Langley, Monica, and Charles F. McCoy. 1986. "Regulators to Ease Accounting Rules for Certain Loans." *Wall Street Journal*, March 12.

Mariano, Ann. 1986. "Foreclosures in the U.S. Near Record Rate: Little Sign of Slowdown as Sales Boom." *Washington Post*, March 15.

Mortgage Bankers Association of America. 1983. "Seasonally Adjusted Delinquency and Foreclosure Ratios: U.S. Totals and Census Regions." *National Delinquency Survey*.

————. 1986. *National Delinquency Survey*. Quarterly data series.

Nash, Nathaniel C. 1986. "Regulation of Banking on the Rise." *New York Times*, February 18.

Ohio Legislature Budget Committee. 1986. "Cost Estimate for HB 556, A Proposed Home Foreclosure Prevention Program." Draft report.

Perin, Constance. 1977. *Everything in Its Place: Social Order and Land Use in America*. Princeton: Princeton University Press.

Ritter, Lawrence S., and William L. Silber. 1983. *Principles of Money, Banking, and Financial Markets*. 4th rev. ed. New York: Basic Books.

Sternlieb, George, and James W. Hughes. 1982. "The Evolution of Housing and the Social Compact." *Urban Land* 41: 17–22.

Stone, Michael. 1978. "Housing, Mortgage Lending, and the Contradictions of Capitalism." In William K. Tabb and Larry Sawers (eds.), *Marxism and the Metropolis*. New York: Oxford University Press. 179–208.

———. 1983. "Housing and the Economic Crisis: An Analysis and Emergency Program." In Chester Hartman (ed.), *America's Housing Crisis: What Is to Be Done?* Boston: Routledge & Kegan Paul. 99–150.

Thompson, Terri. 1985. "The Secondary Mortgage Market's Crisis of Confidence." *Business Week*, September 16, 112–113.

Tremblay, Kenneth R., Jr., and Don A. Dillman. 1983. *Beyond the American Housing Dream*. Lanham, Md.: University Press of America.

U.S. Bureau of the Census. 1960, 1970, 1980. *Census of Population and Housing: 1960, 1970, 1980*.

———. 1980–85. *Current Housing Reports*. Series H-111. *Housing Vacancy Survey*.

U.S. League of Savings Institutions. 1985. *News*, November 15.

Wall, Matthew. 1985. "Owning a Home: A Dream Persists." *New York Times*, February 28.

Wright, Gwendolyn. 1983. *Building the Dream: A Social History of Housing in America*. Cambridge, Mass.: MIT Press.

9

Cooperative and Condominium Conversions

BRIAN J. O'CONNELL

Conversions of multifamily properties from legal ownership by landlords to multiple ownership were virtually unknown until the mid-1970s. By the late 1970s conversion was a critical factor in many urban real estate markets. While the conversion trend has slowed in the 1980s, areas with significant amounts of rental housing will still be subject to large-scale conversion when certain demographic and economic factors converge.

A landmark study of the conversion trend was published in 1980 by the U.S. Department of Housing and Urban Development (hereafter, HUD, 1980). It is used by people on all sides of the controversy as a reference and source of information, although its conclusions are debated. The report is cited here not only as a basic source of definitions and pre-1980 information for this chapter, but as an important part of the history of conversion because it critically framed the options for the monitoring, taxing, and regulating policies of government.

A condominium is a housing unit in a multifamily building or complex owned by an individual, who also owns a partial interest in the common areas of the building or complex. A cooperative is a nonprofit housing corporation in which individual households own shares entitling them to live in a particular unit in a multifamily building or complex and to use the common areas and facilities of the building or complex (HUD, 1980). The key practical distinctions between condominium and cooperative forms of ownership are the lower initial costs for the cooperative purchases and the greater amount of control given to the "board of directors" and the manager of cooperatives. The board of the cooperative usually has strict controls over the choice of new buyers, subletting, alterations, and resale. Sometimes conflict arises between the board and the other shareholders. The bylaws of a condominium may give the "board of managers" some minimal control over resale of units, usually limited to a right of first refusal or of matching the bid of purchasers. The vast majority of conversions have been to condominium ownership, with the exception of New York area conversions.

Many converted units remain rental because the units are bought only for investment or tax-shelter purposes. About 17 percent of the units in converted buildings remained rentals with new investor owners (HUD, 1980), while another 20 percent remained unsold and under the control of the converter. Because of these investor owners, and because many new condominiums, particularly in Sunbelt vacation areas, are rented, the total impact of condominium and cooperative building and conversion activity on rental housing supply has to be measured carefully (Eilbott, 1985).

Another kind of "conversion" is partially and sometimes confusingly related to condominium and cooperative conversion. It is the conversion of industrial or commercial space to residential space, often known as "loft conversion." The big upsurge in these loft conversions occurred in the late 1970s at the same time as the upsurge in condominium and cooperative conversion (Zukin, 1982; Hudson, 1984). The net result in the SoHo area of Manhattan is that 50 percent of the units are owned and 50 percent are rented. Some lofts are first rented to an "artist" type and later turned into cooperatives or condominiums.

An important variation of cooperative ownership is occurring more in the 1980s. It is the "limited-equity" or "low-equity" cooperative, the bylaws of which regulate the resale value of membership shares, guaranteeing that any public subsidies the cooperative may have used and the savings it has generated are passed on to new members (Hartman, Keating, and LeGates, 1981). Shareholders cannot keep capital appreciation when they sell. These are usually government-subsidized conversions in deteriorated or tax-foreclosed buildings. Depending on local laws, there are court-appointed administrators of quasi-cooperative or alternative management programs that slowly turn control to the tenants. Some state housing trust funds are now assisting nonprofit sponsors of such conversions to rehabilitate and create cooperatives or condominiums for moderate-income earners.

HISTORICAL DEVELOPMENT

The first known conversion of a multiple-family building to multiple ownership took place in the borough of Queens in New York City in 1966. In 1976, 20,000 units were converted in the United States, and this escalated to 135,000 units in 1979. About 60 percent of the converted units were in the 12 largest standard metropolitan statistical areas (SMSAs). Contrary to the impressions of many people, 51 percent of conversions have been in the suburban jurisdictions of SMSAs (HUD, 1980).

The 1980 HUD report projected that the most likely scenario for the 1980–85 period would be an increase in the number of conversions each year, but with yearly increases at successively smaller rates. This would mean 1,139,732 converted units in five years. This was a linear trend adjusted for possible limits on the potential supply of rental units appropriate for conversion, household types and income restrictions, and some economic factors.

In the first four years of the decade, however, only 200,000 to 250,000 conversions have been reported (*National Real Estate Investor*, 1985b). Only eight metropolitan areas had significant conversions in 1984, led by New York with 45,000, Boston with 15,000, and six other cities with 1,000 to 4,200 each. Various reasons for the downturn were offered in a multicity survey by the *National Real Estate Investor* (1985a). There is an enormous oversupply in the Sunbelt metropolitan areas that provided 60 percent of the conversions in 1979. Buyers were paying more attention to the economies of the purchase and cash flow than to tax shelters. There was increased building and purchasing of rental properties, due in part to the very short depreciation schedule and the tax credits for rental housing rehabilitation in the 1981 tax revision. The buildings that were prime candidates for conversion were largely depleted. The young urban professionals and empty nesters who could have been cooperative or condominium buyers were content with rentals or scared off by the high interest rates and inflated housing costs. A National Association of Homebuilders study shows that many of the people with the resources to buy their own housing are trading up and are usually looking for more space (Meagher, 1985). It is unlikely that they would find this space in condominiums or cooperatives.

New York City stands as the major exception to the trend. Filings for conversions with the state attorney general numbered fewer than 15,000 units annually in the 1970s. In 1985 there were applications for 46,292 units (Gutis, 1986). Boston is also an exception to the trend. In both instances it is partially a catch-up phenomenon. In the 1970s many cities converted more than 5 percent of the rental units. The Boston metropolitan area converted only 2.37 percent of its rental units, and New York only 0.72 percent. Both have very large stocks of rental housing in all income categories. Thus as conversions go beyond the luxury rental category, New York and Boston have many candidates for conversion.

CURRENT STATUS OF NEIGHBORHOOD, BUILDING TYPE, AND BUYERS

Neighborhood Types and Conversion

Condominium and cooperative conversion takes different forms in revitalizing and nonrevitalizing neighborhoods. Revitalizing neighborhoods are those that have experienced disinvestment in the past but are currently experiencing significant new public or private reinvestment. The nonrevitalizing neighborhoods have experienced steady private investment. The 1980 HUD report found conversion in nonrevitalizing neighborhoods in both central cities and suburbs. These neighborhoods tend to have median incomes and housing values that are higher than average. Turnover rates did not jump with conversion. The only difference between the central city and suburban neighborhoods in this category was the higher percentage of townhouses and garden apartments in the suburbs.

Conversion activity took place in revitalizing neighborhoods in one-third of the 37 SMSAs in the 1980 HUD study. The revitalization pattern started with renovation of single-family homes, then rehabilitation and perhaps conversion of small multiunit buildings. The revitalizing neighborhoods where conversion was taking place were predominantly white, with many professionals among them. Vacancy rates remained low during the conversion, and only slight changes were noticed in the postconversion residents, with somewhat fewer blacks and a smaller percentage of elderly people.

Various models of the stages of neighborhood transition seem unable to predict revitalization or the progress of it. Speculation and price fluctuations are not in predictable patterns (DeGiovanni, 1983). The link between revitalization and conversion will be discussed later, but like revitalization, conversion is difficult to link to patterns of neighborhood change.

Loft conversion has been explained by an extension of the Burgess invasion-succession model. Hudson (1984) and Zukin (1982) both show the indigenous business operations failing to renew themselves with replacements for companies that left the SoHo area of New York in the 1960s. Hudson focuses on the competitive forces operating to reach a new equilibrium. Zukin emphasizes the political power of the developers who shaped zoning and tax abatements to make the loft conversions profitable. Cooperative and condominium conversion fits in the third stage of loft conversion (Zukin, 1982). Zukin found initial settlers similar to the "pioneers" in other revitalizing neighborhoods who do not have much money and who do not stay long (DeGiovanni and Paulson, 1984). In the loft conversions these are often artists. They are replaced by a more affluent gentry, who can afford to purchase some equity in the rapidly appreciating property. Cooperative and condominium arrangements are more common at this stage.

Building Types and Conversion

High-rise buildings constructed in the last 20 years with rents over 50 percent of the area median are the prime targets for conversions (HUD, 1980). More than 75 percent of the conversions are accompanied at most by cosmetic rehabilitation. The few major rehabilitations accompanying conversions occur in revitalizing neighborhoods.

In New York 40 percent of the buildings involved are pre-1947 buildings (Stegman, 1985). There are also increasing instances of rental landlords choosing cooperative conversion at the point where major repairs are necessary (Hinds, 1985). Some landlords blame rent control restrictions on increases for improvements. Many traditional landlords bow out at this point, and converters are the only buyers in many instances. Later in this chapter it will be shown that the end of the period of large tax shelters from accelerated depreciation and the expiration of 10-year balloon mortgages with all the principal due often converge at points where major rehabilitation is needed. These are further pressures for the landlord to sell off. Whether New York is a forerunner of what will happen to older rental stock in other cities remains to be seen.

Buyers and Nonbuyers

Apart from isolated bits of evidence from single building conversions, little information is available on buyers and nonbuyers of converted units. The HUD report (1980) included a survey of 861 households in 12 SMSAs that experienced high conversion rates from 1977 to 1979. This data revealed that 22 percent of the preconversion residents bought into the cooperative or condominium, while 58 to 66 percent moved. That leaves 12 to 20 percent who remained as renters. New York had higher percentages of buyers, perhaps because of laws that required converters to get certain percentages of renters to agree to buy before the conversion would take place.

Diskin and Taschian (1984) provide good descriptions of the types of tenants likely to purchase (inside buyers). The elderly, the higher-income tenants, and those with children are more likely to stay and purchase. Some higher-income younger tenants stay if they cannot put together down payments for their own homes. But the most notable reason for purchase for both insiders and outsiders was a desire for a "low maintenance life style." For the elderly, this may be from physical necessity. But for younger people, some do not want to be slaves to the lawn cutting, painting, and other chores required of single homeowners.

Information on those who moved out at the time of conversion is even sketchier than the data on those who stayed. Sumka (1978) presents results from convenient and nonrandom samples of out-movers from buildings in various cities. There were reasons from unaffordability to seizing the opportunity to move to the suburbs. There are contradictory claims on the proportion of displaced people who found places in the same neighborhood in the studies reported by Sumka and the HUD report. This is probably the result of different kinds of samples. There is agreement, however, that most found housing of similar cost and size, except for some accounts of poorer minority families "paying more for less space." The HUD national household sample found that 90 percent of all the movers were satisfied with their new housing (HUD, 1980).

The study of out-movers and in-movers is complicated by the high rates of mobility in rental housing. Stability depends on replacement by similar people. The movers may have been replaced by people very different from themselves. In New York, for example, the elderly population of converted units dropped from a preconversion 8.2 percent to a postconversion 5.2 percent three years later (Stegman, 1985). As the elderly die or go into nursing homes, it is unlikely that other elderly people will buy into the cooperative or condominium.

In New York the data on preconversion and postconversion racial composition show that blacks occupied 10 percent of the units before conversion and 13 percent after conversion. Stegman (1985) concludes that conversion may have opened up ownership opportunities for blacks that they might not have had otherwise. But the net changes cover individual variations. The data show that 19.7 percent of preconversion units originally occupied by blacks were occupied by whites after conversion. A poor black group may have suffered in displacement, while a more affluent black group moved into the postconversion units.

Single-person households exercise strong demand for all types of condominium and cooperative housing. A National Association of Realtors survey in 1984 showed that 49 percent of condominium buyers were single women with no dependents (Dingle, 1985). The HUD report (1980) showed that 28 percent of the outside buyers of converted units were single-person male households and 29 percent were single-person female households. Thus when conversions occasion large numbers of vacancies, the single-person household may dominate quickly.

MAJOR THEMES AND ISSUES

Causes of Conversion

Conversion of rental housing happened so quickly that it caught people, even policymakers, by surprise. A search for causes is necessary in order to appreciate the dynamics of the housing market and to formulate public policy.

Demographics

The shift in household structure surely shapes the housing situation. From 1960 to 1990 the percentage of households headed by married couples is projected to drop from 74.8 percent to 54.9 percent, and even these married couples will have fewer children living with them (Masnick and Bane, 1980). Households headed by single males are projected to jump from 8.1 percent to 16 percent. Households headed by never-married or divorced/separated women are projected to jump from 7.5 percent to 17.1 percent. Households headed by widowed women are projected to jump from 9.7 percent to 11.9 percent. Some adaptation had to occur to provide housing to the singles and the smaller households, and the evidence of demand for condominiums and cooperatives by single-person households cited earlier shows that this is one of the accommodations the housing market did make.

Unprofitable Rental Markets

Through the 1960s and 1970s rents did not rise as quickly as incomes, and the rental sector did not match the inflation that took place in the value of owned homes (U.S. Department of Housing and Urban Development, Task Force, 1978). This relative slowness in rent increases does not prove the rental sector's unprofitability, but it certainly raises the question of its attractiveness to investors. Whether the relative slowness is due to the inability of renters to pay or to regulation, the comparative value of rental housing as an investment suffers. It is interesting to note that families headed by married couples dropped from 54 percent to 35 percent of the renter population between 1970 and 1980 (Mandel, 1986). Demand-side factors are often overlooked in the economic literature. Rent controls often take the blame for conversion decisions (Harter, 1979). The key question is whether areas without rent control have less conversion than areas with rent control. When similar questions are asked about the linkages of abandonment, maintenance expenditures, and the building of new rental housing to the presence of rent controls, no clear relationships are found (Mandel, 1986). In national comparisons no differences have emerged in conversion patterns between cities with and without rent control (HUD, 1980). In New York conversions are disproportionately concentrated in the newer rent-stabilized inventory (Stegman, 1985). But the buildings in question are post-1947 luxury high-rises that are under the weaker form of New York rent regulations. To judge from experiences in other cities, these buildings would have been prime candidates for conversion even if they were not rent regulated.

Inflation in the Housing Market

Inflation of housing values and the high interest rates that usually accompany inflation feed the demand for condominiums and cooperatives. Those desiring ownership may not be able to afford the severely inflated costs of the single home and are further deterred by the high carrying costs from high interest. But the inflation also makes equity in real estate an attractive hedge against inflation. When these factors converge with the increase in the number of small and single households that do not need the size of the single home, the less expensive cooperative or condominium is in great demand. There are upper limits to this as well. When loans for cooperatives started bumping the 20 percent range in the early 1980s, demand lessened.

From the viewpoint of the converter, the high interest is an incentive not to face long-term debt, as would be the case with rental housing. One New York developer, Daniel Brodsky, puts the threshold at 9 percent interest. Some buildings in New York planned as condominiums when interest rates were 12 percent are now being announced as rentals. Brodsky said that when the interest "turns out to be 9 percent, it becomes workable as a rental" (Oser, 1986).

Avarice of Converters

There are conversion "specialists" who purchase buildings for the purpose of converting them to multiple ownership. Usually these are local real estate people, but there are some national companies like American Invsco that convert luxury buildings across the country.

One concern to residents and community people is the quick profit some of these converters make, along with some of the tactics they use to get rid of tenants. In an interchange between Congressman Benjamin Rosenthal and Aaron Ziegelman, a developer in Queens, at a congressional hearing, the congressman asked Mr. Ziegelman to confirm the following figures about his filing for conversion: "35–50 78 Street, your cash investment is $500,000, and your anticipated profit is $1 million; 35–25 77 Street, your cash investment is $672,373, and your anticipated profit is $1,665,000." To these and a series of similar statistics, Mr. Ziegelman said, "Yes, sir" (U.S. House of Representatives, 1982). In fact, not all of these high-risk conversion plans work, but it is a high-profit game.

While it is beyond the scope of this chapter to investigate the profits and procedures of these converters, there are both legal and competitive factors that can or do restrain their harmful activities. Tenant protections can be legislated. When there are profits to be made, the long-time landlords will find ways of converting themselves rather than selling to conversion specialists. The conversion specialist, avaricious or not, is more a creation of the market forces than a primary cause of the conversion phenomenon.

Taxes

When the depreciation allowance was accelerated for residential real estate in 1954, it created a rapid turnover of landlords. In practical terms it meant that 50 percent of the actual value of the real estate could be depreciated in seven years, even if the property appreciated in value. By the 1970s the rental real estate market had become dominated by the players in the tax-shelter game. Even the traditional landlords got into the frequent selling and trading game to start new periods of tax depreciation. It made little sense to hold properties more than 8 to 10 years (O'Connell, 1985).

Most owners of rental properties had 10-year "balloon mortgages." After 10 years most if not all of the principal was due. This was another incentive to sell off. But in the 1970s some of the traditional players moved the capital into more lucrative investments, for instance, shopping centers, office buildings, and overseas investments. With many buildings coming on the market and fewer traditional buyers, conversion to multiple ownership started to occur at all levels of the rental market.

It is significant to note that the shortening of the depreciation period and the tax credit for renovation of rental housing in the first tax bill under President Reagan brought new investment back into the rental market and slowed the conversion process (*National Real Estate Investor*, 1985a). This shows the importance of tax factors.

Tax factors affect purchasers as well and are used in marketing. In late 1985 a Manhattan cooperative offered cost estimates to prospective share purchasers. For someone in a 50 percent tax bracket on a $70,000 purchase price with $17,500 down, the monthly carrying charges for mortgage and maintenance would be $1,166. But there would be a tax saving of $474 each month, leaving a real cost of $692 each month. Tax factors are quite influential at the upper end of the income scale.

Conversion's Role in Revitalization and Dislocation

In its study of conversion in revitalizing neighborhoods, the HUD report (1980) found that reinvestment, both public and private, started two to five years before the first conversion activities. It concluded that "conversion activity lags behind, rather than acts as a catalyst for revitalization." That conclusion has not been challenged, nor has it been contradicted by any evidence since 1980.

The first stage of revitalization (or gentrification) often touches the single-family and smaller multiunit buildings. The pioneers of this stage, often enterprising young people or artists without much money, move on quickly (De-Giovanni and Paulson, 1984). Even though conversion does not play much of a role in the initial stage of revitalization, it often does at a later stage. It is at this later stage that dislocation can be a problem.

Here the greatest gap in research data is encountered. There are many "invisible evictions" (Hartman, 1979) from threats, arson, and other forms of harassment. There is an enormous increase in legal evictions in many cities, and Hartman finds most of these in revitalizing neighborhoods. Except in the case of single-room-occupancy shut-downs, it is unlikely that other converters would enforce legal evictions, either because of violations of tenant-protection laws or the fear of negative publicity. But the increasing numbers of homeless must make us look at the "invisible evictions" that result in the turmoil that often precedes formal conversion.

The Advantage of a New Form of Homeownership

From experience with conversions in various countries, Alison Woodward raises the issue of whether ownership has advantages over renting in multiunit housing (Woodward, 1981). The advocates of conversion in the European countries foresee lower costs, democratic tenant control over the building, the disappearance of "bad" landlords, and neighborhood stability.

Woodward found mixed results in her extensive data from Sweden and limited data from other countries. It was rare that lower costs were achieved. But converters and tenants who buy the units are happy with the arrangement. Nonbuyers often experience high rent increases and have difficulties dealing with their multiple landlords. Apart from some common concerns about grounds, the purchasing tenants avoided meetings and participation in management. While the decisions were left to a few, Woodward does not describe conflicts between the board and other residents like those that have occurred in the United States. Other than a general feeling of satisfaction, it was difficult to pinpoint changes in the attitude toward dwelling.

SUCCESSES AND FAILURES: ARE PEOPLE
BETTER HOUSED?

Among tenants who purchase at conversion, there are high levels of satisfaction. More of their income is used for housing, but they are content that it is giving them equity. Between 58 and 66 percent of the tenants choose to move. More than half of the former residents are "angry" about the conversion. The vast majority (90 percent) are satisfied with their new housing. Many improve their housing, demonstrated in the fact that 23 percent become owners elsewhere. Among those who rent elsewhere, 28 percent pay at least 25 percent more than they did in the preconversion building, while 30 percent pay less than they did previously (HUD, 1980). Most former residents adjust, but the statistics show a minority hurt by the experience. The sampling here may not pick up the "invisible evictions" that accompany some conversions.

About 2 percent of the nation's rental units have been converted in the last 15 years. In some metropolitan areas the figure is greater than 5 percent. Given the severe downturn in the new construction of rental units, there are fears about the disappearance of rental housing. The worry about the effect of conversion is very localized in the mid-1980s. In the borough of Queens in New York City, owners have filed for the conversion of 60,000 units in the 1980s, which is 15 percent of the rental stock. In a single year in an area of Jackson Heights in Queens, owners filed to convert 3,079 units of the 19,139 units of rental housing (U.S. House of Representatives, 1982). This is a middle- and working-class area. In the 1970s conversion affected mainly luxury housing. The question is whether the conversion now happening in some Jackson Heights–type communities in older and larger cities will spread to other middle-class and working-class areas. The demographic forces and the building stock could be ripe for it. Whether it happens would depend on the tax situation, interest rates, and other factors that shape the decisions of investors.

PROBLEMS AND POLICY ISSUES

Boards and Managers

Conflicts are breaking out between boards of cooperatives and condominiums and the residents. Board members have to be willing to spend long hours. Often weekly meetings are necessary. Conflicts are intensified in buildings with investor or absentee owners. In the beginning stages of conversion the converter controls the board until 50 percent of the units are sold, not allowing the self-determination some buyers desire.

Boards of cooperatives often have strict controls, which help to preserve a preferred life-style, but which some residents find intrusive. The actions have ranged from monitoring alterations to prohibiting guests in the host's absence. The politics of boards are pushing some buyers to condominiums.

Management is another source of conflict, particularly when the converter arranges a long-term maintenance contract. But competition is helping create management firms with reasonable fees and efficient service, and boards are doing careful shopping for managerial services.

The Federal Role

The 1984 Tax Reform Act reduced interest in tax shelters by requiring all shelters to be registered with the Internal Revenue Service before the sale and by rewriting the rules for treating accrued but unpaid interest (Smith, 1985). The Tax Reform Act of 1986 further reduced the lure of tax shelters. The depreciation period was extended from 18 to 27.5 years, the acceleration formula was removed, and passive or accounting losses can no longer be charged off against other ordinary income.

These cumulated changes could shift investor interest away from the multiunit market to the single-home market, where little impact of the reform is anticipated. In the multiunit market investors could shift some interest to the condominium-cooperative sector, in which the tax shelter is not an important factor for the developer or converter. In the short run investors may shun the rental market. One estimate of the effect of extending the depreciation period beyond 25 years would be a 10 percent drop in the value of housing (*National Real Estate Investor*, 1985a). But in the long run this could set the stage for the return of the traditional landlord who makes a profit on cash flow more than on tax shelters and could reduce the quick turnover in landlords seeking maximum depreciation allowances. An exception in the 1986 tax act favors the small landlord-manager by allowing $25,000 of accounting losses against other ordinary income. In the short run there may well be a sudden upturn in conversions. But in the long run there may be renewed health in the rental market.

A critically important way in which the federal government supports the condominium and cooperative sector is through secondary mortgage market operations of purchasing mortgages and loans from conventional lenders in order to provide an adequate supply of funds for new buyers. It was in the late 1970s that the Federal Home Loan Mortgage Corporation and the Federal National Mortgage Association bought condominium mortgages (Eisman, 1980). Without this backup support the condominium explosion might never have happened. It was only in 1985 that the Federal National Mortgage Association started purchasing cooperative loans.

It is relatively easy for the federal government to assist the lower-income rental sector, especially with rehabilitation tax credit and advantageous depreciation schedules. It is not so easy to help the limited-equity cooperative to serve moderate-income people. There could be tax credits passed along to shareholders for rehabilitation, secondary mortgage market support, and perhaps subsidies. The continuance of tax-free bonds issued by local and state governments to provide financing would be a critical help.

The State and Local Role

The list of tenant protection possibilities is long. In broad categories, they include advance notification of tenants, antiharassment laws, the provision of moving expenses for those who leave, requirements of approval from certain percentages of tenants, and special exemptions from eviction for vulnerable people like the elderly.

The legality of conversion controls is being fought in the courts. One opinion holds that laws that directly protect the rights of specific tenants or purchasers, for instance saving tenants from abrupt evictions, are legitimate. But the establishment of certain conditions for conversion like an acceptable vacancy rate or tenant consent are not legitimate (*Michigan Law Review*, 1979). In this view due process is denied, and the owner is forced to forgo a highly profitable use. In practice, only permanent prohibitions of conversions have been declared unconstitutional (Hartman, Keating, and LeGates, 1981). Clear patterns of court decisions are not available on temporary moratoria or other conversion controls.

Property tax abatements can be targeted toward limited-equity cooperatives and away from luxury conversions. Local governments might also target buildings early in the deterioration process with quick tax foreclosure and assistance to the tenants who form limited-equity cooperatives and do light or moderate rehabilitation.

STATE OF RESEARCH

The 1980 HUD report is an unusually comprehensive and thorough study that lays out policy options well. Currently there is need of study on conversion in middle- and moderate-income communities. Tax factors ought to be researched more both on the part of the converter and the buyer. Claims of rent control bringing on conversion ought to be disregarded unless evidence is shown that there is more conversion in areas with rent control than without it.

The displacement issue is the hardest to research. There are some aspects of it that stare us in the face, but there are others, especially the "invisible evictions," that will be difficult if not impossible to study. Long-term intensive case studies of areas with high conversion rates may be the only way to get significant new data.

One area needs research before we jump into the Public Housing Home Ownership Demonstration proposed by President Reagan. This would mean the selling of public housing, presumably to create some cooperative ownership. It is built on the premise that it will change people's attitude toward dwelling. The Swedish case (Woodward, 1981) does not yield clear evidence, and data from American low- and moderate-income groups is lacking. Some data on attitude toward dwelling may come from limited-equity cooperatives now emerging in the United States.

THE FUTURE

Tax factors and the support of the secondary mortgage market may be the critical factors in determining whether owners convert. The small and single households will be there to seek multiple-ownership housing, but in the right kind of market this demand can be satisfied with rentals. The future of limited-equity cooperatives will depend on government support.

The rental market is showing new signs of strength in the 1980s, with a corresponding drop in conversions. This may be reversed for a short term by a squeezing of tax shelters. But in the long run the rate of conversion will depend on whether the rental market is healthy in a new tax and interest rate climate.

REFERENCES

DeGiovanni, Frank. 1983. "Patterns of Change in Housing Market Activity in Revital-izing Neighborhoods." *Journal of the American Planning Association* 49 (Win-ter):22–39.

DeGiovanni, Frank, and Nancy Paulson. 1984. "Household Diversity in Declining Neigh-borhoods." *Urban Affairs Quarterly* 20, no. 2: 211–232.

Dingle, D. J. 1985. "There's No Place like a Condo or a Co-op." *Black Enterprise* 15 (July):31–32.

Diskin, B. A., and A. Taschian. 1984. "Application of Logit Analysis to the Deter-mination of Tenant Absorption in Condominium Conversion." *Journal of the American Real Estate and Urban Economics Association* 12 (Summer): 191–205.

Eilbott, Peter. 1985. "Condominium Rentals and the Supply of Rental Housing." *Urban Affairs Quarterly* 20: 389–399.

Eisman, Eugene. 1980. "Leveraging Maximizes the Effectiveness of State and Federal Housing Program Funds." *Journal of Housing* 37: 552–556.

Gutis, Philip S. 1986. "Eviction Plans Fading Fast as a Road to Conversion." *New York Times*, February 2, sec. R, 7.

Harter, T. R. 1979. "Rent Controls Forcing Condominium Conversions." *Mortgage Banker* 39 (July): 46–47.

Hartman, Chester. 1979. "Comment on Neighborhood Revitalization and Displacement: A Review of the Evidence." *Journal of the American Planning Association* 45 (October): 488–490.

Hartman, Chester, Dennis Keating, and Richard LeGates. 1981. *Displacement: How to Fight It*. Berkeley: National Housing Law Project.

Hinds, Michael de Courcy. 1985. "Conversion of a Rental Developer." *New York Times*, July 28, sec. R, 6–14.

Hudson, James R. 1984. "SoHo: A Study of Residential Invasion of a Commercial and Industrial Area." *Urban Affairs Quarterly* 20: 46–63.

Mandel, Michael. 1986. "A Real Look at Rent Control." *City Limits* 11 (May): 10–14.

Masnick, G., and M. J. Bane. 1980. *The Nation's Families, 1960–1990*. Cambridge, Mass.: Joint Center for Urban Studies.

Meagher, J. D. 1985. "Condo Bust: Investors Bail Out, Leaving Sun Belt Glut." *Barrons* 65 (April 29): 49.

Michigan Law Review. 1979. "Note: The Validity of Ordinances Limiting Condominium Conversion." *Michigan Law Review* 78 (November): 121–141.

National Real Estate Investor. 1985a. "Apartment/Condominium Markets." *National Real Estate Investor* 27 (July): 53–76.

National Real Estate Investor. 1985b. "Stacked Condos in Sun Belt are Slumping." *National Real Estate Investor* 27 (July): 24.

O'Connell, Brian J. 1985. "The Stages of Rental Housing Ownership: Accelerated Depreciation and the Rapid Turnover Syndrome." *Housing and Society* 12, no. 1: 21–31.

Oser, Alan S. 1986. "With Rates Down, Builders Consider 'Going Rental.' " *New York Times*, April 20, sec. R, 7–24.

Smith, David. 1985. "Tax Shelter Topics." *Real Estate Review* 14 (Winter): 14–21.

Stegman, Michael. 1985. *Housing in New York*. New York: New York City Department of Housing Preservation and Development.

Sumka, Howard J. 1978. "Displacement in Revitalizing Neighborhoods." In R. Boynton (ed.), *Occasional Papers in Housing and Community Affairs*, vol. 2. Washington, D.C.: U.S. Department of Housing and Urban Development.

U.S. Department of Housing and Urban Development. 1980. *The Conversion of Rental Housing to Condominiums and Cooperatives: A National Study of Scope, Causes, and Impacts*. Washington, D.C.: Government Printing Office.

———. Task Force on Housing Costs. 1978. *Final Report*. Washington, D.C.: Government Printing Office.

U.S. House of Representatives. Commerce, Consumer, and Monetary Affairs Subcommittee. 1982. *Condominium and Cooperative Conversion: The Federal Response*. Pt. 4, *Queens Regional Hearing*. Washington, D.C.: Government Printing Office.

Woodward, Alison. 1981. "Winners and Losers in the Conversion Game: Some Swedish Data." Paper presented at the annual meeting of the American Sociological Association, Toronto, August 25.

Zukin, Sharon. 1982. *Loft Living: Culture and Capital in Urban Change*. Baltimore: Johns Hopkins University Press.

PART III

HOUSING SUBSIDY PROGRAMS AND TENANT CONCERNS

10

Housing Subsidy Strategies in the United States: A Typology

R. ALLEN HAYS

Since its first involvement in housing in the 1930s, the federal government in the United States has employed numerous strategies to aid the poor in obtaining decent housing within their ability to pay. As each program has been tried, its political and technical shortcomings have stimulated a search for new alternatives, either as supplements or as replacements for it. Simultaneously, the level of overall political support for public subsidies for housing (and other social welfare measures) has ebbed and flowed, and these trends have also affected choices of program design. The purpose of this chapter is to review the types of subsidy programs that have emerged from this process. In this review both the political and technical strengths and weaknesses of each element in subsidy design will be examined, although a complete treatment of each program is beyond the scope of this chapter.

The primary focus will be on programs designed to aid low-income persons. However, one cannot view these efforts in proper perspective without an awareness of the numerous housing subsidies that have flowed to middle- and upper-income groups in the United States during the twentieth century. During the Great Depression the near collapse of the housing finance system led the federal government to intervene with a program of federally insured, long-term, low–down payment mortgages administered by the Federal Housing Administration (FHA). Prior to this time, homeownership had been restricted to those with enough income to afford short-term loans, often with "balloon" repayments of the principal at the end of the loan term. The FHA's inspections, appraisals, and most importantly, federal mortgage insurance gave private lenders enough security to stretch out the term of repayment and to fully amortize the debt. These changes had the ultimate impact of putting homeownership within the reach of a large segment of the American middle class, and the FHA (along with the Veterans Administration [VA] program set up along similar lines) financed the construction of millions of single-family suburban homes, particularly in the years following World War II.

By spreading homeownership to a much larger group, the FHA and VA programs also helped transform the existing federal income tax deduction of mortgage interest and local property taxes into one of the largest and most widely utilized of federal tax deductions. In 1984 these deductions amounted to approximately $32 billion in federal revenues foregone, an amount roughly three times the expenditures for low-income housing subsidies in the same year (Dolbeare, 1985). In addition, the entire rental housing market in the United States, not just the lower end, has become heavily dependent upon federal tax provisions that shelter an investor's income. Costs, which have risen faster than rents, have made rental housing less and less profitable based on rent revenues alone, so that without tax shelters few investors would find it attractive. The poor benefit indirectly from these across-the-board subsidies on rental housing, but in the aggregate these plus homeowner tax breaks add up to far greater subsidies to the middle class than to the poor.

This caveat having been entered, let us now turn our attention to subsidy programs explicitly designed to serve the poor. Table 10.1 indicates, on its horizontal dimension, the basic types of choices available in designing a subsidy strategy. (Obviously, some of the more complex design choices have been omitted.) The vertical dimension lists some of the major subsidy programs initiated since the 1930s. This list is not exhaustive; several programs of shorter duration or smaller impact have been omitted. However, it provides a good overall picture of the American housing subsidy effort.

OWNERSHIP

Public Ownership: The Public Housing Program

The first choice to be made in designing a subsidy program is whether ownership of the units will be public or private. Public ownership means that some unit of government both owns and operates the housing as a public service to low-income tenants. The first federal low-income housing subsidy program in the United States, the public housing program created in 1937, utilizes public ownership. Due to the strong tradition of political decentralization in the United States, units are owned and operated by local housing authorities created by state enabling legislation and subject to control by local governments. (The exact legal arrangements vary from state to state.) These authorities enter into payment contracts with the federal government and thus are subject to numerous federal regulations. The federal government initially paid only construction and financing costs, leaving operating and maintenance costs to be covered by the rents charged. However, in the 1960s these costs began to increase rapidly, leading to deferred maintenance and/or higher rents. As a result, Congress placed a cap of 25 percent (now 30 percent) of tenant income on the rents that could be charged and began to provide operating subsidies to local housing agencies. (Good accounts of the difficulties of the public housing program are provided by Meehan, 1979; and by Mandelker, 1973; see also the chapter by Pit and Van Vliet— in this book.)

Table 10.1
Dimensions of Subsidy Choice by Program

Program	Date Begun	I. Ownership			II. Nature of Subsidy				III. Primary Source of Units		
		Public	Private		Reduced Rent	Direct Govt. Loan	Interest Subsidy to developer or owner	Rent Subsidy	New Construction	Rehabilitation	Existing Units
			Rent	Owner							
Public Housing	1937	X			X				X		
Section 221(d)(3)	1961		X			X			X		
Section 312	1964			X		X				X	
Section 235	1968			X			X		X		
Section 236	1968		X				X		X		
Section 8 New Construction	1974		X					X	X		
Section 8 Existing Housing	1974		X					X			X
Section 8 Substantial & Moderate Rehabilitation	1974		X					X		X	
Housing Vouchers	1982		X					X			X

The public housing program was the only major low-income housing subsidy program in the United States from 1937 to 1961. It generated intense political opposition that, while unable to kill it, was able to keep its scope relatively small. Private realtors and builders opposed it on both pragmatic and ideological grounds. Local governments ran into bitter neighborhood opposition when they tried to locate projects anywhere but in preexisting slums, and many built extremely high density developments to minimize costs. Location restrictions led, in turn, to an increasing stigma, and public housing came to be occupied only by the poorest of the poor. The resulting maintenance, management, and security problems contributed to a further decline in the public image of the program. (Good general histories of the public housing program through the late 1960s are provided by Freedman, 1969; and by Friedman, 1968.)

Yet in spite of these liabilities, the public nature of its ownership has contributed to the program's ability to serve the needs of persons who could not find housing elsewhere. Large, low-income families (often female-headed) are drawn to it as "housing of last resort," and waiting lists have remained long. In addition, a large number of public housing units are designated for the elderly and provide an important source of standard housing for those elderly persons with extremely low incomes. Moreover, contrary to the image generated by well-publicized disasters such as the demolition of the Pruitt-Igoe project in St. Louis, most public housing units continue to provide better accommodations than those available to the poor on the private market. Finally, there has been a tacit recognition by most federal and local decisionmakers that the approximately 1.3 million units of public housing represent a substantial, permanent public investment that should be maintained. Thus operating subsidies have been preserved, even in the Reagan era of drastic retrenchment (U.S. Congressional Budget Office, 1983, provides a recent analysis of the current state of public housing).

Private Ownership of Subsidized Units

In the early 1960s the liberal Kennedy and Johnson administrations wanted to expand the subsidized units available to the poor and to include in subsidy programs a segment of the low-income population considered "too well-off" for public housing. They were aware of the great political resistance to public housing and wished to make some elements of the private housing industry into political allies, not adamant opponents, of subsidy programs. Therefore, they shifted to the option of private-sector ownership of subsidized units, as is indicated in Table 10.1. From then on, though public housing would continue to expand as a source of units, the new federal programs all involved privately owned units.

Section 235: Homeownership for the Poor

Once housing subsidy programs moved into the realm of private-sector ownership, a number of complex program design choices presented themselves. One choice was between subsidies to investor-owned rental units and subsidies that would enable low-income persons to purchase their own homes, much as the middle class had been helped to do by FHA. The bulk of subsidy efforts have been directed at rental units, but in the late 1960s one major program, the Section 235 program, was developed to provide the opportunity for low-income homeownership. The argument was made that homeownership would give the poor a sense of pride and responsibility with regard to their own dwellings and neighborhoods. By giving them this piece of the American dream, it was argued somewhat paternalistically, it might be possible to put them on the road to "responsible" middle-class citizenship.

This program produced about half a million units and served most of its low-income clients reasonably well. However, in a few cities it generated major scandals that tarnished the image of housing subsidy programs in general. These scandals resulted from careless or corrupt FHA administrators who allowed unscrupulous real estate speculators to sell poorly constructed or dilapidated housing to the poor, housing that was often abandoned by its new owners in a short time. Problems also resulted from a lack of counseling of low-income buyers about the responsibilities of homeownership and from the buyer's lack of income reserves to deal with major maintenance problems. Restrictions on participation were gradually tightened in the mid-1970s, and the program was phased out in the early 1980s. (A succinct account of the difficulties of the Section 235 program may be found in McClaughry, 1975.)

Privately Owned Rental Units

In subsidy programs directed at private rental units, choices as to the nature of the subsidy provided become very important, since these choices help to define the structure, impact, and costs of the program. In public housing the subsidy is fairly straightforward. It consists of the difference between the reduced rent paid by the tenants and the government's costs in financing, building, operating, and maintaining the units. No investors are being paid a return on their investment, other than the purchasers of the tax-free bonds issued by the local housing agencies. In contrast, investors in privately constructed units do expect a return on their investment, and they cannot build housing that is affordable to low-income persons and that provides them that return without a government subsidy. (It should be noted by way of qualification that most programs have placed limits, albeit ineffective ones, on private investors' rate of return and that some programs have attracted significant numbers of private nonprofit sponsors, such as religious organizations.) Therefore, to explore more fully the nature of private rental subsidy programs, it is best to move to the next section of the typology, the nature of the subsidy provided.

THE NATURE OF THE SUBSIDY

From Direct Loans to Interest Subsidies

Section 221(d) (3)

The federal government's initial private rental program, the Section 221(d) (3) program created in 1961, used the mechanism of direct loans from the government at below-market interest rates. The lower interest costs were to be passed on to the tenants through lower rents. The first problem of this approach was that the lower interest rates alone did not reduce rents enough to benefit very low income persons. The program helped mainly the "near poor" (or, in the prevalent and somewhat dubious terminology of federal decisionmakers, the "moderate-income" group). The second problem was a budgetary one. Even though direct loans cost the government less in the long run than other subsidy mechanisms, their immediate impact on budget outlays was large, since the money was lent in a lump sum. This made it more difficult politically to get legislative approval for substantial numbers of units. (Milton Semer's essay in U.S. Department of Housing and Urban Development, 1976, provides a thorough account of early subsidy efforts.)

Section 236

As a result, the Johnson administration developed a new program, Section 236, in which an interest subsidy is paid to private lenders on behalf of developers that brings the effective rate paid by the developer down to 1 percent. As market interest rates rose in the early 1970s, this became a substantial subsidy, but it still did not lower rents enough to benefit the very poor. As a partial corrective to this, at least 20 percent of the units in each Section 236 project were reserved for very low income persons, and an additional rent subsidy was provided for these units. Also, it should be kept in mind that Johnson intended the program to be a supplement to public housing, which was still envisioned as the primary source of housing for the very poor. Nevertheless, the Section 236 program was widely criticized for not serving the "truly needy."

Continued Use of Direct Loans in Rehabilitation

In spite of the fact that direct government loans fell out of favor as a subsidy mechanism for large multifamily projects in the mid-1960s, they continued to provide an important mechanism for subsidizing the rehabilitation of existing units. In 1964 the Section 312 program was enacted to provide an alternative to demolition of less deteriorated structures in urban renewal areas. It provided 3 percent, 20-year loans primarily to low-income homeowners, though rental units were also served. The Section 115 program was subsequently added to provide cash grants as a supplement to or in place of loans for those with very limited incomes. Though the aggregate number of units affected by these programs was relatively small, they helped to soften the "federal bulldozer" image of urban renewal. Moreover, the basic strategy of direct, low-interest loans and grants has been adopted by most localities operating rehabilitation loan programs with Community Development Block Grant (CDBG) funds. These programs account for approximately 40 percent of total CDBG expenditures.

Subsidies Based on Rents

The principal alternative subsidy strategy to direct loans or interest subsidies is a direct subsidy to the rent paid by the tenant. Such a subsidy is usually based on the difference between (1) a certain portion of the tenant's income considered by the federal government to be a "reasonable" burden (25 percent was the official criterion until the Reagan administration, which persuaded Congress to change it to 30 percent) and (2) a total rent that will cover the builder's or owner's costs and profits and that is comparable to rents charged for similar units in the surrounding community. Since this type of subsidy is directly tied to tenant income, it enables a program to serve a wide range of income levels, down to the very lowest. Also, since the upper limit is tied to construction and operating costs (although also influenced by local market conditions), it is more flexible in response to inflationary increases in these costs. Such flexibility is desirable in that it avoids some of the cost squeeze that threatened the viability of many Section 236 projects in the 1970s. However, rapid increases in subsidy costs can also hurt a program of this design by stimulating political opposition.

This is precisely what happened to the major new construction program that was designed in this fashion, Section 8 New Construction. Created in 1974, this program proved very popular with developers, in part as a result of its flexibility, and it generated hundreds of thousands of new units in the late 1970s. However, as construction costs and maintenance costs increased with the high inflation of the period, these increases were reflected in the program's upper limits (or, as they are officially called, fair market rents.) This generated much criticism of the program's "skyrocketing" costs, criticism that contributed to congressional willingness to go along with Reagan's proposals for drastic cuts in this program. Funding for new units under this program has now been all but eliminated, with the exception of a few units for the elderly and handicapped (President's Commission on Housing, 1982, presents Reagan's principal arguments against such programs; an earlier study by the U.S. General Accounting Office, 1978, provides a more detailed discussion of cost problems).

Tax Subsidies

The choice and rejection of this subsidy mechanism cannot be fully understood without also examining the related choice between new and existing housing as the main source of subsidized units. However, before leaving the topic of subsidy mechanisms, it is well to consider the important additional subsidy to low-income housing provided by the U.S. tax code. The U.S. tax system allows investors in rental housing to count depreciation losses on their investment at an accelerated rate (that is, at a faster rate than for other types of depreciation write-offs) against their taxable income. Upon sale of the property, any difference between the depreciated value and the actual sales price of the property is subject to capital gains taxation, but for high-income investors, this is a much lower rate than that on income (a study by the U.S. Congressional Budget Office, 1977, provides a succinct description of tax shelters in rental housing).

As was noted earlier in this chapter, rental housing of any type would not be an attractive investment without this tax-sheltering feature, but it has been even more critical to investment in subsidized housing because of the higher risks perceived by investors. Furthermore, in the majority of newly constructed units under Section 236 and Section 8, additional cost savings through the tax system have been required to stimulate private-sector participation. These involve the sale of tax-exempt bonds by state housing development agencies or by local public housing authorities. The latter tax subsidy, created by Section 11b of the Housing Act of 1937, is an extension of a tax subsidy provided to public housing in order to reduce direct government costs (U.S. General Accounting Office, 1980).

Congress in 1986 passed a major tax bill that virtually abolished these investor subsidies. The resulting curtailment in all rental construction, and particularly in moderate- to low-income units, seems likely to be drastic, but the extent of the downturn will not be known for several years.

THE SOURCE OF SUBSIDIZED UNITS: NEW CONSTRUCTION VERSUS EXISTING HOUSING

Table 10.1 indicates that a third major choice must be made in establishing housing subsidy programs: the decision whether to provide the units through new construction, through rehabilitation of existing units, or through utilization of existing units already in suitable condition for occupancy. The public housing program was initiated with the goal of replacing dilapidated slum dwellings with new, if spartan, quarters for the poor. Later, both public housing and subsidized private construction were used to replace housing demolished by urban renewal. Even where direct replacement of dilapidated units was not the goal, the prevailing philosophy of housing subsidy programs until the early 1970s was to add to the stock of standard housing available to lower-income persons through new construction.

In the 1970s, however, three important objections were raised to the use of new construction for low-income housing. The first was a philosophical one. Milton Friedman and other conservative economists argued that if the government feels it must improve living conditions for the poor, it should do so through direct cash grants to the poor, not by providing the desired goods or services itself or granting "in-kind" subsidies tied to specific, privately produced goods. Cash grants, it was argued, allow the free market to distribute goods to the poor more efficiently, and they allow the poor the freedom to choose how to allocate their funds.

The second objection was based on the practical consideration of housing availability. Various statistical analyses, including the Annual Housing Survey initiated by the U.S. Census Bureau and the Department of Housing and Urban Development in 1973, showed a steady improvement in housing conditions in the 1970s, even among lower-income persons. It was argued, therefore, that the main problem of the poor was not housing conditions but housing cost. The poor were widely seen as living in better housing but as paying a disproportionate share of their income to do so. This made a cash subsidy the apparent strategy of choice (perhaps the most widely cited analysis showing this trend is Frieden and Solomon, 1977).

The third objection to the new construction of subsidized units was based on the rapidly increasing costs of such construction, which were alluded to earlier. If an increased supply of reasonably good housing was in fact becoming available, would it not be cheaper to provide cash subsidies to the poor so that they could shop for existing housing, rather than to build new units for them? The answer, of course, was that it would be. This answer was reinforced by an extensive experiment with cash housing subsidies during the 1970s, the Experimental Housing Allowance Program (EHAP), in which poor tenants were very often willing to move to cheaper quarters and divert their cash grants to other purposes if given the chance (thorough description and analysis of the Experimental Housing Allowance Program is provided by Struyk and Bendick, 1981).

The Section 8 Existing Housing Program

Wide acceptance of all three of these arguments led to increased support for housing allowances (cash grants) as a strategy for aiding the poor. In 1974 Congress passed the Housing and Community Development Act, which reoriented federal housing efforts in this direction. The Section 8 New Construction program, though still focused on new units, is closer to the cash allowance concept in its emphasis on a direct rent subsidy to the tenant rather than indirect interest subsidies. However, the clearest embodiment of the housing allowance concept is the Section 8 Existing Housing program. Here, eligible tenants are permitted to "shop" for a unit or even to stay in their present unit if it is found to be in good condition. Their selection is, of course, subject to the willingness of the landlord to enter into a subsidy contract with the local housing agency; however, tenants are given more locational choice than in a program where subsidies are available only to those living in specific housing projects. The amount of their rent subsidy is based on the difference between 25 percent (later 30 percent) of their income, which they pay as rent, and the federally determined fair market rent for existing units in the surrounding community. These fair market rents are usually substantially lower than those for new construction.

Housing Vouchers

Though it substantially incorporated the housing allowance concept, the Section 8 Existing Housing program was still not a sufficiently "pure" housing allowance to suit the free-market conservatives in the Reagan administration. The subsidy was still closely tied to the specific unit through a 15-year contract signed with the landlord. Moreover, the landlord had no incentive to charge less than the fair market rent, and the tenant had no incentive to look for a cheaper unit with subsidies keyed to that preestablished amount. With the EHAP results showing that many tenants might spend less on housing than the levels prescribed by the federal government if they were allowed to use the differences for other things, the Reagan administration saw the potential for gradual reductions in housing subsidy levels in a less restricted housing allowance situation. More than anything else, Reagan and his advisors were passionately concerned with reductions in domestic expenditures.

As a result of these considerations, Reagan proposed a housing voucher program to replace both the Section 8 New Construction and the Section 8 Existing Housing programs. Under this program tenants could pay more than the fair market rent if they chose to spend more of their own funds on housing, or they could pay less and keep the difference if they found a unit in suitable condition. The subsidy contract was for only five years and could move with the tenant to a new dwelling (President's Commission on Housing, 1982). However, this very flexibility proved to be a political liability in Congress, where it was perceived as too little control over how federal subsidies were being expended. Congress was willing to shift the emphasis of housing subsidies from new construction to existing units, but it did so mainly by shifting funds from Section 8 New Construction to Section 8 Existing Housing. To date, it has provided much more limited funding to housing vouchers than Reagan has requested. (Nenno, 1983, provides an explanation and critique of Reagan's housing policies).

Rehabilitation as a Source of Units

This discussion has so far neglected the third major source of subsidized units: rehabilitation of existing structures that are moderately deteriorated but structurally sound. The Section 312/115 program has already been mentioned as a significant rehabilitation effort that has been supplemented and, in recent years, virtually replaced by CDBG programs modeled after it. In addition, all the major subsidy programs since Section 221(d) (3) have made some provision for rehabilitation as a strategy for producing units. Nevertheless, the number of units produced has consistently remained a small fraction of new construction or existing housing.

Perhaps the major reason for this is the high financial risk involved in rehabilitated units. Rehabilitation can often be nearly as costly as new construction,
yet unless the surrounding neighborhood has also been substantially upgraded,
rehabilitated units often cannot command sufficient rents to recover the investment, even when subsidies are provided. This fact is reflected in the much higher
foreclosure rate among Section 236 rehabilitiation projects than among Section
236 projects involving new construction. The Section 8 program contains sub-
programs for substantial rehabilitation and moderate rehabilitation, and these
developments have been pursued somewhat more cautiously than under other
programs in order to prevent failure. Also, the deep rent subsidy helps their
financial viability. Nevertheless, they have remained a small element in the
overall subsidy effort.

The Reagan administration has persuaded Congress to phase out even these
limited programs and to substitute a new program, rental rehabilitation. A grant
of $5,000 per unit to investors for improvement of their property is linked to an
allocation of housing vouchers to low-income tenants who wish to occupy the
renovated units. Though this program is too new for an accurate assessment of
its long-term impact, one feature of it seems likely to prove problematic. Even
though the housing vouchers are initially attached to the renovated units, they
leave the unit with the tenant if he or she moves out. Thus the landlord must
either find other subsidized tenants or have units that will attract tenants who
can pay unsubsidized rents. Given the class segregation typical of American
housing, this prospect seems a slender thread upon which to hang the economic
viability of federally subsidized units.

Subsidized rehabilitation has historically been most successful in programs
that are directed primarily at homeowners and in which a concerted effort to
revitalize an entire neighborhood at once is made. Rehabilitation loans and grants
have been a popular use of CDBG funds because the goal of this program is
neighborhood upgrading, not just the provision of units for individuals. These
programs provide a less disruptive way to improve neighborhoods than the
clearance strategy prevalent under the older urban renewal program. On the
negative side, such programs produce units at a very slow pace, and their impact
is restricted to slightly better-off neighborhoods and to the approximately 40
percent of persons in poverty (largely elderly) who own their own homes.

HOUSING SUBSIDIES IN THE LARGER POLITICAL
ENVIRONMENT

As noted at the beginning of this chapter, the choice of housing subsidy
strategies cannot be isolated from overall trends in political support for the basic
goal of government provision of housing for the disadvantaged. In general,
political liberals have advocated increased efforts in housing, as well as in other
aspects of social welfare, and have sought housing subsidy strategies that would
maximize support for more units. Political conservatives have either opposed

government involvement outright or have sought to limit and contain the impact of housing subsidy programs.

The public housing program was part of the burst of liberal New Deal legislation that created and defined the American welfare state. Yet from the beginning it suffered from the concerted, articulate opposition of the private housing industry, which made every effort to portray it as the most "subversive" and "socialistic" of the New Deal programs. Its lobby, along with members of Congress who opposed the program on philosophical grounds, succeeded in keeping appropriations for new units small throughout the 1940s and 1950s. In addition, their efforts to restrict locations, per unit construction costs, and operating subsidies helped make the negative image of public housing, in part, a self-fulfilling prophecy. The liberal Truman administration pushed through a massive authorization of 850,000 units in 1949, but Eisenhower's lack of enthusiasm and congressional opposition resulted in only half of those actually being built by 1960 (Freedman, 1969; Friedman, 1968).

Therefore, John F. Kennedy, who as a liberal sought an expansion of federal efforts, rather quickly adopted a new subsidy strategy, one involving a public-private partnership. This strategy was continued by Lyndon Johnson, although both Kennedy and Johnson also expanded the public housing program. They succeeded in winning the support of a substantial segment of the private housing industry, and their programs contributed to an unprecedented boom in subsidized housing construction in the early 1970s. By that time, however, leadership had passed to a more conservative Nixon administration. While initially supporting subsidized housing, Nixon later used the scandals and problems associated with public housing and Section 235 as justification for calling a halt to the boom. He declared a moratorium on all subsidized housing construction in 1973 and pushed through the Housing and Community Development Act of 1974 in the waning days of his administration. With this program he hoped to change the approach of housing subsidy programs and also to limit their scope.

After a two-year decline in production due to the moratorium and to the slow start-up of the new Section 8 programs, subsidized housing construction plus allocations of subsidies for existing units gradually increased during the moderate Ford administration and the moderate/liberal Carter administration, even though neither Ford nor Carter supported them with great enthusiasm. By 1980 annual funding for new units had reached levels equal to or exceeding those of the early 1970s.

The election of Ronald Reagan in 1980 signaled the beginning of drastic cutbacks in funding for housing subsidy programs. Throughout the 1970s Reagan and other conservatives had repeatedly attacked housing and other social welfare programs as inefficient and ineffective. They attributed federal deficits and inflation to the growth of spending for such programs and characterized such programs as a drag on the productivity of the whole society. Subsequent, more careful examination of housing subsidies and other social programs has indicated that such blanket condemnations were exaggerated and inaccurate, although serious problems have existed in many programs. Moreover, the great conservative concern with deficit spending seemed to fade once the purposes of federal spending were shifted in the direction of increased national defense. Nevertheless, Reagan's election was widely perceived by other decisionmakers as a public endorsement of his anti–social welfare stance, and Congress proved willing to accede to many, if not all, of his requested reductions. In the ongoing battle over the extent of domestic spending reductions that has characterized congressional decisionmaking during Reagan's time in office, housing subsidy programs have been particularly vulnerable to spending cuts. There are at least two reasons for this.

First, housing subsidies did not, in the years prior to Reagan, become established as a basic entitlement for the poor or middle class, as have social security, Aid to Families with Dependent Children (AFDC) (the basic cash welfare program), medical care programs, food stamps, and unemployment benefits. All of the aforementioned programs are structured such that benefits must be made available to all who are eligible, and Congress must either restrict eligibility (a politically unpopular move) or appropriate funds to meet these open-ended obligations. In contrast, the availability of subsidized housing units has always been considered a discretionary matter subject to the mood of Congress at any given time. Historically, no attempt has been made to meet the total need or demand for housing by low-income persons, as is evidenced by the long waiting lists for such units that exist in most communities. As a result, in a congressional decisionmaking process that is increasingly dominated by battles over the federal budget as a whole, rather than consideration of individual programs on their merits, housing programs have been treated as "discretionary" spending, and allocations of new units have been cut much more drastically than have social welfare entitlements.

The second reason is that housing subsidy cuts are less direct in their impact than other types of social welfare cuts. Most housing subsidy programs involve long-term contractual commitments, ranging from 15 to 40 years. The budget cuts in the Reagan era have so far been mainly directed at funding for additional units. Reagan has made some attempts to reduce these long-term commitments, such as shortening the landlord agreements in his housing voucher program to five years, but there has not been any dramatic selling-off of publicly owned units or displacement of tenants due to subsidy cancellations, either of which events might precipitate a major public outcry. Instead, the cuts made by Congress at Reagan's urging will be felt gradually over 10 years or more, as subsidy contracts from older projects expire, and there are no new units to replace them. Unless federal priorities change drastically after Reagan leaves office, the approximately 4 million units of subsidized housing currently available will suffer from gradual but substantial attrition.

CONCLUSION

This chapter has described, albeit very briefly, the extensive experimentation in housing subsidy strategies that has occurred in the United States over the last

50 years. If there is any lesson to be learned from a review of this experimentation, it is that no one housing strategy can serve the needs of all low-income persons and communities. Each of the programs described has been successful where local economic, political, and social conditions were right for it. Problems have emerged where programs have been administered carelessly or have been applied to inappropriate populations or neighborhoods. An optimal housing subsidy effort would involve the sophisticated and selective application of a range of subsidy alternatives to different communities.

It is also clear that the United States has never made the commitment to adequate housing as a basic human need and right that some other developed, industrial countries have made. In societies with sufficient aggregate wealth, the absence of such a commitment is a result of ideology and politics, not of a lack of resources to carry it out. In this author's view, it is unfortunate that such a commitment has not been made in the United States, but with strong political forces currently pushing away from, rather than toward, such a commitment, it is not at all clear when or if it will be made.

REFERENCES

For a comprehensive bibliography of sources on housing subsidy programs, please see R. Allen Hays, *The Federal Government and Urban Housing: Ideology and Change in Public Policy* (Albany: State University of New York Press, 1985). The following works have been referenced in this chapter in an annotated fashion to provide guidance to some of the most useful primary and secondary sources.

Dolbeare, Cushing N. 1985. *Federal Housing Assistance: Who Needs It? Who Gets It?* Washington, D.C.: National League of Cities.
Freedman, Leonard. 1969. *Public Housing: The Politics of Poverty.* New York: Holt, Rinehart & Winston.
Frieden, Bernard J., and Arthur P. Solomon. 1977. *The Nation's Housing, 1975 to 1985.* Cambridge, Mass.: Joint Center for Urban Studies of MIT and Harvard University.
Friedman, Lawrence. 1968. *Government and Slum Housing: A Century of Frustration.* Chicago: Rand McNally.
Mandelker, Daniel R. 1973. *Housing Subsidies in the United States and England.* Indianapolis: Bobbs-Merrill.
McClaughry, John. 1975. "The Troubled Dream: The Life and Times of Section 235." *Loyola University Law Journal* 6: 1–45.
Meehan, Eugene. 1979. *The Quality of Federal Policymaking: Programmed Failure in Public Housing.* Columbia: University of Missouri Press.
Nenno, Mary K. 1983. "The Reagan Housing, CD Record: A Negative Rating." *Journal of Housing* 40: 135–141.
President's Commission on Housing. 1982. *The Report of the President's Commission on Housing.* Washington, D.C.: Government Printing Office.
Struyk, Raymond J., and Marc Bendick, Jr. (eds.) 1981. *Housing Vouchers for the Poor: Lessons from a National Experiment.* Washington, D.C.: Urban Institute Press.

U.S. Congressional Budget Office. 1977. *Real Estate Tax Shelter Subsidies and Direct Subsidy Alternatives*. Washington, D.C.: Government Printing Office.

————. 1983. *Federal Subsidies for Public Housing: Issues and Options*. Washington, D.C.: Government Printing Office.

U.S. Department of Housing and Urban Development. 1976. *Housing in the Seventies: Working Papers: National Housing Policy Review*. Vol. 1. Washington, D.C.: Government Printing Office.

U.S. General Accounting Office. 1978. *Section 236 Rental Housing: An Evaluation with Lessons for the Future*. Washington, D.C.: Government Printing Office.

————. 1980. *Evaluation of Alternatives for Financing Low and Moderate Income Rental Housing*. Washington, D.C.: Government Printing Office.

11

Public Housing in the United States

FENNA PIT AND WILLEM VAN VLIET—

Intervention by the federal government in housing has always been controversial. The two main positions have involved on the one side those who argue that the production, allocation, and management of housing should be left to private market mechanisms, and on the other side those who deny that private enterprise can provide enough housing units at a sufficiently low cost to serve the low-income population. Underlying this controversy are potentially legitimate, yet conflicting functions of the state more generally, namely, the promotion of economic growth by stimulating private enterprise versus the achievement of greater equity by redistributing some of the nation's wealth.

While the political economy forms an essential context for the analysis of public housing, it is not the concern of this chapter. In keeping with the mission of this book we will paint a broad picture of public housing and provide a historical overview that brings into focus only the more salient developments and issues. Space limitations do not afford this selective treatment of the subject the detail that it warrants, and where appropriate, references will be given to more comprehensive or in-depth coverage elsewhere. Although much of the information provided in this chapter is factual and beyond dispute, other parts will reflect an interpretation of these facts within a political economy framework.

The chapter is structured as follows: We first review some basic aspects, including the definition of public housing, its ideological position, and its scope. A historical sketch then traces public housing from its antecedents through its inception up to the present. A discussion of major approaches taken to public housing is then followed by a selective overview of major problems that have plagued public housing in the United States. The chapter concludes with comments regarding future directions of research and policy.

AN INITIAL DEFINITION

It is important to clarify what we mean by "public" housing in this chapter. A simple public-private dichotomy in which "private" refers to homeownership and "public" to federally funded rental tenure does not reflect the reality of a complex system of housing subsidies, allowances, tax breaks, and secondary mortgage markets (see Bourne, 1981, and the chapters by Hays and Harloe in this book).

There are three main interpretations of the term "public" in public housing. In its most limited and traditional sense public housing refers to housing units constructed, owned, or managed by national or local governments. Often "public housing" is also used interchangeably with "assisted" or "social housing." However, these terms imply a more liberal interpretation that includes all housing directly subsidized by the government. An example is the Section 8 housing program. In a third interpretation, not widely used, "public" refers to housing that in one way or another benefits from public money, that is, a vast majority of the nation's housing units.

Public support for housing may be very direct, as in the case of conventional public housing projects in which the government acts as the landlord. More indirect (and significant) public housing expenditures are mortgage interest reliefs, property tax deductions, and other homeowner tax breaks. As a result of the latter, the federal government currently incurs $40 to $50 billion in lost tax revenues each year (Bratt, 1985). One simple statistic suffices to put these figures into further perspective: "The total of all the assisted housing payments ever made under all HUD programs, from the inception of public housing in 1937 through 1980, was less than the cost to the federal government of housing-related tax expenditures in 1980 alone" (Bratt, 1985: 171; see also the chapter by Hays).

This is not the place to add to the arugment about what constitutes public housing; it suffices here to note the divergent interpretations. This chapter examines the development and nature of public housing chiefly in its traditional meaning, but it will occasionally refer to broader interpretations of public housing. The second interpretation, embraced by the government as its principal framework for providing housing assistance to low-income families, underlies programs discussed in other chapters in this book. Public housing for the elderly is covered in the chapter by Huttman and Gurewitsch.

BASIC INFORMATION

Public housing is a means-tested, non–cash transfer program. A household's income needs to be below a specific standard in order for the household to qualify. In many European countries less restrictive policies have in the past permitted the participation of higher-income families than has been the case under the means-tested policy of the United States. (Huttman and Huttman, 1970). Although income limits for occupancy are constrained by federal guidelines, actual standards vary locally. Assignment policies differ according to the priorities of the more than 3,000 local housing authorities: racial integration, financial solvency by promoting an economic mix of tenants, or sheltering the neediest (Kaplan, 1985).

When it created the national public housing program in 1937, Congress combined federal financing with local responsibilities. It decreed that if a community desired public housing, it must first create a municipal corporation called a local housing authority (LHA) that would both develop and manage the housing units. Thereafter, it became necessary for these communities to abate real estate taxes for any public housing units, accepting only a payment in lieu of taxes (PILOT), generally equal to 10 percent of annual gross tenant rents minus utility payments, while at the same time agreeing to provide full services to the tenants of those units. Federal assistance would be provided in the form of a cash payment pursuant to an annual contributions contract (ACC) that would amortize both the principal and the interest on any bonds issued by the LHA to finance the housing project (National Center for Housing Management, 1973: 19–20).

Nationwide about 3.4 million people are living in 1.2 million public housing units, less than 1.5 percent of the nation's housing stock (U.S. General Accounting Office, 1985). There is no nation in the Western industrialized world with so little public housing. The insignificant proportion of public housing in the United States, comparable to that found in Canada and Australia, contrasts sharply with that of most European countries. In Britain, for example, public (council) housing made up more than 35 percent of that nation's housing stock before the Thatcher government enacted the "right to buy" legislation. Likewise, in 1977, 36 percent of Sweden's housing stock consisted of public housing (Bourne, 1981).

Table 11.1 compares the number of public and private housing starts in the United States for the years 1965–85. It shows a dramatic decrease in the starts of publicly owned housing. Between 1965 and 1985 annual starts of public housing went down from 36,900 to 3,100 units, a drop of 91.6 percent. In contrast, the starts of privately owned housing during that period increased by 17.7 percent, from 1,472,800 to 1,732,800 units per year. In 1965 the ratio of publicly owned starts over privately owned starts was 12.5 times as large as in 1985. The years following 1982 show a particularly sharp decline in public construction, chiefly a result of policies of the Reagan administration to which we will return later. The diminished importance of public housing in the United States is further confirmed by Table 11.2. It shows that for fiscal year 1985 only 5,000 of the 100,000 newly assisted units involved newly constructed or substantially rehabilitated conventional public housing units.

Public housing was originally intended for families who were temporarily poor as a consequence of the economic depression. From the 1930s through the early 1950s tenants were primarily white and somewhat mobile (Hartman, 1975). After this period the public housing clientele changed: the number of female-headed and elderly households increased, whereas the number of white tenants decreased (Meehan, 1979). Since the early 1970s most public housing starts have been specifically for the elderly. Predominant in the changes has been the shift from the temporary poor to the permanent poor.

Table 11.1
New Housing Units Constructed, 1965–85 (Thousands of Units)

Year	Publicly Owned	Privately Owned	Ratio Publicly Owned/ Privately Owned
1965	36.9	1,472.8	.025
1966	30.9	1,164.9	.027
1967	30.3	1,291.6	.023
1968	37.8	1,507.6	.025
1969	32.8	1,466.8	.022
1970	35.4	1,433.6	.025
1971	32.3	2,052.2	.016
1972	21.9	2,356.6	.009
1973	12.2	2,045.3	.006
1974	14.8	1,337.7	.011
1975	10.9	1,160.4	.009
1976	10.1	1,537.5	.007
1977	14.6	1,987.1	.007
1978	15.8	2,020.3	.008
1979	14.8	1,745.1	.008
1980	20.4	1,292.2	.016
1981	16.1	1,084.2	.015
1982	9.8	1,062.2	.009
1983	9.4	1,703.0	.006
1984	6.3	1,749.5	.004
1985	3.1	1,732.8	.002

Source: U.S. Bureau of the Census, 1986.

Table 11.2
New Activity in HUD-Assisted Housing, Fiscal Year 1985

Program	Number of New Units
New Construction/Substantial Rehabilitation	
Public Housing (Conventional)	5,000
Public Housing (Indian)	2,000
Public Housing (Elderly/Handicapped)	12,000
SUB TOTAL	19,000
Existing Housing	
Section 8 Certificates (Regular)	37,500
Section 8 Certificates (Moderate Rehabilitation)	5,000
Housing Vouchers	38,500
SUB TOTAL	81,000
TOTAL	100,000

Source: HUD Budget Summary, FY 1986
(Nenno and Sears, 1985: 176).

Current data on the composition of public housing occupants could not be made available to us.[1] The most recent information comes from the Department of Housing and Urban Development's (HUD) Statistical Yearbook of 1979 (it ceased to be published after that year). In 1979, 247,090 families resided in public housing, 66 percent of whom did not have at least one gainfully employed member. About 78 percent were headed by single adults; 71 percent were headed by females. The median income was about $4,247, compared to $12,600 for all American families, or 34 percent of the median U.S. family income in 1979, versus 37 percent in 1970 and 47 percent in 1960 (Hartman, 1975). In 1978, 46 percent of all units were occupied by elderly. Bratt (1985) puts the figure for nonwhite occupants at 71 percent without, however, specifying the year or source for her information. In 1984, 62 percent of all households in the more inclusive category "publicly owned or other subsidized renter-occupied housing" were without any earnings, and the proportion living below the poverty level increased to 53.8% (U.S. Bureau of the Census, 1985: 2, 33).

Another noteworthy aspect of public housing in the United States is the stigma attached to it. As mentioned, public housing is currently occupied by tenants whose demographic and socioeconomic composition differs sharply from that of the general population. In addition, the generally institutional appearance of the poorly designed, commonly high-rise projects, their frequently undesirable location, and unsatisfactory management all contribute to the low reputation of public housing in the United States. We do not want to add to existing useful discussions of the public housing stigma (see Becker, 1977; Huttman, 1972). The point we wish to emphasize is that when housing officials, tenants, and the public at large hold an image of public housing, that image (fact or fiction) is going to influence their actions.

In 1982 millions of eligible low-income people were on the housing authorities' waiting lists. In New York City, where over 165,000 households are on the waiting list, people wait 18 years for a vacancy (Bratt, 1985; Rodgers, 1984). Nationwide, however, vacancies appear to be a problem. Although up-to-date and reliable data are not available, a recent report prepared by the U.S. General Accounting Office (1985) found an overall vacancy rate of 5.8 percent, with 1,250 (41 percent) of the public housing authorities (PHAs) exceeding rates of 3 percent. Twenty-five large PHAs accounted for 46 percent of the vacancies. Interviews with PHA officials suggested turnover, modernization and demolition, physical deterioration, poor management, and inadequate demand as reasons for the vacancies. In fiscal year 1985 HUD provided PHAs with a total of about $4.5 billion in assistance, including $1.2 billion in operating subsidies. Vacant units (some 70,000 of them) are also currently eligible for full operating subsidies, accounting for about $179 million annually. HUD's proposals to reduce its financial obligations to PHAs with vacancies in excess of 3 percent are anticipated by PHA officials to have little effect or a negative impact (U.S. General Accounting Office, 1985).

HISTORICAL DEVELOPMENT

The first part of this section discusses the origins and development of public housing up to the Housing Act of 1949. Afterwards, assistance to low-income families was increasingly provided in forms different from conventional public housing. Although they are not the topic of this chapter, it is important to touch on these as a link to fuller discussion of them elsewhere in this book. We will do this in the second and third parts of this section as we follow the fate of U.S. public housing in more recent decades (for more extensive historical overviews, see Fisher, 1959; Friedman, 1968; Freedman, 1969; Fish, 1979).

1900–1949

Although legislation established the public housing program only in 1937, its foundations were laid before. Around 1900 restrictive legislation (such as building codes) existed, aimed at the improvement of housing conditions. Investors, builders, and landlords were required to construct safe and healthy accommodations and to improve existing units. While the lack of enforcement disappointed housing reformers, such laws did direct attention at the slums and deplorably substandard housing (Lubove, 1969; Andrachek, 1979).

During World War I federal agencies built and supervised the construction of public dwelling units for workers in (private) defense industries. A third attempt to improve the nation's low-income housing situation took place in the years 1934–35, when the depression caused a serious decrease in living standards. During this period the Housing Division of the Public Works Administration, established under the National Industrial Recovery Act, constructed about 22,000 homes for the poor (Fisher, 1959). In the years 1934–38, inclusive, the New York City Housing Authority built 35 percent of that city's total new units; for the period 1934–41 public housing formed 23 percent of all its completed units (Marcuse, 1986: 354).

Efforts to make low-rent public housing a permanent governmental responsibility resulted in the Housing Act of 1937, which created the U.S. Housing Authority. The initiative came from liberal reformers, the National Housing Conference, the National Association of Housing Officials, and labor pressure groups. It was acknowledged that private enterprise did not fulfill the shelter needs of the lowest-income population. Building housing for the poor was not a profitable business. However, the public housing program was meant to serve several purposes: to assist the depressed construction industry, to reduce unemployment, to weed out slums, and to make cheap housing available to low-income families. Public housing was not the only or even the central issue. Rather, it was seen as a way to improve the stagnant economy of the 1930s. The elimination of slums, however, was given major attention, since the larger (middle-class) society felt threatened by them. The concentration in slums of problems such as poverty, disease, and broken families was viewed as injurious to the health, safety, and morals of citizens. Moreover, the act was seen as a temporary measure. It was expected that once free enterprise operated profitably, the poor would be able to assume their own (housing) responsibilities.

Fewer than 40,000 public housing units had been constructed when World War II intervened. Production efforts were then directed at the war, leaving the nation with a serious housing shortage. A firm federal involvement in housing was feared and hoped for at the same time by different interest groups who became increasingly antagonistic.

The proponents of public housing were organized along similar lines as for the 1937 Housing Act. The American Federation of Labor/Low-income Housing Committee (AFL/LHC) had a double interest: it was committed to employment as well as to low-cost housing opportunities for its members. Additional support came from returning veterans, who were confronted with a housing shortage after the war.

The opposition represented wealthy and powerful interests such as the National Association for Real Estate Boards (NAREB), the U.S. Savings and Loan League, and the U.S. Mortgage Bankers Association. They found extensive governmental involvement in housing an undesirable, socialist activity, threatening the future of their respective enterprises. They did not really mind the clearance of slums as long as the cleared land would be made available primarily for offices, cultural centers, hospitals, and other lucrative usages.

The battle about the enactment of legislation for public housing and urban redevelopment had begun already during the war. Many proposals and bills failed before finally, in 1949, a compromise was reached (for more extensive coverage, see Parson, 1982; Fish, 1979). The new housing act was intended to eliminate substandard housing, to stimulate housing construction, and to provide a "decent home and suitable living environment for every American family." Title I of the act included both a commitment to urban redevelopment and a renewed commitment to public housing. Within six years 810,000 units were to be constructed (Lord, 1977).

Private enterprise was not entirely pleased with the act, since it tied urban redevelopment and public housing together (both under the Federal Housing Administration [FHA]), but a victory for this group was the inclusion of alternative options for slum clearance, which was no longer exclusively tied to public housing: although redevelopment still had to be "predominantly residential" (over 50 percent of the completed projects had to be residential), commercial and industrial uses were also permitted.

1950–80

After 1949 private interests increasingly succeeded in appropriating funds for urban renewal at the cost of public housing. They acquired increasing support to use federal subsidies for the clearance of slum areas and their preparation for private construction. The use of public money was legitimized by the reasoning that the whole nation should be held responsible for the slums it created. Private redevelopment would also create additional tax benefits for the whole municipality, while under public housing schemes the subsidies would go to individual (undeserving) tenants.

At the local level, business interests were also successful in sidestepping federal public housing contracts, some already signed by city councils (for an illustration of counterattacks by business at the local level, see Parson, 1982: 400–402). The influential activities of these private interests were a major factor behind the failure to construct the 810,000 new public housing units within the designated six-year period. This goal was not reached until 1972, 23 years later (Mitchell, 1985; Domhoff, 1978; Parson, 1982).

The public housing program ran into more trouble after 1949 when it lost some of its active proponents. During the Cold War the AFL-CIO and the veterans were forced into a defensive position by a variety of red-baiting tactics. In addition, with the growing post-war prosperity many AFL members could afford a private dwelling (outside the central city). The unions supported the FHA and Veterans Administration (VA) programs that provided mortgage insurance (for lenders, not households) on suburban subdivisions. The Federal Highway Act and the decentralization of industry further reinforced suburbanization. These processes contributed to a spatial separation of middle-class suburbs from public housing in the inner city, occupied by low-income, nonwhite, nonunion workers and welfare families. The withdrawal of the labor unions left the unorganized potential clientele of public housing without a powerful promoter of their housing needs (Parson, 1982).

The Housing Act of 1954 contained no major changes. Eisenhower's Republican administration aimed at less federal involvement and placed more reliance on private enterprise and local initiative. In order to be eligible for federal funds for public housing, slum clearance, or urban renewal, local governments were required to develop a workable program for community development. New public housing contracts were conditional upon slum clearance and urban renewal projects. Units were to be provided to those displaced by urban renewal. This last provision was, in fact, the new public housing commitment of the 1954 act. Mayors and the National Association of Housing and Renewal Officials (NAHRO), among others, criticized the workable program requirement since it would delay public housing construction, as was borne out by later developments (Cole, 1979). In practice there were more units that were demolished than there were newly constructed ones.

The 1954 act also allowed the use of 10 percent of the federal funds for nonresidential construction. Subsequent acts raised this percentage and even dropped the "predominantly residential" clause. For all intents and purposes, the 1954 act was the formal beginning of a steadily declining commitment to conventional public housing, reinforced in the mid-1950s by the separation of the housing and the urban renewal agencies, which enabled private interests in the latter to take precedence over the former. Ever since, the federal government has made no major commitments to construct conventional public housing. Housing policies for low-income groups increasingly emphasized the use of existing housing.

During the 1960s many blacks migrated from the rural South, wher the number of jobs decreased due to the mechanization of farming, to central cities in the North. In the mid-1960s the central cities contained about 56 percent of the black population. However, housing legislation remained focused on demands of middle- and upper-income families in the suburbs (Shannon, 1983). Among the housing acts passed during this period with important implications for low-income groups was the 1965 Housing Act, which created the U.S. Department of Housing and Urban Development (HUD), combining housing at cabinet level in one department with the formerly separate redevelopment agency. Also, several rental assistance programs were initiated: for example, the rent supplement program, which provided for payments directly to the nonprofit and limited-dividend sponsors and owners of new or rehabilitated low-income multifamily housing insured by the FHA to make up the difference between one-fourth of the tenants' income and market rentals (Section 101), and the Section 23 leasing program, which amended the 1937 act to allow local housing authorities to lease existing housing and rent it to low-income households (Hays, 1985; Meeks, 1980).

The pressure of urban disturbances helped create the Housing and Urban Development Act of 1968. It included Sections 235 and 236. Section 235 was a homeownership assistance program. Through mortgage insurance and interest subsidies on loans for the purchase of new, existing, or rehabilitated housing, it did reach a number of low-income families, but the program became implicated in various scandals. Section 236 was a low-income rental housing assistance program. HUD originally insured multifamily mortgages and paid interest subsidies to lenders in order to reduce rents. Sponsors included nonprofit corporations, cooperatives, and private builders who, after construction, sold the units to nonprofit or limited-profit corporations or cooperatives. Since 1974 HUD has paid additional subsidies to help cover operating costs, as tenants have contributed no more than 25 percent of their adjusted income. The program was suspended in 1973 and currently honors previous commitments. While 650,000 such units were subsidized in 1977, the Section 236 program was plagued by problems and failed to reach the poorest families (Rodgers, 1984).

During the 1970s general disillusionment regarding the public housing program prevailed. Neither traditional liberal and intellectual circles nor the unions nor political powers provided significant support. Rapid inflation, the energy crisis, Watergate, and the general abandonment of central cities strongly affected housing production and policy (Sullivan, 1979). In 1970 trials began of an experimental program that provided housing allowances consisting of the difference between the fair market rental of a unit and 25 percent of the tenant's income (Lord, 1977; Sullivan, 1979). Assessments of the appropriateness of these and other housing allowances diverge widely (see Hartman, 1980, 1985; Struyk and

Bendick, 1981; Friedman and Weinberg, 1983; and the chapter by Frieden in this book; see also Oxley, 1987, for a recent international analysis).

In 1973 Nixon's housing moratorium halted many federal programs. An evaluation of existing programs was undertaken in order to establish priorities. Sections 235 and 236 were judged to be inefficient, costing the federal government more than recipients realized in benefits. These sections had also been connected with major public scandals involving corrupt FHA officials, real estate agents, and bankers. Overappraised and overfinanced homes had been sold or rented to the poor. Real estate speculation had gone uncontrolled by the Federal Housing Administration. To remedy these anomalies, the Housing and Community Development Act of 1974 strongly expanded direct subsidies to low-income and poor households rather than to contractors and landlords. Section 23 was replaced by Section 8, which consisted of a program oriented to new construction and substantially rehabilitated units and another program using existing housing, intended to enable low-income households to "shop" for the most desirable housing (for further discussion of Section 8, see the chapter by Hays).

It is safe to conclude that during this period public housing and housing assistance programs failed to serve more than a small proportion of those eligible and in need. The lack of popularity of and political support for publicly owned and managed housing hampered new construction. Section 8 assistance was proposed as an alternative to conventional public housing and meant a major shift in the federal role in the provision of housing. The importance of the government as landlord declined and centralized control decreased. These changes carried over into the housing policies of the Reagan administration.

1981–85

In 1981 the Reagan administration determined that housing assistance consumed too much of the federal budget. Government's involvement in housing could be reduced since the intended economic growth would stimulate the creation of jobs, which in turn would decrease the need for housing assistance for low-income households. It was recognized that there were inequities between federal funds spent for tenants of public housing and those in otherwise-assisted housing units. Also, only a small proportion of eligible households participated in federal housing programs (Struyk, Mayer, and Tuccillo, 1983; Roistacher, 1984). The 1981 Housing Act introduced changes based on two key elements: efficiency and equity. A higher degree of efficiency was necessary to direct the limited resources to the "truly needy." Three measures were taken:

1. The contribution of the assisted tenant was raised from 25 percent to 30 percent of his or her household income, both for Section 8 and public housing tenants. In 1982 HUD estimated that more than three-quarters of the relatively better-off households would leave public housing, while the poorest would remain (Struyk, 1983). However, the concomitant reduction in rental income also made it more difficult for management to maintain a desired level of services.

2. Eligibility for participation in public housing became more targeted to the poorest by reserving only 10 percent of the available resources for assisted households with relatively higher incomes.

3. A third change introduced a uniform calculation of income contribution for Section 8 and public housing programs. The decrease in federal housing spending was accelerated by lowering the fair market rent ceiling in Section 8 and by lowering the cost limits and design standards for public housing. These regulations substantially reduced the number of additionally assisted households compared to that of the Carter period (Struyk, 1983).

In 1983 Congress passed the Housing and Urban-Rural Recovery Act. Section 8 was strongly cut back and complemented by the Housing Payments program. No funds were appropriated for the construction of new public housing, except for the small Indian program, and for the elderly and handicapped (Section 202). The justification was that the existing housing stock would be less costly to operate and that an adequate supply of housing in most markets made new construction superfluous. Eligible households received direct housing subsidies in the form of housing vouchers. These represented a modification of the Section 8 Existing Housing program and housing allowances (Roistacher, 1984). It was reasoned that public housing too often was the last resort, while housing vouchers would offer the prospective tenants an opportunity to shop around for better-quality housing in "better" neighborhoods. The voucher program was introduced in 1983 in an experiment intended to reach 15,000 families (Roistacher, 1984).

A reduction of the existing public housing stock is suggested by several developments. First, the 1983 act changed regulations regarding the demolition and sale of public housing. Demolition is authorized when (1) modernization is not economically feasible; (2) factors such as physical condition and location cause the project to be unusable; or (3) a project can be made usable again by partial demolition. The act also determined that public housing could be sold when (1) changes in the surrounding area make the project unhealthy, unsafe, or economically infeasible; (2) the sale frees money for development or rehabilitation of potentially more efficient lower-income projects; or (3) other factors occur that in HUD's opinion would best serve the interests of the tenants and the public housing authority (Connerly, 1986). Obviously, these conditions for demolition and sale are open to multiple interpretation. It is too early to assess the effects of the new law. It may well be, however, that it will benefit primarily housing authorities (eager to get rid of a "troublesome" project) and HUD rather than low-income households (for a more extensive evaluation, see Connerly, 1986).

A second point concerns the stipulation that modernization funds for public housing projects will only be provided if the projects show long-term viability, that is, for at least 20 years. Since the 1983 act made sale and demolition easier, the question of how viability is assessed becomes critical to the future of the public housing stock. Although HUD developed criteria to determine viability (for example, a vacancy rate of less than 15 percent and the absence of locational or structural problems; see Connerly, 1986), they are sufficiently flexible to suit the administration's policy of decreasing the public housing inventory.

A third point meriting attention is HUD's Public Housing Homeownership Demonstration Program, announced in fall 1984, to sell 1,305 public housing units to tenants at low prices (U.S. Department of Housing and Urban Development, 1985, 1986). Debt-service payments and management service will be provided, but participants will need to cover operating costs. The experience of several European countries, notably Britain, with similar initiatives has prompted a number of comparative analyses. Lessons emerging from these studies include the observations that selling public housing may be an important means of expanding homeownership among low- and moderate-income households; the best housing is sold first; household income and gainful employment are major determinants of take-up rates; substantial discounts (in Britain 33 to 60 percent of market values) are an important incentive; financial overcommitment by low-income families, with subsequent foreclosure, is a real danger; and the quality and quantity of the remaining public housing stock will inevitably decline (Howenstine, 1985; see also Roistacher, 1985; Silver, 1986). Howenstine (1985) has also identified different models for the conversion of public rental housing to ownership: individual ownership, shared equity between government or an association and an individual, condominium associations, co-ownership, and non-equity cooperatives. It remains to be demonstrated, however, how any of these models could avoid adverse consequences as observed in Britain, including, for example, the residualization of public housing whose tenants increasingly consist of the poorest segments of the population (Bentham, 1986; Crook, 1986; Hamnett, 1984; Sewel, Twine, and Williams, 1984). This concern is especially salient in light of the stigma already attached to public housing tenants in the United States and considering their relatively more marginal economic position (a median income of less than 25 percent of the national median, as compared to British council tenants, whose income was 50 percent of that country's median income; Roistacher, 1985).

In an analysis of the political aspects of privatization in general and the sale of public housing in the United States and Britain in particular, Silver (1986) has argued that a failure to maintain a coalition of marginal and productive strata under the formula of the welfare state has led to the political isolation of the poor. Lack of space does not permit us to engage this issue. However, in the more limited context of policies intended to promote private homeownership among the low-income population, it would be appropriate to consider alternatives to the sale of public housing, such as the sale of FHA-foreclosed dwellings to public housing tenants, whose units would thus remain available for new tenants rather than be taken away from the existing stock.

In summary, the Reagan administration has succeeded in dramatically reforming housing assistance policies. Struyk, Mayer, and Tuccillo (1983:76) characterize the new housing philosophy as "freeing public housing to compete with the private sector.'' However, no funds for additional public housing units are being granted, units are being sold and demolished, and the percentage of a tenant's income to be paid for rent has been increased. Under the banner of efficiency and equity considerations, housing programs established since 1937 have been eliminated or curtailed. The positive impacts of these changes, along with cuts in other social programs for the poor, remain to be demonstrated.

MAJOR APPROACHES

Three interrelated changes characterize the provision of low-income housing since the Housing Act of 1937: (1) from a large-scale to a scattered-site approach; (2) from public to private ownership; and (3) from new construction to the use of existing housing (Mitchell, 1985a). In this section we briefly review each of these shifts.

Initially, housing reformers and several presidential committees emphasized the need for large-scale rebuilding of slums. The rebuilt developments would be economical, modern, and efficiently designed, a good investment, and require only a low rent. It was also recognized that bad housing was often found on a neighborhoodwide basis, and it was thought that new, small projects would be dominated by the surrounding distress. Catherine Bauer (1934), a fervent proponent of large-scale public housing, advocated the neighborhood unit as the basic planning unit built according to guidelines such as those given by Perry's (1939) classic neighborhood formula. Early public housing did include a number of well-designed, large-scale projects, often in the form of townhouses, garden apartments, or medium-rise buildings (Polikoff, 1978). Indeed, the very fact that early public housing in New York blended in so well with existing patterns and resembled nonpublic housing provides an important angle for the historical analysis of public housing (Marcuse, 1986).

However, most (later) public housing combined interior-space deficiencies, unimaginative exterior designs, and poor site planning (Bauer, 1957; Stewart, 1979). Problems were exacerbated in the late 1950s and 1960s when economizing measures contributed to increasingly "functional" designs that often failed to take account of the sociobehavioral needs of the tenants. The infamous Pruitt-Igoe project, an award-winning design in St. Louis, condemned and dynamited 18 years after the first residents moved in, was only one of many similar social and economic failures (Yancey, 1971; Cole, 1979; Meehan, 1979).

The process of suburbanization that had accelerated during the 1950s created an additional problem. A mass exodus to the suburbs of households with adequate resources left central-city public housing for the dependent poor. The isolation of the poor was further reinforced by policies requiring public housing tenants with incomes above given levels to move out (Meehan, 1979). In addition, land that was reasonably priced and of sufficient size to accommodate large projects became increasingly scarce, and higher standards regarding, for example, low noise levels and freedom from commercial traffic, allegedly for the benefit of prospective poor residents, effectively excluded many potential sites (Starr, 1985). These problems led to a scattered-site approach that gradually became the cornerstone of federal housing policies after 1965 (Cole, 1979). This change in emphasis notwithstanding, a recent analysis of Chicago shows that while, in that city at least, subsidized housing may have become more dispersed during the last decades, it still remains heavily concentrated (Warren, 1986).

The scattered-site approach went hand in hand with efforts to enlist the private sector in the provision of subsidized low-income housing (Roistacher, 1984; Mitchell, 1985; Sullivan, 1979). Although it was agreed early that private enterprise would not provide the housing needed by low-income groups, opinions differed regarding the appropriate degree of government intervention (Domhoff, 1978; Parson, 1982). The 1937 act designed a system of public ownership in which the federal government subsidized local housing authorities. However, as noted before, since that time private real estate interests have been quite successful in limiting the construction of public housing and public ownership of housing. To enlist private enterprise in the low-income housing market, it has been necessary to create incentives and to improve prospects for making profit. In 1961 mortgage insurance and interest rate subsidies were provided to nonprofit and limited-dividend sponsors, but rising interest rates prevented a major increase in low-income housing (Mitchell, 1985).

A basic problem with conventional public housing had been the inordinate amount of time it took from project inception until construction completion. HUD approval was needed at every step along the way, as in land acquisition, plan preparation, and the awarding of contracts. In 1965, in an effort to develop a more expeditious system of providing public housing, HUD devised the turnkey approach. Under this format the developers/builders purchase the site, retain their own architect, and sell the project to a LHA upon its completion at a stipulated price. Private enterprise played a major role, and government supervision and control were minimal. The turnkey method became a favorite of private lenders (which financed construction) and the National Association of Home Builders, previously strongly opposed to public housing. Practice, however, often diverged from the theoretical model (National Center for Housing Management, 1973: 29–39). The 1974 Housing and Community Development Act abolished the restriction of limited-dividend ownership, established under the 1968 Housing and Urban Development Act, with the effect of undermining public ownership further.

The third shift, from new construction to the use of the existing housing stock, was also especially stimulated by real estate interests (Mitchell, 1985; Struyk, Mayer, and Tuccillo, 1983). Already in the late 1930s the real estate business referred to the existence of high vacancy rates in the housing market to argue that federal subsidies for rent certificates would be more appropriate than new construction. However, high vacancy rates did not exist in the low-income segment of the urban housing market. During the suburbanization of the 1960s vacancy rates in the central city increased, making the use of existing housing seem more efficient. Rental assistance programs since that time have been heavily oriented toward existing housing.

MAJOR PROBLEMS AND ISSUES

A clear-cut categorization of public housing problems is practically impossible, since many of these problems are interrelated and also connected to issues outside the housing arena. In this section we can only provide a summary treatment of selected issues grouped under the broad headings of spatial-physical and economic aspects. Several other aspects are covered elsewhere in this volume (see, for example, the chapters by Pearce and Hays).

Spatial-Physical Aspects

As noted, some early public housing had been relatively well designed and blended in with the surrounding neighborhoods. The assumption of that time was deterministic in nature: adequate shelter, located in decent neighborhoods, was believed to produce decent and respectable residents.

During and after World War II more advanced industrial technologies were used in order to reduce the housing shortage. Increasingly, standardization was applied in the construction of mass housing (Stewart, 1979). The result was an institutional appearance that reinforced the public housing stigma discussed earlier. To reduce federal expenses, public housing was to be designed with a minimum of space and no frills. A justification for this approach was that no luxurious amenities should be provided to people who did not use the opportunities to climb the social ladder. Real estate interests especially wanted public housing projects to look as different as possible from middle-class dwellings.

In addition to the exterior appearance of public housing, its location and site design also were often implicated in the problems that were observed. The powerful resistance of middle-class citizens and real estate interests to public housing in established neighborhoods relegated such projects to undesirable locations (even though research failed to find adverse effects on property values; Nourse, 1963). Sites might be in areas where access to jobs and needed services and facilities was poor (Shannon, 1983), or they might be in blighted areas where one slum unit was to be demolished for every new unit constructed.

Inadequacies of design are illustrated by Yancey's analysis of Pruitt-Igoe (1971). The lack of "wasted space" deprived residents of semipublic opportunities for informal contact and neighborly relations. Under these conditions it was very difficult for them to establish and maintain the local social support system that is so critical in the coping styles of low-income populations. The ensuing social, economic, and physical breakdown of the project was in part a function of its design characteristics.

Following President Nixon's moratorium on subsidized housing in 1973, the number of housing starts in structures with five or more units as a proportion of all starts plummeted from 39 percent to 17.6 percent in 1975 (Sternlieb and Hughes, 1986: 7). Within the political and economic constraints surrounding the design of public housing, approaches were developed to ameliorate the environment of existing, troubled projects and to enhance new construction of low-income housing. These approaches tended to be informed by insights into the sociobehavioral implications of the built environment, generated by the newly developing field of environment-behavior studies (reviewed by Studer elsewhere in this book). Much of the concern centered on the safety of tenants and the prevention of vandalism (Farley, 1982). In keeping with notions regarding crime prevention through environmental design developed by Jeffrey (1971), Newman (1976) proposed the concept of "defensible space," which could be attained by the application of principles of physical design intended, for example, to improve opportunities for surveillance and to augment tenants' proprietary attitudes so as to deter intruders.

Some critics accused Newman of an unfounded faith in physical determinism. A good deal of discussion and research followed (Greenberg and Rohe, 1984; Merry, 1981; Booth, 1981; Wood, 1981), in response to which Newman (1980) espoused a broadened perspective recognizing more explicitly the role of social factors in effectuating a match between residents and their housing environment. HUD's own concern with housing security paralleled these efforts as it conducted an extensive literature review, convened conferences, and contracted for a detailed four-part manual dealing with various facets of the problem (U.S. Department of Housing and Urban Development, 1978, 1979a). Notwithstanding the salience of crime and vandalism in the public image of public housing, research shows that a remarkable proportion of tenants find their situation satisfactory (Bratt, 1985; Francescato et al., 1979).

Economic Aspects

Since its inception public housing has been dominated by an array of economic questions. At issue have been, for example, its role to regulate levels of unemployment, its impact on private profit making, its budgetary situation, and the income levels of tenants. Treatment of any one of these questions obviously requires more space than a short chapter section. Here we discuss selected aspects of housing authority budgetary concerns (see also the chapters by Hays and Pearce).

Financial difficulties of public housing authorities have been attributed, in part, to poor management practices. In response, HUD has developed ameliorative programs and has attempted to establish comprehensive performance standards (Decision Information Systems Corporation, 1985; Struyk, 1980). However, inadequate management is only part of the picture. Federal decisions concerning financial support and eligibility of tenants aggravated the financial problems of local housing authorities. Until 1961 federal funds only backed bonds (which the authorities were authorized to sell) and annual subsidies for mortgage payments. All other expenses, including capital replacements and major repairs, had to be met from collected rent. In addition, local burdens, such as utility payments and a limit to the accumulations of cash reserves, decreased the authorities' budget (see Meehan, 1985). Rent levels were set in such a way that housing authorities would be able to cover their operating costs. Tenants whose income rose above a certain level had to move out. John Macey (1972), an English housing consultant, strongly advised HUD to eliminate income limits, based on his experience that an income mix will produce both social advantages and a higher potential income for housing authorities to supplement public funds.

During and after World War II the financial situation of public housing authorities had been relatively good (Meehan, 1979). However, the upwardly mobile left public housing projects for the suburbs, where conditions for purchasing a dwelling were relatively attractive. By the 1960s public housing tenants were mainly composed of the dependent poor whose lack of education or training, minority status, or family conditions banished them to housing of last resort. In addition, operating costs increased faster than the already-low incomes of the tenants (Meehan, 1985; Mitchell, 1985). Under pressure from vehemently protesting tenants, the basis for determining rent levels was changed in 1969 by the Brooke amendments. The maximum rent that could be charged was set at 25 percent of tenant income. As a consequence, housing authorities could no longer cover expenses from received rent.

The federal government eventually acknowledged the necessity of providing operating subsidies based on a performance funding system (Struyk, 1980). However, older public housing structures had already begun to deteriorate as a result of deferred maintenance, increased vandalism, and poor design and construction. While modernization did occur during the 1970s, funds appropriated in the late 1970s for modernization and routine repairs (not necessitated by inadequate management) were restricted under the Reagan administration to long-term viable projects. According to one critical analysis, "The fiscal arrangements made by Congress were the most important single factor in the eventual breakdown of the conventional public housing program" (Meehan, 1985: 297; see also Rodgers, 1984; Fuerst and Petty, 1979).

FUTURE TRENDS

Research

In the United States public housing is insignificant, both as a proportion of the housing stock and in terms of federal housing policies. Nor is there at the local level a constituency that would make it into a politically significant issue. Existing conventional public housing is a remnant of the past. Its prospects for survival are bleak, especially now that sale and demolition have become part of formal policies. The critical questions need to be addressed in the political and economic arena, not in an academic forum. Theoretical recommendations for public housing research display no urgency or relevance.

There are studies galore that have evaluated public housing and identified its problems. A recent, very partial bibliography lists more than 500 references (Vance, 1982; see also Fisher, 1959). These countless reports and huge amounts of accumulated data have contributed little to the improvement of public housing. Burger (1981) suggests that there often exists a gap between the by-and-large theoretical research of low-income housing and its application in the real world. For example, research recommendations that design, construction, and management practices should be similar to those in the private sector have rarely been implemented. Many reports have apparently ended up in oblivion. Moreover, many data have been on an aggregate level, not reflecting the variations among and within cities to which policies should respond.

Several studies have stressed the difficulties in assessing the performance of public housing that was never intended as a primary goal in a multipurpose program (see Domhoff, 1978; Meehan, 1979). In addition, the goal of a decent home and a suitable living environment has never been operationalized in measurable terms.

Many studies have asked one-sided research questions and produced simple prescriptions dealing with design, construction, tenant satisfaction, or management. This one-sidedness can, in part, be explained by the multitude of problems associated with public housing; analytically it is more attractive to tackle one aspect at a time. It is also easier to attribute the "failure" of public housing to its physical characteristics, its many problem tenants, the malfunctioning of housing authorities, and so on. However, several authors point to a few causes underlying the multiple manifest problems (Meehan, 1979; Struyk, 1980; Hays, 1985; Hartman, 1983). During the almost 50 years of its existence public housing has generally faced opposition from private enterprise and an economic and political climate that has worked against the development of a healthy public housing system. The prerequisite of an ideological and financial commitment in the nation's housing policies to low-income households has never come about. HUD and its predecessors have served as a distributing agency for resources known to be inadequate (Meehan, 1979). Under the Reagan administration such a commitment seems more unlikely than ever. The goal of decent housing and a suitable living environment for every family has not been compatible with the private profit orientation that has dominated the American political economy (Hartman, 1983). The same can be said about the quality of education, transportation, and social services, all of which can be considered as test cases for a nation's ability and willingness to help the less fortunate.

Policy

Given the current and projected situation, what could be done with the public housing program? Based on criteria of tenant satisfaction, management, costs, and accessibility of public services and facilities, Bratt (1985) concludes that public housing fulfills the needs of millions of low-income persons. She pleads against privatization and demolition, and for more resources and support for both existing and additional units. These views are echoed by Burger (1981) and Connerly (1986). However, aid at the federal level should not be expected. Alternative support could come from nonprofit community development organizations. Available evidence indicates that such organizations, as created under the Neighborhood Self-Help Development program during the Carter administration, have been quite successful in housing rehabilitation. Expansion of low-income housing would require additional grants for development, operation, and technical assistance, possibly by state and local governments. Nevertheless, given HUD's initiatives regarding sale and demolition and considering the prevailing general lack of a policy context, the outlook for public housing in the United States is not good.

In the coming years many efforts will be directed at the survival of the existing public housing stock. In this connection, management, always a central issue, has recently received more focused attention. HUD's concern with effective management practices is reflected in a recent series of case studies of public housing agencies, covering in six volumes aspects of security, general administration, finance and accounting, rental and occupancy, maintenance and custodial services, and procurement and inventory (Decision Information Systems Corporation, 1985). Various authors have proposed ways to improve public housing management practices. Bollinger (1981), for example, has argued that local housing authorities should operate more as a private business, with qualified public officials recruited on the basis of higher standards and training. These officials should adopt innovative attitudes, anticipating potential problems rather than merely taking remedial measures. Public relations are seen as essential for developing a positive image of public housing among the public (see also Kolodny, 1984). Besides improved management, Struyk (1980) has stressed the importance of applying selection criteria to change tenant profiles. This could be partially accomplished through the strategic use of other housing programs. Lower project density, for example, can be achieved by serving large families through the Section 8 Existing Housing program and by filling vacancies in public housing projects with smaller families. In addition, experiments with the participation of tenants in the management of public housing projects are continuing. Some such experiments, as described by Rigby (1985), have been successful in that tenants have developed a sense of purpose and competence that appears to be valuable in addressing a range of interrelated community problems. Recent research by Arias (1988), using data from a nationwide sample of 719 public housing projects, also shows that measures of tenant participation are better indicators of housing quality than such physical characteristics as project size, age, and location.

Finally, Welfeld (1985), an advocate of "individual choice in a free market," has argued that public housing should be placed in the housing "mainstream" to expand opportunities for poor households. In his opinion, good management by public housing authorities is hampered by restrictions. The basic problem, in his analysis, is the federally imposed uniform rent policy: rent does not react to signals in the housing market. He proposes a pricing system reflecting differences in cost and quality of the units, just as in the private market. Tenants should be considered as consumers who have choices rather than as passive receivers of "benefits" and should be given buying power according to a scheme that would have to be acceptable to taxpayers, yet would provide housing authorities with adequate income and households with freedom of choice (for details, see Welfeld, 1985).

There is no space here to discuss the relative merits of these and other proposals. Nor need such discussion be pivotal to the provision of housing for low-income groups. As noted, public housing in the United States is insignificant in the overall scheme of things. Realistically, there are no signs that this situation is going to change drastically, other than that it will become even more insignificant. Public housing, however, is not a goal in and of itself, but rather one possible means of providing the low-income population with affordable and decent housing. In the present U.S. context, efforts to that end may be more efficacious when directed at alternative mechanisms, some of which are discussed elsewhere in this book.

NOTES

Our thanks are due to Monica Allebach and Nancy Johnson for contributions beyond the call of duty in transforming illegible scribbles into flawlessly typed script and for facilitating iterative integration of the chapter while we were in different locations. Elizabeth Huttman made helpful comments on an earlier version.

1. The American (Annual) Housing Survey only distinguishes between occupants of owner- or renter-occupied units; Current Population Reports provide data for the combined residents of publicly owned or other subsidized renter-occupied housing.

REFERENCES

Andrachek, Steven E. 1979. "Housing in the United States: 1890–1929." Gertrude S. Fish (ed.), *The Story of Housing*. New York: Macmillan. 123–176.
Arias, E. G. 1988. "Resident Participation and Residential Condition in U.S. Public Housing. Ph.D. diss., Department of City and Regional Planning, University of Pennsylvania.
Bauer, Catherine. 1934. *Modern Housing*. Boston: Houghton Mifflin.
———. 1957. "The Dreary Deadlock of Public Housing." *Architectural Forum*. May, 140.
Becker, F. D. 1977. *Housing Messages*. Stroudsburg, Pa.: Dowden, Hutchinson & Ross.
Bentham, Graham. 1986. "Socio-tenurial Polarization in the United Kingdom, 1953–83: The Income Evidence." *Urban Studies* 23: 157–162.
Bollinger, Stephen J. 1981. "Public Housing Today and Tomorrow: A Director's Perspective." *Journal of Property Management* 46, No. 4: 188–190.
Booth, Allan. 1981. "The Built Environment as a Crime Deterrent: A Reexamination of

 i tx

Defensible Space." Department of Sociology, University of Nebraska. An abbreviated version appears in *Criminology* 18, no. 6: 557–570.

Bourne, Larry S. 1981. *The Geography of Housing*. New York: John Wiley & Sons.

Bratt, Rachel G. 1985. "Controversy and Contributions: A Public Housing Critique." *Journal of Housing* 42, no. 5:165–174.

Burger, Eugene J. 1981. "Low- and Moderate-Income Housing: Does the Perception Match the Reality? President's Letter." *Journal of Property Management* 46, no. 4: 187.

Cole, Albert M. 1979. "Federal Housing Program." In Gertrude S. Fish (ed.), *The Story of Housing*. New York: Macmillan. 277–335.

Connerly, Charles E. 1986. "What Should Be Done with the Public Housing Program?" *Journal of the American Planning Association* 52, no. 2: 142–155.

Crook, A. D. H. 1986. "Privatisation of Housing and the Impact of the Conservative Government's Initiatives on Low-Cost Homeownership and Private Renting between 1979 and 1984 in England and Wales: Impact and Evaluation of Low-Cost Homeownership Policy." *Environment and Planning A* 18: 901–911.

Decision Information Systems Corporation. 1985. *Case Studies of Effective Management Practices within Public Housing Agencies*. 6 vols. Washington, D.C.

Domhoff, G. William. 1978. *Who Really Rules? New Haven and Community Power Reexamined*. Santa Monica, Calif.: Goodyear Publishing.

Farley, J. E. 1982. "Has Public Housing Gotten a Bum Rap?" *Environment and Behavior* 14, no. 4: 443–477.

Fish, Gertrude S. (ed.). 1979. *The Story of Housing*. New York: Macmillan.

Fisher, Robert Moore. 1959. *Twenty Years of Public Housing*. New York: Harper & Brothers.

Francescato, G., S. Weidemann, J. R. Anderson, and R. Chenoweth. 1979. *Residents' Satisfaction in HUD-assisted Housing: Design and Management Factors*. Washington, D.C.: U.S. Department of Housing and Urban Development.

Freedman, Leonard. 1969. *Public Housing: The Politics of Poverty*. New York: Holt, Rinehart & Winston.

Friedman, Joseph, and Daniel M. Weinberg (eds.). 1983. "The Great Housing Experiment. Housing Allowances (1973–1982); Seventeen Essays." *Urban Affairs Annual Reviews* 24.

Friedman, Lawrence M. 1968. *Government and Slum Housing: A Century of Frustration*. Chicago: Rand McNally.

Fuerst, J. S., and Roy Petty. 1979. "Public Housing in the Courts: Pyrrhic Victories for the Poor." *Urban Lawyer* 7, no. 1: 496–513.

Greenberg, Stephanie W., and William M. Rohe. 1984. "Neighborhood Design and Crime: A Test of Two Perspectives." *Journal of the American Planning Association* 50, no. 1: 61–74.

Hamnett, Chris. 1984. "Housing the Two Nations: Socio-tenurial Polarization in England and Wales, 1961–81." *Urban Studies* 21: 389–405.

Hartman, Chester W. 1975. *Housing and Social Policy*. Englewood Cliffs, N.J.: Prentice-Hall.

———. 1980. "Realities of the Federal Housing Allowance." In Richard Plunz (ed.), *Housing Form and Public Policy in the United States*. New York: Praeger. 121–128.

————. 1983. (ed.). *America's Housing Crisis: What Is to Be Done?* Boston: Routledge & Kegan Paul.

————. 1985. "Housing Allowances: A Bad Idea Whose Time Has Come." In J. Paul Mitchell (ed.), *Federal Housing Policy and Programs: Past and Present.* New Brunswick, N.J.: Center for Urban Policy Research, Rutgers University. 383–389.

Hays, R. Allen. 1985. *The Federal Government and Urban Housing: Ideology and Change in Public Policy.* Albany: State University of New York Press.

Howenstine, E. J. 1985. "Selling Public Housing to Individuals and Cooperatives: Lessons from Foreign Experience." *Urban Law and Policy* 7, no. 1: 1–31.

Huttman, Elizabeth D. 1972. "Pathology of Public Housing." *City Magazine*, Fall.

Huttman, J., and E. Huttman. 1970. "Public Expenditures and Income Redistribution: A Case Study of Public Housing." *Annals of Regional Science* 4, no. 1:26–35.

Jeffrey, C. R. 1971. *Crime Prevention through Environmental Design.* Beverly Hills: Sage.

Kaplan, Edward H. 1985. "Tenant Assignments: How PHAs Fill Their Units." *Journal of Housing* 42, no. 1: 13–20.

Kolodny, Robert. 1984. *What Happens When Tenants Manage Their Own Housing?* Washington, D.C.: National Association of Housing and Redevelopment Officials.

Lord, Tom Forrester. 1977. *Decent Housing: A Promise to Keep: Federal Housing Policy and Its Impact on the City.* Cambridge, Mass.: Schenkman.

Lubove, Roy. 1969. *Twentieth-Century Pittsburgh: Government, Business, and Environmental Change.* New York: John Wiley & Sons.

Macy, John. 1972. *Publicly Provided and Assisted Housing in the USA.* Urban Institute Working Paper 209–1–4. Washington, D.C.: Urban Institute.

Marcuse, P. 1986. "The Beginnings of Public Housing in New York." *Journal of Urban History* 12, no. 4:353–390.

Meehan, Eugene J. 1979. *The Quality of Federal Policy Making: Programmed Failure in Public Housing.* Columbia: University of Missouri Press.

————. 1985. "The Evolution of Public Housing Policy." In J. Paul Mitchell (ed.), *Federal Housing Policy and Programs: Past and Present.* New Brunswick, N.J.: Center for Urban Policy Research, Rutgers University. 287–318.

Meeks, Carol B. 1980. *Housing.* Englewood Cliffs, N.J.: Prentice-Hall.

Merry, Sally E. 1981. "Defensible Space Undefended: Social Factors in Crime Control through Environmental Design." *Urban Affairs Quarterly* 16, no. 4: 397–422.

Mitchell, J. Paul. 1985a. "From Public Housing to Housing Allowances, 1930s to 1980s." Paper delivered at the 27th Annual Conference of the Association of Collegiate Schools of Planning, Atlanta, November 1, 1985.

————. 1985b. "The Historical Context for Housing Policy." In J. Paul Mitchell (ed.), *Federal Housing Policy and Programs: Past and Present.* New Brunswick, N.J.: Center for Urban Policy Research, Rutgers University.

————. 1985c. "Historical Overview of Direct Federal Housing Assistance." In J. Paul Mitchell (ed.), *Federal Housing Policy and Programs: Past and Present.* New Brunswick, N.J.: Center for Urban Policy Research, Rutgers University. 187–206.

National Center for Housing Management. 1973. *Report of the Task Force on Improving the Operation of Federally Insured or Financed Housing Programs*, vol. 2, *Public Housing.* Washington, D.C.: NCHM.

Nenno, Mary K., and Cecil E. Sears. 1985. "Rental Housing: Outlook for the Low-Income." *Journal of Housing* 42, no. 5: 174–176.

Newman, Oscar. 1976. *Design Guidelines for Creating Defensible Space.* Washington, D.C.: Law Enforcement Assistance Administration, National Institute of Law Enforcement and Criminal Justice.

———. 1980. *Community of Interest.* Garden City, N.Y.: Anchor Press.

Nourse, H. O. 1963. "The Effects of Public Housing on Property Values in St. Louis." *Land Economics* 39: 433–441.

Oxley, M. J. 1987. "The Aims and Effects of Housing Allowances in Western Europe." In Willem van Vliet—(ed.), *Housing Markets and Policies under Fiscal Austerity.* Westport, Conn.: Greenwood Press. 165–178.

Parson, Don. 1982. "The Development of Redevelopment: Public Housing and Urban Renewal in Los Angeles." *International Journal of Urban and Regional Research* 6, no. 3: 393–413.

Perry, C. A. 1939. *Housing for the Machine Age.* New York: Russell Sage Foundation.

Polikoff, Alexander. 1978. *Housing the Poor: The Case for Heroism.* Cambridge, Mass.: Ballinger.

Rigby, Robert J. 1985. "A Community Based Approach to Salvaging Troubled Public Housing: Tenant Management." In Niels L. Prak and Hugo Priemus (eds.), *Post-War Public Housing in Trouble.* Delft, The Netherlands: Delft University Press.

Rodgers, Harrell R., Jr. 1984. "American Housing Policy in a Comparative Context: The Limits of the Positive State." In Harrell R. Rodgers, Jr. (ed.), *Public Policy and Social Institutions.* Greenwich, Conn.: JAI Press. 155–182.

Roistacher, Elizabeth A. 1984. "A Tale of Two Conservatives: Housing Policy under Reagan and Thatcher." *Journal of the American Planning Association* 50, no. 4: 485–492.

———. 1985. "Selling Public Housing: Should We Try? Who Will Buy? Lessons from Britain." Testimony before the Subcommittee on Housing and Community Development of the Committee on Banking, Finance, and Urban Affairs, U.S. House of Representatives, March 14.

Sewel, J., F. Twine, and N. Williams. 1984. "The Sale of Council Houses: Some Empirical Evidence." *Urban Studies* 21: 439–450.

Shannon, Thomas R. 1983. *Urban Problems in Sociological Perspective.* New York: Random House.

Silver, Hilary. 1986. "The Politics of Privatization: Selling Public Housing in Britain and the United States." Paper presented at the International Research Conference on Housing Policy, National Swedish Institute of Building Research, Gävle, Sweden, June.

Starr, R. 1985. "Twenty Years of Housing Programs." *Public Interest* 81 (Fall): 82–93.

Sternlieb, George, and James W. Hughes. 1986. "Demographics and Housing in America." *Population Bulletin* 41, no. 1 (January): 1–34.

Stewart, K. Kay. 1979. "Twentieth Century Housing Design from an Ecological Perspective." In Gertrude S. Fish (ed.), *The Story of Housing.* New York: Macmillan. 449–497.

Struyk, Raymond J. 1980. *A New System for Public Housing: Salvaging a National Resource.* Washington, D.C.: Urban Institute Press.

Struyk, Raymond J., and Marc Bendick, Jr. (eds.). 1981. *Housing Vouchers for the*

Poor: Lessons from a National Experiment. Washington, D.C.: Urban Institute Press.

Struyk, Raymond J., Neil Mayer, and John A. Tuccillo. 1983. *Federal Housing Policy at President Reagan's Midterm*. Washington, D.C.: Urban Institute Press.

Sullivan, Donald G. 1979. "Housing in the 1970s." In Gertrude S. Fish (ed.), *The Story of Housing*. New York: Macmillan. 382–399.

U.S. Bureau of Census. 1985. *Characteristics of Households and Persons Receiving Selected Noncash Benefits, 1984*. Current Population Reports, Consumer Income, Series P-60, no. 150. Washington, D.C.: Government Printing Office.

———. 1986. Construction Reports "Housing Starts," Series (20–86–82). Washington, D.C.: Government Printing Office.

U.S. Department of Housing and Urban Development. 1978. *Crime in Public Housing: A Review of Major Issues and Selected Crime Reduction Strategies*. 2 vols. Washington, D.C.: Government Printing Office.

———. 1979. *Planning for Housing Security: Assessing the Social Environment (A); Household Safety and Security Survey (B); Site Security Analysis Manual (C)*; and *Site Elements Manual (D)*. Washington, D.C.: Government Printing Office.

———. 1979. *Statistical Yearbook*. Washington, D.C.: Government Printing Office.

———. 1985. "HUD Ceremony Marks First Occupant Purchase of Public Housing Unit." *Recent Research Results*, August. Washington, D.C.: Government Printing Office.

———. 1986. "Public Housing Homeownership Demonstration Sites." *Recent Research Results*, August. Washington, D.C.: Government Printing Office.

U.S. General Accounting Office. 1985. *Public Housing Vacancies and the Related Impact of HUD's Proposal to Reduce Operating Subsidies*. Report GAO/RCED-85–93. Washington, D.C.: GAO.

Vance, M. 1982. *Public Housing: A Bibliography*. Architecture Series A-823. Monticello, Ill.: Vance Bibliographies.

Warren, E. 1986. "The Dispersal of Subsidized Housing in Chicago." *Urban Affairs Quarterly* 21, no. 4: 484–500.

Welfeld, Irving. 1985. "Public Housing: Managing or Mainstreaming." Paper presented at the International Conference on "Housing Policy and Research Issues in an Era of Fiscal Austerity," International Sociological Association, Ad Hoc Group on Housing and the Built Environment Conference, Amsterdam, June.

Wood, D. 1981. "In Defense of Indefensible Space." In Paul J. Brantingham and Patricia L. Brantingham (eds.), *Environmental Criminology*. Beverly Hills: Sage. 77–95.

Yancey, William L. 1971. "Architecture, Interaction, and Social Control: The Case of a Large-Scale Public Housing Project." *Environment and Behavior* 3, no. 1: 3–21.

12

Tax Subsidies: Their Effect on the Rate of Homeownership

IRVING WELFELD

Federal assistance to housing can be tendered directly or indirectly. The assistance can also be a result of design and intelligence or the lack thereof. Paradoxically, most commentators agree that America's most successful housing policy is a result of the latter process. As William Baer has written:

Successful results in social programs can . . . be accomplished through ineptness and ignorance, and . . . this success can be maintained through "benign neglect." . . . An almost perfect and beautiful program . . . is subtle in its workings, robust in its adaptability, and powerful in its social impact. Yet it was deliberately designed by no one: It was an accident. I am speaking of the homeowner deduction provisions in the federal income tax. The provisions comprise a housing subsidy program which makes the deliberately created direct housing programs look feeble in impact, and inept in program effectiveness. (Baer, 1975: 80–81)

The housing policy being discussed is the fostering of homeownership. The mechanism is the tax subsidy. A tax subsidy is a special provision in the tax code that allows a taxpayer who engages in a specific activity to make a smaller tax payment than another taxpayer in the same economic situation. As a result, an added burden is placed—in terms of higher tax rates—on other taxpayers, who must make up the revenue loss of this tax subsidy.

ARE TAX EXPENDITURES SUBSIDIES?

The definition of tax subsidies is deceptively simple. Other subsidies discussed in this book involve a payment made by the government. Here we are dealing with a payment not received by the government. Tax reformers find the location of the subsidy strange.

The Federal income tax system consists really of two parts: one part comprises the structural provisions necessary to implement the income tax . . . ; the second part comprises a system of tax expenditures under which . . . assistance programs are carried out through special tax provisions rather than through direct governmental expenditures. The second system is simply grafted on to the structure of the income tax . . . ; it has no basic relation to that structure. (Surrey, 1972: 49)

Social philosophers find strange the notion that anyone is being subsidized:

Many economists and tax experts—Stanley Surrey, most notably—favor subsidies rather than tax incentives, and argue persuasively for them. . . . So they come quickly to refer to all exemptions and allowances in our tax law as ''tax subsidies'' or even ''tax expenditures.'' But note what happens when you . . . start using such terms. *You are implicitly asserting that all income covered by the general provisions of the tax laws belongs of right to the government, and what the government decides . . . not to collect in taxes constitutes a subsidy.* Whereas a subsidy used to mean a governmental expenditure for a certain purpose, it now acquires quite another meaning—i.e., a generous decision by the government not to take your money. (Kristol, 1974: 14–15; emphasis in original)

Since the issue is not one that can be resolved here, the remainder of this chapter will deal with more down-to-earth matters:

1. What are the major homeowner incentives and how did they come to be?
2. How ''costly'' are they, and do these deductions significantly alter the progressive nature of the income tax?
3. Do these incentives explain the high rate of homeownership in the United States?
4. If not, why do they exist?

A MINIHISTORY

The three main tax incentives to homeownership are the deductions allowed for mortgage interest and real estate taxes, and the noninclusion of the net rental value of the home in the calculation of income.[1]

Mortgage Interest Deduction

Homeowners were first allowed to deduct mortgage interest payments made on their homes for purposes of the federal income tax under the Revenue Act of 1864. Deductions, however, were limited to the extent that the taxpayer had interest income. For example, if a person had interest income of $100 and mortgage interest of $200, only $100 could be deducted. The Revenue Act of 1870 repealed the 1864 act and only allowed the deduction of mortgage interest if it was business related. The Tariff Act of 1894 restored the mortgage interest deduction. Homeowners have been able to deduct the entire interest payment since the Tariff Act of 1913. The basic Internal Revenue Code provision has remained unchanged from 1913 to the present. Section 163(a) of the code at present allows all interest paid or accrued within the taxable year on indebtedness to be deducted from adjusted gross income.

Property Tax Deduction

Homeowners have been able to deduct the real property taxes that they pay on their homes under every federal income tax that the United States has had since 1865. Section 164(a)(1) of the code allows all state, local, and foreign real property taxes to be deducted from adjusted gross income.

Net Imputed Rent

Net imputed rent on an owner-occupied house is equal to the income the owner could obtain by renting his residence to another household or by investing his equity interest in the house in another capital asset. At one point in the Civil War net imputed rent was includable in income for tax purposes. However, in the revenue acts of 1864 and 1870 net imputed rent was specifically excluded from gross income. At present, net imputed rent is not included in taxable income. In contrast, the 1863 Revenue Act permitted tenants to deduct their non-business-related rental payments. However, the Tariff Act of 1894 and all subsequent revenue acts have not permitted a deduction for non-business-related rent.

THE COST

The Treasury Department in an analysis included in the 1986 budget estimated that the federal government would suffer large revenue losses as a result of homeowner tax incentives. The tax expenditure for the mortgage interest deduction was estimated at $24.9 billion in 1985 and $27.3 billion in 1986. For property taxes, the comparable numbers were $9.7 billion and $10.7 billion.

The amount of the tax expenditure is computed by adding the amount of the deduction back to the taxpayer's taxable income and applying the appropriate marginal tax rate. Since the repeal of the provision might result either in lower rates or some other offsetting changes in the tax code, the resulting revenue loss is not necessarily the amount of additional revenue to the government. The sum of the tax expenditure for the two deductions would also exceed the potential revenue gain from repealing both deductions, since more taxpayers would shift to the standard deduction.

Although the Treasury does not calculate the forgone revenue for not including imputed rent in "income" for tax purposes, the National Housing Policy Review in the early seventies characterized it as "the most costly benefit." The estimated revenue loss for 1973 was approximately equal to the total cost of the deductions for mortgage interest and property taxes in 1972 (U.S. Department of Housing and Urban Development [HUD], 1974: 36–37).

In 1982 approximately 34 percent of all tax returns claimed the homeowner deductions, with an average expenditure of $844. As can be seen from Table 12.1, there was a strong relationship between the income of the taxpayer and the amount of his tax savings.

Table 12.1

Expenditures for Homeowner Deductions by Income Class: Returns with Home-owner Deductions, 1982

Income Class	Number of Returns	Percent of Returns	Average Incentive	Total Incentive
Under 10	3,142	9.1	89	280
10 - 15	3,086	22.8	187	576
15 - 20	3,508	31.7	347	1,216
20 - 30	8,811	51.1	592	5,248
30 - 50	10,001	74.9	1,119	11,190
50 - 100	2,895	88.0	2,241	6,487
100+	598	90.6	3,528	2,111
Total	32,041	34.3	844	27,108

Source: HUD, 1974: 36–37.

Affluent households (those with incomes above $50,000), although they constitute 7 percent of all households (U.S. Bureau of the Census, 1984: 461), walk away with almost 32 percent of all the benefits. It is this sharp tilt toward the wealthy that is the heart of the objection of reformers. As Assistant Treasury Secretary Surrey, a law professor by trade, hypothesized when the top tax rate was at 70 percent:

If HUD came up to Congress and said, ''We have a program to assist people who own homes and this is our program. If there is a married couple with more than $200,000 of income why for each $100 of mortgage they have, HUD will pay that couple $70. . . . If there is a . . . couple with an income of $10,000, then . . . HUD will pay only $19. And, of course, if they are too poor to pay an income tax then we are not going to pay them anything . . . It is quite obvious no HUD Secretary would come up with a program as outrageous as this, and yet that is the tax assistance program that we have for owner-occupied homes. (Surrey, 1972: 45)

How can such an outrageously unfair and regressive ''program'' coexist with a progressive tax system? The truth is that it is the very essence of any system that has graduated rates and allows for exemptions and deductions. Is the child of a wealthy person more valuable than the child of a lower-income person because the $1,000 exemption involves a tax savings of $500 to the former and only $100 to the latter? Does the sovereign prize more highly the $1,000 con-

Table 12.2
Tax Payments by Income Groups, 1983

Income Class	Taxes Paid	Percent of
Under 15,000	21,037	7.4
15,000 - 30,000	67,000	23.6
30,000 - 50,000	84,736	29.8
50,000 - 100,000	55,179	19.4
Over 100,000	55,781	19.6

Source: Internal Revenue Service, cited in Veeder and Galloway, 1985: 18.

tribution from the millionaire than the $1,000 from the tithing family? The greater benefit accrues even to the higher-income household that does not itemize its deductions but instead chooses to take the standard deduction (which is larger than the sum of its itemized deductions).

The bottom line on the question of the fairness of the tax system is how it allocates the cost of government among the various income strata in the population. Although there is no political consensus as to the ideal allocation (the question is rarely asked), the present outcome does not fall into the "outrageously unfair" category. Affluent Americans received 32 percent of the benefits from the homeowner deductions. Nevertheless, they paid 39 percent of all taxes in 1983 (Table 12.2). Although it receives an average benefit of $2,400 from the deductions, the average household with an annual income over $50,000 pays over $20,000 in federal taxes.

The Tax Reform Act of 1986 made major changes. Congress did not dare a direct assault on the homeowner tax deductions. However, the combination of changes—an increase in the standard deduction, the increase in personal exemptions, and a sharp decrease in the tax rates—will result in the phenomenon that 75 percent of the homeowners will not itemize their interest and property tax deductions. Nevertheless, the rate of homeownership will not decrease. If the homeownership rate in the United States is so high, there must be a better explanation.

IS IT A PERFECT AND BEAUTIFUL PROGRAM?

How effective are the tax incentives as a social program? Do they explain the high rate of homeownership in the United States? There is no question that after

Table 12.3
Percentage of Owner-Occupancy by Decade

Year	Percentage
1940	43.6
1950	55.0
1960	61.9
1970	62.9
1980	65.6

Source: U.S. Bureau of the Census, 1984.

the imposition of a mass income tax in World War II there was a sharp increase in the rate of ownership in the following decades (Table 12.3). There is, however, a question whether it is "unmistakable that the important tax savings under the higher and more pervasive individual income tax of the World War II and postwar period have been a major factor" (Slitor, 1976:907).

Are these two factors a sufficient explanation for the high rate? To what extent is the desire for homeownership even driven by economic motives? A survey by the United States Savings and Loan League (1971:45) during the late sixties found that the dominant reason was noneconomic by a margin of 62 to 38 percent.[2] The economic motives fell into three main categories: 22 percent were buying to build an equity in real estate, 10 percent wanted something more to show for their money than rent receipts, and 6 percent thought that owning was cheaper than renting. The noneconomic reasons included a better environment for the children, privacy, freedom to improve the property, and the need for more space. The cause may be even deeper. To quote noted housing economist Lou Winnick, "It's like the sex drive, to own my own home on my piece of land" (Mayer, 1978: 5). It may be noted that the Ten Commandments prohibit coveting a neighbor's house and a neighbor's wife.

A closer look at the economics of the increase in homeownership shakes the explanatory power of the homeownership deductions. A great deal has changed since pre–World War II depression years in the financing and the affordability of housing. There has been a revolution in housing financing. The typical home-buyer in the twenties had to make a down payment of at least 25 percent and received a loan for approximately half the value of the home. The balance was covered by second or even third mortgages at progressively steeper interest rates. Most of the mortgages were not amortized and ran for rather short periods— usually five years or less. When the mortgages became due, they had to be renewed frequently at considerable trouble and expense. The high rate of fore-closures in the depression resulted in the creation of the Federal Housing Admin-istration's insurance of low–down payment long-term amortized loans that greatly

Table 12.4
Percentage of Owners by Income Level

1935-1936		1980	
Income Level	Owners	Income Level	Owners
($)	(%)	($)	(%)
Under 500	20.9	Under 3,000	44
500 - 750	21.4	3,000 - 7,000	47
750 - 1,000	21.3	7,000 - 10,000	53
1,000 - 1,250	27.5	10,000 - 15,000	57
1,250 - 1,500	31.0	15,000 - 20,000	66
1,500 - 1,750	33.5	20,000 - 25,000	75
1,750 - 2,000	36.9	25,000 - 35,000	83
2,000 - 2,500	43.7	35,000 - 50,000	90
2,500 - 3,000	50.5	50,000 - 75,000	92
3,000 - 4,000	54.0	Over 75,000	92
4,000 - 5,000	59.3		
5,000 - 10,000	63.8		

Sources: Riley, 1959: 70, 72 (Table 55); U.S. Bureau of the Census, 1981: 1 (Table A-1).

increased the flow of financing into home mortgages; made it possible for young families with small savings to be brought into the housing market; and brought moderate-income families, when general income conditions improved, into the market.

President Hoover's Conference on Home Building and Home Ownership concluded: "It is obvious that the existing distribution of incomes throughout the American population renders impossible, under present conditions, the purchase of homes for a very large number of American families" (President Hoover's Conference, 1932:52). What the statement assumes is that there is a very strong relationship between income and the rate of homeownership. Table 12.4 indicates that the statement was true even at a time when tax rates and therefore tax breaks were extremely low—the effective tax rate in 1936 for a household with a net income of $10,000 was 3.4 percent (Surrey and Warren, 1960:27, Table 5).

The end of the war saw an unparalleled period of prosperity and a major shift in income distribution that vastly increased the number of moderate-income families. Table 12.5 compares the income distributions in 1929 and 1963 (in constant 1963 dollars).

Table 12.5
Income Distribution by Percentage (1963 Dollars)

Income Level	1929	1963
Under 2,000	30	11
2,000 - 4,000	38	18
4,000 - 6,000	16	20
6,000 - 8,000	7	18
8,000 - 10,000	3	12
Over 10,000	6	21

Source: Fitzwilliams, 1965: 2.

When conditions changed, when prosperity came to America, when the suburbs became accessible, homeownership came to moderate-income families. The first 3,000 families that moved out to Levittown, New Jersey, between October 1958 and June 1960 had a median income of $7,125. Sixty percent had been renters before the move. They were buying housing well within their means. Although their housing costs increased, the average Levittowner devoted only 21 percent of income to housing at the time of his arrival. They came for house-related reasons (need for more space, desire for homeownership and a freestanding house), community-related reasons (inadequacy of schools, racial change in the neighborhood) and job-related reasons (transfer by employer) (Gans, 1967: chap. 2).

A look at the international scene also brings into question the importance of the tax subsidies. Canada has a comparable homeownership rate to that of the United States (64 percent in 1981). Yet it does not have comparable homeownership deduction provisions. On the other side of the ocean, West Germany allows the deduction of the principal as well as the interest. Nevertheless, the ownership rate in 1978 was only 36 percent. If there is an explanation for the difference, it seems to lie with the relatively low cost of the single-family home on this continent.

Although the homeownership deductions may have had a marginal effect on the rate of ownership, they have had a greater impact on the price of housing. Upper-income buyers are more prone to buy luxury and vacation homes because of the tax breaks. This is illustrated on a grand scale by the case of condominium conversions. The arrival of condominiums to the United States meant that even the lowly apartment could be upscaled into a home. Converters were willing to sell the apartments at the higher price. Ironically, the higher price usually represented the sale to the buyer of the capitalized value of his own tax breaks (so that after all of the tax breaks the cost was often only slightly higher than if the buyer had remained a renter).

The typical buyer was a young professional or manager with a relatively high income and a small household—a yuppie. With the inflationary increase in housing prices in the seventies, many of the buyers saw housing as an investment. The main reason for their purchase was economic. As a HUD report on the condominium-conversion phenomenon concluded, "Nearly two-thirds of all owner-occupants decided to purchase their unit for essentially economic reasons such as the following: to provide a hedge against inflation; to stabilize their rising costs; to obtain tax shelters and investments; to purchase in lieu of the higher costs of single-family homes; and to take advantage of the discount on the price of the unit offered by the converter (for tenant buyers only)" (HUD, 1980: VI-8). In terms of the overall scene there is much less to the condominium boom than meets the eye—in 1980 they represented 2 percent of all owner-occupied units in the country.

WHY DO THEY EXIST?

The obvious question is why the provisions remain in the tax code if they do not foster homeownership. The answer is that they were not inserted to provide special treatment to homeowners. Rather, the Internal Revenue Code is not discriminating against the homeowner.

Before tax reform, mortgage interest was deductible in the same manner as the interest on the purchase of all consumer goods. The interest on the purchase of the home on credit was treated in the same way as the interest on the installment sale of a sofa, car, or sailboat. The government got its cut on the transaction since the borrower's interest deduction was taxed as the lender's income. To ask for more would be bad form. As Martin Mayer has written, "Taking two bites from a single income stream . . . is generally considered bad manners from the government" (Mayer, 1978: 408).

How do we explain the retention of the mortgage interest deduction in light of Congress's decision to phase out and ultimately eliminate the consumer interest deduction? The distinction is that the finance charge does not much influence the price of the product. In contrast, the elimination of the mortgage interest deduction would almost immediately decrease the value of every home in the United States.

The payment of a property tax is no different from the payment of a local or state income tax. Although Congress did eliminate the sales tax deduction on the belief that it was a matter of small concern (most taxpayer's relied on the I.R.S.–provided table to calculate their deduction), as a general rule, to tax a citizen on the money he pays to support his state, county, or local government would be an egregious form of double taxation in a federal system. Granted, not every state has an income tax, so that not all taxpayers have a chance to take advantage of the deduction. It is, nevertheless, true that in most fiscal years the "high-tax" states send more tax money to Washington than they receive and, therefore, in a manner subsidize the residents who do not share the privilege of paying local income taxes.

The exclusion of the net imputed rent from income is entirely consistent with the fact that we do not have a consumption tax. The amount of the benefit is not peculiar to housing. As Richard Slitor has written, "Motor cars, yachts, speedboats, expensive furniture and home furnishings, camping and sports vehicles, personal libraries . . . luxury wardrobes, hi-fi sets, television receivers, and . . . electronic equipment are some of the important and expensive personal property items that would cost large rentals if such property were leased rather than owned" (Slitor, 1976:928).

Taxing imputed income from owner-occupied homes has a long and inglorious history in other countries. Not only has it not added substantial sums to the revenue base, but in Sweden deficits are reported because the rental value estimates tend to be too low, while expense deductions are more current and realistic. Britain, Australia, and Austria have all abolished taxing of imputed rent in recent years (Slitor, 1976:930–931).

In conclusion, the tax breaks to homeowners have been high in profile and low in performance. They have been far less effective than their critics and supporters have claimed. They are, however, so embedded in the Internal Revenue Code that they cannot be surgically removed without substantially altering many other features of our current tax system or grossly discriminating against homeownership. As even the most popular of American presidents has learned, tax reform has its limits.

NOTES

The author is a senior analyst at the Department of Housing and Urban Development. The views expressed in this chapter are his own.

1. There are a number of other incentives for homeownership tucked away in the recesses of the tax code. They include the treatment as capital gains of the profit made on the sale of a home; the ability to defer the tax if the owner buys another residence of greater value; the exclusion from income, if the seller is over age 55, of the first $125,000 of gain; and the exclusion of interest on state and local housing bonds.

Rental housing also has had its incentives (U.S. Department of Housing and Urban Development, 1972). The Tax Reform Act of 1986, lengthening the depreciation period, was opposed by owners and developers of rental housing, and the claim is being made that rents will have to be increased by 25 percent to provide the same return on investment as under the old tax law (*Housing Affairs Letter*, 1985: 2).

2. In a more recent New York Times/CBS poll "pleasure of ownership" was the most appealing aspect of homeownership (48%), followed by "freedom/independence/space" (24 percent). Only 8 percent said "investment," and only 5 percent cited "deductions/taxes as their main motive (*Builder*, May 1985: 126).

REFERENCES

Baer, William. 1975. "On the Making of Perfect and Beautiful Social Programs." *Public Interest* 39: 80–81.

Fitzwilliams, Jeanette. 1965. "Size Distribution of Income." In Task Force on Economic Growth and Opportunity, *First Report: The Concept of Poverty* Washington, D.C.: Chamber of Commerce of the United States.

Gans, Herbert. 1967. *The Levittowners*. New York: Pantheon.

Housing Affairs Letter. 1985. "The Tax Reform Bill." December 6.

Kristol, Irving. 1974. "Taxes, Poverty, and Inequality." *Public Interest* 38: 14–15.

Mayer, Martin. 1978. *The Builders*. New York: Norton.

President Hoover's Conference on Homebuilding and Homeownership. 1932. *Homeownership, Income, and Types of Dwelling*. Washington, D.C.: Government Printing Office.

Riley, H. 1959. "Housing Costs and Family Income." *Study of Mortgage Credit*. Senate Subcommittee on Housing. 85th Cong., 1st sess. Washington, D.C.: Government Printing Office. Appendix.

Slitor, Richard. 1976. "Rationale of the Present Tax Benefits for Homeowners." In U.S. Department of Housing and Urban Development, National Housing Policy Review. *Housing In The Seventies; Working Papers*. Washington, D.C.: Government Printing Office. 2:907–913.

Surrey, Stanley. 1972. "Prepared Statement." *The Economics of Federal Subsidy Programs*. Joint Economic Committee Hearings. 92d Cong., 1st Sess. Washington, D.C.: Government Printing Office.

Surrey, Stanley, and William Warren. 1960. *Federal Income Taxation*. Brooklyn: Foundation Press.

U.S. Bureau of the Census. 1981. *Annual Housing Survey, 1980. Part C. Financial Characteristics of the Housing Inventory*. Washington, D.C.: Government Printing Office.

———. 1984. *Statistical Abstract*. Washington, D.C.: Government Printing Office.

U.S. Department of Housing and Urban Development. 1972. *Study of Tax Considerations in Multi-Family Housing Investment*. Washington, D.C.: Government Printing Office.

———. 1974. *Housing in the Seventies*. Washington, D.C.: Government Printing Office.

———. 1980. *The Conversion of Rental Housing to Condominiums and Cooperatives*. Washington, D.C.: Government Printing Office.

Veeder, R., and L. Galloway. 1985. "Soaking the Rich through Tax Cuts." *Wall Street Journal*, March 21.

13

The Housing Allowance as a
Subsidy Approach

Housing allowances are one type of subsidy approach. In the United States this approach was tested on a large scale in the Department of Housing and Urban Development's Experimental Housing Allowance Program, which began with great fanfare in 1973 and ended quietly in 1979–80. It involved more than 25,000 families in 12 metropolitan areas at a cost adding up to over $160 million.

This chapter focuses on the housing allowance experiment. The rationale for the experiment was that the best way to help families who needed better housing was to give them money that they could use on their own, instead of building subsidized housing for them. Direct payments to the poor would bypass the project sponsors and other middlemen who were draining off so large a share of the federal housing dollar. Families with cash in hand would be able to make their own decisions about where to live, instead of being limited to designated projects or locations. Rather than having to use their money for costly new housing, they could shop around to find less expensive existing homes. Eligible families would not have to be excluded because they happened to live in communities where developers were not making use of federal housing programs. In addition, direct cash payments could be scaled according to a family's income, rather than following the complicated and regressive formulas that resulted from an attempt to stimulate new construction.

HISTORY OF THE HOUSING ALLOWANCE

The housing allowance idea had caught the attention of top policymakers in the 1960s. President Johnson's Committee on Urban Housing (the Kaiser Committee) in its 1968 report had argued the case for housing allowances. The committee was concerned, however, that a massive housing allowance system could lead to inflation in the general cost of housing and also doubted whether housing allowances would work effectively without parallel measures to counter racial discrimination and provide effective consumer education. It proposed an experimental program to find out.

Limited trials of the housing allowance idea began in 1970 under the auspices of federally funded Model Cities programs in Kansas City, Missouri, and Wilmington, Delaware. The Department of Housing and Urban Development (HUD) began preliminary studies and designs for a systematic national experiment in 1970 and 1971, and then organized its Experimental Housing Allowance Program.

In January 1973 the Nixon administration suspended almost all existing federal housing subsidies for the poor and announced its intention to search for more effective programs. The housing allowance experiment, then getting under way in 12 selected cities, took on special importance as part of that search.

In all areas the basic requirements were the same. The program was open to families of two or more people and to single individuals who were elderly or handicapped. To receive a housing allowance, a family had to have an income below a ceiling that took into account the local cost of adequate housing and the size of the household. For a family of four, the upper income limit was generally below $7,000. Allowance payments in most cases were set to equal the difference between the estimated cost of adequate housing and one-fourth of the family's income; payments averaged $75 per month. Families in the program were free to spend more or less than the estimated amount for rent, but they had to live in or move to housing that met minimum quality standards set for each part of the experiment. The last requirement was relaxed only for two experimental groups in Pittsburgh and Phoenix that could receive the allowance without meeting any standards of housing quality.

In designing the rent allowance experiment, HUD was concerned with specific questions about how poor families would make use of their housing allowances, how local housing markets would respond to the increased demand generated by direct cash payments, and how different administrative arrangements would influence the results. Accordingly, the program was divided into three parts: a demand experiment, a supply experiment, and an administrative-agency experiment.

In the demand experiment (conducted in Pittsburgh and Phoenix), the research focused on the extent to which eligible families took part in the experiment, changes in housing expenditures for participating families, the choices people made with respect to the quality and location of their housing, and their satisfaction with these choices.

The supply experiment (in Green Bay, Wisconsin, and South Bend, Indiana) was designed to test how a large-scale outlay of housing allowance dollars in a single housing market would affect the cost and quality of housing, the behavior of landlords and realtors, and patterns of residential mobility. The supply experiment offered open enrollment to homeowners as well as renters whose incomes were within the established ceilings, and set no limit on the number of families that would be permitted to enroll. (Other parts of the experiment were open to renters only, and the number of participants was limited in advance.)

The administrative-agency experiment selected eight different agencies to carry out housing allowance programs—local housing authorities in Salem, Oregon, and Tulsa, Oklahoma; metropolitan government agencies in Jacksonville, Florida, and San Bernardino County, California; state community development agencies in Peoria, Illinois, and Springfield, Massachusetts; and the state welfare departments in Durham, North Carolina, and Bismarck, North Dakota. In these communities research focused on the administrative performance of such functions as screening and enrolling applicants, certifying eligibility, providing counseling, and making household inspections.

Problems with Past Programs

The housing allowance approach was attractive because it seemed to offer a way of avoiding the problems of past subsidy programs. The underlying cause of the housing allowance experiment was disillusionment with the conventional approach to subsidizing housing for the poor. Ever since the mid-1930s, housing reformers and their political allies had favored a construction strategy. This meant using federal subsidies to build new housing that was then made available to poor people at below-market rents. A series of housing acts from 1937 through the mid-1960s had first established low-rent public housing and then several variations of it, all following essentially the same approach. Yet the flooding tide of housing legislation produced only a trickle of housing. The main problem with this strategy (as has also been said of Christianity) was not that it had been tried and found wanting, but that it had never been tried—at least not on a scale large enough to put it to a real test. In the special political climate of the late 1960s Congress enacted the landmark Housing Act of 1968, interpreted by many as a memorial to Martin Luther King. This act set up two important construction programs backed by the usual federal subsidies. One (known as Section 236) offered rental housing; the other (Section 235) offered homeownership opportunities for low- and moderate-income families. Both were designed to attract developers and investors in the hope that private-sector involvement would generate a high volume of construction commensurate with the country's needs. The 1968 act, in fact, set a target of 2.6 million subsidized housing units to be built within 10 years.

Beginning in 1969, HUD Secretary George Romney gave top priority to putting the new programs into operation and meeting the ambitious targets of the 1968 act. Between 1969 and 1972 the federal government sponsored more subsidized construction than in the preceding 35 years combined. Yet as the HUD programs, together with their rural counterparts in the Farmers Home Administration, grew to a volume of 400,000 starts per year, both their financial and political costs became troublesome. The new housing required annual federal contributions to help the residents pay the rent or the cost of homeownership. By the early 1970s yearly outlays began to approach $2 billion. Although this figure was no more than one-fifth of the total cost of federal tax benefits given to middle-income homeowners, it was a natural target for a conservative administration looking for places to cut the federal budget. In addition, poor administration of these programs led to widespread corruption within the Federal Housing Administration that escaped full notoriety only because Watergate created a bigger scandal. President Nixon's annual report on national housing goals for 1972 complained about the rapid growth of future housing subsidy commitments, then estimated at some $12 billion merely to cover housing already approved. These programs were expensive and getting more so. Worse still, the President's report also noted that the programs were failing to reach the lowest-income families.

Housing experts sponsored by the House of Representatives Subcommittee on Housing were also finding serious faults with these large-scale programs. A group of researchers at the Massachusetts Institute of Technology estimated that from one-fifth to one-half the total federal subsidy was not reaching the residents of the new housing, but went for federal and local administrative expenses and for tax benefits to investors. The same study found that subsidy arrangements were regressive, with greater assistance going to families at the upper end of the eligibility range than to low-income families at the bottom. The programs were serving mainly families above the poverty level in lower middle-income brackets. Further, the families themselves had little freedom of choice in deciding where to live. To get federal housing assistance, they had to move to a designated development whose sponsor had been selected by the local FHA field office. As a result, the allocation of subsidized housing to communities across the country did not correspond as much to the needs of low-income residents as it did to the energy, activity, and political muscle of local sponsors.

An underlying reason for these problems was that the programs were designed to achieve two different purposes that were partially in conflict with each other. One purpose was to encourage new construction; the second was to give financial help to families who could not afford good housing on their own. The construction objective overrode the housing-assistance purpose at many critical points. The high cost and the generous payments to middlemen were part of the construction strategy, as was the reliance on local sponsors to make key decisions about where to locate projects and whom to admit. Ceilings on the subsidy per family made it hard to bring the cost down low enough for the very poor and therefore tipped the balance of effort toward families who were better off. The logic of this critique of production subsidies led toward the conclusion that direct cash payments to low-income families might well be a more effective form of housing assistance.

Other analyses presented to the House Subcommittee on Housing pointed in the same general direction. The New York City Rand Institute had made some startling discoveries in its detailed analyses of the New York City housing market during the 1960s. From year to year a large volume of sound housing was deteriorating in quality, and more than 30,000 units per year were being taken off the market through demolition, conversion to nonresidential use, or outright abandonment. Between 1965 and 1968 housing losses were greater than new construction by a substantial margin. The main reason for this rising volume of deterioration and abandonment was that a large number of the city's low-income families were unable to pay enough rent to cover the rising costs of operating and maintaining rental property. Landlords who were unable to earn a competitive return were cutting back on maintenance and, in time, walking away from their buildings.

Ira S. Lowry (1971) of the Rand Institute staff concluded from the Rand studies that the most effective way to meet the housing needs of low-income families in New York City was to raise the level of maintenance in existing buildings while they were still in good condition. He estimated that a rent increase of from $400 to $700 per year was needed to support moderate renovation and good maintenance in typical older apartments. Even these small increases, however, were beyond the means of low-income families. Lowry (1971) accordingly proposed a housing allowance plan that would make available rent certificates at an average cost of little more than $600 per family.

Criticisms of the Housing Allowance

One reason for a cautious approach to the housing allowance idea was that the public welfare program, which provided families with cash income intended to cover housing costs as well as other expenses, had many of the characteristics of a housing allowance program. Yet a national survey showed that welfare families had severely inadequate housing, a majority of them living in either substandard or overcrowded conditions. The low level of welfare support did not fully explain this situation. Other families in the same income brackets lived in better housing than those on welfare. It was possible, therefore, that money given to poor families through transfer payments might not open up the same access to housing markets that most people already enjoyed.

As the experiment got under way, policy analysts carried on a lively debate over the merits of housing allowances. One school of thought held that housing markets were so restricted and defective that making more money available would still not enable poor people to find decent housing. Others believed that housing markets would respond to a moderate boost in rent levels by increasing the supply of decent, well-maintained housing.

Among the skeptics was Chester Hartman, a long-time critic of federal housing programs, who contended in an article with Dennis Keating that "the shortcomings of the past programs are inherent in the nature of the housing market itself" (1974: 33). The key assumptions were that little housing is available for the poor, markets are noncompetitive, and landlords are dominant. In Hartman's view the housing allowance approach "pays insufficient attention to the vast shortage of decent, moderate-rent housing in most urban and suburban areas, particularly for groups the market now serves poorly, such as large families" (1975: 156). Because of this shortage, he contended, "few doubt that the introduction of housing allowances into a static supply of housing will lead to rent inflation (on a short-term basis at least), not only for recipients, but also for other low- and moderate-income households competing for the same units'' (1975: 156).

In contrast to this view of a captive market, a series of empirical studies in the 1960s found that landlords were in a precarious position themselves, caught between increasing operating costs and limited rental income. George Sternlieb's study of Newark *(The Tenement Landlord* [1966]) and Michael Stegman's study of Baltimore *(Housing Investments in the Inner City* [1972]) went a long way toward revising the stereotyped image of the powerful slum landlord who reaped great profits by milking his properties and plundering his tenants. As Stegman described the situation, ''Many inner-city landlords are today as victimized as are those to whom they provide inadequate shelter'' (1972: 91).

Although a casual look at inner-city rent levels might indeed suggest that landlords were succeeding in charging exorbitant and discriminatory rents while giving little service, Stegman found the reality to be different. Inner-city landlords were incurring high operating costs as a result of such factors as nonpayment of rent, high vacancy rates, and vandalism to their property. These costs were much higher than in middle income areas and helped to explain why prevailing rent levels were neither profitable to most landlords nor adequate to provide good maintenance:

Over 10 percent of cash inflow—an amount equal to about 80 percent of net income—is dissipated on expenditures that do not contribute directly to maintaining or improving resultant flows of housing services. This is why apparently high rents with respect to housing quality can result in little or no profit to the investor. In part, this also explains why housing quality in the inner-city is inferior to that obtainable elsewhere in the city at comparable or only slightly higher rents. (Stegman, 1972: 260)

The shortfall between rent collections and maintenance demands suggested that lack of rent money was one of the most important reasons why inner-city housing markets were failing to meet the needs of the poor. Stegman's careful analysis of Baltimore led to conclusions remarkably similar to those of the New York City Rand Institute (1970). Although Stegman himself did not endorse a housing allowance strategy, his findings (1972: 91) gave strong support to the view that inner-city housing markets were not locked under the control of powerful slumlords and that public policy initiatives could indeed create more effective incentives for responsible management.

SUCCESSES AND FAILURES OF THE HOUSING ALLOWANCE

Reduction of Excessive Rent Burdens

Many people live in housing that meets reasonable physical standards but spend one-third or more of their income for rent—either because low-cost slums are no longer available as an option for the poor or because they have chosen to make financial sacrifices in order to live in better houses.

Low-income families who took part in the housing allowance experiment were originally spending an exorbitant part of their income for housing. Among the 12 cities in the entire program, the median share of total income committed to rental payments varied from 34 percent to 53 percent.

Housing allowance payments did succeed in reducing the share of family income going for rent. In almost all cities the median rent burden for families who received housing allowances was below 25 percent, with the median in individual cities ranging from 17 to 30 percent. But even with the allowance payments, about half the participating families still spent more than the generally accepted norm of 25 percent of gross income for rent.

The rent burden came down because most families who received housing allowances chose to stay where they were already living and decided not to spend much of the allowance money for improved housing. In order to qualify for housing allowance payments, families had to find housing that conformed to the minimum quality standards established for each part of the experiment. A substantial number of families met these requirements without moving from the places where they were living before they enrolled. Of those families that were able to join the program without having to move, most were living in apartments that met the quality standards as soon as they were inspected, but a minority had to make repairs (or get the landlord to make repairs) in order to pass the inspection. The proportion of housing allowance recipients who stayed put, with or without repairs, ranged from 55 percent in the eight cities of the administrative experiment to 83 percent in the two cities of the supply experiment. Families who stayed where they were paid only minor rent increases. (U.S. Department of Housing and Urban Development, 1979).

This pattern of decisions meant that people in the program were using housing allowances mainly to substitute for money of their own that they formerly had spent for rent, rather than using it to make a substantial boost in their housing outlays. In Pittsburgh families in the program used only 9 percent of their payments for rent increases above the normal increase paid by a control group; and in Phoenix 27 percent of the housing allowance dollars went for housing expenditures above normal increases. The great bulk of the payments went to free family income for other expenses.

Ability to Reach Low-Income and Minority Groups

The housing allowance experiment, like other federal housing programs, established income ceilings and payment formulas intended to cover only people who could not afford the cost of decent housing on their own. In other programs, however, project sponsors and local administrators have often screened out those families likely to be most troublesome or most costly to house and have favored people from the high end of the eligible range. As a result, a chronic complaint has been that few of the benefits reached people who were most seriously disadvantaged: the very poor, racial minorities, female-headed households, welfare recipients, large families, and the elderly. The housing allowance program has had great success in reaching these groups, particularly in comparison with earlier federal housing programs (Frieden, 1980).

Opponents of housing allowances argued that many families were "hard to house" because of discriminatory practices and would be unable to use housing allowances effectively for this reason. Yet the housing allowance experiment was conspicuously successful in including minority groups, female-headed families, and people on welfare, which meant that a large number of "hard-to-house" people were able to find places of acceptable quality as required by the program.

Minority families—defined here as black or Hispanic—took part in the program fully in proportion to their eligibility. Female-headed families and those getting welfare assistance were the main participants in the housing allowance program. Households headed by women were about half the eligible families, but were half to three-quarters of those receiving payments in the various cities. Welfare families in the experimental cities ranged from 13 to 31 percent of the eligible families, but accounted for one-fifth to one-half of all those who received housing allowances. Large families with limited incomes are also hard to house, but they took part in the housing allowance program in proportion to their eligibility. Only the aged participated in lesser proportion than were eligible, possibly because they are less likely to move than other groups.

Improvement of Housing Quality

A central purpose of the experiment was to find out whether housing allowances would bring about improvement in the quality of the housing supply. Although a high proportion of participating families lived in housing that met the program's quality standards from the beginning, many did not and either had to make repairs or move in order to qualify. In the eight cities of the administrative experiment an average of 57 percent of recipients either moved or upgraded their prior housing (Temple et al., 1976); in Pittsburgh and Phoenix 61 percent either moved or upgraded (Merrill and Joseph, 1979); and in Green Bay and South Bend 48 percent either moved or upgraded (Rand Corporation, 1978). The housing standards that families had to meet varied somewhat in different parts of the experiment, but they were generally in line with local housing codes, model codes recommended by building code administrators, and standards developed by public health organizations.

In order to meet these standards, most families in the program did improve the quality of their housing, either by moving or by repairing their current residences. The substantial minority who upgraded without moving did so mainly by making minor repairs at low costs. Typical repairs involved fixing windows or installing handrails on stairs; some work was also done on structural components, plumbing, and heating systems. In Green Bay and South Bend landlords and tenants split the work about evenly, using professional contractors for only about 10 percent of repairs. Three out of four below-standard dwellings were brought up to an acceptable level at cash costs of less than $25 in Green Bay and less than $30 in South Bend.

A survey of how participating families in Pittsburgh and Phoenix felt about their housing shows that they valued the quality improvements resulting from the program, but it also reveals a deep-seated reluctance to move in order to get quality improvements (Merrill and Joseph, 1979). Of the families who failed to meet housing standards at the beginning, the most satisfied of all were those who later met them by improving the places where they already lived: 70 percent of these families were "very satisfied" with their housing. But the second most satisfied group were the families who stayed where they were and failed to meet the standards for receiving housing allowances: 45 percent of these were "very satisfied," compared to 30 percent of those who moved and passed and 19 percent of those who moved and failed. The families in the program were strongly attached to their homes. They were pleased if they could make them better at small cost, but giving them up for higher physical standards somewhere else yielded little satisfaction. For those who could not easily meet the standards where they were, the program required a move that was often unwelcome and unsatisfying. The program's objective of bringing everyone into housing of standard quality was out of touch with the preferences and priorities of many of the families who took part.

Improvement of Neighborhood Location

Earlier housing programs usually offered a very restricted choice of neighborhood location, since people who wanted to use the program had to move to designated projects, and as a result of local political pressures the projects were usually concentrated in the worst neighborhoods of the city. The housing allowance strategy, in contrast, promised to open much wider options for neighborhood choice. People in the program could search out moderate-cost housing wherever it was located, and families moving one by one were unlikely to arouse the political protests that kept subsidized projects out of many desirable neighborhoods. A general reluctance to move undercut chances for widespread neighborhood mobility, but a sizable minority of families did move: 45 percent in the administrative experiment cities, 39 percent in Pittsburgh and Phoenix, and 16 percent in Green Bay and South Bend.

The housing allowance experiment produced only scattered information on neighborhood conditions, but what there is shows that people who moved tended to go into better neighborhoods than the ones they left (Weinberg et al., 1977). As the Rand Corporation's report summarizes the experience in Green Bay and South Bend, "The worst neighborhoods in each site lost program participants who moved, on balance, to better neighborhoods'' (Rand Corporation, 1978: 133).

Similarly, in the administrative experiment cities most people who moved went into census tracts with a higher socioeconomic index rating (based on resident income, education, and employment) than the places they left. Of black households who moved, 30 percent moved to areas with lower minority concentrations than their original neighborhoods.

The housing allowance program did not add significantly to opportunities for poor families to live in suburbia. In Pittsburgh 18 percent of the families originally in the central city moved to the suburbs, and 12 percent of those originally in the suburbs moved to the city.

Housing allowances, then, may have widened the locational options open to poor people, but very few took the opportunity to move to different neighborhoods, and most families in the program chose not to move at all. For those who did move, the program did not improve access to the suburbs, but it did help them move to better and less segregated neighborhoods in the cities.

Inflationary Impact

The most troublesome fear raised by the idea of a housing allowance program was that pumping new money into malfunctioning central-city housing markets would drive up housing costs both for people in the program and for low-income renters in general. The supply experiment in Green Bay and South Bend was organized above all to investigate the possible inflationary effects of a housing allowance. All those who were eligible in terms of income were invited to apply, the availability of housing assistance was well publicized, and payments were assured for a full 10 years. The intent was to saturate the housing markets in both cities with housing allowances and then to analyze changes in rent levels.

The results were clear and unequivocal: there was virtually no effect on housing costs. Rents in Green Bay and South Bend increased less rapidly than either regional or national rent averages. Gross rents in Green Bay increased by an average of 7 percent a year from 1974 through 1977, and in South Bend by 5 percent. Higher fuel and utility costs accounted for most of the change in both places.

With hindsight it is easy to see why housing allowances had no inflationary impact. The tendency of families to stay in their previous homes, plus their reluctance to spend more for rent, meant that allowance payments injected few new dollars into local housing markets. In addition, even with open enrollment in Green Bay and South Bend, relatively few families took part in the program; even in the supply experiment, housing allowances went to only 8 percent of the households in the area.

Cost of the Program

In the 10 cities for which information is available, allowance payments per family averaged from $888 to $1,632 per year. Administrative costs averaged from $152 to $429 in addition, excluding the cost of research and analytical work commissioned for the experiment. The average cost per household was about $1,150 in 1976 dollars—$900 in cash payments and $250 for administration.

The average cost of $1,150 compares very favorably with the cost of the two earlier programs for comparable income groups, in which public housing cost an average of $1,650 per family, and rent supplements $1,310, both in 1972 dollars. HUD's current Section 8 program is also more expensive than housing allowances. By 1976 estimates, the Section 8 existing-units program—which is most comparable to housing allowances—costs $1,150 per family, and Section 8 new or rehabilitated units cost more than $4,000. HUD budget projections for 1980 placed the cost of Section 8 existing units at $2,700 per family and new or rehabilitated units at more than $4,500 per family.

Shortcomings

To the surprise of many housing experts, less than half the families eligible for housing allowances actually participated in the program. There are many plausible reasons why poor families who were eligible for housing aid failed to enroll for it or enrolled but failed to qualify for payments. Case studies indicate that some people who were attached to their homes doubted whether they could pass inspection or whether the landlord would agree to rent to people in the program. Others avoided the program out of pride: they viewed housing allowances as something like welfare, or they feared the agency staff would treat them in demeaning ways. Searching for a new place to live was almost always troublesome; it usually meant having to arrange for baby-sitters, getting listings, finding transportation, and dealing with landlords. Often the search had to be completed quickly while places were still available in the local program, and many people had little free time. Even people in the selected groups that were not required to meet any housing standards still had to agree to be interviewed from time to time and to file reports on their finances and their housing. Some people were unwilling to go through the administrative procedures, and some were overwhelmed with other problems.

Families who were able to meet the housing standards where they were already living had the best prospects for getting payments once they enrolled. In a few cities many families never did succeed in meeting the housing standards, perhaps confirming the view of critics who had argued in advance that supply shortages would prevent housing allowances from working satisfactorily. In Pittsburgh 78 percent of the families failed to meet housing standards when they first enrolled, and of these, 73 percent still failed to meet them two years later.

An important factor influencing participation in the housing allowance program was the severity of the housing standards families had to meet: the tougher the standards, the fewer families took part. In Green Bay and South Bend, where housing standards were moderately demanding, about 40 percent of the eligible renters received payments. In Pittsburgh and Phoenix, in the group forced to meet the most stringent housing standards, only 30 percent and 45 percent of those offered enrollment actually received payments. The most likely explanation for this trade-off between standards and participation is that most low-income families are reluctant either to pay higher rent or to move in order to upgrade their housing conditions.

One group—minority families—had an especially hard time qualifying for payments. In the administrative experiment minority families were less likely than other enrollees to meet the standards for payment. This minority experience partly confirms the views of skeptics who argued that discrimination and short-ages of standard housing would offset the value of cash payments to the hard-to-house. But there was also minority experience to the contrary. In Pittsburgh eligible blacks enrolled to a greater extent than other eligible families, and once enrolled, did as well as others in meeting program standards.

Before the housing allowance experiment conventional wisdom held that in-creases in the income of poor families would lead to nearly proportional increases in their housing expenditures—that a 10 percent increase in income would gen-erate a 10 percent increase in rent payments. But in Green Bay and South Bend a 10 percent increase in income for renters led to only a 1.9 percent increase in rent payments. Elasticities estimated for other cities in the housing allowance program were also low.

An implication is that if families who receive housing allowances are free to decide how much of their payment to spend for housing, they will not increase their rent outlays very much above the prior level. But if rent payments do not increase, giving cash to the poor is not likely to prompt landlords to spend much money for property improvements or better maintenance, as Lowry (1971) had anticipated when he proposed housing allowances as a solution to New York City's problems of deterioration and abandonment. Letting consumers make their own decisions regarding how much to spend for rent works against the goal of improving the quality of housing.

The housing allowance program was truly exceptional in allowing for spending on other items. Most housing programs sponsor construction to a predetermined standard and require the families involved to use most of their subsidy to pay for a level of housing quality chosen by an administrator. In the case of housing allowances, federal officials expected the typical family to move to better ac-commodations and to spend most of its subsidy for higher rent. The reality was that most families stayed put, made minor repairs if they were required to meet program standards, got marginally adequate housing if they did not have it to begin with, and used most of the payment to free their own funds for nonhousing expenses. As a result, the program had only limited impact on the quality of the housing supply and on mobility; but these were unavoidable consequences of respecting the wishes of families in the program.

THE FUTURE OF HOUSING ALLOWANCES

The housing allowance experiment did not fully resolve the debates about the nature of inner-city housing markets. The results certainly did not bear out skeptics' fears of widespread inflation and unavailability of housing. Contrary to their predictions, the hard-to-house were able to find adequate housing through the allowance program or had already found reasonable places earlier. Female-headed and welfare families especially were able to make good use of housing allowances. But there were also results to confirm the skeptics' doubts. In some cities enrolled families had severe problems finding adequate housing, depending to a great extent on the standards they had to meet. Minority groups in many cities did not fare as well as others, bearing out the argument that discrimination would blunt some of the desired effects of cash payments for housing.

It turned out that letting the poor make their own decisions led to results that ran counter to the goals of federal housing administrators. The Department of Housing and Urban Development has traditionally given top priority to improving the quality of housing, both for the country at large and for the people who take part in its programs. Marc Bendick, Jr., and James P. Zais of the Urban Institute, in their assessment of the housing allowance experiment, argue persuasively that allowances do not serve the stated goals of HUD policy: "They have failed to generate substantial expansion of the housing stock, dramatic revitalization of cities, or major increases in freedom of choice in housing" (Bendick and Zais, 1978: 2).

Similar results of another housing program are putting HUD's traditional commitments to the test. The Section 8 Existing Housing program has many of the characteristics of a housing allowance and also allows families to use federal subsidies in existing apartments that meet prescribed standards. About half the participants in Section 8 Existing Housing do not move from where they lived before, and they use their financial assistance mainly to reduce their rent burden. This program has had great success in reaching the poor, female-headed families, minorities, and the elderly; but it has done little to improve the quality of the housing supply. Not surprisingly, HUD has begun to slow down the Existing Housing program and to shift most of its housing-assistance activity to a different Section 8 program for new construction or substantial rehabilitation.

HUD should have other missions than quality, ones that encompass the range of housing problems and possess a capacity to use the right tool for each purpose. There is still need for construction programs, since they are likely to be more effective than housing allowances for such purposes as helping minority families in tight housing markets or opening up suburbs to the poor. But housing allowances are the right tool for many problems, such as the emerging concern for the victims of "gentrification." The widely heralded rediscovery of city neighborhoods, which is prompting affluent families to refurbish charming brownstones and townhouses, is also pushing many poor renters out of their homes. Housing allowances would probably be highly effective in helping these families find other places to live nearby while coping with rising rents.

The most valuable contribution of social experiments may be that they raise new and troublesome questions about the purposes of public policy. The housing allowance experiment began by trying to find answers to questions about the design of a national program of cash assistance for housing. But its operation brought to the surface a serious conflict between the priorities of the poor and those of housing program administrators.

The poor do not give housing quality the high priority that program administrators do. In the long history of housing reform in the United States, this is the first time that the beneficiaries of a program have been able to make their views known on how the money should be spent. The views of the reformers have always dominated; in fact, we know almost nothing about whether earlier generations of slum-dwellers would rather have had the cash than either model tenements or public housing projects. But the poor of this generation, at least, have spoken clearly through the housing allowance experiment. Their main problem, as they see it, is cost, not quality. Interestingly, a household survey commissioned by HUD just before the housing allowance experiment began also suggested that housing quality was not a serious problem for the urban poor (de Leeuw, Schnare, and Struyk, 1976). In three cities surveyed in 1972, fully 84 percent of the households with incomes below $5,000 rated their housing units as "excellent" or "satisfactory." The housing allowance experience confirms and amplifies this finding. The poor still have serious housing problems, but they are not the ones most public programs address.

The real test of whether the housing allowance experiment was a success will be whether policymakers reexamine the purposes of government action in the light of its unexpected results. An important question for the next wave of housing programs is: Who should decide how much housing a family ought to consume and where it ought to live, the family or an administrator who sets the standards? (The higher the standards are set, the fewer people will take part.) There may conceivably be public benefits involved that would justify overriding the preferences of the poor themselves and requiring them to pay for better housing than they would otherwise choose to do. If that is so, federal officials have a responsibility to present the case for setting aside the wishes of the poor.

At a minimum, the housing allowance experiment calls into question those housing goals that are based mainly on the weight of tradition or on the organizational mission of an established federal agency. It offers instead a rare opportunity to recognize the changing needs of the clients.

NOTE

Parts of this chapter are revised versions of my article, "Housing Allowances: An Experiment That Worked," *Public Interest*, no. 59 (Spring 1980):15-35. Many individuals associated with the organizations responsible for the housing allowance experiment generously gave of their time and made available reports and other information. I would like to thank especially Jerry J. Fitts and Howard Hammerman of the Department of Housing and Urban Development, Ira S. Lowry of the Rand Corporation, and Clark Abt and Helen Bakeman of Abt Associates.

REFERENCES

Bendick, Marc, Jr., and James P. Zais. 1978. *Incomes and Housing: Lessons from Experiments with Housing Allowances.* Washington, D.C.: Urban Institute.
de Leeuw, Frank, Anne B. Schnare, and Raymond J. Struyk. 1976. "Housing." In William Gorham and Nathan Glazer (eds.), *The Urban Predicament.* Washington, D.C.: Urban Institute.
Frieden, Bernard J. 1980. "What Have We Learned from the Housing Allowance Experiment?" *Habitat International* 5: 227–254.
Hartman, Chester. 1975. *Housing and Social Policy.* Englewood Cliffs, N.J.: Prentice-Hall.
Hartman, Chester, and Dennis Keating. 1974. "The Housing Allowance Delusion." *Social Policy* 4 (January–February): 31–37.
Lowry, Ira S. 1971. "Housing Assistance for Low-Income Urban Families: A Fresh Approach." In U.S. Congress, House Committee on Banking and Currency, *Papers Submitted to Subcommittee on Housing Panels*, 92d Cong., 1st sess. Part 2. 489–523.
Merrill, Sally, and Catherine A. Joseph. 1979. *Draft Report on Housing Improvements and Upgrading in the Housing Allowance Demand Experiment.* Cambridge, Mass.: Abt Associates.
Rand Corporation. 1970. *Rental Housing in New York City.* New York: New York City Housing and Development Administration.
———. 1978. *Fourth Annual Report of the Housing Assistance Supply Experiment.* R2302-HUD. Santa Monica, Calif., May.
Stegman, Michael A. 1972. *Housing Investments in the Inner City: The Dynamics of Decline.* Cambridge, Mass.: M.I.T. Press.
Sternlieb, George. 1966. *The Tenement Landlord.* New Brunswick, N.J.: Rutgers Urban Studies Center.
Temple, Frederick W., William L. Holhouse, Jr., M. G. Trend, David W. Budding, and Mireille L. Ernst. 1976. *Third Annual Report of the Administrative Agency Experiment Evaluation.* Cambridge, Mass.: Abt Associates.
U.S. Department of Housing and Urban Development. 1979. *Experimental Housing Allowance Program: A 1979 Report of Findings.* Washington D.C.: Office of Policy Development and Research, Division of Housing Research.
Weinberg, Daniel, Reilly Atkinson, Avis Vidal, James Wallace, and Glen Weisbrod. 1977. *Locational Choice.* Pt. 1, *Search and Mobility in the Housing Allowance Demand Experiment.* Cambridge, Mass.: Abt Associates.

14

Rent Control in the United States

KENNETH BAAR AND DENNIS KEATING

In contrast to Western European nations, where national rent control laws have been standard, the national housing policies of the United States generally have not included rent control. To the extent that rents have been controlled in the United States, their regulation has been imposed by state and local governments (except during World War II and under federal price controls in effect from August 1971 through January 1973). All of the current rent control laws have been adopted by cities, with the exception of New York laws, which have been adopted by the state. In some states cities cannot enact rent controls without specific state authorization, while in other states cities have broad home rule powers that include the power to adopt rent regulations.

Approximately one-third of U.S. households rent, rather than own, their dwellings. In urban areas the percentage of tenant households is substantially higher. Presently, approximately 3 million of the 28 million rental units in the United States are subject to some type of state or local rent regulation. Rent controls are in effect in cities in California, Massachusetts, New Jersey, New York, and in Washington, D.C.

HISTORICAL DEVELOPMENT

World War I–Era Rent Controls

Rent controls were first adopted in the United States at the end of World War I. During the war public pressure, engineered by local anti-profiteering committees, was targeted at "excessive" rent increases. After the war rent control laws were adopted in many cities, including New York City and Washington, D.C.

The ordinances of that era, rather than setting objective standards for rent increases, permitted tenants to raise excessive rent increases as a defense in eviction actions for nonpayment of rent. In considering rent disputes, the courts held that landlords were constitutionally entitled to fair return on the market value of their property, although a few courts concluded that a return-on-market-value approach to fair return was circular.

During that era laissez-faire and freedom of contract among private parties were viewed by the U.S. Supreme Court as central constitutional rights. In 1921 the Court took the position that rent controls were only constitutional when justified by emergency conditions (*Block* v. *Hirsh* and *Marcus Brown Holding Company* v. *Feldman*, 1921). Three years later the Court ruled that conditions created by World War I could no longer serve as a basis for claiming an emergency that justified rent controls (*Chastleton Corp.* v. *Sinclair*, 1924).

World War II–Era Regulations

In 1942, just after the United States entered World War II, federal rent regulations were instituted in designated "defense areas" as part of a national policy of wage and price controls. (The defense areas contained most of the nation's rental units.) Under the legislation rents were rolled back to their prewar levels, and the Office of Price Administration (OPA) was granted the authority to establish standards for across-the-board increases and individual building rent adjustments. Pursuant to these powers, the OPA authorized regional across-the-board increases designed to cover operating cost increases and individual adjustments for capital improvements, operating expense increases, and special circumstances (such as non-arm's-length transactions). Evictions were limited to specified grounds, such as nonpayment of rent, damage to the premises, or owner-occupancy.

The constitutionality of the federal rent controls was challenged. However, since the legal challenges of the 1920s the constitutional setting had changed. During the 1930s, in the face of national and local economic regulation designed to deal with the economic crisis of the depression, the U.S. Supreme Court had retreated from its prior position that laissez-faire and freedom of private contract were constitutionally required. In 1934 it had ruled that price controls were valid as long as they had some rational basis (*Nebbia* v. *New York*).

In response to constitutional challenges during and after World War II, the courts ruled that rent controls were justified by a war-generated emergency, rather than addressing the question of whether or not such regulations, like other types of price regulations, were valid as long as they had a rational basis. This development had substantial implications for state court consideration of the constitutionality of local rent controls in subsequent peacetime periods. In regard to fair return, the federal courts ruled that return-on-value approaches were nonsensical and circular in the context of price regulations (*Wilson* v. *Brown*, 1943).

After World War II the federal rent controls were annually renewed with accompanying resolutions that they were temporary measures. In 1953 the federal rent control legislation expired. In some areas state or local controls were adopted. In several instances local controls were terminated by state court rulings that rent control measures were invalid because they no longer had an emergency justification. The state courts reached this conclusion notwithstanding the depression-era changes in federal judicial doctrines applicable to price regulations. By 1956 all state and local rent control regulations had been terminated, with the exception of those in New York City, where over 80 percent of the residents were tenants.

New York City Rent Controls

The New York City experience with rent controls from 1950 through 1969 played a major role in creating a negative image for rent regulation. Under the New York City laws that were in effect until 1969, (1) no annual across-the-board increases were permitted; (2) 15 percent increases were permitted upon vacancies; (3) there were extensive provisions for individual adjustments for capital improvements and service increases; and (4) units constructed after February 1947 were exempted from regulation.

The combination of the failings in the design of New York City's rent control standards and of its severe urban housing problems served to give rent control a particularly bad reputation. Limiting increases to vacancy gave an incentive to landlords to harass tenants and reduce maintenance in order to stimulate turnover, while serving as an economic incentive for tenants not to move. The vacancy increase policy resulted in situations where rents for comparable units, even within the same building, varied tremendously.

Widespread abandonment of properties by landlords was attributed to the rent controls, notwithstanding the facts that abandonment rates were as high in other cities (Bartelt and Lawson, 1986). and that under the New York rent regulations landlords had a right to a 6 percent net return on the value of their properties.

In 1969 and 1970 New York City amended its rent control law (Keating, 1987) to provide for annual across-the-board increases under its rent control law and adopted a rent stabilization ordinance that applied to units constructed between 1947 and 1969 and later to rent-controlled units that had become vacant since the repeal of vacancy decontrol in 1974. Under the rent control law annual across-the-board increases of 7.5 percent are permitted, while under rent stabilization annual increases are determined on the basis of studies of increases in apartment operating costs. In some years additional increases were permitted for rent-stabilized units that became vacant. Since 1974 rent-controlled units have been transferred upon vacancy to the rent stabilization system. By 1986 about 90 percent of the regulated units were covered by the rent stabilization law.

The Emergence of Peacetime Rent Controls (1970–85)

At the beginning of the 1970s, for the first time in U.S. history, rent controls that were not justified by a war-created emergency were adopted outside of New York. Boston and several neighboring suburbs adopted rent controls after the state legislature authorized local controls in 1970. Approximately 100 New Jersey municipalities adopted ordinances pursuant to their home rule powers after the state legislature failed to adopt a state law. Rent controls were also adopted in Maryland; Berkeley, California; Miami Beach, Florida; and Washington, D.C. However, the Maryland and Miami Beach controls expired by the mid-1970s.

Massachusetts

Under the Massachusetts local regulations, across-the-board increases are permitted periodically based on operating cost studies. Under individual-adjustment fair-return standards, owners have been entitled to increases in net operating income tied to all or part of the increase in the cost of living. In 1976 Boston added a "total" vacancy decontrol provision under which units that become vacant after that date are exempted from regulation. As a result, most of the units in that city are exempted.

New Jersey

New Jersey municipal ordinances originally permitted annual across-the-board increases tied to the cost of living and in addition allowed pass-throughs of property tax increases. In response to the steep inflation of the mid-1970s, the ordinances were amended to limit annual increases to a fixed percentage (usually about 5 percent) or a percentage of the increase in the cost of living (usually 50 percent–75 percent). New Jersey ordinances use a variety of types of individual-adjustment fair-return standards.

In the late 1970s and early 1980s a substantial number of the ordinances were amended to include vacancy decontrol provisions. The latter development was largely spurred by landlord stimulation of homeowner fears that rent controls would lead to a reduction in rental properties' share of the property tax base and therefore increase the property tax burden of homeowners. This fear emerged even in communities where apartments were only a small fraction of the property tax base. In fact, it was impossible to attribute any shifts in the property tax base to particular causal factors (Baar, 1984). While the homeowner majority has not felt a direct stake in the impacts of rent controls on rents, landlords' profits, maintenance, and new construction, it has been particularly sensitive to the spectre of increased property taxes.

California

While New Jersey rent controls have been significantly weakened by the property tax issue, in California property tax reform has acted as an important stimulant to the rent control movement. In 1978, in response to spiraling property values and property assessments, California voters passed an amendment to the state constitution (Proposition 13) that limited local property tax rates to 1 percent (about one-third of prior rates) and rolled back assessments to their 1975 levels, with reassessments at market value only occurring when properties are sold.

Tenants, who were accustomed to hearing landlords claim that their rent increases were justified by property tax increases, expected that landlords would reduce their rents after the passage of Proposition 13. Instead, rents continued to increase at an exceptional rate consistent with the spiraling property values and housing-shortage conditions of that period. In 1978 and 1979 rent controls were adopted by Los Angeles, San Francisco, San Jose, Berkeley, and Santa Monica.

In the following years a major mobile-home rent control movement emerged. (Presently, California has approximately 380,000 mobile homes.) Mobile-home owners are in a particularly difficult position. They own their mobile homes, which typically cost from $20,000 to $50,000, but the land on which their mobile homes are situated is usually in mobile-home parks where spaces are rented.

In fact, the mobile ("manufactured") homes are not mobile. Moving these homes typically costs from $5,000 to $10,000. Furthermore, park owners commonly exclude the entry of older mobile homes. The combination of the substantial investments made by mobile-home–park tenants, the demographic make-up of mobile-home–park tenantry (primarily senior citizens), and their concentration in parks that typically have several hundred units, has resulted in a particularly powerful political bloc. Presently, approximately 40 California cities regulate mobile-home space rents.

Approximately 13 cities regulate apartment rents. In a number of cities tenant-sponsored rent control initiatives have been defeated. On the other hand, a 1980 landlord-sponsored statewide initiative that would have substantially circumscribed local powers to design rent regulations was defeated (Keating, 1985b).

The rent control ordinances of the larger cities (Los Angeles, San Francisco, and San Jose) include vacancy decontrol provisions. Typically, annual across-the-board rent increases are tied to the cost of living. Fair-return standards in California rent control ordinances commonly guarantee landlords the right to an increase in net operating income at a percentage of the increase in the cost of living.

Other States

Efforts to institute rent controls have been rejected by local governments in some major cities. Rent control initiatives have been defeated in other cities. In a few cities measures passed by the voters have been invalidated by the courts (Baltimore and Miami Beach). As an alternative to rent control, some communities have adopted voluntary rent mediation programs, which have not had a major impact on rent increases.

In response to the successful local efforts for rent controls, national and statewide counterefforts have emerged. On a national level opponents of rent control have introduced legislation that would penalize localities with rent regulations. Proposed penalties have included the loss of federal housing entitlements or federal mortgage insurance (President's Commission on Housing,

1982). Several states, including Arizona, Florida, Michigan, Texas, and Washington, have banned local rent ordinances.

THE DESIGN OF RENT CONTROL ORDINANCES

Rent control ordinances vary substantially in design. Frequently they have been amended. In this section some of the ordinances' principal characteristics and significant variations are described (see also Baar, 1983).

Coverage

Ordinances typically contain the following exemptions: owner-occupied dwellings with four or fewer units; care facilities; bona fide nonprofit institutions; and government-owned or subsidized units. Some ordinances exempt single-family dwellings, luxury units (typically defined as units renting for above a specified amount as of a pre–rent control date), or substantially rehabilitated units.

Virtually all rent control laws exempt new construction. These exemptions follow one of two principal forms: either they exempt all units built after a designated date approximating the date of passage of the ordinance, or they permit the landlord to set the base rent for the newly constructed unit but subject subsequent increases to regulation.

Base-Date Rollbacks and Across-the-Board Increases

Rent control laws usually establish as legal base rents those rents that were in effect for each unit at a designated date prior to the adoption of the ordinance (usually a year or less prior to adoption). An annual across-the-board increase is the principal rent increase mechanism under most ordinances. There are three principal types of across-the-board increase mechanisms:

1. Fixed percentage increases (for example, 5 percent or 7 percent per year)
2. Percentage increases equal to 50 percent or more of the annual percentage increase in the Consumer Price Index (CPI), all items
3. Increases determined by a city commission based on an apartment operating cost study

The concept of tying annual increases to the Consumer Price Index has commonly run into strong opposition from either landlords or tenants based on particular inflation trends at the time the ordinance was adopted. Some laws have placed a floor and/or a ceiling on increases tied to the CPI (such as a 3 percent minimum and a 7 percent maximum) in order to alleviate the most severe consequences of using such an approach.

Under the operating cost study methodology a weighted index of apartment operating costs is used in lieu of the CPI in order to calculate allowable rent increases. The advantage of the operating cost methodology is that it may be superior to the CPI as an indicator of apartment operating cost increases, since the CPI reflects the market basket of all types of goods and services that are purchased by a typical urban household rather than the operating expenses associated with renting apartments. Two types of apartment operating costs, utilities and property taxes, are often subject to far more dramatic fluctuations than the CPI.

The operating cost approach requires fairly complex annual data collection and analysis, which can be the subject of intense political debate. As a result of the complexity of the data analysis, it may be reformulated by a public commission in order to obtain a desired result. Whether or not a "political reanalysis" process takes place, the final outcome is seen as a political decision by a rent board. In contrast, the CPI methodology is generally seen as credible and nonpolitical because it is beyond the control of the administering agency.

Across-the-board increase regulations commonly authorize additional increases for landlords who pay for heat and/or electricity. Some laws have permitted dollar-for-dollar pass-throughs of property tax increases (which often vary greatly among properties).

Individual Adjustments for Fair Return, Capital Improvements, Reductions in Services or Inadequate Maintenance

Fair-Return Adjustments

The courts have concluded that landlords are constitutionally guaranteed the right to a "fair return" under rent controls. However, the question of what constitutes a fair return has been the subject of an unresolved 60-year-long debate within the judiciary, rent boards, and legislative bodies.

Virtually all rent control laws authorize individual adjustments for fair return and capital improvements (Keating, 1985a). While in most rent-controlled jurisdictions only a small percentage of landlords rely on individual fair-return adjustments, in some jurisdictions individual adjustments are used to set rents for a substantial portion of regulated units. Under California mobile-home space rent control ordinances that do not permit across-the-board increases, the individual fair-return mechanism has been the sole rent increase mechanism.

Five principal types of fair-return standards have been used:

Cash Flow

Fair Rent = Operating Expenses + Mortgage Interest

Under this standard landlords are entitled to rents that are adequate to cover their operating expenses and mortgage payments. (Issues related to this standard

are discussed in the following section in combination with the discussion of the
return-on-investment standard.)

Return on Investment

$$\text{Fair Rent} = \text{Operating Expenses} + \text{Mortgage Interest} + x\% \text{ of Cash Investment}$$

Under this standard landlords are entitled to rents that are adequate to cover
mortgage payments and mortgage interest and yield a designated rate of return
on cash investment.

The cash-flow and return-on-investment standards assure the right to a profit
(or at least to an even cash flow), no matter what investment and mortgage
interest expenses are incurred. These standards are commonly subject to the
proviso that increases in investment or mortgage payments after the adoption of
rent regulations will not be considered. These types of standards discriminate
against long-term owners, who typically have mortgage interest and investments
that are low by current standards, while favoring recent purchasers who were
relying on substantial rent increases in order to obtain an adequate return. Recently, the concept of indexing original investment for inflation has been introduced in some jurisdictions that use a return-on-investment standard.

Return on Value

$$\text{Fair Rent} = \text{Operating Expenses} + x\% \text{ of Value}$$

Under this standard landlords are entitled to rents that are adequate to cover
operating expenses and yield a designated rate of return on value. Mortgage
payments are not considered under this standard because a return is allowed on
the whole value of the property rather than just on the cash investment.

The value of a property is determined by its rental income. Therefore, it is
circular to use the value in order to determine what rental income should be
permitted. When return-on-value standards have been used in eastern states,
value has usually been defined as assessed value in order to avoid protracted
and expensive debates over the value of the property.

Percentage Net Operating Income

$$\frac{\text{Net Operating Income}}{\text{Gross Income}} \geq x\%$$

Under this standard landlords are guaranteed that their net operating income will
equal a designated percentage (typically 40 to 50 percent) of gross income. The

principal weakness of the standard is that net operating income/gross income ratios normally vary among properties according to their age and the desirability of their location. These differences are reflected in differences in purchase price.

Maintenance of Net Operating Income

Fair Rent = Base-Period Net Operating Income +
Current Operating Expenses

Under this standard a landlord has a right to preserve the net operating income level that a building had as of a designated "base" period. When this type of approach is used, fair net operating income is typically defined as base-period net operating income adjusted by a designated percentage of the percent increase in the CPI. (For example, a standard may guarantee the right to a net operating income that has increased by at least half the inflation rate over base-period levels.) The maintenance-of-net-operating-income approach has become widespread in recent years (except in New Jersey). It is consistent with the underlying concept of rent controls, which is to stabilize rent and profit levels.

Capital Improvements Adjustments

Capital improvement standards permit landlords to pass through to tenants the amortized cost of capital improvements. Amortization schedules vary substantially among jurisdictions and often are a critical determinant of the volume of petitions for capital improvement adjustments. Other critical determinants of the volume of rent increase applications based on capital improvements are whether applications are approved administratively or after a hearing, whether interest expenses are considered as a cost of the capital improvement, and whether other issues such as building maintenance are considered.

Rent Decreases for Inadequate Maintenance or Reductions in Services

Some rent control laws authorize the administering agency to reduce rents for individual buildings or units in situations where services or amenities have been reduced since the adoption of rent controls or where maintenance has been inadequate. There is little documentation and analysis on the use of such mechanisms.

Vacancy Decontrol

A substantial portion of U.S. rent control laws contain vacancy decontrol provisions. Under the most common type of vacancy decontrol, when a unit becomes vacant, the landlord sets the initial rent for the subsequent tenant. Thereafter, rent increases are subject to regulation until the unit becomes vacant again. Some laws permit only limited increases upon vacancies (for example, 5 or 10 percent). Under a few laws units that become vacant after a specified date are no longer subject to rent regulation.

Landlords have seen vacancy decontrols as the key to making rent controls reasonable, while tenant groups have taken the position that vacancy decontrols undercut the effective operation and a major purpose of rent controls. Under rent regulations that include vacancy decontrols, rent increase patterns tend to parallel those in unregulated markets, in which substantial rent increases are usually reserved for the time when units become vacant. However, rent controls with vacancy decontrols do prevent the common practice by new owners of passing through increases in financing costs caused by the purchase.

Arguments in favor of vacancy decontrols have been based on claims that they are necessary to permit landlords to obtain sufficient rent increases to maintain and improve their properties, and that prospective tenants do not need rent protections because they are free to accept or reject the rent level demanded by the landlord. Vacancy decontrols have been opposed on the basis that they provide an incentive to landlords to stimulate vacancies by reducing maintenance or harassing tenants. Opponents of vacancy decontrols have also claimed that market rents are unreasonably high in housing-shortage areas and that it is essential to control rent increases for vacant units in order to maintain the overall affordability of rental units.

Just Cause for Eviction

Under U.S. state landlord-tenant laws "just cause" is not required for evictions, except in rent-controlled jurisdictions (and the state of New Jersey). Typically, in the absence of a lease providing otherwise, 30 days' notice of termination is all that is required before commencing an eviction proceeding.

Under laws that require just cause for evictions, reasons for eviction commonly include failure to pay rent, violation of the rental agreement (other than a promise to vacate the premises by a certain date), nuisance or disturbance of other tenants, use of the premises for an illegal purpose, refusal to provide reasonable access for repairs or to show the premises to prospective buyers, subletting without the landlord's approval, major repairs or renovation, and occupancy by the owner or a close relative. Just-cause-for-eviction requirements have been considered central to rent regulation. Without them the security-of-tenure objectives of rent regulations would not be accomplished, and the threat of eviction could be used to obtain illegal rents.

In recent years many rent control ordinances have been amended in order to address abuses stemming from evictions and threats of eviction. Owner- and relative-occupancy eviction provisions have enabled landlords to move in temporarily and then rerent their units at a much higher rent. Responses to eviction abuses have included limitations on the frequency of owner-occupancy evictions within a building, permitting owner-occupancy evictions only in smaller buildings, penalties for bad-faith evictions, and requirements for relocation payments.

Administration

Rent controls are usually administered by local boards that are appointed by the mayor and city council of the municipality. In two cities, Berkeley and Santa Monica, California, the rent boards are elected. Boards' primary responsibilities may include determining annual across-the-board rent increases based on operating cost studies, promulgating fair-return regulations, and reviewing individual landlord and tenant applications for rent adjustments.

Financing

The administration of rent control programs is often financed by annual apartment unit registration fees imposed on landlords, which may be passed through to tenants on a pro rata monthly basis. Fees for individual rent adjustment petitions are also common.

In New Jersey municipal ordinances are typically administered by volunteer boards without staff (other than a secretary). In other states administration expenses range from $5 to $72 per year per unit.

Conversion and Demolition Controls

During the past decade condominium and cooperative conversions have decreased the supply of rental housing in some cities. In response to these developments, many rent-controlled jurisdictions have restricted conversions, have not permitted owner-occupancy as a just cause for eviction from units that have been converted, or have required very substantial notice periods and relocation benefits. In 1984 the U.S. Court of Appeals upheld a New Jersey statute that granted life tenancy to low- and moderate-income senior citizens occupying units that are converted after the passage of the state law (*Troy* v. *Renna*).

Demolition restrictions have been adopted in some jurisdictions where it is profitable to purchase apartment buildings, demolish them, and replace them with condominium units or other uses. Restrictions on demolitions are in effect in New York City; Berkeley and Santa Monica, California; and Brookline and Cambridge, Massachusetts. Legal challenges to demolition restrictions have been rejected by the U.S. Supreme Court (*Fresh Pond Shopping Center* v. *Cambridge Rent Control Bd.* and *Nash* v. *City of Santa Monica*).

THE DEBATE OVER RENT CONTROLS

A housing policy that has an immediate impact on rents and the fortunes of a multitude of investors is bound to lead to intense controversy. The controversy has been accentuated by the fact that the view that rents should be controlled conflicts with the prevailing American ideology that the marketplace provides the best solution to housing supply and price problems.

Debate over Impacts

The principal arguments against rent controls have been the following:

1. They deter new rental construction, and therefore, by limiting supply, hurt rather than help the interests of tenants in the long run.
2. They lead to undermaintenance of rental units, thereby shortening their life, and in some cases they even lead to abandonment.
3. They lead to the conversion of rental housing to more profitable uses.
4. They lead to inefficient and expensive administration.
5. They disproportionately benefit middle-income tenants at the expense of low-income tenants. This occurs because when rents are held below market levels, landlords tend to choose single persons and higher-income households.
6. They shift the property tax burden to homeowners.

While the thrust of the arguments against rent controls has been that they hurt tenants, especially low-income tenants, the proponents of the arguments have not included tenant groups.

The debate over the impact of rent controls has not been a model of high-quality analysis. Generally, conclusions about the impacts of rent controls have been based on anecdotes, econometric equations, or ideological pronouncements by economists, rather than on empirical data. For example, the arguments that rent controls deter new apartment construction almost uniformly fail to provide any new construction data (President's Commission on Housing, 1982; Rydell, 1981), or the data is insufficient to provide a reasonable basis for analysis. The analyses also fail to compare the rent increases that are permitted in rent-controlled jurisdictions with the rent increases that are occurring in the balance of the nation.

In any case, it is particularly difficult to determine the impact of rent regulation. There are a multitude of other variables that may have an impact on housing production and maintenance. These include zoning, mortgage interest rates, real estate investment tax benefits, location, code enforcement, and trends in the rates of return in alternative investments. Quantifying and controlling for these variables can be a virtually impossible task.

Trends in housing maintenance are extremely hard to measure. Also, it is often difficult to draw causal conclusions from data. For example, a reduction in landlord maintenance expenditures may reflect either a reduction in expenditures that affect long-term housing quality, a reduction in costs due to a reduction in turnover, a reduction in cosmetic types of maintenance that do not affect the life of a dwelling, or a shift in interior maintenance costs (such as painting) to the tenant.

The most comprehensive studies of rent control have been undertaken in New York City, where a triennial study is required in order to prove that there is still a housing emergency that justifies the extension of rent controls. Studies by Sternlieb (1972) and the Rand Corporation (1970), which concluded that the New York rent controls of the 1960s did not permit rent increases adequate to cover operating cost increases, helped provide impetus for the introduction of across-the-board increases in the 1970s. Other major case-study evaluations of the impact of rent controls include studies of rent control in Massachusetts (Selesnick, 1974; Sternlieb, 1974) and Los Angeles.

Analyses of the impact of rent control on new construction in New Jersey have included Gruen, Gruen and Associates' (1977) projection that significant negative impacts would develop and Gilderbloom's (1981b) and Baretto's (1985) findings that there have been no significant impacts.

Ideological Debates

Ideological positions range from the view that housing is a basic right that can only be assured by insuring that rents are maintained at affordable levels to the view that rent control unreasonably forces landlords to subsidize tenants. In 1982 the President's Commission on Housing concluded:

Moreover, rent control essentially yields an income redistribution from landlords to tenants by implicitly taxing landlords for the benefit of tenants. In general such a tax is inefficient and inequitable. Rental property owners are often small-scale investors who do not have large financial resources. More importantly, such a tax ignores the fact that individuals can move to another area to avoid or take advantage of local redistribution programs. (President's Commission on Housing, 1982: 92)

This statement is consistent with historic biases against regulations that benefit tenants. In fact, depending on one's point of view, terms such as ''inequitable,'' ''taxation,'' or ''income redistribution'' may be selected to describe a panopoly of U.S. ''institutions'' that alter the housing market, including mortgage interest and property tax deductions from income taxes for homeowners, zoning restrictions that severely restrict the amount of land that is available for multifamily rental construction, and apartment owners' tax depreciation allowances. Each of these policies has ''redistribution'' consequences.

Rent controls have also been criticized on the basis that they benefit all tenants within a rent-controlled jurisdiction, rather than being limited to low- and moderate-income tenants who are especially in need of protection. This argument subjects rent control to a means test that federal policies designed to assist homeowners could not meet. Mortgage interest and property tax deductions are not targeted toward households that need the most assistance. In fact, the inverse is true: the higher the income of the household, the greater the benefit of the deductions. Zoning and local land-use policies are commonly designed to exclude types of housing that are affordable to low-income households (*NAACP* v. *Mt. Laurel*, New Jersey Supreme Court, 1975 and 1983).

ASSESSMENT OF FUTURE TRENDS

Increasing rents may lead to greater political pressure for rent controls. In the past few years U.S. rents have increased at a greater rate than the cost of living (Consumer Price Index, all items). From January 1980 to January 1986 the residential rent index increased by 41 percent, while the Consumer Price Index, all items, increased by 49 percent. However, rents and rent increase patterns have varied enormously among regions. Therefore, it is difficult to project whether or not rent controls will become more or less widespread in the future.

National rent control legislation is extremely unlikely. Tenants' greatest political strength is at the local level, and therefore rent controls will most probably continue to be adopted only by states and municipalities.

REFERENCES

Extensive bibliographies (listed separately) have already been published. These references are more recent publications and sources cited in this article.

Baar, Ken. 1983. "Guidelines for Drafting Rent Control Laws: Lessons of a Decade." *Rutgers Law Review* 35: 721–885.
———. 1984. "Rent Controls and the Property Tax Base: The Political-Economic Relationship." *Property Tax Journal* 3: 1–20.
Baretto, Felix. 1985. "Rental Housing Production and the Fiscal Effects of Rent Control." Ph. D. dissertation, University of Texas, Arlington.
Bartelt, David, and Ronald Lawson. 1986. "Rent Control and Abandonment in New York City: A Look at the Evidence." In Rachel G. Bratt, Chester Hartman, and Ann Meyerson (eds.), *Critical Perspectives on Housing*. Philadelphia: Temple University Press. 180–201.
Gilderbloom, John. 1981a. "Moderate Rent Control." *Urban Affairs Quarterly*. 17: 123–142.
——— (ed.). 1981b. *Rent Control: A Source Book*. Santa Barbara, Calif.: Foundation for National Progress.
Gruen, Gruen and Associates. 1977. *Rent Control in New Jersey*. San Francisco: Gruen, Gruen and Associates.
Keating, Dennis. 1985a. "The Elmwood Experiment: The Use of Commercial Rent Stabilization to Preserve a Diverse Neighborhood Shopping District." *Journal of Urban and Contemporary Law*. 28: 107–194.
Keating, Dennis. 1985b. "Rent Control: Dispersion and Adaptation." In Paul L. Niebanck (ed.), *The Rent Control Debate*. Chapel Hill: University of North Carolina Press. 61–62.

————. 1987. "Landlord Self-Regulation: New York City's Rent Stabilization System, 1969–1985." *Journal of Urban and Contemporary Law* 31: 77–134.

President's Commission on Housing. 1982. *Report.* Washington, D.C.: Government Printing Office.

Rand Corporation. 1970. *Rental Housing in New York City.* New York: New York City Housing and Development Administration.

Rydell, Peter, et al. 1981. *The Impact of Rent Control on the Los Angeles Housing Market.* Santa Monica, Calif.: Rand Institute.

Selesnick, Herbert. 1974. *A Study of Rent and Eviction Controls in the Commonwealth of Massachusetts.* Boston: Harbridge House.

Sternlieb, George. 1972. *The Urban Housing Dilemma.* New York: New York City Housing and Development Administration.

————. 1974. *The Realities of Rent Control in the Greater Boston Area.* Boston: Greater Boston Area Real Estate Board.

BIBLIOGRAPHIES

Keating, Dennis. 1976. *Rent and Eviction Controls: A Selected Annotated Bibliography.* Chicago: Council of Planning Librarians.

Levin, Marc. 1981. *Rent Control in the United States: An Annotated Bibliography and Guide to the Literature.* Chicago: Council of Planning Librarians.

15

Tenants' Movements in the United States

JOHN I. GILDERBLOOM

In a recent essay Peter Dreier (1982b) laments the fact that since the founding of American sociology, tenants have been virtually ignored as a social group. In a lengthy criticism Dreier (1982b: 179) contends that sociology treats tenants as virtually nonexistent as a group, with little known about renters as agents of social change. According to a recent article by S. S. Duncan (1981: 251), very little is known about the kind of impact renters can have: "Our understanding of the effects of housing reform on social relations and political consciousness is left notably deficient. We are unable to say much about political action or even about class conflict on the economic level."

This chapter will attempt to fill this gap by conducting a review of theoretical and empirical research on tenants' movements and housing policy. It will provide a detailed overview of the tenants' movement in the United States, covering the causes, consequences, goals, and the future of the renters' revolt in the United States.

HISTORICAL OVERVIEW

Historically tenants have not participated in the political process, especially in the area of electoral politics. Alan Heskin in his recent book, *Tenants and the American Dream* (1983), argues that the status of a tenant in the United States is that of a second-class citizen. When the first settlers came to America, non–property owners could not vote or seek elected office (Heskin, 1981: 95). Tenants did not have the right to vote in federal elections until 1860 (Martin, 1976). Even after tenants became eligible to cast a ballot, landlords in certain parts of the East could control a large block of tenant votes (Flanigan and Zingale, 1979: 12). Today tenants are still barred from voting in certain property bond, tax, and special district elections. Even when tenants are allowed to vote in elections, the turnout of tenants is low. In a study done by the U.S. Bureau of the Census (1979), homeowners voted twice as much as renters. In the November 1978 election only 46 percent of the eligible voters turned out. Of those who turned out, 59 percent of the homeowners voted, compared to only 28 percent of the renters. According to the U.S. Census Bureau study (1979: 1), of all the variables related to voting (age, income, region, sex, and race), housing status "appeared to have the strongest relationship with voting." Interviews conducted by the U.S. Census Bureau (1979: 84) found that the most prominent reason given by renters—39 percent of them—for why they did not vote was because they were "not interested, they did not care."

Tenants do, however, take collective action when housing is at stake. History has shown that severe shortages in low-income housing can eventually lead to "violent confrontations between citizens and authorities, and even revolutions, when societies and their governments failed to provide adequate housing" (Rosentraub and Warren, 1986). This is persuasively demonstrated in Roger Friedland's comprehensive study of black urban riots during the 1960s that left 100,000 arrested, 10,000 injured, and 300 dead. He concluded that "local public policies played an important role in conditioning the city's level of black political violence" (1982: 162). Conducting a regression analysis to discover determinants of aggregate riot severity in U.S. cities, Friedland found that—all else being equal amount of urban renewal and lack of low-rent housing relative to demand were positively correlated with riot severity. Between 1949 and 1974 urban renewal demolished 500,000 low-income housing units; only 100,000 units were replaced, and most of these were for middle-income people rather than the poor (Shipnuck, Keating, and Morgan, 1974). Even traditionally conservative observers anticipate "a major housing calamity," as one of the rental housing industry's most prominent spokesman put it (Preston Butch, cochair of the National Multi-Housing Council, quoted in Betz, 1981). During the late 1970s and early 1980s in West Germany, Holland, Switzerland, and England, riots broke out over the lack of affordable and decent housing (Hall, 1981: 15–16; Glen and Shearer, 1980)

CURRENT STATUS

During the seventies and early eighties tenants responded to the affordability crisis by demanding rent control in a growing number of communities across the United States (Gilderbloom, 1981a, 1983, 1984). Rent control has become the principal organizing strategy of most tenants' unions, who see in this issue a concrete demand with immediate and tangible results. The past few years have witnessed the creation of hundreds of locally based tenants' unions, statewide organizations in California, Michigan, Massachusetts, New Jersey, Texas, and Illinois, and a National Tenants' Organization (see Dreier, Gilderbloom, and Appelbaum, 1980; Gilderbloom, 1980; Gilderbloom and Keating, 1982; Dreier and Atlas, 1980). Roughly 130 cities and counties in the United States currently have some form of rent regulation, including over 100 municipalities in New Jersey, as well as cities and counties in Massachusetts, New York, Virginia, Maryland, Alaska, Connecticut, and California. Over half of all rental units in

California, New York, Massachusetts, and New Jersey are presently rent controlled; an estimated 10 percent of the nation's housing stock is covered by some form of rent control. Many other cities are now considering some form of rent control to put the brakes on runaway rental housing costs.

Although the causes of the renters' movement have not been tested empirically with reliable research and statistical procedures, social movement theory provides certain plausible explanations for the rise and development of the tenants' movement in the United States. While these theories often compete with each other for dominance in the arena of social movement theory, all shed a certain amount of light on the rise of the renters' movement (Chafetz and Dworkin, 1986; Wood and Jackson, 1982).

Renters' movements, whether reformist or radical, are dependent upon the degree of structural strain within society (Smelser, 1963). The successful passage of rent control occurred in cities with relatively high rent levels tied together with high home prices (Gilderbloom and Keating, 1982). During the 1970s rents soared, increasing at twice the rate of tenants' wages. In 1970 one-third of all renters paid more than a quarter of their income for rent; by 1983 this figure had risen to almost one-half of all renters (Gilderbloom and Appelbaum, 1988). Tenants in middle-class communities organized for rent control because high home prices forced them to remain as renters rather than become owners. Moreover, a development of consciousness that views landlords as both a class and as exploitive was also critical in developing support for rent control from both tenants and homeowners (Capek, 1985). Capek (1985: 219) declares that a successful tenants' movement must develop the power to redefine historical identities of both landlord and tenant. She says that, moreover, tenants must frame the issues of "fairness" and "democracy" from their perspective; in other words, tenants must gain symbolic control over the definition of the renters' movement. As Ron Lawson (n.d.: 9) has noted, "Leaving aside the owner of the sweatshop, the landlord has a worse reputation in American urban mythology than the employer."

Ecological explanations are helpful in gaining an understanding of the renters' movement. A majority of the cities that enacted rent control tended to be dense, slow-growing cities. The existence of previous social movements also appears to have planted the seeds for the renters' movement. Many rent-controlled cities are located near areas (San Francisco, Boston, New York, and Washington, D.C.) of major anti-war organizing that took place during the sixties.

Resources also played a critical role in the development of the rent control movement. Rent control campaigns were dependent on philanthropic foundations and government agencies to fund staff and support services. Both Vista Volunteers and Legal Services played a crucial role in the rise of the tenants' movement (see Capek, 1985; Dreier, 1982b). The renters' movement appears to have risen not only from "objective conditions" but from "funding and other sources in the external environment" (Dreier, 1982b: 191; see also Zald and McCarthy, 1979).

The success of the tenants' ability to pass legislation on their behalf depends largely on the degree of tenant consciousness shared by their fellow renters. In a movement for even the mildest kind of government-imposed rent restrictions comes a rise in "tenant consciousness." Tenant consciousness develops when the following conditions are met: (1) tenants view themselves as a group sharing similar problems; (2) they have a common understanding of the causes of their problems; and (3) they have a collective political purpose that responds effectively to these problems (Heskin, 1981: 1; Atlas and Dreier, 1981: 34). Allan Heskin (1981: 1), who has done extensive research on the concept of tenant consciousness, argues that tenants with high consciousness tend to view the market as incapable of supplying decent and affordable housing; they feel that government must regulate the housing market by either limiting rent increases or by developing more public housing, and that renters must become politically organized and active in politics. The tenant who takes this view contrasts sharply with the tenant whom Heskin characterizes as "a landlord lover." These are the tenants who take the side of landlords on all housing issues: they oppose any form of rent control; they view supply and demand as the cause for rising rents; they feel that landlords have the right to raise rents any amount; and they oppose any kind of political actions against the landlord. Among tenants, class distinctions appear to exist.

Heskin argues that tenant consciousness develops through political action on housing issues. Efforts for better housing reveal that capitalism by itself cannot solve the housing problem and that government is needed to intervene directly in the housing market. The market cannot provide affordable housing for the poor because of the high capital cost of new housing, speculation, high interest rates, and landlord cartels (Marcuse, 1981; O'Connor, 1979; Dreier, Gilderbloom, and Appelbaum, 1980). Demands for government intervention range from mild forms of limits on allowable rent increases to more extreme measures such as producing on a massive scale nonmarket forms of housing—limited-equity housing or "human-scale" public housing (Hartman and Stone, 1980).

People will participate in the electoral system when they are organized around an issue that affects them directly. Not surprisingly, housing is one of those issues that tenants consider important. Of the many actions tenants could take, rent control generates the most mass involvement. Other actions do not create the support necessary for renters' movements to be successful. Rent strikes or squatting involve a high degree of personal risk—arrest, loss of possessions, legal costs, fines and perhaps even imprisonment. Campaigns to lower interest rates or increase housing subsidies are "too remote in their targets, too long term in their potential results, too indirect and diffuse in their impact and at least in the United States today, too little" (Marcuse, 1981: 86). Rent control, on the other hand, if restrictive enough, can have a direct and immediate effect on rent and involves little personal risk.

When tenants organize for better housing conditions, they learn that simply protesting is not enough to meet their needs. They find that they must involve themselves directly in the electoral system if they wish to see long-term change occur (Hayden, 1980; Booth, 1981). Tenant activists also learn a valuable ideological lesson: ordinary people working collectively can effect significant change in terms of gaining greater control over the conditions of their lives. Winning one reform can spark demands for even more fundamental changes.

MAJOR THEMES

Rent control laws provide protection against extreme rent increases, unjust evictions, and poor maintenance (Gilderbloom, 1981b). These kinds of protections usually do not exist for tenants in the absence of controls. Within the United States three major forms of rent control laws exist: stringent, strong, and moderate. Stringent rent control laws set rents without regard to landlords' returns on their investments. In postwar New York City, the classic example, rent control laws virtually froze rents for over two decades. Stringent rent controls, most studies have found, have resulted in disinvestment in rental housing—a decline in construction, maintenance, and overall rental property value.

Attempts to avoid these problems resulted in the introduction of moderate rent controls during the early 1970s. Moderate rent controls guarantee a "fair and reasonable return" competitive with other kinds of investments with similar risks. In order to meet this criterion of guaranteeing a "fair return" (Baar and Keating, 1981), most moderate rent control ordinances share the following features as well: exemption of new construction, a requirement of adequate maintenance as a condition of rent increases, guaranteed annual increases as necessary to cover increases in operating costs, and provisions for "pass-through" of major capital cost increases (Baar, 1983). Moderate rent control allowed for rent increases that were close to increases in the Consumer Price Index. The rent control board generally consisted of two landlords, two tenants, and one homeowner appointed by the city council. Administration of the law was generally underfunded and understaffed.

A third form of rent regulation, known as strong rent control, arose during the late 1970s (Gupta and Rea, 1984) because moderate controls simply "stabilized" rents, resulting in the maintenance of excessive rent burdens for many tenants covered by moderate regulations. Tenant activists noted that moderate rent control had only "stabilized" rents and had failed to produce a reduction in the proportion of income going into rent. Strong rent control called for rent increases that were approximately one-half of the Consumer Price Index, no vacancy decontrol, and a well-funded administration. The rent control board was made up of members sympathetic to tenant needs over landlord interests. Finally, strong rent controls were the result of mass-based tenants' movements that focused on taking over the reins of power for the entire city.

SUCCESS OR FAILURE?

Rent control is perhaps the most popular program advocated by tenants to reduce rent levels in U.S. cities (Atlas, 1982; Atlas and Dreier, 1980; Harvey, 1981; O'Connor, 1981; Lowe and Blumberg, 1981; Heskin, 1983; Gilderbloom, 1981b; Gilderbloom and Capek, n.d.). An examination of rent control as a social movement to redistribute wealth from landlord to tenant demonstrates the kind of gains renters can achieve through collective action as well as certain structural limitations to challenging existing private property relations. What kind of power do tenants have to change existing rent levels? In what ways can the social organization of tenants affect rent levels? To what extent can organized tenants alter existing economic relations between landlords and themselves? It is well known that tenants have historically been disorganized and have been a relatively ineffective force in affecting the general conditions under which they live (Heskin, 1981; Marcuse, 1981; Dreier and Atlas, 1980). What happens when renters become organized?

The success or failure of tenants' movements and of their objective of getting tenants a lower rent through rent control is generally dependent on the kind of rent control enacted. Most of the cities that have adopted rent regulation during the past 15 years have opted for moderate rent controls. Moderate rent control has not caused significant rent relief for tenants. Gilderbloom, Gottschalk, and Amory (1986) examined the mean rents for 1970 and 1980 for the 26 rent-controlled and 37 non-rent-controlled cities from Gilderbloom's original study (1984). The data show that the average percentage rent increase between 1970 and 1980 was almost identical for the rent-controlled cities (105 percent) and non-rent-controlled cities (106 percent). Using multiple regression analysis, Gilderbloom (1984) attempted to predict rents as a function of city population, 1970 median rent, income, percentage housing rental, and population increases, as well as rent control. He found that in three of the four equations tested rent control did not have a statistically significant effect on 1980 mean rents. In the one equation where rent control was statistically significant, the unstandardized regression coefficient indicated that mean monthly rents were $39 higher in rent-controlled cities. Similar results were found by Heffley and Santerre (1985) in their study of New Jersey rent controls. Heffley and Santerre (1985: 22) examined 101 rent-controlled cities in New Jersey and found that the average price per room was 8 percent higher in rent-controlled cities. No statistically significant difference exists between rent-controlled cities and overall median contract rent. These data suggest that the impact of New Jersey's rent control law on rents has been to simply match rent increases with those in the noncontrolled sector.

Studies done on the impact of the tenants' movements' efforts through rent controls to reduce rents in other parts of the country with moderate rent control have come up with similar conclusions. Mollenkopf and Pynoos (1973: 71) in their early study of Cambridge, Massachusetts, claimed that not only had rent control failed to reduce rents, but controls had also resulted in "some cases [in] increasing rates of returns to landlords." Daugherbaugh (1975: 2) found that Alaska's rent control programs in Anchorage and Fairbanks were ineffective in holding down rents because of the structure and administration of the law.

Cities that have adopted strong rent control ordinances, such as Berkeley and Santa Monica, demonstrate that redistribution of wealth between landlords and tenants has taken place. In a study of Santa Monica, California, David Shulman (1980) estimates that under rent controls rents increased from $281 in 1978 to $320 in 1980, a rise of 14 percent. If no controls had existed during that same time period, he estimates that rents would have risen to an average of $446 a month, an increase of almost 59 percent in two years. Shulman (1980: 13) calculates that as a result of rent control the amount of rent lost to landlords and the amount of income gained by tenants was roughly $108 million over this 24-month period, thus showing a success for the strong tenant movement in the city.

Santa Monica provides an interesting case study of a strong tenants' movement and the kinds of political and economic gains tenants can win by organizing themselves as a collective force. Until 1978 Santa Monica was run like most other American cities. A local growth machine made up of the local newspaper, banks, real estate interests, and commercial interests had the final say on most political matters, especially development issues (Molotch, 1976). Political analysts could safely label the town as conservative (Capek, 1985).

When rising rents became an issue, tenants organized to put rent control on the ballot. The first time the issue was voted on, rent control proponents lost by a narrow margin. The tenants' pro–rent control campaign was poorly funded and organized, and landlords were able to successfully argue that the answer to tenant woes was not rent control but Proposition 13, which cut landlord taxes by at least half. When Proposition 13 failed to deliver the promised reduction in rents, rent control was again put on the ballot, and victory for the renters' coalition soon followed. After the rent control ordinance was put on the books, a slate of pro–rent control candidates was elected to the city's rent control board and city council. The central theme of these victorious candidates was to defend the rent control law from landlord court challenges.

The renters who wrested control of the city council from the city's conservative probusiness faction won not just rent control by itself but a progressive political program that would have tangible benefits for the city's tenants, who made up 70 percent of the population. It was this progressive political program that spoke to the needs of tenants and inspired them to vote. According to Derek Shearer, campaign coordinator for the victorious Renters Rights Coalition, "I think it shows that the vote for Reagan was not a conservative vote. It was a vote against inflation and wishy-washy, middle of the road, Carter-type Democrats. When Democrats and local activists ran on a progressive program very clearly spelled out, there was a lot of support for it" (Cockburn and Ridgeway, 1981). The Renter's Rights Coalition, a politically progressive platform on the local level, campaigned for rent controls, cooperative housing, limited commercial expansion, inclusionary zoning programs, farmers' markets, food cooperatives, neighborhood anticrime efforts, and controls on toxic wastes. The city council, now dominated by the tenants' movement leaders, attempted to democratize city hall by funding numerous neighborhood organizations, appointing citizen task forces and commissions, and making extensive use of public hearings.

Tenants have also been instrumental in electing progressive candidates in other parts of the country. In March 1981 the voters of Vermont's largest city, Burlington, voted out of the mayor's office a five-term conservative Democrat and elected Bernard Sanders, a tenants' movement supporter and a self-proclaimed "socialist." Sanders focused on the basic issues confronting Burlington's heavily blue-collar population: high rents, unchecked development, property taxes, and neighborhood preservation. Sanders' victory was largely attributed to his pro-tenant stand, which drew together a coalition of tenants, senior citizens, municipal unions, and liberal homeowners. During the election Sanders appealed to their votes by proclaiming:

We have a city that is trying to help a developer build $200,000 luxury waterfront condominiums with pools and health clubs and boutiques and all sorts of upper middle class junk blocks away from an area where people are literally not eating in order to pay their rent and fuel bills. . . . The issue here is that people have been exploited, thrown out of houses. In Burlington a tenant has no rights at all. Hundreds of people have been forced to move from apartments in Burlington because of rent increases. It's about time tenants have legal protection. (McKee, 1981: 8)

Similar kinds of appeals to the "tenant vote" have been successfully used in electing David Sullivan to the Cambridge City Council and Peter Shapiro, backed by the tenants' movement, to the powerful position of Essex County executive in New Jersey (Krinsky, 1981: 10; Atlas and Dreier, 1981: 8). Shapiro was nominated the Democratic candidate for governor of New Jersey for 1985. More recently, the successful election of Mayor Ray Flynn in Boston was won, in part, on the basis of a strong protenant identification. Peter Dreier, whose academic and political work with tenant organizing and legislation is well known, was one of Flynn's chief campaign organizers and is now a top aide of Mayor Flynn.

Tenants have also played a role in pushing through reforms in archaic landlord-tenant laws. This has been especially true in New Jersey, which has the most progressive landlord-tenant law in the United States today. Through the efforts of the 60,000 dues-paying members of the New Jersey Tenants Organization (NJTO), over 100 cities currently have rent control (Atlas and Dreier, 1981: 34). The NJTO has pushed through numerous protenant laws on security deposits, eviction for just cause, receivership, state income tax credits, and landlord disclosure of ownership. Victories in passing protenant legislation have contributed to the continual growth of the NJTO. The laws that have been won by the NJTO have been copied by other tenants' groups and successfully passed in cities and states around the nation.

Tenants' movements for rent control, in addition to giving tenants protection against arbitrary rent increases, can also lead to the building of a continuing broad-based tenants' coalition that works not only for election of protenant officials, but also for reform of landlord-tenant laws (Lawson, 1983; Capek, 1985). This coalition usually consists of seniors, blue-collar workers, and minorities (Jacob, 1979; Leight et al., 1980; Kirschman, 1980). This coalition cuts across age, race, and sex lines. Women often play a prominent leadership role in tenants' movements. During the past 10 years women have been elected president of the statewide tenants' associations in New Jersey and California, while many citywide organizations are also headed by females. It has been these age, race, and sex divisions that have traditionally hampered low- and moderate-income persons from having political clout. The uniting of working and non-working people in the struggle for better housing is particularly significant since conservative politicians have historically used the nonworking poor as a scapegoat for the working person's problems (O'Connor, 1981: 3). Tenants' movements have the support of progressive homeowners.

The debate over whether a city should adopt a rent control ordinance is centered around the rights of landlords versus the rights of tenants. A particularly tough issue that creates tensions between low- and moderate-income persons is the amount rents should be reduced by the proposed rent control ordinance (Heskin, 1981; Marcuse, 1978). In Berkeley, for example, the lack of active support by several key community organizations that felt that the ordinance was too moderate was one reason a proposed rent control ordinance lost at the polls in the late 1970s. While groups can find a common consensus that "rent control is needed," it is almost impossible to find consensus on the kind of rent control necessary (Hartman, 1979; Renters Alliance, 1980; Kirschman, 1980). The argument is usually centered over whether a landlord should be guaranteed a "fair rent" versus guaranteeing a tenant a "fair rent." According to Heskin (1981: 5), this can create sharp divisions among renters:

Another activist said the division in the tenant movement (and society) manifested itself in what was called a "racist" City of Los Angeles rent control law. The law limits general rent increases helping the white population gain control over the problem of rapidly rising rents, but it allows the pass through of the cost of repairs that are necessitated by housing code violations. The law does not relieve the affordability problem for minority tenants, who are now threatened with increasing rents if they demand even the minimum conditions of habitability required by law.

ASSESSMENT OF FUTURE TRENDS

An analysis of the existing tenants' movement in the United States shows how certain economic and political gains can be made. While it is certainly true that the economic gains made by the tenants' movement have been moderate here, it seems likely that more radical rent reduction programs will be on future government agendas. It should also be kept in mind that the tenants' movement in the United States is relatively new. In 1969 there was very little tenant activity in the United States; only a few cities had rent control or tenants' unions. Today the tenants' movement is a force that politicians are only beginning to reckon with. Its inroads to gain decent and affordable housing have barely started. Social policy is not simply an instrument of class domination but of class conflict. Government policies and programs, especially those of a distributional nature, are "an object of class struggle" between propertied and nonpropertied groups. The fight for decent housing has helped to build the bridges linking various disenfranchised groups into an organized body demanding even greater economic and political change in all spheres of life. Unlike most housing reforms that are sponsored by real estate interests to accommodate their profits, programs pushed by the tenants' movement directly challenge these entrenched interests.

Rent control is one such program. Decent and affordable housing is debated before the public. The issue of rent control raises important political and economic questions of how housing is produced and distributed. The central question in this debate is one of "property rights versus human rights."

The debate over rent control therefore makes an important political impact. It has taught tenants that in order for housing conditions to improve, they must get involved in the political system. They must vote for referendums and elect political candidates that promote their interests. Traditionally, tenants have been apathetic toward the political system, but when they have an issue that directly affects them, they have responded by participating in political activities. Participation of tenants in politics can also affect other political matters.

The evidence in this chapter suggests that the movement for rent control in the United States has had more of a political than an economic impact. In regard to rent control's distributional impact, it appears that most rent control ordinances have worked only to prevent exorbitant or extravagant rent increases. They have also provided protection against arbitrary evictions and incentives for maintenance of rentals and have allowed the tenant to know what kind of rent increase to expect in the future. Certainly, this is an improvement for tenants who have had none of these protections in the unfettered market. They have not, however, brought rents down to a level that is affordable to the majority of tenants. Recognizing this problem—and the public's acceptance of government intervention in the marketplace—numerous tenants' groups are pushing for even tougher rent restrictions and an array of other "nonmarket" housing programs. How successful these attempts will be depends on whether the tenants' movement can continue to grow.

Because the future of rent control as housing policy seems cloudy, and the benefits are often small, given the magnitude of shelter poverty, while the efforts required to enact and maintain them are enormous (Stone, 1980b), many tenant organizers have come to question the efficacy of rent control as the chief objective of the tenants' movement and are now pushing other innovative housing programs in addition to rent control. Large-scale cooperative housing programs for low-

and moderate-income persons are becoming the main organizing theme of many tenants' rights groups (Gilderbloom, 1981b: 212–260; Lawson, 1984). Rent control advocacy groups appear to be waging a defensive campaign to preserve the existence of rent control rather than an offensive campaign of spreading the law to other cities. Real estate groups have launched a well-financed attack on rent control, lobbying for and passing legislation that undermines the potency of current moderate rent control laws.

On the other hand, rent control might continue to be a part of housing policy if the Reagan administration continues to sharply cut back on low- and moderate-income housing programs aimed primarily at subsidizing the income of poor renters and building public housing. President Reagan has already cut $26 billion in low- and moderate-income housing funds from the budget. The pipeline for those needing housing assistance is beginning to run dry, with a severe reduction anticipated beginning in 1990 (Herbers, 1985: 1). Moreover, important tax incentives to build low- and moderate-income rental housing were removed in the 1986 federal tax law. Professional real estate analysis suggests that rents might increase anywhere from 15 percent to 20 percent to make up for the loss of tax shelters. Landlords' efforts to have strong rent ordinances outlawed were dealt a setback when the Supreme Court declared that such laws are constitutional. Coupled with this are demographic projections predicting that during the 1980s some 42 million people will reach age 30, compared to only 30 million during the last decade. With federal housing programs being sharply cut, tenants and tenants' movements will have to look to local solutions; rent control could rejuvenate itself, but the debate will simmer around the issue of whether it is symbolic or redistributional politics (Edelman, 1964).

NOTE

Special thanks are due to the comments made by Janet Chafetz, Russel Curtis, Mimi Hinnawi, Patricia Gilderbloom, and Richard Appelbaum for comments on an earlier draft, and to Susan Erwin and Beth Huttman for their detailed comments.

REFERENCES

Atlas, John. 1982. "National Tenants' Union Platform: Rent Control Plank Draft." East Orange, N.J.: National Tenants' Union.
Atlas, John, and Peter Dreier. 1980. "Legislative Strategy: Fighting for Rent Control." *Shelterforce* 5 (October 4).
———. 1981. "Making Tenant Votes Count in New Jersey." *Social Policy* (May/June).
Baar, Kenneth. 1983. "Guidelines for Drafting Rent Control Laws: Lessons of a Decade." *Rutgers Law Review* 35, no. 4: 721–885.
Baar, Kenneth, and Dennis Keating. 1981. *Fair Return Standards and Hardship Appeal Procedures: A Guide for New Jersey Rent Leveling Boards*. Berkeley, Calif.: National Housing Law Project.

Betz, J. 1981. "Rental Housing Crisis Called 'Calamity.' " *Los Angeles Times*, October 4, sec. 8, 23.

Booth, Heather. 1981. "Left with the Ballot Box." *Working Papers for a New Society* 8 (May/June): 3.

Capek, Stella. 1985. "Urban Progressive Movements: The Case of Santa Monica." Ph.D. diss., Department of Sociology, University of Texas.

Chafetz, Janet, and Anthony Gary Dworkin. 1986. *Female Revolt*. Totowa, N.J.: Rowman & Allanheld.

Cockburn, Alexander, and James Ridgeway. 1981. "Tenant Coalition Sweeps Local Elections." *Village Voice*, April 22–28.

Daugherbaugh, Debbie. 1975. *Anchorage Rent Review Program*. Anchorage, Alaska: Alaska Public Interest Group.

Dreier, Peter. 1982a. "Dreams and Nightmares." *Nation* 232, no. 5: 141–146.

———. 1982b. "The Status of Tenants in the United States." *Social Problems* 30 (December): 179–199.

Dreier, Peter, and John Atlas. 1980. "The Housing Crisis and the Tenants Revolt." *Social Policy* 2 (January): 13–24.

Dreier, Peter, John I. Gilderbloom, and Richard P. Appelbaum. 1980. "Rising Rents and Rent Control: Issues in Urban Reform." In Pierre Clavel, John Forester, and William Goldsmith (eds.), *Urban and Regional Planning in an Age of Austerity*. New York: Pergamon. 154–176.

Duncan, S. S. 1981. "Housing Policy, the Methodology of Levels, and Urban Research: The Case of Castells." *International Journal of Urban and Regional Research* 5, no. 2: 251.

Edelman, Murray. 1964. *The Symbolic Use of Politics*. Urbana: University of Illinois Press.

Flanigan, William H., and Nancy H. Zingale. 1979. *Political Behavior of the American Electorate*, 4th ed. Boston: Allan & Bacon.

Gilderbloom, John I. 1980. *Moderate Rent Control: Experiences of U.S. Cities*. Washington, D.C.: National Conference on Alternative State and Local Public Policies.

———. 1981a. "Moderate Rent Control: Its Impact on the Quality and Quantity of the Housing Stock." *Urban Affairs Quarterly* 18, no. 2: 123–142.

———. 1981b. *Rent Control: A Source Book*. San Francisco: Foundation for National Progress.

———. 1983. "The Impact of Moderate Rent Control in New Jersey: An Empirical Study of 26 Rent Controlled Cities." *Urban Analysis: An International Journal* 7, no. 2: 135–154.

———. 1984. "Redistributive Impacts of Rent Control in New Jersey." Paper presented at the annual meeting of the American Sociological Association, San Antonio, Texas, August.

Gilderbloom, John I., and Richard Appelbaum. 1988. *Rethinking Rental Housing*. Philadelphia: Temple University Press.

Gilderbloom, John I., and Stella Capek. In press. *Gimme Shelter: The Tenants' Movement and the Battle for Community*. Albany: State University of New York Press.

Gilderbloom, John I., and Dennis Keating. 1982. *An Evaluation of Rent Control in Orange, New Jersey*. San Francisco: Foundation for National Progress, Housing Information Center.

Gilderbloom, John I., with Simon Gottschalk and Nora Amory. 1986. "The Impact of

Housing Status on Radical Beliefs." Paper presented at the annual meeting of the American Sociological Association, New York, August 28.

Glen, Maxwell, and Cody Shearer. 1980. "Reagan and Rent Control." *Sacramento Bee*, December 11.

Gupta, Dipka, and Louis Rea. 1984. "Second Generation Rent Control Ordinances: A Quantitative Comparison." *Urban Affairs Quarterly* 19, no. 3 (March): 395–408.

Hall, Peter. 1981. "Squatters Movement Solidifies." *Rolling Stone*, September 17.

Hartman, Chester. 1979. "Landlord Money Defeats Rent Control in San Francisco." *Shelterforce* 5: 3.

Hartman, Chester, and Michael Stone. 1980. "A Socialist Housing Program for the United States." In Pierre Clavel, John Forester, and William Goldsmith (ed.) *Urban and Regional Planning in an Age of Austerity*. New York: Pergamon.

Harvey, David. 1981. "Rent Control and a Fair Return." In John I. Gilderbloom (ed.), *Rent Control: A Source Book*. San Francisco: Foundation for National Progress. 80–83.

Hayden, Tom. 1980. *The American Future: New Visions beyond Old Frontiers*. Boston: South End Press.

Heffley, Dennis, and Rex Santerre. 1985. "Rent Control as an Expenditure Constraint: Some Empirical Results." Paper presented at the annual meeting of the Eastern Economic Association, Pittsburgh, Pennsylvania, March 23.

Herbers, John. 1985. "Housing-Aid Debate Focuses on Question of U.S. Duty to Poor." *New York Times* May 4, sec. 1, 1.

Heskin, Allan David. 1981. Tenants and the American Dream: The Ideology of Being a Tenant. Los Angeles: University of California, School of Urban Planning and Architecture. Mimeo.

———. 1983. *Tenants and the American Dream*. New York: Praeger.

Jacob, Mike. 1979. *How Rent Control Passed in Santa Monica, California*. Oakland, Calif.: Housing Action and Information Network. May.

Kirschman, Mary Jo. 1980. *Winning Rent Control in a Working Class City*. Baltimore: Rent Control Campaign.

Krinsky, Steve. 1981. "Tenant Activist Wins City Council Seat." *Shelterforce* 6, no. 2 (Spring): 10.

Lawson, Ronald. 1983. "A Decentralized But Moving Pyramid: The Evolution and Consequences of the Structure of the Tenant Movement." In Jo Freeman (ed.), *Social Movements of the Sixties and Seventies*. New York: Longman.

———. 1984. *Owners of Last Resort: An Assessment of the Track Records of New York City's Early Low Income Housing Cooperative Conversions*. New York: Department of Housing Preservation and Development, Office of Program and Management Analysis.

———. N.d. "Labor Unions and Tenant Organizations: A Comparison of Resource Mobilization, Strategic Leverage, and Impact." Flushing: Urban Studies Department, Queens College, City University of New York. Typescript.

Leight, Claudia, Elliot Lieberman, Jery Kurtz, and Dean Pappas. 1980. "Rent Control Wins in Baltimore." *Moving On* (Chicago: New American Movement), 4, no. 8: 15–20.

Lowe, Carey, and Richard Blumberg. 1981. "Moderate Regulations Protect Landlords as Well as Tenants." In John I. Gilderbloom (ed.), *Rent Control: A Source Book*. San Francisco: Foundation for National Progress.

McKee, Cindy. 1981. "Tenants Help Elect Progressive Mayor." *Shelterforce* 6, no. 2 (Spring 1981): 22.

Marcuse, Peter. 1978. "The Political Economy of Rent Control: Theory and Strategy." *Planning* 7 (New York: Columbia University Division of Urban Planning).

————. 1981. "The Strategic Potential of Rent Control." In John I. Gilderbloom (ed.), *Rent Control: A Source Book*. San Francisco: Foundation for National Progress.

Martin, Phillip. 1976. "The Supreme Court's Quest for Voting Equality on Bond Referenda." *Baylor Law Review* 28: 25–37.

Mollenkopf, John, and Jon Pynoos. 1973. "Boardwalk and Park Place: Property Ownership, Political Structure, and Housing Policy at the Local Level." In Jon Pynoos, Robert Schafer, and Chester Hartman (eds.), *Housing Urban America*. Chicago: Aldine. 55–74.

Molotch, Harvey. 1976. "The City as a Growth Machine: Toward a Political Economy of Growth." *American Journal of Sociology* 82, no. 2 (September): 309–332.

O'Connor, James. 1979. "Rent Control Is Absolutely Essential." *City on a Hill Press* (University of California, Santa Cruz), March 1, 3.

————. 1981. "The Fiscal Crisis of the State Revisited." *Kapitalistate: Working Papers on the Capitalist State* 9.

Renters Alliance. 1980. "Analysis of a Campaign." *Shelterforce* 5, no. 3 (Summer).

Rosentraub, Mark, and Robert Warren. 1986. "Tenants Associations and Social Movements: The Case of the United States." Paper presented at the Urban Affairs Association meetings, Fort Worth, Texas, March 8.

Shipnuck, Leslie, and Dennis Keating, with Mary Morgan. 1974. *The People's Guide to Urban Renewal*. Berkeley: A Community Defense Manual.

Shulman, David. 1980. "Real Estate Valuation under Rent Control: The Case of Santa Monica." Los Angeles: University of California, Business Forecasting Project. Mimeo.

Smelser, Neil J. 1963. *Theory of Collective Behavior*. New York: Free Press of Glencoe.

Stone, Michael. 1980a. "Housing and the American Economy: A Marxist Analysis." In Pierre Clavel, John Forester, and William W. Goldsmith (eds.), *Urban and Regional Planning in an Age of Austerity*. New York: Pergamon.

————. 1980b. "The Housing Problem in the United States: Origins and Prospects." *Socialist Review*. 10, no. 2 (July-August: 65–119).

U.S. Bureau of the Census. 1979. "Voting and Registration in the Election of November 1978." *Current Population Reports*. Series P-20, no. 344. Washington, D.C.: Government Printing Office.

Wood, James L., and Maurice Jackson. 1982. *Social Movements: Development, Participation, and Dynamics*. Belmont, Calif.: Wadsworth.

Zald, Mayer N., and J. D. McCarthy. 1979. *The Dynamics of Social Movements*. Cambridge, Mass.: Winthrop Publishers.

PART IV

GROUPS WITH SPECIAL HOUSING NEEDS

16

Women's Housing and Neighborhood Needs

KAREN FRANCK

This chapter reviews the recent literature on women's housing and neighborhood needs in the United States. It focuses primarily on women in the early and middle period of their lives who have children, whether or not they are married. Some attention is also given to women heads of household without children.

Neither women in general nor women with children form homogeneous groups; other background characteristics create important differences in the type and degree of need. Women do, however, have needs that can be distinguished from those of men; these have to do primarily with women's caretaking responsibilities for other people and for dwellings. When women have children, these responsibilities are even more extensive. This chapter assumes the commonality of the needs that arise from caretaking and distinguishes between subgroups according to income, geographic location, presence of children, and employment and marital status when the research evidence being reviewed warrants such distinctions.

HISTORICAL DEVELOPMENT

Discussions of women's housing and neighborhood needs have long revealed two somewhat independent themes: the need for housing and communities designed to address the particular needs of women as a group and the need for adequate, affordable housing for low-income women. During the first period of discussion of these issues, from the mid-nineteenth century to the Great Depression, attention was focused more on the first theme than on the second. One of the earliest and most influential writers during this period was the architect Catherine Beecher Bauer, who idealized women's domestic role and their isolation in the single-family house (Hayden, 1981a, 1984). In contrast, three generations of "material feminists" devoted their efforts to creating alternative forms of housing, socialized housework, and child care in order to achieve equality for women (Hayden, 1981a).[1] Those concerned with housing for low-income women focused more on the needs of the family than of women per se.

These included Catherine Bauer, Edith Elmer Wood (Birch, 1983), and Elizabeth Coit (Stevens, 1977).

The second period of discussion, from the early 1970s through the present, first reflected an interest in women's environmental needs, with few distinctions between subgroups (Hapgood and Getzels, 1974; Wekerle, Peterson, and Morley, 1980; Stimpson et al., 1981; Keller, 1981a).[2] It is only more recently that considerable attention has been directed at the housing needs of low-income women (Birch, 1985a), homeless women (Watson and Austerberry, 1986; Stoner, 1986), and women in transition (Sprague, 1986).

CURRENT CIRCUMSTANCES

In accord with this division of interests, current circumstances are reviewed in terms of the need for affordable, adequate housing for low-income women and the need for housing and neighborhoods designed to meet the particular needs of women.

Need for Affordable Housing

Today in the United States women heads of household with and without children are more poorly housed than ever before. The number of homeless single people and homeless families has been increasing as a result of deinstitutionalization, unemployment, domestic violence, rising housing costs, cutoffs in disability benefits, and loss of low-cost housing. In January 1986 New York City sheltered 4,067 homeless families in shelters and welfare hotels (Basler, 1986). In October 1984 over 3,100 families were quartered in emergency shelters in New York each night; this figure was twice that of the previous year (Hopper and Hamberg, 1984). Many of the families seeking shelter in the Northeast are headed by women (Hopper and Hamberg, 1984). In New York City most homeless families are housed in welfare hotels (Basler, 1986) where the conditions are horrific (Simpson, Kilduff, and Blewet, 1984). Based on a survey of emergency shelters across the country, the U.S. Department of Housing and Urban Development (HUD) (1984) estimated that 21 percent of those seeking shelter in the winter of 1983–1984 were family members and 13 percent were single women. One author (Stoner, 1986) has noted that homeless women receive harsher judgments by society and less adequate services than homeless men, are more vulnerable to crime and rape, and are subjected to pressure for sexual favors in return for food and shelter. There is some evidence that the causes of homelessness and the particular needs of homeless people may differ between women and men (Stoner, 1986; Watson and Austerberry, 1986). One example is homelessness among women caused by domestic violence and the consequent, acute need for psychological support and physical security.

Women heads of household with and without children who have permanent housing are often burdened by other housing problems: poor physical conditions, overcrowding, and high rental costs. When housing quality is measured by a combination of these factors, the 1981 National Housing Survey by the U.S. Department of Housing and Urban Development shows that 40 percent of the 23 million households who are ill-housed in the United States are headed by women (Birch, 1985b). A female head of household with children is more than twice as likely to have a housing problem than other American households (Birch, 1985b). Other research (Ahrentzen, 1985) indicates that low-income single mothers are more likely to live in physically inadequate housing while also paying a higher proportion of their income for rent than are two-parent families.

Homelessness and the poor quality of the housing that many women heads of household occupy are, in part, consequences of the "feminization of poverty." In 1980 two out of every three adults whose income fell below the official poverty level were women, and more than half of all poor families were headed by women (Stallard, Ehrenreich, and Sklar, 1983). Responsibility for supporting themselves and their children when they are not married, low-paying jobs, and wage discrimination against women all contribute to this situation. Again, economic circumstances among single mothers are particularly severe: they have lower family incomes and are more likely to be unemployed, live in the central city, and rent their living quarters than single fathers and two-parent families (U.S. Bureau of the Census, 1985a). Understandably, low-income single mothers experience significantly more stress than do other groups (Pearce and McAdoo, 1981). No-fault divorce laws intended as enlightened reform have actually contributed to the impoverishment of divorced women and their children. According to Weitzman's research (1985), divorced women and their children experience a 73 percent decline in their standard of living, while their ex-husbands experience a 42 percent rise. Many of these women who were accustomed to a middle-income life-style prior to and during marriage are forced to apply for welfare after divorce (Sidel, 1986).

Need for Housing to Meet Women's Needs

The variety of household types has increased dramatically in the United States in recent years. In 1970 the most frequent household type was the prototype family for the single-family house: 40.3 percent of all households consisted of a married couple with children under eighteen (U.S. Bureau of the Census, 1985b). By 1984 this type had decreased to 28.5 percent. The largest increase was in the proportion of non-family households, people living alone or with unrelated others. This type increased from 18.8 to 27.4 percent. The greater variety in type was also created by an increase in single-parent families with children. When considered as a proportion of all family households, this type rose from 12.9 to 25.7 percent between 1970 and 1984. Women are far more likely than men to head these families: 83 percent of all single-parent households are headed by women. Women are also more likely than men to live completely alone: 63 percent of all one-person households were composed of women in 1984.[3]

Women are now more likely to be employed outside the home. Between 1960 and 1980 women's participation in the labor force grew from 35.4 to 51.4 percent (Hacker, 1983). Even in the traditional two-parent family with children where the husband is employed, the wife is also likely to be employed: in 1984 this was true of 57 percent of all such households.

The design of housing and neighborhoods has not responded to these changes in household composition and activities. Single-family homes in suburban locations are still designed according to the earlier prototype family of employed father, homemaking mother, and young children, despite sales brochures and marketing efforts directed at other household types (Franck, 1985a).

While some household circumstances have changed, others have not. Wives continue to carry the primary responsibility for all homemaking and child care tasks (Vanek, 1974; Berk, 1981; Hartman, 1981; Miller and Garrison, 1982; Schooler et al., 1984; Michelson, 1985). This seems to be true regardless of employment of the wife, number of children, or level of education or income. The home is also a place where women care for the sick and the elderly (Finch and Groves, 1983). Women are also more dependent on public transportation than men (Cichoki, 1981; Mazey and Lee, 1983; Pickup, 1984; Fox, 1985; Michelson, 1985). Women's triple responsibilities for wage earning, homemaking, and caring for others and their greater dependency on public transportation all suggest the inadequacy of the suburban single-family home for women. These responsibilities also indicate women's need for good support services and facilities near the home and workplace and for scheduling flexibility in services and employment.

Crime and fear of crime are additional problems for women, who report higher levels of fear than do men and are more likely to engage in self-protective behaviors, including curtailing their activities outside the home (Gordon et al., 1981). The design of housing, neighborhoods, and services must be sensitive to these issues as well. Women also face problems of physical abuse from their spouses: a woman is beaten every 18 seconds in the United States (Grossholtz, 1983). While this chapter deals primarily with permanent housing, one essential housing need is for emergency shelters for battered women (Roberts, 1981) and for transitional housing (Sprague, 1986).

MAJOR APPROACHES IN THE LITERATURE

Three different approaches to women's housing and neighborhood needs can be detected in the recent literature: (1) conceptualizing the relationships between women and their physical and social environments; (2) appraising existing housing and neighborhoods and assessing women's needs; and (3) proposing alternative house and neighborhood forms.

Conceptual Approach

Central to most theoretical discussions of women and housing is an acknowledgment of the social, spatial, and gender divisions so pervasive in industrialized societies. The public domain of wage work and social gathering is separated from the private domain of homemaking, child rearing and family interaction. Men are assigned to the former domain, women to the latter. Davidoff, L'Esperance, and Newby (1976) describe the growth of the "beau ideal" of the house and housewife providing a peaceful domestic retreat from the competitive public realm of men and business. This was an ideal that denied the isolation of the wife and the single-family house, the tyranny of the husband, and the frequency of households without husbands or with employed wives. Others analyze the relationship between production and reproduction, the relationship of these processes to gender and spatial divisions, and the dependency of the patriarchal/ capitalist system upon those divisions (Markusen, 1981; McDowell, 1983; MacKenzie and Rose, 1983). These analyses show how the growth of industrial capitalism generated an ever-increasing distance between workplace and home and helped place men in the former and women in the latter. The industrial capitalist system thrived on these arrangements through the psychological renewal and biological reproduction of its male work force in the home environment and through the extensive purchase of consumer goods necessitated by the single-family home model (Miller, 1983).

The process of creating a spatial division between home and work reached its zenith in the American suburb, where zoning restrictions forbid integration of commercial spaces with residential spaces and where building types are often restricted to single-family houses with a required amount of acreage and square footage, characteristics so dear to the "beau ideal" of rural domestic retreat. This extreme spatial and land-use separation between the city and the suburb reflects and enforces the work life/domestic life, male/female dichotomies (Saegert, 1981; McDowell, 1983; MacKenzie and Rose, 1983; Hayden, 1981a, 1984; Franck, 1985a, 1986).

Appraisal and Assessment

The dichotomies of home/work, female/male, and suburb/city are cultural symbols (Saegert, 1981) that direct design and policy decisions and the activities and attitudes of household members. Despite the realization of these symbols in the physical form of housing and communities and in some daily events, the polarities are a fiction. This contradiction between the ideal and the reality of most daily life is a fundamental problem for women. Women, even full-time homemakers, do not remain at home all the time. In pursuing homemaking and child care tasks, they venture into the public realm for shopping, transporting family members, visiting health care facilities, and other services. The ideology of separation not only misrepresents the real activities, even of full-time homemakers, but makes those activities difficult to pursue because of the spatial distances the ideology has generated. When mothers are employed, the difficulties multiply.

The public/private dichotomy also prescribed the privatization of the suburban house and thereby the isolation of the individual housewife. She is separated not only from places of work and public life but also from people in general as she pursues tasks of homemaking and child care in a complete, self-sufficient, and separate domicile (Hayden, 1981a; Franck, 1985a).

Alternative Housing and Communities

Housing and community alternatives attempt to resolve the problems created by spatial and gender divisions and by women's dual responsibilities for wage earning and homemaking. Hayden (1981a) documents many historical alternatives, both proposed and built. Her recent book (1984) describes contemporary examples that also seek integration between domains and that are designed to meet the needs of different household types, including single people, single-parent families, and employed mothers. Leavitt (1985b), Soper (1981), Sprague (1985, 1986), France (1985), and Klodawsky and Spector (1985) all describe proposed or built examples of housing for single parents, either transitional or permanent, as does Hayden (1984). Hayden (1981b) proposes the redesign of 40 conventional suburban single-family homes to create a more cooperative, socially integrated, mixed-use community. MacKenzie (1985) imagines a suburban community sometime in the future where women themselves have fully integrated home and work by developing cottage industries and exchange of services. The most utopian alternative of all is Piercy's community of Mattapoisett (1976), where no gender divisions exist even for childbearing and nursing and where the social and spatial organization of life encourages high levels of integration between activities and cooperation between community members (Franck, 1986).

MAJOR FINDINGS IN THE LITERATURE

Major empirical findings include those that document the poor housing conditions women experience, which were reviewed earlier, and those generated by the appraisal approach. This approach generally employs the criterion of how well particular housing and neighborhood arrangements allow women to pursue their many different activities relatively easily and in an integrated way. According to this criterion, conventional suburbs, some new towns in England and the United States, and planned unit developments receive the lowest ratings because they create divisions and distances between spheres of different activities, between individual households, and between different household types. In contrast, high density, mixed-use housing environments receive the highest ratings for decreasing these divisions and distances. Low-rise buildings are added to the list of positive attributes to avoid the problems that high-rise living may entail, particularly for households with children.

The empirical research supporting these ratings often involves an urban/suburban comparison, with the urban location having the supportive characteristics and the suburban location lacking them. Sometimes the research also entails a male/female comparison. Empirical research involving locational and gender comparisons suggests that women favor the urban location more than do men for the variety of functions it provides (Michelson, 1977). In this study women in suburban single-family homes were the least satisfied with how they spent their time, while men in these settings were the most satisfied. Saegert and Winkel (1980) review research indicating that men find the retreat and recreational aspects of the suburban home more satisfying than do women. Their own research indicates that married women in the city had more friends within walking distance than did men, whereas men in the suburbs were more likely than women to be living near their friends. Fava (1985) has found that in describing considerations that led to their present choice of dwelling, women put greater emphasis on proximity to friends and relatives, convenient shopping, neighborhood safety, and mass transportation than did men. Similarly, gender comparisons within the urban setting show that women are more likely than men to praise the ease of accessibility to services and the ease of making social contacts; they also enjoy those contacts more than do men (MacKintosh, 1985).

Other research has focused on women in different types of suburban or other nonurban settings. In a study of women with children in suburbs in San Jose, Rothblatt, Garr, and Sprague (1979) found that density of their present residential location had positive effects on indexes of satisfaction with community services and with group participation. Distance from the city center showed a negative relationship to satisfaction with transportation services and measures of companionship. Many women preferred multifamily housing with maintenance and security services in proximity to cultural and entertainment activities over single-family houses.

That women in suburbs may experience isolation and boredom gains support from Keller's study (1981b) of the first planned unit development in New Jersey. Sixty percent of the women Keller interviewed felt bored; twice as many housewives as employed wives felt bored "very often." Forty percent of the women also reported that it was hard to meet people like themselves in the community.

The findings become less supportive of the conclusion that "a woman's place is in the city" (Wekerle, 1984) when possible differences in the preferences of different household types are directly addressed. Banner, Berheide, and Greckel (1982) studied the housing preferences of homebuyers in the metropolitan area of Louisville, Kentucky. The authors found that two-parent familes with children were more likely to have chosen a house for its suburban or rural location than were other household types. The greater the number of children, the more likely the family was to regard suburban location as a very important reason for its choice. Households with employed wives differed significantly from households with full-time homemaking wives in preferring a house near the wife's job and in viewing suburban location as unimportant. Single parents expressed no significant preference for a particular type of location; income and time constraints dominated their decisions (Banner, Berheide, and Greckel, 1982). In studying the search for housing among low-income female-headed households, Ahrentzen (1985) found that such households expressed greater concern over access to public transportation than did two-parent households.

Evidence that women do not prefer the central city or "urban" location per se but rather some characteristics that that location possesses is provided by Fava's research (1985). Almost half of the women in that national sample preferred to live in a small city, town, or village not in the suburbs, whereas only 16 percent chose a large city and 12 percent chose a "medium-sized city in the suburbs." The leading reason given for the choice of their current residence was neighborhood safety (69 percent), something urban neighborhoods are less likely to have than suburban ones. Another drawback of the urban residence is dwelling size. Saegert and Winkel (1980) report that compared to suburban respondents, urban respondents were more dissatisfied with their homes. The authors attribute this to smaller dwelling units and lower sense of safety in the urban setting. Finally, those seeking single-family detached homes are not going to find them in urban centers, and this house form still holds great sway in the United States. In a 1981 survey of visitors to builders' model homes in eight metropolitan areas, two-thirds of the shoppers were looking for a detached house on its own lot (Gers, 1985).

EVALUATION AND SUGGESTIONS FOR FUTURE RESEARCH

The present design of American urban and suburban communities makes it very difficult to separate women's preferences for a particular type of location from preferences for the characteristics that those locations possess. While urban locations often possess attributes supportive of women's needs, which women themselves may or may not realize, they also present problems, including small dwelling size, crime, and few detached houses. Even though characteristics of the house and community may be more important in determining preference than location, as Fava (1985) suggests, the two are presently unavoidably linked. This confounding of location and community characteristics should be considered in future research and discussion.

The presence of children in the household plays an important part in residential choice. The apparent preference for locations outside the central city evidenced in some of the research (Banner, Berheide, and Greckel, 1982; Berheide and Banner, 1981; Fava, 1985) may be due to the perception that suburbs, towns, or rural locations are the best places to raise children. Locational preferences and benefits may be different, if not conflicting, for different household members. This issue is not adequately addressed, much less resolved, in the existing literature even when differences in the preferences of men and women are documented.

Differences and possible conflicts between preferences may also exist between women at different stages of the life cycle and between women of different socioeconomic classes. Piven (1974) argues forcefully that sex roles cannot be understood separately from the context of race and class and that what middle-income women need is not what low-income women need. In some cases the two sets of needs may clash, as in the revitalization of cities, which may benefit middle-income women with the provision of rehabilitated housing and specialized services but may destroy the low-cost housing and services that benefit low-income women (Holcomb, 1984). With few exceptions, differences and possible conflicts between the needs of different groups of women are not addressed in the literature.

Another issue is the possible contradiction between what people perceive to be the best alternative and what will actually best meet their needs. Even though suburbs are often perceived to be ideal for raising children, they may have detrimental effects on children's lives, providing fewer social contacts than urban neighborhoods (Boocock, 1981; Van Vliet—, 1981) and generating a dependency upon adults for transportation and stimulation (Franck, 1985a). Both residents and researchers make assumptions about how the needs of different family members are met, or not met, by the physical and social design characteristics of the single-family house and neighborhood. While research can often show that these assumptions are not warranted empirically, the power of the "beau ideal" (Davidoff, L'Esperance, and Newby, 1976) and of urban/suburban symbolism (Saegert, 1981) is so strong that people's beliefs may persist nonetheless. The persistence of the ideal and the symbolism merits further research.

Another topic for future research is the issue of time with respect to type and location of housing, employment, transportation, and the scheduling of jobs and services. Michelson's research (1985) demonstrates very well the time pressures employed mothers experience and the importance of considering the temporal characteristics of services and employment opportunities. Future research on women and housing might do well to consider the temporal dimensions of women's lives along with the spatial dimensions.

More research attention could also be given to the design of the interior of the dwelling. The research reviewed here deals almost exclusively with type of housing, location, and neighborhood characteristics. Studying women's needs with respect to the interior of the house is rarer. The discussions that do exist are often historical (Rock, Torre, and Wright, 1981), cross-cultural (Ardener, 1981), or purely descriptive (Franck, 1985b, 1986). Contemporary, empirical research on the design and use of interior space is certainly warranted.

One way to study both interior and community design and to develop a clearer view of possible improvements is to document the design and behavioral and attitudinal consequences of alternative house and community forms. Popenoe (1977) has done this in comparing the communities of Levittown, New Jersey, and Vällingby in Sweden, demonstrating the problems posed by the former and the benefits of the latter for women. While other alternatives are also described by Hayden (1980b, 1984), Leavitt (1985a, 1985b), Franck (1985b, 1986) and others, these are descriptions without empirical evidence of behavioral or attitudinal consequences, which would be good topics for future research. Such research might focus on shared housing, housing for single parents, alternative designs for the private dwelling, or speciality housing such as shelters for battered women or life care communities.

RECOMMENDATIONS FOR FUTURE POLICY AND DESIGN

This chapter has identified two sets of housing problems for women in the United States. The first is lack of adequate housing and lack of income to pay for adequate housing when it is available. At the very least, emergency shelter must be provided, leading perhaps to a national homeless-relief program, and attention must be given to the particular needs of women with and without children. Transitional housing should also be considered. Long-term measures require provision of low-cost housing through new construction and rehabilitation and improved levels of public assistance indexed to cost-of-living trends (Hopper and Hamberg, 1984). This will require intensive advocacy efforts. Sternlieb and Hughes (1983) point out that the housing needs of the poor have lost their "political potency" and that a reformation of broad-based housing constituencies is needed. Cash allowances to low-income households are not sufficient if low-cost housing is unavailable. Although employment is also not a sufficient answer, since most women are likely to continue to work in low-paying occupations (Noble, 1985), it is essential to end employment and wage discrimination against women (Sidel, 1986) and to couple housing programs with economic development programs (Hayden, 1984). One policy change not directly related to housing that will improve the financial circumstances of divorced women is the alteration of no-fault divorce proceedings to provide better standards of property division, alimony, and child support (Weitzman, 1985). Improving public policy, including the welfare system, to address the needs of low-income women and children is yet another necessity (Sidel, 1986).

One difficult question to be addressed in developing programs and policies to improve housing conditions for women is whether the focus should be on "families" or on "women." Suggestions for a "U.S. family policy" (Sidel, 1986) would not benefit the large number of low-income women without children who are ignored by programs directed toward families (Watson and Austerberry, 1986). In either case it is important that programs and policies do not further encourage the flight of husbands and fathers from the nuclear family (Ehrenreich, 1983).

Housing and economic development programs to improve women's housing situation need not take the standard, centralized, bureaucratic forms of intervention. Women in many neighborhoods work cooperatively and independently to save housing and to take over and manage deteriorated housing (Leavitt and Saegert, 1984). Future intervention programs should draw upon the social ties, feelings of community attachment, and skills these women have and should encourage cooperation rather than competition. These are two of the feminist planning principles Saegert (1985) proposes.

The second set of problems identified in this chapter is the lack of housing and communities designed with social and spatial connections between home, employment, and services and between households. The integration of services with housing is a top priority (Wekerle, 1985; Leavitt, 1985b; Hayden, 1984; Saegert, 1985). Location and hours of operation should be considered (Michelson, 1985; MacKenzie and Rose, 1983). Home-based services are one option and could include day care, after-school care, and respite care for children or the elderly (Hare and Price, 1985).

Some have recommended that women with young children might do computer-based work at home. However, this option poses some difficulties. Juggling child care with work responsibilities within the same space and time context generates stress (Olson and Primps, 1984; Christensen, 1985). Lack of employment benefits, the possibilities of exploitation, and low visibility in the organization are additional drawbacks to this solution. Also, this arrangement only serves to further the isolation of the individual housewife. The split between home and paid work can be bridged in other ways by making scheduling more flexible through flextime or job sharing (Boneparth and Stoper, 1983) and by locating places of employment closer to residential neighborhoods.

The latter suggestion speaks to the need for greater integration of land uses. Yet this is counter to the original and continuing tenet of suburban zoning. One of the most significant policy changes for meeting women's housing needs would be the revision of zoning ordinances to permit home-based services, local shopping and health care facilities in residential areas, accessory apartments in single-family homes, and dwellings shared by several unrelated people.

Other recommendations concern the dwellings themselves. Designers and policymakers should consider the particular needs of different types of households rather than envisioning an idealized and temporally fixed prototype of parents and young children (Franck, 1985a, 1985b). Dwellings can also be designed to facilitate the household work of all household members (Rock, Torre, and Wright, 1980) and to change over time to allow for changes in the use of spaces and in household size and composition (Franck, 1987). Such changes and the greater integration of land uses will require changes in images and in regulations. The present social and physical design of the American house and community is governed by idealized, static images of the home and family and is enforced by zoning ordinances, building codes, and lending policies based on those images. If the conditions of women's lives are to be improved, both the images and the regulations have to change. Central to that process will be a new understanding of the desirable relationships between home, work, and services and between private and public domains.

NOTES

1. Women's housing and neighborhood needs were also considered in various utopian communities in nineteenth-century America. See Wright (1981) and Hayden (1976).

2. Planners were the first to address this topic in print with the proceedings of a HUD conference (Hapgood and Getzels, 1974). Interest among architects surfaced in 1974 with conferences on women and architecture that resulted in the formation of the Women's School of Planning and Architecture (Weisman and Birkby, 1983), the Women's Development Corporation (Adam, Aitcheson, and Sprague, 1981), and the Women's Institute for Housing and Economic Development (Sprague, 1984). Women's contributions to architecture were documented in a volume edited by Torre (1977) and in a special issue of *Heresies* (1981). Interest among psychologists and sociologists was signaled by a review article in the journal *Environment and Behavior* (Peterson, Wekerle, and Morley, 1978). Edited volumes with contributions from planners, architects, and social scientists followed (Wekerle, Peterson, and Morley, 1980; Stimpson et al., 1981; Keller, 1981a). The most recent work includes special issues of the journals *Ekistics* and *Sociological Focus* in 1985 and new books by Hayden (1984), Birch (1985a), and Michelson (1985).

3. For further discussion of changes in household composition, see Glick (1984) and Pampel (1983).

REFERENCES

Adam, Katrin, Susan E. Aitcheson, and Joan Forrester Sprague. 1981. "Women's Development Corporation." *Heresies* 3: 19–20.

Ahrentzen, Sherry. 1985. "Residential Fit and Mobility among Low-Income, Female-Headed Households in the United States." In Willem van Vliet—, Elizabeth Huttman, and Sylvia Fava (eds.), *Housing Needs and Policy Approaches*. Durham, N.C.: Duke University Press.

Ardener, Shirley (ed.). 1981. *Women and Space*. New York: St. Martin's Press.

Banner, Mae E., Catherine Berheide, and Fay Greckel. 1982. "Housing Preferences in Louisville." *Housing and Society* 9:95–110.

Basler, Barbara. 1986. "State to Require Private Rooms in City Shelters." *New York Times*, February 1.

Berheide, Catherine W., and Mae G. Banner. 1981. "Making Room for Employed Women at Home and at Work." *Housing and Society* 7:153–163.

Berk, Sarah F. 1980. "The Household as Workplace." In Gerda R. Wekerle, Rebecca Peterson, and David Morley (eds.), *New Space for Women*. Boulder, Colo.: Westview. 65–81.

Birch, Eugenie. 1983. "Women Made America." In D. Krueckeberg (ed.), *The American Planner*. New York: Methuen. 149–178.

———. (ed.). 1985a. *The Unsheltered Woman*. New Brunswick, N.J.: Center for Urban Policy Research, Rutgers University.

———. 1985b. "The Unsheltered Woman: Definition and Needs." In Eugenie Birch (ed.), *The Unsheltered Woman*. New Brunswick, NJ: Center for Urban Policy Research, Rutgers University. 21–45.

Boneparth, Ellen, and Emily Stoper. 1983. "Work, Gender, and Technological Innovation.'' In Irene Diamond (ed.), *Families, Politics, and Public Policy.* New York: Longman. 265–278.

Boocock, Sarane S. 1981. ''The Life Space of Children.'' In Suzanne Keller (ed.), *Building for Women.* Lexington, Mass.: D. C. Heath. 93–116.

Christensen, Kathleen E. 1985. ''Impacts of Computer-mediated Home-based Work on Women and Their Families.'' New York: City University of New York. Unpublished paper.

Cichoki, Mary K. 1981. ''Women's Travel Patterns in Suburban Development.'' In Gerda R. Wekerle, Rebecca Peterson, and David Morley (eds.), *New Space for Women.* Boulder, Colo.: Westview. 151–163.

Davidoff, Leonore, Jean L'Esperance, and Howard Newby. 1976. ''Landscape with Figures.'' In Juliet Mitchell and Ann Oakley (eds.), *The Rights and Wrongs of Women.* New York: Penguin.

Ehrenreich, Barbara. 1983. *The Hearts of Men.* Garden City, N.Y.: Anchor.

Fava, Sylvia. 1985. ''Residential Preferences in the Suburban Era.'' *Sociological Focus* 18:109–117.

Finch, Janet, and Dulcie Groves (eds.). 1983. *A Labour of Love.* London: Routledge & Kegan Paul.

Fox, Marion B. 1985. ''Access to Workplaces for Women.'' *Ekistics* 52: 69–76.

France, Ivy. 1985. ''Hubertsusvereniging.'' *Women and Environments* 7: 20–22.

Franck, Karen A. 1985a. ''Social Construction of the Physical Environment: The Case of Gender.'' *Sociological Focus* 18: 143–170.

———. 1985b. ''Together or Apart: Sharing and the American Household.'' Paper presented at the annual meeting of the Association of Collegiate Schools of Architecture, Vancouver. March 7.

———. 1986. ''At Home in the Future: Feminist Visions and Some Built Examples.'' Paper presented at the annual meeting of the Association of Collegiate Schools of Architecture, New Orleans. November.

———. 1987. ''Shared Spaces, Small Spaces, and Spaces That Change.'' In Willem van Vliet—, H. Choldin, W. Michelson, and D. Popenoe (eds.), *Housing and Neighborhoods.* Westport, Conn.: Greenwood Press. 157–172.

Gers, Barbara. 1985. ''Housing Preferences.'' In Eugenie Birch (ed.), *The Unsheltered Woman.* New Brunswick, N.J.: Center for Urban Policy Research, Rutgers University. 79–82.

Glick, Paul C. 1984. ''American Household Structures in Transition.'' *Family Planning Perspectives* 6: 205–211.

Gordon, Margaret Y., Stephanie Riger, Robert K. LeBailly, and Linda Heath. 1981. ''Crime, Women, and the Quality of Urban Life.'' In Catharine Stimpson, Elsa Dixler, Mantha J. Nelson, and Kathryn B. Yatrakis (eds.), *Women and the American City.* Chicago: University of Chicago Press. 141–157.

Grossholtz, Jean. 1983. ''Battered Women's Shelters and the Political Economy of Sexual Violence.'' In Irene Diamond (ed.), *Families, Politics, and Public Policy.* New York: Longman. 59–69.

Hacker, Andrew. 1983. *U.S.: A Statistical Portrait of the American People.* New York: Viking.

Hapgood, Karen, and Judith Getzels (eds.). 1974. *Planning, Women, and Change.* Washington, D.C.: U.S. Department of Housing and Urban Development.

Hare, Patrick H., and Gail A. Price. 1985. "Services Begin at Home." *Planning*, September, 24–25.

Hartman, Heidi. 1981. "The Family as the Locus of Gender, Family, and Political Structure." *Signs* 6: 366–394.

Hayden, Dolores. 1976. *Seven American Utopias*. Cambridge, Mass.: MIT Press.

———. 1981a. *The Grand Domestic Revolution*. Cambridge, Mass.: MIT Press.

———. 1981b. "What Would a Non-Sexist City Be Like?" In Catharine Stimpson, Elsa Dixler, Martha Jo Nelson, and Kathryn B. Yatrakis (eds.), *Women and the American City*. Chicago: University of Chicago Press.

———. 1984. *Redesigning the American Dream*. New York: W. W. Norton.

Holcomb, Briavel. 1984. "Women in the Rebuilt Environment." *Built Environment* 10: 18–24.

Hopper, Kim, and Jill Hamberg. 1984. *The Making of America's Homeless*. New York: Community Service Society.

Keller, Suzanne (ed.). 1981a. *Building for Women*. Lexington, Mass.: D. C. Heath.

———. 1981b. "Women and Children in a Planned Community." In Suzanne Keller (ed.), *Building for Women*. Lexington, Mass.: D. C. Heath. 67–75.

Klodawsky, Fran, and Aaron Spector. 1985. "Mother-Led Families and the Built Environment in Canada." *Women and Environments* 7: 12–13.

Leavitt, Jacqueline. 1985a. "A New American House." *Women and Environments* 7: 14–16.

———. 1985b. "The Shelter Service Crisis and Single Parents." In Eugenie Birch (ed.), *The Unsheltered Woman*. New Brunswick, N.J.: Center for Urban Policy Research, Rutgers University. 153–176.

Leavitt, Jacqueline, and Susan Saegert. 1984. "Women and Abandoned Buildings." *Social Policy*, Summer, 32–39.

McDowell, Linda. 1983. "Towards an Understanding of the Gender Division of Urban Space." *Environment and Planning* 1:59–72.

MacKenzie, Suzanne. 1985. "No One Seems to Go to Work Anymore." *Canadian Women's Studies* 5: 5–8.

MacKenzie, Suzanne, and Damaris Rose. 1983. "Industrial Change, the Domestic Economy, and Home Life." In J. Anderson, S. Duncan, and R. Hudson (eds.), *Redundant Spaces in Cities and Regions*. London: Academic Press. 157–199.

MacKintosh, Elizabeth. 1985. "Highrise Family Living in New York City." In Eugenie Birch (ed.), *The Unsheltered Woman*. New Brunswick, N.J.: Center for Urban Policy Research, Rutgers University. 101–119.

Markusen, Ann. 1981. "City Spacial Structure, Women's Household Work, and National Urban Policy." In Catharine Stimpson, Elsa Dixler, Martha J. Nelson, and Kathryn B. Yatrakis (eds.), *Women and the American City*. Chicago: University of Chicago Press. 20–41.

Mazey, Mary Ellen, and David R. Lee. 1983. *Her Space, Her Place*. Washington, D.C.: Association of American Geographers.

Michelson, William. 1977. *Environmental Choice, Human Behavior, and Residential Satisfaction*. New York: Oxford University Press.

———. 1985. *From Sun to Sun*. Totowa, N.J.: Rowman & Allanheld.

Miller, Joanne, and Howard H. Garrison. 1982. "Sex Roles." *Annual Review of Sociology* 8: 237–262.

Miller, R. 1983. "The Hoover in the Garden." *Environment and Planning D* 1: 73–87.

Noble, Kenneth. 1985. "Low Paying Jobs Foreseen for Most Working Women." *New York Times*, December 12, A20.

Olson, Margrethe H., and Sophia Primps. 1984. "Working at Home with Computers." *Journal of Social Issues* 40: 97–112.

Pampel, Fred C. 1983. "Changes in the Propensity to Live Alone." *Demography* 20: 433–448.

Pearce, Diana, and Harriette McAdoo. 1981. *Women and Children*. Washington, D.C.: National Advisory Council on Economic Opportunity.

Peterson, Rebecca, Gerda R. Wekerle, and David Morley. 1978. "Women and Environments." *Environment and Behavior*. 10: 511–534.

Pickup, Laurie. 1984. "Women's Gender Role and Its Influence on Travel Behavior." *Built Environment*. 10: 61–68.

Piercy, Marge. 1976. *Woman on the Edge of Time*. New York: Fawcett.

Piven, Frances F. 1974. "Planning for Women in the Central City." In Karen Hapgood and Judith Getzels (eds.), *Planning, Women and Change*. Washington, D.C.: U.S. Department of Housing and Urban Development. 57–62.

Popenoe, David. 1977. *The Suburban Environment*. Chicago: University of Chicago Press.

Roberts, Albert. 1981. *Sheltering Battered Women*. New York: Springer.

Rock, Cynthia, Susana Torre, and Gwendolyn Wright. 1980. "The Appropriation of the House." In Gerda R. Wekerle, Rebecca Peterson, and David Morley (eds.), *New Space for Women*. Boulder, Colo.: Westview. 83–100.

Rothblatt, Donald N., Daniel J. Garr, and Jo Sprague. 1979. *The Suburban Environment and Women*. New York: Praeger.

Saegert, Susan. 1981. "Masculine Cities and Feminine Suburbs." In Catharine Stimpson, Elsa Dixler, Martha J. Nelson, and Kathryn B. Yatrakis (eds.), *Women and the American City*. Chicago: University of Chicago Press. 93–108.

———. 1985. "The Androgenous City." *Sociological Focus* 18: 161–176.

Saegert, Susan, and Gary Winkel. 1980. "The Home." In Gerda R. Wekerle, Rebecca Peterson, and David Morley (eds.), *New Space for Women*. Boulder, Colo.: Westview. 41–63.

Salerno, Dan, Kim Hopper, and Ellen Baxter. 1984. *Hardship in the Heartland*. New York: Community Service Society.

Schooler, Carmi, Joanne Miller, Karen Miller, and Carol Richard. 1984. "Work for the Household." *American Journal of Sociology* 90: 97–124.

Sidel, Ruth. 1986. *Women and Children Last*. New York: Viking.

Simpson, John H., Margaret Kilduff, and C. Douglas Blewet. 1984. *Struggling to Survive in a Welfare Hotel*. New York: Community Service Society.

Soper, Mary. 1981. "Housing for Single Parent Families." In Gerda R. Wekerle, Rebecca Peterson, and David Morley (eds.), *New Space for Women*. Boulder, Colo.: Westview. 319–322.

Sprague, Joan. 1984. *A Development Primer*. Boston: Women's Institute for Housing and Economic Development.

———. 1985. "Transitional Housing, Planning, and Design." *Ekistics* 52: 51–55.

———. 1986. *A Manual on Transitional Housing*. Boston: Women's Institute for Housing and Economic Development.

Stallard, Karin, Barbara Ehrenreich, and Holly Sklar. 1983. *Poverty in the American Dream*. Boston: South End Press.

Sternlieb, George, and James W. Hughes. 1983. "Housing the Poor in a Postshelter Society." *Annals of the American Academy of Political and Social Science*. 465: 109–122.

Stevens, Mary Otis. 1977. "Struggle for Place: Women in Architecture, 1920–1960." In Susana Torre (ed.), *Women in American Architecture*. New York: Whitney Library of Design. 88–102.

Stimpson, Catharine, Elsa Dixler, Martha J. Nelson, and Kathryn B. Yatrakis (eds.). 1981. *Women and the American City*. Chicago: University of Chicago Press.

Stoner, Madeleine. 1986. "The Plight of Homeless Women." In Jon Erickson and Charles Wilhelm (eds.), *Housing the Homeless*. New Brunswick, N.J.: Center for Urban Policy Research, Rutgers University. 279–292.

Torre, Susana (ed.) 1977. *Women in American Architecture*. New York: Whitney Library of Design.

U.S. Bureau of the Census. 1985a. *Current Population Reports: Population Characteristics*. Series P 20, no. 399.

———. 1985b. *Current Population Reports: Household and Family Characteristics*. Series P-20, no. 398.

U.S. Department of Housing and Urban Development. 1984. *A Report to the Secretary on Homelessness and Emergency Shelters*. Washington, D.C.: Government Printing Office.

Van Vliet—, Willem. 1981. "Neighborhood Evaluations by City and Suburban Children." *American Planning Association Journal* 47: 458–466.

Vanek, Joann. 1974. "Time Spent in Housework." *Scientific American* 231: 116–120.

Watson, Sophie, and Helen Austerberry. 1986. *Housing and Homelessness: A Feminist Perspective*. London: Routledge & Kegan Paul.

Weisman, Leslie, and Noel P. Birkby. 1983. "The Women's School of Planning and Architecture." In Charlotte Bunch and Sandra Pollack (eds.), *Learning Our Way*. Trumansburg, N.Y.: Crossing Press. 224–245.

Weitzman, Lenore. 1985. *The Divorce Revolution*. New York: Free Press.

Wekerle, Gerda R. 1984. "A Woman's Place Is in the City." *Antipode* 16: 11–19.

———. 1985. "From Refuge to Service Center." *Sociological Focus*. 18: 79–95.

Wekerle, Gerda R., Rebecca Peterson, and David Morley (eds.). 1980. *New Space for Women*. Boulder, Colo.: Westview.

Wright, Gwendolyn. 1981. "The Woman's Commonwealth." *Heresies* 3: 24–27.

17

Minorities and Housing Discrimination

DIANA PEARCE

Racial discrimination in housing is a means to an end, with the end that of residential segregation. Residential segregation, in turn, is itself one means to the end of maintaining racial inequality. Despite the near universality of racial inequality, however, neither housing segregation nor housing discrimination are universal. A society may have racial inequality without either housing segregation or discrimination; thus in the South until the mid-twentieth century school segregation and socioeconomic segregation maintained racial inequality without resort to residential segregation; indeed, without modern transportation, residential segregation was an unnecessary inconvenience. Likewise, though less clearly racial, India's caste system of inequality does not rely on residential exclusion as a mainstay. A society may also have housing segregation without housing discrimination to maintain it; the ghettoes of Eastern Europe and the "quarters" of Middle Eastern cities are historical examples of segregation without discrimination in housing. In modern societies South Africa's apartheid maintains segregation under apartheid laws. What these historical and cross-cultural examples suggest is that housing discrimination is found only in modern, urbanized societies that are characterized by class rather than caste systems of inequality, or what Van den Berghe (1967) would call "competitive race relations."

A second characteristic of housing discrimination and the resulting segregation is its close interaction with economic inequality. While residential segregation may cause economic inequality, for example, through limiting access to educational and occupational opportunities, in analyzing patterns of residential segregation, economic inequality is not seen as problematic. To the extent that housing segregation is economically rather than racially based, it is seen as indicative of a healthy free enterprise system. Thus if the minority group's lesser resources result in poorer housing, which is located in less expensive, different geographic areas than the housing of the more affluent majority, that is the "natural" result of the market system operating. Not only are economic differences and their consequences seen as normal, but economic disadvantage is seen, at least in part, as the result of individual differences in effort, and therefore "deserved."

For all these reasons, separating out race-based from economics-based discrimination and segregation has dominated the analysis of housing discrimination from the start. From the early discussions of the property value issues to current analysis of the disadvantaged position of families with children, racial segregation in housing has been viewed as the joint product of rational/economic and irrational/racial differential treatment. By way of contrast, analysis of voting rights discrimination begins with the assumption that rich and poor have equal rights to vote; each eligible adult who is prevented from voting is an instance of unequivocal discrimination. There is no rational/economic factor to separate out from the "pure" or "real" voting discrimination. In voting rights discrimination research the null hypothesis is the dictum of "one man, one vote"; the equivalent in housing discrimination—"one family, one house"—would be seen as absurd without examination of the role of economics.

The third characteristic of housing discrimination in the American context is the lack of intermediary institutions. American housing discrimination is a peculiar blend of state action—or often, inaction—and individual action to produce discriminatory results. An extreme example of this is the condoning or ignoring by police and authorities of mob or individual action against black families who move into white neighborhoods. Although the mix of state and individual discriminatory action to maintain housing segregation has shifted over time from more state to more individual, the lack of institutional intermediaries continues to give housing discrimination its distinctive character. This characteristic is most apparent in the area of the dismantling of segregation. The kinds of social science studies that are found in the area of school desegregation, for example, which focus on community dynamics, school officials, or federal courts, are absent in the study of housing discrimination, for it lacks similar mediating institutions. Federal courts do not have the kind of jurisdiction over the housing market that they have over school districts, nor are there housing superintendents or boards, with powers akin to school superintendents or boards, who can mandate where people shall live. Even employment discrimination is more centralized than housing, due to the hierarchical structure of most organizations and to relatively large employee groups. One court case may affect thousands if it involves employment discrimination, hundreds if it involves schools, but only a handful of people if housing discrimination is at issue. Housing discrimination involves literally thousands of separate actors, the majority of whom are "amateurs" with no ongoing responsibility beyond the single, even once-in-a-lifetime, decision.

A fourth characteristic that distinguishes American housing "discrimination" is its interaction with ethnic segregation. Sometimes this is referred to as "self-segregation." Some separation of minorities from majority whites is seen as the result of preference on the part of minorities as well as the majority to "live with their own kind." As with the economic factor, the self-segregation factor has been deemed important to take account of, especially in analyzing the impact of particular discriminatory practices on segregation levels. Just as some racial segregation in housing is considered a product of economic differences, some is considered to be the result of individual preference for same-race neighbors.

All four of these characteristics—the class nature of American housing discrimination, its intertwining with economic inequality, the lack of intermediary institutions, and the self-segregation preferences are continuing themes from the earliest to the most recent discussions of housing discrimination and segregation. In this chapter the study of racial discrimination falls into three distinct eras, which parallel the legal and societal changes in civil rights. In the pre–civil rights era, which ends in the mid- to late 1960s, social science analysis documented the extent of racial segregation and described the racial practices and processes that resulted in racial segregation. Not until the 1970s, however, after the passage of civil rights laws and seminal Supreme Court cases, did social science conceptualize housing discrimination as a phenomenon in its own right and begin to analyze its nature and quantify its extent. Finally, in the 1980s analysis of housing discrimination has begun to focus on such issues as the changing nature of housing discrimination and its relationship to other types of discrimination as both cause and effect (for example, school segregation and employment discrimination).

THE HISTORICAL DEVELOPMENT OF HOUSING DISCRIMINATION STUDIES

There is broad agreement today, both within and outside of social science, that racial discrimination is differential treatment on the basis of race (by either an individual or a collective agent) that is both negative (to the racial/ethnic minority) in its consequences and contrary to civil rights laws (broadly speaking). While differential or discriminatory treatment could theoretically be positive for minorities, efforts to define positive differential treatment on the basis of race as discrimination have been unsuccessful, as in the attempt to reconceptualize affirmative action (in employment or university admissions) as "affirmative discrimination." In short, racial discrimination in housing is understood today as differential treatment by race that is negative and illegal.

Before the era of civil rights, this or any concept of housing discrimination was absent. To get to our modern understanding required not only new civil rights law and litigation, but even more fundamentally, documentation of both the existence of differential treatment by race and ethnicity and its negative consequences for minorities. Thus the early studies in this area concentrated on two tasks: (1) documenting how black (only much later were other minorities included) as compared to white housing consumers were treated differently by housing agents, landlords, homesellers, and so on, and (2) describing the development of modern ghettoes and segregated housing patterns, including their negative effects on minority opportunities.

A number of authors have detailed the ways in which segregated enclaves for blacks were created. Although some maintain that for a brief period of time blacks in some cities were allowed to settle outside of segregated areas, few would disagree that when significant numbers of blacks began to migrate to the city, policies and practices arose that confined blacks to segregated ghettoes (see, for example, Spear, 1967, on Chicago, W. E. B. Du Bois, 1899, on Philadelphia, Green, 1967, on Washington, D.C., Kusmer, 1976, on Cleveland, and Osofsky, 1963, on Harlem). Some authors reject the "numbers threat" hypothesis and trace the roots of residential segregation, particularly in the South, to the growth of Jim Crow laws that mandated "separate and unequal" in virtually every area of public life, including public accommodations, voting, and schools (Woodward, 1957).

While each of the case studies cited above describes instances of housing discrimination, the most comprehensive study is Rose Helper's classic *Racial Policies and Practices of Real Estate Brokers*. Although it was not published until 1969, the basic research was done in the 1950s in Chicago. Based on extensive interviews, it exhaustively details the ways in which real estate brokers shape communities in the communities' own image.

Helper's study as well as those of other social scientists (for example, Palmer, 1955), describes not only the ways in which blacks were differentially treated—ways that were not yet conceptualized as discrimination—but also the context in which these acts occurred. First, these studies document how state action enforced individual actions, although usually indirectly. Governments at all levels rarely directly mandated segregation, as European cities designated areas as ghettoes for Jews, or the South African government has designated townships or homelands under apartheid as black. Efforts to do so, as in Virginia's 1912 statute that permitted towns to designate neighborhoods as black or white, were overturned by the Supreme Court in 1917 (*Buchanan* v. *Warley*) on the grounds that such designations interfered with property rights. Restrictive covenants to accomplish the same end on a property-by-property basis rather than by block or neighborhood were used until they too were ruled unenforceable by the Supreme Court in 1948 (*Shelley* v. *Kraemer*; see Farley, 1985).

Rather, as Helper and others have documented, government has reinforced housing discrimination in many indirect ways. An important example of this was the practice of real estate boards of sanctioning, even expelling, members who broke racial barriers, for example, by selling a home to a black family in a white neighborhood. The authorities basically delegated to real estate boards their policing duties. Equally important, although rarely discussed in the housing discrimination literature, was local government action, through the police, that tacitly permitted mob action to enforce racial barriers the local government was unwilling to enforce directly. A common instance of this was the firebombing or other damage of a home bought by a black family in a previously white area, which led to no arrests, much less convictions. In this vacuum of leadership it is not surprising that in both Helper and the case studies real estate brokers are seen, and see themselves, as the gatekeepers of the community. Thus the brokers' actions are taken to defend what they see as in the community's best interest.

Complementing these descriptive studies of housing agent practices is the pioneering work of the Taeubers that detailed the consequences of these racial practices, the highly segregated housing patterns that characterize American cities. Using the block data for census years beginning with 1940, they calculated the index of dissimilarity for each city, a time-consuming and tedious task in the days before the computer (Taeuber and Taeuber, 1965).[1] Their findings, updated and refined (Sørenson, Taeuber, and Hollingsworth, 1975; Van Valey, Roof, and Wilcox, 1977; Taeuber, 1983), have set out our basic understanding of the shape and shaping of American cities' residential patterns in the mid-twentieth century. One of their most important findings was that segregation increased as cities grew in the post–World War II era, reaching its zenith on the segregation index in 1950 in the North and in 1960 in the South (which was slower to make the transition from caste-type to class-type race relations). Most importantly, this measure, with a range of 0 (no segregation) to 100 (complete segregation) made clear that housing segregation was very high by 1940 (the first year with block-level data), with very little change in subsequent decades. Even during the seventies, the decade with the biggest change of any decade and the biggest decrease in segregation levels, the average level of segregation in American cities fell only 6 points, from a score of 87 to 81 (intercensal comparisons should be taken as approximate, for racial measures changed from nonwhite to Negro/black and from white to nonblack, and which cities were included changed with each decade as America urbanized and census definitions changed).

Finally, a third set of studies, often utilizing the case-study approach (rather than national data sets), looked at a key stage in the segregation process, that of the neighborhood undergoing racial transition. The development of suburbs and the increasing urbanization of Americans, white as well as black, meant that maintaining high levels of segregation required converting successive neighborhoods from white to black as white families moved to the suburbs, adding them to areas of black concentration, the ghetto. The issue that occupied many social scientists of the time was whether or not this process of racial transition was "normal." A number of studies posited a model of "ecological succession," likening racial transition to the process whereby, for example, sand dunes were converted into deeply wooded hills as successive groups of plants succeeded each other. By definition, ecological succession is "natural." It is also irreversible, following inevitably an orderly pattern. Likewise, Molotch (1972) compared the rates of buying and selling of homes in neighborhoods undergoing racial transition with rates in otherwise similar neighborhoods not undergoing racial change and found that they were comparable.

Two aspects of this racial transition process have received particular attention. First, the empirical question was raised and studied, but still not definitively answered, of whether or not there is a universal "tipping point," a threshold of a specific percentage at which the racial transition process either accelerates or becomes inevitable (Stinchcombe, McDill, and Walker, 1969; Schelling, 1971; Farley et al., 1978). Second, the issue of how much the racial transition process is the result of normal economic forces, the market at work, and how much it is the product of housing agent practices such as blockbusting was raised particularly by economists. The flight of whites from neighborhoods undergoing transition could be explained as an economically rational response to the real or feared fall of property values. It was more difficult to explain the higher prices (compared to either comparable housing or even to the selling price of the same house to the intermediary or broker a short time before) paid by incoming black families for the same housing until the development of the idea of a dual housing market. Under this model black housing consumers operate in a much more constrained market, with the result that they have fewer options than whites and are forced to accept less for their dollars than whites can buy for the same amount.

Perhaps the most imaginative methodology that documented the way in which the dual housing market reinforced racial inequality within the racial transition process was that of Lansing, Clifton, and Morgan (1969). Starting with the occupants of brand-new houses, they traced the "chain of moves" triggered by the creation of a new housing unit until it ended (for example, with the formation of a new household or the destruction of a housing unit). They found that while the creation of new, usually more expensive houses did "trickle down" economically, eventually benefiting moderate- or low-income households, the "chains" rarely crossed racial lines; in short, whites and blacks buy housing in two different markets, with the black market characterized by more demand and less supply, resulting in higher prices for black housing consumers. Finally, several studies indirectly documented the operation of the dual housing market by showing that homeownership rates of blacks were below those of whites in the same income bracket, suggesting barriers to homebuying other than lack of the economic wherewithal (Kain and Quigley, 1975; Hermalin and Farley, 1973).

Contrasting views of the role of individual preference and normal/natural processes were presented by the Taeubers on the one hand and Lieberson on the other. To the natural, ecological models, Lieberson (1963) added the factor of ethnic self-segregation, asserting that the ethnic and racial groups that succeeded each other in a given neighborhood did so as a group because they desired to settle and move together. To Lieberson, the benchmark for examining levels of racial segregation should not be the zero score on the index of dissimilarity, but rather the indexes of dissimilarity found between other ethnic groups, such as between Eastern Europeans and Southern Europeans. Because they presumably experience little or no discrimination, their levels of residential segregation are assumed to reflect the natural levels of segregation that ethnics impose on themselves voluntarily. On the other hand, the Taeubers (1963) argue that the ways in which violence and the threat of violence, individual or mob, maintain segregation belie the normal or natural character of racial transition and resegregation. As they point out, the possibility of violent consequences being visited on those who would break racial barriers makes it impossible to know how voluntary the segregation of blacks actually is. Even the words used to describe some real estate agent practices, such as blockbusting, suggest destruction, panic, and fear that are psychologically if not physically violent and hard to describe as just normal operations of the housing market.[2]

HOUSING DISCRIMINATION IN THE CIVIL RIGHTS ERA

Defining differential treatment on the basis of race as discrimination was basically a political process and an outcome of the open-housing movement (Saltman, 1971). Using protests, marches, and other actions often aimed at local and state authorities, the fair-housing movement sought to define housing discrimination as a violation of one's civil rights. Social science documented this change in opinion polls, tracking individual views. Interestingly, questions in this area of race relations were often carefully worded to eliminate the economic factor, for example, "If a Negro of the same education and income as you moved next door, would you mind . . . a lot, a little, or not at all?" Such caveats were usually absent when questions were asked in other areas (schools, employment, and so on).

In 1968, within a single month, the U.S. Congress and the Supreme Court both made discrimination in housing transactions illegal. Because the law upheld by the Supreme Court had no exemptions, the Court case, *Jones* v. *Mayer*, is broader in application; Title VIII of the civil rights law, on the other hand, bars discrimination on bases not covered by the Fourteenth Amendment (which is restricted to race), such as discrimination because of gender, source of income, religion, and national origin.

Because discrimination was not defined in any specific terms in the law, or in the court case beyond the case specifics, and because the U.S. Department of Housing and Urban Development (HUD) has never issued regulations under the law, what is and is not illegal housing discrimination remains unclear. Court cases brought under Title VIII or the Constitution have tended to be the most blatant or extreme instances of discrimination, as when the minority person is simply refused the housing altogether; only occasionally have more subtle measures been used (such as whether the financial terms were equal), and not always successfully.

The development of the audit was probably the most important event during the seventies in the study of housing discrimination. In the course of documenting discrimination to develop the case for local, state, and national open-housing laws, advocates developed the technique of testing: black and white testers (individuals or couples) would seek housing from the same housing agent, presenting roughly the same financial resources and family situation and differing essentially only in race. Each tester would write down his or her experiences, and these would be compared; evidence of differential treatment unfavorable to the black tester would be presented to a judge, or other relevant authority.

From both a legal and social science point of view, the audit neatly "controlled" for two factors historically considered relevant, as discussed earlier: economics and preference. By design the black and white testers presented equal (though, for obvious reasons, not identical) financial resource pictures and by definition sought the "same" housing.[3] The original means of documentation, usually a one- or two-page, largely unstructured "log" or journal-type description, became less and less useful as housing agents became less blatant in their means of racial discrimination. Pearce's dissertation (1976), which used social science techniques of behavior measurement drawn from the literature of field experiments and attitude-action research, developed a highly structured, highly differentiated, detailed, and quantified set of measures that resulted in a nine-page form (plus additional pages for housing actually inspected).

By far the largest study of housing discrimination was the HUD-sponsored Housing Market Practice Survey (HMPS), conducted in 40 cities in the spring and summer of 1977. Using the revised and honed audit form, over 1,600 audits were conducted in both the rental and sales markets. According to the only published analysis of the entire study, black homeseekers who go to four housing agents will encounter discrimination 72 percent of the time in the rental market and 48 percent of the time in the sales market (not counting racial steering in the latter) (HUD, 1979).

Complementing this documentation of actual racial practices of housing agents toward white and black housing consumers was the racial attitude data on preferences. Studies of whites found increasingly large majorities who accepted housing integration (although often with the economics-controlling caveat that the black neighbor be of similar socioeconomic status) and decreasing numbers who would uphold property rights at the expense of rights of minorities to live where they wished and could afford. Studies of blacks found high majorities, depending upon the exact question wording, who preferred racially mixed to all- or predominantly black neighborhoods.

Squaring this dramatic acceptance, even preference, of housing integration by both blacks and whites with the reality of little change in the traditionally high levels of segregation was partially due to the unique study done in Detroit by Farley, Bianchi, and Colasanto (1979). By using a series of cards that depicted schematically neighborhoods of differing racial compositions, ranging from token to 50/50 to predominantly black, they made clear the very real differences by race in preference and acceptance of integration. Roughly summarized, they found that for whites, acceptable integration was largely confined to token levels, but for blacks, the ideal neighborhood was closer to 50/50. Moreover, while whites were willing to pay a substantial premium for a house located in a suburban neighborhood with little or no integration, compared to the same house in the city proper, blacks were not willing to pay such a premium. In dynamic terms this means that as neighborhoods move from the token-integration levels attractive to whites to the proportions desired by blacks, white demand drops off, making the racial transition process inevitable.

HOUSING DISCRIMINATION IN THE EIGHTIES

Social science research in the eighties built on the increased knowledge of the seventies, elaborating our understanding of the housing discrimination process itself and the way in which it is linked to the larger context of racial segregation and inequality generally. In particular, three areas received attention. First, a number of local studies, using the form developed for the 1977 HUD study or similar instruments, documented continuing racial discrimination against minorities, Hispanics as well as blacks, in both rental and sales markets. Second, attention began to focus on the growing discrimination in the rental market against families with children. Third, the link between housing and school segregation/ desegregation was explored.

While some of the post-HMPS studies varied the methodology, for example, alternating whether the white or black tester visited the rental agent first, their main contribution was to document the continuing differential treatment of minority housing consumers compared to otherwise similar majority homeseekers. At the same time, they made clear that while discrimination in housing has persisted, its practice is covert and subtle. Many of these studies were done pursuant to federal grants for housing, with the goal that federal housing subsidies should not increase or maintain housing segregation. Others were carried out by voluntary fair-housing groups. Cities covered ranged from Boston to Los Angeles.

Particularly in California, Texas, and the growing states of the South and West, a new phenomenon became more and more apparent: discrimination against families with children is not only increasing, but effectively replacing racial/ethnic discrimination in some areas. That is, because minority households are considerably more likely to have children in them and are more likely to be confined by lower incomes to less expensive or rental housing, excluding families with children has become a legal way to exclude many minority households. Moreover, even when state or local laws bar total exclusion of families with children, limitations on the number, ages, and even gender of the children serve to severely constrain the housing opportunities of many families. Today, one out of four rental units excludes children altogether, and another two out of four restrict families with children. The result is the growth of (largely minority) "children's ghettoes," with particularly strong impact on school segregation for obvious reasons.

The Supreme Court over 15 years ago noted the reciprocal relationship between housing and school segregation. While most have observed that segregated neighborhoods result in segregated schools, social science research has documented that segregation of schools, in the South through law and in the North through gerrymandering of school attendance zones and other measures, helped promote and perpetuate housing segregation. Hawley and Rock (1973) have called this reciprocal relationship the web of urban racism. Pearce (1979) has documented the way in which segregated schools undergird housing discrimination practices by facilitating steering of housing consumers along racial lines. Moreover, several studies have shown that school desegregation, particularly at the metropolitanwide (for example, countywide) level, leads to steady and long-term declines in housing segregation levels (Farley, Richards, and Wurdock, 1980; Pearce, 1980; Pearce et al., 1984).

Some issues, however, have received little systematic exploration to date. For example, there is very little documentation of the impact of housing discrimination on employment opportunities of minorities; while empirically it may be less than, for example, the relationship between housing and school discrimination/segregation, it may also be more difficult to delineate. Conceptualization is also weaker in this area: if housing is denied on the basis that two children of the opposite sex would be sharing a bedroom, is that "discrimination"?

Such issues of conceptualization and unexplored questions also point to an important factor in this area of social science inquiry, which is that the nature of the phenomenon being studied, housing discrimination, is changing in fundamental ways. To a certain extent, the study of housing discrimination is a classic case of the measurement of the phenomenon affecting the phenomenon itself. The development of the audit, its use in a national study, and its subsequent use under Title VIII of the Civil Rights Law (and the Supreme Court case, *Jones* v. *Mayer*) in hundreds of local court cases have resulted in more sophisticated and more subtle patterns of practice than those originally documented. Thus the future of social science research on housing discrimination is a challenging one, combining the documenting of its relationship to other urban processes with describing its changing nature.

NOTES

1. The index of dissimilarity ranges from 0 to 100, representing no segregation to complete segregation. It compares the distribution of two groups across a set of units, such as city blocks. It is unaffected by variation in population totals between units, and larger units contribute proportionately more to the total index. It can be thought of as the percentage of one of the two groups who would have to move to reduce the index to zero (no segregation).

2. Ironically, the violent terminology, such as "blockbusting" and "invasion group," is applied to those most likely to be victims rather than perpetrators of violence.

3. In some audits the testers bring in or refer to the same property or properties advertised by the agency being tested; in others they present themselves as (new) homebuyers, with a very general idea of what they want. Still other audit designs fall between these two extremes.

REFERENCES

Du Bois, W. E. B. 1899. *The Philadelphia Negro.* Philadelphia: University of Pennsylvania Press.

Farley, Reynolds. 1985. "The Residential Segregation of Blacks from Whites: Trends, Causes, and Consequences." Ann Arbor: Population Studies Center, University of Michigan.

Farley, Reynolds, Suzanne Bianchi, and Diane Colasanto. 1979. "Barriers to the Racial Segregation of Neighborhoods: The Detroit Case." *Annals of the American Academy of Political and Social Sciences* 441: 97–113.

Farley, Reynolds, Toni Richards, and Charles Wurdock. 1980. "School Desegregation and White Flight: An Investigation of Competing Models and Their Discrepant Findings." *Sociology of Education* 53: 123–129.

Farley, Reynolds, Howard Schuman, Suzanne Bianchi, Diane Colasanto, and Shirley Hatchett. 1978. "Chocolate City, Vanilla Suburbs: Will the Trend toward Racially Separate Communities Continue?" *Social Science Research* 7: 319–344.

Green, Constance M. 1967. *The Secret City: A History of Race Relations in the Nation's Capital.* Princeton: Princeton University Press.

Hawley, Amos, and V. Rock (eds.). 1973. *Segregation in Residential Areas.* Washington, D.C.: National Academy of Science.

Helper, Rose. 1969. *Racial Policies and Practices of Real Estate Brokers.* Minneapolis: University of Minnesota Press.

Hermalin, Albert I., and Reynolds Farley. 1973. "The Potential for Residential Integration in Cities and Suburbs: Implications for the Busing Controversy." *American Sociological Review* 38: 595–610.

Kain, John F., and J. M. Quigley. 1975. *Housing Markets and Racial Discrimination: A Microeconomic Analysis.* New York: National Bureau of Economic Research.

Kusmer, Kenneth L. 1976. *A Ghetto Takes Shape: Black Cleveland, 1870–1930.* Urbana: University of Illinois Press.

Lansing, John B., Charles W. Clifton, and James N. Morgan. 1969. *New Homes and Poor People: A Study of Chains of Moves.* Ann Arbor: Institute for Social Research, University of Michigan.

Lieberson, Stanley. 1963. *Ethnic Patterns in American Cities.* New York: Free Press of Glencoe.

Molotch, Harvey L. 1972. *Managed Integration.* Berkeley and Los Angeles: University of California Press.

Osofsky, Gilbert. 1963. *Harlem: The Making of a Ghetto: Negro New York, 1890–1930.* New York: Harper & Row.

Palmer, Stuart. 1955. "The Role of the Real Estate Agent in the Structuring of Residential Areas: A Study in Social Control." Ph.D. diss. Yale University.

Pearce, Diana. 1976. "Black, White, and Many Shades of Gray: Real Estate Brokers and Their Racial Practices." Ph.D. diss. University of Michigan.

———. 1979. "Gatekeepers and Homeseekers: Individual and Institutional Factors in Racial Steering." *Social Problems* 26: 325–342.

———. 1980. "Breaking Down Barriers: New Evidence on the Impact of Metropolitan School Desegregation on Housing Patterns." Final Report on Grant #G-78–91–25 to the National Institute of Education. Washington, D.C.

Pearce, Diana, Robert L. Crain, Reynolds Farley, and Karl Taeuber. 1984. "Lessons Not Lost: The Impact of School Desegregation on the Racial Ecology of Large American Central Cities." Paper presented at the American Educational Research Association annual meeting, New Orleans, October 21.

Saltman, Juliet Z. 1971. *Open Housing as a Social Movement: Challenge, Conflict, and Change*. Lexington, Mass: Heath Lexington Books.

Schelling, Thomas. 1971. "On the Ecology of Micromotives." *Public Interest* 25: 61– 98.

Sørenson, Annemette, Karl E. Taeuber, and Leslie J. Hollingsworth. 1975. "Indexes of Racial Residential Segregation for 109 Cities in the United States, 1940 to 1970." *Sociological Focus* 8: 125–142.

Spear, Allan H. 1967. *Black Chicago*. Chicago: University of Chicago Press.

Stinchcombe, Arthur L., Mary McDill, and Collien Walker. 1969. "Is There a Racial Tipping Point in Changing Schools?" *Journal of Social Issues* 25: 11–35.

Taeuber, Karl E. 1983. *Racial Residential Segregation, 28 Cities, 1970–80*. CDE Working Paper 83–12. Madison, Wis.: Center for Demography and Ecology, University of Wisconsin.

Taeuber, Karl E., and Alma F. Taeuber. 1965. *Negroes in Cities*. Chicago: Aldine.

U.S. Department of Housing and Urban Development. 1979. *Measuring Racial Discrimination in American Housing Markets*. Washington, D.C.: Government Printing Office.

Van den Berghe, Pierre. 1967. *Race and Racism: A Comparative Perspective*. New York: Wiley.

Van Valey, Thomas L., Wade Clark Roof, and Jerome E. Wilcox. 1977. "Trends in Residential Segregation, 1960–1970." *American Journal of Sociology* 82: 826– 844.

Woodward, C. Vann. 1957. *The Strange Career of Jim Crow*. New York: Oxford University Press.

18

The Housing and Living Arrangements of Young People in the United States

WILLEM VAN VLIET—

Stage in the life cycle is, together with social class and ethnic origin, among the most important correlates of individual housing behavior and residential conditions. However, whereas there has been extensive research on social class and ethnic origin in relation to housing, there appears to be no comparable literature on the role of age or stage in the life cycle. At best, there exists an uneven distribution of research on housing as a context for the human condition across the life span. Much has been written, for example, about housing for the elderly (see the chapter by Huttman and Gurewitsch in this volume). Likewise, changes in life-cycle stage have been examined in relation to residential mobility and homeownership (Speare, 1970; Pickvance, 1973). The literature, however, is scattered and noncumulative and lacks an overarching conceptualization of the ways in which stage in the life cycle, in conjunction with other relevant factors, interfaces with a broader spectrum of housing questions related to, for example, preferences for housing type, residential location, residential choice, tenure status, maintenance, and management practices. Also required is an empirical documentation of conditions, processes, and trends vis-à-vis these considerations. This chapter contributes to the latter and makes observations and interpretations to identify factors that potentially have a bearing on the development of a more comprehensive framework for the study of housing across the life span.

Specifically, this brief chapter covers the housing and living arrangements of young people. The first section clarifies the term "young people," distinguishes between their "housing" and their "living arrangements," and provides some basic information. The second section reviews the living arrangements of young people. It is followed by a discussion of their housing situation. The conclusion points out several policy issues and argues for further research that links housing across the life span with various contextual considerations.

DEFINITION AND BASIC INFORMATION

Needless to say, there is no clear-cut criterion defining when someone begins or ceases to be young. This difficulty of definition exists not only in a developmental sense, but also in regard to questions related to housing. Age in and of itself is a meaningless criterion. It takes on significance only in relation to age-linked entitlements and role repertoires (for example, those associated with marriage, parenthood, and work) that introduce new opportunities and requirements with respect to housing. Sometimes official definitions clash with reality. In Australia, for example, legislated age restrictions have been shown to function with the effect of excluding homeless youth from needed shelter (Low and Crawshaw, 1985). On the other hand, there are children who, out of choice or lack thereof, continue to live through much of their adult life in their parents' home.

While acknowledging these limitations, I will adopt as a frame of reference the 15 to 34 age group. The life span between 15 and 34 is a period when major life events with implications for housing typically occur. For example, it is during this time that most people leave the parental home, set up their own household, and, in the United States, buy their first home. Another reason for this delineation is largely pragmatic: it encompasses a number of different age breakdowns used in the literature and conveniently corresponds to much of the available statistical information.

Housing, in this chapter, refers to aspects of shelter. Questions in this connection concern, for example, the type of housing in which young people live, the cost and quality of their housing, their tenure status, and their residential preferences. Living arrangements refer to aspects of household organization that are accommodated by and have implications for given housing situations. Relevant trends relate to, for example, age at leaving home, number of children per household, divorce rates, and so on.

Changes in living arrangements reflect a number of demographic, cultural, and economic factors. High unemployment rates, for example, may lead young people to postpone marriage or to delay leaving their parents' home (Eversley, 1983), and various class-related variables were found to be significant by Leppel (1987) and Jones (1987). Housing is also among the factors impacting on living arrangements. Tight housing markets may act to discourage divorces (Morton, 1985). Tenure status has been found to be related to average number of live births per family (Murphy, 1984; Murphy and Sullivan, 1985). Rising housing costs have also been linked to reduced fertility rates (Myers, 1983), as have crowded living conditions (Felson and Solaun, 1975; Morton, 1974), although it is not clear what the critical level is above which such effects would show up (Edwards and Booth, 1977). On the other hand, new life-styles emerging in conjunction with rising levels of affluence may find expression in preferences for innovative housing designs and alternative forms of housing management. Thus while housing and living arrangements are closely intertwined, they are not identical. Rather, the two must be seen as constituting a complex matrix, with some of the cells contained therein having more congruence than others.

What is the significance of young people in the housing market? Studies addressing this question are conspicuous by their absence. However, a few statistics are informative. In 1985 people between the ages of 18 and 34 made up more than 40 percent of the U.S. adult population (U.S. Bureau of the Census, 1985h: 27). In March 1984 households headed by adults under 35 years of age comprised 30 percent of all households nationwide (U.S. Bureau of the Census, 1985e: 215). The demographic significance of these numbers becomes magnified in the housing market. The bulk of housing transactions in the United States are precipitated by residential relocation, and among movers people under 35 dominate. In 1980 they made up more than half of all moving owner-occupiers and more than 68 percent of all renters who moved (U.S. Bureau of the Census, 1985c: 47, 50). In 1985 this same age group made up 46 percent of all mortgage borrowers, 52 percent of all homebuyers, and 71 percent of all first-time buyers (U.S. League of Savings Institutions, 1986: 7, 18).

Obviously, these figures conceal more than they reveal. However, they suffice to indicate that the housing of people under 35 years of age merits our attention. There are numerous questions regarding the housing conditions and residential behavior of this age group, the relation to behaviors in other life spheres and in later life stages, and factors impinging on these behaviors. The aim of this chapter is not to try and answer these questions, but to raise some of them while documenting an initial information base.

LIVING ARRANGEMENTS

The U.S. Bureau of the Census uses three main categories to classify the living arrangements of young adults. The distribution of people under 35 across these categories for the 1960–1985 period is shown in Table 18.1. In 1985, in the 18 to 24 age group about 60 percent of the men were children of householders, that is, living with one or both parents. The proportion of men in this category had increased only slightly between 1960 and 1970 and remained stable in the next decade, but it rose by more than 5 percent between 1980 and 1985. Since 1970 the proportion of family householders among men in this age group has dropped from 30 percent to 16 percent. However, the increase in male nonfamily householders seen during the 1970s has been halted and has, in fact, been followed by a slight decline. Among women, the same trends have prevailed, although the pattern differs in that women, on the average marrying at a younger age than do men, are less often living with their parents and more often as a family householder. Although the relative numbers differ, the direction of the trends is very similar among the 25 to 34 age group. Most noticeable among both men and women is a continuing decline in family householders and a corresponding rise in nonfamily households.

The basic patterns shown in Table 18.1 reflect and are related to various other demographic trends that impact on household formation. Among these trends are the following:

1. *Delays in first marriage.* Median age at first marriage steadily declined during the first part of this century, reaching a low in the mid-1950s of 22.5

Table 18.1
Living Arrangements of Young Adults

Living Arrangements	1985	1980	1970	1960
Adults 18 to 24 years				
Male:				
Child of householder	59.7	54.3	54.3	52.4
Fam. householder or spouse	16.4	21.3	30.0	31.6
Nonfamily householder	9.6	11.1	5.4	2.7
Other	14.3	13.3	10.3	13.4
Female:				
Child of householder	47.8	42.7	41.3	34.9
Fam. householder or spouse	32.0	36.2	44.7	51.1
Nonfamily householder	6.9	8.1	4.2	2.2
other	13.3	13.1	9.7	11.8
Adults 25 to 34 years				
Male:				
Child of householder	13.3	10.5	9.5	10.9
Fam. householder or spouse	60.1	66.4	79.3	78.5
Nonfamily householder	16.1	15.3	6.5	3.7
Other	10.5	7.9	4.8	6.9
Female:				
Child of householder	8.0	7.0	6.6	7.4
Fam. householder or spouse	75.5	78.1	86.1	86.1
Nonfamily householder	9.7	8.8	3.5	2.1
Other	6.7	6.2	3.9	4.4

Source: U.S. Bureau of the Census, 1986b: 74.

years for men and 20.1 years for women. Since that time this trend has reversed itself, most notably in the last ten years. In 1985 the estimated median age at first marriage for women reached the all-time high of 23.3 years, while the average of 25.5 years for men is nearing the highest level of 26.1, recorded for 1890, the first year for which data are available (U.S. Bureau of the Census, 1986b).

The delay in first marriage is also apparent in increases in the proportion of men and women under 35 who have never married. Between 1970 and 1985 the proportion of never-married men and women in the 20 to 24 age group increased by more than 20 percent to 76 percent and 59 percent, respectively. During the same period the corresponding numbers for men and women in their late twenties and early thirties doubled (Table 18.2).

2. *Changes in homeleaving age.* The proportion of persons aged 18 to 29 who were living with their parents reached a high point near the end of the economic depression of the 1930s. Following World War II it started to decline. A recent analysis used data from a Rhode Island sample, thought by the authors to be comparable to the U.S. population during the 1920–79 period, to suggest that this decline in homeleaving age is a continuing trend (Goldschneider and LeBourdais, 1986). However, U.S. census data show that since about 1970 there has been an increase in the number of young adults living with their parents. In 1984, 43 percent of the men and 31 percent of the women from 18 to 29 years of age lived with their parents (U.S. Bureau of the Census, 1985g). Glick and Lin (1986), among others, have examined the characteristics of these people.

Homeleaving may involve intermediate stages of semiautonomy (Goldschneider and DaVanzo, 1986) and is caused by a complex set of factors, including choices by young people to continue their education, get a paid job, and marry. The last variable continues to play a major role in homeleaving decisions (Goldschneider and DaVanzo, 1985; Heer, Hodge, and Felson, 1985). Of course, decisions regarding schooling, work, and marriage are not taken in a vacuum. The reversal in the decline in homeleaving age would seem to be related to, for example, increased housing costs and higher unemployment rates among young people, raising the question of housing affordability, to which we will return later.

3. *Changes in the number of persons living alone.* The number of people living alone has increased by more than 90 percent since 1970, as compared to a 37 percent rise in the number of all households (U.S. Bureau of the Census, 1985f). In part, the one-person households are formed by young adults choosing to live alone for some time after leaving their parents' home and by young couples who divorce after a short marriage. However, after nearly doubling between 1970 and 1980, the number of persons under 25 living alone has since declined by 3 percent. A similarly strong increase of singles in the 25 to 34 age group during that decade was followed by only slight increases for both men and women, suggesting a growing tendency among young adults to postpone (the costs of) setting up their own households.

Table 18.2
Percent Never Married by Age and Sex

Age	Women			Men		
	1970	1980	1985	1970	1980	1985
20 to 24 years	36	50	59	55	69	76
25 to 29 years	11	21	26	19	33	39
30 to 34 years	6	10	14	9	16	21

Source: U.S. Bureau of the Census, 1985f: 8.

4. *Increase in divorces*. The continuing increase in the propensities for marriages to be dissolved by divorce has been well documented. In the present context it is significant that divorce rates have risen fastest among young adults. In 1960 the number of divorced men under 30 was less than one-fifth of the 90 (per 1,000 married with spouse present) recorded for 1984. Among women in this age group the 1984 figure of 116 is more than four times as much as that for 1960 (U.S. Bureau of the Census, 1986b). Similar sharp increases have occurred among men and women aged 30 to 34 (in 1984, the respective rates were 137 and 168).

5. *Increase in single-parent families*. In 1970 married-couple families made up 71 percent of all households. By 1985 this proportion had dropped to 58 percent. This decline was accounted for chiefly by the drop in families with own children under 18 (from 40 percent to 28 percent). During the same period the number of families headed by a lone parent increased from less than 2 million to more than 10 million. A majority of these families include children under 18, and women outnumber men as household heads by a ratio of five to one (U.S. Bureau of the Census, 1985f: 7). In 1979 women under 35 heading families with children increased their proportion of all such families to 54 percent (U.S. Bureau of the Census, 1980: 6). Their income was about half the median of that of their male counterparts.

6. *Increase in unmarried couples*. Unmarried-couple households consist of two unrelated adults of the opposite sex, with or without children under 15 years old. Between 1970 and 1984 such households increased by 280 percent; in 70 percent of them the partners were less than 35 years old. Among those with no children present, the proportion with householders under 25 was 23 percent in 1984, and householders aged 25 to 34 increased their share to more than 40 percent (U.S. Bureau of the Census, 1985g: 7). Their dramatic increase notwithstanding, it should be remembered that the number of unmarried couples in the United States still amounts to only about 4 percent of all couples (U.S. Bureau of the Census, 1985f: 3).

7. *Decrease in fertility*. The number of births per women has decreased to 1.8 from 3.8 in 1957. In 1980 the number of births to date per 1,000 women from 18 to 34 had declined to 1,127, down by 11 percent from 1976. The number of expected live births also declined during the same period, while births for married women decreased by 30 percent between 1967 and 1980 (U.S. Bureau of the Census, 1986b).

8. *Declining household and family size*. The average household and family size in the United States has steadily declined from 3.67 and 3.76 persons, respectively, in 1940 to 2.69 and 3.23 in 1985. These smaller household and family sizes are attributable to a number of factors. Several of these factors reflect changes among young adults, including the tendency to have fewer children. This trend is also seen in a continuing drop in the average number of children under 18 per household (1.09 in 1970, .72 in 1985) and per family (1.34 in 1970, .98 in 1985).

Obviously, the preceding thumbnail sketch of living arrangements among young adults and trends impacting on them is only a partial representation of all relevant factors. The discussion is also limited to descriptive information. As such, it reflects the nature of demographic research on this topic in the United States, which has speculated about but not conclusively studied the linkages between the observed demographic changes and broader developments in the national political economy.

Nevertheless, in spite of these limitations, even a cursory examination of these trends suggests significant implications for the housing situation of young people. There are, first of all, important questions of demand and supply simply in terms of absolute numbers of required and available dwelling units according to current and projected figures (for recent reviews, see Burns and Grebler, 1986; Sternlieb and Hughes, 1986). Beyond the provision of shelter, there are important issues having to do particularly with short- and long-term effects of tenure and affordability, as discussed in the next sections.

HOUSING

Against the background of the preceding sketch of young adults' living arrangements, this section examines selected aspects of their housing situation. The discussion is divided into three parts. The first part is concerned with housing type and tenure, as well as location. This logically leads into questions of affordability taken up in the second part. The final part deals with aspects of housing quality.

Housing Type, Location, and Tenure

Most Americans aspire to a privately owned single-family home. There is also a general preference for suburban types of environments, which is where most such houses are found. Hence in the United States housing type, location, and tenure are highly interrelated, a factor that should be borne in mind in the following discussion that treats each in turn.

Housing Type

Table 18.3 shows the distribution of households by age across housing types in 1980, broken down according to tenure status. The data show that even among 15- to 19-year-old householders single-unit detached dwellings form the largest share (22 percent) of any of the housing types distinguished in the census of housing. However, if grouped together, the various categories of multifamily housing account for a large majority of the households in this age group. The proportion of households living in freestanding, single units rapidly increases for each subsequent age group, reaching 62 percent among those in their early thirties. Excepting single attached units (with a constant share of about 4 percent), occupancy of all other housing types steadily decreases with age.

Table 18.3
Housing Type by Age of Householder and Tenure, 1980

	Age of Householder					
Housing Type	15 to 19 yrs	20 to 24 yrs	25 to 29 yrs	30 to 34 yrs	15 yrs and over
One unit detached	22.0%	31.0%	48.2%	62.4%	62.9%
owned	6.4	14.9	33.8	51.2	53.8
rented	15.6	16.1	14.4	11.2	9.1
One unit attached	4.2	4.5	4.7	4.5	4.1
owned	.3	.8	1.7	2.2	2.3
rented	3.9	3.7	3.0	2.3	1.8
Two units	9.4	9.5	8.0	5.9	6.1
owned	.3	.6	1.0	1.2	1.9
rented	9.1	8.9	7.0	4.7	4.2
3 or 4 units	12.0	10.1	7.5	5.1	4.9
owned	.2	.3	.6	.7	.8
rented	11.8	9.8	6.9	4.4	4.1
5 to 9 units	11.2	9.4	7.0	4.7	4.3
owned	.1	.2	.4	.5	.5
rented	11.1	9.2	6.6	4.2	3.8

Table 18.3 (Continued)

Housing Type	Age of Householder				
	15 to 19 yrs	20 to 24 yrs	25 to 29 yrs	30 to 34 yrs	15 yrs and over
10 to 19 units	12.5	10.8	7.4	4.8	4.5
owned	.1	.2	.3	.4	.4
rented	12.4	10.6	7.1	4.4	4.1
20 to 49 units	8.6	7.2	4.8	3.2	3.4
owned	.1	.1	.2	.2	.3
rented	8.5	7.1	4.6	3.0	3.1
50 or more units	9.3	8.0	5.9	4.5	5.1
owned	.1	.2	.3	.4	.5
rented	9.2	7.8	5.6	4.1	4.6
Mobile homes, trailers, etc.	10.5	9.0	6.3	4.6	4.8
owned	4.5	5.8	4.7	3.6	3.8
rented	6.0	3.2	1.6	1.0	1.0
Total (x1,000)	624	5,972	9,118	9,166	80,390

Source: U.S. Bureau of the Census, 1984: 3–19.

Within each housing type there are parallel developments in tenure, as renters become fewer and owners proportionately increase in older age groups. This pattern prevails even though the absolute number of owners may decrease. Exceptions are found in mobile-home ownership and single detached units in rental tenure, both of which reach their peak among people in their early twenties (Table 18.3).

Data from the U.S. Bureau of the Census (1984: 3–19), not presented here, also show that in 1980 single detached units dominated among owners of all age groups. Their share steadily increased, from 52 percent among owners aged 15 to 19 to 85 percent among owners 30 to 34 years old. Mobile homes and trailers housed 37 percent of 15- to 19-year-old owners, their proportion steadily decreasing to 6 percent of those in their early thirties. All other housing types (including condominiums) represent only a fraction of owners.

Among renters there is a tendency to live in structures with fewer units as they get older. Albeit less dramatically than among owners, the proportion of renters in single detached dwellings also goes up with age, from 18 percent (15 to 19 years) to 28 percent (30 to 34 years). Mobile homes are much less prevalent among renters than among owners, with a share that declines from 7 percent among 15- to 19-year-olds to 3 percent among people in the 30 to 34 age group (U.S. Bureau of the Census, 1984: 3–19).

Location

The preceding data reveal a differential distribution of housing types and tenure across age. A different age-related pattern exists with respect to residential location, at least among married-couple families (no suitable age breakdown is available for other types of households). Table 18.4 indicates that in 1980 a majority of married-couple families under 25 were urban renters (51 percent). Even among such households headed by persons in their late twenties, urban renters outnumbered owners in both rural and urban areas (as well as rural renters).

Closer examination of the figures in Table 18.4 brings out two further points. First, in 1980 the total proportion of married-couple households (renters plus owners) living in urban areas was constant in the various age groups (around 64 percent). In light of the urbanization of the suburbs and the gentrification of selected inner-city areas, it would be interesting to see the distribution of this group across suburbs and cities, particularly as it might have changed over time. Unfortunately, such data were not available. It is noteworthy, however, that in a national survey conducted for the U.S. Department of Housing and Urban Development (HUD) (1978: 181), 31 percent of those in the 25 to 34 age bracket and 49 percent of those under 25 believed that the best housing is in the city. In the same survey 18 percent and 19 percent, respectively, listed a large city as their first choice as a place to live, more than any other age group, but considerably less than the more than 25 percent who preferred a rural area (HUD, 1978: 560).

Another point that stands out in Table 18.4 is the differential increase in

Table 18.4
Married-Couple Families by Age of Householder, Residential Location, and Tenure, 1980

Families	Owners		Renters		Total (x1,000)
	urban	rural	urban	rural	
Total	46.9%	30.1%	16.8%	5.9%	50,521
Age of Householder					
under 25 years	13.3	17.7	51.1	17.8	2,394
25 to 29 years	29.9	23.1	34.4	12.6	5,234
30 to 34 years	42.3	27.9	21.7	8.1	6,467

Source: U.S. Bureau of the Census, 1985d: E4.

homeownership with age among urban and rural households, while the urban/ rural ratio among renters remains stable around three to one at all age levels. Rural ownership grows from 18 percent among married-family householders under 25 to 28 percent among those 30 to 34 years of age. The corresponding increase in urban areas is much sharper: from 13 percent (less than rural owners and urban as well as rural renters) to 42 percent (far more than any other category).

The greater scarcity of rental housing in rural areas limits the number of rural renters in general, but it does not explain why rental tenure is disproportionately more common among young urbanites. Without further study one can only speculate about the reasons for this age-related pattern. However, it is likely that a strong contributing factor is the much higher cost of private homeownership, which people can only carry when they advance in their careers and get higher incomes (assuming that urban-rural differences in housing costs are not offset by urban-rural income differences).

Shifts in Tenure

The preceding discussion has shown how, with very few exceptions, ownership increases with age within any given housing type and in urban as well as rural areas. Not surprisingly, the same pattern exists for each of the various household types shown in Table 18.5. However, between 1976 and 1986 several significant changes took place.

First, whereas homeownership in older age groups increased during that period, it declined among householders under 35, reversing a long trend. Second, among young people the drop in homeownership rate increases with age. Third, the decrease in owning husband-wife families alone is responsible for the entire decline in ownership among all young households. Ownership in single-parent and nonfamily households, in fact, rose slightly (although clearly less than in older age groups). Overall, however, ownership rates remain low for single-parent households, although they are higher for men (less than 25 years: 27 percent; 25–29 years: 40 percent; 30–34 years: 52 percent) than for women (less than 25 years: 6 percent; 25–29 years: 23 percent; 30–34 years: 32 percent).

Data restricted to families indicate a similar trend (Table 18.6). From 1976 to 1984 homeownership is again found to have declined among those under 35, whereas it rose in older age groups. Table 18.6 also shows the larger than average proportion of young families renting public housing. The proportion of female-headed families in public housing is much higher yet; in 1979 it was 14 percent among householders under 25, and among blacks in that age group it was 23 percent (U.S. Bureau of the Census, 1980). While overall the proportion of families headed by a person under 30 in public housing constitutes only a fraction of all young families, it is significant that their number has increased between 1976 and 1984. This increase in "last-resort" housing points to a growing problem of housing affordability, to which we return in the next section (see also the chapter by Hartman in this book).

Some observers manage to project housing trends for people under 35 without

Table 18.5
Households by Age, Type, and Tenure

Households	1976				1984			
	under 25 yrs	25 to 29	30 to 34	all households	under 25 yrs	25 to 29	30 to 34	all households
Owners	21.1%	43.6%	62.3%	65.1%	17.6%	38.4%	54.4%	64.6%
Family Households								
husband-wife	17.0	37.6	54.4	49.3	11.2	29.4	43.0	45.5
male head, no wife present	.5	.4	.6	1.3	.7	.9	1.0	1.4
female head, no husband present	.7	2.2	4.0	4.9	1.3	2.5	3.7	5.5
Nonfamily Households								
male	2.1	2.2	2.5	2.9	2.8	3.9	4.7	4.2
female	.8	1.1	.8	6.8	1.7	1.7	2.0	8.1
Renters	78.9	56.4	37.7	34.9	82.4	61.6	45.6	35.4
Family Households								
husband-wife	37.3	30.4	18.9	15.6	30.0	26.2	19.2	13.2
male head, no wife present	1.2	.7	.6	.7	2.5	1.6	1.2	1.0
female head, no husband present	10.8	7.6	8.6	5.2	13.5	10.0	9.0	6.1
Nonfamily Households								
male	16.2	10.9	6.3	6.1	19.8	14.2	9.2	7.3
female	13.4	7.0	3.4	7.3	16.5	9.6	7.0	7.9
N(x 1000)	5,877	8,298	7,212	72,867	5,510	9,848	9,960	85,407

Source: U.S. Bureau of the Census, 1977: 135; 1985e: 215.

Table 18.6
Families by Age of Householder and Tenure

Tenure	1976				1984			
	under 25	25 to 29	30 to 34	All families	under 25	25 to 29	30 to 34	All families
Owners	27.2%	50.9%	67.7%	71.9%	22.2%	46.5%	61.9%	72.1%
Renters								
Public	4.6	2.4	2.6	1.9	5.2	3.6	2.7	2.1
Private	68.3	46.7	29.8	26.2	72.6	49.8	35.5	25.8
N (in thousands)	4,042	6,589	6,296	56,245	3,257	6,952	7,680	61,997

Source: U.S. Bureau of the Census, 1977: 49; 1985e: 31.

Figure 18.1
1980 National Expectation of Life by Occupied State at Age X

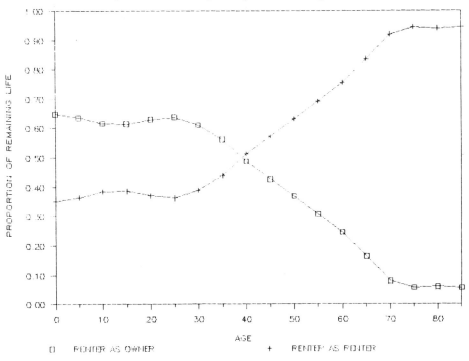

Source: Morrow-Jones, 1986. Reprinted with permission.

regard for the recent decline in homeownership in this age group (Sternlieb and Hughes, 1986). Others suggest that the decline has created a pent-up demand for ownership that will be released when the baby-boom generation moves into its peak-earning stage (Dahmann, 1985). However, tenure transitions are affected by conjuncturally sensitive considerations of consumption (Plaut, 1987), and these indifferent and optimistic assessments contrast with probabilities of the rent-to-own transition calculated for different age groups by Morrow-Jones (1986). Using data from the Annual Housing Survey of 1980, she determined the number of years an individual can expect to live beyond a given age as a renter or an owner, depending on his or her tenure at that age. The results of the analysis, shown in Figure 18.1, indicate that after about age 30 the proportion of remaining life that renters, on the average, will live as owners drops off steadily and fairly rapidly. In other words, if people have not yet bought a home by that age, statistically their chances diminish quickly.

Affordability

Convention has it that it is reasonable for households in the United States to spend between 20 and 25 percent of their budget on housing. This criterion is quite arbitrary, as it does not take into account many factors, including the quality of the dwelling, its surroundings, and the level of household income. Households with very low incomes will have difficulty spending even 10 percent on housing, because they need the money for expenses on food, clothing, and medical care. Against this background, what proportion of their income do young adults spend on housing? The emphasis in the following discussion is on owners, but we first briefly review the situation of renters.

Renters

When examining the housing costs of renters, it is more useful to consider gross rent than contract rent. Payments of tenants to their landlord may include utilities and/or fuel costs. Gross rent comprises these costs plus contract rent and therefore enhances the comparability of the figures that are obtained.

It is at once evident from Table 18.7 that households headed by persons under 35 tend to pay considerably more than what has traditionally been deemed reasonable. Median gross rent for householders 25 to 34 years of age ranges from 23 to 29 percent of household income. For younger age groups, housing costs are much higher yet. Blacks consistently spend a greater portion of their income on housing than do whites, especially in the younger age groups. Among whites in large, multifamily structures there is a tendency to have higher costs than do those renting single detached units and mobile homes. In some categories it is not uncommon to find more than 60 percent of the households spending 25 percent or more of their income on housing.

In considering the figures in Table 18.7, it should be remembered that young adults also tend to have incomes below the national median, leaving them with fewer resources for other necessities. Moreover, renters (who, as shown later, also live in more crowded dwellings) have much lower incomes than do owners. In 1983 the median income of renters was 56 percent of that for owners (U.S. Bureau of the Census, 1985a: 19). One wonders, then, are young owners indeed much better off?

Owners

Before examining the housing costs of young owners, it is useful to emphasize the importance of private homeownership in U.S. society. Not only does it provide shelter that is relatively more secure than that afforded by rental dwellings; it is also seen as a symbol of success and accomplishment, expressed in its interior, exterior, and locational characteristics. A private homeowner is

Table 18.7
Median Gross Rent as Percentage of Household Income in 1979 of Renter-Occupied Housing Units by Housing Type, Race, and Age, 1980

Age	one-unit detached		20 to 49 units in structure		50 or more units in structure		mobile homes, trailers, etc.	
	black	white	black	white	black	white	black	white
15 to 19 years	49	33	50+	41	47	43	49	35
20 to 24 years	32	25	33	29	31	30	34	27
25 to 29 years	28	23	26	24	24	24	29	24
30 to 34 years	28	24	24	23	23	23	28	24

Source: U.S. Bureau of the Census, 1984: 501, 513, 515, 517, 519, 531, 533, 535.

viewed as someone who "has made it," in contrast to renters who are typically viewed as transients, still on their way to make it or, when in public housing, stigmatized as an underclass. Private homeownership also confers significant financial advantages on owners in terms of tax breaks, helps to provide security during retirement, and has been found to benefit the housing situation of the next generation.

Needless to say, none of these advantages is inherent in homeownership per se; all have been so construed by a complex of ideological factors and political and economic interests (Kemeny, 1981). Here it is only possible to note these antecedents and to acknowledge a reality in which private homeownership is greatly desired. Results of a recent nationwide survey commissioned by the *Professional Builder* led this organization to the conclusion that "homeownership is still the American dream" (1984: 67). This conclusion cannot come as a great surprise, considering that the sample consisted of prospective purchasers "who said they plan to buy a house in the next six months" (1984: 65). However, more impartial studies also point to the overriding importance that continues to be attached to homeownership. In response to a question about what is part of the good life asked by the Roper Organization in national polls in 1975, 1978, and 1981, homeownership was most frequently mentioned each year (Myers, 1985b: 319).

The desire for ownership does not appear to be any less strong among the younger generation. In a Louis Harris survey conducted in 1978, 84 percent of the respondents in the 25 to 34 age range listed an owned single detached house as their first dwelling choice, more than any other age group, with an additional 5 percent selecting ownership of other housing types (HUD, 1978: 641). Among a sample of college students, Hohm (1983b: 65) found that 86 percent rated homeownership as being important to them. An overwhelming majority (69 percent) of those who expected to buy a home indicated a single-family detached dwelling as their choice (Hohm, 1983a: 29), and 48 percent would limit their number of children to afford a home (Hohm, 1984). However, the same study also found a significant discrepancy between the housing payments projected by the respondents and the payments that would be realistically required (Hohm, 1985: 52).

In 1985, according to data published by the U.S. League of Savings Institutions (1986: 22), first-time buyers spent 23 percent (median) of their household income on housing. While this does not seem to be an excessive figure, it is useful to look at the proportional distribution of housing expenses. Table 18.8 presents this information, broken down by age group. The data show that in 1980 even among owners in their early thirties, 38 percent spent more than 25 percent of the household income on housing. This percentage increases as owners are younger, reaching 61 percent among the youngest age group. Although not strictly comparable, these figures contrast sharply with 1950, when only 2.6 percent and 2.9 percent of the owners with FHA- and VA-insured mortgages,

Table 18.8
Selected Monthly Owner Costs as Percentage of Monthly Income for Owners of Detached Single Dwellings by Age Group, 1980

Age	less than 10%	10 to 14%	15 to 19%	20 to 24%	25 to 29%	30% or more
15 to 19 years	3.9	7.8	10.4	12.5	11.2	50.2
20 to 24 years	3.0	10.2	18.9	20.9	16.0	31.0
25 to 29 years	3.1	11.8	21.6	22.3	15.9	25.3
30 to 34 years	4.0	14.6	22.8	20.9	14.4	23.3
All owners	11.6	20.9	20.7	15.9	10.3	20.6

Note: Costs include the sum of payments for mortgages, deeds of trust, or similar debts on property, real estate taxes, fire and hazard insurance on the property, utilities (gas, water, electricity), and fuels. Totals may not add up to 100 percent because of uncomputed proportions.

Source: U.S. Bureau of the Census, 1984: 587.

respectively, paid 30 percent or more for principal and interest (U.S. Bureau of the Census, 1952: 290–291).

Available data were used to plot the relation between household income and house prices from 1950 through 1984, broken down by age. Figure 18.2 shows that the median sales price of existing one-family dwellings and median household income increased steadily and remained more or less parallel to each other from 1950 through 1970. Since that time, however, sales prices of existing and new one-family dwellings have increased exponentially, whereas incomes have risen at a much slower pace. During that period gains in the 15 to 24 age group also began increasingly to lag behind income increases for households in the 25 to 34 age range.

Of course, the relation between income and housing prices should be adjusted for the effects of inflation, interest rates, capital gains, and the deductability of interest payments and property taxes from income. Kain (1983: 141, 145), after reviewing the evidence regarding after-tax costs, suggested that affordability is a problem for first-time buyers. The decline in homeownership among young people only, in spite of persistent ownership preferences, supports this conclusion. Trends noted earlier (the delay in first marriage and the reversals of both the decline in homeleaving age and the rise in the number of young people living alone) are also in line with the interpretation that homeownership has become less accessible to young people. In spite of declining interest rates and new mortgage arrangements, the signs are that this trend will continue. One indicator, for example, is that FHA- and VA-financed housing transactions, typically around 20 percent of the annual total, grew to 30 percent in 1985–86 (Smith, 1986: 21). Unemployment among young people, particularly in minority groups, continues to rise, and rents are expected to go up even more as a result of the new tax law changes, leaving young people with less money for growing upfront purchase costs. Finally, private homeownership has become increasingly dependent on a total household income based on two earners. This important point is illustrated by the fact that in 1985 a second income accounted for more than 10 percent of total household income for more than 68 percent of all first-time buyers consisting of households with two adults; for about one-third of them it contributed between 40 and 50 percent of total household income (corresponding figures for repurchasers were, respectively, 53 percent and 18 percent; U.S. League of Savings Institutions, 1986: 19).

Housing Quality

A recent public opinion poll conducted among a nationwide sample inquired about people's satisfaction with their housing situation. In the 18 to 29 age group, 56 percent of the respondents was found to be "highly satisfied" (Gallup, 1983: 18). While this figure suggests that a majority have little to complain about, it is lower than for any other age group (for example, 80 percent of those above 65 were highly satisfied). It also does not reflect the finding, reported by

Figure 18.2
Sales Price of New and Existing One-Family Dwellings and Median Income of Families by Age Group, 1950-84

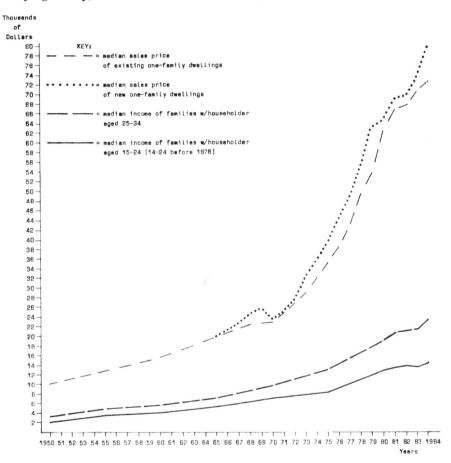

Source: U.S. Bureau of the Census, 1980a, 1985h; and *Current Population Reports,* Series P-60,
    Money Income of Households, Families, and Persons in the U.S., nos. 9, 24, 37, 51, 80,
    103, 137, 146, 151 (various years).

Michelson (1977), that young households may seek out and be satisfied with one housing type in the face of prospects for very different dwelling (a detailed house) during a later life-cycle stage in which they would consider a continuation of their previously satisfactory housing situations as wholly inadequate. Furthermore, global measures summarizing subjective perceptions do not reveal anything about specific aspects of the actual housing situation. Unfortunately, information in that regard is sparse.

Winter (1980) compared the housing quality of owners under 35 with that of older owners and nonowners among a stratified random sample of Iowa households. Results of this study showed that, compared to older owners, young owners had significantly fewer bathrooms, but differed little with respect to plumbing facilities and defects in walls, floors, roofs, and heating systems. The housing quality of young owners was superior to that of young nonowners. Interpretation of these findings is difficult, however, because nonowners included also owners of dwellings other than single detached dwellings, while owners consisted of owners of mobile homes and owners of single-family detached houses, two quite distinct categories.

One common measure of housing quality is crowding, in the United States generally thought to exist at a level of 1.01 persons per room and above. In 1980, of about 3.5 million crowded dwellings nationwide, 55 percent were occupied by families with children under six. Most of them lived in central cities (U.S. Bureau of the Census, 1983). Table 18.9 further shows that crowding is not a rare occurrence in some categories. It is, not surprisingly, more common among married-couple families than single-parent families and among families headed by persons in their late twenties and early thirties than among those with heads under 25, who generally have fewer children. Crowding is also uniformly more frequent among renters than owners. Among owners it is more common in central cities, whereas among renters the opposite holds true. Also, black families live much more often under crowded conditions than do white families. In fact, among renters one of every five black married-couple families lived in crowded housing in 1980.

Another indicator of housing quality may be the number of dwelling units removed from the housing inventory. Such dwellings are usually condemned because their substandard conditions have made them unfit for human habitation or because they were located in undesirable sites where they were liable to be and indeed were destroyed by fire, flooding, or other hazards. The most recent American (Annual) Housing Survey (U.S. Bureau of the Census, 1985d) gives 1973 characteristics of units removed from the inventory in 1983. From these data it appears that owners and renters under 30 accounted for 29 percent and 35 percent, respectively, of the affected two-or-more-person households with a male head with a wife present and no nonrelatives. A comparison of these figures with the proportion of such households in the overall population in 1973 (U.S. Bureau of the Census, 1975: 3) shows that renters under 30 were underrepresented among households whose dwellings were removed from the inventory (35 percent

Table 18.9
Crowded Households by Type, Age, Tenure, Race, and Residential Location, 1980

Households	Owners				Renters			
	Black	White	Central Cities of SMSA's	Outside SMSA's	Black	White	Central Cities of SMSA's	Outside SMSA's
Married-couple families Age of Householder								
15 to 24 years	8.2	2.0	2.7	2.0	14.9	5.1	9.8	5.7
25 to 34 years	9.6	3.0	3.9	5.2	19.9	8.3	15.4	11.1
Male Householders, no wife present								
15 to 24 years	5.0	.9	1.8	1.6	5.1	2.3	3.9	2.4
25 to 34 years	3.7	.8	1.1	1.9	4.3	1.4	2.8	2.2
Female Householders, no husband present								
15 to 24 years	10.4	1.1	3.2	3.8	10.2	2.1	5.2	4.0
25 to 34 years	8.3	1.3	2.9	4.6	12.6	2.6	7.0	7.2

Note: Crowded means 1.01 or more persons per room.
Source: U.S. Bureau of the Census, 1985b: 41, 43, 72, 74.

versus 41 percent), whereas owners were overrepresented (29 percent versus 12 percent). This comparison suggests that young family owners tend to live in housing of a lesser quality than do those in older age groups, while, as shown earlier, they also typically spend a larger share of their income on housing.

FUTURE DIRECTIONS

Policy

There can be little question that affordability will remain a salient issue in debates regarding the housing of young people. Some have tried to document that affordability is a problem, whereas others have argued that higher house prices are offset by tax breaks and more flexible mortgage mechanisms. However, several observers have pointed out that the question is not whether there is an affordability problem, but for whom there is an affordability problem (Rudel, 1985; Morrow-Jones, 1986). Data reviewed earlier suggest that young adults, especially first-time buyers, are among the groups for whom it is a problem, a problem that is worse among female-headed families, blacks, and persons of Spanish origin. Homebuying is becoming more difficult yet according to plans that call for tightened income requirements for FHA and VA loans and an increase in down payment from 5 to 10 percent (Smith, 1986: 21).

Murphy and Sullivan (1986) have shown a relation between employment status and tenure for Britain. However, a polarization between renters and owners in terms of social class and a gradual residualization of the rental sector have been found not only for Britain (Hamnett, 1984; Bentham, 1986), but also for Australia (Paris, 1984), Canada (Pratt, 1986; Hulchanski and Drover, 1987) and Italy (Tosi, in press). Indeed, Harloe (1984) has suggested that these developments are a feature of all advanced industrial capitalist societies. Data available at this time show that from 1980 through 1983 unemployment in the United States increased in all age groups under 35, among men as well as women (U.S. Bureau of the Census, 1985a: 395; 1986a: 383). The proportion of young families below the poverty line also increased. These trends do not point to a narrowing of the gap between those who already own homes and those who do not.

While there is no space here to consider the merits of proposals that have been put forth to facilitate access to homeownership, it is perhaps useful to point out that questions related to such proposals are formulated within an accepted framework with a given distribution of costs and benefits associated with the different tenure forms. However, the question of housing affordability must not be asked narrowly in terms of the affordability of homeownership; it must be extended to inquire about the costs of housing per se. Data presented in this chapter show how many young renters face more serious problems of housing affordability than do young owners. It is in order, therefore, to explore possibilities for restructuring the housing system to attain alternative arrangements that address the issue of affordability more inclusively.

A second issue in the future housing of young people concerns innovations in housing type and management. The share of single units (including detached single-family houses as well as attached units like ground-level townhouses) in total private housing starts dropped from 77 percent in 1975 to 62 percent in 1984. During that same period starts of dwellings in structures with five or more units increased from 18 percent to 31 percent (Sternlieb and Hughes, 1986: 7). Of course, these changes are greatly affected by economic factors. However, new life-styles and trends in household formation are creating a growing demand for alternatives to the privately owned single-family dwelling. These alternatives include aspects of design (interior and structure), tenure, and location vis-à-vis community support functions. Several such innovations are reviewed by Franck (1987), who also details alternative forms of tenure that are being developed in tandem.

Franck also makes the important observation that the innovations often require changes in local zoning ordinances, building codes, bank financing practices, and federal subsidies, all of which tend to be designed with the effect of protecting the interests of the owners and builders of single dwellings by discouraging or prohibiting alternative housing. The argument is not that detached homes are an outdated form of housing no longer desired by the present generation, but rather that there is a need to accommodate also alternative preferences (Baum, 1986). Holland (1986) reports how in Australia state government intervened when a local authority issued demolition orders for alternative housing built in contravention of existing regulations. The Technical Assistance Group that it set up is an example of ways in which innovative practices could be supported rather than resisted.

A third issue is the discrimination in rental housing against families with children. A recent national study conducted for HUD found that the proportion of rental apartments in the surveyed buildings that exclude children had increased by 50 percent in the 1974–80 period, making one out of every four rental units inaccessible to families with children (Marans and Colten, 1985). These practices, often coupled with exclusionary zoning (Calvan, 1979), and in the case of many female-headed families additionally exacerbated by sexual harassment by landlords (Fuentes and Miller, 1986; Lee, 1987) further hamper an often already-difficult search by young families seeking rental housing. Curtailment of these practices should clearly be placed on the policy agenda. However, it is unlikely that it will; given the lack of any family policy at all on the part of the U.S. government, initiatives with respect to the housing of young families are not likely to be forthcoming.

Research

Future studies will continue to examine the links between demographic trends, life-style developments, and housing. Lack of space did not permit discussion of young people's life-styles in this chapter. There is a need, however, for better qualitative insights into the day-to-day housing experiences of, for example, students, the unemployed, single parents, and dual-earner couples among the young, along with an improved understanding of how these life-styles are culturally and structurally anchored in choice and constraint. There will also be further research on the economic, psychological, and sociobehavioral aspects of young people's housing and living arrangements. It is impossible to lay out a complete research agenda here, but one line of inquiry should be mentioned. In addition to ongoing work, further studies are needed on the context of young people's housing. Such contextual studies should cover at least four aspects.

First, there is the temporal context. We need better insights into the linkages over time between the sequential housing conditions of a given individual or household. A good example of research in this vein is the analysis by Morrow-Jones (1986) of the transition from renting to owning a home. Her original application of multistate methodology to housing would lend itself well for use with a longer time span.

A second important context could be called developmental. Forrest and Kemeny (1982) proposed the term "housing career" to denote a more historical integration of analyses of housing and household structure. There are, however, at least three main dimensions of the developmental context of housing careers: the household life cycle, human development, and labor career. Each inevitably comes into focus when studying housing across people's life paths. Research has clearly established housing implications of household formation and of changes in its composition over time. However, it is useful to include also an intergenerational perspective. Studies have found significant associations (not causation) between the housing preferences of young adults and their residential experience during childhood (Montgomery and Kivlin, 1962; Hohm, 1983a) and also between the housing expenditure, tenure, and density of parents and their children (Jenkins and Maynard, 1983; Henretta, 1984). Further research is needed to determine to what extent these are genuine intergenerational housing continuities rather than spurious relationships explained by external variables.

Another aspect of the developmental context with implications for housing deals with differences in mental and physical abilities. There are distinct literatures on the housing needs of developmentally disadvantaged and handicapped people (Dear and Taylor, 1982; Okolo and Guskin, 1984; Rostron, 1984) and numerous assessments of how housing requirements change during childhood (Pollowy, 1977) and in old age, as people's faculties become impaired and diminish in performance (Lawton, 1980; Altman, Lawton, and Wohlwill, 1984).

Yet another aspect of the developmental context deals with the linkage between housing and labor careers. This connection has long been recognized with respect to residential mobility (Bartel, 1979), but there are other interfaces that have been neglected. Researchers in Britain, for example, have examined the interrelationships between housing pathways and patterns of socioeconomic stratification (Payne and Payne, 1977; Sullivan and Murphy, 1984). Similar studies are lacking for the United States. It is also necessary to examine more carefully the processes of residential decisionmaking in households with multiple members, described by one author as "muddling through" (Park, 1982), especially in light of the increased reliance by families on two incomes for the payment of housing expenses, a trend with policy implications in itself (Myers, 1985a).

The discussion so far suggests research of housing sequences as they intertwine with developments along three main dimensions. Housing careers are also impacted by characteristics associated with the spatial context. In the Netherlands, for example, Linde, Dieleman, and Clark (1986) found that the housing situation of "starters" varied not only according to age, marital status, income, and other personal attributes, but also according to regional housing market differences. Rudel (1985) and Morrow-Jones (1986) have made similar observations for the United States. Of course, the spatial context of a household includes other elements besides the housing stock. Also important are, for example, the labor market and the demographic and socioeconomic composition of the population competing for opportunities in the housing and job markets.

A final aspect to be mentioned here concerns the regulatory context. The housing conditions and choices of young adults are, in part, molded by a complex set of private and public regulations. Earlier parts of the discussion referred to rental practices restricting housing access for families with children and noted how building codes, zoning ordinances, and other regulations often discourage alternative housing aspired to by young people. On the other hand, banks may target young people for special incentives in the form of designated savings schemes or adjusted mortgage arrangements, and government policies may include selected subsidies and tax advantages. While some other countries have perhaps given more deliberate attention to the housing of young people and have developed a fuller arsenal of relevant instruments (Hungary, Ministry of Building and Urban Development, 1977; Haywood, 1984; Van Vliet—, 1985), research in the United States should also incorporate policy and other regulatory considerations in analyses of young people's housing.

NOTE

I am grateful to Hazel Morrow-Jones, who commented on a previous version and kindly gave permission to use Figure 18.1, and to Allen Harlow for helping produce Figure 18.2.

REFERENCES

Altman, I., M. P. Lawton, and J. Wohlwill (eds.). 1984. *Elderly People and the Environment*. New York: Plenum Press.

Bartel, A. P. 1979. "The Migration Decision: What Role Does Job Mobility Play?" *American Economic Review* 69: 775–786.

Baum, Frances. 1986. "Shared Housing: Making Alternative Lifestyles Work." *Australian Journal of Social Issues* 21, no. 3 (August).

Bentham, Graham. 1986. "Socio-tenural Polarization in the United Kingdom, 1953–83: The Income Evidence." *Urban Studies* 2: 157–162.

Booth, A. and J. N. Edwards. 1976. "Crowding and Family Relations." *American Sociological Review* 41, no. 2: 308–321.

Burns, L. S., and L. Grebler. 1986. *The Future of Housing Markets: A New Appraisal.* New York: Plenum.

Calvan, R. 1979. "Children and Families—The Latest Victims of Exclusionary Land Use Practices." *Challenge* 10, no. 11: 26–28.

Dahmann, D. C. 1985. "The Demographics of Homeownership in America Today: A Deferred Dream for Younger Households?" Unpublished paper. Abbreviated note appeared in *American Demographics* (November): 47.

Dear, M. J., and S. M. Taylor. 1982. *Not on Our Street.* London: Pion.

Edwards, J. N., and A. Booth. 1977. "Crowding and Human Sexual Behavior." *Social Forces* 55, no. 3: 791–808.

Eversley, David. 1983. "The Family and Housing Policy: The Interaction of the Family, the Household, and the Housing Market." In *The Family.* British Society for Population Studies Occasional Paper 31. London: Office of Population Censuses and Surveys. 82–95.

Felson, M., and M. Solaun. 1975. "The Fertility-inhibiting Effects of Crowded Apartment Living in a Tight Housing Market." *American Journal of Social Science* 80: 1410–1427.

Forrest, R., and J. Kemeny. 1982. "Middle-Class Housing Careers: The Relationship between Furnished Renting and Homeownership." *Sociological Review* 30, no. 2: 208–222.

Franck, K. 1987. "Shared Spaces, Small Spaces, and Spaces That Change: Examples of Housing Innovation in the United States." In Willem van Vliet—, H. Choldin, W. Michelson, and D. Popenoe (eds.), *Housing and Neighborhoods: Theoretical and Empirical Contributions.* Westport, Conn.: Greenwood Press. 157–172.

Fuentes, A., and M. Miller. 1986. "Unreasonable Access: Sexual Harassment Comes Home." *City Limits,* June/July, 16–22.

Gallup, G. H. 1983. *The Gallup Poll: Public Opinion, 1982.* Wilmington, Del.: Scholarly Resources.

Glick, P. C., and S. L. Lin. 1986. "More Young Adults Are Living with Their Parents: Who Are They?" *Journal of Marriage and the Family* 48: 107–112.

Goldschneider, F., and J. DaVanzo. 1985. "Living Arrangements and the Transition to Adulthood." *Demography* 22, no. 4: 545–563.

———. 1986. "Semiautonomy and Leaving Home in Early Adulthood." *Social Forces* 65, no. 1: 187–202.

Goldschneider, F., and C. LeBourdais. 1986. "Growing Up and Leaving Home: Variation and Change in Nestleaving Patterns, 1920–1979." *Sociology and Social Research* 70, no. 2: 143–145.

Hamnett, C. 1984. "Housing the Two Nations: Socio-tenural Polarization in England and Wales, 1961–81." *Urban Studies* 43: 389–405.

Harloe, M. 1984. *Private Rented Housing in the United States and Europe.* London: Croom Helm.

Haywood, I. 1984. "Housing in Denmark." In M. Wynn (ed.), *Housing in Europe.* London: Croom Helm.

Heer, D. M., R. W. Hodge, and M. Felson. 1985. "The Cluttered Nest: Evidence That

Young Adults Are More Likely to Live at Home Now Than in the Recent Past.'' *Sociology and Social Research* 69, no. 3: 436–441.

Henretta, J. C. 1984. "Parental Status and Child's Homeownership." *American Sociological Review* 49, no. 1: 131–140.

Hohm, C. F. 1983a. "Expectations for Future Homeownership." *Housing and Society* 10, no. 1: 25–35.

———. 1983b. "On the Importance of Homeownership: Correlates of Differential Attitudes." *Housing and Society* 10, no. 2: 61–71.

———. 1984. "Housing Aspirations and Fertility." *Sociology and Social Research* 68: 351–363.

———. 1985. "The Financial Commitment to Homeownership: Attitudes of Future Homebuyers." *Social Science Journal* 22, no. 3: 47–55.

Holland, G. E. 1986. "Planning and Building Regulations and Alternative Lifestyles." *Journal of Architectural and Planning Research* 3: 65–77.

Hulchanski, J. David, and Glenn Drover. 1987. "Housing Subsidies in a Period of Restraint: The Canadian Experience." In Willem van Vliet— (ed.), *Housing Markets and Policies under Fiscal Austerity*. Westport, Conn.: Greenwood Press. 51–70.

Hungary. Ministry of Building and Urban Development. 1977. "Directives for the Establishment of Living Units Suitable for Young Couples, Pensioners, or Single Persons." In United Nations (ed.), *Housing for Special Groups*. New York: Pergamon Press. 169–172.

Jenkins, S. P., and A. K. Maynard. 1983. "Intergenerational Continuities in Housing." *Urban Studies* 20: 431–438.

Jones, Gill. 1987. "Leaving the Parental Home: An Analysis of Early Housing Careers." *Journal of Social Policy* 16, no. 1: 49–74.

Kain, J. F. 1983. "America's Persistent Housing Crisis: Errors in Analysis and Policy." *Annals of the American Academy of Political and Social Sciences* 465 (January), 136–148.

Kemeny, P. J. 1981. *The Myth of Home-Ownership: Private versus Public Choices in Housing Tenure*. London: Routledge & Kegan Paul.

Lawton, M. P. 1980. *Environment and Aging*. Monterey, Calif.: Brooks/Cole.

Lee, Elliott D. 1987. "Female Tenants Battle Increased Sex Harassment." *Wall Street Journal*, January 30.

Leppel, Karen. 1987. "Income Effects on Living Arrangements: Differences between Male and Female Householders." *Social Science Research* 16: 138–153.

Linde, M. A. J., F. M. Dieleman, and W. A. V. Clark. 1986. "Starters in the Dutch Housing Market." Paper presented at the International Research Conference on Housing Policy, National Swedish Institute for Building Research, Gävle, Sweden, June.

Low, N. P., and B. W. Crawshaw. 1985. "Youth without Housing: Patterns of Exclusion." *Australian Quarterly* 57, no. 1–2: 77–84.

Marans, Robert, and Barbara Colten. 1985. "U.S. Rental Housing Policies affecting Families with Children." In Willem van Vliet—, Elizabeth Huttman, and Sylvia Fava (eds.), *Housing Needs and Policy Approaches: Trends in Thirteen Countries*. Durham, N.C.: Duke University Press.

Michelson, W. 1977. *Environmental Choice, Human Behavior, and Residential Satisfaction*. New York: Oxford University Press.

Montgomery, J. E., and J. E. Kivlin. 1962. "Place of Residence as a Factor in Housing Desires and Expectation." *Rural Sociology* 27: 484–491.

Morrow-Jones, H. A. 1986. "A Multistate Analysis of the Transition from Renting to Owning a Home in the United States." Working Paper WP-8–10. Boulder: Population Program, Institute of Behavioral Science, University of Colorado.

Morton, H. W. 1974 "What Have Soviet Leaders Done about the Housing Crisis?" In H. W. Morton and R. L. Tokes (eds.), *Soviet Politics and Society in the 1970's*, New York: Free Press.

———. 1985. "The Housing Game." *Wilson Quarterly*, Fall, 61–73.

Murphy, M. J. 1984. "The Influence of Fertility, Early Housing-Career, and Socioeconomic Factors on Tenure Determination in Contemporary Britain." *Environment and Planning A* 16: 1303–1318.

Murphy, M. J., and O. Sullivan. 1985. "Housing Tenure and Family Formation in Contemporary Britain." *European Sociological Review*, 1 no. 3: 230–243.

———. 1986. "Unemployment, Housing, and Household Structure among Young Adults." *Journal of Social Policy* 15, no. 2: 205–222.

Myers, D. M. 1983 "The Impact of Rising Homeownership Costs on Family Change." Paper presented at the annual meeting of the Population Association of America, Pittsburgh, April.

———. 1985a. "Reliance upon Wives' Earnings for Homeownership Attainment." *Journal of Planning Education and Research* 4, no. 3: 167–176.

———. 1985b. "Wives' Earnings and Rising Costs of Homeownership." *Social Science Quarterly* 66, no. 2: 319–329.

Okolo, C., and S. Guskin. 1984. "Community Attitudes toward Community Placement of Mentally Retarded Persons." *International Review of Research in Mental Retardation* 12: 26–66.

Paris, C. 1984. "Private Rental Housing in Australia." *Environment and Planning A* 16: 1079–1098.

Park, C. Whan. 1982. "Joint Decisions in Home Purchasing: A Muddling Through Process." *Journal of Consumer Research* 9: 151–162.

Payne, J., and G. Payne. 1977. "Housing Pathways and Stratification: A Study of Life Changes in the Housing Market." *Journal of Social Policy* 6, no. 2: 129–156.

Pickvance, C. G. 1973. "Life Cycle, Housing Tenure, and Intraurban Residential Mobility: A Causal Model." *Sociological Review* 21: 279–297.

Plaut, Steven E. 1987. "The Timing of Housing Tenure Transition." *Journal of Urban Economics* 21: 312–322.

Pollowy, Anne-Marie. 1977. *The Urban Nest*. Stroudsburg, Pa.: Dowden, Hutchinson & Ross.

Pratt, Geraldine. 1986. "Housing Tenure and Social Cleavages in Urban Canada." *Annals of the Association of American Geographers* 76, no. 3: 366–380.

Professional Builder. 1984. "What 1985 Buyers Want in Housing." Eleventh Annual Consumer Survey, December, 65–81.

Rostron, J. 1984. "The Physically Disabled: An International Audit of Housing Policies." *Public Health* 98: 247–255.

Rudel, T. K. 1985. "Changes in Access to Homeownership during the 1970s." *Annals of Regional Science* 19, no. 1: 37–49.

Smith, D. A. 1986. "Demographic Shifts in Housing Demand." *Real Estate Review* 16, no. 3: 18–22.

Speare, A. 1970. "Homeownership, Life Cycle Stage, and Residential Mobility." *Demography* 7: 449–458.

Sternlieb, G., and J. W. Hughes. 1986. "Demographics and Housing in America." *Population Bulletin* 41, no. 1: 1–34.

Sullivan, O., and M. J. Murphy. 1984. "Housing Pathways and Stratification: Some Evidence from a British National Survey." *Journal of Social Policy* 13, no. 2: 147–165.

Tosi, A. In press. "Housing in Italy." In Willem van Vliet— (ed.), *International Housing*. Westport, Conn.: Greenwood Press.

U.S. Bureau of the Census. 1952. *Census of Housing: 1950*. Vol. 4. *Residential Financing, Mortgaged Nonfarm Properties*. Washington, D.C.: Government Printing Office.

———. 1975. *Current Housing Reports*. Series H-150–73A. *General Housing Characteristics, Part A, Annual Housing Survey, 1973*. Washington, D.C. Government Printing Office.

———. 1977. *Household and Family Characteristics, March 1976*. Current Population Reports, Population Characteristics, Series P-20, no. 311. Washington, D.C.: Government Printing Office.

———. 1980a. *Construction Reports: Characteristics of New One-Family Homes*. Washington, D.C.: Government Printing Office.

———. 1980b. *Families Maintained by Female Householders, 1970–1979*. Current Population Reports, Series P-23, no. 107. Washington, D.C.: Government Printing Office.

———. 1983. *Census of Housing (1980)*. Vol. 5. *Residential Finance*. Washington, D.C.: Government Printing Office.

———. 1984. *Census of Housing (1980)*. Vol. 3. *Subject Reports*. Chap., 4. *Structural Characteristics of the Housing Inventory*. Washington, D.C.: Government Printing Office.

———. 1985a. *After-Tax Money Income Estimates of Households, 1983*. Current Population Reports, Special Studies, Series P-23, no. 143. Washington, D.C.: Government Printing Office.

———. 1985b. *Census of Housing (1980)*. Vol. 3, chap. 5. Space Utilization of the Housing Inventory. Washington, D.C.: Government Printing Office.

———. 1985c. *Census of Housing (1980)*. Vol. 3, chap. 6. *Mover Households*. Washington, D.C.: Government Printing Office.

———. 1985d. *Current Housing Reports*. Series H-150–83. *Urban and Rural Housing Characteristics for the U.S. and Regions, 1983*. Annual Housing Survey, 1983, Part E. Washington, D.C.: Government Printing Office.

———. 1985e. *Household and Family Characteristics, March 1984*. Current Population Reports, Population Characteristics, Series P-20, no. 398. Washington, D.C.: Government Printing Office.

———. 1985f. *Households, Families, Marital Status, and Living Arrangements, March 1985 (Advance Report)*. Current Population Reports, Series P-20, no. 402, October. Washington, D.C.: Government Printing Office.

———. 1985g. *Marital Status and Living Arrangements, March 1984*. Current Population Reports, Series P-20, no. 399, July. Washington, D.C.: Government Printing Office.

————. 1985h. *Statistical Abstract of the United States, 1986*. 106th ed. Washington, D.C.: Government Printing Office.

————. 1986a. *Earnings in 1983 of Married-Couple Families, by Characteristics of Husbands and Wives*. Current Population Reports, Series P-60, no. 153. Washington, D.C.: Government Printing Office.

————. 1986b. *Marital Status and Living Arrangements, March 1985*. Current Population Reports, Population Characteristics, Series P-20, no. 410. Washington, D.C.: Government Printing Office.

U.S. Department of Housing and Urban Development. 1978. *The 1978 HUD Survey on the Quality of Community Life: A Data Book*. Washington, D.C.: Government Printing Office.

U.S. League of Savings Institutions. 1986. *Homeownership: Returning to Tradition*. Chicago: U.S. League of Savings Institutions.

Van Vliet—, Willem. 1985. "Housing Policy as a Planning Tool." *Urban Studies* 22: 105–117.

Winter, M. 1980. "Managerial Behavior of Young Families in Pursuit of Single-Family Homeownership." *Journal of Consumer Affairs* 14, no. 1: 82–95.

19

The Elderly and Housing

ELIZABETH HUTTMAN AND ELEANOR GUREWITSCH

In discussing special groups in need of housing tailored to their circumstances, the elderly, those 65 and over, stand out as a prime example. For this population of about 28 million, housing assistance must often be more than shelter alone. A package of shelter and services is needed to allow them to keep their independence and avoid premature institutionalization (Thompson, 1978). Many elderly need financial help to allow them to keep their own homes or to meet the affordability problems of private rentals. For the frail and increasingly immobile aged, the need may be for alternative housing: specially designed elderly housing, a granny flat, or shared agency-run housing that offers some supports.

To housing specialists, knowledge of the housing situation of and housing alternatives for the elderly is relevant for a number of reasons. One-fifth of the housing stock in the United States is owned by households headed by an elderly person (13.4 million households in 1985) (American Association of Retired Persons [AARP], 1985). A large part of the federal housing program consists of subsidization of units occupied by the elderly. Several million elderly receive housing assistance (Struyk, 1985), and elderly households are over one-third of those on the Section 8 housing assistance program, one-fourth in Section 236 housing, one-sixth in Section 221(d)(3), and almost half of the households in Section 515 Farmers Home Administration (FmHA) (National Institute of Senior Housing [NISH], 1983–84). The elderly occupy over 80 percent of Section 202 units and have been major recipients of rehabilitation and repair funds through Section 312 and Community Development Block Grants (CDBG).

A substantial amount of new construction over the years has been for the elderly under subsidy programs such as public housing, Section 202, 236, and 221(d) (3); Section 8 new construction; and FmHA Section 515. The supply of for-profit planned housing for middle-income elderly, from Leisure Worlds to simple townhouse complexes, even to manufactured (mobile) homes, is growing. Architectural concerns include the design of housing for this group, with features meeting their special health needs.

Characteristics of the elderly population, including small household size and an increasing number of single households, have an effect on both the supply and the demand for housing. The longer these elderly live, the longer they have this demand and the longer they occupy units that would otherwise trickle down to younger families. Some old-old (75 and over) move from large homes, increasing demand for small rental units, often already in short supply in metropolitan areas. The demand for developments with services already exceeds supply. Waiting lists are long.

Those housing specialists interested in rehabilitation or urban renewal often find their focus is on units occupied by the elderly, since central cities have a high concentration of poor elderly (Huttman, 1981a). Agencies may need to counsel and relocate elderly occupants (Huttman, 1981b) or negotiate with them to take part in rehabilitation/conservation and historic preservation programs. Researchers interested in housing affordability find one group of major concern is elderly renters with burdensome income/housing-cost ratios.

A major focus of research on housing for the elderly is on services in relation to "fit" of the physical environment, including housing, to the needs of the elderly. The largest group of researchers concerned with housing for the elderly is composed of gerontologists who focus on shelter alternatives to institutions such as the nursing home and on supplements to shelter per se that allow the elderly to continue to occupy independent or semi-independent living arrangements. This chapter will also emphasize shelter with services provided, because this is what is special about housing for this particular group. As Gurewitsch (1984) explains, "Some types of environments in later life [with services] seem to be more conducive to the maintenance of independent and semi-independent life [for the elderly] than others" (199).

In this chapter housing alternatives with services are detailed, and their worth versus the nursing home is shown. Since the 1960s the nursing home has dominated as the assumed alternative to fully independent living arrangements. Studies show that as many as one-third of those in such a medical facility could live in more independent housing arrangements if they were available (Thompson, 1978; see also Gurewitsch, 1982). But such alternatives are either totally lacking or in short supply in most communities due to meager government funding—the U.S. Department of Housing and Urban Development) (HUD) has rejected many good non-profit elderly housing projects sponsored by established agencies due to lack of funds (Gurewitsch, 1986). Instead, massive federal funds through Medicaid—over $6 billion in 1983—have gone to subsidize nursing home residents who are low income (Huttman, 1985). In some states even higher per day expenses occur because many elderly are kept in acute-care hospitals awaiting nursing home placement, as in New York State. The expenses under Medicaid—$290 a day in Schenectady County, New York, compared to a $675 monthly cost of the alternative of housing and services for impaired residents under Schenectady's enriched housing program (Gurewitsch, 1986) are an example of this. Experts interested in cost-effectiveness (such as Crystal, 1982, and Heumann, 1984) through semi-independent living for those who can manage under it deplore this situation. But because in the nursing home the government provides legally mandated subsidization of low-income user costs through Medicaid, while it does not provide such an entitlement for sheltered housing, the elderly, their adult children, and their physicians automatically turn to nursing homes when completely independent living seems no longer possible, even though semi-independent living could be possible. Other reasons that some in fully independent arrangements would be better off as residents of congregate housing include no maintenance and a support system. Studies have found that residents of congregate housing have higher morale than those living in private residences (Diamond, Kaye, and Monk, 1986). Older people living in private households are more subject to depression, isolation, and alcoholism than those in regular contact with others (Gurewitsch, 1986). These factors are the ones that have brought gerontologists into the housing field. A continuum of housing alternatives with services available, they feel, is urgently needed. The long waiting lists for the limited number of protected senior housing units provide proof that there is a demand. Many communities, aware that so many of their tax dollars go to Medicaid, are demanding expansion of the more agreeable, humane, and cost-effective alternatives, the different types of protected housing (Gurewitsch, 1986; NISH, 1985c). Even HUD recognizes the cost-effectiveness of these housing alternatives.

This chapter covers the housing situation of the elderly, themes regarding need, and housing alternatives or supports in the community that meet the demand for quality housing and affordable housing and go beyond the provision of shelter alone. It also considers subsidization programs and specially designed housing.

THE HOUSING SITUATION OF THE ELDERLY

Seventy-five percent of elderly households are owner-occupied; only about one-fourth of the 17.9 million households headed by elderly in 1984 were renters. Minorities, especially black households, were somewhat more likely to be renters. Not only do the elderly usually own, but most have mortgage-free homes (83 percent in 1983; AARP, 1985).

Many owners are older women, living alone; almost two-thirds of older households are headed by a woman alone. Few elderly live with children or other relatives, mainly old-old women. However, in general, the old-old (75 and older) stay on in their own homes; 70 percent of those 75 and over own, with half living alone (Newman, 1984).

Housing Conditions

Owners usually underutilize rather than overcrowd space, though they may close off rooms, especially in the winter. Owners in general occupy older units; in 1983 over one-third of the homes owned by older persons were built prior to 1940 (AARP, 1985). Not surprisingly, 8 percent in 1983 had deficiencies that classified them as inadequate. On most of the eight deficiencies that cause a unit to be considered physically inadequate, the elderly were more likely to have them than younger households (Annual Housing Survey analysis, Struyk, 1985). From analysis of a sample of elderly households in the Annual Housing Survey (1979), Struyk and Turner (1984) found almost one-tenth of all elderly owners without a mortgage and 6 percent with one had permanent deficiencies; however, almost one-fifth of elderly rural owner households with a mortgage and 27.4 percent without had deficiencies. Thus of owners, it is the poor, minorities, and the rural elderly, overlapping groups, that have housing deficiencies (see also Struyk and Soldo, 1980).

Renters in rural areas are likely to occupy physically deficient units (40 percent did so according to the 1979 Annual Housing Survey, analyzed in Struyk and Turner, 1984). Black and poor renters were even worse off; almost half of black aged renters were in physically deficient units. Not only do aged black owners usually live in old units and often have housing deficiencies such as exposed electrical wiring, roof leaks, and inefficient and potentially dangerous heat sources (one-third of black older owners did in 1975), but they often lack complete plumbing.

Housing Affordability

The dilemma of many elderly owners is that their major asset, their house, is a nonliquid one that they do not want to sell or mortgage (Chen, 1977); at the same time, they have limited income and a housing affordability problem. To be specific, elderly owners have a house, usually without a mortgage, with a median worth of almost $50,000 (1983) and increasing in appreciation each year, especially in major urban areas (AARP, 1985). Yet many owners are poor. One in every five elderly-headed households had an income of less than $10,000 in 1984. Struyk (1985) estimated that of elderly households not receiving housing assistance, about 15 percent of owners and 28 percent of renters were in poverty. One-third of black, one-fifth of Hispanic, and one-ninth of white elderly are living below the poverty level. Another 2.4 million elderly are nearly poor (with income 125 percent of the poverty level) (AARP, 1985).

Some owners spend an excessive amount of their income as outlay for housing and utilities. While in 1983 elderly owners without a mortgage paid on average 15 percent of their income for housing, those with a mortgage paid 24 percent of their income, and this excludes the high cost of maintenance, repairs, and utilities (AARP, 1985). Struyk and Turner (1984) found from the 1979 Annual Housing Survey data that more than one-fourth of all elderly owners with mortgages and 4.5 percent without had an excessive housing cost (over 30 percent of income). About three-fourths of the owners who were in poverty and had a mortgage paid excessive housing costs; only 17.7 percent of poverty-level owners without a mortgage did. Single elderly owners, often widows, were among the worst off, with 60 percent of those with a mortgage and 23 percent without one in 1976 paying excessive housing costs (Newman, Zais, and Struyk, 1984).

All this data illustrates the difficulty many owners have in keeping their houses, even if mortgage-free; the insurance, maintenance, and utilities cost seniors hundreds of dollars a month, especially in very cold or hot climates, though some states do provide utilities assistance. In addition, property taxes keep going up, although in some localities the poor elderly can avail themselves of property tax exemptions or property tax postponement.

Renters, of course, have more of an affordability problem if they are not in subsidized housing. Struyk and Turner (1984) report from their sample of the 1979 Annual Housing Survey that of all elderly households renting, 55.3 percent had an excessive expenditure on housing. Of Hispanics, Hoover (1981) reports that one-third in the 1975 Annual Housing Survey spent over 35 percent of their income on gross rent. Black elderly and single renters also often have a very excessive housing cost (Herbert, 1983).

Health Conditions

The problems of present housing and the need for suitable housing alternatives relate in a very major way to health conditions of the aged. As life expectancy increases, with the 75 to 84 and 85 and over groups the fastest-growing groups in our society, we obviously have an increasing number of older persons unable to function adequately in their present living arrangements. Many elderly have physical limitations. In the United States nationwide over one-third of the non-institutionalized aged in 1982 assessed their health as only fair or poor; over one-half of black elderly rated their health as such (AARP, 1985). Most elderly had at least one chronic condition in 1982, with half having arthritis, 26 percent a heart condition, and 17 percent orthopedic impairments (AARP, 1985).

What degree of malfunctioning indicates that the elderly person would best be served by moving to alternative housing with services is an issue for debate. Most gerontologists recommend that the elderly stay in their own homes with support help as long as possible. However, they recognize that beyond a certain point it is disadvantageous for the elderly to try to continue in an isolated environment. To decide when impairments are serious enough to warrant a move, Lawton (1972) and others have developed measurements of ability to perform activities of daily living (ADLs) (See also Fitch and Slivinske, 1986).

MAJOR THEORETICAL ORIENTATIONS

Needs Specific to the Dwelling versus Needs Related to Dwelling Use

Needs related to dwelling use by those with the variety of health problems faced by the elderly are one type of shelter need (AARP, 1983). Others are the traditional type of what Struyk (1985) calls "dwelling-specific" needs, that is, deficiencies in the dwelling and overcrowding, and the financial need to avoid spending an excessive share of income on housing. Added to these dwelling-specific needs are others, such as conditions of the neighborhood in which the housing is located. Federal programs normally are directed to dwelling-specific needs.

The other type Struyk gives, "dwelling-use" needs, are those due to activity limitations and other health problems; programs include house modification and repair services in one's present home, or provision of specially designed housing for those with serious limitations, whether congregate housing, shared housing, or other arrangements.

Struyk (1985: 13) says that in regard to dwelling-specific needs, about 1.61 million elderly-headed households lived in physically deficient dwellings in 1979, and 2.58 million spent an excessive share of income on housing. In regard to dwelling-use physical limitations of users, in 1979 about 12 percent of persons 65 and over had need of supportive services (21 percent of those 75 and over did). Struyk also estimated that about a million elderly-headed households needed dwelling modification (besides the 700,000 that already had it).

A Continuum of Housing Alternatives

"Continuum of housing alternatives" is a terminology that gerontologists such as Lawton, Brody, and Turner-Massey (1978) have developed. This continuum of housing, Streib (1984:4) states, should range from living independently and autonomously in a private house or apartment to a full-care institution with 24-hour-a-day skilled nursing care, or from the least supportive to the most supportive environment (see also Huttman, 1986; Streib, 1982). Private accommodations with community supportive services provided and modification of one's own home for physical limitations falls close to the independent end of the continuum. Specially designed apartments, congregate housing, and shared housing would fall in the middle of the continuum (Table 19.1).

Public intervention to provide this continuum, Struyk (1985) recommends, should be a central issue in federal housing policy. This intervention should be "to assist the elderly in making the necessary housing transition in a way that community-based housing becomes an active and integral element in the overall long term care system. Current housing policy for the elderly really gives only passing attention to this issue" (Struyk, 1985:1).

The Congruence/Ecological Theories

The "continuum" approach relates to a major theoretical orientation in research on housing for the elderly concerned with matching the person's housing and physical environment (such as special congregate housing) and its resources to his health and psychological needs. To Lawton, one of the originators of these

Table 19.1
Housing Assistance Alternatives and Physical Limitations of Elderly Users

Housing Assistance	Physical Limitations		
	Well Elderly	Some Limitations	Major Limitations
In Their Own Home			
Home Repairs		X	X
House Modification		X	X
Accessory Units		X	X
Mobile Homes	X		
House Matching		X	
Home Equity Programs	X	X	X
Tax Exemption and Postponement	X	X	X
Renters: Section 8 and Vouchers	X	X	X
In Special Housing			
Shared or Group Housing	X	X	
Apartments	X	X	
Congregate Housing		X	X
Life Care		X	X
Retirement Communities	X	X	

theories, the environment consists of the physical environment, including the buildings and the grounds, the spaces where tenants engage in their daily lives; the personal environment, consisting of the individuals who play particularly significant roles with respect to the tenant, including other tenants and service personnel; and the social environment created by the organizational milieu, ranging from the micro level of local administrative practices in public housing or the like to the macro level of social attitudes, and institutionalized health, and cultural values as exemplified in organizational purposes. (See Lawton, Greenbaum, and Liebowitz, 1980; Kahana, 1975, 1982.)

Congruence/ecological theorists ask what barriers exist in the environment to lessen a satisfactory congruence or ''fit''—that is to impede the person's successful functioning. The lower the person's competence in activities of daily living, the greater the demand on the housing environment to make up for this by provision of facilities and services or a location near them (Lawton and Nahemow, 1971).

Brody (1982) gives as an illustration of such congruence dining areas for group meals. The success of the environment/services fit, Brody says, can be measured by the extent to which the housing environment (1) obviates or minimizes the need for services; (2) facilitates development and delivery of those required; and (3) can be flexible in accomodating to changing service needs of changing elderly in the development.

Lawton and his colleagues have measured different aspects of housing and neighborhood satisfaction to determine to what extent there is congruence between the capacities of the individual and the housing and neighborhood environment with which a person must cope. The objective variables they have used in various studies include central location (near transportation, parks, amenities); distance from shopping facilities; independent household (private television, stove, toilet, refrigerator); and block traffic and condition of the block. In other studies, one on a planned environment (Lawton, Nahemow, and Teaff, 1975) and another using the Annual Housing Survey data (Lawton, Greenbaum, and Liebowitz, 1980), the physical characteristics of an objective nature were building size and height, sponsorship, and community size (1975) and use of structure and length of occupancy (1980). Carp and Carp (1984) include harm avoidance (crime, accidents, health, fire), nox avoidance (inconvenience, noise, air quality), order, privacy, aesthetics, and many psychological needs.

Concerning choice of variables and measurement system, issues that stand out are (1) the need to develop criteria for assessment of whether a person is suitable for a particular environment (criteria for eligibility and continued occupancy); (2) the need for specifying the normal services to provide in a particular environment (Brody, 1982); (3) and from another angle, the need to identify, by comparisons, whether one type of housing setting is more suitable than another, that is, a better fit between need and environment (Carp and Carp, 1984).

Studies have often compared different housing settings; for example, Lawton (1976) looked at differences in outcome following entry into a housing situation with support services as opposed to one requiring independent living. In his 1982 research Lawton includes single-family structures versus hotels versus rooming houses and measures satisfaction of each in relation to health status (see Lawton, Windley, and Byerts, 1978). A major problem that Carp and Carp (1984) see is interpreting what variable in the new planned environment the person moves to gives him satisfaction and meets his needs.

Housing Alternatives and the Willingness of the Elderly to Move

Willingness to move is necessary if the alternative housing choices for the elderly (the housing continuum) are to be of use to those with functional impairments, increasing the congruence or ''fit'' of the environment to needs. The move can end the aged person's burdensome house maintenance and can free the financial assets tied up in the house, permitting use for living expenses (Sumichrast, Shafer, and Sumichrast, 1984). An advantage of the move for the larger society is that it increases the supply of affordable housing for families, helping the trickle-down process.

Yet many elderly are reluctant to move (Yayney and Slover, 1979). Elderly nationwide were half as likely to move as those under 65 between 1975 and 1980, with about one-fifth moving during that period. Most moved within their own town or state (AARP, 1984). Data from the HUD Experimental Housing Allowance showed that very few elderly were willing to move to take advantage of the allowance; they either stayed in their present rental unit and received the allowance, or did not take part (Huttman, 1985; Heumann, 1984).

The elderly often are not psychologically able to leave their old house with its many memories, nor are they able to move from a familiar neighborhood with its known commercial services. They fear the unknown new setting and worry about their ability to function in it. As Markson (1982) points out, the move is seen as going to a place of less control, negatively affecting the person's sense of continuity for maintaining his or her behavior system. Of equal importance, the alternative may not fit the person's natural life-style, or, if congregrate housing, may present an image of housing for sick people (Verderber, 1986).

The elderly also do not want to move because they do not have the energy to sort out and pack up 40 years or more of possessions, or are unwilling to part with any of them to meet the limitations of a smaller unit, as many relocation personnel have found (Huttman, 1981b). The individual's resistance to moving to an optimal setting may also be because the person does not recognize his or her own physical limitations or those of the present housing environment, which often lacks health-related needs such as elevators (Anderson, Chen, and Hula, 1984; Struyk and Zais, 1982).

The elderly often lack detailed knowledge of housing alternatives (Heumann and Boldy, 1982). Because of their immobility, they are unlikely to investigate even known alternatives or search for suitable small units. Often good housing alternatives do not exist or have long waiting lists.

Unwillingness of Agency Personnel to Move the Elderly

Besides the unwillingness of the elderly to move, we have the unwillingness of agency personnel to move their residents, whether in independent or semi-independent housing. This is a factor negatively affecting implementation of the housing continuum of care and the congruence concept. Many gerontologists supporting the congruence theory propose movement of the elderly along the continuum as their health problems escalate; yet some of these experts realize that for many it is preferable to avoid a disruptive move, as studies show that this can have a very negative effect on psychological and physical well-being (Huttman, 1981b). The two values, that of keeping the elderly in their own setting, whether private home or their present special housing arrangement, and the value of providing a housing environment that gives the best fit, can conflict.

Thompson (1978) has pointed out that in many public elderly housing projects there are many residents "aging in place." The "fit" of person to environment is no longer good. The congruence is gone and more services are needed. Yet managers and administrators are unwilling to move the impaired out of the public housing complex, as Sheehan (1986) found in her study. Many administrators do not consider the nursing home a good environment for their low-income residents (Huttman, 1977). Brody (1982) also speaks of this in relation to congregate housing where the limits of person/environmental congruence have begun to be stretched for some. Even for those whose capacities fit with the service pattern, on occasion a richer service pattern will be needed after hospitalization and during convalescence.

Static versus Accommodating Housing Environment

Instead of moving the person from one level of special housing to a more health-oriented level, many experts would say that the housing environment services should be expanded to accommodate the elderly person's needs as they change. Others argue that this is not feasible, and that the person instead should be moved to another housing environment to achieve congruence, while the housing development stays static or constant in what services it provides. Lawton, Greenbaum, and Liebowitz (1980) raise these questions. They point out that the needs of residents change over time and, that what is a perfectly matched environment at one point may not fit the person's needs a few years later.

If a housing complex wants to avoid being an "aging" environment, it needs to move tenants to other accommodations as their health deteriorates. The administrator, besides assessing tenant ability to continue occupancy based on health condition, must have rigid ADL standards and behavioral standards in admittance of new residents. Fowles (1978) suggests that only the youngest elderly be used as tenant replacements. Lawton, Greenbaum, and Liebowitz (1980) say that if the frail are not screened out, potential healthy applicants may screen themselves out, perceiving the environment as only semi-independent. If the local image of the complex is that of a fairly independent environment, they may apply. Removing residents as they become frail is the constant or static model that attempts to preserve the original character of the tenant population, and the housing environment. Because the frail are sent elsewhere, the service needs of the tenants do not change much over the years (Lawton, Greenbaum, and Liebowitz, 1980). Instead, there is a high rate of turnover.

The other approach is to provide an "accommodating" type of environment, which Lawton, Greenbaum, and Liebowitz (1980: 56) say "accommodates administratively by tolerating an extended period of residence of tenants despite growing impairments and by relaxing admission requirements." Accommodation may be of several different types: the complex may start with services already in place, may add services to meet declining tenant competence by altering or adding space for these services; or administration accommodation may occur without expanding services and physical spaces. Brody (1982), in commenting on Lawton's theory, says that if one adds more services, the nature of the facility itself changes.

PROGRAMS AND SUBSIDIES FOR HOUSING THE ELDERLY

Government policy for public intervention in helping the elderly with housing needs has traditionally been in the areas of improving quality of housing and assisting with excessive housing costs. On the supply side the policy has been to promote and finance construction through non-profit groups (Section 202) or public housing authorities, to make guarantees to the private market through insurance coverage against lending risk and allowing tax shelters for investors in low-income housing, or to upgrade and increase units through renovation or recycling of public buildings. On the demand side policy has been to subsidize rents through housing allowance programs, public housing, and below-market interest assistance.

Though renters constitute about one-fourth of the elderly households, the federal subsidies have gone mainly to low-income renters in public housing, the Section 8 program, or Sections 202 or 236 new construction. For owners there is new construction under the Farmers Home Administration Section 502 program, or one-time repair/maintenance/rehabilitation help under the Community Development Block Grants, Section 312, or other programs. In addition, owners have benefited from federal tax regulations such as a $125,000 one-time capital gains exemption for elderly 55 and over on the sale of their primary residence, or from federal income tax deductions for mortgage interest and local property taxes.

History of Special Shelter for the Elderly

The most important aspect of government policy on shelter for the elderly, differentiating it from that of other housing provisions, is special planned housing with services. Thus before we discuss in detail the variety of government subsidies, we outline the history of this particular special type of government aid.

The growth of a program of special housing for the aged is a recent phenomenon, though historically local government has provided some housing especially designated for the elderly—usually called "homes for the aged." These were often "poorhouses" run by local authorities. Nonprofit groups also ran some of better quality. Both had an institutional atmosphere and seldom included private apartment arrangements.

In the postwar period these institutions often disappeared or were improved, becoming less institutional and similar to the new emerging types of specially designated housing for the elderly. But a more medically oriented equivalent of the institutional "old age home," the nursing home, gained prominence. As Langer and Avorn (1982: 24), state "The direction of public policy in the 1960's was to excessively reimburse institutional care and nearly ignore home-based alternatives."

Specially designed housing for the elderly, though receiving less policy support, did from the 1950s onward increase in importance in the public housing program, because from then on the program allowed single elderly to occupy units. In the 1960s the elderly were mixed with families and often were the "white" element in "integrated" public housing, as in the New York City Housing Authority (Huttman, 1977). But increasingly the elderly were housed separately. Every housing act since 1961 has contained programs on housing for the elderly (Thompson, 1978). Because of community opposition to family public housing with its large proportion of poor female-headed households and children, many communities in the 1960s and 1970s voted approval only of the construction of public housing complexes for the elderly. When state programs became active in the 1970s through state bond arrangements, preference again was for housing for the elderly, as in California.

Nonprofit housing also increased in the 1960s. In the 1959 Housing Act assistance was given for nonprofit developments through direct low-cost loans for Section 202 housing exclusively for the elderly and disabled. It began slowly and was not a major program until after 1974, with Section 221(d)(3) and then Section 236 for new rental housing being more popular. The 1973 moratorium on housing subsidy programs by the Nixon administration seriously curtailed Section 236 and other programs. However, Section 202 grew from the 1974 Housing Act onward. By 1986, after many Reagan administration housing cutbacks, it was one of the few housing subsidy programs for new construction that remained.

Housing acts in the 1970s began giving some support to congregate-type housing, though non-profit groups had long done so. HUD made agreements with the Department of Health, Education and Welfare (HEW), now the Department of Health and Human Services (HHS), for some services to public housing tenants. The U.S. Senate Committee on Aging in 1976 held hearings on the advantages of congregate housing. While HUD continued to see its role primarily as provider of housing and not services, it allowed some communal facilities in public housing and even more in Section 202 complexes. With public housing residents "aging in place" (Thompson, 1978), more was needed. In 1984 HUD took a new turn and sponsored the Congregate Housing Demonstration Project for service provision to selected frail elderly in 50 to 60 projects serving about 1,800 residents in public housing and Section 202 (Nachison, 1985). By the mid-1980s private profit-making congregate-type complexes, often life care ones, were increasing in number and considered a good investment.

By the 1980s gerontologists were becoming more pronounced in their support of these housing programs, considering them a better fit for many impaired elderly than the nursing home (Pynoos, 1984). Congregate housing may increasingly expand to provide a cost-effective alternative to nursing homes; Heumann (1984) estimates that equivalent services in congregate-type shelter for those needing less than nursing home care can cost about one-third less than in longterm care facilities. Struyk (1985) envisions the goal of "public intervention to assist the elderly to make the necessary housing transition in a way that community-based housing becomes an active and integral element in the overall long term care system." He suggests "in-place" house changes whenever possible, rather than moves, and a housing policy of flexible response to varied needs. He urges innovative housing alternatives and describes several—shared (group) housing, modification of present home, and congregate housing. (On innovative housing, see also Hare and Huske, 1983–84; Brody and Liebowitz, 1981.)

Many elderly have dwelling-specific problems, so one must discuss not only special housing with services, but many other programs, including ones for those in their own homes (Lawton, 1985). One cannot abandon traditional government programs to improve housing quality and to lower excessive housing costs. At present, traditional subsidy programs cover only a small proportion of those elderly in need. About 2 million elderly households, mostly renters, participated in housing assistance programs other than one-time repair or rehabilitation assistance in 1985 (Struyk, 1985). Of those eligible for means-tested programs, Struyk says a million or more are not receiving assistance. Let us now discuss all these different programs in detail, starting with those in a person's own home (see also Lawton and Hoover, 1981) and then those in special housing.

Programs and Subsidies for Those in Their Own Homes

Home Repairs

Owners are helped by community repair programs, often funded through Community Development Block Grants (now being phased out) and revenue-sharing monies with low-interest loans or grants. This work may be painting, fixing a leaky roof, or doing minor electrical repairs; the workers may be unemployed workers under a special program. Major renovation and rehabilitation may be done to bring the housing up to code, often as part of area rehabilitation/historic preservation, under Section 312, CDBGs, or local government bonds. If owners are in rural areas, they are helped by the Farmers Home Administration (FmHA) Section 504 repair and rehabilitation grants, for seniors with low income, or loans, for those of higher income, to remove health hazards.

House Modification

A "dwelling-use" program that is especially useful where there is an impaired person in the house is the housing modification program. CDBG funds have supported these. Struyk and his colleagues, in studying modifications done in households with an impaired aged person, found from the 1978 Annual Housing Survey that extra handrails or grab bars were the most common modifications. Others were sink, faucet, and cabinet adjustments, light switch adaptations, elevators and lift chairs, specially equipped telephones, ramps, and extra-wide doors (Struyk and Zais, 1982). In another study of seven central cities, Struyk and Katsura (1985) found that 5 percent of the elderly household sample had changed the use of a room in the last two years, and 10 percent had done a dwelling modification to assist an impaired person.

Accessory Units in Owner-Occupied Residences

The addition of an accessory unit, a second unit in the house, or an adjacent echo (elderly) housing, or granny flat as the Australians call them, can be useful housing alternatives for the aged, giving a support source and, for the homeowner who subdivides his or her house, a rent income. Such a program is definitely a supply-side one.

We need more small units, which this program can provide. The University of Michigan National Policy Center on Housing and Living Arrangements for Older Americans has warned that as the old-old, mainly singles, move out of their homes in large numbers, we need 235,000 new units each year up to the year 2000 for these elderly households. They recommend a change in zoning ordinances to allow a second unit in single-family residential areas and increased use of manufactured homes, with legal status and financing provided in the same way as for other homes (*Aging*, 1983–84d). Forceful lobbies such as the AARP and the Gray Panthers have pushed for second-unit ordinances. Many communities in Connecticut, New York, and California permit them, and towns in Virginia, Colorado, and Minnesota are considering ordinances (Hare and Hollis, 1983). Most ordinances provide that an owner must live on the premises and an elderly household must be included. If a detached removable unit in the backyard, called echo housing, or a granny flat, is allowed the city may limit use to the period when the elderly parent is using it.

The AARP (1983) lists as a major advantage of the parent-child arrangement that of having a close relative nearby to provide a personal support system. For the elderly owner who subdivides his or her home into a second unit, this may mean a tenant who can do maintenance and provide the safety and security desired as well as rent income. For the general society, as Hare and Hollis (1983) point out, this division of the home into two units gives young families with limited financial resources a greater chance of moving into a good suburban neighborhood, either housing an elderly parent (and getting rent from him or her) or renting from an elderly owner. Subsidies for subdividing and for house matching may come from local nonprofit agencies, often using Older Americans Act monies or state housing agency funds.

Manufactured or Mobile Homes

Recent state regulation changes have increased the likelihood of small-unit inexpensive ownership of manufactured homes for use as a detached echo unit, an independent living arrangement in an adult mobile home, or on an individual, usually rural, lot. In recent years many elderly homesellers have turned to this relatively cheap option; it is estimated that one-fifth of the manufactured-home residents are 55 and over (Pastalan, 1984). About 3 percent of the elderly in 1976 lived in mobile homes (Welfeld and Struyk, 1978). This housing is now of respectable size and quality. The National Mobile Home Construction and Safety Standards Act of 1974 required rigid building standards and HUD inspection. Most are double-size and hardly mobile. In a number of states these manufactured homes, when placed on permanent foundations, can be put in the same neighborhood as conventional homes (with most meeting local building code requirements) (Pastalan, 1984). In the late 1970s manufactured homes became eligible for FHA and VA mortgages, opening the way to conventional financing (Pastalan, 1984). Recent laws in some states have moved mobile homes from personal to real property and tax them accordingly.

Adult mobile-home parks on pleasant clean sites often offer special recreational facilities and provide companionship, security, and low maintenance. There are disadvantages (AARP, 1983). Long-term costs have been estimated to be higher than for conventional homes due to short life span (usually less than 15 years), though for many elderly this is acceptable (Cottin, 1979). Other disadvantages are high site costs in mobile-home parks, the difficulty of finding park sites after the mobile home has aged, quick depreciation, and higher financing costs. Mobile homes are known to develop structural defects in some instances and to be unsuitable in cold and windy areas.

House Matching

Housing matching or senior matching occurs when a single elderly person invites another person to share housing, as the National Council on Aging (NCOA) defines it. In some of the literature this is considered shared housing, but the NCOA considers the latter to be when an agency purchases or rents a home for seniors to share the facilities (Streib, Folts, and Hilker, 1984); the

AARP (1983) describes shared housing as three to seven individuals living together in a large house, sharing living expenses and housekeeping.

House matching is organized by many agencies serving seniors or by housing groups. Housing counselors assist elderly people who live alone to find another single to share their home; this renter may or may not be elderly and may or may not provide some services, such as maintenance work or cooking, in return for reduced rent. The arrangement means that the single elderly person has a supportive person on the premises and receives some rent income. However, many elderly are reluctant to give up their privacy and to share facilities.

An *Aging* article (1983–84b) describing one house-matching effort, a Memphis Share-A-Home program, stated that the agency tried to match different generations—the aged home provider and the young, often student, house seeker. The agency required a trial period of sharing before permanent arrangements were made. One problem with such sharing is that it effects Supplementary Security Income (SSI) benefits.

Other Subsidies to Older Owners

One of the few homeownership loan programs available to seniors is the Farmers Home Administration (FmHA) Section 502 homeownership loan program, with direct loans at low interest rates to low- and lower moderate-income families who cannot get credit elsewhere; they can be used for new construction, existing housing rehabilitation, or repairs. In the late 1970s about one-third of the borrowers were elderly (Noll, 1981). Another assistance in most states is property tax exemption or postponement for low- moderate-income persons. A federal help is exclusion of the first $125,000 of capital gains on sale of a house for individuals 55 or over.

Home-Equity Conversion

Home-equity conversion programs are being pushed by nonprofit groups serving the elderly, in coordination with banks. AARP (1983) defines home-equity conversion as "an option allowing homeowners to convert the asset represented by the value of their homes (equity) into cash while retaining certain ownership rights, specifically *use* and *possession*." Such programs allow the elderly to draw money from their major asset and use it for everyday expenses. Unlike equity-based second mortgage loans, these programs do not require immediate monthly payback. Repayment may be postponed for a set number of years or for life.

Home-equity conversion programs take a variety of forms; reverse annuity mortgages (RAMs) are best known (Garnett and Guttentag, 1984). Others are deferred-payment loans and sale-leasebacks. Under the sale-leaseback contract, the elderly owner sells the home to the investor and pays a rent agreed upon at the sale to continue occupancy of the unit. The former owner no longer pays property tax, insurance, or even maintenance costs, but does not get full appraised value, as the investor's rental/income is restricted by the lease.

Reverse annuity mortgages and deferred-payment loans, that is, a lump-sum loan, vary in type. RAMs can give the owner a fixed monthly amount for a specific length of time; the owner then begins repaying the principal and the interest at the end of a period of 5 or 10 years. At that time, if the owner wants to stay in the home, there is a very large payback. If other assets are lacking, the owner must sell the house. A life-term RAM avoids this problem, but because the bank is gambling on the elderly person's life expectancy, the annuity is lower and, for a deferred-payment loan, 80 percent or less of home value (Pastalan, 1983). Heirs of the estate will not get a house free of liens; this is a major concern of most elderly. That or the terms of the fixed-contract repayment plan have discouraged many from using these programs, according to the San Francisco Foundation in its major demonstration project with a local bank (Huttman, 1985).

Many experts such as Jacobs (1986), in his *Gerontologist* article on his major study of home-equity conversion, support RAMs. He states: "Analysis revealed that reverse mortgage loans could have a substantial impact on the budgets of many elderly homeowners, with impressive percentage increases in income . . . [and] also contribute to older owners' capacity to keep up with housing expenses or finance long-term care" (496). However, Pastalan (1983), in reviewing Jacobs' earlier report (1980), finds that the life-term type offers such a low income increase (about $100 a month) that other housing alternatives might be preferable. Among agencies, much interest in home-equity programs exist, as a 1983 conference showed (*Aging*, 1983–84a).

Renters: Section 8 Housing Assistance

Section 8, introduced in 1974, is financial assistance for shelter, a traditional dwelling-specific program. The Section 8 Existing Housing program gives rent help to over 200,000 aged (end of 1980), one-third of the assisted tenant population (Newman, 1984). The Section 8 Existing Housing program is for low-income families and the elderly, with the latter getting a special allocation; those in Section 202 new construction elderly housing also get a special Section 8 allocation.

Section 8 in recent years has been directed at those at 50 percent (previously 80 percent) of the median income of the area. It covers the part of their allowable "fair market rent" over 30 percent of the household income. The unit must qualify as a standard-quality private or non-profit unit. For the elderly who qualify, 65 percent do so in their current homes (Newman, 1984).

Besides the Existing Housing program, there is a Section 8 New Construction program, supplying rental apartments with rent assistance to tenants, and a Section 8 Rehabilitated Housing program that does the same. The former has higher allowable rents than for existing private units. Developers of new construction get funding for the building from a variety of sources, such as Section 202, the Government National Mortgage Association, state or local agencies (for example, through exempt bonds), or from private sources investing in the buildings as a tax shelter. At least 20 percent of the units must be allocated to Section 8 tenants. Developers and HUD sign a long-term annual contributions contract.

Special Housing for the Elderly with Supportive Services

The Section 8 New Construction subsidies, here related to rent subsidies, are only one way of providing housing especially for the elderly; Section 202 and public housing for the elderly are other ways. They differ from all the other programs mentioned in the previous section in that they are for buildings constructed, rehabilitated, or renovated to meet the needs of somewhat-impaired elderly, who need a more protective environment with a bundle of varying services (Regnier, 1986). Apartments with few services, shared housing, "congregate" living arrangements, life care developments, and retirement communities are all part of the continuum of care.

Type and Degree of Services and Facilities

In special housing for the elderly, bricks and mortar are only a part of the total living environment. To varying degrees, services are provided (Sherwood et al., 1985). In public housing in the United States and Canada (Huttman, 1977) services are usually very limited and sporadic, coming from the community; there is little or no staff or only maintenance staff on site. Facilities are usually only one communal room, perhaps with an adjacent kitchenette and small office for community providers. In some public housing a Title III meals program is run. Private luxury apartments may have many more services, usually of a recreational nature.

"Congregate" housing is a term referring to housing for the elderly with a number of services; it usually includes meal service and housekeeping service, some recreational and education activities, and likely some minor medical assistance such as a part-time nurse or visiting doctor. Facilities usually include a dining room, recreation rooms, a library, medical service facilities (often with an infirmary and occupational and physical therapy rooms), and perhaps a chapel. While congregate housing often has hotel-type rooms, even shared ones, many more luxurious complexes have apartments with small kitchenettes. Those of the "life care" type even have full apartments or townhouses. In this nonsubsidized luxury life care community one buys an apartment and is guaranteed housing and services for life. There is a high monthly maintenance payment. This type usually has an infirmary, the services and facilities previously mentioned, and a nursing home. Some are run by religious groups; many are private for-profit enterprises, even chains. A number have been known to go bankrupt, leaving the person without his purchase money or housing (a number of states now regulate life care; see U.S. Senate, Select Committee on Aging, 1983). The Section 202 rental type usually has a number of nonmedical services and facilities and is sponsored by churches and nonprofit groups. More expansive owner-occupied retirement communities such as Leisure Worlds have been privately developed for profit. The marketing focus is on recreational facilities, golf, tennis, and many clubs for the 50–55 age group.

However, residents have "aged in place." In the Rossmoor, California, Leisure World, founded in 1964, by 1980 half the residents were widows; the average age was over 80 (Huttman, 1985). Such support systems as a medical clinic (with its separate fee), homemaker and home health services, community meals-on-wheels, and transportation services receive heavy use.

This discussion indicates that it is hard to make clear-cut distinctions between apartment and congregate forms of developments. Not only do numbers of facilities and services vary, but whether the development or the community provides most of these services. Even the distinction between public housing apartments and normal congregate developments with services is not always valid, as the HUD and state congregate service programs are now giving services to selected frail elderly in public housing.

Another type of development is the multilevel facility. Different buildings or wings are devoted to apartments for independent living, congregate housing for the semi-independent, and nursing homes for dependent care. The continuum of housing alternatives is contained in one complex. Some retirement communities have all three, and some congregate developments have a nursing home nearby. Huttman (1982) found many such complexes in her World Health Organization (WHO) study of Danish and Dutch facilities. In Denmark municipalities and housing associations in the postwar years or earlier built nursing homes; in the 1970s they added service flats in the form of small modern apartments with a communal dining room and an infirmary for that wing. These complexes also include an adult day-care center. The Dutch have "residential homes"—congregate housing, with a nursing home often adjacent, run by a separate Ministry of Health.

Driehoven, in Amsterdam, has apartments, congregate housing, and nursing homes. The advantages are easy movement from one wing to another; medical staff in the nursing wing; and cost economies of one kitchen and joint administrative staff. The disadvantage, as with any "accommodating" housing, is that residents are not happy to have the sick of the nursing wing nearby. Even with enriched housing, some residents resist this program, as it means keeping on those who are frail (Gurewitsch, 1986).

In specially planned housing the question arises of staff on the site; many public housing projects have only maintenance staff on site. Yet the elderly often have emergency needs (Lawton, Moss, and Grimes, 1985). Should the community or the development provide services? Community services are cheaper, but if one has many frail elderly, it may be better to have services on site.

Shared or Group Housing

Shared or group housing is usually converted conventional residential housing, even mansions, that are used as semicommunal living arrangements for a small group of unrelated people, often fewer than 15 persons, with common space and facilities but private apartments or rooms. Definitions differ somewhat; the AARP (1983) and Struyk (1985) emphasize sharing of housekeeping and other tasks by residents, but Streib (1984), through his case studies, points out that many shared-housing programs employ one or more persons and also use agency volunteers.

In shared housing such services as meals and nursing assistance, the latter through community agencies, are usually provided. The program may be sponsored by a church or other small group, by a large multiservice nonprofit agency for the aged, or by a county authority. In Phoenix the board of supervisors created a senior village out of a cluster of nine empty houses it had acquired as part of a flood-control program. It remodeled them through use of revenue-sharing funds and an Administration on Aging grant and is housing 45 elderly. The program is supervised by the County Health Department/Long Term Care Program, partly because it focuses on servicing those formerly in nursing homes.

Instead of a cluster of adjacent houses, the program may be houses scattered throughout the city or be one house. Many shared-housing programs have a cost advantage that is reflected in their rents. Streib in his case studies (1984) indicates low monthly rents around $335, $445, and for a multiservice agency with many services, $875. Struyk (1985) sees the savings as potentially great for those who might otherwise need a nursing home.

The disadvantages are that the number of services offered may not be enough for all of the residents; any housekeeping requirements may be too much effort for some residents. Great care is needed in selecting participants who can take part in such communal living arrangements and who will not be dissatisfied with the lack of privacy. Another barrier to shared housing is local government zoning ordinances.

Reuse of Public and Private Buildings

Reuse of public and private buildings for shared housing, for apartments, for single-room-occupancy (SRO) hotels or for congregate housing is now popular (Reilly, 1983–84). Some cities, using federal, state, or local funding, are now renovating public or private buildings, often obtaining free the land under them. They are recycling schools, hospitals, hotels, and other structures. In a Conference of Mayors survey (NISH, 1985c), one-third of 361 cities responding said that they had reuse projects and 86 more said that they were working on them. Federal funding used included Community Development Block Grants, Section 202, Urban Development Area Grants and Section 8. The city governments also used bonds, tax incentives, and general revenues. Besides public buildings, an old paper mill in Turner Falls, Massachusetts, turned into senior housing by the county housing authority and a seminary into a senior center in Centerville, Ohio, are examples of use of private buildings (NISH, 1985c). Another is agency purchase and management of SRO hotels, as in Long Beach, New York (Felton, Lehmann, and Adler, 1981).

Public Housing for the Elderly

Public housing for the elderly is more typically housing constructed specifically for this group's use. This program is meant to be a traditional dwelling-specific type, providing a standard unit at a low rent, with rent further reduced in relation to income (30 percent of income) (see the chapter by Pitt and Van Vliet—). These complexes, found in most large communities and even in many small ones, though less often in rural areas, are run by local city or county housing authorities with a federal subsidy. This subsidy consists of federal loans from HUD directly to the local public housing authority for construction of the units, and in a few cases for rehabilitation of housing for such use. HUD also helps with operating costs, though these should be covered from rents. Eligibility for this housing is by a means test, with the low low-income given preference.

About 440,000 households in public housing are low-income elderly, over 37 percent in 1980. During that year over one-third of all units constructed were for the elderly (U.S. Congress, Senate, 1982; Newman, 1984). By 1985 a majority of the construction was elderly units (see the chapter by Pit and Van Vliet—).

These elderly projects are architecturally more pleasing and better located than public housing for poor families, although some of the high-rise buildings were originally used for families until such occupancy was considered undersirable. Typically, special facilities have been limited to a communal room and office, with services provided by community agencies. However, for some tenants, HUD's new demonstration Congregate Housing Service Program Project is changing this.

Section 202 Senior Housing

Like public housing, HUD's Section 202 is both a supply-side program to provide new construction in the form of quality rental units for the elderly and a program of financial subsidy through low rents due to government assistance on the mortgage and use of Section 8 rent assistance in such housing. This dwelling-specific program is one of federal assistance through direct loans to nonprofit groups for construction or rehabilitation of rental housing at low interest rates; it is directed exclusively to the elderly and handicapped. There were about 40,000 Section 202 units occupied by the elderly at the end of 1980 (Newman, 1984). In addition, one-fourth of those in the similar earlier below-market interest subsidy program, Section 236, are elderly, and 12.5 percent in an even earlier similar program, Section 221(d)(3) (NISH, 1986).

In these programs the government assumes that support facilities will be included, but it limits their space to keep costs down and to insure that rents will not only be at or below fair market, but within federal limitations (Gelfand, 1984). The government has placed sharp limitations on health care facilities and services in Section 202 (Newman, Zais, and Struyk, 1984). Due to these requirements, HUD design specifications, and local planning regulations, it usually takes three to five years to implement a project, with five stages of the application process, even if the nonprofit group uses an experienced developer (Gelfand, 1984).

In 1974 an effort was made to increase the number of low-income in these nonprofit projects by making the rent more affordable through the use of a Section 8 set-aside allocation for each unit built and thus to insure that at least 20 percent of the participants were very low income. Section 202 has continued even in the period of federal housing cutbacks in 1984 and 1985 to receive new construction allocations by Congress.

Farmers Home Administration Section 515 Rental Housing Program

Another supply-side program of providing new rental units for the elderly is FmHA, the Farmers Home Administration Section 515 rural rental housing program. Almost 300,000 units have been built under the program, with somewhat less than half for the elderly (NISH, 1986). The program provides subsidized (90 percent of loans) and unsubsidized loans for construction of multifamily rental projects. The subsidy mechanism is an interest credit, with the tenant paying rent based on his income and with the mortgage interest rate ranging from 1 percent up to the market interest rate. The developer is often a nonprofit organization or a housing authority. Section 515 can be used in combination with HUD's Section 8 under a special FmHA rental assistance program brought forth in 1977. The service area for FmHA 515 crosses metropolitan lines and includes communities of up to 20,000 (Noll, 1981).

Private Market-Rate Housing Projects' Federal Insurance Coverage

For market-rate housing projects, mostly developed by the private sector, the federal government has facilitated their ability to get mortgages by insuring the mortgage. FHA insures such projects designed for elderly occupancy and, since 1983, congregate housing facilities, board and care facilities, and "life care centers" with services beyond those provided in congregate facilities (Struyk, 1985). The insurance has also been useful in making the mortgages marketable to secondary financial facilities such as the Government National Mortgage Association (GNMA) and the Federal National Mortgage Association (FNMA), making these mortgages more attractive to loan originators.

State Housing Programs

Many states now have state housing and development agencies and provide funds for construction of rental housing or approve of cities in their state providing bond issues for developing housing. A major focus has been on elderly housing projects. The state housing agency may provide mortgage money directly to developers, generating these general funds through sales of notes and bonds, often tax-exempt. The funds may be for construction financing of a short duration (3 years) or may be for permanent financing by sale of 40-year bonds. The private developer gets a lower mortgage rate than for traditional mortgages, and this can mean charging lower rents.

These tax-exempt bonds have been a major source of lower-cost mortgage financing in recent years, attracting investors to financing of low-income housing both through state and city bonds and by direct investment in elderly housing. However, the new tax reform law (1986) discourages this. For passive investors investing directly in housing, that is, limited partners who are putting equity into rental housing, the loss generated from such an investment cannot offset other income, as in the past. This act also decreases tax losses by lengthening the depreciation period on such housing (NISH, 1986).

Tax-exempt incentives are only part of state and local efforts. To fund congregate services in housing, a variety of funding sources are used. State housing agencies and departments of elderly affairs have been leaders in providing such congregate services. In 1983 Massachusetts was funding services for 1,500 units; the state housing agency did the development and management of the congregate housing, but the Department of Elderly Affairs funds the services. Home health aides and nursing services were paid for by Medicaid (NISH, 1985b). In Maine the state also funds congregate services programs, and in Maryland it funds sheltered housing. New Jersey has an extensive congregate housing services program, funded through the state division on aging, subsidized from the casino revenue funds (Day, 1983).

The New York State Enriched Housing Program provided services to selected tenants at 34 sites, mainly public housing, in 1985, with a total participation of around 300 (Gurewitsch, 1986). The New York State law limits the number of people to be covered in any given enriched housing project, whether public or not-for-profit housing, to 15 percent of all residents, so that the senior housing complex will not gradually take on the character of a health-related facility. Selected for participation are those with functional impairments. In the absence of the enriched housing program they would be precluded from independent living. Low-income participants have the services paid for by a state supplement to SSI. Examples of services the sponsoring agency secures are, in the Ten Eyck public housing, lunch in a special studio unit for the 10 participants, help in apartment cleaning and laundry, and transportation to appointments. An aide helps with bathing, dressing, and medications (Gurewitsch, 1986).

Local Nonprofit Housing Groups' Funding Initiatives

Because federal and state funding is limited and HUD is turning down more good projects than it subsidizes (Gurewitsch, 1986), local nonprofit housing groups have to obtain a "package" of financial assistance, bringing together funding from many sources. An example is Eden Housing, Inc., in the California Bay Area; it has sponsored over a dozen projects. Its first venture (1973) was a rental housing complex for the elderly under Section 236 subsidies, with rent supplements for low-income tenants and with use of Comprehensive Employment and Training Act (CETA) workers for the meals program. Two other projects were built under Section 202, with one of these planned with Bay Area Japanese-American groups. Another financial arrangement was a Section 202 project for the disabled, developed with an Independent Living group and owned by a limited partnership affiliate of Eden Housing, with investors putting in money and getting a tax advantage for 12 to 14 years (Eden Housing, Inc., 1986; Broder, 1982).

Their other financing arrangements have included a limited-equity nonprofit housing cooperative of townhouses; a hybrid of owning and renting under the State of California Rental Housing Construction Program, in this case for families; and two joint ventures with private developers, in each case with a certain number of Section 8 rental assistance units. For one of these there was below-market permanent mortgage financing through the GNMA tandem fundings program and a tax-exempt revenue bond for a below-market interest rate construction loan issued by the city of Hayward. For another project, with one-fifth low-income units (guaranteed for 20 years), some for the handicapped, Eden Housing not only got low-interest mortgage revenue bonds for construction, issued by Union City, but low land costs due to use of a former school site.

Funding to acquire and rehabilitate three low-income apartment houses (1981) came through a local foundation grant for planning, CDBG monies for acquisition, and Section 8 moderate rehabilitation program funds for renovation. Section 8 rental assistance helped keep rents down. Long-term financing of the acquired units was from FHA 203(k) monies. Funding for two innovative self-help programs, where users contribute their labor under the supervision of a licensed contractor, thus cutting costs (eliminating down payments and permitting lower mortgage payments), came from city mortgage bond monies and Section 235, seldom used in recent years.

Local initiators of elderly housing include not only nonprofit groups such as this one, but churches, service clubs, and local government. Blackie (1983) describes a totally locally funded elderly project in Northville, Michigan. The city council, bothered by HUD's requirement of low-income occupancy for subsidized elderly housing and various other regulations, took on the job itself, issuing a building authority bond (1977), obtaining a low-interest mortgage, and providing the balance of the project money from the city Improvement Fund (money from a tax on a local race course). It saw that low-income tenants got rent assistance through the Michigan State Housing Development Authority or trust fund monies, as well as local property tax credits.

FUTURE TRENDS IN HOUSING FOR THE ELDERLY

"In the United States, legislation passed in 1965 made care in an institutional setting an *entitlement program* for the medically indigent frail elderly. Adequate protected housing for frail old-old seniors is not yet considered worthy of *entitlement* status. The result: a disproportionate amount of public funds spent to maintain people 65 and over in high cost institutional settings; long waiting lists for protected housing" (Gurewitsch, 1987). The prospect that "the average period of diminished physical vigor will decrease, that chronic disease will occupy a smaller proportion of the typical life span, and that the need for medical care in later life will decrease" (Fries, 1980) means that shelter can be more in terms of protected housing for seniors if more widely available, and less in terms of nursing homes. Legislation at the state and national level making it attractive or mandatory for pension funds to invest a portion of their massive financial resources in protected housing for seniors would greatly improve prospects for construction of new housing.

Programs that bring an element of protection and socialization into existing private, middle-income housing complexes with large numbers of old-old residents will develop. It is unlikely that protected housing for frail, old-old seniors will become an entitlement program in the foreseeable future. However, due to the exorbitant costs of the nursing home alternative, public- and private-sector development of expanded protected senior housing strategies will achieve much the same purpose. Future generations of seniors will demand an opportunity to live in settings that minimize prospects that their final days will be spent in an institutional environment.

States will see this housing as cost-effective. As a St. Paul, Minnesota, spokesman told the U.S. House of Representatives Select Committee on Aging hearings in relation to the HUD Congregate Housing Service Program (NISH, 1985a), the program can cost only one-third as much as a nursing home and can stop premature institutionalization.

There are, of course, barriers at the present time to funding, such as the federal deficit and increasing construction costs, meaning higher rents, especially if Section 8 or its equivalent is not expanded. Another problem is loss of existing subsidized units to low-income users presently in them because under the mortgage arrangements, certain owners can repay the mortgage after 20 years; for example, among the FmHA Section 515 rural rental units built before 1979, over 123,000 units can be repaid now, and under the old Section 221(d)(3) and Section 236 programs 217,500 units are eligible between 1986 and 1995. While the subsidized housing sector may suffer these short-term setbacks, the profitable private sector will grow as the number of affluent elderly increases (Gelwicks and Dwight, 1982).

Assistance to elderly in the community, whether in their own homes or in alternative housing, will be needed more than ever, as only a fraction of the somewhat-impaired elderly can be served in special housing. Local communities need to try more innovations. Repair programs will also flourish in the future. Home-equity plans, with more appealing provisions, will finally take hold.

REFERENCES

Aging. 1983–84a. "Conference on Home Equity." December–January, 41.
———. 1983–84b. "Experience Exchange: Memphis Share-A-Home." December–January, 26.

————. 1983–84c. "Group Living in Style." December–January, 28.

————. 1983–84d. "University of Michigan Study." December–January, 34.

American Association of Retired Persons. 1983. *Housing Choices for Older Homeowners.* Washington, D.C.: AARP.

————. 1984. *A Profile of Older Americans, 1984.* Washington, D.C.: AARP.

————. 1985. *A Profile of Older Americans, 1985.* Washington, D.C.: AARP.

Anderson, Elaine, Alexander Chen, and Richard Hula. 1984. "Housing Strategies for the Elderly: Beyond the Ecological Model." *Journal of Housing for the Elderly* 2 (Fall): 47–58.

Blackie, Norman. 1983. "Allen Terrace—No HUD Money Here!" *Journal of Housing for the Elderly* 3 (Fall): 77–82.

Broder, James. 1982. "Nonprofit Housing for the Elderly: A Primer for Sponsors." In Robert Chellis, James Seagle, Jr., and Barbara Seagle (eds.), *Congregate Housing for Older People.* Lexington, Mass.: Lexington Books.

Brody, Elaine. 1982. "Service Options in Congregate Housing." In Robert Chellis, James Seagle, Jr., and Barbara Seagle (eds.), *Congregate Housing for Older People.* Lexington, Mass.: Lexington Books.

Brody, Elaine, and Bernard Liebowitz. 1981. "Some Recent Innovations in Community Living Arrangements for Older People." In M. Powell Lawton and Sally Hoover (eds.), *Community Housing Choices for Older Americans.* New York: Springer.

Carp, Frances, and Abraham Carp. 1984. "A Complementary Congruence Model of Well-Being." In I. Altman, J. Wohwill, and M. P. Lawton (eds.), *The Physical Environment and the Elderly.* New York: Plenum Press.

Chen, Y. P. 1977. "Housing Assets as Potential Income: Implications for Income-Conditioned Programs." In *The Treatment of Assets and Income from Assets in Income-Conditioned Government Benefit Programs.* Washington, D.C.: Federal Council on the Aging. 149–176.

Cottin, Lou. 1979. *Elders in Rebellion: A Guide to Senior Activism.* New York: Anchor Press.

Crystal, Stephen. 1982. *America's Old Age Crisis: Public Policy and the Two Worlds of Aging.* New York: Basic Books.

Day, Suzanne. 1983. *Market Considerations and Utilizations of the Congregate Housing Services Program: Why Don't All Eligible Enroll?* New Jersey: New Jersey Department of Community Affairs.

Diamond, B. E. L., W. Kaye, and A. Monk. 1986. "Enriched Residential Housing Stock for the Elderly." *Gerontologist* 26: 238A. Abstract.

Eden Housing, Inc. 1986. *Report.* Hayward, Calif. (Partly prepared by William Vanderbergh, president).

Felton, Barbara, Stanley Lehmann, and Arlene Adler. 1981. "Single-Room Occupancy Hotels: Their Viability as Housing Options for Older Citizens." In M. Powell Lawton and Sally Hoover (eds.), *Community Housing Choices for Older Americans.* New York: Springer. 267–285.

Fitch, V., and L. Slivinske. 1986. "The Effect of Age on Self-Perception of Health and Well-Being of Elderly Individuals Living in Retirement Communities: A Preliminary Investigation." *Gerontologist* 26: 237A. Abstract.

Fowles, D. G. 1978. "A Model for Creating a Stable Population in Congregate Housing Residences." In W. T. Donahue, P. H. Pepe, and P. Murray (eds.), *Assisted*

Independent Living in Residential Congregate Housing for Older People. Washington, D.C.: International Center for Social Gerontology.

Fries, James. 1980. ''Aging, Natural Death, and the Compression of Morbidity.'' *New England Journal of Medicine*, July 17, 130.

Garnett, R., and J. Guttentag. 1984. ''The Reverse-Shared-Appreciation Mortgage.'' *Housing Finance Review* 3: 63–84.

Gelfand, Donald. 1984. *The Aging Network: Programs and Services*, 2d ed. New York: Springer.

Gelwicks, Louis, and Maria Dwight. 1982. ''Programming for Alternative and Future Models.'' In Robert Chellis, James Seagle, Jr., and Barbara Seagle (eds.), *Congregate Housing for Older People*. Lexington, Mass.: Lexington Books. 69–87.

Gurewitsch, Eleanor. 1982. *Reducing Requirements for Long Term Institutional Care: Results of a Retrospective Study*. Bern: Association for the Care of the Elderly.

———. 1984. ''Reduced Requirements for Long-Term Institutional Care: Results of a Retrospective Study.'' *Gerontologist* 24, no. 2: 199–204.

———. 1986. ''Enriched Housing in New York State: No Place like Home.'' Unpublished paper.

———. 1987. ''Enriched Housing Programs.'' Paper presented at the International Symposium on Normal Aging and Clinical Problems in the Elderly, Monteaux, Switzerland, March 30.

Hare, Patrick, and Linda Hollis. 1983. ''Saving the Suburbs for Schoolchildren.'' *Journal of Housing for the Elderly* 1 (Fall): 69–76.

Hare, Patrick, and Margaret Huske. 1983–84. ''Innovative Living Arrangements.'' *Aging*, December–January, 3.

Herbert, A. W. 1983. ''Enhancing Housing Opportunities for the Black Elderly.'' In R. L. McNeely and J. L. Colen (eds.), *Aging in Minority Groups*. Beverly Hills: Sage. 123–136.

Heumann, Leonard. 1984. ''Rent Subsidies and the Elderly.'' *Journal of Housing for the Elderly* 2 (Fall): 71–87.

Heumann, Leonard, and Duncan Boldy. 1982. *Housing for the Elderly*. New York: St. Martin's Press.

Hoover, Sally. 1981. ''Black and Spanish Elderly: Their Housing Characteristics and Housing Quality.'' In M. Powell Lawton and Sally Hoover (eds.), *Community Housing Choices for Older Americans*. New York: Springer. 65–89.

Huttman, Elizabeth. 1977. *Housing and Social Services for the Elderly*. New York: Praeger.

———. 1981a. *Introduction to Social Policy*. New York: McGraw-Hill.

———. 1981b. ''Social Work Services in the Housing Field.'' In Neil Gilbert and Harry Specht (eds.), *Handbook of the Social Services*. Englewood Cliffs, N.J.: Prentice-Hall.

———. 1982. ''Multi-Level Housing Facilities for the Elderly in Denmark and Holland.'' *Housing and Society* 9: 20–30.

———. 1985. *Social Services for the Elderly*. New York: Free Press.

———. 1986. ''Continuum of Care.'' In George Maddox (ed.), *Encyclopedia of Aging*. New York: Springer.

Jacobs, Bruce. 1980. ''The Potential Anti-Poverty Impact of RAMs and Property Tax Deferral.'' In K. Cholen and Y. P. Chen (eds.), *Unlocking Home Equity for the Elderly*. Cambridge, Mass.: Ballinger. 50–60.

————. 1986. "The National Potential of Home Equity Conversion." *Gerontologist* 26:496–504.

Kahana, Eva. 1975. "A Congruence Model." In P. G. Windley, T. O. Byerts, and F. G. Ernst (eds.), *Theory Development in Environment and Aging*. Washington, D.C.: Gerontological Society.

————. 1982. "A Congruence Model of Person-Environment Interaction." In M. P. Lawton, P. Windley, and T. Byerts (eds.), *Aging and the Environment*. New York: Springer.

Langer, Ellen, and Jerry Avorn. 1982. "Impact of the Psychosocial Environment of the Elderly on Behavioral and Health Organizations." In Robert Chellis, James Seagle, Jr., and Barbara Seagle (eds.), *Congregate Housing for Older People*. Lexington, Mass.; Lexington Books. 15–26.

Lawton, M. Powell. 1972. "Assessing the Competence of Older People." In D. R. Kent, R. Kastenbaum, and S. Sherwood (eds.), *Long Term Care*. New York: Behavioral Publications. 122–143.

————. 1975. *Planning and Managing Housing for the Elderly*. New York: Wiley.

————. 1976. "The Relative Impact of Congregate and Traditional Housing on Elderly Tenants." *Gerontologist* 16:237–242.

————. 1985. "Housing and Living Environments of Older People." In Robert Binstock and Ethel Shanas (eds.), *Handbook of Aging and the Social Sciences*, 2d ed. New York: Van Nostrand Reinhold. 450–478.

Lawton, M. Powell, and Sally Hoover (eds.). 1981. *Community Housing Choices for Older Americans*. New York: Springer.

Lawton, M. Powell, and L. Nahemow. 1971. "Ecology and the Aging Process." In C. Eisdorfer and M. Powell Lawton (eds.), *The Psychology of Adult Development and Aging*. Washington, D.C.: American Psychological Association.

Lawton, M. Powell, E. Brody, and P. Turner-Massey. 1978. "The Relationship of Environmental Factors to Changes in Well-Being." *Gerontologist* 18:137.

Lawton, M. Powell, Maurice Greenbaum, and Bernard Liebowitz. 1980. "The Lifespan of Housing Environments for the Aging." *Gerontologist* 20:56–63.

Lawton, M. Powell, M. Moss, and M. Grimes. 1985. "The Changing Service Needs of Older Tenants in Planned Housing." *Gerontologist* 25:258–264.

Lawton, M. Powell, L. Nahemow, and J. Teaff. 1975. "Housing Characteristics and the Well-Being of Elderly Tenants in Federally Assisted Housing." *Journal of Gerontology* 30:601–607.

Lawton, M. Powell, P. G. Windley, and T. O. Byerts (eds.). 1982. *Aging and the Environment: Theoretical Approaches*. New York: Springer.

Markson, Elizabeth. 1982. "Placement and Location: The Elderly Congregate Care." In Robert Chellis, James Seagle, Jr., and Barbara Seagle (eds.), *Congregate Housing for Older People*. Lexington, Mass.: Lexington Books. 51–66.

Nachison, J. S. 1985. "Who Pays? The Congregate Housing Question." *Generations*, Spring, 34–35.

National Institute of Senior Housing. 1983–84. *NISH News*. December–January.

————. 1985a. "Housing Services Program." *NISH News* 2 (August): 4.

————. 1985b. "Massachusetts Congregate Housing Program." *NISH News* 2 (August): 6.

————. 1985c. "U.S. Conference of Mayors." *NISH News* 2 (August): 5.

————. 1986. "Prepayment Threatens Older Tenants." *Senior Housing News* 1, no. 4:1.

Newman, Sandra J. 1984. "The Availability of Adequate Housing for Older People: Issue Areas for Advocates." *Journal of Housing for the Elderly* 2 (Fall): 3–14.

Newman, Sandra J., J. Zais, and R. Struyk. 1984. In I. Altman, J. Wohwill, and M. P. Lawton (eds.), *The Physical Environment and the Elderly*. New York: Plenum Press.

Noll, Paul. 1981. "Federally Assisted Housing Programs for the Elderly in Rural Areas: Problems and Prospects." In M. Powell Lawton and Sally Hoover (eds.), *Community Housing Choices for Older Americans*. New York: Springer. 90–108.

Pastalan, Leon. 1983. "Housing Equity Conversion: A Performance Comparison with Other Housing Options." *Journal of Housing for the Elderly* 3 (Fall): 83–90.

————. 1984. "Manufactured Housing for the Elderly: A Viable Alternative." *Journal of Housing for the Elderly* 2 (Fall): 89–91.

Pynoos, Jon. 1984. "Selling the Elderly Housing Agenda." *Policy Studies Journal* 13: 173–184.

Regnier, Victor. 1986. "Design Trends and Resident Preferences in Congregate Housing." *Gerontologist* 26: 239A. Abstract.

Reilly, Pat. 1983–84. "Old Buildings." *Aging*, December–January, 12.

Sheehan, Nancy. 1986. "Aging of Tenants: Termination Policy in Public Senior Housing." *Gerontologist* 26: 505–509.

Sherwood, S., J. N. Morris, C. C. Sherwood, S. Morris, E. Bernstein, and E. Gorstein. 1985. *Final Report on the Evaluation of the Congregate Housing Services Program*. Boston: Hebrew Rehabilitation Center.

Streib, Gordon. 1982. "The Continuum of Living Arrangements." In G. Lesnoff-Caravaglia (ed.), *Aging and the Human Condition*. New York: Human Services Press.

————. 1984. "Choices and Constraints: The U.S. Experience." Paper presented at the conference on "Accommodations for the Elderly," Perth, Australia, August 28.

Streib, Gordon, W. Edward Folts, and Mary Anne Hilker. 1984. *Old Homes—New Families: Shared Living for the Elderly*. New York: Columbia University Press.

Struyk, Raymond. 1985. "Current and Emergent Issues in Housing Environments for the Elderly." Paper presented at the Institute of Medicine Symposium, December 9–12.

Struyk, Raymond, and H. Katsura. 1985. *Aging at Home: How the Elderly Adjust Their Housing without Moving*. Urban Institute Report 3166–03. Washington, D.C.: Urban Institute.

Struyk, Raymond, and Beth Soldo. 1980. *Improving the Elderly's Housing*. Cambridge, Mass.: Ballinger.

Struyk, Raymond, and M. Turner. 1984. "Changes in the Housing Situation of the Elderly." *Journal of Housing for the Elderly* 2 (Spring): 3–20.

Struyk, Raymond, and J. Zais. 1982. *Providing Special Dwelling Features for the Elderly with Health and Mobility Problems*. Washington, D.C.: Urban Institute.

Sumichrast, Michael, Ronald Shafer, and Marika Sumichrast. 1984. *Planning Your Retirement Housing*. Washington, D.C.: American Association of Retired Persons/ Scott, Foresman.

Thompson, Marie McGuire. 1978. *Assisted Residential Living for Older People*. Washington, D.C.: International Institute of Gerontology.

U.S. Congress. Senate. Select Committee on Aging. 1982. *Developments in Aging.* Washington, D.C.: Government Printing Office.

———. 1983. *Life Care Communities: Promises and Problems.* Hearings. 98th Cong., 1st sess. Washington, D.C.: Government Printing Office.

Verderber, S. F. 1986. "Adaptable Housing Environments for the Elderly: A Comparative Analysis of Research-Based Design Prototypes." *Gerontologist* 26:238A. Abstract.

Welfeld, I. H., and Raymond Struyk (eds.). 1978. *Housing Options for the Elderly.* Occasional Papers in Housing and Community Affairs, vol. 3. Washington, D.C.: Government Printing Office.

Yawney, R., and D. Slover. 1979. "Relocation of the Elderly." In A. Monk (ed.), *The Age of Aging: A Reader in Social Gerontology.* Buffalo, N.Y.: Prometheus Books.

20

The Problem of Homelessness in the United States

CHARLES HOCH AND MARY JO HUTH

WHAT IS THE PROBLEM?

Deciding who counts as a homeless person in the United States of the 1980s provides an important point of departure for mapping the contours of the problem of the homeless. According to officials from the U.S. Department of Housing and Urban Development (HUD), the homeless include those people who inhabit public or private emergency shelters, or who use for shelter structures that were not designed for that purpose (HUD, 1984: 7–8). This definition uses the absence of a permanent residential shelter as the primary criterion for classifying the homeless. For instance, people sheltered by institutions for purposes of treatment or who live in overcrowded conditions with relatives are considered to be sheltered according to this definition, and are therefore not counted among the homeless.

Recent studies indicate, however, that the homeless come from poor households subjected to the double economic pressures of stable or declining income and rising housing costs. The loss of inexpensive rental units to demolition, abandonment, and conversion, especially in urban areas, has reduced the stock of inexpensive rental housing and driven up rents, while unemployment, low wages, and inadequate public assistance benefits provide insufficient income for increasing numbers of the poor to afford to rent even the cheapest dwellings. The homeless on the street may be only the most visible portion of a growing population of poor people whose economic vulnerability leaves them frequently at risk of losing their hold on permanent shelter (Hopper and Hamberg, 1984; Salerno, Hopper, and Baxter, 1984).

The homeless person in the United States not only lacks a decent and regular place to live, but social standing as well. In addition to their miseries of poverty and lack of shelter, the homeless experience social isolation and even the indignity of blame from others with better incomes and adequate housing. As economically weak and socially vulnerable inhabitants of U.S. cities, the homeless have become subject to the power and authority of others responsible for maintaining public order or providing emergency services, including shelter. The homeless "count" only when harbored in a shelter, when recorded by those providing relief, or when arrested for a criminal offense. It is these counts that agencies like HUD use to classify and describe the homeless.

THE HISTORY OF THE HOMELESS PROBLEM IN THE UNITED STATES

The story of homeless people in the United States reflects the pathways followed by different groups of poor people in their search for accommodations at the periphery of the market for shelter. It also reveals how these pathways were blocked, modified, and in some cases improved by the intervention of public or private officials. Moreover, it indicates that the definition of the homeless has changed many times since the colonial period, reflecting major shifts in the economic and social structure of American society as well as changing conceptions of social order. We have identified and will now discuss three prominent perceptions of the homeless in the United States since the eighteenth century: the homeless as vagrants, as deviants, and as victims.

The Homeless as Vagrants

Laws governing vagrancy were imported from England and were developed for the purpose of outlawing unemployed transients, forcing the homeless to return to their place of origin to obtain relief (Chambliss, 1964). In early eighteenth-century Boston, Philadelphia, and New York, for example, poor laws enabled local constables to warn off strangers by requiring able-bodied transients to labor in a communal workhouse (Nash, 1979: 126–127). Thus in preindustrial America vagrancy laws were used by local governments to cope with the wandering poor. By the end of the century, however, the increasing mobility of the general population as well as of transients rendered local solutions inadequate. For example, in the emerging social order of late eighteenth-century Massachusetts, which defined transients as deviants from the cultural and economic norms of family life, residential stability, and secure employment, banishment was no longer considered a satisfactory solution to the problem of homelessness (Jones, 1984:48).

Rapid industrialization of American society in the nineteenth century generated not only a much larger number of wandering poor, but a different variety as well. While the preindustrial homeless included a relatively large proportion of families and single women (Clement, 1984), by the time of the first major industrial economic recession of 1873 the composition of the wandering poor had changed to include mainly young, single males searching for work. At the end of the century hundreds of thousands of these tramps traveled across the United States, especially in the Western States, mining, lumbering, herding, harvesting, building, and otherwise laboring to provide a crucial but overlooked economic contribution. Most tramps were white, law-abiding workers, including a substantial minority of foreign-born immigrants.

Poorhouses and police stations sheltered tramps whose meager wages did not afford them the luxury of paying much rent. From the Civil War to the turn of the century, police practice focused on controlling the "dangerous classes," which meant not only fighting crime, but controlling disease, poverty, and homelessness as well. However, the police spent more time managing the mobile, homeless poor than criminals because the ranks of the former could grow much more rapidly and unpredictably than the number of criminals, threatening the basic social order of the city (Monkkonen, 1981:86).

Police lodgings in Detroit, for instance, increased ninefold between 1865 and 1880. Ninety-five percent of the lodgers were men. New York's police department was furnishing almost 150,000 lodgings annually by 1890. Police stations were overrun with tramps at night. Until bunks were provided in 1875, lodgers at Detroit's central police station had to sleep on the floor. That was still the case in some Chicago stations at the turn of the century. Police lodgings had become an urban scandal. (Schneider, 1984:221)

One historian estimates that as many as one in five households possessed a member who had lodged in a police station between 1867 and 1883 (Monkkonen, 1981: 94). But police control of the tramp did not go uncontested. Middle- and upper-class social reformers criticized police provision of shelter and relief, arguing that no matter how well intentioned, such largesse promoted indolence and dependence. The leaders of philanthropic organizations eventually mobilized sufficient legislative support for programs to replace permissive police lodgings. Thus, in 1880 the New York State Tramp Act disallowed payments from county funds to overseers of poorhouses who gave lodging to tramps (Bremner, 1980: 175).

After the closing of police stations to tramps, municipal lodging houses and rescue missions emerged as the predominant forms of shelter for tramps between 1880 and 1910. Municipal lodging houses were usually little more than squalid residential warehouses that offered a bunk with little privacy and even less cleanliness in return for manual labor, like cutting wood or filling potholes. Rescue missions required attendance at religious services, offering spiritual conversion in exchange for a small donation (Schneider, 1984: 222). The homeless poor resisted administrative changes that forced them "to beg, save enough for commercial lodging houses, or go to municipal lodging houses with their work tests" (Monkkonen, 1981: 108). At the same time, the mobility and social independence of the tramp made such anarchistic resistance to local authorities a viable life-style, giving fellow travelers a shared sense of dignity (Anderson, 1923; Harring, 1977; Taft, 1960). But the rebellious spirit of tramps also stimulated community fears, helping to justify the proposal and adoption of work rules and labor camps (Gillin, 1929; Kelly, 1908) whereby the line between the unworthy vagrant and the worthy transient was drawn on moral grounds, leaving responsibility for social privation with the homeless individual. Ironically, the failure of labor tests to instill an appropriate work ethic among tramps did not discredit the rigid individualism of the reform perspective, but actually encouraged further diagnosis of the causes and motivations of the individual's choice to tramp, using the new social science disciplines of psychology and sociology.

The Homeless as Deviants

Professional attention to the problem of the homeless at the beginning of the twentieth century focused on the geographic concentration of transients and the poor in the high-density rooming houses of the urban slum. Structural shifts in the economy were undermining the livelihood of transient workers. Increasing mechanization in the agricultural and extraction industries, for example, reduced the demand for unskilled workers (Gilbert and Healy, 1942; Haymer, 1945; Schneider, 1984), and as such job opportunities contracted (especially in the 1920s), the number of transient homeless persons also dwindled. The fortunate found work and became residentially stable, while the less fortunate succumbed to the problems of poverty: illness, petty crime, and drunkenness. Social work professionals trained in the scientific diagnosis of social pathology identified and classified this distress. Indirectly, through programs of environmental improvement (Boyer, 1978), and directly, through the counseling and education of individuals, these professional caretakers tried to "cure" the maladjusted and promote their rehabilitation (Hoy, 1928; Klein, 1923: 88–127; Lilliefors, 1928).

The Homeless as Victims

The profound economic dislocations imposed by the Great Depression of the 1930s increased dramatically the number of homeless poor and transients in the United States. Overwhelmed by the sheer scale of economic hardship and by the diversity of its victims, local governments, charities, and professional caretakers were forced to acknowledge the link between economic circumstances and the social problems of the transient population. Mobilization of national resources through New Deal programs provided shelter facilities, social insurance programs, and work relief projects for the unemployed (Sutherland and Locke, 1936: 184). These welfare-state reforms rationalized the provision of relief under the control of social service professionals who now incorporated earlier practices within an overall framework of entitlement.

Conscription for World War II, the demand for labor in the war industries, and the postwar economic prosperity reduced economic hardship in the United States and lowered the incidence of homelessness. The composition of the homeless narrowed from the wide range of households and people displaced by the massive unemployment of the Great Depression to include mainly older, single males surviving on pensions and marginal employment in the aging hotels and flophouses of skid row. However, extensive studies of skid row residents between

1950 and 1980 documented not only the decline in the number of skid row residents (Bahr, 1967; Bogue, 1963; Lee, 1980; Rooney, 1973; Wallace, 1968), but a growing consensus among professional caretakers that homelessness is less a matter of lacking shelter than a form of disaffiliation (Bahr, 1973; Caplow, 1940; Lee, 1978). Thus the social stigma associated with the powerless residents of skid row areas was classified as a social illness characterized by homelessness (Blumberg, Shipley, and Barsky, 1978).

CURRENT STATUS OF THE PROBLEM

Who Are the New Homeless?

Historical interpretations of the homeless remain relevant today as officials, professionals, and reporters for the various media use these concepts to define and explain the "new homeless." Conservatives appropriate the definition of the homeless as immoral vagrants or social deviants tempted into indolence by the largesse of the welfare state, while liberals split into two camps. One emphasizes the physical vulnerability of the homeless due to age, illness, or addiction; the other focuses on the economic vulnerability of the homeless based on unemployment, underemployment, and inadequate public aid payments. Despite their obvious differences, all these interpretations share a common belief in the desirability of individual autonomy that places homeless individuals at the center of the problem—either as misguided and willful deviants or as vulnerable and unwilling victims. Ironically, however, the recovery of individual autonomy by the homeless, whether justified by conservative or liberal ideals, still requires the intervention of an outside authority.

The marginality of the homeless once again became an important social issue in the early 1980s when the worst economic recession since the 1930s hit at the same time as a newly elected president initiated unprecedented cutbacks in public assistance programs funded by the federal government (Hopper and Hamberg, 1984). Segments of the working and middle classes seriously hurt by the economic hardships of the Great Depression were insulated from the trauma of unemployment in this recent recession by Social Security, Medicare, and unemployment insurance programs. The growing ranks of the working poor, however, were not so fortunate, as cutbacks in welfare programs during 1981 not only reduced the levels of support for the Aid to Families with Dependent Children (AFDC), Food Stamp, and child nutrition programs, but intensified the means-testing apparatus.

According to a 1983 national survey of shelter managers conducted by the Department of Housing and Urban Development, the profile of the new homeless contrasts sharply with that of the skid row resident. Whereas skid row homeless are overwhelmingly male, one in ten shelter tenants is a woman and another two out of ten are families. Moreover, while the average age of those using shelters is 34 years (only 6 percent are over 60 years of age), the homeless on skid row usually average about 20 years older. Finally, while skid row homeless are usually white, more than half (56 percent) of shelter users are minority persons (blacks, Hispanics, or Asians). In brief, the new homeless are a younger and more socially diverse category than skid row derelicts.

Why Are They Homeless?

The 1983 HUD-sponsored survey also reviewed studies conducted by shelter providers in various cities across the United States. These studies indicate that while most (about 60 percent) of the homeless have been unemployed for many years, 20 to 25 percent are employed on a part-time or irregular basis. The ranks of the new homeless have been filled mainly from this category of the working poor whose irregular and marginal jobs make them vulnerable to economic downturns. Shelter-provider studies also show that while 30 to 35 percent of the homeless are recipients of some form of public assistance or welfare, 40 to 50 percent subsist by selling blood, collecting and selling cans, scavenging, and panhandling.

Not only does the poverty of the new homeless make renting a dwelling virtually impossible, but at the same time, the buildings offering the least expensive single-room accommodations are being destroyed at an unprecedented rate by private urban renewal efforts in many older, low-income neighborhoods (Hoch, 1986; National Trust for Historic Preservation, 1981). Such efforts displace many households that are ill-equipped to afford the economic risks of moving by converting low-rent housing into high-rent apartments or condominiums (Clay, 1979; Reed, 1979). Many evicted households, unable to find affordable replacement housing, join the homeless in emergency shelters. Moreover, since 1981 the Reagan administration has relentlessly pursued a policy of dismantling federal housing programs that serve low- and moderate-income households (U.S. General Accounting Office, 1985: 23). The annual amount committed by HUD to assisted housing declined 78 percent between 1980 and 1983 (Hopper, 1984). New construction programs have been stopped, and rent subsidy programs have been cut back, the subsidy per household having been reduced from the difference between market rent and 25 percent of household income to the difference between market rent and 30 percent of household income. Many for whom subsidized housing offered a last resort now end up without any shelter at all. Persons suffering from illness, addiction, or personal crises are especially vulnerable to the loss of shelter attributable to poverty and the scarcity of affordable housing. Although the wealthy may endure similar illnesses, addictions, or crises, they avoid the privations of the streets and the indignities of dependence by purchasing the care their savings or insurance benefits afford them.

Local shelter-provider studies have identified relatively high levels of mental illness and addiction among the homeless. At one extreme is a study of 193 Philadelphia shelter users that claimed that 84 percent suffered from some form of mental illness (Arce et al., 1983). By contrast, HUD findings, based on interviews with emergency-shelter operators across the country, indicate that only 22 percent of the homeless are judged to be mentally ill, while 40 percent are considered addicted to either alcohol or drugs (HUD, 1984). It is probable, however, that if the hard-core "street people" who tend to shun shelters were included in the estimates, more than half of the homeless would be found to suffer from one or both of these chronic disabilities (Baxter and Hopper, 1984; Brown et al., 1983; City of Boston Emergency Shelter Commission, 1983; Ropers and Robertson, 1984).

Between 1963 and 1981 the population of mental hospitals nationally declined from 505,000 to 125,000 due to a policy of planned deinstitutionalization authorized by the Community Mental Health Centers Act of 1963 (Crystal, 1984; Katz, Lipton, and Sabatini, 1983). During the same period, the Veterans Administration reduced the number of psychiatric beds from 59,000 to 28,500 (City of New York, 1982). Initiated as a reform to protect the human rights of patients and to reduce the harmful effects of institutional dependence, deinstitutionalization rapidly gained momentum as governors and state legislators recognized the enormous cost savings it made possible. However, because support for community care facilities and programs did not match the enthusiasm for deinstitutionalization, many patients discharged from large mental hospitals did not receive adequate community-based care. These mental patients, combined with those who have become mentally ill since the deinstitutionalization policy was initiated, have overburdened community care programs and have forced many of the mentally ill to become urban nomads (Appleby and Desar, 1985).

Critical situations such as divorce and domestic violence are other factors that frequently lead to separations between vulnerable individuals or family groups and their places of residence. The negative effects of divorce, for example, fall most heavily on women, who usually retain custody of the children and thus responsibility for their daily care without adequate income. In fact, one-third of all female-headed households (50 percent among black female heads) subsist on incomes at or below the poverty line (Parrillo, Stimson, and Stimson, 1985). Domestic violence and sexual abuse also frequently lead to homelessness, as many victims—notably children and wives—seek escape by leaving their residences or cities without adequate means of support. Recent statistics show that 14 out of every 100 children and 16 out of every 100 spouses suffer from violent attacks each year in the United States, and that 9 percent of male children and 19 percent of female children are sexually abused annually (Parrillo, Stimson, and Stimson, 1985).

PROGRAMS FOR THE HOMELESS

Unexpected increases in the number of homeless people in American cities after 1980 produced visible evidence of increased poverty and suffering in the midst of the worst recession since the Great Depression. Although Congress responded to the rise in social misery in 1983 by enacting Public Law 98–8, which established the Federal Emergency Management Agency (FEMA), the federal government itself did not take a leading role in providing relief. FEMA distributed about half of the $475 million appropriated between 1983 and 1985 to national nonprofit religious and philanthropic agencies such as the United Way, the National Council of Churches, and the American Red Cross to help fund their efforts to shelter the homeless. The other half of the funds has gone to the states to distribute to their local governments for the purpose of sheltering and in other ways serving the homeless (Executive Office of the President, 1985). Thus about 60 percent of the city and county government officials interviewed by HUD in its 1983 survey reported offering operating subsidies to private shelter operators, and 50 percent admitted providing vouchers to the homeless for temporary housing in hotels, motels, or apartments when shelters are full. While only 20 percent of city and county governments use locally generated revenues to provide such financial assistance to the homeless (HUD, 1984: 46), many local governments rehabilitate and subsequently lease public buildings at minimum cost to nonprofit shelter operators for use as shelters. It is not surprising, therefore, that the 1983 HUD survey found that 94 percent of shelters for the homeless are operated by private nonprofit organizations, 40 percent of which are religious groups. Since 1983, however, several state governments—those of California, Massachusetts, New Jersey, and New York—have begun to finance their own programs to house the homeless because federal funds have proven woefully inadequate and are in constant jeopardy of being eliminated altogether, while the number of the homeless continues to increase. But as is true of local governments, state governments typically leave responsibility for directly serving the homeless to private nonprofit agencies.

HUD officials estimated from shelter-operator reports in 1983 that about 111,000 homeless persons could be sheltered on any given night in the United States, including 12,000 runaway youths and 8,000 battered women (HUD, 1984: 34). Although most shelters remain open year-round, occupancy rates vary, reflecting seasonal weather conditions as well as the mismatch between admission criteria and the characteristics of homeless persons. For example, in 1983 the emergency-shelter voucher system in Denver administered by the Department of Social Services during the day and the Police Department at night restricted eligibility to the elderly, the disabled, and to families in need of shelter (Salerno, Hopper, and Baxter, 1984: 139). Similarly, rescue missions designed specifically for male residents of skid row do not shelter families, women, youths, or the mentally disabled.

Besides a place to sleep, most shelters offer food, clothing, showers, and laundry facilities. However, receipt of such services is usually contingent upon the homeless resident's attending religious services, performing certain chores, receiving counseling, or fulfilling other "house rules." In some cases shelter staff even encourage residents to share responsibility for providing services and maintaining order with the intent of strengthening the autonomy and self-respect of the homeless. The same rationale motivated the Burnside Community Council in Portland, Oregon, to provide not only shelter, but employment for the homeless in a recycling center, auto repair shop, and day labor service (U.S. Department of Health and Human Services [HHS], 1984: 70). In Philadelphia three homeless men, with the help of a few organizational advocates, formed the Committee for Dignity and Fairness for the Homeless, which applied for and received FEMA funds to help start and complete plans for a shelter operated by and for the homeless. The committee now operates a 40-bed shelter that offers food, counseling, and an open-door policy to anyone regardless of sex, age, or other personal characteristics (HHS, 1984: 77). Far more common, however, are those shelters that insist upon a regimented (if well-intentioned and compassionate) system of providing basic necessities to the homeless. The large size of many shelters, combined with the fact that 40 percent do not allow residents to stay during the day, precludes the formation of social attachments that might make possible the development of a secure and mutually supportive residential environment. Emergency shelters are designed to treat the homeless condition as a temporary problem, even though the number of homeless continues to grow.

Efforts to increase the number of shelters have encountered resistance from potential neighbors who place political pressure on local elected officials to use zoning and building code regulations to exclude the construction of shelters (National Coalition for the Homeless, 1983). Moreover, lack of government leadership in the design and development of quality standards for emergency shelters has left the responsibility for innovations to service providers whose inexperience in housing proves a formidable handicap (Greer, 1985). However, most shelter operators and other social service providers who aid the homeless recognize the gap between needs and available resources and acknowledge the inadequacies of the emergency assistance they offer. They also realize that for many of their clients, homelessness is not temporary. As a result, service providers and advocates for the homeless have formed coalitions in many cities across the country to take steps that go beyond short-term shelter to long-term housing for the poor.

PLANNING FOR THE HOMELESS

One plan that integrates both short- and long-term solutions to the problem of homelessness involves three residential tiers: emergency shelter, transitional shelter, and permanent low-cost housing (Brown et al., 1983; Kaufman, 1984). Emergency shelter gets the homeless off the street for a few weeks, while transitional shelter provides not only housing, but a variety of services (counseling, job training and so on for up to nine months) designed to help the resident become self-sufficient. Finally, the availability of low-rent housing remains crucial for people leaving a transitional environment whose slim resources can be quickly exhausted by market-rate rents. Unfortunately, media attention to the problem of homelessness has tended to emphasize its extraordinary and dramatic aspects, focusing on the physical and social difficulties of the homeless (Nelson, 1983: 25). Such accounts build public support for emergency aid provided by professionals, but do not tie the plight of the homeless to the lack of low-rent housing or to unemployment. Similarly, justifying the three-tier residential plan primarily on the basis of a service need paradoxically strengthens the status of the professionals while weakening the status of the homeless, because the first two tiers of the plan rest on a politics of compassion—a politics in which the professional altruists aid the weak homeless. While the third tier of the plan relies on a politics of entitlement by which citizens receive their due and the homeless earn respect, such a politics requires leadership that will tie the fate of everyone in our society to that of the disenfranchised homeless. This involves not only pointing out how the homeless resemble the nonhomeless, but also emphasizing the precarious hold that many Americans have on the shelter they occupy. But it is unlikely that such leadership will come from social service professionals, since their authority does not extend into the political arena of housing entitlements. In other words, they cannot secure the low-income housing necessary to make possible long-term shelter autonomy for the homeless. Moreover, implementation of the three-tier residential plan in the present context of weak public support and fiscal retrenchment promises to produce fragmented rather than integrated outcomes.

Unlike the tramps of the 1890s and the wandering unemployed of the 1930s, however, the new homeless pose no serious threat to the integrity of the social fabric. Although more socially diverse than their skid row predecessors, they share the kind of social marginality that inspires professional scrutiny and compassion while it encourages public curiosity and contempt. The increased provision of emergency and transitional shelters may meet the basic needs of the poor, but it will likely institutionalize the social marginality of the homeless as well. Perhaps, if spread broadly enough, these shelter services will eventually instill expectations of a right to decent shelter among the homeless, nurturing a clientele who will take unified actions to demand better housing. The privations of the homeless, combined with the structure and diversity of shelters, however, undermine such a hope. The homeless will resist regimentation and control as did their predecessors, but the prospects that such efforts will reduce shelter uncertainty among the poor in the United States appear grim.

REFERENCES

Anderson, N. 1923. *The Hobo: The Sociology of the Homeless Man*. Chicago: University of Chicago Press.
Appleby, L., and P. N. Desar. 1985. "Documenting the Relationship between Homelessness and Psychiatric Hospitalization." *Hospital and Community Psychiatry* 36: 732–737.
Arce, Anthony, Marilyn Tadlock, Michael J. Vergare, and Stuart H. Shapiro. 1983. "A

Psychiatric Profile of Street People Admitted to an Emergency Shelter.'' *Hospital and Community Psychiatry* 34: 812–817.

Bahr, H. M. 1967. ''The Gradual Disappearance of Skid Row.'' *Social Problems* 15 (Summer): 41–45.

——— (ed.). 1973. *Skid Row: An Introduction to Disaffiliation*. New York: Oxford University Press.

Baxter, Ellen, and Kim Hopper. 1984. ''Troubled on the Streets.'' In John A. Talbott (ed.), *The Chronic Mental Patient*. New York: Grune & Stratton.

Blumberg, L. T., T. E. Shipley, Jr., and S. F. Barsky. 1978. *Liquor and Poverty: Skid Row as a Human Condition*. New Brunswick, N.J.: Rutgers Center of Alcohol Studies.

Bogue, D. J. 1963. *Skid Row in American Cities*. Chicago: Community and Family Study Center, University of Chicago.

Boyer, Paul. 1978. *Urban Masses and Moral Order in America, 1820–1920*. Cambridge, Mass.: Harvard University Press.

Bremner, Robert. 1980. *The Public Good*. New York: Alfred A. Knopf.

Brown, C., S. McFarlane, R. Paredes, and L. Stark. 1983. *The Homeless of Phoenix: Who Are They and What Should Be Done?* Phoenix, Ariz.: South Community Mental Health Center.

Caplow, Theodore. 1940. ''Transiency as a Cultural Pattern.'' *American Sociological Review* 5: 731–739.

Chambliss, W. F. 1964. ''A Sociological Analysis of the Law of Vagrancy.'' *Social Problems* 12 (Summer): 67–77.

City of Boston Emergency Shelter Commission. 1983. *The October Project: Seeing the Obvious Problem*. Boston: City of Boston Emergency Shelter Commission.

City of New York. 1982. *Soldiers of Misfortune: A Memorandum*. New York: New York City Research and Liaison Unit, Office of the Comptroller, November 11.

Clay, Phillip L. 1979. *Neighborhood Renewal*. Lexington, Mass.: Lexington Books.

Clement, P. F. 1984. ''The Transformation of the Wandering Poor in Nineteenth Century Philadelphia.'' In Eric Monkkonen (ed.), *Walking to Work: Tramps in America, 1790–1935*. Lincoln: University of Nebraska Press.

Crystal, Stephen. 1984. ''Homeless Men and Homeless Women: The Gender Gap.'' *Urban and Social Change Review* 17, no. 2: 2–6.

Gilbert, J. G., and J. C. Healy. 1942. ''The Economic and Social Background of the Unlicensed Personnel of the American Merchant Marine.'' *Social Forces* 21: 40–43.

Gillin, J. L. 1929. ''Vagrancy and Begging.'' *American Journal of Sociology* 35: 424–432.

Greer, N. R. 1985. *Housing the Homeless*. Conference Proceedings. Washington, D.C.: American Institute of Architects.

Harring, Sidney L. 1977. ''Class Conflict and the Suppression of Tramps in Buffalo, 1892–1894.'' *Law and Society Review* 11: 873–911.

Haymer, N. S. 1945. ''Taming the Lumberjack.'' *American Sociological Review* 10: 217–225.

Hoch, C. J. 1986. *SROs, an Endangered Species: Single Room Occupancy Hotels in Chicago*. Chicago: Jewish Council on Urban Affairs.

Hopper, K. 1984. ''Whose Lives Are These Anyway?'' *Urban and Social Change Review* 17: 12–13.

Hopper, K., and J. Hamberg. 1984. *The Making of America's Homeless: From Skid Row to New Poor*. New York: Community Service Society.

Hoy, W. R. 1928. "Case of the Homeless in St. Louis." *Family* 9: 209–219.

Jones, D. L. 1984. "The Beginning of Industrial Tramping." In Eric Monkkonen (ed.), *Walking to Work: Tramps in America, 1790–1935*. Lincoln: University of Nebraska Press.

Katz, Steven E., Frank R. Lipton, and Albert Sabatini. 1983. "Down and Out in the City: The Homeless Mentally Ill." *Hospital and Community Psychiatry* 34: 817–821.

Kaufman, N. K. 1984. "Homelessness: A Comprehensive Policy Approach." *Urban and Social Change Review* 17: 21–22.

Kelly, E. 1908. *The Elimination of the Tramp*. New York: G. P. Putnam's Sons.

Klein, P. 1923. *The Burden of Unemployment*. New York: Russell Sage Foundation.

Lee, B. A. 1978. "Residential Mobility on Skid Row: Disaffiliation, Powerlessness, and Decisionmaking." *Demography* 15: 285–300.

———. 1980. "Disappearance of Skid Row: Some Ecological Evidence." *Urban Affairs Quarterly* 16: 81–107.

Lilliefors, M. 1928. "Social Casework and the Homeless Man." *Family* 9: 291–294.

Monkkonen, Eric H. 1981. *Police in Urban America, 1860–1920*. Cambridge, England: Cambridge University Press.

Nash, G. B. 1979. *The Urban Crucible: Social Change, Political Consciousness, and the Origins of the American Revolution*. Cambridge, Mass.: Harvard University Press.

National Coalition for the Homeless. 1983. *Downward Spiral: The Homeless in New Jersey*. New York: National Coalition for the Homeless.

National Trust for Historic Preservation. 1981. *Rehabilitating Residential Hotels*. Information from the National Trust for Historic Preservation, no. 31. Washington, D.C.: National Trust for Historic Preservation.

Nelson, Bryce. 1983. "Mental Illness Cited among Many Homeless." *New York Times*, October 2, 25.

Parrillo, Vincent N., John Stimson, and Ardyth Stimson. 1985. *Contemporary Social Problems*. New York: John Wiley & Sons.

Reed, Richard E. 1979. *Return to the City*. Garden City, N.Y.: Doubleday.

Rooney, J. F. 1973. "Societal Forces and the Unattached Male: An Historical Review." In B. Howard (ed.), *Disaffiliated Man*. Toronto: University of Toronto Press.

Ropers, Richard, and Marjorie Robertson. 1984. *Basic Shelter Research Project*. Los Angeles: Psychiatric Epidemiology Program, School of Public Health, University of California at Los Angeles.

Salerno, D., K. Hopper, and E. Baxter. 1984. *Hardship in the Heartland*. New York: Community Service Society.

Schneider, J. C. 1984. "Tramping Workers, 1890–1920: A Subcultural View." In Eric Monkkonen (ed.), *Walking to Work: Tramps in America, 1790–1935*. Lincoln: University of Nebraska Press.

Sutherland, E. H., and H. J. Locke. 1936. *Twenty Thousand Homeless Men*. Chicago: J. B. Lippincott.

Taft, P. 1960. "The IWW in the Grain Belt." *Labor History*, Winter, 53–67.

U.S. Department of Health and Human Services. 1984. *Helping the Homeless: A Resource Guide*. Washington, D.C.: Government Printing Office.

U.S. Department of Housing and Urban Development. 1984. *A Report to the Secretary on the Homeless and Emergency Shelters*. Washington, D.C.: Department of Housing and Urban Development, Office of Policy Development and Research.

U.S. General Accounting Office. 1985. *Homelessness: A Complex Problem and the Federal Response*. Washington, D.C.: General Accounting Office, Research Division, April.

U.S. Office of Management and Budget. 1985. *Appendix, Budget of the United States Government, Fiscal Year 1986*. Washington, D.C.: Government Printing Office.

Wallace, S. E. 1968. ''The Road to Skid Row.'' *Social Problems* 16: 92–105.

PART V

HOUSING IN URBAN, SUBURBAN, AND NEW COMMUNITIES

21

The Traditional American Suburban House and Environment: Social Effects

DAVID POPENOE

This chapter presents a review and discussion of social science, mainly socio-logical, knowledge about the social effects on residents of living in the traditional American suburban house and built environment. However significant they may be, the consequences of suburbs and suburbanization for broader economic, political, and social realities, such as racial problems, fiscal crises, metropolitan fragmentation, or urban decline, are not considered here. Even with this limi-tation, the review will be brief and only major sources will be cited.

It should be stated at the outset that in general the social effects of housing and the built environment are relatively weak, transitory, and often indirect (Ittelson, et al., 1974; Michelson, 1976). Changing one's environment would not have nearly the same social consequences, for example, as changing one's social class, religion, ethnic background, sex, age, family origin, or biological makeup. Nevertheless, there are some noteworthy effects, albeit modest, and the importance of these effects is magnified by the fact that unlike most of the social and biological variables just mentioned, housing and the built environment can be and often are rearranged and modified through human agency (Gutman, 1972).

Gaining valid knowledge of these social effects, moreover, is no easy task. Unlike animals in a laboratory experiment, people cannot be shifted around to see how various environments affect them, and the range of research approaches to this area is narrow (Michelson, 1976; Zeisel, 1981). The same people can be monitored as they move from environment to environment, a before-and-after longitudinal study, but this is expensive and does not control for the fact that the people themselves may change for other reasons. More commonly, people new to an environment can be asked to compare it with previous environments in which they have lived, with all the subjectivity that this implies. Similar people living in different environments can be compared, the cross-sectional study; but are they really similar? Finally, different people in different environ-ments can be compared, with an attempt made to create similarities among the people through statistical means.

An additional complexity to be faced in each of these approaches is whether by "effects" one means objective, overt behavior or subjective reality such as emotions. In either case it is normal to ask people how they are acting, or have acted in the past, or how they feel, or have felt in the past, and in both cases a strong element of subjectivity enters in. Because of such methodological difficulties, firm conclusions in this area are few, and most generalizations are not without an element of speculation. This is true, however, of most social science knowledge.

If a suburb is defined as "a community that lies apart from a city but is adjacent to and dependent on it," a common definition, then suburbs are historically nearly as old as cities themselves. But the word suburban has become almost synonymous with the post–World War II pattern of urban development in the Unites States, and that is the sense in which it is used in this chapter (Muller, 1981). By world standards, this now-traditional U.S. suburban pattern has been almost unique, consisting as it does largely of detached, owner-occupied, single-family houses in homogeneous residential areas, built at very low densities and tied to the city by the automobile.

Suburban development is surely found in other nations. Indeed, such development could probably be called the master urban trend of the twentieth century in the sense of urban areas expanding in a centrifugal manner and "spilling over their borders" (Light, 1983). Made possible by a particular configuration of technological, economic, and governmental factors, however, together with the availability of land, the proliferation of low-density suburban development found in the United States is not common in other countries; the only possible competitors are Australia, Canada, and New Zealand (Clawson and Hall, 1973). From a subjective point of view, the postwar suburban environments have been geared to the strong preference of most Americans for a detached dwelling rather than a row house or apartment, for rural life over urban life, and for owning instead of renting. Americans in the suburban era were prohibited from achieving the rural ideal, but in their new suburban homes they found at least a taste of the countryside (Jackson, 1985).

After the war Americans moved to the new suburban environments in large numbers, first the middle class and later the working class. They were usually upwardly mobile young families, caught up in the postwar baby boom. The early suburban dwellers came from the cities; they were soon followed by persons moving from rural area to suburb without passing through the city, and finally by persons moving from suburb to suburb, the pattern most common today. In the late 1940s and 1950s the suburban residential environment was a relatively new experience for most people, the suburban population in the United States in 1940 having been only 17 percent of the total population. Over the following decades the suburban environment almost became the universal national environment, and one could talk about the suburbanization of the United States (Jackson, 1985). In the 1980 U.S. census over 40 percent of Americans were classified as living in suburban areas, a higher percentage than lived either in cities or in rural areas, and many others not classified as suburban actually lived in suburbanlike environments, especially in the metropolitan areas of the ever-growing Sunbelt. Today the total number of suburban and suburbanlike dwellers undoubtedly stands at well over 50 percent of the population.

Because the suburban environment is today so common, the study of its social and behavioral consequences has become problematic; the unique geographic niche this environment once occupied has seriously eroded. Also, the suburban areas themselves have changed greatly since their early postwar days (Gans, 1970). They have become much less socially homogeneous as new waves of residents have moved in and large pieces of the cities' commercial and industrial sectors have moved out, turning many suburban areas into new minicities and making them much less dependent on the urban centers from which they initially sprang (Masotti and Hadden, 1973; Schwartz, 1976; Muller, 1981).

In addition, many suburban areas are no longer bastions of large, detached houses constructed at very low densities; they have become the habitat for many low-rise, high-density, and often rental housing units, especially those called by Americans garden apartments and townhouses (Sternlieb and Hughes, 1986). For America as a whole, detached houses as a percentage of all new housing starts dropped from 75 percent in 1975 to 54 percent in 1982, the result of higher land and housing costs, less personal disposable income, and smaller household sizes. Such trends have prompted some experts to descry for the coming generation the end of "the American dream," the dream of eventually owning a detached, single-family house in the suburbs (Sternlieb, 1972).

To a large extent, then, the American residential suburb in the late twentieth century is receding ever further with each passing year from its traditional form, and the study of this form may even now be of mainly historical interest. This fact should be borne in mind in the following discussion, which will focus primarily on the effects of the American suburb as a relatively pure type, the low-density, homogeneous residential environment described earlier. Of course, thousands of environments around the nation still closely resemble the proto-typical pattern, and it is also probable that this pattern continues to loom large as an environmental ideal for many Americans.

HISTORY OF SUBURBAN STUDIES

Before World War II there were virtually no sociological or other investigations of suburban life, and as late as 1952 one urban sociology textbook devoted only two pages to a discussion of the subject (Riemer, 1952). The focus of sociology had been either on big cities and especially on their perceived evils, or on small towns. The first people to target the postwar suburbs for special attention were journalists. In a spate of books and magazine articles in the mid-1950s the new suburbs were attacked, mostly by city-dwelling intellectuals, in what one commentator later called "a critical onslaught of monumental, and largely nonsens-ical, proportions" (Donaldson, 1969: 1). The viewpoint of these books was that the new suburbs fostered overconformity, hyperactivity, anti-individualism, conservatism, momism, dullness and boredom, and status seeking, plus a host of more serious psychological ills including alcoholism, sexual promiscuity, and mental illness. Nonsensical or not, this view of the suburbs—a mostly negative hypercommunity—came to permeate the culture of the urban elite of the time.

This outpouring of negativism soon engaged the attention of sociologists. Although with more sophisticated reasoning and scholarly flourish, the first sociological commentaries on the suburbs tended to support the views of the journalists (Riesman, 1957; Seeley, Sim, and Loosley, 1956). But soon most sociologists were calling the alleged negative effects of suburban living "a myth." In the book *Working Class Suburb* (1960) Bennett M. Berger analyzed the move of a group of auto workers to a California suburb and found that their lives had changed little after two years. Some of the negative traits of suburban life may be characteristic of the middle class in general, he felt, but there was very little about the suburban environment per se that had much effect on these working-class residents. This study was soon followed by Herbert Gans's *The Levittowners* (1967), the study of a prototypical New Jersey suburb, which reached very similar conclusions. "Few changes can be traced to the suburban qualities of Levittown" (Gans, 1967: 288).

The conclusions of these books, together with a growing "anti–environmental determinism" sentiment among urban planners, left many sociologists in the 1960s and 1970s with the idea that "it doesn't make much difference where you live, there are so many more important social factors that shape our lives." The social factor that loomed largest in the minds of most sociologists, including Berger and Gans, was social class.

While recognizing that the effects of the built environment are relatively weak, however, a new generation of environmentally oriented social scientists in the 1970s and 1980s began to overturn the glib conclusions of sociologists like Berger and Gans that the built environment was of little importance (Altman and Chemers, 1980; LaGory and Pipkin, 1981; Porteous, 1977). They utilized more sensitive and comparative approaches for isolating environmental impacts. Yet the amount of solid research done on this topic is still very meager.

COMPARISONS WITH THE CITY

At least implicit in any analysis of the social effects of the built environment is the question of how the behavior, attitudes, emotions, and overall life-style of the residents of a given environment would be different if these people lived somewhere else, that is, in a different kind of residential environment. In modern societies the most common alternative residential environments to suburbs are cities and small towns, and these will be the main foci of comparison used here. Sociologists' assessments of suburban characteristics depend very much on whether a comparison is being made with cities or with small towns. The traditional comparison has been with cities; in such a comparison, for example, suburbs have shown high degrees of neighboring (Fava, 1959). Yet a comparison with small towns will show that suburbs have a relatively low degree of neighboring. It is important when looking at residential environments, therefore, always to keep in mind the full range of environmental variation.

Starting with the suburban/city comparison, many studies have shown that a certain type of person chooses to live in the suburbs rather than the city, and there is no doubt that this selectivity of people affects the suburban way of life (Choldin, 1985; Fischer, 1984). In general, people who move to suburbs are better off than most city dwellers and desire a more familistic life style. That suburban residents are more family oriented than city dwellers is surely a result of the fact that more suburbanites have families; and that suburbanites are rather consumption and status oriented compared to the urban working class surely is a result of their middle-class status (Gans, 1970).

Because they can afford to do so, middle-class families move to the suburbs partly to get away from what they perceive as the noise, congestion, and pollution of the city, and partly to get more housing space. The price in opportunity costs that suburban residents must pay for a relatively large house in a pleasant environment is distance from jobs and services. This trade-off is consciously perceived by most residents, and they are more than willing to live in a less accessible location if they can have a nice house in a pleasant environment. By and large, suburbanites coming from the city express a high level of satisfaction with their environment, and few ever return.

There are some intrinsic physical characteristics of the suburban environment that also shape the lives of people there, however, no matter what their class level or stage of life cycle. Although environments are mostly experienced by individuals as a single entity, it is important for research purposes to isolate each of the main physical elements of any environment. The principal elements of the traditional American suburb are owned, single-family detached homes built at very low densities; socially homogeneous, all-residential environments of relatively small scale and detached from city life; and reliance on the automobile as the only means of transportation.

The first and perhaps most obvious social consequence of these elements of the suburban environment relates to leisure time. The large owned house with yard, together with distance from city leisure facilities, means that the suburban leisure style is much more home centered, with such activities as gardening, backyard barbecues, and entertaining at home being relatively common (Michelson, 1977). Compared to the city, a second consequence is increased contact among neighbors (Fischer, 1982). This is affected by many nonphysical factors (for example, neighboring is higher among families with children), but the physical factors that are especially important are the large (owned) house and yard, which require constant maintenance and bring people outdoors, and the distance from commercial facilities and services, which generates some neighborhood cooperation and sharing (Keller, 1968). A third consequence is a slightly higher level of community participation, a result of the small scale of the community and the fact that one's personal home and property interests are intimately tied up with suburban community political issues (Choldin, 1980). These elements are all combined in the term suburban localism, which refers to a social life that is directed toward the immediate locality and its residents (Fischer et al., 1977).

A final aspect of suburban life that should be mentioned is the lack of social differentiation and variety. Partly due to the small scale of suburban environments and the homogeneity of house types, suburbs tend to have less social diversity than comparable urban areas. There are fewer minority groups, fewer social deviants, and a narrower spectrum of social classes. This is regarded by most suburban residents as an advantage, but by most (urban-dwelling and egalitarian) sociologists as a disadvantage.

COMPARISONS WITH SMALL TOWNS

In most of these respects the suburb differs from the city in the direction of the small town. Metropolitan residents, in their social and geographic trade-offs, are basically looking for small-town elements within a metropolitan orbit. Comparisons with the city, however, which is the kind of comparison most sociologists have made, can be misleading. If suburban residents are really looking for a small-town environment, then perhaps that is the more relevant comparison.

How newcomers experience the suburbs, for example, depends very much on where they come from in addition to their class level. The working-class person coming from a small town can find suburban life to be rather formal and unfriendly (Popenoe, 1977). This is not only because most suburbs are middle class, and middle-class people tend to be more formal in their dealings with others than working-class people, but also because of some intrinsic suburban environmental elements that differ from those of the small town. To a middle-class person coming from the city, in contrast, the suburb will appear informal and friendly.

Suburbs have less neighboring, less community participation, and less localism in general than small towns, and such traits generate a suburban life-style that is comparatively formal, privatized, and anonymous. The environmental condition probably most responsible for this difference is that suburban communities are less complete, more specialized communities than small towns. Suburbs typically represent but one piece of a "whole" community, the residential piece. Residents must go outside the local community for work, shopping, and leisure. This tends to retard the development of the kind of dense, overlapping social networks that are found in small towns, where people who live together are more likely also to work and shop together (Fischer, 1982). For the same reason, suburbs also tend to have less "public life" than small towns, in the sense of public events as well as street life. One negative aspect of the suburban lifestyle is weakened informal social control mechanisms, a factor that helps to account for the fact that suburbs have higher crime and delinquency rates than small towns (Hirschi, 1969; Podolefsky, 1983; Popenoe, 1987).

INDIVIDUAL CONGRUENCE

The social world of the suburbs also looks quite different if one examines the lives and satisfactions not of suburbanites in general but of residents of certain types. We have noted that the suburban environment seems generally satisfactory for middle-class families moving from the city, but what if, rather than using these general categories, we look at people in terms of such categories as gender and age and see how people in these categories "fit" in the suburban setting? Perhaps the best way to socially examine any environmental setting is to look at the way it meshes, or is congruent, with the personal needs and desired life-styles of the range of people who live there (Michelson, 1976). In such an approach one must keep in mind that every environment represents a trade-off; if you live in the city, you can't expect too many trees, and if you live in the countryside, you can't expect too many shops. But the concept of congruence points up the degree to which particular trade-offs that a given environment represents are desired by or suitable for a certain category of person.

There is good reason to believe that suburbs are more congruent with men than with women, which is ironic because men spend much less time there than do women. Because a man's work life ordinarily takes him out of the area, to him the suburb can be a satisfying nest or refuge from the tense environment of the work day, and the small scale and lack of variety in the suburban community are not perceived as a great disadvantage (Michelson, 1977). Moreover, he is the most mobile of the family members, having maximum access to the auto-mobile, and he therefore does not have the same problems of accessibility that others may have. In addition, the owned house provides the man with a useful diversion in his leisure time, the activities of home maintenance and repair.

At almost the opposite extreme stands the woman, particularly the typical "suburban housewife." Being in the local community all day, she finds the lack of variety in the local community and the lack of public life more of a drawback. Being in the home all day, she finds the size of the house and its need for daily care more of an impediment. Since she often has less access to an automobile, the inaccessibility of the suburb for her is much more real. For the working wife, there are the additional problems of having to take care of the large house while also holding down a job, and, with her lower mobility, encountering a considerably restricted range of job opportunities (Michelson, 1985). For all of these reasons, the American suburbs have become a favorite subject for feminist analysis (Hayden, 1984; *Signs*, 1980; Wekerle, Peterson, and Morley, 1980).

An even more "deprived" type in the suburb may be the teenager (Wynne, 1977). Teenagers have much less mobility than housewives; their social lives must be lived almost entirely within the local community. The lack of suburban variety and public life causes many suburban teenagers to think of their communities as boring (Popenoe, 1977). For teenagers, the city (if reasonably safe) often is put forth as a more desirable environmental form.

Another relatively disadvantaged group in suburban areas is the elderly, who suffer from a lack of public transportation due to the suburb's extreme automobile orientation and sometimes from a lack of suitable housing because of the suburb's single-family house homogeneity. Similarly, the poor in general find it harder to make ends meet in suburbia because it is oriented to middle-class persons and relies heavily on private expenditures for services and facilities. A final group that expresses some displeasure with suburban life, mainly due to lack of scale and variety, is single persons. Nevertheless, all of these groups of people often choose to live in the suburbs over the city because of their perception that the suburbs have a safer and less noxious environment.

CONCLUSION

While the early critiques of the postwar suburbs suggested that they were hypercommunities with a forced sociability and conformity, the first generation of sociological studies concluded that the suburbs have few independent effects at all; the suburban life-style is what residents voluntarily choose and represents an expression of such fundamental sociological characteristics as class, age, and stage of the life cycle. These studies also found, in comparison with the cities, what they felt was evidence of a strong localism and community life and a very satisfied population. For reasons suggested in the last two sections, many recent studies and critiques of the suburban environment have found there a kind of anticommunity (Michelson, 1977, 1985; Popenoe, 1979, 1985; Schwartz, 1980; Wynne, 1977). In these studies suburbs are seen as residential environments attempting to be "real" communities but without all of the pieces in place, and as areas with some real social drawbacks. The anticommunity theme can also be seen in at least one recent critique of an American life in general that has become increasingly suburbanized (Bellah et al., 1985).

One has the sense in America today that the era of the proliferation of low-density urban development is nearing an end. At the same time, there appears to be a growing national consensus around the need to strengthen local communities. These provide the opportunity for suburban change. Much American suburban development, unlike that of its European counterparts, has consisted of little more than building houses, with roads to connect them. For the suburban development of the future, perhaps further research on housing and the built environment will underscore the importance of building not just housing but communities as a whole. This means housing for a diversity of people that is closely linked to workplaces, shopping, and a wide array of social, cultural, and recreational facilities. It means built environments that have clearer boundaries and focal points, so as to foster a more contained local community life. These are all elements in which the traditional American suburb, despite its many virtues, has been found wanting.

REFERENCES

Altman, Irwin, and Martin M. Chemers. 1980. *Culture and Environment*. Monterey, Calif: Brooks/Cole.

Bellah, Robert N., R. Madsen, W. M. Sullivan, A. Swidler, and S. M. Tipton. 1985. *Habits of the Heart: Individualism and Commitment in American Life*. Berkeley and Los Angeles: University of California Press.

Berger, Bennett M. 1960. *Working-Class Suburb*. Berkeley and Los Angeles: University of California Press.

Choldin, Harvey. 1980. "Social Participation in Suburban Apartment Enclaves." In Clare Ungerson and Valerie Karn (eds.), *The Consumer Experience of Housing*. Westmead, England: Gower. 116–127.

———. 1985. *Cities and Suburbs*. New York: McGraw-Hill.

Clawson, Marion, and Peter Hall. 1973. *Planning and Urban Growth*. Baltimore, Md.: Johns Hopkins University Press.

Donaldson, Scott. 1969. *The Suburban Myth*. New York: Columbia University Press.

Fava, Sylvia. 1959. "Contrasts in Neighboring: New York City and a Suburban County." In W. M. Dobriner (ed.), *The Suburban Community*. New York: Putnam. 122–131.

Fischer, Claude S. 1982. *To Dwell among Friends: Personal Networks in Town and City*. Chicago: University of Chicago Press.

———. 1984. *The Urban Experience*. 2d ed. San Diego, Calif.: Harcourt Brace Jovanovich.

Fischer, Claude S., R. M. Jackson, A. A. Stueve, K. Gerson, L. M. Jones, and M. Baldassare. 1977. *Networks and Places: Social Relations in the Urban Setting*. New York: Free Press.

Gans, Herbert J. 1967. *The Levittowners*. New York: Pantheon.

———. 1970. "Urbanism and Suburbanism as Ways of Life: A Re-evaluation of Definitions." In Robert Gutman and David Popenoe (eds.), *Neighborhood, City, and Metropolis*. New York: Random House. 70–84

Gutman, Robert. 1972. *People and Buildings*. New York: Basic Books.

Hayden, Dolores. 1984. *Redesigning the American Dream*. New York: W. W. Norton.

Hirschi, Travis. 1969. *The Causes of Delinquency*. Berkeley and Los Angeles: University of California Press.

Ittleson, William H., H. M. Proshansky, L. G. Rivlin, and G. H. Winkel. 1974. *An Introduction to Environmental Psychology*. New York: Holt, Rinehart & Winston.

Jackson, Kenneth T. 1985. *Crabgrass Frontier: The Suburbanization of the United States*. New York: Oxford University Press.

Keller, Suzanne. 1968. *The Urban Neighborhood*. New York: Random House.

LaGory, Mark, and John Pipkin. 1981. *Urban Social Space*. Belmont, Calif.: Wadsworth.

Light, Ivan. 1983. *Cities in World Perspective*. New York: Macmillan.

Masotti, Louis H., and Jeffrey K. Hadden (eds.). 1973. *The Urbanization of the Suburbs*. Beverly Hills: Sage.

Michelson, William. 1976. *Man and His Urban Environment*. Reading, Mass.: Addison-Wesley.

———. 1977. *Environmental Choice, Human Behavior, and Residential Satisfaction*. New York: Oxford University Press.

———. 1985. *From Sun to Sun*. Totowa, N.J.: Rowman & Allenheld.

Muller, Peter O. 1981. *Contemporary Suburban America*. Englewood Cliffs, N.J.: Prentice-Hall.

Podolefsky, Aaron. 1983. *Case Studies in Community Crime Prevention*. Springfield, Ill.: Charles C. Thomas.

Popenoe, David. 1977. *The Suburban Environment: Sweden and the United States*. Chicago: University of Chicago Press.

———. 1979. "Urban Sprawl: Some Neglected Sociological Considerations." *Sociology and Social Research* 63: 255–68.

———. 1985. *Private Pleasure, Public Plight: American Metropolitan Community Life in Comparative Perspective*. New Brunswick, N.J.: Transaction Books.

———. 1987. "Suburbanization, Privatization, and Juvenile Deliquency: Some Possible Relationships." In Willem van Vliet—, Harvey Choldin, William Michelson, and David Popenoe (eds.), *Housing and Neighborhoods: Theoretical and Empirical Contributions*. Westport, Conn.: Greenwood Press. 119–137.

Porteous, J. Douglas. 1977. *Environment and Behavior*. Reading, Mass.: Addison-Wesley.

Riemer, Svend. 1952. *The Modern City*. Englewood Cliffs, N.J.: Prentice-Hall.

Riesman, David. 1957. "The Suburban Dislocation." *Annals of the Association of Political and Social Sciences*. 123–46.

Schwartz, Barry (ed.). 1976. *The Changing Face of the Suburbs*. Chicago: University of Chicago Press.

———. 1980. "The Suburban Landscape: New Variations on an Old Theme." *Contemporary Sociology* 9, no. 6: 640–50.

Seeley, John R., A. Sim, and E. W. Loosley. 1956. *Crestwood Heights*. New York: Basic Books.

Signs: Journal of Women and Culture in Society. 1980. Vol. 5, no. 3, Supplement.

Sternlieb, George. 1972. "Death of the American Dream House." *Society* 9: 39–42.

Sternlieb, George, and James W. Hughes. 1986. "Demographics and Housing in America." *Population Bulletin* 41, no. 1: 1–34.

Wekerle, Gerda R., R. Peterson, and D. Morley. (eds.). 1980. *New Space for Women*. Boulder, Colo.: Westview Press.

Wynne, Edward A. 1977. *Growing Up Suburban*. Austin: University of Texas Press.

Zeisel, John. 1981. *Inquiry by Design*. Monterey, Calif.: Brooks/Cole.

22

Urban Redevelopment

NORMAN FAINSTEIN AND SUSAN FAINSTEIN

Since the latter part of the nineteenth century and the construction of the street railways, American metropolitan areas have spread out from their early port and manufacturing centers. Peripheral expansion resulted in the decay of old cores. The process accelerated with the halt of private investment during the Great Depression and World War II and the postwar in-migration of low-income blacks displaced from the rural South. The failure of the private market to improve the condition of central cities led eventually to a public role. But the history of public programs for urban redevelopment in the United States is relatively short and uneven compared to that in other wealthy nations. This chapter concerns itself with federal programs for the physical improvement of central cities and the local response to changes in the level of federal activity. It first traces the history of federal redevelopment policy, then evaluates its impacts. Finally, it roots policy in the American political economy.

THE HISTORY OF URBAN REDEVELOPMENT POLICY

As was the case for many interventionist policies, federal involvement began with the Great Depression, when the national government, through its public works employment programs, granted funds to cities for infrastructural development. After World War II a number of interests converged to push for the Housing and Urban Renewal Act of 1949, which formed the framework for redevelopment policy during the next 25 years. The context of this seminal legislation included, first, the general concerns of policymakers that military demobilization would bring back widespread unemployment. Construction programs for housing and public works were viewed as a means to ameliorate this problem. Second, real estate and financial institutions with large fixed investments in central cities, along with downtown businesses, feared that suburban expansion and obsolescence of core areas would destroy the value of their holdings. Third, housing advocates hoped, by combining urban redevelopment and housing legislation, to overcome the resistance of real estate groups to subsidized housing and assumed that such housing could be developed to replace units destroyed through slum clearance efforts (Gelfand, 1975: chaps. 4–6; Hays, 1985: chap. 7; Wilson, 1966).

Urban Renewal and Model Cities

Title 1 of the 1949 housing act was the legislative mandate for the federal urban renewal program until 1974 (Gelfand, 1975). Under this approach to removing urban "blight," local authorities used the power of eminent domain to acquire privately held land; once a site appropriate for redevelopment had been aggregated and prepared, they turned the land over to a public agency or private developer at a lower price. The federal government paid for between two-thirds and three-quarters of the net project cost (the difference between the purchase price and selling price of the land plus costs of demolition and improvements). The local share could either be a cash payment or in-kind contribution—for example, the construction of a police station or school on the project site. Although the act declared that the redevelopment area should be predominantly residential in character and that all displaced families must be relocated in suitable accommodations, it included no mechanism to induce private developers to build housing for low-income households.

The underlying rationale for Title 1 came from a diagnosis of the causes of central-city decay that argued that failure to invest in the urban core resulted from its lack of cost competitiveness with suburban land. This analysis attributed the high price of urban reinvestment to the costliness of aggregating the large sites required by modern business in locations characterized by multiple ownership of small parcels. The problem was aggravated by the existence of obsolete structures that inflated the value of sites beyond their worth to developers who were only interested in cleared land. Moreover, once a developer started putting together a site, holdouts would seek to extort an unreasonable payment for the remaining land. Consequently, a subsidy was required to bring down the cost of cleared land to that of its suburban counterpart, and the power of eminent domain was needed in order to deal with holdouts. A further, largely unspoken argument for using eminent domain was the desire to remove low-income households and marginal businesses from the periphery of the central business district (CBD) so as to enhance its appeal to middle-class shoppers and elite office users.

The vision of the modern city that dominated the minds of urban renewal planners during the decades following the 1949 act was of a high-rise suburbia. Designed to accommodate the automobile, and incorporating the open spaces and segregation of uses that gave the suburbs their attractiveness, the renewed metropolis would be accessible by superhighway, would have ample parking space, and would possess widely separated buildings, permitting their occupants to enjoy light, air, and attractive views. Architecturally the model was Le Corbusier's Radiant City; in terms of land use it imitated the suburban master plan but incorporated higher densities (see Jacobs, 1961).

In its initial formulation the urban renewal law provided little protection for existing occupants of land designated as blighted. Compensation for homeowners was inadequate to cover the costs of a new domicile; renters received at best a small sum to cover moving expenses; little replacement housing was built, and that only after long time lags; and despite exhortations in the law, few received any kind of relocation services (Hartman, 1971). Between 1950 and 1971, 293,068 families and 157,297 single individuals, mostly poor and black, were relocated by local renewal authorities. An additional 102,012 businesses also were displaced (Sanders, 1980: 119). Many more households and businesses left renewal areas without benefit of official assistance.

The social objectives of urban renewal, expressed in the preamble to the 1949 act, which called for "a decent home and suitable living environment for all Americans," clashed with the actual content of the legislation. The statute gave dominant roles in the renewal process to private enterprise and to local rather than federal officials. Restriction of government's role to land preparation and subsequent reliance on private developers caused renewal planning to conform to business goals. The categorical and discretionary nature of the federal grant-in-aid process allowed those local urban renewal authorities who were able to write successful grant applications to control a steady flow of funds insulated from the regular municipal budget process. The autonomy of the renewal authorities and their responsiveness to corporate interests meant that neither affected neighborhoods nor the national liberal forces that supported the housing component of the original legislation had much influence over the implementation of the program.

Criticisms of the urban renewal program, particularly of its destruction of usable structures within project areas and its creation of "bombed-out" districts in the hearts of cities, led to subsequent modifications of the 1949 legislation. In 1954 incentives for rehabilitation rather than wholesale clearance were added; and the requirement of a "workable program," that is, a redevelopment plan, was imposed. In 1968 urban renewal authorities were required to set up project-area committees to represent community residents. The 1970 passage of the Uniform Relocation Assistance Act increased relocation payments to realistic levels (Hays, 1985: 185).

Within the general context of 1960s unrest, neighborhood resistance to urban renewal, along with a crescendo of criticism by intellectuals (Jacobs, 1961; Fried, 1966; Anderson, 1964; Gans, 1966) caused the Johnson administration to rethink the idea that slums could be eliminated through displacing their occupants. Without terminating the urban renewal program, which continued to be used for downtown redevelopment, Congress passed the Demonstration Cities Act of 1966 (subsequently called Model Cities) to redirect the thrust of activity in poor neighborhoods toward community preservation (Frieden and Kaplan, 1975). The new emphases were on the coordination of physical and social planning; rehabilitation rather than demolition; community participation; and a focus on target neighborhoods.

The 1974 Housing and Community Development Act

Both Model Cities and urban renewal ended with the 1974 passage of the Housing and Community Development Act (HCDA), which introduced the Community Development Block Grant (CDBG) (Dommel et al., 1980; Fainstein et al., 1983). Part of President Nixon's "new federalism" of special revenue sharing and increased authority for local governments, CDBG supplanted seven previous categorical programs. CDBG funds were distributed on a formula rather than a project basis, with the bulk going to approximately 540 entitlement cities larger than 50,000 in population; the remainder was distributed to urban counties. The allocation formula was originally based on population size and poverty; it was revised in 1977 to provide further assistance to older cities with large stocks of obsolete housing and declining populations. Local elected officials were responsible for setting community priorities in physical improvements and neighborhood-based social services. While initially the Model Cities intent of combining physical and social services was retained in the program, the social service component was gradually dropped in most cities.

During the course of the CDBG program, the extent of federal involvement shifted from minimal under President Ford to extensive in the Carter administration. Between 1977 and 1980 federal regulations required targeting to low- and moderate-income groups, concentration of grant spending within designated neighborhoods, and a citizen participation plan (Fainstein and Fainstein, 1980). But even under these more stringent regulations CDBG offered few benefits to renters, who could not take advantage of rehabilitation funds typically limited to owner-occupied housing; and it gave no guarantee that residents would not be displaced from "upgraded" neighborhoods. Thus even though CDBG did not cause the massive displacement that occurred under urban renewal, its limitations meant that it was not a potent instrument for improving conditions in very poor neighborhoods. Most of the Carter regulations concerning types of uses and citizen participation were eliminated under Reagan, and federal oversight lapsed as the application and reporting requirements for cities were drastically curtailed.

The years after 1974 saw an increasing emphasis on using private investment to redevelop cities. For cities that had drawn heavily on urban renewal financing, CDBG represented a considerable decline in government funding available to support redevelopment efforts. In 1977, in order to provide more funding for specific projects, Congress added the Urban Development Action Grant (UDAG) program to the HCDA. UDAGs were provided on a discretionary basis for the sole purpose of fostering economic development (Gist, 1980). As in the urban renewal program, funds were frequently used for land clearance. Different from urban renewal, however, UDAG moneys could only be spent if the private component were committed in advance. Essentially UDAG represented a subsidy to business for coming to or remaining in economically distressed areas.

The description of federal redevelopment activity in terms of two principal programs (urban renewal and CDBG) extending over a nearly 40-year period obscures the inconsistencies of the federal role. Regulations concerning demolition versus rehabilitation, minimum size of projects, citizen participation, low-income targeting, and relocation changed constantly. Moreover, the federal intervention was afflicted with inadequate and perpetually fluctuating levels of funding (Fainstein et al., 1983: chap. 1; Hays, 1985: 208–217). While federal outlays for urban redevelopment increased from $8 million in 1951 to a high of $5.1 billion 30 years later, in real dollars they peaked in 1969 and wound down in an oscillating pattern thereafter (Table 22.1). Federal expenditures in this category never exceeded 1.5 percent of total outlays and rarely topped 1 percent. Ultimately the amount of federal support directed at any one locality became too small to fund major efforts, and cities began to look to other sources for financing development projects. In particular, they sought to devise locally generated inducements to private investment.

Local Investment Incentive Programs

In order to enhance their limited resources, city governments have worked out a group of ingenious mechanisms for "leveraging" private investment (Peltz and Weiss, 1984). Among those most frequently used are various kinds of tax inducements. In addition to tax abatements, whereby property tax exemptions are granted for a period of years after new construction, there are methods by which tax revenues are directed toward specified ends rather than the general fund (Mandelker, Feder, and Collins, 1980). Usually in the central business district, but also in industrial and port areas, municipal governments have set up special assessment and tax districts whereby a proportion of property taxes levied on structures within the area is returned to it. Funds so raised may be used for further capital expenditure, as backing for loans, or for services such as special security forces. Somewhat similarly, tax-increment financing employs any increase in property taxes resulting from a redevelopment project, such as a hotel or parking garage, to pay back the bonds used to finance the investment or to reinvest further in the area (Holcomb and Beauregard, 1981). Free trade or enterprise zones combine tax reductions with exemption from various regulations to firms operating within designated areas. All these measures, justified as producing economic development and employment, undercut what was one of the original arguments for government-sponsored redevelopment projects— that they would add to the municipal tax base and thereby support the level of services required by cities with large dependent populations.

Municipalities requiring large amounts of capital for major projects resort to state-sponsored revenue bonds. Current federal law allows tax exemption for interest on these bonds even if the funds raised are lent to private investors. Since repayment is tied to revenue streams from the development generated, these bonds are usually exempt from the referendum requirements of general obligation bonds. Types of projects funded in this way range from convention

Table 22.1
Federal Government Outlays for Urban Redevelopment, Excluding Housing Expenditures, in Current and Constant (1967) Dollars

Year	Current $	Constant $	Year	Current $	Constant $
1951	8	10	1969	2786	2538
1952	15	19	1970	2171	1867
1953	45	56	1971	2486	2048
1954	37	46	1972	2878	2300
1955	56	70	1973	3100	2331
1956	4	5	1974	3000	2034
1957	49	58	1975	3100	1925
1958	78	90	1976	2800	1644
1959	108	124	1977	3500	1929
1960	130	147	1978	3300	1690
1961	162	181	1979	4000	1844
1962	261	288	1980	4900	1989
1963	222	242	1981	5100	1871
1964	306	329	1982	4600	1592
1965	420	444	1983	4353	1458
1966	446	458	1984	4520	1455
1967	561	561	1985	4598	1462
1968	1277	1225			

Sources: U.S. Bureau of the Census, 1953–83 (various years); Office of Management and Budget, 1986.

centers to industrial parks to large, mixed-use developments such as Battery Park City in New York, which combines expensive office and residential structures.

Yet another method of developing financing for large projects such as sports arenas or parking garages is lease financing, whereby a state or city agency leases the facility to an operator, who usually pledges a percentage of the profits as rent (Hartman and Kessler, 1978: 156). The difference between the rent and the annual debt service is paid from public funds. Such arrangements may require no initial outlay by the public agency since the original funding comes from private lenders. But if profits do not in fact reach anticipated levels, the public ends up paying most or all of the debt.

The loss of direct federal grants has stimulated neighborhood groups, often with assistance from city and state governments, to seek new sources of funding. The usual vehicle for doing so is the nonprofit community development corporation, which permits businesses and neighborhood organizations to use the various tax advantages, loan funds, and capital grants available within distressed urban districts (Mier and Wiewel, 1983). In addition to having access to the tax devices listed above, such corporations, as well as individual firms, may be able to draw on funds raised through revenue bonds to finance commercial and industrial development or housing. The necessity of proving creditworthiness and demonstrating efficiency causes these kinds of community organizations to be businesslike and staff dominated rather than political mobilization devices or community spokespersons. They thus differ from the organizations spawned by urban renewal and Model Cities.

THE EVALUATION OF REDEVELOPMENT PROGRAMS

Very few governmental programs are evaluated in any kind of systematic way (Aaron, 1978); urban redevelopment efforts have been no exception. The very nature of these programs has raised serious technical problems for the conduct of scientific evaluations. Even more importantly, during four decades redevelopment programs have constantly changed in scope and character, reflecting shifts in national and local balances of political power. With these shifts have come new consensuses among policymakers as to the appropriateness of governmental intervention, the importance of the federal role, and the criteria by which programmatic successes and failures should be evaluated. Therefore, were all the technical problems to be overcome, the evaluation of redevelopment would still depend upon the political perspectives of the evaluators and the historical period in which the evaluation was conducted.

Methodological Problems

In general, redevelopment programs have been designed to affect the built environment and urban economy by influencing the behavior of businesses and households. For this reason there is a long chain of causality between a governmental action and its ultimate consequence. At every point along this chain, factors other than the original program may significantly influence ultimate results: for example, differing economic conditions in thousands of localities, the efficiency and biases of local governments and renewal authorities, and the behavior of particular private developers and leading businesses. Scholars trying to disentangle the final effects (or impacts) of federal urban programs inevitably comment upon the difficulty of controlling for external factors that influence program effectiveness (Glickman, 1980).

Their efforts have been undermined by continuously changing regulations and administrative styles, and perhaps more significantly, by the interaction among government programs with quite disparate objectives. For example, during the sixties a given city might be undergoing redevelopment simultaneously as a result of urban renewal, the construction of public housing, neighborhood rehabilitation under Model Cities, and national interstate highway projects. Of all these interventions, the most money almost certainly would have been spent for highway construction, and clearance for highways would likely have displaced more households than the other programs combined. Under these circumstances, identification of the unique effects of urban renewal would have been impossible. In fact, compared with activities of the private sector and the interstate highway program, all of the federally sponsored urban redevelopment efforts were relatively weak treatments in terms of how much money they spent and their ultimate consequences for urban development.

Except for Anderson's (1964) pathbreaking effort to apply cost-benefit analysis to the urban renewal program, there were few evaluations of federal redevelopment programs, and none on a national scale, until the seventies. During that decade, and particularly during the years of the Carter administration, efforts were made to evaluate CDBG, UDAG, and various programs of the Economic Development Administration (EDA) of the Department of Commerce (see Jacobs and Roistacher, 1980). The studies of CDBG, of which the Brookings Institution conducted the most important (Dommel et al., 1980), concentrated on the distribution of benefits and problems of implementation in what was a complex program of intergovernmental revenue sharing. The Brookings studies found, in general, that low- and moderate-income groups received the largest portion of benefits, as mandated by Congress. But the studies were limited in that they interpreted anything done to a lower-income neighborhood or household as benefiting it. Moreover, while they identified the ostensible beneficiaries of CDBG, the types of program activities, and the character of citizen participation under it, they were unable to measure the impacts of the program, that is, its ultimate effects on the quality of urban life.

Studies of programs with explicit economic development objectives, particularly of the UDAG program, have examined such impacts as jobs created and private capital leveraged. The results have been impressive, with leveraging ratios of more than five to one for UDAG (Gist, 1980). But here again, some serious methodological problems limit the inferences that can be drawn. For one thing, the data about job creation or private investment originate with the program applicants, who only receive grants in the first place if they meet high leveraging criteria. Moreover, these and similar studies are unable to specify how much investment might have taken place without public subsidies, or the extent to which private firms substitute public funds for their own capital in qualifying projects.

At any particular moment these and other technical problems make evaluation difficult. But what if we wanted to evaluate the impacts of redevelopment programs over time, say over the last 30 years or so? Such a historical interpretation would require a much broader scope than any of the policy evaluations that were actually undertaken. From a technical perspective, it would have to determine how much lag time should be allowed between, for example, the clearance of a site and construction upon it. Many urban renewal projects took 10 or more years to produce results. Should effects that are not felt until years later be attributed to the original urban renewal effort?

In addition, from a historical perspective, the "secondary" effects of federal redevelopment projects may have been more important than the primary impacts on the sites defined as the program target areas. Urban renewal displaced hundreds of thousands of people, many of whom were poor and black. These population movements within and between jurisdictions profoundly affected the overall development of cities. Yet another "secondary" result of federal programs over time was to stimulate social movements (usually with local governments as the targets) among affected residents (Fainstein et al., 1983; Mollenkopf, 1983). These movements dramatically influenced the whole course of urban and national politics and helped produce the frequent changes in program character that made technical evaluation difficult in the first place. Ultimately, in fact, political reaction to the programs played a significant role in reshaping policymakers' views about the part government should play in urban redevelopment. Consequently, even if the technical problems could be overcome, the possibility of conducting an "objective" evaluation of redevelopment programs collides with the inherently political nature of such an undertaking.

Changing Bases for Policymakers' Evaluations

Perceptions by policymakers of urban redevelopment strategies may have little relationship to objective social science policy evaluation, but they have everything to do with the rise and fall of different social interests and their relative success at placing their problems on the political agenda. Changing interpretations of urban development problems and ameliorative programs can thus be traced to the overall political climate of the time (Stone, 1976; Friedland, 1983).

The Fifties and Early Sixties

The housing objectives of the coalition that supported urban renewal in the forties were quickly subverted with the demise of the Truman administration. Physical redevelopment (defined as wholesale clearance) and private investment became the main criteria of program success. But private investment was constrained by the need to select sites for redevelopment according to planning rather than market criteria and by the requirement that developers be chosen after sites were cleared. Thus urban renewal was viewed by most policymakers as a nonpolitical program whose main shortcoming lay in implementation (that is, in producing adequate private investment). Its critics on the right claimed that the program was not cost-effective and that it amounted to the confiscation of private property. On the left, criticisms centered on the destruction of neighborhoods, the undemocratic character of the program, and its particularly negative effect on black people.

Mid-Sixties to Mid-Seventies

Black mobilization and the reforms of the Great Society substantially modified urban renewal, strengthening citizen participation, allowing for more rehabilitation, and providing substantial compensation to displaced residents. Just when urban renewal began meeting more of the objectives of its liberal critics, however, it started to lose business support, in large part for that very reason. As the program became more sensitive to lower-class interests and increasingly the target of mass protest, it became less effective as a vehicle for depoliticizing government-sponsored redevelopment. While urban renewal was very popular with local officials, block grants proved even more popular since they gave mayors greater program control and more freedom from federal oversight than urban renewal and the other categorical programs.

The Carter Years

The Carter administration rearranged the programs aimed at economic development and at the social and physical reconstruction of urban lower-income communities. The former objective was to be obtained through UDAG. This program solved the implementation problem of urban renewal by eliminating almost every planning requirement, effectively allowing developers to select sites on which they could make a profit with moderate levels of public subsidy after clearance. A series of court decisions affirmed the authority of local governments to take property from one business and sell it to another with a federal UDAG subsidy. As noted, UDAG was evaluated using purely economic criteria, according to which it appeared very successful.

CDBG was a more complicated program, with multiple and often conflicting objectives. Social welfare criteria continued to be employed in its evaluation. But CDBG also aimed at eliminating "blight" through economic development, whose beneficiaries did not need to be stated. Moreover, because CDBG was supposed to achieve its social objectives (improving the lot of the poor) through physical transformations, program evaluators, especially within the federal government, inferred that lower-income groups benefited whenever they were affected by CDBG, even if their housing was demolished.

Together, UDAG and CDBG buried the contradictions that entangled urban renewal once resident populations were politically strong enough in the sixties to incorporate some of their interests in the program. The Carter administration gave the "communities" CDBG and business UDAG, each to be judged by quite different criteria. But both were firmly in the hands of the mayors, for whom the main agenda was increasingly economic growth rather than social stability or social welfare.

The Reagan Approach

The Reagan administration rejected federal leadership for urban redevelopment and governmental planning at all levels. In keeping with the logic of its political attack on the welfare state, it found that previous urban programs were lacking precisely because they failed to benefit the most needy. Thus urban renewal displaced the poor and enriched a few businesses. UDAG funds were insufficiently targeted to those cities in the greatest economic distress. CDBG allowed local governments to spend federal funds on objectives that should be met locally, or not at all, by government. Accordingly, the administration let CDBG and UDAG languish as it diverted national resources away from urban programs and lower-income groups.

In this context the evaluation of extant federal programs virtually halted. At the local level, programs to subsidize businesses through tax incentives were widely supported without much objective evaluation as to their costs and benefits, to some extent because such evaluations were technically difficult. But popular support also resulted because of the absence of major federal programs at a time when economic growth was consensually viewed by policymakers as the paramount criterion for effective government. Local governments, operating in a mercantilist environment enhanced by a national programmatic vacuum, were politically evaluated on their effort to attract investment. The level of effort was inferred from the extent to which municipalities subsidized business.

The parallel to urban renewal in the fifties is evident. The difference in evaluative criteria was between the amount of private investment in the eighties versus acres cleared in the fifties. In each case, however, the criterion for the political evaluation of governmental efforts was a proxy measure of benefit to business. The reason for the parallel was the ascendancy of business objectives within the political sphere, and thereby in the evaluation of redevelopment programs.

HISTORICAL INTERPRETATION OF REDEVELOPMENT

Any theoretical explanation of the history of redevelopment programs in the United States must take into account the decentralized character of its political system and the continual presence of class and race conflict in the determination of governmental strategies. Local governments have always had considerable impact on determining the character of redevelopment programs, both through their influence on federal policies and through the ways in which they implemented those policies, And they have always been highly responsive to the interests of their business communities. Yet despite business influence and local autonomy, common national factors external in origin to particular municipalities functioned to produce similar changes in many cities at about the same time.

U.S. postwar history has involved only a single interlude of popular mobilization, extending from the mid-sixties to the mid-seventies. Before 1965 urban governments planned large-scale redevelopment, which initially was directly sponsored by them. These administrations, which we call directive, operated with little effective opposition. They were succeeded by concessionary administrations, which were forced by the uprisings of the sixties to be more responsive to popular interests than were governments before or afterwards. In the mid-sixties, during a period of super economic growth and minority rebellion, relatively liberal business leaders established a conciliatory corporate response. Thus there was a rapid expansion in federal programs for social welfare, citizen participation, and racial integration.

Reinforced by the continuity of federal programs, business interests in urban redevelopment remained basically the same in both the directive and concessionary periods. The emphasis was on restructuring land use through governmental planning and orchestration of development. While the concessionary period saw the emergence of program mixes involving more preservation and less clearance, as well as coherent strategies for the functional conversion of old cities, the role of government remained active and central.

The most recent period, marked by both the counterattack of business at all levels of government and by popular acquiescence, witnessed the emergence of yet a third type of local administration. This last type, extending from 1975 to the present, was neither directive nor concessionary, but conserving—conserving in the senses of being politically conservative, of emphasizing the fiscal stability of local government, yet of retaining, ultimately at a greatly reduced scale, many of the programs developed during the concessionary period.

The decline of black militance in the seventies changed the character of political pressure and therefore the kinds of accommodations that had to be made. By 1975 inflation, declining personal income, and profit squeeze caused sharp drops in governmental revenues. With political order taken for granted, the urban problem became redefined from social welfare to economic growth. The conservative reorientation of the national government reinforced the power of local governments in relation to racial minorities and community organizations.

The years after 1975 were marked by an increasing depoliticization of urban class conflict. As government ceased to be the direct agent of redevelopment, it became a less important target for class conflict over the use of the city. This conflict was now played out in a disaggregated manner between landlords and tenants, working-class residents and gentrifiers, and small shopkeepers and big developers. Even where popular forces were strongest, local governments could claim correctly that they had only limited control over private-market actors.

There was a redirection of economic growth strategies around 1975. The completion of most CBD clearance efforts, combined with the new national emphasis on enhancing business profits, resulted in the primacy of economic development over land-use strategies. Business pressed successfully for contraction in government activity as a prerequisite to development, one outcome of which was privatized control over land use. With private businesses now directing urban redevelopment, though heavily subsidized by government through tax expenditures, most of the gains of economic growth were channeled back into further subsidy programs for business.

By the mid-1980s economic recovery meant that many cities were no longer undergoing fiscal crisis. But their increased capabilities did not result in a renewal of the efforts at social amelioration and physical transformation that had marked the concessionary period. Although a number of cities, including many of the largest, now had mayors drawn from minority groups, the combination of federal retrenchment and continued local quietude meant that the conserving period had gradually become a genuinely conservative one. The emphasis on economic growth and subsidies to business continued; the effort to preserve the social programs of the sixties had so faded as to be almost forgotten.

REFERENCES

Aaron, Henry. 1978. *Politics and the Professors.* Washington, D.C.: Brookings Institution.

Anderson, Martin. 1964. *The Federal Bulldozer.* Cambridge, Mass.: MIT Press.

Dommel, Paul, Victor E. Bach, Sarah F. Liebschutz, and Leonard S. Rubinowitz. 1980. *Targeting Community Development.* Third Report of the Brookings Institution Monitoring Study of the Community Development Block Grant Program. Washington, D.C.: U.S. Department of Housing and Urban Development.

Fainstein, Susan S., and Norman I. Fainstein. 1980. "Mobility, Community, and Participation: The American Way Out." In William A. V. Clark and Eric G. Moore (eds.), *Residential Mobility and Public Policy.* Beverly Hills: Sage. 242–262.

Fainstein, Susan S., Norman I. Fainstein, Richard Child Hill, Dennis Judd, and Michael Peter Smith. 1983. *Restructuring the City.* New York: Longman.

Fried, Marc. 1966. "Grieving for a Lost Home: Psychological Costs of Relocation." In James Q. Wilson (ed.), *Urban Renewal: The Record and the Controversy.* Cambridge, Mass.: MIT Press. 359–379.

Frieden, Bernard J., and Marshall Kaplan. 1975. *The Politics of Neglect.* Cambridge, Mass.: MIT Press.

Friedland, Roger. 1983. *Power and Crisis in the City.* New York: Schocken.

Gans, Herbert. 1966. "The Failure of Urban Renewal." In James Q. Wilson (ed.), *Urban Renewal: The Record and the Controversy.* Cambridge, Mass.: MIT Press. 537–557.

Gelfand, Mark I. 1975. *A Nation of Cities.* New York: Oxford University Press.

Gist, John R. 1980. "Urban Development Action Grants: Design and Implementation." In Donald B. Rosenthal (ed.), *Urban Revitalization.* Beverly Hills: Sage. 237–252.

Glickman, Norman. 1980. "Methodological Issues and the Prospects for Urban Impact Analysis." In Norman Glickman (ed.), *The Urban Impacts of Federal Policies*. Baltimore: Johns Hopkins University Press. 3–32.

Hartman, Chester. 1971. "Relocation: Illusory Promises and No Relief." *Virginia Law Review* 57: 745–817.

Hartman, Chester, and Rob Kessler. 1978. "The Illusion and Reality of Urban Renewal: San Francisco's Yerba Buena Center." In William K. Tabb and Larry Sawers (eds.), *Marxism and the Metropolis*. New York: Oxford University Press.

Hays, R. Allen. 1985. *The Federal Government and Urban Housing*. Albany: State University of New York Press.

Holcomb, H. Briavel, and Robert A. Beauregard. 1981. *Revitalizing Cities*. Washington, D.C.: Association of American Geographers.

Jacobs, Jane. 1961. *Death and Life of Great American Cities*. New York: Vintage.

Jacobs, Susan, and Elizabeth Roistacher. 1980. "The Urban Impacts of HUD's Urban Development Action Grant Program." In Norman Glickman (ed.), *The Urban Impacts of Federal Policies*. Baltimore: Johns Hopkins University Press. 335–362.

Mandelker, Daniel, Gary Feder, and Margaret R. Collins. 1980. *Reviving Cities with Tax Abatement*. New Brunswick, N.J.: Center for Urban Policy Research, Rutgers University.

Mier, Robert, and Wim Wiewel. 1983. "Business Activities of Not-for-Profit Organizations: Surviving the New Federalism?" *Journal of the American Planning Association* 49: 316–325.

Mollenkopf, John. 1983. *The Contested City*. Princeton: Princeton University Press.

Office of Management and Budget. 1986. *Budget of the United States Government, Fiscal Year 1987*. Washington, D.C.: Government Printing Office.

Peltz, Michael, and Marc A. Weiss. 1984. "State and Local Government Roles in Industrial Innovation." *Journal of the American Planning Association* 50: 270–279.

Sanders, Heywood T. 1980. "Urban Renewal and the Revitalized City: A Reconsideration of Recent History." In Donald B. Rosenthal (ed.), *Urban Revitalization*. Beverly Hills: Sage. 103–126.

Stone, Clarence. 1976. *Economic Growth and Neighborhood Discontent*. Chapel Hill: University of North Carolina Press.

U.S. Bureau of the Census. 1953–83 (various years). *Statistical Abstract of the United States*. Washington, D.C.: Government Printing Office.

Wilson, James Q. (ed.). 1966. *Urban Renewal: The Record and the Controversy*. Cambridge, Mass.: MIT Press.

23

Gentrification, Revitalization, and Displacement

J. JOHN PALEN

PATTERNS OF NEIGHBORHOOD CHANGE

Patterns of community and neighborhood change have been a major topic of urban research and theory since the days of Park, Burgess, and McKenzie (1925), Burgess (1924), and Wirth (1938). Among those topics given the greatest attention has been discussion of how neighborhoods filter down as a consequence of the invasion and succession of new land uses and population groups. Massive post–World War II suburbanization and consequent softening of central-city housing markets led by the 1970s to widespread lamentations about urban crisis and death of the city (Sternlieb, 1977). Disinvestment, deterioration, and demolition were seen as virtually inevitable. The established wisdom held that middle- and upper middle-status populations having residential choice could be induced to return to central-city residence only through constructing new housing in planned urban renewal areas (Hauser, 1960).

In the late 1970s a new myth began appearing. In place of inevitable inner-city blight and decline, the new orthodoxy was one of a city of urban regeneration and neighborhood revival. However, as old neighborhoods began to undergo revitalization, new questions and concerns arose. What impact was revitalization having on central cities? How extensive was and is rehabilitation? Which neighborhoods are affected and which are not? Who is involved in revitalization? Does revitalization mean gentrification? Does gentrification mean displacement of the indigenous residents? Thus far our answers to these questions have been largely tentative. This is partially because of the complexity of the questions asked, and partially because revitalization activity largely is the product of the last decade. Both these urban changes and the research done on them are still in an emergent state. Still, there is now enough data to provide a reasonable state-of-the-art report.

DEFINITIONS, IMAGERY, AND MYTHS

First, it should be noted that what is being discussed here is neighborhood revitalization as a consequence of private housing market activity, rather than as the conscious consequence of federal, state, or municipal government policy. Moreover, this revitalization, whether gentrification or incumbent upgrading, initially occurred against a backdrop of perceived central-city decline and decay. Early central-city revitalizers often perceived municipal governments more as being the problem than as providing solutions. To protect their perceived interests, in-movers organized to protest failure to enforce local building codes, poor police protection, inadequate garbage pickup and sanitation, and general non-maintenance of neighborhood lights, streets, sidewalks, and parks (Palen, 1987: 257). In a few cases the initially residential occupancy was illegal, as in SoHo in New York, where old manufacturing and commercial tenants were replaced by loft apartments (Hudson, 1984; Simpson, 1981; Zukin, 1982). By the mid-1970s some cities were de facto encouraging gentrification, while others were seeking to stop its spread. An example of the latter was legislation introduced in Washington, D.C., to restrict gentrification—and thus involuntary displacement—through special taxes on housing speculation (Zeitz, 1979). More recently, government attitudes have become more positive, but the impetus for revitalization was and remains overwhelmingly private investment rather than public policy.

Second, before discussing what is occurring, it is necessary to attempt some conceptual and linguistic clarity.[1] The rhetoric of urban revitalization uses terms such as gentrification, renewal, rehabilitation renovation, and reinvasion (Clay, 1979; Laska and Spain, 1980). Often these terms are not defined and appear to describe the same phenomenon. The plethora of terms, however, reflects more than terminological entrepreneurship. The terms used often reflect theoretical and ideological perceptions and positions regarding what is occurring and how it should be evaluated. The term "gentrification," for example, is often used to imply a not wholly positive change. It has come to imply displacement of existing residents. The terms renovation or revitalization, by contrast, project a more positive imagery.

The imagery may also contain substantial dollops of myth. The commonly used term, gentrification, was borrowed from British usage (Glass, 1964) and technically suggests the return of landed proprietors of upper or noble class to the inner city. This is an inaccurate reflection of reality on several counts. First, American central-city in-movers are hardly gentry. In fact, initial in-movers are often economically marginally middle class. They are attracted to the area because their economic resources are limited and other alternatives are beyond reach. Since their expectations outrun their incomes, they often provide a major segment of their investment in sweat equity. This may be meritorious, but it badly distorts the dictionary definition of gentry.

Similarly, the implied suggestion of return from suburbs or countryside does not conform to the data in spite of the popular conception that gentrification reflects a back-to-the-city movement (Laska and Spain, 1980). It is now evident that no such widespread migratory movement exists. Census data confirms that central-city revitalizers are not dissatisfied suburbanites fleeing from supposed suburban conformity and blandness (Long, 1980). Numerous studies indicate that most in-movers are already city dwellers who are being retained within the city (Gale, 1984; Nachmias and Palen, 1982; Schill and Nathan, 1983). Generally, less than one-fifth have moved to their current address from the suburbs.

As misleading as the back-to-the-city myth is the belief that gentrification is an irresistible wave that is transforming city neighborhood after neighborhood. It is true that urban revitalization is a widespread phenomenon found in all areas of the country and in all sizes of cities (Lipton, 1977; Clay, 1979; Black, 1980; U.S. Department of Housing and Urban Development [HUD], 1981; Palen and London, 1984). Cities with high levels of white-collar employment and substantial suburban commuting distances are especially likely to be experiencing neighborhood revival (Lipton, 1977). However, to date, "Gentrification neighborhoods account for only a tiny fraction of any city's neighborhoods and housing stock" (Clay, 1979: 17). Revitalization has only occurred in a handful of any given city's neighborhoods. Middle- and upper middle-class revitalization often is still a risk-taking enterprise involving substantial investments of time and energy as well as money. Of the limited number able to make such commitments, only a smaller fraction are interested in so doing. Not everyone wishes to reside in restored inner-city housing. Suburbia is still the location of preference for most homebuying adults (Sumka and Cicin-Sain, 1979).

Moreover, only a minority of any city's neighborhoods have the combination of characteristics that encourage revitalization. Urban neighborhoods that have been most prone to middle-class in-movement generally have possessed in some combination the advantages of historic location, attractive architecture, and access to amenities. Unfortunately, most cities' supply of such housing is limited. If revitalization is confined to the so-called gentrification of one or two previously elite neighborhoods that, having fallen on darker days, now are being rehabilitated by young professionals, the changes will have more meaning for the media than the city at large. For the city per se to be affected, revitalization activity must spill over into the "ordinary" residential areas that compose the bulk of the housing. The extent and form in which this is occurring will be addressed later in this chapter.

The stereotypical image of gentrifiers is one of white, college-educated, middle-class, young adults having professional, technical, or managerial occupations (Gale, 1984: 10–12). This is in substantial part an accurate characterization. Gentrifiers additionally are more likely than their suburban compatriots to be single or unmarried to the person with whom they are living, and if married, without children. Some gentrifying areas within New York, Chicago, San Francisco, and other cities also have a substantial representation of gays. As a group, in-movers are likely to share an ideology that places high value on symbols of urban diversity and on the superior virtue of older rather than newer housing (Allen, 1984). Bound with this there often is an explicit rejection of "suburbanism" as a way of life.

There is far less controversy over the physical consequences of revitalization than over the social ramifications. Physically the consequences are almost uniformly positive; homes are refurbished and upgraded, housing code violations decrease, and municipal service and maintenance improve. Most importantly from the perspective of municipal officials, home values appreciate, and thus tax revenues increase. The controversy is whether or not these advantages are occurring at the cost of displacing poorer and less advantaged neighborhood residents.

THEORETICAL CONSIDERATIONS

Current discussions of urban renovation, revitalization, and gentrification are posited upon theoretical assumptions, but excepting Marxist perspectives, these undergirdings usually are not explicitly detailed. Empirical description rather than theoretical discussion is the focus. However, a review of the literature suggests that research efforts can be placed into one (or more) of five alternative categories or approaches. These categories are (1) demographic-ecological, (2) sociocultural, (3) political-economic, (4) community networks, and (5) social movements. When reading the following paragraphs, one should keep in mind that the categories are not mutually exclusive and that this is merely an outline rather than a complete and logically well-developed statement of any given theory.

Demographic-Ecological

A number of demographic-ecological variables are often cited in discussing gentrification. The first of these is simply the increase in numbers of those of prime homebuying ages (Clay, 1979). Baby boomers are now 25 to 40, and this is placing heavy demand on the housing market. Some of this demand will be met by the "recycling" of inner-city dwellings and neighborhoods. Other important demographic factors affecting a decision to seek central-city housing include rising age at first marriage, low fertility, the later birth of the first child, increases in married women participating in the labor force, and a rising number of dual-income families. Taken together, these factors may represent a decline in the "familism" that spurred post–World War II suburbanization (Bourne, 1977; Kern, 1977). To the extent that relatively affluent, dual-income, child-free couples, without concerns about quality of central-city schools, tend to choose to live closer to downtown jobs and adult amenities, demographic factors can be said to partially explain urban revitalization.

In terms of urban ecology it appears that Burgess' concentric-ring urban growth model (Burgess, 1924) is being turned inside out, with centrally located neighborhoods experiencing upper middle-class invasion and succession. It has been documented that such reinvasion is positively correlated with white-collar administrative activity in the central business district (CBD) and negatively associated with blue-collar or industrial activity (Lipton, 1977). This would suggest that cities high in white-collar economic activities and low in blue-collar activities are most likely to experience urban revitalization.

It is reasonable to speculate that cities having substantial employment in high-tech firms, government agencies, universities, and professional groups are likely sites for revitalization. Gentrification to date has been most common in such cities, which serve as diversified advanced service centers (Gale, 1984: 153–157). However, some newer cities in this category, having much of their economic growth in outer areas, have not yet been major sites for revitalization (Berry, 1987). Los Angeles, Houston, Phoenix, and Miami, for example, are not usually mentioned as locations of major revitalization activity. Given the recent trends toward decentralization of industry and the increasingly corporate nature of the nation's major CBDs, ecological relationships take on additional significance and require further empirical examination.

Sociocultural

A second theoretical direction in the literature on revitalization is sociocultural orientation. Here the focus is not on aggregate or structural characteristics of areas or populations, but rather on attitudes, beliefs, ideas, and choices as factors affecting revitalization decisions. The distinction in focus between sociocultural and demographic-ecological approaches mirrors the long-standing debate within human ecology between the "materialist/neoclassical" and "nonmaterialist/sociocultural" ecologists (Bailey and Mulcahy, 1972; Berry and Kasarda, 1977). The sociocultural approach suggests that no urban ecological change, including revitalization, can be fully understood without reference to the learned cultural values that motivate human behavior. Firey's examination (1945) of land-use patterns in central Boston is the classic study emphasizing "sentiment and symbolism" as ecological variables.

Under the sociocultural heading falls the whole series of life-styles, choices, values, and motives that favor central-city living. Allen (1984) suggests that gentrification in particular has undertones of ideology and utopia in seeking a transcendent community experience. Certainly during the 1980s, being an "urban pioneer" has an "inner-city chic" not associated with the current portrayals of suburbia. Engaging in restoring an urban home may reflect new urban values or may be a new way of realizing older dominant values of self-identity and the symbolizing of material success (Fusch, 1978). In either case it throws into question the conventional assumptions regarding the pervasiveness of an American antiurban ideology or value system (Allen, 1984). For at least that segment of the population caricatured as "yuppies," it is clear that prourban sociocultural factors strongly influence their participation in urban gentrification.

Political-Economic

The third category, political-economic, moves sharply back to macro-level explanations. Analyses fall into both traditional and Marxist explanations. The former emphasize competition and supply-and-demand market efficiency, while the latter focus on power relationships and the uneven costs and benefits of neighborhood change. Certainly for single individuals or two-income households, central cities offer locational advantages in terms of access to both employment and adult-oriented amenities and services. In the same fashion, suburban housing meets the needs of families with children for open play spaces and adequate schooling. For some childless couples, rising suburban construction costs and taxes, plus generally higher (in time and money) suburban maintenance and heating/cooling costs, together with higher commuting costs (again in time and money) have acted to tip the balance in favor of revitalized city housing. Redoing an older home can be less expensive than building anew in the suburbs. Political changes, such as tax advantages for residing in historic districts, and civil rights legislation have also contributed to mortgage funds now available for central areas formerly redlined.

Marxist explanations, by contrast, are less likely to look to indirect political and economic market forces and more to direct conscious manipulation. Smith and Le Faivre suggest that capitalists actively plan "devalorization" of neighborhoods (1984). Once a neighborhood has been abandoned, a rent gap develops between current economic rent and what could be obtained after redevelopment and gentrification. The suggested pattern is one of selected disinvestment and managed reinvestment.

In the Marxist model consumer demand is less important than the systematic and planned disinvestment and reinvestment in neighborhoods in order to maximize profit (Smith and Le Faivre, 1984). Gentrification thus is not so much a sociocultural life-style choice or a social movement as it is the consequence of decisions made by land-based interest groups manipulating the real estate market. Upper-class groups benefit most from such decisions, while the urban underclass pays the highest cost in terms of displacement (Hartman, 1984). The image of the city as a growth machine designed to encourage the return of the middle class through "boosterism" is appropriate here (Molotch, 1976).

Links between the stages of capital accumulation and urban form are posited by Gordon (1978), who suggests that commercial, industrial, and corporate stages of urban capital formation are conducive to different distributions of people and functions in space. While the industrial stage is characterized by the polarization of cities and suburbs by race and class, the corporate city is noted for the decentralization of industry, the dispersal of working-class areas, and the proliferation of the service sector. These stages parallel in some respects the relationship noted earlier (Lipton, 1977) between the amount of administrative service activity and the extent of gentrification.

Community Networks

Viewing the local community as an interactive social group has a distinguished sociological history. Classics such as *Street Corner Society* (Whyte, 1943), *The*

Urban Villagers (Gans, 1962), and *Tally's Corner* (Liebow, 1967) examined neighborhoods as microsocieties. Indeed, critics have charged that "urban sociology has tended to be *neighborhood sociology*" (Wellman and Leighton, 1981: 80; emphasis in original). Going back to the Chicago School, the community approach directly addresses the question of how groups interact and maintain personal ties within what often appears to be a hostile larger social system stressing competition and division of labor. Community studies thus occupy a critical juncture between macro-level demographic-ecological and micro-level sociocultural approaches. As such, community studies address questions relating to the persistence and viability of kinship, social networks, and types of community involvement.

The classic Chicago School approach has been summarized in Louis Wirth's much-quoted essay "Urbanism as a Way of Life" (1938). Emphasizing the destruction of local attachments, this approach has been characterized as the "community lost" perspective (Hunter, 1978). Technological changes—especially in communication and transportation—are seen as supplanting the locally bound local community with mass-society political and social organizations (Greer, 1962). With the role of the neighborhood becoming more circumscribed (Fischer, 1984), the future is seen as one of "minimalist" or "liberated" neighborhoods (Wellman and Leighton, 1981).

An alternative to these views is the "community saved" or "emergent" perspective. This more optimistic perspective sees a resurgence rather than a breakdown of community commitment, involvement, and activity (Hunter, 1978; Suttles, 1972). Since voluntary community networks and involvement can be increased as well as decreased, the question is whether local networks are becoming more extensive, tightly knit, and clustered. Are local crime watches, community betterment associations, and block parties producing an increasing sense of gemeinschaft?

Central-city neighborhood revitalization has been associated with heightened participation in voluntary community organizations (Nachmias and Palen, 1982; Maher et al., 1985). Upgrading areas also place considerable emphasis on identifying and demarcating their areas by a specific name. At least on the superficial level, there is increased identification with a named and bounded community. To what extent this shared symbolism reflects shared sentiments is the important question for those taking a community networks perspective.

Social Movements

While there are disagreements over the definition of what constitutes a social movement, most suggest that such movements have an ideological base, are oriented toward change, and are socially organized, often in terms of leader-follower relationships. Earlier social movements such as postwar suburbanization or the new-towns movements were often based—at least implicitly—on antiurban ideologies (Donaldson, 1969; Gans, 1967; Palen, 1987). These ideologies often had at their core a rejection of the supposed slums, crime, and confusion of cities in search for a simpler and more "natural" way of life. Federal policies such as Federal Housing Administration (FHA) loans and new expressways subsidized this movement, much to the economic advantage of land developers, builders, and lending institutions.

Urban revitalization and especially gentrification is a social movement setting new life-style criteria for inner-city chic. Gentrifier prourban cultural tastes are buttressed by a changing land economics that suggests that the profits of inner-city reinvestment can be considerable, while the economic risks are far less than in the past. Political-economic elites encourage the gentrifying movement in order to promote their investments and profits. Redlining is replaced by investment strategies that encourage the transformation of deteriorating areas into trendy gentrifying neighborhoods. Newcomers mobilize to enhance their investments by obtaining historic-district designation, enforcing compliance with housing codes, and in general making the neighborhood more comfortable and advantageous for middle-class residents.

Incumbent residents threatened with displacement sometimes form their own countermovements to defend their turf (Hartman, 1984) and limit elitist incursions. However, the nonsystematic impression is that these low-power groups have not been noticeably more successful than earlier indigenous grass roots groups were in their attempts to halt urban renewal projects (Henig, 1982).

DISPLACEMENT

The most controversial issue regarding neighborhood revitalization is that of potential displacement of incumbent residents. Specifically, is there forced involuntary dislocation of households with low economic and political power such as the poor, minorities, and the aged? Data on this question is contradictory. In some instances ideology expressly affects interpretation and inferences, while in other instances it plays a less visible role.

Amount of Displacement

Part (but only part) of the dispute over the role of displacement is due to confusion over what is being included. Grier and Grier (1980) provide a useful service by distinguishing three types of displacement: disinvestment displacement, market competition displacement, and private reinvestment displacement. While the precise effects of each may be hard to distinguish since all may be occurring in the same neighborhood, they are analytically separate. Disinvestment displacement occurs not as a consequence of housing-quality improvement, but because dwellings decline and run down to the point where they may be abandoned and demolished. Residents are forced out by the nonmaintenance of housing. Displacement through disinvestment remains by far the major cause of central-city displacement.

Market competition displacement refers to overall national changes in the housing market such as rising costs, limited new construction, and demographic changes in number of households. Increased housing costs displace some, particularly those at the bottom. While sometimes confused with reinvestment displacement, market displacement simply forces marginal properties to turn over in occupancy without any physical improvement in the properties.

Reinvestment displacement takes place when the former residents are displaced, and then the deteriorated properties are substantially upgraded for occupancy by occupants of higher socioeconomic status. This process is commonly referred to as gentrification.

Annual Housing Survey (AHS) estimates indicate that between .8 and 1.1 percent of U.S. households (1.7 to 2.4 million persons) are displaced annually for all three of the these categories (HUD, 1981: iii). The higher figure, according to the HUD report, is "upwardly biased due to the inclusion of ambiguous cases which do not clearly represent displacement" (HUD, 1981: iii). Reinvestment displacement would represent only a minority of displacements. Based on examination—but not research—of 22 cities, Grier and Grier (1980: 260–61) suggest that the number of people displaced by private-market rehabilitation would be only 100 to 200 persons per year in most cities. In cities such as San Francisco or Washington, D.C., where displacement is more common, the estimate of annual displacement is "in the low thousands at most" (Grier and Grier, 1980: 261). Research commissioned by HUD from the Institute of Social Research at the University of Michigan similarly found that displacement affects relatively few households (HUD, 1981). On the other hand, LeGates and Hartman (1981) estimate a minimum of 2.5 million persons displaced each year for all causes.

The Department of Housing and Urban Development concluded on the basis of its review of the literature and its own studies of 12 revitalizing neighborhoods in 6 cities that relatively few households are affected by reinvestment displacement (1981). Schill and Nathan's study of displacement in 9 neighborhoods undergoing change also found that displacees were a minority of those moving (1983). This is the consensus of most researchers in the area, although there are some strong dissents, particularly among researchers taking a Marxist perspective (Smith and Le Faivre, 1984).

Characteristics of the Displaced

Even if displacement is limited nationally, it is nonetheless true that it can have a substantial impact on local areas (Baldassare, 1984; DeGiovanni and Paulson, 1984; Gale, 1984; Hudson, 1984; Lee and Hodge, 1984; Maher et al., 1985; Palen and London, 1984; Schill and Nathan, 1983). Displacement has been particularly severe in some cities—for example, Washington, D.C., and San Francisco. Also, basic to any discussion of displacement effects is the question of the characteristics of those displaced. There is a general belief that involuntary moves are not evenly distributed, and that the burden falls disproportionately on households that are poor, elderly, black, and female headed. This "underclass hypothesis" (Lee and Hodge, 1984) derives support from a number of neighborhood-level case studies (Clay, 1979; Cybrinski, 1978; Goldfield, 1980; City of St. Paul, 1981; Gale, 1980; Hartman, 1984; Henig, 1984).

Research directly focused on the question of who is displaced, however, suggests that the underclass hypothesis needs further examination and qualification. Using AHS data, Lee and Hodge (1984) found that displacement moves of all types occurred disproportionately among elderly and lower-income movers. However, they also reported that households with black and female heads "experience levels of displacement only marginally higher than their advantaged white and male counterparts" (Lee and Hodge, 1984: 161).

Schill and Nathan's examination (1983) of 9 neighborhoods in the cities of Boston, Cincinnati, Denver, Richmond, and Seattle also found the popular image of the displaced to be flawed. Income and employment status were found to be the strongest predictors of displacement. By contrast, neither age nor race was a significant predictor of displacement.

These findings are in line with HUD's conclusions based on its commissioned University of Michigan Institute of Social Research study. HUD's studies in six cities (particularly in San Francisco) and review of the literature indicate that renters, short-term residents (three years or less), those with household heads working less than full-time, poorer families, and minorities were most likely to be displaced. However, when socioeconomic variables of income, education, and welfare dependency were controlled, minorities were not more likely to be displaced than were whites (HUD, 1981: 40). Displacement was not found to have a disproportionate effect on the elderly (HUD, 1981: 41).

Schill and Nathan (1983) also suggested that those displaced were generally pleased with their replacement housing. Similarly, a study of involuntary movers in Seattle reported that of those displaced, 72 percent found the new neighborhood as good or better and 70 percent found their new dwellings as good or better (City of Seattle, 1979). This agrees with Palen's interviews (1983) of 142 former residents of a revitalizing Milwaukee working-class neighborhood, where it was discovered that movers generally reported themselves to be happier with their new housing and neighborhoods. The only significant problem reported was that of higher housing costs. It has been suggested by Schill and Nathan (1983) that displacement is not necessarily negative, and that it may be a means of forcing a family to adjust its housing to its current needs. In any case, recent research, as opposed to media imagery, supports the earlier conclusion of HUD that residential displacement may not be as serious a problem as sometimes portrayed (HUD, 1981).

NONGENTRY UPGRADING

Literature on revitalization generally focuses on two processes and groups. The first and most discussed group is the upper middle-class newcomers who "invade" an area and upgrade its housing—the so-called gentrifiers. The second group is older residents who reinvest in their own neighborhoods, a process that is usually referred to as "incumbent upgrading" (Clay, 1979). This is attractive imagery. The difficulty with this latter category is the modifier "incumbent," which implies that long-term residents remain and upgrade their residences. In reality, working-class neighborhoods continually undergo residential movement. At any given time a substantial proportion of residents are likely to be newcomers (less than three years in the area). This is particularly true of renters, where turnovers in excess of 40 percent a year are not unusual.

What maintains an area's character is not as much the lack of mobility as that in-movers have characteristics substantially similar to those who are leaving. Stable central-city neighborhoods—particularly ethnic neighborhoods—have retained their character over time, not as much through lack of population turnover as through the social, economic, and ethnic compatibility of those moving in and those moving out. One difference is that younger in-movers to older central-city neighborhoods are more likely to be employed in white-collar positions than older residents, but the in-movers' positions are usually white-collar jobs of lower pay and status (Nachmias and Palen, 1986). Moreover, such newcomers enter the neighborhood as individual families rather than through a block-by-block "invasion" as is often the case in gentrifying areas. Thus the newcomers are perceived as "new blood" for the neighborhood, not as a radical threat to its existence. Consequently, displacement is not usually an issue in upgrading working-class neighborhoods.

Most city neighborhoods are not potential targets for gentrification, nor should they be. These neighborhoods are primarily older working-class areas that were constructed to house "ordinary" populations. As such, the housing is often solidly built but rarely architecturally or historically outstanding. Often the post–World War II city's problems are mirrored in these neighborhoods. Economically, the property in older working-class neighborhoods may be undervalued, particularly in comparison to both outlying suburban areas and gentrifying areas. The affordability of nongentrifying central-city neighborhoods is perhaps their major attraction (Nachmias and Palen, 1986).

The future of the city as a place of residence depends on what occurs in such ordinary neighborhoods of the city. If the city is to prosper as a site of locational choice, there must be upgrading housing activity in other than gentrifying areas. There are some suggestive indicators that this is occurring (Nachmias and Palen, 1986). External signs of change, however, usually are less visible to a casual observer in an older established neighborhood than in a gentrifying one. In the former, incidents of upgrading and improvement are often gradual and undramatic. Rather than extensive external renovation, efforts are more likely to be directed toward improved upkeep and repair. To save expense, internal renovations are often done by the owner himself or by a local handyman, with the result that building permits—which raise assessments—are rarely obtained. Thus established areas may have far more renovation activity than official records suggest. Characterizing such areas as stable traditional neighborhoods partially distorts reality. Rather, these areas are undergoing change.

As Ernest Burgess noted over half a century ago, neighborhood stability has never been a characteristic of the American city (Burgess, 1924). During this century inner-city neighborhoods were first displaced by commercial expansion of the central business district and by industrial plant development, and then, following World War II, by programs of urban renewal and urban expressway construction. What is new today is not that some low-power and vulnerable groups are being displaced, but that they are sometimes now being replaced by middle-class newcomers living in the same—albeit upgraded—housing. What is also new is that old houses and old neighborhoods are not being torn down and replaced with new structures.

Meanwhile, some urban working- and lower middle-class neighborhoods appear to quietly be undergoing a process of reinvestment and repair. If this pattern becomes more widespread, it is possible that cities may reverse their post–World War II slide toward being the residence of those either having wealth or on welfare. It is possible that cities may be developing into more complex forms where residents are socially, racially, and economically more diverse.

The urban crisis and death of the city visions of a score of years ago have proved to be wide of the mark. While prognosticating the city's future has always been a dubious and dangerous activity, urban neighborhoods, at least for the present, are demonstrating unexpected vitality. The extent of urban revitalization should not be exaggerated, but neither should its potential for urban change be cavalierly underestimated.

NOTES

1. Portions of the material present here appeared in earlier form in J. John Palen and Bruce London (1984: 6–22).

REFERENCES

Allen, Irving L. 1984. ''The Ideology of Dense Neighborhood Redevelopment.'' In J. John Palen and Bruce London (eds.), *Gentrification, Displacement, and Neighborhood Revitalization*. Albany: State University of New York Press.

Bailey, K. D., and P. Mulcahy. 1972. ''Sociocultural versus Neoclassical Ecology: A Contribution to the Problem of Scope and Sociology.'' *Sociological Quarterly* 13: 37–41.

Baldassare, Mark. 1984. ''Evidence for Neighborhood Revitalization: Manhattan.'' In J. John Palen and Bruce London (eds.), *Gentrification, Displacement and Neighborhood Revitalization*. Albany: State University of New York Press.

Berry, Brian. 1987. ''Island of Renewal—Sea of Decay: The Evidence of Inner-City Gentrification.'' In P. Peterson (ed.), *The Future of the City*. Chicago: University of Chicago Press.

Berry, Brian, and John Kasarda. 1977. *Contemporary Urban Ecology*. New York: Macmillan.

Black, J. T. 1980. "Private-Market Housing Renovation in Central Cities." In Shirley B. Laska and Daphne Spain (eds.), *Back to the City*. Elmsford, N.Y.: Pergamon Press.

Bourne, L. S. 1977. *Perspectives on the Inner City: Its Changing Character, Reasons for Decline, and Revival*. Research Paper no. 94. Toronto: University of Toronto Centre for Urban and Community Studies.

Burgess, Ernest W. 1924. "The Growth of the City: An Introduction to a Research Project." *Publication of the American Sociological Society* 18: 85–97.

City of St. Paul. 1981. "Displacement in St. Paul." Division of Planning, Department of Planning and Economic Development, January.

City of Seattle. 1979. "Seattle Displacement Study." Seattle Office of Policy Planning, Physical Planning Division, October.

Clay, Phillip L. 1979. *Neighborhood Renewal: Middle-Class Resettlement and Incumbent Upgrading in American Neighborhoods*. Lexington, Mass.: Lexington Books.

Cybrinski, Roman. 1978. "Social Aspects of Neighborhood Change." *Annals of the Association of American Geographers* 68: 17–33.

DeGiovanni, Frank, and Nancy Paulson. 1984. "Housing Diversity in Revitalizing Neighborhoods." *Urban Affairs Quarterly* 20: 211–232.

Donaldson, S. 1969. *The Suburban Myth*. New York: Columbia University Press.

Firey, Walter. 1945. "Sentiment and Symbolism as Ecological Variables." *American Sociological Review* 10: 140–48.

Fischer, Claude S. 1984. *The Urban Experience*, 2d ed. San Diego: Harcourt Brace Jovanovich.

Fusch, R. 1978. "Historic Preservation and Gentrification: A Search for Order in the Urban Core." Paper read at the American Association of Geographers meeting, New Orleans, November 19.

Gale, Dennis. 1980. "Neighborhood Resettlement: Washington, D.C." In Shirley B. Laska and Daphne Spain (eds.), *Back to the City: Issues in Neighborhood Renovation*. Elmsford, N.Y.: Pergamon Press.

———. 1984. *Neighborhood Revitalization and the Postindustrial City*. Lexington, Mass.: Lexington Books.

Gans, Herbert J. 1962. *The Urban Villagers*. New York: Free Press.

———. 1967. *The Levittowners*. New York: Vintage Books.

Glass, Ruth. 1964. "Introduction." In Centre for Urban Studies (ed.). *London: Aspects of Change*. London: McGibbon & Kee.

Goldfield, D. R. 1980. "Private Neighborhood Redevelopment and Displacement in Washington, D.C." *Urban Affairs Quarterly* 15: 453–469.

Gordon, D. M. 1978. "Capitalist Development and the History of American Cities." In W. K. Tabb and L. Sawers (eds.), *Marxism and the Metropolis*. London: Oxford University Press.

Greer, Scott. 1962. *The Emerging City*. New York: Free Press.

Grier, George, and Eunice Grier. 1980. "Urban Displacement: A Reconnaissance." In Shirley B. Laska and Daphne Spain (eds.), *Back to the City: Issues in Neighborhood Renovation*. New York: Pergamon Press.

Hartman, Chester. 1984. *The Transformation of San Francisco*. San Francisco: Rowman & Allanheld.

Hauser, Philip M. 1960. *Population Perspectives*. New Brunswick, N.J.: Rutgers University Press.

Henig, Jeffrey R. 1982. "Neighborhood Response to Gentrification: Conditions of Mobilization." *Urban Affairs Quarterly* 17: 343–58.

———. 1984. "Gentrification and Displacement of the Elderly: An Empirical Analysis." In J. John Palen and Bruce London (eds.), *Gentrification, Displacement and Neighborhood Revitalization*. Albany: State University of New York Press.

Hudson, James R. 1984. "SoHo, A Study of Residential Invasion of a Commercial and Industrial Area." *Urban Affairs Quarterly* 20: 46–63.

Hunter, Albert. 1978. "Persistence of Local Sentiments in Mass Society." In David Street and Associates (ed.), *Handbook of Contemporary Urban Life*. San Francisco: Jossey-Bass.

Kern, D. R. 1977. "High Income Neighborhoods in the City: Will the New Demography Guarantee Their Future?" Paper read at the Regional Science Association meeting, Philadelphia, November 7.

Laska, Shirley, and Daphne Spain (eds.). 1980. *Back to the City: Issues in Neighborhood Renovation*. New York: Pergamon Press.

Lee, Barret A., and David C. Hodge. 1984. "Social Differentials in Metropolitan Residential Displacement." In J. John Palen and Bruce London (eds.), *Gentrification, Displacement and Neighborhood Revitalization*. Albany: State University of New York Press.

LeGates, Richard, and Chester Hartman. 1981. *Displacement*. San Francisco: Legal Services Anti-Displacement.

Liebow, Elliott. 1967. *Tally's Corner*. Boston: Little, Brown.

Lipton, S. Gregory, 1977. "Evidence of Central City Revival." *Journal of the American Institute of Planners* 36 (April): 136–47.

Long, Larry. 1980. "Back to the Countryside and Back to the City in the Same Decade." In Shirley B. Laska and Daphne Spain (eds.), *Back to the City*. Elmsford, N.Y.: Pergamon Press.

Maher, T., A. Hass, B. Levine, and J. Liell. 1985. "Whose Neighborhood? The Role of Established Residents in Historic Preservation Areas." *Urban Affairs Quarterly* 21: 267–81.

Molotch, Harvey. 1976. "The City as a Growth Machine: Toward the Political Economy of Place." *American Journal of Sociology* 82: 309–32.

Nachmias, Chava, and J. John Palen. 1982. "Membership in Voluntary Neighborhood Associations and Urban Revitalization." *Policy Sciences* 14: 179–93.

———. 1986. "Neighborhood Satisfaction, Expectations, and Urban Revitalization." *Journal of Urban Affairs* 8: 51–62.

Palen, J. John. 1987. *The Urban World*, 3d ed. New York: McGraw-Hill.

———. 1983. "Neighborhood Revitalization in Working Class Neighborhoods." Washington, D.C.: National Institute of Mental Health. NIMH Grant II ROIMH 35526.

Palen, J. John, and Bruce London (eds.). 1984. *Gentrification, Displacement, and Neighborhood Revitalization*. Albany: State University of New York Press.

Park, Robert E., Ernest Burgess, and R. D. McKenzie. 1925. *The City*. Chicago: University of Chicago Press.

Schill, Michael, and Richard Nathan. 1983. *Revitalizing America's Cities: Neighborhood Reinvestment and Displacement*. Albany: State University of New York Press.

Simpson, C. R. 1981. *SoHo: The Artist in the City*. Chicago: University of Chicago Press.
Smith, Neil, and Michele Le Faivre. 1984. "A Class Analysis of Gentrification." In J. John Palen and Bruce Condon (eds.), *Gentrification, Displacement and Neighborhood Revitalization*. Albany: State University of New York Press.
Sternlieb, George. 1977. "The City as Sandbox." In J. John Palen (ed.), *City Scenes*. Boston: Little, Brown.
Sumka, Howard, and B. Cicin-Sain. 1979. "Displacement in Revitalizing Neighborhoods: A Review and Research Strategy." *Occasional Papers in Housing and Community Affairs* (Washington, D.C.: Department of Housing and Urban Development) 2: 134–167.
Suttles, Gerald. 1972. *The Social Construction of Communities*. Chicago: University of Chicago Press.
U.S. Department of Housing and Urban Development, 1981. *Residential Displacement: An Update Report to Congress*. Washington, D.C.: Office of Policy Development and Research, Department of Housing and Urban Development, October.
Wellman, Barry, and Barry Leighton. 1981. "Networks, Neighborhoods, and Communities." In J. John Palen (ed.), *City Scenes*, 2d ed. Boston: Little, Brown.
Whyte, William F. 1943. *Street Corner Society*. Chicago: University of Chicago Press.
Wirth, Louis. 1938. "Urbanism as a Way of Life." *American Journal of Sociology* 44: 1–24.
Zeitz, Eileen. 1979. *Private Urban Renewal*. Lexington, Mass.: Lexington Books.
Zukin, Sharon. 1982. *Loft Living: Culture and Capital in Urban Change*. Baltimore: Johns Hopkins University Press.

24

New Communities in the United States

ELIZABETH HUTTMAN

New communities are characterized as large-scale, distinct, well-planned entities with residential, commerical, and industrial sectors. The development of new towns was a major planning focus of the 1960s and 1970s in Europe and the United States. Although the British Garden Cities movement began at the turn of the century under Ebenezer Howard, and in the United States there were the World War I congressionally funded developments and the New Deal Greenbelt towns, (Eden and Alanen, 1983; Miller, 1981) it was in the post–World War II period that the movement became a major one. By the 1960s the British Mark I new towns, built in the early postwar period, were occupied, thriving developments (Nicholson, 1961; Huttman, 1985a), observed and commented on by planners, architects, social scientists, and policymakers. In the late 1960s the Mark II new towns, such as Milton Keynes, were being planned and built, bringing the number of British new towns to 27 (Huttman, 1969).

In Sweden and France the first round of new towns had been built, and in the Netherlands Lelystad and other new towns had been getting under way. The literature on all these European towns was voluminous. The fever caught on in the United States (Fava, 1987). New towns offered a vision of careful and efficient planning and environmental soundness that contrasted very favorably with the ills and shortcomings of the city (Choldin, 1985; Jackson, 1985). As Alonso and McGuire (1972) state, this image, with these attributes and "a more modest and therefore richer scale of social interaction, a social balance which is consistent with social justice," was the reason the new towns held "such profound fascination for planners, architects, and interested laymen." These people saw the new town as "a second chance, a redemption, to live a new life unencumbered by the sins of the past" (Alonso and McGuire, 1972: 76).

In the United States in the 1960s private developers began planning and building new towns (Eichler and Kaplan, 1967). In 1968 and especially in the 1970 New Communities Act the federal government provided guarantees for bonds for 13 privately developed new towns, plus some grant monies for 3 more. Hopes were high for success for these privately developed communities, in some cases partially federally subsidized. They were an innovative developer-planner response to the unplanned suburban communities that mushroomed in the United States after World War II (Popenoe, 1985a; R.L. Lindquist, as quoted in Shashaty, 1983), giving attention to aesthetic, ecological, and social concerns (Burby and Weiss, 1976). By the 1970s over 40 private new towns existed in the United States for the University of North Carolina Center for Urban and Regional Studies to survey. Many researchers, including the author (Huttman, 1975), studied them, praised their goals, and were optimistic about their future. Yet built in the economic recession period of the 1970s, these new communities ran into financial troubles (O'Mara, 1983), and the federal government did little to save them from the default, refinancing, and resale problems (Mitchell, 1985). Government policymakers (R.L. Lindquist as quoted in Shashaty, 1983; U.S. Department of Housing and Urban Development [HUD], 1983) and some academic researchers proclaimed the new-town solution unworkable, a failure, and by the late 1970s these professionals seldom focused on this housing and planning concept (as the lack of research journal articles indicated).

Yet these American new towns and their European predecessors have not disappeared from the scene (Potter, 1982; Underhill, 1983) and in many cases have prospered, as Fava (1987) and Grubisich and McCandless (1985) show for Reston, Virginia, 20 years after its opening, and as Wireman (1978) does for Columbia, Maryland. Others, such as Irvine, California, and Foster City, California, while having housing affordability and other problems (Baldassare, 1986; Hill, 1980; Huttman, 1985a) are becoming lively large developments. Woodlands, Texas, in the early 1980s was the model of a fast-growing successful new town until the oil recession hit Texas.

In northern Europe new towns are now long-established parts of the urban scene (Donnison and Ungerson, 1982). The Mark I British new towns around London, such as Stevenage, are thriving, often engulfed by surrounding suburbs, while the disastrous economic situation in the north of Britain has decreased employment opportunities in both Mark I and Mark II towns, and government fiscal austerity has decreased subsidies (Forrest and Murie, 1987) and stimulated selling of government-owned industrial plants, land, and office building. In Sweden the traditional-architecture early postwar new towns, such as Vällingby, with their small units, are in high demand, while the later new towns, more distant from Stockholm, with their poorer-quality, high-density buildings, are unpopular and have high immigrant populations (Huttman, 1978, 1985a). In the Netherlands the new towns' success is also mixed. The early new town, Emmeloord, on the north polder and the very new Almere, within easy reach of Amsterdam, are prospering (see note), but Lelystad, more remote, lacking a railroad line until recently, without sufficient businesses, and being heavily occupied by welfare recipients, and the Bijlmer development near Amsterdam (Van Kempen, 1985) suffer from unappealing architecture of the high-density buildings and from having a heavy representation of immigrant families. Government policy is to keep subsidizing housing (Priemus, 1985; Van Weesep, 1982).

Some experts are still enthusiastic about new towns as the wave of the future, better solutions than the unplanned piecemeal suburbs. As Shostak (1975) has exclaimed, they will be needed as solutions to our urban chaos and to provide social mix: "Almost alone they [the new towns] present housed, cheek by jowl, the social class, life-style, and interracial types that stuffy 'know-nothings' have long insisted cannot be harmoniously mingled." As R. L. Allen, a new community planner (Soul City, North Carolina) adds, they are a valid concept, an alternative to sprawl, and they have important regional impact; Soul City has provided a water system that has made industrial expansion possible in the three-county area (Allen quoted in Shashaty, 1983).

HISTORY OF NEW TOWNS

In Britain the Garden Cities movement was spearheaded by Ebenezer Howard and F. J. Osborn (see Osborn and Whittich, 1963) and put into effect by the developing of such cities as Letchworth (1903) and Welwyn (1919). It became an internationally acclaimed planning approach, which soon took hold in the United States. Such privately developed new towns as Radburn, New Jersey (1928) were constructed under this impetus as well as the Greenbelt towns built under the New Deal monies in Maryland, Ohio, and Wisconsin in the 1930s and the 25 developments funded by Congress in 1918. They became familiar to planners through the extensive literature on them. In addition, special-purpose planned cities were developed, such as the World War II and postwar cities of science, Los Alamos, New Mexico, and Oak Ridge, Tennessee.

It was after the war that northern European countries turned to new towns as one of the solutions to their serious housing needs. New-town housing generated a special appeal in Britain, where the existing stock of housing was inadequate in both supply and quality. The shortage of housing was critical; the alternatives to planned communities were increased congestion of existing urban areas, random expansion, suburban sprawl, speculative inflation of land values, and maldistribution of resources. Planned communities offered prospects for stimulating growth through the provision of housing for workers and the achievement of transfer and site location efficiencies, and by supplying modern physical plants for firms that had been destroyed in the war.

Government policy in Britain was that new towns were to be self-contained, with people working and living there, and were to have a socially balanced population. In the early days most of the housing was rental units owned by the new town's corporation, though some clusters of executive housing were built. After 1966 half was to be owner-occupied. In the 1980s the Thatcher government started selling off the rental units (Forrest and Murie, 1987).

Many of the postwar new-town sites—for example, Stevenage, Crawley, and

Harlow—were in the vicinity of London, and it was widely assumed in the early postwar days that the process of housing London's overspill population in them would facilitate social balance. This was not achieved to the extent envisioned (as described later), and eventually the goal of meeting new industry job needs was substituted for that of providing housing for the city poor. Relocation of industry to new towns was encouraged. Official policy promoted the establishment of new towns in economically stagnant areas to stimulate growth, though there were also London-area new towns to stop urban sprawl.

Some Dutch new towns were established to divert population growth from already-overpopulated Amsterdam to the southeastern polder, reclaimed land of Holland's IJsselmeer near Amsterdam, to avoid further urban sprawl. The national government was the developer of two major new towns, Lelystad, founded in 1967, and Almere, the southern polder town developed in the 1980s closer to Amsterdam, with a large projected population. Another Dutch new town, Emmeloord, was developed earlier on the northern polder, and major large-scale housing developments such as Bijlmer were built by the government adjacent to Amsterdam. While they are not entirely self-contained, they do include industry, office, shopping, and residential areas.

Around Stockholm such developments, not self-contained, with commuters to the city, but otherwise representing a new town, have been constructed in several waves by the national government. The same has happened around Paris, Bordeaux, Marseille, and other French cities (Tullen, 1983).

In the United States, in contrast, private developers in the postwar period, aware of the European developments and the U.S. prewar Greenbelt cities, and seeing the appeal of planned versus unplanned large developments, moved into this activity with massive private financing. These merchant builders, such as Bob Simon and Jim Rouse, developed mammoth plans with a number of villages within the town, industrial areas, recreational areas, and a complete infrastructure of service buildings. For example, Jonathan, developed by a Minnesota merchant builder in the 1970s, was planned to have half a dozen villages and an industrial area on 8,142 acres. As Huttman found in her three-year study, within the only village ever developed in Jonathan (due to financial problems), there are seven neighborhoods, one having Section 236 housing and another Section 235 housing, a village center, a large man-made lake with a beach house, bike paths, a theater, and stables. Several miles away there is a large industrial park (Huttman, 1975).

In the 1960s and 1970s HUD tried to spur the development of these large new communities, first through the vehicles of the 1966 Demonstration Cities and Metropolitan Development Act, then through Title IV of the 1969 Housing and Urban Development Act, and most importantly through Title VII of the 1970 Urban Growth and New Communities Development Act, which created the New Communities Development Corporation (NCDC) and authorized it to guarantee taxable bonds by developers of new towns (usually up to $50 million), make grants, and give housing and other assistance necessary for the orderly devel-

Table 24.1
Subsidized New Communities in the United States, December 31, 1982

	Initially Planned Population at Buildout in 7 to 30 years	Present Population	Commercial/ Industrial Space (in square feet)
Cedar Riverside, MN[1]	30,000	3,100	50,000
Flower Mound, TX	65,000	2,300	15,000
Gananda, NY	56,000	700	63,000
Harbison, SC	23,000	2,500	97,000
Jonathan, MN	50,000	3,125	1,220,000
Maumelle, AR	45,000	2,490	960,550
Newfields, OH[2]	32,000	232	9,000
Park Central, TX	12,000	3,000	597,000
Park Forest South, IL	110,000	6,300	1,020,000
Radisson, NY	18,000	3,500	1,355,000
Riverton, NY	26,000	1,200	8,000
Roosevelt Island, NY	18,000	5,500	40,000
Shenandoah, GA	70,000	750	2,800,000
Soul City, NC	30,000	180	73,000
St. Charles, MD	70,000	16,700	504,000
The Woodlands, TX	160,000	16,000	2,900,000

[1]A new-town-in-town in Minneapolis, Minnesota.
[2]Now called Sycamore Woods.
Source: New Communities Development Corporation, 1983.

opment of well-planned, diversified, and economically sound new communities, including major additions to existing communities, in a manner that would rely to the maximum extent on private enterprise.

Ultimately, 13 new communities were designated to receive loan guarantees by the federal government, guarantees that were intended as front money to help the developments through the extensive, costly period of purchasing land, building infrastructure, shopping and other commercial establishments, and housing, and attracting business, industry, and residents. Three additional communities received direct financial help only (without guarantees) (See Table 24.1).

However, this federal money was not enough to hold off the financial problems these developers experienced in the economic recession period of 1973–75, just when they needed buyers and investors (McGuire, 1975). Nine of the new communities defaulted on their guaranteed debentures, and the NCDC foreclosed and acquired their assets and liquidated them. Three others (Harbison, Maumelle, and St. Charles) had trouble meeting their debt-service obligations but worked out financial arrangements to avoid foreclosure, and as of the mid-1980s were considered somewhat successful and even growing. With three others HUD terminated its relationship but not financial guarantees. Woodlands, Texas, until the oil recession crisis, was considered the most financially stable and a growth town. Of the nonsubsidized new towns (HUD did not take on any new ones after 1975 and closed the NCDC in 1983), many have been sold to large corporations, for example, Reston to Gulf (Shashaty, 1983).

In the 1980s the federal government has eliminated provisions for almost all subsidized housing and is less interested in racially integrated housing, taking a less aggressive stance in interpreting and enforcing civil rights legislation; this has made the financial and social balance situation even worse in new towns (Struyk, Mayer and Tucillo, 1983; Hays, 1985). This cutoff of government support makes it hard to judge the potential for success of new towns. As Fava (1985:22) states, "Because the scenario for federally assisted new communities was never 'played out' it is impossible to assess how they might have achieved one of their goals—the diversity of residential population." Nevertheless, we must try to assess how well new towns meet their goals, for their worth is in fulfilling these objectives for a better physical environment, as seen by Ebenezer Howard, F. J. Osborn, and many planners.

MAJOR OBJECTIVES OF NEW TOWNS

Definition

The definition of what an American new town is, or should be, is not clear. As Alonso and McGuire (1972: 74) have said:

A modal definition would have it housing somewhere between 30,000 and 100,000 inhabitants, containing shopping and employment commensurate with this population. It should be a recognizable focus of urbanization, somewhat separated or distinct from other urbanized areas. Its development should be rapid, following a well-defined general plan, which should preferably embody such design features as a hierarchical sub-delineation of neighborhoods and villages, separation of vehicle from pedestrian traffic, and ample provision of green spaces and other amenities. It should be socially integrated in terms of class, race, and age.

They add that what is called a new town can cover a surprising range; because the concept is fashionable, many developers and planners have tried to attach the label to rather ordinary large subdivisions, and urban renewal projects have often laid claim to the title. Even HUD includes categories not thought of as conventional new towns in Europe because they are not separate entities, such as "new-towns-in-town."

The conventional view of a new town is of a development having a careful and often prize-winning physically planned character with a high level of urban design, respect for the environment, and access to nature and a sense of community and social balance. Unlike their European counterparts, these new communities have not been developed by a national government (although some received up-front federal subsidies and included subsidized housing). However, unlike most American suburban towns, new towns are formed by a single developer following a master plan; his development organization comprehends the town as a system, and in contrast to the many different builders in the normal suburb, he can make decisions and optimize for the whole system (Alonso and McGuire, 1972).

A Planned Community as a Goal

As indicated, the main goal among many has been to have a large well-designed physically planned community, with thought given to the most appropriate layout for neighborhoods, shopping areas, recreational facilities (Marans, 1971), roadways, and even bike paths to avoid use of the car (or Radburn plans to best place these roads). Fava (1987), describing Reston, says that "the Residential Planned Community zoning passed by Fairfax County for Reston in 1962 enabled Reston to have very innovative planning that preserved the natural environment and mixed a wide variety of residential types with business, industry, shopping, schools, and outdoor recreational and leisure facilities." She adds that the architecture was very attractive, with many units winning awards, and this helped the total effect—that of the smallest details considered and planned for in Reston. This has made the new town a place of striking beauty, one with many amenities. Another example of good environmental design is Jonathan, a planned community where emphasis was put on natural outdoor living and a related life-style. It has rolling hills, tree-covered slopes, and a great deal of open space, and the village is designed to be a walking community.

In European new towns a major consideration has been the attractiveness of the town itself. Like British new towns, the Dutch new town Lelystad has a large and bustling central mall for pedestrians, with shops, dining establishments, and professional offices; other features include a spacious town park, a community center, an indoor recreational hall, youth centers easily accessible by pedestrian and cyclist paths, and pleasant-looking separate industrial parks. The imaginative planning of the total environment in Lelystad, like that for all European new towns, has been made possible by the role of government as sole landowner at the outset of the project (Huttman, 1969, 1978; Netherlands Polder Development Authority, 1970).

Goal of Self-Containment and Employment Opportunities

In addition to planned development, a goal stressed for British new towns was self-containment and provision of employment opportunities. In the American 1970 Urban Growth and New Communities Development Act this was also mentioned, but less stress has been put on it, as is also true for the Swedish and French new towns.

The major purpose in establishing new towns is to avoid urban sprawl. To British planners, the solution was freestanding cities located away from major established urban centers, with the entirety of local jobs matched to the talents of the resident work force; this could ideally mean that the population would not travel elsewhere to work, and local jobs would be reserved for residents.

Positions in a new town must be matched with needed skills. Although in Britain workers initially were required to arrange for local jobs to secure housing, as new towns grew older, some residents shifted to employment in nearby cities. As the children of residents entered the labor force, they continued to live with their families or even obtained housing of their own in the new town while commuting to jobs. This meant that many new towns in Britain were far from self-contained in reality (Grieco, 1985; Huttman and Huttman, 1974), although in the early 1970s Stevenage had only about 15 percent commuting out.

The experience of British new towns indicates the difficulties encountered in perpetuating self-containment as the community matures and economic changes occur. Some new towns' industries in the United Kingdom turned out to be less stable than originally conceived, placing jobs in jeopardy. Walter Bor (1965) president of the Town Planning Institute, has questioned the feasibility of perpetuating the self-containment of new towns and has argued for a broader interpretation of new-town functions in a regional context. He says concerning British new towns:

Over the years it had come to be realized that the tidy pattern of complete equilibrium [between jobs and homes] could not be achieved. Human beings made their own decisions and did not always do what the planners arranged for them. Some change was taking place in that, whereas our new towns had been tied to particular existing towns by over-spill agreements, we were reaching a more open-ended situation where we were less in control of where people lived and worked. Not everybody who moved to a new town necessarily both lived and worked there. The proportion who did not do so might be about 15 per cent. There was a change from the old idea of new towns as being inwardly-looking self-contained units, satellites of parent cities; we now regard them as parts of the whole complex of a region. (73–74)

For the United States, the goal of jobs and residence in the same town has been espoused by some developers, such as Bob Simon for Reston, and to some degree by the government. This has only been achieved to a fair degree in Reston (42 percent working and living there), Columbia, Woodlands, and other cities that have become regional centers, including centers for shopping activities. Irvine in California has also become such a center and in addition has benefited from the existence of a major branch of the University of California located there. This does not mean that types of jobs and residents always synchronize. In the American successful towns people now commute in to work; in the unsuccessful ones many commute out (as was the case in the early days of the successful new towns, when firms were just starting to establish there and service opportunities were limited due to population size. This is true, for example, in the unsuccessful Jonathan new town; in addition, many workers in the Jonathan firms live in rural areas or in the town where the firms were previously located. Only about one-fifth of Jonathan's residents lived and worked in Jonathan in the mid-1970s. In American new towns this is considered acceptable. In Foster City, California, while employment opportunities are increasing as more business comes in and the service sector expands, many commute out, especially to employment associated with the nearby San Francisco International Airport.

Size, of course, can influence the amount of employment and the types of jobs, with larger communities offering jobs for unskilled and semiskilled workers in the expanding service sector. There has always been a debate over size of new towns in Britain, with the early Mark I new towns limited in the 1970s to 60,000 to encourage intimate relations and a sense of belonging and local community, to avoid transportation congestion, and to fit in with the infrastructure provided. By the late 1960s British planners decided that larger new towns were more advantageous (150,000 for Milton Keynes and other Mark II towns). In the Netherlands Lelystad and later Almere on the Flevoland polder were envisioned as growing to 150,000–200,000 (see note). But Lelystad, like the Welsh new towns and some French ones (Tullen, 1983), has had slower growth. American new towns have also usually been planned for large populations, but many have failed to attract residents or industry due to poor location (Shashaty, 1983), for example, Jonathan, which is not in the area of major suburban outward growth around Minneapolis (Copperman, 1987) (see Table 24.1).

In European new towns the national government, as developer of these planned communities, has seen fit to induce industry to come in with incentives or to place its own activities in the new towns. In Britain development corporations have had the authority to build factories for rental or sale to industries contemplating location in the new towns, especially in developing areas, and to lease office space to provide headquarters and administrative facilities for newly located firms. These are now being offered for sale, as is rental housing (Forrest and Murie, 1987; Hamnett, 1987).

In the Netherlands encouragement to industry and service firms to settle in new towns such as Lelystad has taken several forms, including reduction in rents during early years for shops and money incentives to industry, such as per worker payments. Another inducement was housing, generally still in short supply in the Netherlands in the 1970s. Further incentives have included low land costs as compared to costs elsewhere in the Netherlands and the availability of an industrial hall where firms can rent floor space. The Dutch government also brought in its own activities. For Lelystad, located along the seaward side of the polder, initial sources of employment were the power plant for the polder and various government services, such as the polder's development authority and a government scientific animal research clinic. These were all moved to Lelystad to increase the town's residential and work opportunities. The same is happening in Almere. In British new towns the national government brought in many different activities, such as the internal revenue service in East Kilbride and the national university correspondence program (open university) in Milton Keynes (Huttman and Huttman, 1973).

In the United States in some new towns some government activities also have moved in, for a variety of reasons. These include the U.S. Geological Survey in Reston, Howard Community College in Columbia, and a branch of the University of California in Irvine.

Goal of Innovative Social Services

The promotional literature of new towns stressed innovative measures in social services. This is a sharp deviation from the approach of the typical residential developer, who seeks no such relationship with the prospective homeowners (McGuire, 1975). Such innovations as day care, health care, transportation, adult education programs, and cultural enrichment programs were promoted in the new town by the development corporation.

In Jonathan the developer provided a youth center, a social activities center with university lectures and monthly socials for newcomers, a theater, and an art center. Reston and Columbia have a variety of services, including for children, a theater, movie houses, and many recreational facilities. Keller (1981) describes services in her New Jersey PUD. The new-town developer and later community groups have to produce an environment that is responsive to crucial social concerns, and herein lies one strength of the new town. In Columbia the village board was a sounding board for concerns from different parts of the community, bringing together residents of different classes and social backgrounds (Wireman, 1978). This also helped the goal of community spirit.

Goal of Community Spirit and Feeling of Belonging

Early British new-town proponents such as Erin Bevin saw the new town as a village where the squire lived next to the poor man; he talked of new towns being an equalitarian setting to lead the way to breaking down British class lines. There was to be a "gemeinschaft" relationship. In the United States some new-town developers, such as James Rouse, carried on the idea in such new towns as Columbia, Maryland.

Goal of Social Balance and Resident Diversity

The goal of social balance is potentially viable within the new-town environment. Social balance implies that the new town contains a cross section of society encompassing diversity of income, occupation, social status, age, education, religion, race, and ethnic groups. Social balance is advocated by planners who believe that a heterogeneous population strengthens the prospect for alleviating social tension. The new town offers opportunities for social integration frequently lacking in deteriorating urban areas (Ahlbrandt, 1984). Grisson (1971) points out that one reason for considering the "balanced community concept" is that new jobs are being created primarily in the suburbs and new towns, while the chronically unemployed and underemployed population is increasingly concentrated in the inner city. This separation makes it more and more difficult for the poor and members of minority groups to achieve full employment in decent jobs. He adds that if there were more housing for the poor in the suburbs or new towns, they could be nearer job opportunities. Grisson also points out that for the United States, balanced communities should mean a decrease in the number of segregated schools.

Grisson (1971: 2) gives a third reason for balanced communities.

Perhaps most important, the "balanced community" concept explicitly seeks to achieve a single nation rather than accepting the present movement toward a split society. The development of this concept would enable us to at least begin reversing the profoundly divisive trend already so evident in our metropolitan areas. "Balanced communities" should provide the opportunity for real housing choices to all citizens regardless of racial, ethnic or socio-economic status. Such communities would enable families to establish their homes on the basis of job location, commercial and recreational facilities, space needs, and general convenience rather than being narrowly restricted because of race and economic level.

In Britain balance has been espoused as a major goal of British new towns, with diversity of residents considered an essential ingredient by the postwar Labour governments supporting new towns. Efforts to include the very poor, to train them for new-town jobs, and to give them low-cost housing were continually pushed by Labourites. However, because the degree of social balance realized in the new town is to a large degree determined by labor force requirements of the types of firms attracted, this goal was hard to meet. In Britain employment opportunities were limited for less skilled, low-income workers, especially since most newly located firms were capital-intensive. Economic growth considerations resulted in higher priority being accorded to technological sophistication of new industry than to having a wide occupational distribution.

In the Swedish and Dutch new towns social balance was not a major goal, though some like Grunfeld (1985) of the Netherlands espoused it. Unsuccessful new towns have had sizable immigrant populations (Swedish outer-area towns, Bijlmer in the Netherlands) or welfare populations (Lelystad) (Van Kempen, 1985; Huttman, 1978, 1985a); successful ones, such as Vällingby and other older Swedish towns and the new developing Almere in the Netherlands, have had mainly skilled workers, technicians, and managerial personnel.

In America the concept of social balance, the utopian idea of mix of income and racial/ethnic groups, has been discussed by a number of sociologists, such as Gans in his article on the "Balanced Community" (1961) and Keller in her article on "Social Class in Physical Planning" (1966). American new communities have been seen as offering possibilities to experiment with new approaches to housing for low- and moderate-income households; they should demonstrate how families and individuals of a wide variety of incomes and ethnic attributes can live together. Some view new towns as the potential demonstration ground to show that exclusionary housing is not the mode for the future. As Burby and Weiss (1976) reported in their book on the major new-town research study by the University of North Carolina, "One of the most persistent elements of the new community concept has been the belief that new communities, as microcosms of larger cities, will promote social diversity—including class and racial integration." Lansing, Marans, and Zehner (1970) also mention this goal. Some new-town developers, such as Bob Simon of Reston, James Rouse of Columbia, and the Jonathan developers, set themselves the goal of diversity, and the federal new-town legislation supported it.

Federal Role in the Policy of Social Balance

American legislators in the Urban Growth and New Communities Development Act of 1970 stressed the need for these communities to have a diversity of social class and ethnic groups. As Fava (1976: 208) pointed out:

The Congressional hearings on the 1968 housing bill and such organizationally-sponsored presentations as the book *The New City* make it clear that many groups would not support the expenditure of public funds if New Towns did not achieve balance and diversity. The key fact disturbing many individuals and groups is the momentum toward "two societies" represented in the residential segregation of whites and blacks in metropolitan areas.

Summarizing the views of the late 1960s and early 1970s, she noted that "although not all proponents of New Towns believed such communities could substantially alter the residential separation of racial groups in American society, all organized New Town support holds that New Towns themselves should be racially open and balanced" (see also Perloff, 1973; Alonso, 1973).

The integration goal was reflected in the guidelines for rendering financial assistance to "new communities" under Title IV of the 1968 Housing Act (Fava, 1974, 1976). The general criteria for new communities stated that they "must be designed for the fullest possible range of people and families of different compositions and incomes and must be open to all members of all national, ethnic, and racial groups." The specific criteria stated in the Federal Register of April 23, 1970, included the requirements that a new community must contain a variety of housing types for "all incomes, ages and family composition, including a substantial amount for people of low and moderate income," and further required the "location and distribution of housing types and price ranges so as to prevent segregation and afford full access to facilities, and participation in activities, of the community and neighborhood by groups, families, and individuals of different economic, social, and racial background."

These racial themes were reiterated in Title VII of the 1970 Housing Act. The HUD guidelines stated that the racial composition of the new community should represent that of the general population.

Another pressure on the new-town developers came from numerous regional "fair share" or housing-allocation schemes that called for dispersal of low- and moderate-income families into suburban areas (McGuire, 1975). Relocation of federal facilities also provided stimulus for the provision of moderate-income housing. Executive Order 11,512 required that the sites for federal installations have an adequate supply of decent and nonsegregated housing within the area of expected residency and within price ranges affordable by an agency's employees. Burby and Weiss (1976) reported that when the U.S. Geological Survey announced its proposed relocation to Reston, the Washington Metropolitan Housing Authority and the Housing Opportunities Council brought a class-action suit against the General Services Administration (GSA) and Gulf-Reston for noncompliance with this order. The suit resulted in an agreement by Gulf-Reston to provide 688 more subsidized housing units in the community. HUD continually monitored new communities receiving loans under Title VII of the 1970 act. It tried to pressure Park Forest, Illinois, and some other towns to build more subsidized housing. These pressures meant that the new-town developer had to find an optimal housing-mix solution that would satisfy HUD and advocates of low- and moderate-income housing and still be consistent with profit-maximizing criteria (McGuire, 1975).

The availability of subsidized housing funds and the initiative to get them is a major factor in providing low- and moderate-income housing (University of North Carolina, 1974). HUD wanted one-fifth of the housing units in new towns to be subsidized housing. Jonathan was one of the very few that had that much. Another was Woodlands, where over 1,000 units of low-income housing were built out of a total (1983) of 6,597 housing units, though few of these were occupied by minorities, since the population was only 5 percent minority (Shashaty, 1983).

With the present decrease in federal subsidies and other support for low- and moderate-income housing (Hays, 1985; Hartman, 1986), only very small amounts of housing for these groups can be added to the existing stock, meaning few low-income households, as Alonso (1973) long ago predicted. Federal programs for realistic job training and welfare restructuring are also important as are encouragement of firms providing jobs for semiskilled workers and efforts to expand the town so that there will be service jobs (Fava, 1987). Bringing in minorities, including those of the middle class, is related not only to government pressure for nonsegregated housing but to the attitude of the private new-town developer and ultimately to the attitudes of residents.

Attitude of the Private New-Town Developer

In the United States the initiator of the social balance, above all, is the developer of the private new town. In Jonathan the new-town corporation put Section 236 rental housing for low- and moderate-income families and Section 235 low-income homeownership housing in its first village, a total of 153 units (1975). Reston, Virginia, also included low-income housing units, but Fava's review of the situation in 1985 on the occasion of Reston's 20th anniversary shows that Reston can no longer add subsidized units because federal funds are no longer available. Even middle-income groups are being priced out of the Reston housing market because Reston has become the "victim of its own success'' at being a beautifully planned community and in attracting jobs (Fava, 1987). The jobs have been concentrated in high-tech firms and offices because with the completion of the Dulles access road Reston is only minutes away from the airport. Incoming executives and professionals have driven up the price of housing.

Fava also raises the question of whether current Restonians are as committed to economic and racial integration as the early Restonians. Robert Simon, the original developer of Reston, made diversity of various kinds—housing types, age groups, economic levels, races—a cornerstone of his plan. Current management, although saying that it is committed to carrying out Simon's original goals, focuses on amenities for leisure and "the good life" in its advertising, rarely, if ever, mentioning racial minorities or low-income groups (Fava, 1987). Using census data, Fava concludes that Reston has more economic and racial diversity than suburban Fairfax County, in which it is located, but far less than its metropolitan area, Washington, D.C. (Urban Land Institute, 1976). She finds that economic and racial integration are well established in Reston as a result of early policies, but that only upper middle-income blacks and whites can afford to move there now (Fava, 1987). Lenore Blackwell confirms this, stating, as head of the local chapter of the National Association for the Advancement of Colored People and an 11-year Reston resident, that there is little overt racism and no "racial steering" (Witherspoon, 1984). This may support the early opinion, based on Foster City new-town research, that class is more important than race for residential acceptance (Werthman, Mandel, and Diensfrey, 1965).

Limits to Social Mix

Social balance or mix can be in terms of mix in the whole town but not on the block. A number of writers, including Gans, feel that at the same time that people have a positive attitude to mix on a community level, they want homogeneous blocks and neighborhoods. In other words, there are limits to diversity. Gans, one of the advisors to James Rouse on the development of Columbia, Maryland, has pointed out:

Conflict between neighbors is ever present, and since they are spatially tied to each other, it must be minimized . . . much conflict is based on class differences. Block homogeneity is necessary; putting well-educated with poorly educated people or working-class with upper-middle class people creates such conflicts. One cannot segregate by education or by child-rearing values, so price, which reflects income, is the only form of leverage. Mixing rich with poor puts terrible pressures on the latter to keep up, especially since children make demands they learn on the block . . .

The more homogeneous the block, the greater the opportunity for heterogeneity in the neighborhood and in community institutions, although even here, social stratification will develop . . . Higher-priced houses probably need their own neighborhood, both because of property-value considerations and because their purchasers are buying status and must be socially and physically separate from lower-priced houses. (1961: 48)

Fava comments on this: "In effect, Gans was proposing for Columbia a method for achieving some heterogeneity while maintaining economic and social viability within the widespread American pattern of homogeneity. This kind of advice has apparently been heeded" (1976: 208). As with most American new towns, in Jonathan mix has not existed at the neighborhood level; there are specific Section 236 and Section 235 neighborhoods, and most other neighborhoods have one house type and a narrow range of prices for housing. This neighborhood homogeneity is a pattern planners have felt most suitable even in Britain, as Heraud points out:

The concept of social balance was never spelt out in detail by planners, but it was hoped that New Towns would recruit inhabitants from all social classes. Each town would be divided into neighborhoods, self-sufficient for day-to-day needs. Most plans stopped short of actual cheek-by-jowl mixing of different types of housing. They put together similar dwellings in groups of 100 to 300 families. Actual social mixing in the neighborhoods was to be based more on certain facilities. (1968)

In some new towns, however, such as Lelystad in Holland and in Jonathan, the upper-income housing is put in several small areas, rather than segregated in one area; and in some, such as Jonathan, some scattering of low-income housing is likewise done.

Neighborhood Location

If one is going to have homogeneous neighborhoods, to facilitate community mixing, one must carefully plan location of these neighborhoods. In Jonathan one area of subsidized housing was isolated on one fringe of the village, and the other was on another fringe, not as isolated, but placed next to the highest-priced housing neighborhood, with very few children. Not surprisingly, when residents of subsidized housing in Jonathan were asked about changes to improve arrangement of housing, 37 percent called for more diversity and mixing in the location of subsidized homes (See Fuller interviews in Huttman, 1975). Fava (1987) reports that Reston's internal location or structure has shown some socioeconomic, racial, and life-style separation. The Dulles access road divides Reston into the two Restons—the wealthier portion south of the Road and the portion north of the Road, which is less affluent. Fava (1985: 6) notes that "there are seven villages in Reston and each contains a range of expensive single-family homes, townhouses and, sometimes, rental apartments. There is no residential racial segregation in Reston, except for that associated with the location of two low-income subsidized housing apartment complexes in the same section of Reston."

Evidence of Contact between Diverse Residents

Some researchers have pointed out that social balancing in new towns or physical placement of diverse social groups adjacent to each other on the assumption that they will mix may show too naive a faith in physical determinism, too much a visionary hope that "by putting people together . . . they will interact socially" (Fava, 1976: 230; see also Gans, 1973; 1982; Perloff, 1973; Gruen and Gruen: 1973). Studies of social interaction give us some indication of the actual situation.

In class-bound Britain Heraud's opinion (1968: 47) for the new towns was that "the hoped-for intermingling of classes in their home neighborhood remains a dream." For American new towns, scholars feel that there is some degree of class mixing. As Smookler (1976: 121) says: "The results show that economic integration is feasible, both politically and economically, and that it is beneficial for low income families." She adds that this "feasibility of socio-economic integration is firmly established." Evidence of contact between residents of subsidized housing and other residents in new towns is given by Burby and Weiss (1976) in their main report on the University of North Carolina data. Reporting on their samples in five new towns with subsidized housing, they say of these residents and their degree of social integration into the community:

Occasional concern has been expressed that lower income residents living in the midst of affluent, high social status communities may achieve the benefits of superior community facilities and services funded by their more affluent neighbors, at the cost of extreme social isolation. However, subsidized housing residents living in new communities did not appear to be at all isolated . . . also did not see their higher income neighbors as hostile. Over 80 per cent reported that "it was easy to make new friends in the community."

Finally, there was only a 7 percent difference between new-community subsidized-housing residents (49 percent) and nonsubsidized-housing residents (56 percent) who felt a part of what went on in their communities (See also Blum and Kingston, 1984).

Data on class interaction in Jonathan show a generally positive situation of mixing in a setting where one-fifth of the community population (1975) was moderate income and where these moderate-income people were in segregated subsidized-housing neighborhoods within the community. Certain characteristics of these moderate-income households (in Section 235 and Section 236 housing) were probably conductive to mixing, such as the fact that they were of the same racial group and age bracket as most other residents, were upwardly mobile, and, above all, had middle-class life-styles and recreational interests, causing social mixing (see Catton, 1972). Residents of the subsidized housing also had a fairly high level of education, were usually in the work force, and had incomes that were not that far below incomes of many non-subsidized-housing residents. On the other hand, some of their characteristics were less conducive to mixing: these families had a large number of young children, while private renters often had none, and in the Section 236 housing area there were a number of female-headed households. The mixing was mainly between those in subsidized housing and higher-income private homeowners, while the young renters in the unsubsidized units had a low level of participation in all activities.

Evidence of actual mixing between these moderate-income households in subsidized housing and the rest of the population was provided by an analysis of membership lists of many adult and children's organizations (Huttman, 1975). In the 30 adult organization lists analyzed, most showed fair to medium representation of moderate-income households. They made up two-fifths of the Jonathan Community Church membership, one-fifth of the Interim Players and of the activities committee of the Jonathan Association, and a large proportion of the couples softball players and the Teen Center supervisors. Evidence from the survey of residents also proved that subsidized-housing residents' organizational participation was high, one-fourth to one-fifth in some groups and one-tenth in many others. Fuller's data (1974) also showed high participation for Section 236 subsidized-rental residents and informal visiting across socioeconomic neighborhoods, with 40 percent of these residents visiting friends in privately owned housing. In Jonathan, Huttman's analysis of lists of participants in children's organizations showed even more of a mixing of children in subsidized and nonsubsidized housing. One-third of the popular ice hockey team members and the summer archery group, one-fifth of those in the swimming program, and two-thirds of the Teen Center participants were children from subsidized housing. In subsidized-housing households with children, one-third of the children were in three or more organizations.

Interaction and integration of black residents in five subsidized new towns covered by the University of North Carolina were also positive:

A significantly higher proportion of black respondents than nonblack respondents (63 per cent versus 52 per cent) said they felt a part of what went on in their communities. Three fourths of respondents reported that it was no harder to call on their neighbors in time of need than in their former communities. For all of these measures—calling on neighbors, making new friends, and feeling a part of the community—new community black residents indicated a higher degree of social integration than the black residents of the two suburban conventional communities. (Burby and Weiss, 1976)

In Columbia being from a racial minority or a subsidized-housing neighborhood did not limit one's participation in the always-shifting community alliances (Burkhart, 1981). Wireman (1982) found participation by racial minorities in the Columbia Village; in Reston black leaders were vocal participants in community issues related to the black population. However, for Columbia and for Reston, more intimate interaction between racial groups was found to be less likely by Wireman (1978) than by Burby and Weiss (1976). Interaction was limited more to community organizations. (On general barriers to integration, see Farley, Bianchi, and Colasanto, 1979; Gelber, 1985.)

CONCLUSION

American new towns have been successful in many cases as examples of outstanding planning. They have proved highly satisfactory to their residents (Hillman, 1975; Burby and Weiss, 1976). Some, such as Woodlands, Jonathan, Reston, and Columbia, have had a considerable mix of income groups due to existence of subsidized housing, and some, such as Reston and Columbia, have had a significant representation of minority groups. Many, unfortunately, have had neither low-income nor minority representation to any degree.

Few have been self-contained, but most have been distinct entities, with some becoming regional centers, though many have stagnated (see Table 24.1 for populations). Some actually have become just part of the suburban scene, instead of a model for the future, as has also happened for some British new towns. Others have suffered from the opposite problem, not having the right location to be in the path of urban growth (Copperman, 1987, on Jonathan; Lindquist, in Shashaty, 1983).

A major problem for any new such ventures, as new-community developers such as James Todd of Reston and Lester Gross of Harbison point out, is the difficulty of assembling so much land; of having such massive up-front costs; of promising too many up-front amenities; and, in general, of having millions of dollars of expenses before one resident arrives. Some of the present new towns were in trouble before they even got out of the planning stage, and as J. Stuart of St. Charles new town says (as quoted in Shashaty, 1983), they were hit with two major downturns in the economy, a rise in interest rates (Florida, 1986), and three real estate crises just when they were trying to get started (Baldassare, 1985). The federal government also caused trouble, but gave little help: financial support was poor, later refinancing was often not given, much red tape existed, and time periods for federal decisions on financing were long (Shashaty, 1983). Finally, some new towns suffered from poor management and bad marketing decisions ("Community Builders," 1983).

NOTE

The research by the author mentioned in this chapter included a three-year study of Jonathan new town, Minnesota, under a National Institute of Mental Health (NIMH) grant. The study included a survey of 114 residents in a stratified sample, interviews with many town leaders, and continual contact with the Jonathan Association staff, use of their statistics, and use of data on Jonathan from the University of North Carolina large study. The author has observed European new towns from 1966 to date in a three-year doctoral study of British subsidized housing, 1966–69, and revisits in 1973, 1979, and 1985; a study of Dutch new towns, especially Lelylstad in 1970 and 1971, with revisits in 1975 and 1985; and Almere in 1985 and Swedish new towns, especially Vällingby, in 1968 and 1978 and in a revisit in 1986.

Sylvia Fava has provided data from her 1985 study of Reston new town and has provided useful comments for editing this chapter.

REFERENCES

Ahlbrandt, Roger, Jr. 1984. *Neighborhoods, People, and Community*. New York: Plenum Press.

Alonso, William. 1973. "The Mirage of New Towns." *Public Interest* 19 (Spring) 13–15.

Alonso, William, and Chester McGuire. 1972. "Pluralistic New Towns." *Lex et Scientia* 9, no. 3: 74–84.

Baldassare, Mark. 1985. "The Housing Crisis in Suburbia." Paper presented at the American Sociological Association meetings, Washington, D.C., August.

———. 1986. *Trouble in Paradise*. New York: Columbia University Press.

Blum, Terry C., and Paul W. Kingston. 1984. "Homeownership and Social Attachment." *Sociological Perspectives* 27, no. 2: 159–180.

Bor, Walter. 1965. "The Changing Concept of New Town Development." *Housing Review* 20, no. 3: 72–74.

Burby, Raymond, and Shirley Weiss. 1976. *New Communities U.S.A.* Lexington, Mass.: Lexington Books.

Burkhart, Lynne. 1981. *Old Values in a New Town: The Politics of Race and Class in Columbia, Maryland*. New York: Praeger.

Catton, William, Jr. 1972. "Leisure and Social Stratification." In G. Thielbar and S. Feldman (eds.), *Issues in Social Inequality*. Boston: Little, Brown.

Choldin, Harvey. 1985. *Cities and Suburbs*. New York: McGraw-Hill.

Clapp, James. 1971. *New Towns and Urban Policy*. New York: Dunellen.

———. "Community Builders Comment on the New Communities Program." 1983. *Urban Land* 42, no. 6: 8–9.

Copperman, David. 1987. Telephone interview with author. April 15.

Donnison, David, and Clare Ungerson. 1982. *Housing Policy*. Harmondsworth: Penguin Books.

Eden, Joseph, and Arnold Alanen. 1983. "Looking Backward at a New Deal New Town: Greendale, Wisconsin, 1935–1980." *American Planning Association Journal* (Winter): 40–58.

Eichler, Edward, and Marshall Kaplan. 1967. *The Community Builders*. Berkeley and Los Angeles: University of California Press.

Farley, Reynolds, Suzanne Bianchi, and Diane Colasanto. 1979. "Barriers to the Racial Integration of Neighborhoods: The Detroit Case." *Annals of the American Academy of Political and Social Science* 441: 97–113.

Fava, Sylvia F. 1974. "Blacks in American New Towns: Problems and Prospects." *Sociological Symposium* 12: 111–135.

———. 1976 "New Towns in the United States: Some Sociological Aspects of Policies and Prospects." In J. V. Ferreira and S. S. Jha (eds.), *Essays on Urbanization in Memory of Patrick Geddes*. Bombay, India: Popular Prakashan.

———. 1985. "Building Housing and Building Community: Lessons from New Communities in the U.S." Paper presented at the International Sociological Association Ad Hoc Committee on Housing and the Built Environment conference, Amsterdam, June.

———. 1987. "Diversity in New Communities: A Case Study of Reston at Age Twenty." In Willem Van Vliet—, H. Choldin, W. Michelson, and D. Popenoe (eds.),

Housing and Neighborhoods: Theoretical and Empirical Contributions. Westport, Conn.: Greenwood Press.

Florida, R. L. 1986. "The Political Economy of Financial Deregulation and Reorganization of Housing Finance in the United States." *International Journal of Urban and Regional Research* 10, no. 2: 207–231.

Forrest, Ray, and Alan Murie. 1987. "Fiscal Reorientation, Centralization, and the Privatization of Council Housing." In Willem Van Vliet— (ed.), *Housing Markets and Policies under Fiscal Austerity.* Westport, Conn.: Greenwood Press.

Gans, Herbert. 1961. "Balanced Community." *Journal of the American Institute of Planners*, 47–61.

———. 1973. "The Possibility of Class and Racial Integration in American New Towns." In Harvey Perloff and Neil Sandberg (eds.), *New Towns: Why and for Whom?* New York: Praeger.

———. 1982. *The Levittowners: Ways of Life and Politics in a New Suburban Community.* 2d. ed. New York: Columbia University Press.

Gelber, B. S. 1985. "Race-Conscious Approaches to Ending Segregation in Housing." *Rutgers Law Review* 1: 921–960.

Grieco, M S. 1985. "Corby: New Town Planning and Imbalanced Development." *Regional Studies* 19, no. 1: 9–18.

Grisson, LeRoy. 1971. "Toward Balanced Suburbs: The San Diego Experience." Paper presented at the American Institute of Planners convention, San Diego, November.

Grubisich, Tom, and Peter McCandless. 1985. *Reston: The First Twenty Years.* Reston, Va.: Reston Publishing Company.

Gruen, Nina, and Claude Gruen. 1975. "Housing Policy and Class Integration." Paper presented at the Western Regional Science Association meeting, San Diego, February.

Grunfeld, F. 1985. "The Problem of Spatial Segregation and the Preservation of an Urban Society." In Willem Van Vliet—, Elizabeth Huttman, and Sylvia Fava (eds.), *Housing Needs and Policy Approaches: Trends in Thirteen Countries.* Durham, N.C.: Duke University Press.

Hamnett, Chris. 1987. "Conservative Government Housing Policy in Britain, 1979–1985." In Willem Van Vliet— (ed.), *Housing Markets and Policies under Fiscal Austerity.* Westport, Conn.: Greenwood Press.

Hartman, Chester. 1986. "Housing Policies under the Reagan Administration." In Rachel Bratt, Chester Hartman, and Ann Meyerson (eds.), *Critical Perspectives on Housing.* Philadelphia: Temple University Press.

Hays, R. Allen. 1985. *The Federal Government and Urban Housing.* Albany: State University of New York Press.

Heraud, B. J. 1968. "Social Class and the New Towns." *Urban Studies* (February): 33–58.

Hill, Gladwin. 1980. "Big But not Bold." *Planning* (American Planning Association) 51: 16–20.

Hillman, Arthur. 1975. "New Communities: Are Residents Satisfied?" *Sociological Focus*, April, 161–170.

Huttman, Elizabeth. 1969. "Stigma in Public Housing: Britain and the U.S." Ph.D. diss., University of California, Berkeley.

———. 1975. *Class Mix in a New Town: Jonathan.* Report to NIMH. Hayward: California State University at Hayward.

————. 1978. "Suburban and New Town Density and Transportation Fit for Different Types of Residential Populations: Observations from Sweden, Finland, Holland, Britain, and France." Unpublished paper.

————. 1985a. "Policy Approaches to Social Housing in Northern and Western Europe." In Willem Van Vliet—, Elizabeth Huttman, and Sylvia Fava (eds.), *Housing Needs and Policy Approaches: Trends in Thirteen Countries*. Durham, N.C. Duke University Press.

————. 1985b. "Transnational Housing Policy." In Irving Altman and Carol Werner (eds.), *Home Environments*. New York: Plenum Press.

Huttman, John, and Elizabeth Huttman, 1973. "Dutch and British New Towns: Self-Containment and Socio-Economic Balance." *Growth and Change*, January, 30–37.

————. 1974. "New Towns Grow Old: Reshaping of Land Use, Size, and Transportation in Maturing British and Dutch 'New Towns.' " *Sociological Symposium* 12: 131–136.

Jackson, Kenneth. 1985. *Crabgrass Frontier: The Suburbanization of the United States*. New York: Oxford University Press.

Keller, Suzanne. 1966. "Social Class in Physical Planning." *International Social Science Journal* 10: 494–522.

————. 1981. "Women and Children in a Planned Community." In Suzanne Keller (ed.), *Building for Women*. Lexington, Mass.: D. C. Heath.

Lansing, J. B., R. W. Marans, and R. B. Zehner. 1970. *Planned Residential Environments*. Ann Arbor: Institute for Social Research, University of Michigan.

McGuire, Chester. 1975. "Operational Problems of New Communities." *Journal of Sociology and Social Welfare* 10 (November): 136–140.

Marans, Robert. 1971. "Determinants of Outdoor Recreation Behavior in Planned Residential Environments." Ph.D. diss., University of Michigan.

Miller, Zane. 1981. *Suburb: Neighborhood and Community in Forest Park, Ohio, 1935–1976*. Knoxville: University of Tennessee Press.

Mitchell, J. Paul (ed.). 1985. *Federal Housing Policy and Programs, Past and Present*. New Brunswick, N.J.: Center for Urban Policy Research, Rutgers University.

Netherlands Polder Development Authority. 1970, 1973. *Flevoland: Facts and Figures*. Den Haag: Rijksdienst voor de IJsselmeerpolders.

Nicholson, J. H. 1961. *New Communities in Britain: Achievements and Problems*. London: National Council of Social Services.

O'Mara, W. P. 1983. "New Towns in the United States." *Urban Land* 42 no. 6:4–5.

Osborn, F., and A. Whittich. 1963. *The New Towns: The Answer to Megalopolis*. London: Leonard Hill.

Perloff, Harvey. 1973. "Social Aspects of New Towns." In Harvey Perloff and Neil Sandberg (eds.), *New Towns: Why and for Whom*. New York: Praeger.

Popenoe, David. 1985a. "Post-war Suburbanization and Social Control: The Role of Housing and the Built Environment." In Leon Deben and Dick van der Vaart (eds.), *International Conference on Housing Research and Policy Issues in an Era of Fiscal Austerity*. Amsterdam: Gestructurveede Samenwerking.

————. 1985b. *Private Pleasure, Public Plight: American Metropolitan Community Life in Comparative Perspective*. New Brunswick, N.J.: Transaction Books.

Potter, S. 1982. "The Last of the New Towns." *Planners News*. (London), June 7–12.

Priemus, Hugo. 1985. "Economic and Demographic Stagnation, Housing Policy, and

Housing Research: The Case of the Netherlands (1974–1984).'' Paper presented at the International Sociological Association Ad Hoc Committee on Housing and the Built Environment Conference, Amsterdam, June.

Shashaty, Andre. 1983. "HUD Terminating Its New Communities Program." *Urban Land* 42, no. 6: 2–7.

Shostak, Arthur. 1975. "New Towns and Social Welfare Prospects, 1975–2000." *Journal of Sociology and Social Welfare* November, 131–133.

Smookler, H. V. 1976. *Economic Integration in New Communities.* Cambridge, Mass.: Ballinger.

Struyk, R., N. Mayer, and J. Tuccillo. 1983. *Federal Housing Policy at President Reagan's Midterm.* Washington, D.C.: Urban Institute Press.

Tullen, J. N. 1983. "The Development of French New Towns: An Assessment of Program." *Urban Studies* 20, no. 1: 11–30.

Underhill, J. 1983. "New Communities: A Selected Bibliography, Managing, Planning, Financing, Staffing, Organizing, and Building Large Scale Developments." *ITCC Review* 12, no. 1: 28–36.

University of North Carolina. 1974. *Subsidized Housing Residents in Five New Communities and Two Suburban Control Communities.* Report no. 19. Chapel Hill: University of North Carolina Center for Urban and Regional Studies, New Community Development Project.

Urban Land Institute. 1976. *Washington, D.C. Metropolitan Area Today.* Urban Land Institute Spring Meeting Project Brochure. Washington, D.C.

U.S. Department of Housing and Urban Development. Office of Policy Development and Research. 1983. *New Communities.* Washington, D.C.: Government Printing Office.

Van Kempen, Eva. 1985. *High Rise Estates and the Concentration of Poverty: The Case of Bijlmermeer.* Paper presented at the International Sociological Association Ad Hoc Committee on Housing and the Built Environment conference, Amsterdam, June.

Van Weesep, J. 1982. *Production and Allocation of Housing: The Case of the Netherlands.* Amsterdam: Vrije Universiteit, Geografisch en Planologisch Institute.

Werthman, Carl, Jerry Mandel, and Ted Dienstfrey. 1965. *Planning and the Purchase Decision: Why People Buy in Planned Communities.*

Wireman, Peggy. 1977. "The Meanings of Community: Some Implications from New Towns." Ph.D. diss., American University. Berkeley: Institute of Urban and Regional Development, University of California.

————. 1978. "The Functions of Intimate Secondary Relationships." Paper presented at the World Congress of Sociology, Uppsala, Sweden, August 19.

Witherspoon, Roger. 1984. "Time Hedges Billion Dollar Bet at Reston." *Washington Post*, June 17, 23.

25

Prospects and Issues in U.S. Housing: A Comment

WILLEM VAN VLIET—

An analysis of the problems of and prospects for housing in the United States is an ambitious undertaking. It is fraught with formidable difficulties arising from multiple challenges facing any attempt to address all the relevant issues. Housing, as conceived of in this book, represents a diverse array of functions finding expression along different dimensions and on different levels of aggregation. A complete picture of the housing situation requires contributions from a rare combination of disciplines and professions. The diverse backgrounds of the authors in this book, including sociology, political science, economics, law, architecture, and planning, reflect this requirement. The eminence of the authors notwithstanding, a comprehensive analysis eludes even their collective endeavor in this book. The reason is simple. Almost without exception, each of the chapters constitutes a condensation of a vast body of literature covering a well-established and distinctive domain in the field. The chapters provide excellent guidance regarding the most salient aspects of these subareas. They cannot, however, provide full and detailed coverage of them within the limited space available.

It would be presumptuous to present the conclusion to this book as a review of the points treated in the earlier parts and in other work that could not be included here for lack of space. This is also not the place for a summary, based on the preceding chapters, that lays out an agenda for research and sketches prospective developments. For that purpose, readers are referred to the original chapters, which afford these points fuller discussion than would be possible here and also furnish references for greater in-depth study of the issues. Other discussions that appear elsewhere deal extensively with such aspects as economic and demographic forecasts in relation to future housing demand and supply (Manchester, 1987; Burns and Grebler, 1986) and housing finance (Kane, 1984; Florida, 1986). These, again owing to space constraints, could be given but limited attention in this volume. It is in order, however, to end this book with two observations. They are quite obvious, but they are important enough that they deserve to be reiterated and emphasized.

There is no denying that *on the average*, housing problems in the United

States have diminished since World War II. For example, housing conditions of the general population have steadily improved during this period. In 1940, 49 percent of all occupied dwellings lacked complete plumbing or needed major repairs, and 20 percent of all units were overcrowded (Lindamood and Hanna 1979: 27). In 1947, 33 percent did not have one or more designated facilities, that is electric light, running water, flush toilet, bathtub/shower, or installed cooking facilities for exclusive use of the unit's occupants (U.S. Bureau of the Census, 1950: 738). Housing analysts have repeatedly criticized national census data as measures of housing quality because of their unreliability and tendency to undercount dwelling inadequacies (Pynoos, Schafer, and Hartman, 1973: 3–4). However, there is no doubt that on the whole, physical housing conditions have greatly improved during the last several decades.

At the same time, it is evident that among certain segments of the population there remain very substantial proportions of households living in inadequate housing with defective heating systems, water leakage through holes and open cracks in ceilings, floors, and walls, vermin infestation, and over-crowded and otherwise execrable conditions. No special studies are needed to document this fact. Even a quick examination of information readily obtained from the Census of Housing and the American Housing Survey reveals significant disparities between the housing quality of different population groups. In this connection the growing problem of the homeless should also be mentioned as a sad testimony of a society that is among the world's most affluent and yet gravely lacking in commitment to its most needy citizens.

Overall, nonphysical aspects of housing quality, having to do with, for example, access to opportunities, have also improved in some ways (although they have gotten worse in other ways). Until 1950 the federal government insisted upon discriminatory practices as a prerequisite to government housing aid. The official manuals of the Federal Housing Authority (FHA) cautioned against "infiltration of inharmonious racial and national groups," "a lower class of inhabitants," or the "presence of incompatible racial elements" in new neighborhoods. Zoning was advocated as a device for exclusion, and the use was urged of a racial covenant (prepared by FHA itself) with a space left blank for the prohibited races and religions, to be filled in by the builder as occasion required. The Federal Home Loan Bank Board—the federal agency regulating savings and loans associations—urged similar practices (Abrams, 1965: 61).

Discrimination in federally assisted housing was officially outlawed in 1962. However, in spite of legislative progress (Gelber, 1985; Kmiec, 1986), residential segregation and discrimination remain real issues (Hershfield, 1985; Drinan, 1984; Palm, 1985; see also the chapter by Pearce in this book). Redlining and a variety of exclusionary zoning practices continue almost routinely with the effect of restricting the housing opportunities of large numbers of people, including blacks, persons of Hispanic origin, female-headed households, renters, and families with children (Bullard, 1984; Marans and Colten, 1985; Smith and Thomson, 1987). The housing difficulties of these groups also tend to be ex-

Table 25.1
Overall Rating of Dwelling Quality by Race and Tenure

Rating	Owners		Renters	
	all races	blacks	all races	blacks
1974:				
Excellent	43%	24%	21%	10%
Good	45	50	46	37
Fair	10	22	25	37
Poor	1	4	7	16
1983:				
Excellent	48	31	25	14
Good	42	48	47	41
Fair	8	18	23	34
Poor	1	2	5	10

Note: Totals may not add up to 100% because of nonresponse.
Source: U.S. Bureau of the Census (1974: 6, 18; 1985: E14, E54).

acerbated by affordability problems. In fact, without discounting problems of housing quality and discrimination, which still are very pressing for many Americans, it is the issue of affordability that has greatly gained in significance in the recent period, as indicated by Hartman and others in this book and as also manifested in a growing socioeconomic polarization across tenure lines.

Numerous examples could be given, but there is no need to belabor the point. The examples already given suffice to illustrate the importance of disaggregating the housing picture. In discussing housing in the United States, the first and foremost question must be: *whose* housing? Are we talking about affluent people, people near or below the poverty line, or the growing number of homeless people? About rural or urban areas? Suburbs or central cities? Owners or renters? White people or black people? Men or women? Families with children or elderly households? There are great discrepancies between measures of housing quality, accessibility, and affordability for these different groups. The situation is even more complex because households fall into more than one category and typically in such a way that they are encapsulated by an accumulation of costs *or* benefits (as in the case of single-parent households, whose housing problems are likely worst for those with more than one child and headed by an unemployed, young black woman renting an inner-city high-rise apartment).

Unevenness in objective measures of housing quality, access, and affordability for different population groups is mirrored in the subjective assessments that these groups make of their housing and neighborhood situations. Table 25.1 shows the responses of a nationwide sample of households to a question asking them to rate the overall quality of their dwelling. Clearly, blacks give their homes lower rankings than whites do, and renters are much less satisfied than are owners.

Table 25.2
Rating of Neighborhood Quality by Race and Tenure

	Owners		Renters	
Rating	all races	blacks	all races	blacks
1973:				
Excellent	42%	19%	22%	10%
Good	43	46	47	38
Fair	12	30	25	39
Poor	2	4	5	11
1983:				
Excellent	41	21	23	13
Good	46	51	50	44
Fair	11	24	22	35
Poor	1	3	4	7

Note: Totals may not add up to 100% because of nonresponse.
Source: U.S. Bureau of the Census (1975: 12, 18; 1985: E18, E58)

Moreover, while in all categories ratings went up by a little between 1974 and 1983, the relative differences between them remained rather constant. Table 25.2 indicates an identical pattern for the overall ratings of the neighborhood.

Once we have made the self-evident but important observation that questions of housing must be asked vis-à-vis *specific* population groups, the next observation concerns a set of more generic points to be borne in mind when addressing incongruities in the housing system. It is useful to stress first, that the housing system is neither static nor autonomous, but rather interdependent with other systems (for example, economic, political, cultural), all of which change as they interact with each other. A proper understanding of current housing problems requires a thorough knowledge of prevailing policies, programs, and other relevant factors as they exist at present. However, also needed, beyond an examination of contemporary manifestations, are historical analyses informed by insights into how the present situation has evolved from the dynamics within and between the various systems involved. Such analyses show that the role of given systems in effectuating a housing situation is not constantly dominant or subservient, but fluctuates over time. Furthermore, these studies also indicate that the economic, political, and cultural systems are not internally homogeneous. Rather, they are themselves characterized by divergent interests and values that shift allegiances, compete with each other, and often form cross-system coalitions in attempts to affect outcomes of the housing process, a point well illustrated by Marcuse's analysis (1986) of the beginnings of public housing in New York. Historical research would also demonstrate that the record of housing is not one of monotonic progress. Some problems are resolved, in whole or in part, others are not, and new ones emerge.

Perhaps most salient in historical inquiries would be the observation that housing questions are almost invariably located in the interstices of the public and the private realm. This is so whether one examines the design, planning, construction, financing, management, or use of housing. The appearance, layout, and structural form of dwellings are molded by zoning ordinances articulated by the local community and by building codes and other regulations stipulated by local, state, and federal governments. The location of dwellings relative to community services and facilities is similarly constrained. In the United States direct public building is negligible, but private development and construction firms operate within explicit frameworks of governmental subsidization and taxation policies. To a significant extent, the federal government has also shaped the mortgaging sector, particularly by the establishment of loan guarantees and more recently by the deregulation of housing finance. The tenure system is heavily weighted in favor of private ownership owing to legislated financial benefits not associated with rental tenure. Even domestic space is not immune to public oversight. There are, for example, regulations that limit sound levels, ban the use of wood stoves, and prescribe the types of household members permitted in a dwelling. Recent analyses of attempts at privatization of the housing system in the United States and Britain (Adams, 1986; Forrest and Murie, 1987) show that the modalities and foci of public intervention change, but reaffirm the interplay of public and private interests as a defining characteristic of housing.

REFERENCES

Abrams, C. 1965. *The City Is the Frontier*. New York: Harper & Row.

Adams, Carolyn Teich. 1986. *"The Politics of Privatization."* Paper presented at the International Research Conference on Housing Policy, June, Gävle, Sweden.

Bullard, Robert D. 1984. "The Black Family: Housing Alternatives in the 80's." *Journal of Black Studies* 14, no. 3: 341–351.

Burns, L. S., and L. Grebler. 1986. *The Future of Housing Markets: A New Appraisal*. New York: Plenum Press.

Drinan, R. F. 1984. "Untying the White Noose." *Yale Law Journal* 94, no. 2: 435–443.

Florida, R. L. 1986. "The Political Economy of Financial Deregulation and the Reorganization of Housing Finance in the United States." *International Journal of Urban and Regional Research* 10, no. 2: 207–231.

Forrest, Ray, and Alan Murie. 1987. "Fiscal Reorientation, Centralization, and the Privatization of Council Housing." In Willem van Vliet— (ed.), *Housing Markets and Policies under Fiscal Austerity*. Westport, Conn.: Greenwood Press.

Gelber, B. S. 1985. "Race-Conscious Approaches to Ending Segregation in Housing: Some Pitfalls on the Road to Integration." *Rutgers Law Review/Civil Rights Developments* 1: 921–960.

Hershfield, David C. 1985. "Attacking Housing Discrimination: Economic Power of the

Military in Desegregating Off-Base Rental Housing." *American Journal of Economics and Sociology* 44, no. 1: 23–28.

Kane, Edward J. 1984. "Change and Progress in Contemporary Mortgage Markets." *Housing Finance Review* 3, no. 3: 257–282.

Kmiec, D. W. 1986. "Exclusionary Zoning and Purposeful Racial Segregation in Housing: Two Wrongs Deserving Separate Remedies." *Urban Lawyer* 18, no. 2: 393–422.

Lindamood, S., and S. Hanna. 1979. *Housing, Society, and Consumers*. St. Paul, Minn.: West Publishing.

Manchester, T. 1987. "Inflation and Housing Demand." *Journal of Urban Economics* 21, no. 1.

Marans, Robert, and Mary Colten. 1985. "U.S. Rental Housing Policy effecting Families with Children." In Willem van Vliet—, Elizabeth Huttman, and Sylvia Fava (eds.), *Housing Needs and Policy Approaches: Trends in Thirteen Countries*. Durham, N.C.: Duke University Press.

Marcuse, P. 1986. "The Beginnings of Public Housing in New York." *Journal of Urban History* 12, no. 4: 353–390.

Palm, Risa. 1985. "Ethnic Segmentation of Real Estate Agent Practice in the Urban Housing Market." *Annals of the Association of American Geographers* 75, no. 1: 58–68.

Pynoos, J., R. Schafer, and C. W. Hartman. 1973. *Housing Urban America*. Chicago: Aldine.

Smith, R. L., and L. Thomson. 1987. "Restricted Housing Markets for Female-Headed Households in U.S. Metropolitan Areas." In Willem van Vliet—, H. Choldin, W. Michelson, and D. Popenoe (eds.), *Housing and Neighborhoods: Theoretical and Empirical Contributions*. Westport, Conn.: Greenwood Press.

U.S. Bureau of the Census. 1950. *Statistical Abstract of the United States: 1950*, 71st ed. Washington, D.C.: Government Printing Office.

———. 1975. *Current Housing Reports, Series H-150-73B; Annual Housing Survey: 1973, Part B, Indicators of Housing and Neighborhood Quality*. Washington, D.C.: Government Printing Office.

———. 1985. *Current Housing Reports, Series H-150-83, Urban and Rural Housing Characteristics for the U.S. and Regions, 1983; Annual Housing Survey: 1983, Part E*. Washington, D.C.: Government Printing Office.

Author Index

Aaron, Henry, 137, 146, 152, 163, 409, 415
Abrams, Charles, 456, 459
Adam, Katrin, 296
Adams, Carolyn, 150, 164, 459
Adams, John, 3, 17
Adler, Arlene, 5, 18, 366, 372
Agnew, John, 149, 151, 163
Ahlbrant, Roger, Jr., 46, 51, 55, 442, 451
Ahrentzen, Sherry, 135, 146, 287, 292, 296
Aitcheson, Susan, 296
Alanen, Arnold, 433, 451
Alexander, C., 74, 93
Allen, Irving, 419, 421, 428
Alonso, William, 433, 438–439, 444–445, 451
Altman, Irving, 3, 17, 28, 35, 77, 78, 80, 93, 339–340, 396, 401
American Association of Retired Persons, 5, 347, 349, 351, 355, 360–362, 366, 372
American Public Health Association, 39, 55, 99
Amory, Nora, 274, 280
Anderson, E. N., 100, 107
Anderson, Elaine, 355, 372
Anderson, James, R., 57, 95, 220
Anderson, Martin, 405, 410, 415
Anderson, N., 379, 386
Andrachek, Steven E., 205, 219

Andrews, Frank, 46, 50, 51, 54, 55, 59, 109
Angrist, Shirley, 52, 55, 109
Apgar, William, 7, 17
Appelbaum, Richard, 270, 272, 280
Appleby, L., 383, 386
Appleyard, Donald, 47, 49, 51, 55, 109
Arce, Anthony, 383, 386
Archea, J., 78, 93
Ardener, Shirley, 293, 296
Arias, E. G., 218–219
Arnstein, Sherry, 30, 33
Atkinson, Reilly, 251
Atlas, John, 145–146, 270, 272, 274, 276, 279–280
Avorn, Jerry, 358, 374

Baar, Kenneth, 5, 8, 15, 256, 258, 266, 273
Bach, Victor, 415
Back, K., 42, 57
Baer, William C., 29, 34, 42–43, 55, 60, 225, 234
Bagley, Christopher, 38, 55
Bahr, H. M., 381, 387
Bailey, K. D., 421, 428
Bajic, Vladimir, 7, 17
Baldassare, Mark, 3–4, 29, 33, 49, 55, 99, 101, 104, 106–107, 401, 425, 428, 434, 450–451
Bane, M. J., 172, 179
Banerjee, Tridib, 29, 34, 42–43, 55, 60
Banner, Mae E., 291–292, 296

Mitchell, E. T., 101, 107
Mitchell, J. Paul, 5, 19, 207, 212–213, 216, 221, 434, 453
Mitroff, Ian, 91–94
Mittelbach, Frank, 8, 18
Moen, Elizabeth, 47, 59
Mollenkopf, John, 131, 147, 274, 282, 411, 416
Molotch, Harvey, 275, 282, 305, 311, 422, 430
Monk, A., 349, 372
Monkkonen, Eric, 379, 388
Montgomery, J. E., 339, 342
Montgomery, Roger, 13, 19
Moore, Eric, 29, 34
Moore, G. T., 28, 35, 76, 78, 90, 94
Moore, Gary, 28, 35
Moore, William, 27, 35
Morgan, James, 12, 19, 306, 311
Morgan, Mary, 270, 282
Morley, David, 286, 296, 299–300, 399, 402
Morris, Earl, 7, 19, 77, 94
Morris, N., 375
Morris, S., 375
Morrow-Jones, H. A., 328, 337, 339–340, 343
Mortgage Bankers Association, 116–118, 128, 149, 155, 164
Morton, H. W., 314, 343
Moss, M., 365, 374
Mueller, E., 43–44, 58
Mulcahy, P., 421, 428
Muller, Peter, 394–395, 402
Murie, Alan, 434–435, 441, 452, 459
Murphy, M. J., 314, 343
Murray, Donald, 59
Myers, D. H., 40, 59, 314, 331, 339, 343–344
Myers, D. M., 340, 343
Myers, Dowell, 59

Nachison, J. S., 359, 374
Nachmias, Chava, 419, 423, 427, 430
Nash, G. B., 160, 164, 378, 388
Nash, Nathaniel, 160, 164
Nathan, Richard, 419, 425–426, 430
Nathanson, Constance, 47, 59

Nathemow, L., 354, 374
National Association of Home Builders, 11, 19, 117
National Center for Housing Management, 200, 213, 221
National Coalition for the Homeless, 385, 388
National Institute of Senior Housing, 349, 366–369, 371, 374
National Low Income Housing Coalition, 134–135, 147
National Opinion Research Center, 50–51, 60
National Trust for Historic Preservation, 382, 388
Nelken, D., 143, 147
Nelson, Bryce, 386, 388
Nelson, Martha, 300
Nelson, Stephen, 60
Nenno, Mary, 133–134, 140–141, 147, 192, 196
Netherlands Polder Development Authority, 439, 453
Newby, Howard, 289, 293, 297
Newcomer, Robert, 5, 19
Newman, Dorothy, 123, 128
Newman, Jeanne, 47, 59
Newman, Oscar, 3, 20, 42, 60, 78, 94, 100, 107, 215, 222
Newman, Sandra, 43, 57, 59–60, 349, 351, 363, 367, 375
New York City, 383, 387
Nicholson, J. H., 433, 453
Noble, Kenneth, 294, 299
Noll, Paul, 362, 368, 375
Nourse, H. O., 214, 222

O'Connell, Brian, 4–5, 16, 174, 180
O'Connor, James, 272, 274, 277, 282
O'Donnell, P. M., 95
Ofshe, R., 101, 107
Ohio State Legislature, 160, 184
Okalo, C., 339, 343
Olson, Margrethe H., 295, 299
O'Mara, W. P., 434, 453
Osborn, F., 435, 453
Oser, Alan S., 173, 180
Osofsky, Gilbert, 304, 311

474   Author Index

Whittich, A., 435, 453
Whyte, William Foote, 422, 431
Whyte, William H., Jr., 26, 36
Wiewel, Wim, 409, 416
Wilcox, Jerome, E., 312
Williams, J., 43, 57
Williams, N., 211, 222
Wilner, Daniel, 27, 36, 46, 50–51, 61
Wilson, James, 27, 36, 404, 416
Wilson, R. L., 42, 44, 49, 61
Wilson, Victor, 4, 18
Windley, P. G., 355, 374
Winkel, Gary, 291–292, 299
Winnie, Richard E., 47, 57
Winters, Mary, 7, 19, 77, 94, 345
Wireman, Peggy, 434, 442, 449, 454
Wirth, Louis, 98–99, 108, 417, 423, 431
Witherspoon, Roger, 446, 454
Withey, Stephen B., 46, 50–51, 54–55
Wohlwill, J. F., 77, 93, 96, 339–340
Wolf, Eleanor, 43, 61
Wood, D., 215, 223
Wood, James, 271, 282
Woods, Margaret, 132, 148
Woodward, Allison, 175, 178, 180, 304, 311

Woodward, C. Vann, 304, 312
Worden, Orian, 60
Wright, Gwendolyn, 151, 165, 293, 295–296, 299
Wurdock, Charles, 310–311
Wynne, Edward A., 399–400, 402

Yancey, William, 4, 20, 87, 90, 212, 214, 223
Yatrakis, Kathryn, 300
Yawney, R., 355, 376
Yoon, Bong Joon, 3, 9, 18, 36

Zais, J., 5–6, 20, 249, 251, 351, 355, 360–361, 375
Zald, Mayer, 271, 282
Zawadski, Rick, 52–56
Zehner, Robert, 29, 34, 36, 42–44, 49–51, 58, 444, 453
Zeisel, John, 77–79, 90, 96, 393, 402
Zeitz, Eileen, 418, 431
Zelinsky, Wilbur, 70, 171
Zimring, Craig, 29, 36
Zinglae, Nancy, 269, 289
Zube, E. H., 78, 94
Zuiches, James, 58
Zukin, Sharon, 168, 170, 180, 418, 431

Subject Index

Abandonment, 13, 16, 27, 133, 255
Accessory units, for elderlry, 360–361
Architectural design, 1, 4, 73–79, 404
Architecture: evaluation of, 29, 87, 89;
  public housing, 4, 87, 92. *See also*
  Environmental design

Below-market interest rate subsidies. *See*
  Section 202 elderly housing; Section
  221 (d) 3 rental housing; Section 235
  home ownership program; Section 236
  rental housing
British housing, 270; council housing,
  14, 201; homeownership mortgage foreclosures, 161–162; new towns, 433–
  436, 440–441, 443, 448, 450; ownership, 161; private rental housing, 141–
  143; sale of council housing, 211
Building codes, 4, 8, 10, 11, 64, 295,
  338, 360–361, 459
Building industry, 16. *See also* Housing
  construction

Canadian housing, 246, 342
Central-city housing. *See* Gentrification;
  Rehabilitation; Urban renewal/develop-
  ment
Class and housing. *See* Homeownership;
  Neighborhood; Suburbs and housing
Class mix in housing: new towns, 442–
  450; suburbs, 297
Community contact: neighborhoods, 69–
  71; suburbs, 399

Community Development Block Grant,
  138, 189, 193, 347, 357, 370, 406–
  407, 410, 412–413
Condition of housing, 7, 13, 24–25, 38–
  39, 47, 244–245, 287, 335, 349–350,
  360, 456–457; elderly housing, 349–
  350, 360; female-headed households,
  287; quality as goal, 15–16, 405–407.
  See also Substandard housing
Condominium and cooperative conversion, 2, 4, 16, 133, 135–136, 167–
  178, 232; advantages of ownership,
  167, 175; causes of conversion, 172–
  175, 263; characteristics of buyers,
  167–168, 171–172; definition, 167–
  168; dislocation and conversion, 175;
  economics of conversion, 174–175;
  history, 168–169; neighborhood, building types, and conversion, 168–170;
  number of, 168–169, 173; problems,
  175–177; research on, 178–179; taxes,
  174, 178
Condominiums, 2, 7, 167–168, 232–233
Congruence in housing, 3, 25–29, 92,
  339, 348, 352–357, 399
Cooperative housing, 2, 167–178
Crime and housing, 3, 7, 99, 288
Crowding. *See* Density and crowding

Demographic factors and housing, 2, 7,
  9, 18, 172, 287, 314–320, 338–339
Demolition, 119, 263, 335. *See also* Urban renewal/development

41–42, 44, 46, 69–70; services, 50,
53, 70; women and neighborhoods,
287–288, 295
Netherlands housing, 270, 433–434, 436,
439, 441, 443
New communities, 4, 12, 16, 29, 433–
454; history, 435–438; national government role, 433–438, 441, 444–445,
450; New Communities Act, 433, 436;
new town goals, 438–444; planning,
433, 438–439, 450; satisfaction, 449–
450; social balance, 442–449; social
contacts, 447–448
New York City housing: public housing,
458; rent control, 253, 255, 265
Nonprofit housing, 6; for elderly, 369–
370. *See also* Farmers Home Administration housing programs; Section 202
elderly housing; Section 221 (d) 3
rental housing; Section 236 rental
housing

Planned community (PUD-planned urban
development), 16, 63–70; density, 69;
design, 67; planning, 63–70; townhouse form, 63–70. *See also* New
communities
Politics of housing, 1, 9, 13–14, 186–
176, 204–212, 272, 274–275, 405,
411–414
Poverty and housing, 111–145, 125, 207,
216, 287, 294, 381–383
Price of rental housing, 26, 101, 106
Privacy and housing, 67–69, 78, 101–102
Property tax, 227, 256–257, 264–265
Public housing, 2, 14, 25–26, 87, 92,
100, 119, 137, 178–179, 184–186,
194, 199–219; architecture, 87, 92,
211, 214–215, 217; characteristics of
users, 186, 201, 204, 325; crime, 215;
demolition, 210, 218; description of
program, 186, 194, 200–212; elderly
program, 199–201, 359, 365, 367–368;
finances, 186, 194, 201, 204, 207,
215–216; history, 186, 194, 205–212;
management, 218; modernization, 210,
problems, 162, 186, 194, 207, 211,

214, 218; Public Housing Ownership
Demonstration, 178–179; sale of housing, 210, 218; scattered sites, 194,
212–213; stigma, 204, 211; tenant participation, 218; waiting lists, 204

Quality of housing. *See* Condition of
housing; Substandard housing

Racial integration. *See* Segregation and
discrimination in housing of minorities;
Minorities and housing need
Reagan administration housing policy,
13–14, 121, 137, 189, 192–194, 209–
210, 215, 279, 358, 381–382, 413
Real estate industry and discrimination,
304
Redlining, 456
Rehabilitation, 2, 14, 16, 126, 188–189,
192–193, 293, 348, 359, 405–406,
412. *See also* Gentrification; Urban re-
newal/development
Rental housing, private, 2, 7–8, 111,
114, 131–145, 325–326, 350, 357;
abroad, 131, 141–143; affordability,
111–114, 135, 264; characteristics of
landlords, 7–13, 173; characteristics of
tenants, 133–134; history, 9, 132–136;
investment in, 139–140, 172–173, 177,
241–242, 264–266; landlord neglect,
262; location, 133, 135; profitability,
9, 172, 255; quality, 254, 264; rent increases, 135, 140–142, 144, 172, 254–
267, 274, 279; rural rentals, 138, 325;
submarkets, 135, 306, 324–325, 357,
456–458; tax shelter, 139–141, 174
Rentals: maintenance cost, 241; purchase
price, 140; return on investment, 9,
140, 144, 172–173, 177, 241–242,
264–266; vacancy decontrol, 255–257,
261–262; vacancy rates, 141
Rent burden, 111–114, 140. *See* Housing
affordability for renters
Rent control, 2, 5, 13, 27, 143, 173,
253–267, 270–279; debate over, 263–
266; evictions, 262–263; financing,
263, 266; history, 253–258; New York

Contributors

KENNETH BAAR is an attorney and urban planner in Berkeley, California. He has served as a consultant to cities in California and to the state of New Jersey on rent control issues, taught housing courses at San Francisco State University, and published numerous articles on rent control.

MARK BALDASSARE is Associate Professor in the Program in Social Ecology at the University of California, Irvine. His interests are in urban sociology and specifically in examining the relationship between community features and residential satisfaction. He is the author of several books, including *Residential Crowding in Urban America*.

CHARLES E. CONNERLY is Associate Professor in the Department of Urban and Regional Planning at Florida State University. He has published articles on resident participation in neighborhood life and resident attitudes toward their neighborhood. He has also published research on housing and growth management policy and is currently completing research on housing trust funds.

NORMAN FAINSTEIN is Professor of Urban Affairs and Policy Analysis at the New School for Social Research. SUSAN FAINSTEIN is Professor of Urban Planning and Policy Development at Rutgers University. Together they have collaborated on numerous books and articles on urban redevelopment and urban political economy.

SYLVIA F. FAVA is Senior Research Scholar in the Ph.D. Program in Sociology at the Graduate Center, City University of New York. She has written on urban sociology, new towns, suburban society, and housing. Currently she is conducting studies of the "suburban generation" and the role of gender in community life.

KAREN FRANCK is Associate Professor at the School of Architecture, New Jersey Institute of Technology, Newark, New Jersey. She is currently completing a National Science Foundation project on recent social and spatial innovations in American housing. Additional research interests include the history of public housing design, women and environments, and architecture and social change. Previously she collaborated with Oscar Newman on research about the relationships between housing design, crime, fear of crime, and community instability. She has published articles in the *Journal of Social Issues*, *Population and Environment*, *Sociological Focus*, *Sociological Inquiry*, *Environment and Behavior*, and *Ekistics*.

BERNARD J. FRIEDEN is Chairman of the Massachusetts Institute of Technology Faculty and Class of 1942 Professor in the Department of Urban Studies and Planning. He formerly served as research director of the M.I.T. Center for Real Estate Development and as director of the M.I.T.—Harvard Joint Center for Urban Studies. He has been an advisor on federal housing and community development policy under three presidential administrations. His most recent book, *The Environmental Protection Hustle*, is a study of conflicts between housing and environmental politics. He is the author (with Lynne Sagalyn) of a forthcoming book on the rebuilding of central cities, *Behind the New Downtowns: Politics, Money, and Marketplaces*.

JOHN I. GILDERBLOOM is Assistant Professor of Sociology and Research Associate at the Center for Public Policy at the University of Houston. He is also an Associate Fellow at the Foundation for National Progress in San Francisco, where he directs the Housing Information Center. He has published a variety of articles on rental issues. He is also editor of *Rent Control: A Source Book* and co-author of the forthcoming book, *Gimme Shelter: The Tenant's Movement and the Battle for Community*. His current research examines intercity rent differentials.

ELEANOR GUREWITSCH received her B.A. cum laude in economics from Radcliffe College in 1943 and her Ph.D. from the Union of Experimenting Colleges and Universities in 1981. She is a consultant in gerontology and public health. She is the author of articles in *Aging*, *Perspectives on Aging*, *Gerontologist*, *Modern Maturity*, the *New York Times*, the *Christian Science Monitor*, *Neue Zürcher Zeitung*, and various other newspapers and magazines in the United States and Switzerland. Her book *Reducing Requirements for Long Term Institutional Care*, a joint publication of the International Social Gerontology Center, Riviera Beach, Florida, and the Association for the Care of the Elderly, Bern-Bumpliz, Switzerland, demonstrates the important role that protected housing plays in reducing length of stay in long-term institutions prior to death.

MICHAEL HARLOE, Department of Sociology, University of Essex, is the author of numerous books and articles based on extensive research in housing and urban studies. His present work includes an international study of innovative housing policies and practices as responses to emerging housing crises. He is also the editor of the *International Journal of Urban and Regional Research.*

CHESTER HARTMAN is a Fellow at the Institute for Policy Studies in Washington D.C. He has taught at Harvard, Yale, Cornell, the University of North Carolina, and the University of California (Berkeley). He chairs the Planners Network, a national organization of progressive urban and rural planners. His most recent books are *Critical Perspectives on Housing* (with Rachel Bratt and Ann Meyerson), *The Transformation of San Francisco*, and *America's Housing Crisis: What Is to Be Done?*

R. ALLEN HAYS is Associate Professor of Political Science at the University of Northern Iowa. He has published articles on various housing issues and has written a book on federal housing policy entitled *The Federal Government and Urban Housing: Ideology and Change in Public Policy*. He is currently doing research on the course of housing policy under the Reagan administration and on the structure of public attitudes with regard to housing and other social welfare programs.

BARBARA SCHMITTER HEISLER is Assistant Professor in the Department of Sociology at Cleveland State University. She has been a postdoctoral fellow at Duke University and a visiting assistant professor at the State University of New York at Buffalo. Her research interests center on structural problems of advanced industrial societies, among them unemployment, housing, and immigration. She has published several articles on immigration in Western Europe and recently coedited an issue of the *Annals of the American Academy of Political and Social Science.*

CHARLES HOCH teaches housing and planning courses as an Assistant Professor in the School of Urban Planning and Policy at the University of Illinois (Chicago). He has published several articles on the problem of homelessness in the United States and recently completed a forthcoming book with coauthor Robert Slayton entitled *The New Homeless and the Skid Row SRO.*

LILY M. HOFFMAN is Assistant Professor at Eugene Lang College, New School for Social Research. She was Culpeper Fellow in Urban Studies at Oberlin College, and a postdoctoral fellow at the Rutgers-Princeton Program in Mental Health Research. Her general concern is with the restructuring of advanced industrial societies, specifically, issues related to unemployment, housing, and professional work. She has published several articles in these areas and is currently completing a book, *From Experts to Experts: Activist Movements in Medicine and Planning*. She and Barbara Schmitter Heisler are working on a comparative study of home mortgage foreclosures in the United States and United Kingdom.

MARY JO HUTH is Professor of Sociology at the University of Dayton where she chaired the department from 1965 to 1970. In Washington, D.C., at the Department of Housing and Urban Development, Dr. Huth has been a Public Administration Fellow (1972–73) and a Visiting Scholar (1979–80) and, at the National Bureau of Standards, a research sociologist (1973–74). Her lastest book is *The Urban Habitat: Past, Present, and Future*. She has presented papers on the unique problems of various types of households in the United States and on women in development issues. In recent years Dr. Huth has engaged in research on community development programs and on the status of women in Kenya and Tanzania, and has also studied housing policies and urban/regional planning in France and Switzerland. In 1986 she was a member of the U.S. Delgation to the 74th Session of the United Nations Economic Commission for Europe's Committee on Building, Housing, and the Environment in Geneva, Switzerland.

ELIZABETH HUTTMAN is Professor of Sociology at California State University, Hayward. She has written *Housing and Social Services for the Elderly*, coedited *Housing Needs and Policy Approaches*, and authored "Transnational Housing Policy" in *Home Environments* (edited by Irving Altman and Carol Werner). She is co-organizer of the International Committee of Housing and the Built Environment.

DENNIS KEATING is Associate Professor of Urban Studies and Law at the College of Urban Affairs, Cleveland State University. He has written extensively on housing and community development and has been a consultant to federal, state, and local government and national and local foundations. He has published studies of rent control in California, New Jersey, and New York and is coauthoring a book on rent control in the United States, Canada, and Western Europe. Presently, Professor Keating is acting director of CSU's Center for Neighborhood Development and is participating in a national evaluation of community development corporations.

SUZANNE KELLER is Professor of Sociology at Princeton University, former Vice President of the American Sociological Association, and board member of *Ekistics*. She has had long-time experience in architecture. Her books include *Beyond the Ruling Class*, *Urban Neighborhoods*, and *Planning and Women*. She is currently completing a book on community research.

ROBERT W. MARANS is Professor in the College of Architecture and Urban Planning at the University of Micnigan, a research scientist at the university's Institute for Social Research, and director of the university's Ph.D. program in urban, environmental, and technological planning. He is a licensed architect and